The Editor

NORMAN PAGE is Professor of English emeritus, University of Nottingham and University of Alberta. He is the author of many books, among them *The Language of Jane Austen, Speech in the English Novel, Thomas Hardy, Tennyson: An Illustrated Life,* and *A. E. Housman: A Critical Biography.* He is editor of the *Oxford Reader's Companion to Thomas Hardy* (forthcoming), past editor of the *Thomas Hardy Journal* and the *Thomas Hardy Annual,* and a vice-president of the Thomas Hardy Society.

A NORTON CRITICAL EDITION

Thomas Hardy
JUDE THE OBSCURE

AN AUTHORITATIVE TEXT

BACKGROUNDS AND CONTEXTS

CRITICISM

SECOND EDITION

Edited by

NORMAN PAGE

EMERITUS, UNIVERSITY OF NOTTINGHAM

W · W · NORTON & COMPANY · *New York* · *London*

The text of this book is composed in Electra
with the display set in Bernhard Modern.
Composition by Binghamton Valley Composition.
Manufacturing by Maple-Vail Book Group.
Book design by Antonina Krass.

Library of Congress Cataloging-in-Publication Data

Hardy, Thomas, 1840-1928.
Jude the obscure : an authoritative text : backgrounds and
contexts, criticism / Thomas Hardy ; edited by Norman Page. — 2nd
ed., a Norton critical ed.
        p.   cm.
Includes bibliographical references.

ISBN 0-393-97278-X (pbk.)

1. England—Social life and customs—19th century—Fiction.
2. Man-women relationships—England—Wessex—Fiction.   3. Hardy,
Thomas, 1840–1928.   Jude the obscure.   4. Wessex (England)—Fiction.
I. Page, Norman.   II. Title.
PR4746.A1   1999
823'.8—dc21   98-21563
                               CIP

W. W. Norton & Company, Inc., 500 Fifth Avenue, New York, N.Y. 10110
www.wwnorton.com

W. W. Norton & Company Ltd., Castle House, 75/76 Wells Street,
London W1T 3QT

5 6 7 8 9 0

Contents

Preface to the First Edition

Hardy's last novel, *Jude the Obscure*, is one of the greatest works of late Victorian literature; but it is also something more than that. With courage and sensitivity, Hardy explores some of the most significant social issues of his time—and not only of his time. The intensity of his response to the questions debated and dramatized in the novel derives from their importance being at the same time public and personal. That some at least of his contemporaries recognized the force and originality of its propagandist elements is attested by the comment of one of his earliest critics, an anonymous writer in the *Saturday Review* (February 8, 1896): after quoting from the scene describing the death of Jude, he declares: "That is the voice of the educated proletarian, speaking more distinctly than it has ever spoken before in English literature." And that these qualities are still recognized is suggested by Kate Millett's description of the novel as "a significant contribution to the literature of the sexual revolution" (*Sexual Politics* [New York, 1970], p. 133). It happens, of course, that these two critics, three generations apart, single out quite different facets of Hardy's novel for commendation; and, indeed it is difficult to think of another novel of the period in which such a diversity of vital social and intellectual questions—the class system, inequality of educational opportunity, urbanization and the drift to the towns, and above all questions of marriage and sexual morality—are so vigorously ventilated.

Jude the Obscure occupied Hardy for longer than any of its predecessors. According to the preface he wrote for the first edition, he began making notes in 1887, presumably soon after he had finished *The Woodlanders* and before *Tess of the d'Urbervilles* was started; in 1890 he "jotted down" the "scheme" of the novel, by which he probably meant an outline of the plot as it was at first conceived; in October 1892 he visited Great Fawley, the Berkshire village where his grandmother had lived and which is the prototype of "Marygreen" in the novel; during 1892–93 he wrote the story "in outline," and also visited Oxford, on which "Christminster" is based; and in 1893–94 the novel was written "at full length." The date at the end of the manuscript is March 1895. Like nearly all of Hardy's novels, *Jude the Obscure* was originally published as a serial, appearing simultaneously in England and America in *Harper's New Monthly Magazine* from December 1894 to November 1895. As the preface admits, the serial version was "abridged and modified" from what Hardy had written; these changes, which can be traced in the manuscript and involved (in R. L. Purdy's words) an "amazing sacrifice of art and credibility," were made in response to objections from the editor of the magazine, who had protested that the treatment of Jude's relationships with Arabella and Sue was unsuitable for a family periodical. According to J. Henry Harper, Hardy had originally assured his editor that the new novel "would be a tale that could not offend the most fastidious maiden"; but as work progressed he found himself obliged to admit that "the development of the story was carrying him into unexpected fields," and he was "afraid to predict its future trend." What had happened, in fact, was that a novel about the quest for an education had, in the process of composition, turned into a novel about the much more inflammatory topics of sex and marriage. Study of the manuscript shows that Hardy's enforced bowdlerization involved not only drastic modifications to the action of the novel, but numerous minor verbal revisions—for example, "couch" was substituted at one point for "bed," and "shaking hands" for "kissing."

In November 1895 *Jude* appeared in volume form in London and New York, the cuts and revisions made for serial publication having been largely (though not entirely) eliminated by restoration of the original version. The book was published in a single volume at a relatively low price; it thus broke with the Victorian tradition of the expensive three-volume novel, the format in which most of Hardy's work had appeared. Hardy revised *Jude* for further editions in 1903 and 1912; the latter revision, for the Wessex Edition of his work, also added an important postscript to the preface. This final revision is generally accepted as the definitive text, representing as it does Hardy's final intentions and incorporating numerous corrections prompted by his minute and painstaking scrutiny of the earlier texts. It has been used as the basis of the present edition. I have collated it with the first English edition (dated 1896 on the title page, though actually published, as noted above, before the end of 1895), and have when necessary made reference to the manuscript and the 1903 revision. Hardy's 1912 postscript to the preface, which is actually much longer than the original preface, refers modestly to "a few verbal corrections"; but this is a characteristically Hardyan understatement, and, as Robert C. Slack has shown, there are over two hundred variants between the 1903 and 1912 texts. Though nearly all are of minor significance, they indicate that Hardy, even after his abandonment of fiction, was sufficiently interested in his novel to subject it to a very close revision. A few errors, mainly affecting punctuation, eluded his careful proofreading; and some of them have persisted in modern editions. In the present text, twenty obvious misprints have been silently corrected. The textual history of this novel, including an account of the surviving manuscript, of the pressure brought to bear upon Hardy to bowdlerize his novel, and of the subsequent restoration and revisions, is described in this edition through a series of extracts by Hardy himself, his contemporaries, and modern scholars.

The reception of *Jude* by late-Victorian reviewers in England and America was characterized by vehement, though not unanimous, disapproval. For one lady critic, it was "almost the worst book I have ever read," dealing as it did with the behavior of "pigs—animal and human"; Hardy was accused of attacking "the fundamental institutions of society" and "all the obligations and relations of life which most people hold sacred," and of "wallowing in the mire" and "dabbling in beastliness and putrefaction"; an American reviewer called it "a moral monstrosity" and "a stream of indecency"; one British critic observed that it was "steeped in sex"; and another lady reviewer urged Hardy to avoid coarseness and to return to "the sweet smell of woods and fields." A selection of the more important of the contemporary reviews, favorable and otherwise, is given in this book. Hardy's autobiography, relevant extracts from which are reproduced, cites other responses, ranging from the laudatory to the ludicrous, and records some of his own reactions to this publicity. By the end of his life, the qualities of his novel had won due recognition: one obituary notice called it "the finest sex-novel ever written," and in the following years Ford Madox Ford and others expressed the view that it is Hardy's masterpiece. Recognition was international: before his death it had been translated into German, French, Japanese, and other languages, and since then it has appeared in Italian, Russian, Chinese, and many more. For many modern critics it represents not only the summit of Hardy's achievement in the novel but the beginning of an important tradition in modern British fiction, as the first major novel with a working class hero.

In writing *Jude the Obscure* Hardy drew heavily (perhaps, indeed, more heavily than ever before) on his personal experiences and passionate convictions: this much is clear in spite of his firm declarations to the contrary. I have sought to illuminate some of the sources of the novel by means of extracts from contemporary materials: most importantly, from Hardy's own letters, diaries, poems and journalistic writings. A further section of material presents modern interpretations and evaluations of the novel from various critical standpoints.

Jude is a highly allusive novel, containing abundant evidence of Hardy's eclectic reading and specialized interests. Annotation has therefore necessarily been somewhat fuller than usual, and a glance at the notes brings home rather strikingly certain aspects of Hardy's literary and intellectual equipment. There are, for example, some fifty allusions to the Bible, and thirty to the Greek and Latin classics; about fifty dialect words and expressions; numerous technical terms of architecture; and a wide range of references to English authors from Shakespeare, Milton, and Bunyan to poets of Hardy's own time such as Browning and Swinburne, as well as to French and German authors. I have tried not only to explain any expression or reference that might puzzle the student, but also on occasion to suggest some of the personal and structural undercurrents of the novel.

In the footnotes, *"Life"* indicates F. E. Hardy's *The Life of Thomas Hardy, 1840–1928* (single-volume edition, London, 1962); references to "Hardy's manuscript" are to the manuscript of *Jude the Obscure* now in the Fitzwilliam Museum, Cambridge.

In preparing and annotating the text, I have been indebted to several previous editors of this novel, especially P. N. Furbank, Robert B. Heilman, and F. R. Southerington, as well as to Robert C. Slack's unpublished variorum edition. My thanks are also due to the director and staff of the Fitzwilliam Museum, Cambridge, for allowing me access to Hardy's manuscript, and to Cambridge University Library for providing a copy of an 1891 Plan of Oxford.

NORMAN PAGE

Preface to the Second Edition

Jude the Obscure has celebrated its hundredth birthday since this Norton Critical Edition originally appeared twenty years ago, and the claims made then for its relevance to contemporary issues seem now even stronger than they were in the 1970s. Another generation of rapid social and ideological change has made it even clearer that Hardy's last novel is a key text for the understanding of the modern age that was emerging as he wrote. If *Jude* once seemed to critics and readers to be the last major Victorian novel, it should probably now be seen as the first modern novel. Its engagement with questions of sexual behavior and sexual morality—love and desire, marriage and partnerships outside marriage, the place of children in different kinds of union, gender and androgyny, to give some obvious examples—enables this novel of the closing years of the nineteenth century to speak directly to the closing years of the twentieth. Among the new features of this Second Edition are critical considerations, from different ideological standpoints, of these aspects of a richly multifaceted work.

In a broader context, whereas the rediscovery and revaluation of Hardy was only just getting seriously under way in the 1970s, the past twenty years have seen an astonishing burst of scholarly and critical energy directed at his novels, poems, short stories, and other writings. Within the large and varied Hardy canon, there have inevitably been during these decades shifts of emphasis and revised estimations, and it is probably true to say that *Jude the Obscure* is more highly regarded today than ever before.

At the end of his career as a writer of fiction, Hardy's fourteenth published novel reveals him as prepared to experiment with a new kind of writing: never before, to draw attention to a small but significant point, had he written an opening sentence so starkly direct in its promise of bleak realism and yet so subtle in its wistful implications. Reading on, anyone familiar with the earlier Hardy is bound to be surprised by the rapidly shifting settings, the depiction of urban civilization, and the psychological complexity with which, in particular, Jude Fawley and Sue Bridehead are portrayed. Earlier readers would have been taken aback, too, by the brutal frankness that led an Anglican bishop to claim publicly that he had burned the book in disgust: the episode in which Arabella throws the pig's "pizzle" at the innocent and unworldly Jude is surely without parallel in the fiction of its time.

Genuinely original works of art remain perennially fresh and permanently topical: only the derivative and the second-rate go out of fashion and are forgotten, as some of the best-sellers by Hardy's contemporaries—books that sold far better than his own—have done. Swift's *Gulliver's Travels* is a more remarkably experimental work than most of the experimental writing of our own time; Shakespeare's *Hamlet* is more "relevant" to our individual lives than more resolutely topical works. Hardy once said that he was not a best-seller but was a long-seller, and in the last analysis this is what counts. For many readers today *Jude* is of all his novels the most ambitious, the most powerful, and the most productive of fruitful argument and debate.

NORMAN PAGE

The Text of
JUDE THE OBSCURE

Hardy prepared this map of "Wessex," his fictional territory, in 1895 for a collected edition of his works. Actual names are in solid capitals: BRISTOL, BATH, STONEHENGE. The others are fictitious, the following being the most important in *Jude the Obscure*:

"Marygreen" corresponds to Great Fawley (a village in Berkshire)
"Christminster" corresponds to Oxford
"Aldbrickham" corresponds to Reading

"Melchester" corresponds to Salisbury
"Shaston" corresponds to Shaftesbury
"Alfredston" corresponds to Wantage
"Kennetbridge" corresponds to Newbury

Note that the scale of Hardy's fictional world is small: from "Christminster" to "Melchester," for instance, is only about seventy miles.

Contents of *Jude the Obscure*

Preface to the First Edition

The history of this novel (whose birth in its present shape has been much retarded by the necessities of periodical publication) is briefly as follows. The scheme was jotted down in 1890, from notes made in 1887 and onwards, some of the circumstances being suggested by the death of a woman[1] in the former year. The scenes were revisited in October 1892; the narrative was written in outline in 1892 and the spring of 1893, and at full length, as it now appears, from August 1893 onwards into the next year; the whole, with the exception of a few chapters, being in the hands of the publisher by the end of 1894. It was begun as a serial story in *Harper's Magazine* at the end of November 1894, and was continued in monthly parts.

But, as in the case of *Tess of the d'Urbervilles*, the magazine version was for various reasons an abridged and modified one, the present edition being the first in which the whole appears as originally written. And in the difficulty of coming to an early decision in the matter of a title, the tale was issued under a provisional name, two such titles having, in fact, been successively adopted.[2] The present and final title, deemed on the whole the best, was one of the earliest thought of.

For a novel addressed by a man to men and women of full age; which attempts to deal unaffectedly with the fret and fever, derision and disaster, that may press in the wake of the strongest passion known to humanity; to tell, without a mincing of words, of a deadly war waged between flesh and spirit; and to point the tragedy of unfulfilled aims, I am not aware that there is anything in the handling to which exception can be taken.

Like former productions of this pen, *Jude the Obscure* is simply an endeavour to give shape and coherence to a series of seemings, or personal impressions, the question of their consistency or their discordance, of their permanence or their transitoriness, being regarded as not of the first moment.

August 1895

Postscript

The issue of this book sixteen years ago, with the explanatory Preface given above, was followed by unexpected incidents, and one can now look back for a moment at what happened. Within a day or two of its

---

1. Probably Hardy's cousin, Tryphena Sparks. See his poem "Thoughts of Phena at News of her Death" (*The Complete Poems of Thomas Hardy*, ed. James Gibson [1976] 62).
2. The serial version began as *The Simpletons*, but changed after the first installment to *Hearts Insurgent*.

publication the reviewers pronounced upon it in tones to which the reception of *Tess of the d'Urbervilles* bore no comparison, though there were two or three dissentients from the chorus. This salutation of the story in England was instantly cabled to America, and the music was reinforced on that side of the Atlantic in a shrill crescendo.

In my own eyes the sad feature of the attack was that the greater part of the story—that which presented the shattered ideals of the two chief characters, and had been more especially, and indeed almost exclusively, the part of interest to myself—was practically ignored by the adverse press of the two countries; the while that some twenty or thirty pages of sorry detail deemed necessary to complete the narrative, and show the antitheses in Jude's life, were almost the sole portions read and regarded. And curiously enough, a reprint the next year of a fantastic tale that had been published in a family paper some time before,[3] drew down upon my head a continuation of the same sort of invective from several quarters.

So much for the unhappy beginning of *Jude's* career as a book. After these verdicts from the press its next misfortune was to be burnt by a bishop[4]—probably in his despair at not being able to burn me.

Then somebody discovered that *Jude* was a moral work—austere in its treatment of a difficult subject—as if the writer had not all the time said in the Preface that it was meant to be so. Thereupon many uncursed me, and the matter ended, the only effect of it on human conduct that I could discover being its effect on myself—the experience completely curing me of further interest in novel-writing.

One incident among many arising from the storm of words was that an American man of letters, who did not whitewash his own morals, informed me that, having bought a copy of the book on the strength of the shocked criticisms, he read on and on, wondering when the harmfulness was going to begin, and at last flung it across the room with execrations at having been induced by the rascally reviewers to waste a dollar-and-half on what he was pleased to call 'a religious and ethical treatise.'

I sympathized with him, and assured him honestly that the misrepresentations had been no collusive trick of mine to increase my circulation among the subscribers to the papers in question.

Then there was the case of the lady[5] who having shuddered at the book in an influential article bearing intermediate headlines of horror, and printed in a world-read journal, wrote to me shortly afterwards that it was her desire to make my acquaintance.

---

3. *The Pursuit of the Well-Beloved* was serialized in the *Illustrated London News* in 1892. It was published in volume form in 1897 as *The Well-Beloved*.
4. W. W. How, Bishop of Wakefield. See below, pp. 341 and 390.
5. Jeannette Gilder. See below, pp. 342–44.

To return, however, to the book itself. The marriage laws being used in great part as the tragic machinery of the tale, and its general drift on the domestic side tending to show that, in Diderot's[6] words, the civil law should be only the enunciation of the law of nature (a statement that requires some qualification, by the way), I have been charged since 1895 with a large responsibility in this country for the present 'shop-soiled' condition of the marriage theme (as a learned writer characterized it the other day). I do not know. My opinion at that time, if I remember rightly, was what it is now, that a marriage should be dissolvable as soon as it becomes a cruelty to either of the parties—being then essentially and morally no marriage—and it seemed a good foundation for the fable of a tragedy, told for its own sake as a presentation of particulars containing a good deal that was universal, and not without a hope that certain cathartic, Aristotelian [7] qualities might be found therein.

The difficulties down to twenty or thirty years back of acquiring knowledge in letters without pecuniary means were used in the same way; though I was informed that some readers thought these episodes an attack on venerable institutions, and that when Ruskin College[8] was subsequently founded it should have been called the College of Jude the Obscure.

Artistic effort always pays heavily for finding its tragedies in the forced adaptation of human instincts to rusty and irksome moulds that do not fit them. To do Bludyer[9] and the conflagratory bishop justice, what they meant seems to have been only this: 'We Britons hate ideas, and we are going to live up to that privilege of our native country. Your picture may not show the untrue, or the uncommon, or even be contrary to the canons of art; but it is not the view of life that we who thrive on conventions can permit to be painted.'

But what did it matter. As for the matrimonial scenes, in spite of their 'touching the spot,' and the screaming of a poor lady in *Blackwood* that there was an unholy anti-marriage league afoot,[1] the famous contract—sacrament I mean—is doing fairly well still, and people marry and give in what may or may not be true marriage as light-heartedly as ever. The author has even been reproached by some earnest correspondents that he has left the question where he found it, and has not pointed the way to a much-needed reform.

6. Denis Diderot (1713–1784), French author. The statement appears in his *Encyclopédie* (1751–72).
7. The reference is to Aristotle's treatise on literary criticism, the *Poetics*, in which it is suggested that one of the effects of tragic drama is to produce a *catharsis* or "purgation" of the emotions.
8. Founded in 1899 at Oxford for the higher education of working-class men.
9. A hostile reviewer in Thackeray's *Pendennis* (1848).
1. The reference is to Mrs. Margaret Oliphant's review of the novel in *Blackwood's Magazine* under the title "The Anti-Marriage League": see below, p. 379.

After the issue of *Jude the Obscure* as a serial story in Germany, an experienced reviewer of that country informed the writer that Sue Bridehead, the heroine, was the first delineation in fiction of the woman who was coming into notice in her thousands every year—the woman of the feminist movement—the slight, pale 'bachelor' girl— the intellectualized, emancipated bundle of nerves that modern con- ditions were producing, mainly in cities as yet; who does not recognize the necessity for most of her sex to follow marriage as a profession, and boast themselves as superior people because they are licensed to be loved on the premises. The regret of this critic was that the portrait of the newcomer had been left to be drawn by a man, and was not done by one of her own sex, who would never have allowed her to break down at the end.

Whether this assurance is borne out by dates I cannot say. Nor am I able, across the gap of years since the production of the novel, to exercise more criticism upon it of a general kind than extends to a few verbal corrections, whatever, good or bad, it may contain. And no doubt there can be more in a book than the author consciously put there, which will help either to its profit or to its disadvantage as the case may be.

T. H.

April 1912

Jude the Obscure

epigraph 'The letter killeth'[1]

Part First: At Marygreen[2]

'Yea, many there be that have run out of their wits for women, and
become servants for their sakes. Many also have perished, have erred, *gone wrong*
and sinned, for women. . . . O ye men, how can it be but women
should be strong, seeing they do thus?'

—ESDRAS.[3]

I–1

The schoolmaster was leaving the village, and everybody seemed
sorry. The miller at Cresscombe lent him the small white tilted[4] cart
and horse to carry his goods to the city of his destination, about twenty
miles off, such a vehicle proving of quite sufficient size for the departing teacher's effects. For the school-house had been partly furnished
by the managers, and the only cumbersome article possessed by the
master, in addition to the packing-case of books, was a cottage piano
that he had bought at an auction during the year in which he thought
of learning instrumental music. But the enthusiasm having waned he
had never acquired any skill in playing, and the purchased article had
been a perpetual trouble to him ever since in moving house.

The rector had gone away for the day, being a man who disliked the
sight of changes. He did not mean to return till the evening, when the
new school-teacher would have arrived and settled in, and everything
would be smooth again.

The blacksmith, the farm bailiff, and the schoolmaster himself were
standing in perplexed attitudes in the parlour before the instrument.
The master had remarked that even if he got it into the cart he should
not know what to do with it on his arrival at Christminster, the city

---

1. "For the letter killeth, but the spirit giveth life" (2 Corinthians 3.6).
2. Based on the village of Fawley in Berkshire, where Hardy's paternal grandmother, Mary Head,
   lived as a girl. Hardy visited the village in October 1892 (F. E. Hardy, *The Life of Thomas
   Hardy, 1840–1928* [London, 1962] [hereafter cited as *Life*] 250–51).
3. 1 Esdras 4.26, 27, 32.
4. With a "tilt" or canvas cover.

he was bound for, since he was only going into temporary lodgings just at first.

A little boy of eleven, who had been thoughtfully assisting in the packing, joined the group of men, and as they rubbed their chins he spoke up, blushing at the sound of his own voice: 'Aunt have got a great fuel-house, and it could be put there, perhaps, till you've found a place to settle in, sir.'

'A proper good notion,' said the blacksmith.

It was decided that a deputation should wait on the boy's aunt—an old maiden resident—and ask her if she would house the piano till Mr. Phillotson should send for it. The smith and the bailiff started to see the practicability of the suggested shelter, and the boy and the school-master were left standing alone.

'Sorry I am going, Jude?' asked the latter kindly.

Tears rose into the boy's eyes, for he was not among the regular day scholars, who came unromantically close to the schoolmaster's life, but one who had attended the night school only during the present teacher's term of office. The regular scholars, if the truth must be told, stood at the present moment afar off, like certain historic disciples,[5] indisposed to any enthusiastic volunteering of aid.

The boy awkwardly opened the book he held in his hand, which Mr. Phillotson had bestowed on him as a parting gift, and admitted that he was sorry.

'So am I,' said Mr. Phillotson.

'Why do you go, sir?' asked the boy.

'Ah—that would be a long story. You wouldn't understand my reasons, Jude. You will, perhaps, when you are older.'

'I think I should now, sir.'

'Well—don't speak of this everywhere. You know what a university is, and a university degree? It is the necessary hall-mark of a man who wants to do anything in teaching. My scheme, or dream, is to be a university graduate, and then to be ordained. By going to live at Christminster, or near it, I shall be at headquarters, so to speak, and if my scheme is practicable at all, I consider that being on the spot will afford me a better chance of carrying it out than I should have elsewhere.'

The smith and his companion returned. Old Miss Fawley's[6] fuel-house was dry, and eminently practicable; and she seemed willing to give the instrument standing-room there. It was accordingly left in the school till the evening, when more hands would be available for removing it; and the schoolmaster gave a final glance round.

5. When Christ was crucified, "all his acquaintance . . . stood afar off, beholding these things" (Luke 23.49).
6. Hardy's manuscript in the Fitzwilliam Museum, Cambridge (hereafter referred to as "Hardy's manuscript") shows that Jude's surname gave him considerable trouble: earlier versions were Head, Stancombe, Hopeson, and England.

The boy Jude assisted in loading some small articles, and at nine o'clock Mr. Phillotson mounted beside his box of books and other *impedimenta*,[7] and bade his friends good-bye.

'I shan't forget you, Jude,' he said, smiling, as the cart moved off. 'Be a good boy, remember; and be kind to animals and birds, and read all you can. And if ever you come to Christminster remember you hunt me out for old acquaintance' sake.'

The cart creaked across the green, and disappeared round the corner by the rectory-house. The boy returned to the draw-well at the edge of the greensward, where he had left his buckets when he went to help his patron and teacher in the loading. There was a quiver in his lip now, and after opening the well-cover to begin lowering the bucket he paused and leant with his forehead and arms against the frame-work, his face wearing the fixity of a thoughtful child's who has felt the pricks of life somewhat before his time. The well into which he was looking was as ancient as the village itself, and from his present position appeared as a long circular perspective ending in a shining disk of quivering water at a distance of a hundred feet down. There was a lining of green moss near the top, and nearer still the hart's-tongue fern.

He said to himself, in the melodramatic tones of a whimsical boy, that the schoolmaster had drawn at that well scores of times on a morning like this, and would never draw there any more. 'I've seen him look down into it, when he was tired with his drawing, just as I do now, and when he rested a bit before carrying the buckets home! But he was too clever to bide here any longer—a small sleepy place like this!'

A tear rolled from his eye into the depths of the well. The morning was a little foggy, and the boy's breathing unfurled itself as a thicker fog upon the still and heavy air. His thoughts were interrupted by a sudden outcry:

'Bring on that water, will ye, you idle young harlican!'[8]

It came from an old woman who had emerged from her door towards the garden gate of a green-thatched cottage not far off. The boy quickly waved a signal of assent, drew the water with what was a great effort for one of his stature, landed and emptied the big bucket into his own pair of smaller ones, and pausing a moment for breath, started with them across the patch of clammy greensward whereon the well stood— nearly in the centre of the little village, or rather hamlet of Marygreen.

It was as old-fashioned as it was small, and it rested in the lap of an undulating upland adjoining the North Wessex downs. Old as it was, however, the well-shaft was probably the only relic of the local history

---

7. Baggage, possessions.
8. This dialect word is a corruption of *harlequin*. Hardy's manuscript shows that he first wrote *scamp*. In a letter of 1904 he explained its meaning as "wild-looking urchin, object, scarecrow (as applied to a small boy)."

that remained absolutely unchanged. Many of the thatched and dorm-ered[9] dwelling-houses had been pulled down of late years, and many trees felled on the green. Above all, the original church, hump-backed, wood-turreted, and quaintly hipped,[1] had been taken down, and either cracked up into heaps of road-metal in the lane, or utilized as pig-sty walls, garden seats, guard-stones to fences, and rockeries in the flower-beds of the neighbourhood. In place of it a tall new building of modern Gothic design, unfamiliar to English eyes, had been erected on a new piece of ground by a certain obliterator of historic records who had run down from London and back in a day. The site whereon so long had stood the ancient temple to the Christian divinities was not even recorded on the green and level grass-plot that had immemorially been the church-yard, the obliterated graves being commemorated by eigh-teenpenny cast-iron crosses warranted to last five years.

I–2

Slender as was Jude Fawley's frame he bore the two brimming house-buckets of water to the cottage without resting. Over the door was a little rectangular piece of blue board, on which was painted in yellow letters, 'Drusilla Fawley, Baker.' Within the little lead panes of the window—this being one of the few old houses left—were five bottles of sweets, and three buns on a plate of the willow pattern.

While emptying the buckets at the back of the house he could hear an animated conversation in progress within-doors between his great-aunt, the Drusilla of the signboard, and some other villagers. Having seen the schoolmaster depart, they were summing up particulars of the event, and indulging in predictions of his future.

'And who's he? asked one, comparatively a stranger, when the boy entered.

'Well ye med[1] ask it, Mrs. Williams. He's my great-nephew—come since you was last this way.' The old inhabitant who answered was a tall, gaunt woman, who spoke tragically on the most trivial subject, and gave a phrase of her conversation to each auditor in turn. 'He come from Mellstock, down in South Wessex, about a year ago—worse luck for 'n, Belinda' (turning to the right) 'where his father was living, and was took wi' the shakings for death, and died in two days, as you know, Caroline' (turning to the left). 'It would ha' been a blessing if Goddy-mighty had took thee too, wi' thy mother and father, poor useless boy! But I've got him here to stay with me till I can see what's to be done with un, though I am obliged to let him earn any penny he can. Just now he's a-scaring of birds for Farmer Troutham. It keeps him out of

9. With dormer windows (projecting windows in a sloping roof).
1. With a projecting edge to the roof.
1. Might (dialect).

mischty. Why do ye turn away, Jude?' she continued, as the boy, feeling the impact of their glances like slaps upon his face, moved aside.

The local washerwoman replied that it was perhaps a very good plan of Miss or Mrs. Fawley's (as they called her indifferently) to have him with her—'to kip 'ee company in your loneliness, fetch water, shet the winder-shetters o' nights, and help in the bit o' baking.'

Miss Fawley doubted it. . . . 'Why didn't ye get the schoolmaster to take 'ee to Christminster wi' un, and make a scholar of 'ee,' she continued, in frowning pleasantry. 'I'm sure he couldn't ha' took a better one. The boy is crazy for books, that he is. It runs in our family rather. His cousin Sue is just the same—so I've heard; but I have not seen the child for years, though she was born in this place, within these four walls, as it happened. My niece and her husband, after they were married, didn't get a house of their own for some year or more; and then they only had one till—Well, I won't go into that. Jude, my child, don't *you* ever marry. 'Tisn't for the Fawleys to take that step any more. She, their only one, was like a child o' my own, Belinda, till the split come! Ah, that a little maid should know such changes!'

Jude, finding the general attention again centering on himself, went out to the bakehouse, where he ate the cake provided for his breakfast. The end of his spare time had now arrived, and emerging from the garden by getting over the hedge at the back he pursued a path northward, till he came to a wide and lonely depression in the general level of the upland, which was sown as a corn-field. This vast concave was the scene of his labours for Mr. Troutham the farmer, and he descended into the midst of it.

The brown surface of the field went right up towards the sky all round, where it was lost by degrees in the mist that shut out the actual verge and accentuated the solitude. The only marks on the uniformity of the scene were a rick of last year's produce standing in the midst of the arable, the rooks that rose at his approach, and the path athwart the fallow by which he had come, trodden now by he hardly knew whom, though once by many of his own dead family.

'How ugly it is here!' he murmured.

The fresh harrow-lines seemed to stretch like the channellings in a piece of new corduroy, lending a meanly utilitarian air to the expanse, taking away its gradations, and depriving it of all history beyond that of the few recent months, though to every clod and stone there really attached associations enough and to spare—echoes of songs from ancient harvest-days, of spoken words and of sturdy deeds. Every inch of ground had been the site, first or last, of energy, gaiety, horse-play, bickerings, weariness. Groups of gleaners had squatted in the sun on every square yard. Love-matches that had populated the adjoining hamlet had been made up there between reaping and carrying. Under the hedge which divided the field from a distant plantation girls had given themselves to lovers who would not turn their heads to look at them by the next harvest; and in that ancient corn-field many a man had made love-promises to a woman at whose voice he had trembled by the next seed-time after fulfilling them in the church adjoining. But this neither Jude nor the rooks around him considered. For them it was a lonely place, possessing, in the one view, only the quality of a work-ground, and in the other that of a granary good to feed in.

The boy stood under the rick before mentioned, and every few seconds used his clacker or rattle briskly. At each clack the rooks left off pecking, and rose and went away on their leisurely wings, burnished like tassets[2] of mail, afterwards wheeling back and regarding him warily, and descending to feed at a more respectful distance.

He sounded the clacker till his arm ached, and at length his heart grew sympathetic with the birds' thwarted desires. They seemed, like himself, to be living in a world which did not want them. Why should he frighten them away? They took upon them more and more the aspect of gentle friends and pensioners—the only friends he could claim as being in the least degree interested in him, for his aunt had often told him that she was not. He ceased his rattling, and they alighted anew.

'Poor little dears!' said Jude, aloud. 'You *shall* have some dinner— you shall. There is enough for us all. Farmer Troutham can afford to let you have some. Eat, then, my dear little birdies, and make a good meal!'

They stayed and ate, inky spots on the nut-brown soil, and Jude enjoyed their appetite. A magic thread of fellow-feeling united his own life with theirs. Puny and sorry as those lives were, they much resembled his own.

His clacker he had by this time thrown away from him, as being a mean and sordid instrument, offensive both to the birds and to himself as their friend. All at once he become conscious of a smart blow upon his buttocks, followed by a loud clack, which announced to his surprised senses that the clacker had been the instrument of offence used. The birds and Jude started up simultaneously, and the dazed eyes of the latter beheld the farmer in person, the great Troutham himself, his red face glaring down upon Jude's cowering frame, the clacker swinging in his hand.

'So it's "Eat, my dear birdies," is it, young man? "Eat, dear birdies," indeed! I'll tickle your breeches, and see if you say, "Eat, dear birdies," again in a hurry! And you've been idling at the school-master's too, instead of coming here, ha'n't ye, hey? That's how you earn your sixpence a day for keeping the rooks off my corn!'

Whilst saluting Jude's ears with this impassioned rhetoric, Troutham had seized his left hand with his own left, and swinging his slim

2. Parts of a suit of armor designed to protect the thighs.

frame round him at arm's-length, again struck Jude on the hind parts
with the flat side of Jude's own rattle, till the field echoed with the
blows, which were delivered once or twice at each revolution.

'Don't 'ee, sir—please don't 'ee!' cried the whirling child, as helpless
under the centrifugal tendency of his person as a hooked fish swinging
to land, and beholding the hill, the rick, the plantation, the path, and
the rooks going round and round him in an amazing circular race. 'I—
I—sir—only meant that—there was a good crop in the ground—I saw
'em sow it—and the rooks could have a little bit for dinner—and you
wouldn't miss it, sir—and Mr. Phillotson said I was to be kind to 'em—
O, O, O!'

This truthful explanation seemed to exasperate the farmer even
more than if Jude had stoutly denied saying anything at all; and he
still smacked the whirling urchin, the clacks of the instrument continuing to resound all across the field and as far as the ears of distant workers—who gathered thereupon that Jude was pursuing his business of
clacking with great assiduity—and echoing from the brand-new church
tower just behind the mist, towards the building of which structure the
farmer had largely subscribed, to testify his love for God and man.

Presently Troutham grew tired of his punitive task, and depositing
the quivering boy on his legs, took a sixpence from his pocket and gave
it him in payment for his day's work, telling him to go home and never
let him see him in one of those fields again.

Jude leaped out of arm's reach, and walked along the trackway weeping—not from the pain, though that was keen enough; not from the
perception of the flaw in the terrestrial scheme, by which what was
good for God's birds was bad for God's gardener; but with the awful
sense that he had wholly disgraced himself before he had been a year
in the parish, and hence might be a burden to his great-aunt for life.

With this shadow on his mind he did not care to show himself in
the village, and went homeward by a roundabout track behind a high
hedge and across a pasture. Here he beheld scores of coupled earthworms lying half their length on the surface of the damp ground, as
they always did in such weather at that time of the year. It was impossible to advance in regular steps without crushing some of them at
each tread.

Though Farmer Troutham had just hurt him, he was a boy who
could not himself bear to hurt anything. He had never brought home
a nest of young birds without lying awake in misery half the night after,
and often reinstating them and the nest in their original place the next
morning. He could scarcely bear to see trees cut down or lopped, from
a fancy that it hurt them; and late pruning, when the sap was up and
the tree bled profusely, had been a positive grief to him in his infancy.
This weakness of character, as it may be called, suggested that he was
the sort of man who was born to ache a good deal before the fall of

the curtain upon his unnecessary life should signify that all was well with him again. He carefully picked his way on tiptoe among the earthworms, without killing a single one.

On entering the cottage he found his aunt selling a penny loaf to a little girl, and when the customer was gone she said, 'Well, how do you come to be back here in the middle of the morning like this?'

'I'm turned away.'

'What?'

'Mr. Troutham have turned me away because I let the rooks have a few peckings of corn. And there's my wages—the last I shall ever hae!'

He threw the sixpence tragically on the table.

'Ah!' said his aunt, suspending her breath. And she opened upon him a lecture on how she would now have him all the spring upon her hands doing nothing. 'If you can't skeer birds, what can ye do? There! don't ye look so deedy![3] Farmer Troutham is not so much better than myself, come to that. But 'tis as Job said, "Now they that are younger than I have me in derision, whose fathers I would have disdained to have set with the dogs of my flock."[4] His father was my father's journeyman, anyhow, and I must have been a fool to let 'ee go to work for 'n, which I shouldn't ha' done but to keep 'ee out of mischty.'

More angry with Jude for demeaning her by coming there than for dereliction of duty, she rated him primarily from that point of view, and only secondarily from a moral one.

'Not that you should have let the birds eat what Farmer Troutham planted. Of course you was wrong in that. Jude, Jude, why didstn't go off with that schoolmaster of thine to Christminster or somewhere? But, O no—poor or'nary[5] child—there never was any sprawl[6] on thy side of the family, and never will be!'

'Where is this beautiful city, aunt—this place where Mr. Phillotson is gone to?' asked the boy, after meditating in silence.

'Lord! you ought to know where the city of Christminster is. Near a score of miles from here. It is a place much too good for you ever to have much to do with, poor boy, I'm a-thinking.'

'And will Mr. Phillotson always be there?'

'How can I tell?'

'Couldn't I go to see him?'

'Lord, no! You didn't grow up hereabout, or you wouldn't ask such as that. We've never had anything to do with folk in Christminster, nor folk in Christminster with we.'

Jude went out, and, feeling more than ever his existence to be an undemanded one, he lay down upon his back on a heap of litter near

3. Serious (dialect).
4. Job 30.1.
5. Mediocre, inferior (dialect).
6. Energy, go (dialect).

the pig-sty. The fog had by this time become more translucent, and the position of the sun could be seen through it. He pulled his straw hat over his face, and peered through the interstices of the plaiting at the white brightness, vaguely reflecting. Growing up brought responsibilities, he found. Events did not rhyme quite as he had thought. Nature's logic was too horrid for him to care for. That mercy towards one set of creatures was cruelty towards another sickened his sense of harmony. As you got older, and felt yourself to be at the centre of your time, and not at a point in its circumference, as you had felt when you were little, you were seized with a sort of shuddering, he perceived. All around you there seemed to be something glaring, garish, rattling, and the noises and glares hit upon the little cell called your life, and shook it, and warped it.

If he could only prevent himself growing up! He did not want to be a man.

Then, like the natural boy, he forgot his despondency, and sprang up. During the remainder of the morning he helped his aunt, and in the afternoon, when there was nothing more to be done, he went into the village. Here he asked a man whereabouts Christminster lay.

'Christminster? O, well, out by there yonder; though I've never bin there—not I. I've never had any business at such a place.'

The man pointed north-eastward, in the very direction where lay that field in which Jude had so disgraced himself. There was something unpleasant about the coincidence for the moment, but the fearsomeness of this fact rather increased his curiosity about the city. The farmer had said he was never to be seen in that field again; yet Christminster lay across it, and the path was a public one. So, stealing out of the hamlet he descended into the same hollow which had witnessed his punishment in the morning, never swerving an inch from the path, and climbing up the long and tedious ascent on the other side, till the track joined the highway by a little clump of trees. Here the ploughed land ended, and all before him was bleak open down.

I–3

Not a soul was visible on the hedgeless highway, or on either side of it, and the white road seemed to ascend and diminish till it joined the sky. At the very top it was crossed at right angles by a green 'ridgeway'— the Icknield Street[1] and original Roman road through the district. This ancient track ran east and west for many miles, and down almost to within living memory had been used for driving flocks and herds to fairs and markets. But it was now neglected and overgrown.

The boy had never before strayed so far north as this from the nestling hamlet in which he had been deposited by the carrier from a

1. Ancient road crossing England from Norfolk in the east to Cornwall in the southwest.

railway station southward, one dark evening some few months earlier, and till now he had no suspicion that such a wide, flat, low-lying country lay so near at hand, under the very verge of his upland world. The whole northern semicircle between east and west, to a distance of forty or fifty miles, spread itself before him; a bluer, moister atmosphere, evidently, than that he breathed up here.

Not far from the road stood a weather-beaten old barn of reddish-gray brick and tile. It was known as the Brown House by the people of the locality. He was about to pass it when he perceived a ladder against the eaves; and the reflection that the higher he got, the further he could see, led Jude to stand and regard it. On the slope of the roof two men were repairing the tiling. He turned into the ridgeway and drew towards the barn.

When he had wistfully watched the workmen for some time he took courage, and ascended the ladder till he stood beside them.

'Well, my lad, and what may you want up here?'

'I wanted to know where the city of Christminster is, if you please.'

'Christminster is out across there, by that clump. You can see it—at least you can on a clear day. Ah, no, you can't now.'

The other tiler, glad of any kind of diversion from the monotony of his labour, had also turned to look towards the quarter designated. 'You can't often see it in weather like this,' he said. 'The time I've noticed it is when the sun is going down in a blaze of flame, and it looks like—I don't know what.'

'The heavenly Jerusalem,' suggested the serious urchin.

'Ay—though I should never ha' thought of it myself. . . . But I can't see no Christminster to-day.'

The boy strained his eyes also; yet neither could he see the far-off city. He descended from the barn, and abandoning Christminster with the versatility of his age he walked along the ridge-track, looking for any natural objects of interest that might lie in the banks thereabouts. When he repassed the barn to go back to Marygreen he observed that the ladder was still in its place, but that the men had finished their day's work and gone away.

It was waning towards evening; there was still a faint mist, but it had cleared a little except in the damper tracts of subjacent country and along the river-courses. He thought again of Christminster, and wished, since he had come two or three miles from his aunt's house on purpose, that he could have seen for once this attractive city of which he had been told. But even if he waited here it was hardly likely that the air would clear before night. Yet he was loth to leave the spot, for the northern expanse became lost to view on retreating towards the village only a few hundred yards.

He ascended the ladder to have one more look at the point the men had designated, and perched himself on the highest rung, overlying the tiles. He might not be able to come so far as this for many days. Perhaps if he prayed, the wish to see Christminster might be forwarded. People said that, if you prayed, things sometimes came to you, even though they sometimes did not. He had read in a tract that a man who had begun to build a church, and had no money to finish it, knelt down and prayed, and the money came in by the next post. Another man tried the same experiment, and the money did not come; but he found afterwards that the breeches he knelt in were made by a wicked Jew. This was not discouraging, and turning on the ladder Jude knelt on the third rung, where, resting against those above it, he prayed that the mist might rise.

He then seated himself again, and waited. In the course of ten or fifteen minutes the thinning mist dissolved altogether from the northern horizon, as it had already done elsewhere, and about a quarter of an hour before the time of sunset the westward clouds parted, the sun's position being partially uncovered, and the beams streaming out in visible lines between two bars of slaty cloud. The boy immediately looked back in the old direction.

Some way within the limits of the stretch of landscape, points of light like the topaz gleamed. The air increased in transparency with the lapse of minutes, till the topaz points showed themselves to be the vanes, windows, wet roof slates, and other shining spots upon the spires, domes, freestone-work, and varied outlines that were faintly revealed. It was Christminster, unquestionably; either directly seen, or miraged in the peculiar atmosphere.

The spectator gazed on and on till the windows and vanes lost their shine, going out almost suddenly like extinguished candles. The vague city became veiled in mist. Turning to the west, he saw that the sun had disappeared. The foreground of the scene had grown funereally dark, and near objects put on the hues and shapes of chimæras.[2]

He anxiously descended the ladder, and started homewards at a run, trying not to think of giants, Herne the Hunter,[3] Apollyon[4] lying in wait for Christian, or of the captain with the bleeding hole in his forehead and the corpses round him that remutinied every night on board the bewitched ship.[5] He knew that he had grown out of belief in these horrors, yet he was glad when he saw the church tower and the lights in the cottage windows, even though this was not the home of his birth, and his great-aunt did not care much about him.

Inside and round about that old woman's 'shop' window, with its twenty-four little panes set in leadwork, the glass of some of them

2. Mythical monsters.
3. According to medieval legend, a ghostly hunter who haunted Windsor Great Park.
4. Monster in Bunyan's *Pilgrim's Progress*.
5. In a story by the German romantic writer Wilhelm Hauff (1802–1827).

oxidized with age, so that you could hardly see the poor penny articles exhibited within, and forming part of a stock which a strong man could have carried, Jude had his outer being for some long tideless time. But his dreams were as gigantic as his surroundings were small.

Through the solid barrier of cold cretaceous upland to the northward he was always beholding a gorgeous city—the fancied place he had likened to the new Jerusalem, though there was perhaps more of the painter's imagination and less of the diamond merchant's in his dreams thereof than in those of the Apocalyptic writer.[6] And the city acquired a tangibility, a permanence, and hold on his life, mainly from the one nucleus of fact that the man for whose knowledge and purposes he had so much reverence was actually living there; not only so, but living among the more thoughtful and mentally shining ones therein.

In sad wet seasons, though he knew it must rain at Christminster too, he could hardly believe that it rained so drearily there. Whenever he could get away from the confines of the hamlet for an hour or two, which was not often, he would steal off to the Brown House on the hill and strain his eyes persistently; sometimes to be rewarded by the sight of a dome or spire, at other times by a little smoke, which in his estimate had some of the mysticism of incense.

Then the day came when it suddenly occurred to him that if he ascended to the point of view after dark, or possibly went a mile or two further, he would see the night lights of the city. It would be necessary to come back alone, but even that consideration did not deter him, for he could throw a little manliness into his mood, no doubt.

The project was duly executed. It was not late when he arrived at the place of outlook, only just after dusk; but a black north-east sky, accompanied by a wind from the same quarter, made the occasion dark enough. He was rewarded; but what he saw was not the lamps in rows, as he had half expected. No individual light was visible, only a halo or glow-fog over-arching the place against the black heavens behind it, making the light and the city seem distant but a mile or so.

He set himself to wonder on the exact point in the glow where the schoolmaster might be—he who never communicated with anybody at Marygreen now; who was as if dead to them here. In the glow he seemed to see Phillotson promenading at ease, like one of the forms in Nebuchadnezzar's furnace.[7]

He had heard that breezes travelled at the rate of ten miles an hour, and the fact now came into his mind. He parted his lips as he faced the north-east, and drew in the wind as if it were a sweet liquor.

---

6. The phrase "the new Jerusalem" occurs in Revelation 3.12. The original Greek title of Revelation is *Apocalypsis*.
7. "I see four men loose, walking in the midst of the fire, and they have no hurt" (Daniel 3.25).

'You,' he said, addressing the breeze caressingly, 'were in Christminster city between one and two hours ago, floating along the streets,
pulling round the weather-cocks, touching Mr. Phillotson's face, being
breathed by him; and now you are here, breathed by me—you, the very
same.'

Suddenly there came along this wind, something towards him—a
message from the place—from some soul residing there, it seemed.
Surely it was the sound of bells, the voice of the city, faint and musical,
calling to him, 'We are happy here!'

He had become entirely lost to his bodily situation during this mental leap, and only got back to it by a rough recalling. A few yards below
the brow of the hill on which he paused a team of horses made its
appearance, having reached the place by dint of half an hour's serpen-
tine progress from the bottom of the immense declivity. They had a
load of coals behind them—a fuel that could only be got into the
upland by this particular route. They were accompanied by a carter, a
second man, and a boy, who now kicked a large stone behind one of
the wheels, and allowed the panting animals to have a long rest, while
those in charge took a flagon off the load and indulged in a drink round.

They were elderly men, and had genial voices. Jude addressed them,
inquiring if they had come from Christminster.

'Heaven forbid, with this load!' said they.

'The place I mean is that one yonder.' He was getting so romantically
attached to Christminster that, like a young lover alluding to his mistress, he felt bashful at mentioning its name again. He pointed to the
light in the sky—hardly perceptible to their older eyes.

'Yes. There do seem a spot a bit brighter in the nor'-east than elsewhere, though I shouldn't ha' noticed it myself, and no doubt it med
be Christminster.'

Here a little book of tales which Jude had tucked up under his arm,
having brought them to read on his way hither before it grew dark,
slipped and fell into the road. The carter eyed him while he picked it
up and straightened the leaves.

'Ah, young man,' he observed, 'you'd have to get your head screwed
on t'other way before you could read what they read there.'

'Why?' asked the boy.

'O, they never look at anything that folks like we can understand,'
the carter continued, by way of passing the time. 'On'y foreign tongues
used in the days of the Tower of Babel, when no two families spoke
alike.[8] They read that sort of thing as fast as a night-hawk will whir.
'Tis all learning there—nothing but learning, except religion. And
that's learning too, for I never could understand it. Yes, 'tis a serious-

8. Genesis 11.

minded place. Not but there's wenches in the streets o' nights. . . . You
know, I suppose, that they raise pa'sons there like radishes in a bed?
And though it do take—how many years, Bob?—five years to turn a
lirruping[9] hobble-de-hoy chap into a solemn preaching man with no
corrupt passions, they'll do it, if it can be done, and polish un off like
the workmen they be, and turn un out wi' a long face, and a long black
coat and waistcoat, and a religious collar and hat, same as they used
to wear in the Scriptures, so that his own mother wouldn't know un
sometimes. . . . There, 'tis their business, like anybody else's.'

'But how should you know—'

'Now don't you interrupt, my boy. Never interrupt your senyers.
Move the fore hoss aside, Bobby; here's some'at coming. . . . You must
mind that I be a-talking of the college life. 'Em lives on a lofty level;
there's no gainsaying it, though I myself med not think much of 'em.
As we be here in our bodies on this high ground, so be they in their
minds—nobleminded men enough, no doubt—some of 'em—able to
earn hundreds by thinking out loud. And some on 'em be strong young
fellows that can earn a'most as much in silver cups. As for music, there's
beautiful music everywhere in Christminster. You med be religious, or
you med not, but you can't help striking in your homely note with the
rest. And there's a street in the place—the main street—that ha'n't
another like it in the world. I should think I did know a little about
Christminster!'

By this time the horses had recovered breath and bent to their collars
again. Jude, throwing a last adoring look at the distant halo, turned
and walked beside his remarkably well-informed friend, who had no
objection to tell him as they moved on more yet of the city—its towers
and halls and churches. The waggon turned into a cross-road,
whereupon Jude thanked the carter warmly for his information, and
said he only wished he could talk half as well about Christminster as
he.

'Well, 'tis oonly what has come in my way,' said the carter unboast-
fully. 'I've never been there, no more than you; but I've picked up the
knowledge here and there, and you be welcome to it. A-getting about
the world as I do, and mixing with all classes of society, one can't help
hearing of things. A friend o' mine, that used to clane the boots at the
Crozier Hotel in Christminster when he was in his prime, why, I
knowed un as well as my own brother in his later years.'

Jude continued his walk homeward alone, pondering so deeply that
he forgot to feel timid. He suddenly grew older. It had been the yearning of his heart to find something to anchor on, to cling to—for some
place which he could call admirable. Should he find that place in this
city if he could get there? Would it be a spot in which, without fear

9. Slouching, ungainly (dialect).

of farmers, or hindrance, or ridicule, he could watch and wait, and set himself to some mighty undertaking like the men of old of whom he had heard? As the halo had been to his eyes when gazing at it a quarter of an hour earlier, so was the spot mentally to him as he pursued his dark way.

'It is a city of light,' he said to himself.

'The tree of knowledge grows there,' he added a few steps further on.

'It is a place that teachers of men spring from and go to.'

'It is what you may call a castle, manned by scholarship and religion.'

After this figure he was silent a long while, till he added:

'It would just suit me.'

I–4

Walking somewhat slowly by reason of his concentration, the boy— an ancient man in some phases of thought, much younger than his years in others—was overtaken by a light-footed pedestrian, whom, notwithstanding the gloom, he could perceive to be wearing an extraordinarily tall hat, a swallow-tailed coat, and a watch-chain that danced madly and threw around scintillations of sky-light as its owner swung along upon a pair of thin legs and noiseless boots. Jude, beginning to feel lonely, endeavoured to keep up with him.

'Well, my man! I'm in a hurry, so you'll have to walk pretty fast if you keep alongside of me. Do you know who I am?'

'Yes, I think. Physician Vilbert?'

'Ah—I'm known everywhere, I see! That comes of being a public benefactor.'

Vilbert was an itinerant quack-doctor, well known to the rustic population, and absolutely unknown to anybody else, as he, indeed, took care to be, to avoid inconvenient investigations. Cottagers formed his only patients, and his Wessex-wide repute was among them alone. His position was humbler and his field more obscure than those of the quacks with capital and an organized system of advertising. He was, in fact, a survival. The distances he traversed on foot were enormous, and extended nearly the whole length and breadth of Wessex. Jude had one day seen him selling a pot of coloured lard to an old woman as a certain cure for a bad leg, the woman arranging to pay a guinea, in instalments of a shilling a fortnight, for the precious salve, which, according to the physician, could only be obtained from a particular animal which grazed on Mount Sinai, and was to be captured only at great risk to life and limb. Jude, though he already had his doubts about this gentleman's medicines, felt him to be unquestionably a travelled personage, and one who might be a trustworthy source of information on matters not strictly professional.

'I s'pose you've been to Christminster, Physician?'

'I have—many times,' replied the long thin man. 'That's one of my centres.'

'It's a wonderful city for scholarship and religion?'

'You'd say so, my boy, if you'd seen it. Why, the very sons of the old women who do the washing of the colleges can talk in Latin—not good Latin, that I admit, as a critic: dog-Latin[1]—cat-Latin, as we used to call it in my undergraduate days.'

'And Greek?'

'Well—that's more for the men who are in training for bishops, that they may be able to read the New Testament in the original.'

'I want to learn Latin and Greek myself.'

'A lofty desire. You must get a grammar of each tongue.'

'I mean to go to Christminster some day.'

'Whenever you do, you say that Physician Vilbert is the only pro-prietor of those celebrated pills that infallibly cure all disorders of the alimentary system, as well as asthma and shortness of breath. Two and threepence a box—specially licensed by the government stamp.'

'Can you get me the grammars if I promise to say it hereabout?'

'I'll sell you mine with pleasure—those I used as a student.'

'O, thank you, sir!' said Jude gratefully, but in gasps, for the amazing speed of the physician's walk kept him in a dog-trot which was giving him a stitch in the side.

'I think you'd better drop behind, my young man. Now I'll tell you what I'll do. I'll get you the grammars, and give you a first lesson, if you'll remember, at every house in the village, to recommend Physician Vilbert's golden ointment, life-drops, and female pills.'

'Where will you be with the grammars?'

'I shall be passing here this day fortnight at precisely the hour of five-and-twenty minutes past seven. My movements are as truly timed as those of the planets in their courses.'

'Here I'll be to meet you,' said Jude.

'With orders for my medicines?'

'Yes, Physician.'

Jude then dropped behind, waited a few minutes to recover breath, and went home with a consciousness of having struck a blow for Christ-minster.

Through the intervening fortnight he ran about and smiled out-wardly at his inward thoughts, as if they were people meeting and nodding to him—smiled with that singularly beautiful irradiation which is seen to spread on young faces at the inception of some glorious idea, as if a supernatural lamp were held inside their transparent natures, giving rise to the flattering fancy that heaven lies about them.[2]

---

1. Bad Latin. ("Cat-Latin" seems to be Physician Vilbert's invention.)
2. "Heaven lies about us in our infancy" (Wordsworth, Ode: Intimations of Immortality).

He honestly performed his promise to the man of many cures, in whom he now sincerely believed, walking miles hither and thither among the surrounding hamlets as the physician's agent in advance. On the evening appointed he stood motionless on the plateau, at the place where he had parted from Vilbert, and there awaited his approach. The road-physician was fairly up to time; but, to the surprise of Jude on striking into his pace, which the pedestrian did not diminish by a single unit of force, the latter seemed hardly to recognize his young companion, though with the lapse of the fortnight the evenings had grown light. Jude thought it might perhaps be owing to his wearing another hat, and he saluted the physician with dignity.

science reference (physics)

'Well, my boy?' said the latter abstractedly.

'I've come,' said Jude.

'You? who are you? O yes—to be sure! Got any orders, lad?'

'Yes.' And Jude told him the names and addresses of the cottagers who were willing to test the virtues of the world-renowned pills and salve. The quack mentally registered these with great care.

'And the Latin and Greek grammars?' Jude's voice trembled with anxiety.

'What about them?'

'You were to bring me yours, that you used before you took your degree.'

'Ah, yes, yes! Forgot all about it—all! So many lives depending on my attention, you see, my man, that I can't give so much thought as I would like to other things.'

Jude controlled himself sufficiently long to make sure of the truth; and he repeated, in a voice of dry misery, 'You haven't brought 'em!'

'No. But you must get me some more orders from sick people, and I'll bring the grammars next time.'

Jude dropped behind. He was an unsophisticated boy, but the gift of sudden insight which is sometimes vouchsafed to children showed him all at once what shoddy humanity the quack was made of. There was to be no intellectual light from this source. The leaves dropped from his imaginary crown of laurel; he turned to a gate, leant against it, and cried bitterly.

The disappointment was followed by an interval of blankness. He might, perhaps, have obtained grammars from Alfredston, but to do that required money, and a knowledge of what books to order; and though physically comfortable, he was in such absolute dependence as to be without a farthing of his own.

At this date Mr. Phillotson sent for his pianoforte, and it gave Jude a lead. Why should he not write to the schoolmaster, and ask him to be so kind as to get him the grammars in Christminster? He might slip a letter inside the case of the instrument, and it would be sure to reach the desired eyes. Why not ask him to send any old second-hand copies, which would have the charm of being mellowed by the university atmosphere?

To tell his aunt of his intention would be to defeat it. It was necessary to act alone.

After a further consideration of a few days he did act, and on the day of the piano's departure, which happened to be his next birthday,[3] clandestinely placed the letter inside the packing-case, directed to his much-admired friend; being afraid to reveal the operation to his aunt Drusilla, lest she should discover his motive, and compel him to abandon his scheme.

The piano was despatched, and Jude waited days and weeks, calling every morning at the cottage post-office before his great-aunt was stirring. At last a packet did indeed arrive at the village, and he saw from the ends of it that it contained two thin books. He took it away into a lonely place, and sat down on a felled elm to open it.

Ever since his first ecstasy or vision of Christminster and its possibilities, Jude had meditated much and curiously on the probable sort of process that was involved in turning the expressions of one language into those of another. He concluded that a grammar of the required tongue would contain, primarily, a rule, prescription, or clue of the nature of a secret cipher, which, once known, would enable him, by merely applying it, to change at will all words of his own speech into those of the foreign one. His childish idea was, in fact, a pushing to the extremity of mathematical precision what is everywhere known as Grimm's Law[4]—an aggrandizement of rough rules to ideal completeness. Thus he assumed that the words of the required language were always to be found somewhere latent in the words of the given language by those who had the art to uncover them, such art being furnished by the books aforesaid.

When, therefore, having noted that the packet bore the postmark of Christminster, he cut the string, opened the volumes, and turned to the Latin grammar, which chanced to come uppermost, he could scarcely believe his eyes.

The book was an old one—thirty years old, soiled, scribbled wantonly over with a strange name in every variety of enmity to the letterpress, and marked at random with dates twenty years earlier than his own day. But this was not the cause of Jude's amazement. He learnt for the first time that there was no law of transmutation, as in his innocence he had supposed (there was, in some degree, but the grammarian did not recognize it), but that every word in both Latin and Greek was to be individually committed to memory at the cost of years of plodding.

---

3. "Eleventh birthday," according to Hardy's manuscript.
4. Concerned with consonant changes between related languages; named after Jacob Grimm (1785–1863), German philologist and folklorist.

Jude flung down the books, lay backward along the broad trunk of the elm, and was an utterly miserable boy for the space of a quarter of an hour. As he had often done before, he pulled his hat over his face and watched the sun peering insidiously at him through the interstices of the straw. This was Latin and Greek, then, was it, this grand delusion! The charm he had supposed in store for him was really a labour like that of Israel in Egypt.[5]

What brains they must have in Christminster and the great schools, he presently thought, to learn words one by one up to tens of thousands! There were no brains in his head equal to this business; and as the little sun-rays continued to stream in through his hat at him, he wished he had never seen a book, that he might never see another, that he had never been born.

Somebody might have come along that way who would have asked him his trouble, and might have cheered him by saying that his notions were further advanced than those of his grammarian. But nobody did come, because nobody does; and under the crushing recognition of his gigantic error Jude continued to wish himself out of the world.

I–5

During the three or four succeeding years a quaint and singular vehicle might have been discerned moving along the lanes and by-roads near Marygreen, driven in a quaint and singular way.

In the course of a month or two after the receipt of the books Jude had grown callous to the shabby trick played him by the dead languages. In fact, his disappointment at the nature of those tongues had, after a while, been the means of still further glorifying the erudition of Christminster. To acquire languages, departed or living, in spite of such obstinacies as he now knew them inherently to possess, was a herculean performance which gradually led him on to a greater interest in it than in the presupposed patent process. The mountain-weight of material under which the ideas lay in those dusty volumes called the classics piqued him into a dogged, mouselike subtlety of attempt to move it piecemeal.

He had endeavoured to make his presence tolerable to his crusty maiden aunt by assisting her to the best of his ability, and the business of the little cottage bakery had grown in consequence. An aged horse with a hanging head had been purchased for eight pounds at a sale, a creaking cart with a whity-brown tilt obtained for a few pounds more, and in this turn-out it became Jude's business thrice a week to carry loaves of bread to the villagers and solitary cotters[1] immediately around Marygreen.

---

5. "And the Egyptians made the children of Israel to serve with rigour: And they made their lives bitter with hard bondage . . ." (Exodus 1.13–14).
1. Occupants of cottages belonging to a farm.

The singularity aforesaid lay, after all, less in the conveyance itself than in Jude's manner of conducting it along its route. Its interior was the scene of most of Jude's education by "private study." As soon as the horse had learnt the road and the houses at which he was to pause awhile, the boy, seated in front, would slip the reins over his arm, ingeniously fix open, by means of a strap attached to the tilt, the volume he was reading, spread the dictionary on his knees, and plunge into the simpler passages from Caesar, Virgil, or Horace, as the case might be, in his purblind stumbling way, and with an expenditure of labour that would have made a tender-hearted pedagogue shed tears; yet somehow getting at the meaning of what he read, and divining rather than beholding the spirit of the original, which often to his mind was something else than that which he was taught to look for.

The only copies he had been able to lay hands on were old Delphin editions,[2] because they were superseded, and therefore cheap. But, bad for idle school-boys, it did so happen that they were passably good for him. The hampered and lonely itinerant conscientiously covered up the marginal readings, and used them merely on points of construction, as he would have used a comrade or tutor who should have happened to be passing by. And though Jude may have had little chance of becoming a scholar by these rough and ready means, he was in the way of getting into the groove he wished to follow.

While he was busied with these ancient pages, which had already been thumbed by hands possibly in the grave, digging out the thoughts of these minds so remote yet so near, the bony old horse pursued his rounds, and Jude would be aroused from the woes of Dido[3] by the stoppage of his cart and the voice of some old woman crying, 'Two to-day, baker, and I return this stale one.'

He was frequently met in the lanes by pedestrians and others without his seeing them, and by degrees the people of the neighbourhood began to talk about his method of combining work and play (such they considered his reading to be), which, though probably convenient enough to himself, was not altogether a safe proceeding for other travellers along the same roads. There were murmurs. Then a private resident of an adjoining place informed the local policeman that the baker's boy should not be allowed to read while driving, and insisted that it was the constable's duty to catch him in the act, and take him to the police court at Alfredston, and get him fined for dangerous practices on the highway. The policeman thereupon lay in wait for Jude, and one day accosted him and cautioned him.

---

2. Series of Latin classics originally published in France about 1670.
3. Queen of Carthage who committed suicide after being abandoned by Aeneas: the story is told by Virgil (*Aeneid* 4).

As Jude had to get up at three o'clock in the morning to heat the oven, and mix and set in the bread that he distributed later in the day, he was obliged to go to bed at night immediately after laying the sponge;[4] so that if he could not read his classics on the highways he could hardly study at all. The only thing to be done was, therefore, to keep a sharp eye ahead and around him as well as he could in the circumstances, and slip away his books as soon as anybody loomed in the distance, the policeman in particular. To do that official justice, he did not put himself much in the way of Jude's bread-cart, considering that in such a lonely district the chief danger was to Jude himself, and often on seeing the white tilt over the hedges he would move in another direction.

On a day when Fawley was getting quite advanced, being now about sixteen, and had been stumbling through the 'Carmen Sæculare,'[5] on his way home, he found himself to be passing over the high edge of the plateau by the Brown House. The light had changed, and it was the sense of this which had caused him to look up. The sun was going down, and the full moon was rising simultaneously behind the woods in the opposite quarter. His mind had become so impregnated with the poem that, in a moment of the same impulsive emotion which years before had caused him to kneel on the ladder, he stopped the horse, alighted, and glancing round to see that nobody was in sight, knelt down on the roadside bank with open book. He turned first to the shiny goddess, who seemed to look so softly and critically at his doings, then to the disappearing luminary on the other hand, as he began:

'Phoebe silvarumque potens Diana!'[6]

The horse stood still till he had finished the hymn, which Jude repeated under the sway of a polytheistic fancy that he would never have thought of humouring in broad daylight.

Reaching home, he mused over his curious superstition, innate or acquired, in doing this, and the strange forgetfulness which had led to such a lapse from common-sense and custom in one who wished, next to being a scholar, to be a Christian divine. It had all come of reading heathen works exclusively. The more he thought of it the more convinced he was of his inconsistency. He began to wonder whether he could be reading quite the right books for his object in life. Certainly there seemed little harmony between this pagan literature and the mediæval colleges at Christminster, that ecclesiastical romance in stone.

4. Dough left to ferment for several hours before baking.
5. Latin poem by Horace, written 17 B.C.
6. "Phoebus and Diana, queen of the woods . . ." This invocation to the moon is the opening line of the Carmen Saeculare.

Ultimately he decided that in his sheer love of reading he had taken up a wrong emotion for a Christian young man. He had dabbled in Clarke's Homer,[7] but had never yet worked much at the New Testament in the Greek, though he possessed a copy, obtained by post from a second-hand bookseller. He abandoned the now familiar Ionic[8] for a new dialect, and for a long time onward limited his reading almost entirely to the Gospels and Epistles in Griesbach's text.[9] Moreover, on going into Alfredston one day, he was introduced to patristic literature by finding at the bookseller's some volumes of the Fathers[1] which had been left behind by an insolvent clergyman of the neighbourhood.

As another outcome of this change of groove he visited on Sundays all the churches within a walk, and deciphered the Latin inscriptions on fifteenth-century brasses and tombs. On one of these pilgrimages he met with a hunchbacked old woman of great intelligence, who read everything she could lay her hands on, and she told him more yet of the romantic charms of the city of light and lore. Thither he resolved as firmly as ever to go.

But how live in that city? At present he had no income at all. He had no trade or calling of any dignity or stability whatever on which he could subsist while carrying out an intellectual labour which might spread over many years.

What was most required by citizens? Food, clothing, and shelter. An income from any work in preparing the first would be too meagre; for making the second he felt a distaste; the preparation of the third requisite he inclined to. They built in a city; therefore he would learn to build. He thought of his unknown uncle, his cousin Susanna's father, an ecclesiastical worker in metal, and somehow mediæval art in any material was a trade for which he had rather a fancy. He could not go far wrong in following his uncle's footsteps, and engaging himself awhile with the carcases that contained the scholar souls.

As a preliminary he obtained some small blocks of freestone, metal not being available, and suspendiᵤg his studies awhile, occupied his spare half-hours in copying the heads and capitals in his parish church.

There was a stone-mason of a humble kind in Alfredston, and as soon as he had found a substitute for himself in his aunt's little business, he offered his services to this man for a trifling wage. Here Jude had the opportunity of learning at least the rudiments of freestone-working. Some time later he went to a church-builder in the same

7. Samuel Clarke's edition of Homer was published in 1818. Hardy's own copy of this book still exists (see below, p. 31, note 1).
8. The most important of the ancient Greek dialects.
9. Before he was twenty, Hardy had studied the New Testament in the original Greek from "a new text, Griesbach's, that he had seen advertised as the most correct" (*Life*, p. 29). Griesbach was a German theologian; his edition had been published in 1775.
1. Christian writers of the first five centuries A.D.

place, and under the architect's direction became handy at restoring the dilapidated masonries of several village churches round about.

Not forgetting that he was only following up this handicraft as a prop to lean on while he prepared those greater engines which he flattered himself would be better fitted for him, he yet was interested in his pursuit on its own account. He now had lodgings during the week in the little town, whence he returned to Marygreen village every Saturday evening. And thus he reached and passed his nineteenth year.

1–6

At this memorable date of his life he was, one Saturday, returning from Alfredston to Marygreen about three o'clock in the afternoon. It was fine, warm, and soft summer weather, and he walked with his tools at his back, his little chisels clinking faintly against the larger ones in his basket. It being the end of the week he had left work early, and had come out of the town by a roundabout route which he did not usually frequent, having promised to call at a flour-mill near Cresscombe to execute a commission for his aunt.

He was in an enthusiastic mood. He seemed to see his way to living comfortably in Christminster in the course of a year or two, and knocking at the doors of one of those strongholds of learning of which he had dreamed so much. He might, of course, have gone there now, in some capacity or other, but he preferred to enter the city with a little more assurance as to means than he could be said to feel at present. A warm self-content suffused him when he considered what he had already done. Now and then as he went along he turned to face the peeps of country on either side of him. But he hardly saw them; the act was an automatic repetition of what he had been accustomed to do when less occupied; and the one matter which really engaged him was the mental estimate of his progress thus far.

'I have acquired quite an average student's power to read the common ancient classics, Latin in particular.' This was true, Jude possessing a facility in that language which enabled him with great ease to himself to beguile his lonely walks by imaginary conversations therein.

'I have read two books of the Iliad, besides being pretty familiar with passages such as the speech of Phoenix in the ninth book, the fight of Hector and Ajax in the fourteenth, the appearance of Achilles unarmed and his heavenly armour in the eighteenth, and the funeral games in the twenty-third.[1] I have also done some Hesiod, a little scrap of Thu-

1. This list corresponds exactly to a penciled list of his favorite passages made by the young Hardy in his copy of Clarke's Homer; the book, inscribed "Thomas Hardy 1858," is now in the Dorset County Museum (W. R. Rutland, *Thomas Hardy* [New York, 1938] 21–22).

cydides, and a lot of the Greek Testament. . . . I wish there was only one dialect, all the same.

'I have done some mathematics, including the first six and the eleventh and twelfth books of Euclid; and algebra as far as simple equations.

'I know something of the Fathers, and something of Roman and English history.

'These things are only a beginning. But I shall not make much further advance here, from the difficulty of getting books. Hence I must next concentrate all my energies on settling in Christminster. Once there I shall so advance, with the assistance I shall there get, that my present knowledge will appear to me but as childish ignorance. I must save money, and I will; and one of those colleges shall open its doors to me—shall welcome whom now it would spurn, if I wait twenty years for the welcome.

'I'll be D.D.[2] before I have done!'

And then he continued to dream, and thought he might become even a bishop by leading a pure, energetic, wise, Christian life. And what an example he would set! If his income were £5000 a year, he would give away £4500 in one form and another, and live sumptuously (for him) on the remainder. Well, on second thoughts, a bishop was absurd. He would draw the line at an archdeacon. Perhaps a man could be as good and as learned and as useful in the capacity of archdeacon as in that of bishop. Yet he thought of the bishop again.

'Meanwhile I will read, as soon as I am settled in Christminster, the books I have not been able to get hold of here: Livy, Tacitus, Herodotus, Æschylus, Sophocles, Aristophanes—'

'Ha, ha, ha! Hoity-toity!' The sounds were expressed in light voices on the other side of the hedge, but he did not notice them. His thoughts went on:

'—Euripides, Plato, Aristotle, Lucretius, Epictetus, Seneca, Antoninus. Then I must master other things: the Fathers thoroughly; Bede and ecclesiastical history generally; a smattering of Hebrew—I only know the letters as yet—'

'Hoity-toity!'

'—but I can work hard. I have staying power in abundance, thank God! and it is that which tells. . . . Yes, Christminster shall be my Alma Mater; and I'll be her beloved son, in whom she shall be well pleased.'[3]

In his deep concentration on these transactions of the future Jude's walk had slackened, and he was now standing quite still, looking at the ground as though the future were thrown thereon by a magic lantern. On a sudden something smacked him sharply in the ear, and he

2. Doctor of Divinity.
3. "And lo a voice from heaven, saying, This is my beloved Son, in whom I am well pleased" (Matthew 3.17). The passage is one of several suggesting parallels between Jude and Christ.

became aware that a soft cold substance had been flung at him, and
had fallen at his feet. *he has a sexual dimension*

A glance told him what it was—a piece of flesh, the characteristic
part of a barrow-pig,[4] which the country-men used for greasing their
boots, as it was useless for any other purpose. Pigs were rather plentiful
hereabout, being bred and fattened in large numbers in certain parts
of North Wessex.

On the other side of the hedge was a stream, whence, as he now for
the first time realized, had come the slight sounds of voices and laughter that had mingled with his dreams. He mounted the bank and
looked over the fence. On the further side of the stream stood a small
homestead, having a garden and pig-sties attached; in front of it, beside
the brook, three young women were kneeling, with buckets and platters
beside them containing heaps of pigs' chitterlings,[5] which they were
washing in the running water. One or two pairs of eyes slyly glanced
up, and perceiving that his attention had at last been attracted, and
that he was watching them, they braced themselves for inspection by
putting their mouths demurely into shape and recommencing their
rinsing operations with assiduity.

'Thank you!' said Jude severely.

'I *didn't* throw it, I tell you!' asserted one girl to her neighbour, as if
unconscious of the young man's presence.

'Nor I,' the second answered.

'O, Anny, how can you!' said the third.

'If I had thrown anything at all, it shouldn't have been *that*!'

'Pooh! I don't care for him!' And they laughed and continued their
work, without looking up, still ostentatiously accusing each other.

Jude grew sarcastic as he wiped his face, and caught their remarks.

'*You* didn't do it—O no!' he said to the up-stream one of the three.

She whom he addressed was a fine dark-eyed girl, not exactly handsome, but capable of passing as such at a little distance, despite some
coarseness of skin and fibre. She had a round and prominent bosom,
full lips, perfect teeth, and the rich complexion of a Cochin hen's egg.[6]
She was a complete and substantial female animal—no more, no less;
and Jude was almost certain that to her was attributable the enterprise
of attracting his attention from dreams of the humaner letters to what
was simmering in the minds around him.

'That you'll never be told,' said she deedily.[7]

'Whoever did it was wasteful of other people's property.'

'O, that's nothing.'

'But you want to speak to me, I suppose?'

4. Castrated boar. The "characteristic part" is the penis.
5. Pig's intestines used as food.
6. Type of fowl originally from China.
7. Energetically.

'O yes; if you like to.'

'Shall I clamber across, or will you come to the plank above here?'

Perhaps she foresaw an opportunity; for somehow or other the eyes of the brown girl rested in his own when he had said the words, and there was a momentary flash of intelligence, a dumb announcement of affinity in *posse*,[8] between herself and him, which, so far as Jude Fawley was concerned, had no sort of premeditation in it. She saw that he had singled her out from the three, as a woman is singled out in such cases, for no reasoned purpose of further acquaintance, but in commonplace obedience to conjunctive orders from headquarters, unconsciously received by unfortunate men when the last intention of their lives is to be occupied with the feminine.

Springing to her feet, she said: 'Bring back what is lying there.'

Jude was now aware that no message on any matter connected with her father's business had prompted her signal to him. He set down his basket of tools, picked up the scrap of offal, beat a pathway for himself with his stick, and got over the hedge. They walked in parallel lines, one on each bank of the stream, towards the small plank bridge. As the girl drew nearer to it, she gave, without Jude perceiving it, an adroit little suck to the interior of each of her cheeks in succession, by which curious and original manœuvre she brought as by magic upon its smooth and rotund surface a perfect dimple, which she was able to retain there as long as she continued to smile. This production of dimples at will was a not unknown operation, which many attempted, but only a few succeeded in accomplishing.

They met in the middle of the plank, and Jude, tossing back her missile, seemed to expect her to explain why she had audaciously stopped him by this novel artillery instead of by hailing him.

But she, slyly looking in another direction, swayed herself backwards and forwards on her hand as it clutched the rail of the bridge; till, moved by amatory curiosity, she turned her eyes critically upon him.

'You don't think *I* would shy things at you?'

'O no.'

'We are doing this for my father, who naturally doesn't want anything thrown away. He makes that into dubbin.'[9] She nodded towards the fragment on the grass.

'What made either of the others throw it, I wonder?' Jude asked, politely accepting her assertion, though he had very large doubts as to its truth.

'Impudence. Don't tell folk it was I, mind!'

'How can I? I don't know your name.'

'Ah, no. Shall I tell it to you?'

8. Potentially.
9. Grease used to render leather waterproof.

'Do!'

'Arabella Donn. I'm living here.'

'I must have known it if I had often come this way. But I mostly go straight along the high-road.'

'My father is a pig-breeder, and these girls are helping me wash the innerds[1] for black-puddings[2] and such like.'

They talked a little more and a little more, as they stood regarding each other and leaning against the hand-rail of the bridge. The unvoiced call of woman to man, which was uttered very distinctly by Arabella's personality, held Jude to the spot against his intention— almost against his will, and in a way new to his experience. It is scarcely an exaggeration to say that till this moment Jude had never looked at a woman to consider her as such, but had vaguely regarded the sex as beings outside his life and purposes. He gazed from her eyes to her mouth, thence to her bosom, and to her full round naked arms, wet, mottled with the chill of the water, and firm as marble.

'What a nice-looking girl you are!' he murmured, though the words had not been necessary to express his sense of her magnetism.

'Ah, you should see me Sundays!' she said piquantly.

'I don't suppose I could?' he answered.

'That's for you to think on. There's nobody after me just now, though there med be in a week or two.' She had spoken this without a smile, and the dimples disappeared.

Jude felt himself drifting strangely, but could not help it. 'Will you let me?'

'I don't mind.'

By this time she had managed to get back one dimple by turning her face aside for a moment and repeating the odd little sucking operation before mentioned, Jude being still unconscious of more than a general impression of her appearance. 'Next Sunday?' he hazarded. 'To-morrow, that is?'

'Yes.'

'Shall I call?'

'Yes.'

She brightened with a little glow of triumph, swept him almost tenderly with her eyes in turning, and retracing her steps down the brook-side grass rejoined her companions.

Jude Fawley shouldered his tool-basket and resumed his lonely way, filled with an ardour at which he mentally stood at gaze. He had just inhaled a single breath from a new atmosphere, which had evidently been hanging round him everywhere he went, for he knew not how long, but had somehow been divided from his actual breathing as by

1. Internal organs, viscera.
2. Sausages made from pig's blood and suet.

a sheet of glass. The intentions as to reading, working, and learning, which he had so precisely formulated only a few minutes earlier, were suffering a curious collapse into a corner, he knew not how.

'Well, it's only a bit of fun,' he said to himself, faintly conscious that to common-sense there was something lacking, and still more obviously something redundant, in the nature of this girl who had drawn him to her, which made it necessary that he should assert mere sportiveness on his part as his reason in seeking her—something in her quite antipathetic to that side of him which had been occupied with literary study and the magnificent Christminster dream. It had been no vestal[3] who chose *that* missile for opening her attack on him. He saw this with his intellectual eye, just for a short fleeting while, as by the light of a falling lamp one might momentarily see an inscription on a wall before being enshrouded in darkness. And then this passing discriminative power was withdrawn, and Jude was lost to all conditions of things in the advent of a fresh and wild pleasure, that of having found a new channel for emotional interest hitherto unsuspected, though it had lain close beside him. He was to meet this enkindling one of the other sex on the following Sunday.

Meanwhile the girl had joined her companions, and she silently resumed her flicking and sousing of the chitterlings in the pellucid stream.

'Catched un, my dear?' laconically asked the girl called Anny.

'I don't know. I wish I had thrown something else than that!' regretfully murmured Arabella.

'Lord! he's nobody, though you med think so. He used to drive old Drusilla Fawley's bread-cart out at Marygreen, till he 'prenticed himself at Alfredston. Since then he's been very stuck up, and always reading. He wants to be a scholar, they say.'

'O, I don't care what he is, or anything about 'n. Don't you think it, my child!'

'O, don't ye! You needn't try to deceive us! What did you stay talking to him for, if you didn't want un? Whether you do or whether you don't, he's as simple as a child. I could see it as you courted on the bridge, when he looked at 'ee as if he had never seen a woman before in his born days. Well, he's to be had by any woman who can get him to care for her a bit, if she likes to set herself to catch him the right way.'

I–7

The next day Jude Fawley was pausing in his bedroom with the sloping ceiling, looking at the books on the table, and then at the black

3. Virgin or innocent (from *vestal virgins*: priestesses in the temple of Vesta in ancient Rome).

mark on the plaster above them, made by the smoke of his lamp in past months.

It was Sunday afternoon, four-and-twenty hours after his meeting with Arabella Donn. During the whole bygone week he had been resolving to set this afternoon apart for a special purpose,—the re-reading of his Greek Testament—his new one, with better type than his old copy, following Griesbach's text as amended by numerous correctors, and with variorum readings in the margin. He was proud of the book, having obtained it by boldly writing to its London publisher, a thing he had never done before.

He had anticipated much pleasure in this afternoon's reading, under the quiet roof of his great-aunt's house as formerly, where he now slept only two nights a week. But a new thing, a great hitch, had happened yesterday in the gliding and noiseless current of his life, and he felt as a snake must feel who has sloughed off its winter skin, and cannot understand the brightness and sensitiveness of its new one.

He would not go out to meet her, after all. He sat down, opened the book, and with his elbows firmly planted on the table, and his hands to his temples, began at the beginning:

Η ΚΑΙΝΗ ΔΙΑΘΗΚΗ[1]

•   •   •   •   •   •

Had he promised to call for her? Surely he had! She would wait indoors, poor girl, and waste all her afternoon on account of him. There was a something in her, too, which was very winning, apart from promises. He ought not to break faith with her. Even though he had only Sundays and week-day evenings for reading he could afford one afternoon, seeing that other young men afforded so many. After to-day he would never probably see her again. Indeed, it would be impossible, considering what his plans were.

In short, as if materially, a compelling arm of extraordinary muscular power seized hold of him—something which had nothing in common with the spirits and influences that had moved him hitherto. This seemed to care little for his reason and his will, nothing for his so-called elevated intentions, and moved him along, as a violent schoolmaster a schoolboy he has seized by the collar, in a direction which tended towards the embrace of a woman for whom he had no respect, and whose life had nothing in common with his own except locality.

Η ΚΑΙΝΗ ΔΙΑΘΗΚΗ was no more heeded, and the predestinate Jude sprang up and across the room. Foreseeing such an event he had already arrayed himself in his best clothes. In three minutes he was out of the house and descending by the path across the wide vacant hollow of corn-ground which lay between the village and the isolated house of Arabella in the dip beyond the upland.

1. "The New Testament"(Greek).

As he walked he looked at his watch. He could be back in two hours, easily, and a good long time would still remain to him for reading after tea.

Passing the few unhealthy fir-trees and cottage where the path joined the highway he hastened along, and struck away to the left, descending the steep side of the country to the west of the Brown House. Here at the base of the chalk formation he neared the brook that oozed from it, and followed the stream till he reached her dwelling. A smell of piggeries came from the back, and the grunting of the originators of that smell. He entered the garden and knocked at the door with the knob of his stick.

Somebody had seen him through the window, for a male voice on the inside said:

'Arabella! Here's your young man come coorting! Mizzle,[2] my girl!'

Jude winced at the words. Courting in such a business-like aspect as it evidently wore to the speaker was the last thing he was thinking of. He was going to walk with her, perhaps kiss her; but 'courting' was too coolly purposeful to be anything but repugnant to his ideas. The door was opened and he entered, just as Arabella came downstairs in radiant walking attire.

'Take a chair, Mr. What's-your-name?' said her father, an energetic black-whiskered man, in the same business-like tones Jude had heard from outside.

'I'd rather go out at once, wouldn't you?' she whispered to Jude.

'Yes,' said he. 'We'll walk up to the Brown House and back, we can do it in half-an-hour.'

Arabella looked so handsome amid her untidy surroundings that he felt glad he had come, and all the misgivings vanished that had hitherto haunted him.

First they clambered to the top of the great down, during which ascent he had occasionally to take her hand to assist her. Then they bore off to the left along the crest into the ridgeway, which they followed till it intersected the high-road at the Brown House aforesaid, the spot of his former fervid desires to behold Christminster. But he forgot them now. He talked the commonest local twaddle to Arabella with greater zest than he would have felt in discussing all the philosophies with all the Dons in the recently adored University, and passed the spot where he had knelt to Diana and Phœbus without remembering that there were any such people in the mythology, or that the Sun was anything else than a useful lamp for illuminating Arabella's face. An indescribable lightness of heel served to lift him along; and Jude, the incipient scholar, prospective D. D., Professor, Bishop, or

2. Hurry up (dialect).

what not, felt himself honoured and glorified by the condescension of this handsome country wench in agreeing to take a walk with him in her Sunday frock and ribbons.

They reached the Brown House barn—the point at which he had planned to turn back. While looking over the vast northern landscape from this spot they were struck by the rising of a dense volume of smoke from the neighbourhood of the little town which lay beneath them at a distance of a couple of miles.

'It is a fire,' said Arabella. 'Let's run and see it—do! It is not far!'

The tenderness which had grown up in Jude's bosom left him no will to thwart her inclination now—which pleased him in affording him excuse for a longer time with her. They started off down the hill almost at a trot; but on gaining level ground at the bottom, and walking a mile, they found that the spot of the fire was much further off than it had seemed.

Having begun their journey, however, they pushed on; but it was not till five o'clock that they found themselves on the scene,—the distance being altogether about half-a-dozen miles from Marygreen, and three from Arabella's. The conflagration had been got under by the time they reached it, and after a short inspection of the melancholy ruins they retraced their steps—their course lying through the town of Alfredston.

Arabella said she would like some tea, and they entered an inn of an inferior class, and gave their order. As it was not for beer they had a long time to wait. The maid-servant recognized Jude, and whispered her surprise to her mistress in the background, that he, the student, 'who kept hisself up so particular,' should have suddenly descended so low as to keep company with Arabella. The latter guessed what was being said, and laughed as she met the serious and tender gaze of her lover—the low and triumphant laugh of a careless woman who sees she is winning her game.

They sat and looked round the room, and at the picture of Samson and Delilah[3] which hung on the wall, and at the circular beer-stains on the table, and at the spittoons underfoot filled with sawdust. The whole aspect of the scene had that depressing effect on Jude which few places can produce like a tap-room on a Sunday evening when the setting sun is slanting in, and no liquor is going, and the unfortunate wayfarer finds himself with no other haven or rest.

It began to grow dusk. They could not wait longer, really, for the tea, they said. 'Yet what else can we do?' asked Jude. 'It is a three-mile walk for you.'

'I suppose we can have some beer,' said Arabella.

3. Delilah, loved by Samson, betrayed him to his enemies after making him drunk (Judges 16); the story has an obvious relevance to Jude's situation. For later references, see below, pp. 59 and 297.

'Beer, O yes. I had forgotten that. Somehow it seems odd to come to a public-house for beer on a Sunday evening.'

'But we didn't.'

'No, we didn't.' Jude by this time wished he was out of such an uncongenial atmosphere; but he ordered the beer, which was promptly brought.

Arabella tasted it. 'Ugh!' she said.

Jude tasted. 'What's the matter with it!' he asked. 'I don't understand beer very much now, it is true. I like it well enough, but it is bad to read on, and I find coffee better. But this seems all right.'

'Adulterated—I can't touch it!' She mentioned three or four ingredients that she detected in the liquor beyond malt and hops, much to Jude's surprise.

'How much you know!' he said good-humouredly.

Nevertheless she returned to the beer and drank her share, and they went on their way. It was now nearly dark, and as soon as they had withdrawn from the lights of the town they walked closer together, till they touched each other. She wondered why he did not put his arm round her waist, but he did not; he merely said what to himself seemed a quite bold enough thing: 'Take my arm.'

She took it, thoroughly, up to the shoulder. He felt the warmth of her body against his, and putting his stick under his other arm held with his right hand her right as it rested in its place.

'Now we are well together, dear, aren't we?' he observed.

'Yes,' said she; adding to herself: 'Rather mild!'

'How fast I have become!' he was thinking.

Thus they walked till they reached the foot of the upland, where they could see the white highway ascending before them in the gloom. From this point the only way of getting to Arabella's was by going up the incline, and dipping again into her valley on the right. Before they had climbed far they were nearly run into by two men who had been walking on the grass unseen.

'These lovers—you find 'em out o' doors in all seasons and weathers—lovers and homeless dogs only,' said one of the men as they vanished down the hill.

Arabella tittered lightly.

'Are we lovers?' asked Jude.

'You know best.'

'But you can tell me?'

For answer she inclined her head upon his shoulder. Jude took the hint, and encircling her waist with his arm, pulled her to him and kissed her.

They walked now no longer arm in arm but, as she had desired, clasped together. After all, what did it matter since it was dark, said Jude to himself. When they were half way up the long hill they paused as by arrangement, and he kissed her again. They reached the top, and he kissed her once more.

'You can keep your arm there, if you would like to,' she said gently.

He did so, thinking how trusting she was.

Thus they slowly went towards her home. He had left his cottage at half-past three, intending to be sitting down again to the New Testament by half-past five. It was nine o'clock when, with another embrace, he stood to deliver her up at her father's door.

She asked him to come in, if only for a minute, as it would seem so odd otherwise, and as if she had been out alone in the dark. He gave way, and followed her in. Immediately that the door was opened he found, in addition to her parents, several neighbours sitting round. They all spoke in a congratulatory manner, and took him seriously as Arabella's intended partner.

They did not belong to his set or circle, and he felt out of place and embarrassed. He had not meant this: a mere afternoon of pleasant walking with Arabella, that was all he had meant. He did not stay longer than to speak to her stepmother, a simple, quiet woman without features or character; and bidding them all good night plunged with a sense of relief into the track over the down.

But that sense was only temporary. Arabella soon reasserted her sway in his soul. He walked as if he felt himself to be another man from the Jude of yesterday. What were his books to him? what were his intentions, hitherto adhered to so strictly, as to not wasting a single minute of time day by day? 'Wasting!' It depended on your point of view to define that: he was just living for the first time: not wasting life. It was better to love a woman than to be a graduate, or a parson; ay, or a pope!

When he got back to the house his aunt had gone to bed, and a general consciousness of his neglect seemed written on the face of all things confronting him. He went upstairs without a light, and the dim interior of his room accosted him with sad inquiry. There lay his book open, just as he had left it, and the capital letters on the title-page regarded him with fixed reproach in the grey starlight, like the unclosed eyes of a dead man:

H KAINH ΔIAΘHKH.

•   •   •   •   •   •

Jude had to leave early next morning for his usual week of absence at lodgings; and it was with a sense of futility that he threw into his basket upon his tools and other necessaries the unread books he had brought with him.

He kept his impassioned doings a secret almost from himself. Arabella, on the contrary, made them public among all her friends and acquaintance.

Retracing by the light of dawn the road he had followed a few hours earlier under cover of darkness, with his sweetheart by his side, he reached the bottom of the hill, where he walked slowly, and stood still. He was on the spot where he had given her the first kiss. As the sun had only just risen it was possible that nobody had passed there since. Jude looked on the ground and sighed. He looked closely, and could just discern in the damp dust the imprints of their feet as they had stood locked in each other's arms. She was not there now, and 'the embroidery of imagination upon the stuff of nature' so depicted her past presence that a void was in his heart which nothing could fill. A pollard willow[4] stood close to the place, and that willow was different from all other willows in the world. Utter annihilation of the six days which must elapse before he could see her again as he had promised would have been his intensest wish if he had only the week to live.

An hour and half later Arabella came along the same way with her two companions of the Saturday. She passed unheedingly the scene of the kiss, and the willow that marked it, though chattering freely on the subject to the other two.

'And what did he tell 'ee next?'

'Then he said—' And she related almost word for word some of his tenderest speeches. If Jude had been behind the fence he would have felt not a little surprised at learning how very few of his sayings and doings on the previous evening were private.

'You've got him to care for 'ee a bit, 'nation if you han't!' murmured Anny judicially. 'It's well to be you!'

In a few moments Arabella replied in a curiously low, hungry tone of latent sensuousness: 'I've got him to care for me: yes! But I want him to more than care for me; I want him to have me—to marry me! I must have him. I can't do without him. He's the sort of man I long for. I shall go mad if I can't give myself to him altogether! I felt I should when I first saw him!'

'As he is a romancing, straightfor'ard, honest chap, he's to be had, and as a husband, if you set about catching him in the right way.'

Arabella remained thinking awhile. 'What med be the right way?' she asked.

'O you don't know—you don't!' said Sarah, the third girl.

'On my word I don't!—No further, that is, than by plain courting, and taking care he don't go too far!'

The third girl looked at the second. 'She *don't* know!'

' 'Tis clear she don't!' said Anny.

'And having lived in a town, too, as one may say! Well, we can teach 'ee som'at then, as well as you us.'

'Yes. And how do you mean—a sure way to gain a man? Take me for an innocent, and have done wi' it!'

---

4. With the branches trimmed to encourage growth.

'As a husband.'

'As a husband.'

'A countryman that's honourable and serious-minded such as he; God forbid that I should say a sojer, or sailor, or commercial gent from the towns, or any of them that be slippery with poor women! I'd do no friend that harm!'

'Well, such as he, of course!'

Arabella's companions looked at each other, and turning up their eyes in drollery began smirking. Then one went up close to Arabella, and, although nobody was near, imparted some information in a low tone, the other observing curiously the effect upon Arabella.

'Ah!' said the last-named slowly. 'I own I didn't think of that way! . . . But suppose he *isn't* honourable? A woman had better not have tried it!'

'Nothing venture nothing have! Besides, you make sure that he's honourable before you begin. You'd be safe enough with yours. I wish I had the chance! Lots of girls do it; or do you think they'd get married at all?'

Arabella pursued her way in silent thought. 'I'll try it!' she whispered; but not to them.

I–8

One week's end Jude was as usual walking out to his aunt's at Marygreen from his lodging in Alfredston, a walk which now had large attractions for him quite other than his desire to see his aged and morose relative. He diverged to the right before ascending the hill with the single purpose of gaining, on his way, a glimpse of Arabella that should not come into the reckoning of regular appointments. Before quite reaching the homestead his alert eye perceived the top of her head moving quickly hither and thither over the garden hedge. Entering the gate he found that three young unfattened pigs had escaped from their sty by leaping clean over the top, and that she was endeavouring unassisted to drive them in through the door which she had set open. The lines of her countenance changed from the rigidity of business to the softness of love when she saw Jude, and she bent her eyes languishingly upon him. The animals took advantage of the pause by doubling and bolting out of the way.

'They were only put in this morning!' she cried, stimulated to pursue in spite of her lover's presence. 'They were drove from Spaddleholt Farm only yesterday, where father bought 'em at a stiff price enough. They are wanting to get home again, the stupid toads! Will you shut the garden gate, dear, and help me to get 'em in? There are no men folk at home, only mother, and they'll be lost if we don't mind.'

He set himself to assist, and dodged this way and that over the potato rows and the cabbages. Every now and then they ran together, when he caught her for a moment and kissed her. The first pig was got back promptly; the second with some difficulty; the third, a long-legged creature, was more obstinate and agile. He plunged through a hole in the garden hedge, and into the lane.

'He'll be lost if I don't follow 'n!' said she. 'Come along with me!'

She rushed in full pursuit out of the garden, Jude alongside her, barely contriving to keep the fugitive in sight. Occasionally they would shout to some boy to stop the animal, but he always wriggled past and ran on as before.

'Let me take your hand, darling,' said Jude. 'You are getting out of breath.' She gave him her now hot hand with apparent willingness, and they trotted along together.

'This comes of driving 'em home,' she remarked. 'They always know the way back if you do that. They ought to have been carted over.'

By this time the pig had reached an unfastened gate admitting to the open down, across which he sped with all the agility his little legs afforded. As soon as the pursuers had entered and ascended to the top of the high ground it became apparent that they would have to run all the way to the farmer's if they wished to get him. From this summit he could be seen as a minute speck, following an unerring line towards his old home.

'It is no good!' cried Arabella. 'He'll be there long before we get there. It don't matter now we know he's not lost or stolen on the way. They'll see it is ours, and send un back. O dear, how hot I be!'

Without relinquishing her hold of Jude's hand she swerved aside and flung herself down on the sod under a stunted thorn, precipitately pulling Jude on to his knees at the same time.

'O, I ask pardon—I nearly threw you down, didn't I! But I am so tired!'

She lay supine, and straight as an arrow, on the sloping sod of this hill-top, gazing up into the blue miles of sky, and still retaining her warm hold of Jude's hand. He reclined on his elbow near her.

'We've run all this way for nothing,' she went on, her form heaving and falling in quick pants, her face flushed, her full red lips parted, and a fine dew of perspiration on her skin. 'Well—why don't you speak, deary?'

'I'm blown too. It was all up hill.'

They were in absolute solitude—the most apparent of all solitudes, that of empty surrounding space. Nobody could be nearer than a mile to them without their seeing him. They were, in fact, on one of the summits of the county, and the distant landscape around Christminster could be discerned from where they lay. But Jude did not think of that then.

'O, I can see such a pretty thing up this tree,' said Arabella. 'A sort of a—caterpillar, of the most loveliest green and yellow you ever came across!'

'Where?' said Jude, sitting up.

'You can't see him there—you must come here,' said she.

He bent nearer and put his head in front of hers. 'No—I can't see it,' he said.

'Why, on the limb there where it branches off—close to the moving leaf—there!' She gently pulled him down beside her.

'I don't see it,' he repeated, the back of his head against her cheek. 'But I can, perhaps, standing up.' He stood accordingly, placing himself in the direct line of her gaze.

'How stupid you are!' she said crossly, turning away her face.

'I don't care to see it, dear; why should I?' he replied, looking down upon her. 'Get up, Abby.'

'Why?'

'I want you to let me kiss you. I've been waiting to ever so long!'

She rolled round her face, remained a moment looking deedily aslant at him; then with a slight curl of the lip sprang to her feet, and exclaiming abruptly 'I must mizzle!' walked off quickly homeward. Jude followed and rejoined her.

'Just one!' he coaxed.

'Shan't!' she said.

He, surprised: 'What's the matter?'

She kept her two lips resentfully together, and Jude followed her like a pet lamb till she slackened her pace and walked beside him, talking calmly on indifferent subjects, and always checking him if he tried to take her hand or clasp her waist. Thus they descended to the precincts of her father's homestead, and Arabella went in, nodding good-bye to him with a supercilious, affronted air.

'I expect I took too much liberty with her, somehow,' Jude said to himself, as he withdrew with a sigh and went on to Marygreen.

On Sunday morning the interior of Arabella's home was, as usual, the scene of a grand weekly cooking, the preparation of the special Sunday dinner. Her father was shaving before a little glass hung on the mullion[1] of the window, and her mother and Arabella herself were shelling beans hard by. A neighbour passed on her way home from morning service at the nearest church, and seeing Donn engaged at the window with the razor, nodded and came in.

She at once spoke playfully to Arabella: 'I zeed 'ee running with 'un—hee-hee! I hope 'tis coming to something?'

Arabella merely threw a look of consciousness into her face without raising her eyes.

1. Vertical bar dividing a window into sections.

'He's for Christminster, I hear, as soon as he can get there.'

'Have you heard that lately—quite lately?' asked Arabella with a jealous, tigerish indrawing of breath.

'O no! But it has been known a long time that it is his plan. He's on'y waiting here for an opening. Ah well: he must walk about with somebody I s'pose. Young men don't mean much now-a-days. 'Tis a sip here and a sip there with 'em. 'Twas different in my time.'

When the gossip had departed Arabella said suddenly to her mother: 'I want you and father to go and inquire how the Edlins be, this evening after tea. Or no—there's evening service at Fensworth—you can walk to that.'

'Oh? What's up to-night, then?'

'Nothing. Only I want the house to myself. He's shy; and I can't get un to come in when you are here. I shall let him slip through my fingers if I don't mind, much as I care for 'n!'

'If it is fine we med as well go, since you wish.'

In the afternoon Arabella met and walked with Jude, who had now for weeks ceased to look into a book of Greek, Latin, or any other tongue. They wandered up the slopes till they reached the green track along the ridge, which they followed to the circular British earth-bank[2] adjoining, Jude thinking of the great age of the trackway, and of the drovers who had frequented it, probably before the Romans knew the country. Up from the level lands below them floated the chime of church bells. Presently they were reduced to one note, which quickened, and stopped.

'Now we'll go back,' said Arabella, who had attended to the sounds.

Jude assented. So long as he was near her he minded little where he was. When they arrived at her house he said lingeringly: 'I won't come in. Why are you in such a hurry to go in to-night? It is not near dark.'

'Wait a moment,' said she. She tried the handle of the door and found it locked.

'Ah—they are gone to church,' she added. And searching behind the scraper she found the key and unlocked the door. 'Now, you'll come in a moment?' she asked lightly. 'We shall be all alone.'

'Certainly,' said Jude with alacrity, the case being unexpectedly altered.

Indoors they went. Did he want any tea? No, it was too late: he would rather sit and talk to her. She took off her jacket and hat and they sat down—naturally enough close together.

'Don't touch me, please,' she said softly. 'I am part egg-shell. Or perhaps I had better put it in a safe place.' She began unfastening the collar of her gown.

'What is it?' said her lover.

2. Ancient earthwork, perhaps originally for defense.

'An egg—a cochin's egg. I am hatching a very rare sort. I carry it about everywhere with me, and it will get hatched in less than three weeks.'

'Where do you carry it?'

'Just here.' She put her hand into her bosom and drew out the egg, which was wrapped in wool, outside it being a piece of pig's bladder, in case of accidents. Having exhibited it to him she put it back, 'Now mind you don't come near me. I don't want to get it broke, and have to begin another.'

'Why do you do such a strange thing?'

'It's an old custom. I suppose it is natural for a woman to want to bring live things into the world.'

'It is very awkward for me just now,' he said, laughing.

'It serves you right. There—that's all you can have of me.'

She had turned round her chair, and, reaching over the back of it, presented her cheek to him gingerly.

'That's very shabby of you!'

'You should have catched me a minute ago when I had put the egg down! There!' she said defiantly, 'I am without it now!' She had quickly withdrawn the egg a second time; but before he could quite reach her she had put it back as quickly, laughing with the excitement of her strategy. Then there was a little struggle, Jude making a plunge for it and capturing it triumphantly. Her face flushed; and becoming suddenly conscious he flushed also.

They looked at each other, panting; till he rose and said: 'One kiss, now I can do it without damage to property; and I'll go!'

But she had jumped up too. 'You must find me first!' she cried.

Her lover followed her as she withdrew. It was now dark inside the room, and the window being small he could not discover for a long time what had become of her, till a laugh revealed her to have rushed up the stairs, whither Jude rushed at her heels.

I–9

It was some two months later in the year, and the pair had met constantly during the interval. Arabella seemed dissatisfied; she was always imagining, and waiting, and wondering.

One day she met the itinerant Vilbert. She, like all the cottagers thereabout, knew the quack well, and she began telling him of her experiences. Arabella had been gloomy, but before he left her she had grown brighter. That evening she kept an appointment with Jude, who seemed sad.

'I am going away,' he said to her. 'I think I ought to go. I think it will be better both for you and for me. I wish some things had never begun! I was much to blame, I know. But it is never too late to mend.'

Arabella began to cry. 'How do you know it is not too late?' she said. 'That's all very well to say! I haven't told you yet!' and she looked into his face with streaming eyes.

'What?' he asked, turning pale. 'Not . . . ?'

'Yes! And what shall I do if you desert me?'

'O Arabella—how can you say that, my dear! You *know* I wouldn't desert you!'

'Well then—'

'I have next to no wages as yet, you know; or perhaps I should have thought of this before. . . . But, of course, if that's the case, we must marry! What other thing do you think I could dream of doing?'

'I thought—I thought, deary, perhaps you would go away all the more for that, and leave me to face it alone!'

'You knew better! Of course I never dreamt six months ago, or even three, of marrying. It is a complete smashing up of my plans—I mean my plans before I knew you, my dear. But what are they, after all! Dreams about books, and degrees, and impossible fellowships, and all that. Certainly we'll marry: we must!'

That night he went out alone, and walked in the dark, self-communing. He knew well, too well, in the secret centre of his brain, that Arabella was not worth a great deal as a specimen of woman kind. Yet, such being the custom of the rural districts among honourable young men who had drifted so far into intimacy with a woman as he unfortunately had done, he was ready to abide by what he had said, and take the consequences. For his own soothing he kept up a factitious belief in her. His idea of her was the thing of most consequence, not Arabella herself, he sometimes said laconically.

The banns were put in and published the very next Sunday. The people of the parish all said what a simple fool young Fawley was. All his reading had only come to this, that he would have to sell his books to buy saucepans. Those who guessed the probable state of affairs, Arabella's parents being among them, declared that it was the sort of conduct they would have expected of such an honest young man as Jude in reparation of the wrong he had done his innocent sweetheart. The person who married them seemed to think it satisfactory too.

And so, standing before the aforesaid officiator, the two swore that at every other time of their lives till death took them, they would assuredly believe, feel, and desire precisely as they had believed, felt, and desired during the few preceding weeks.[1] What was as remarkable as the undertaking itself was the fact that nobody seemed at all surprised at what they swore.

Fawley's aunt being a baker she made him a bride-cake, saying bitterly that it was the last thing she could do for him, poor silly fellow;

1. The allusion is to the marriage service of the Anglican church, in which the couple promise to "live together," and to "love" and "honor" each other, "till death us do part."

and that it would have been far better if, instead of his living to trouble her, he had gone underground years before with his father and mother. Of this cake Arabella took some slices, wrapped them up in white note-paper, and sent them to her companions in the pork-dressing business, Anny and Sarah, labelling each packet 'In remembrance of good advice.'

The prospects of the newly married couple were certainly not very brilliant even to the most sanguine mind. He, a stone-mason's apprentice, nineteen years of age, was working for half wages till he should be out of his time. His wife was absolutely useless in a town-lodging, where he at first had considered it would be necessary for them to live. But the urgent need of adding to income in ever so little a degree caused him to take a lonely roadside cottage between the Brown House and Marygreen, that he might have the profits of a vegetable garden, and utilize her past experiences by letting her keep a pig. But it was not the sort of life he had bargained for, and it was a long way to walk to and from Alfredston every day. Arabella, however, felt that all these makeshifts were temporary; she had gained a husband; that was the thing—a husband with a lot of earning power in him for buying her frocks and hats when he should begin to get frightened a bit, and stick to his trade, and throw aside those stupid books for practical undertakings.

So to the cottage he took her on the evening of the marriage, giving up his old room at his aunt's—where so much of the hard labour at Greek and Latin had been carried on.

A little chill overspread him at her first unrobing. A long tail of hair, which Arabella wore twisted up in an enormous knob at the back of her head, was deliberately unfastened, stroked out, and hung upon the looking-glass which he had bought her.

'What—it wasn't your own?' he said, with a sudden distaste for her.

'O no—it never is nowadays with the better class.'

'Nonsense! Perhaps not in towns. But in the country it is supposed to be different: Besides you've enough of your own, surely?'

'Yes, enough as country notions go. But in towns the men expect more, and when I was barmaid at Aldbrickham—'

'Barmaid at Aldbrickham?'

'Well, not exactly barmaid—I used to draw the drink at a public-house there—just for a little time; that was all. Some people put me up to getting this, and I bought it just for a fancy. The more you have the better in Aldbrickham, which is a finer town than all your Christminsters. Every lady of position wears false hair—the barber's assistant told me so.'

Jude thought with a feeling of sickness that though this might be true to some extent, for all that he knew, many unsophisticated girls would and did go to towns and remain there for years without losing their simplicity of life and embellishments. Others, alas, had an instinct

towards artificiality in their very blood, and became adepts in coun-
terfeiting at the first glimpse of it. However, perhaps there was no great
sin in a woman adding to her hair, and he resolved to think no more
of it.

A new-made wife can usually manage to excite interest for a few
weeks, even though the prospects of the household ways and means
are cloudy. There is a certain piquancy about her situation, and her
manner to her acquaintance at the sense of it, which carries off the
gloom of facts, and renders even the humblest bride independent
awhile of the real. Mrs. Jude Fawley was walking in the streets of Alfredston one market-day with this quality in her carriage when she met
Anny her former friend, whom she had not seen since the wedding.

As usual they laughed before talking; the world seemed funny to
them without saying it.

'So it turned out a good plan you see!' remarked the girl to the wife.
'I knew it would with such as him. He's a dear good fellow, and you
ought to be proud of un.'

'I am,' said Mrs. Fawley quietly.

'And when do you expect—?'

'Ssh! Not at all.'

'What!'

'I was mistaken.'

'O Arabella, Arabella; you be a deep one! Mistaken! well, that's
clever—it's a real stroke of genius! It is a thing I never thought o', wi'
all my experience! I never thought beyond bringing about the real
thing—not that one could sham it!'

'Don't you be too quick to cry sham! 'Twasn't sham. I didn't know.'

'My word—won't he be in a taking! He'll give it to 'ee o' Saturday
nights! Whatever it was, he'll say it was a trick—a double one, by the
Lord!'

'I'll own to the first, but not to the second. . . . Pooh—he won't care!
He'll be glad I was wrong in what I said. He'll shake down, bless 'ee—
men always do. What can 'em do otherwise? Married is married.'

Nevertheless it was with a little uneasiness that Arabella approached
the time when in the natural course of things she would have to reveal
that the alarm she had raised had been without foundation. The occasion was one evening at bed-time, and they were in their chamber in
the lonely cottage by the wayside to which Jude walked home from his
work every day. He had worked hard the whole twelve hours, and had
retired to rest before his wife. When she came into the room he was
between sleeping and waking, and was barely conscious of her undress-
ing before the little looking-glass as he lay.

One action of hers, however, brought him to full cognition. Her face
being reflected towards him as she sat, he could perceive that she was
amusing herself by artificially producing in each cheek the dimple

before alluded to, a curious accomplishment of which she was mistress, effecting it by a momentary suction. It seemed to him for the first time that the dimples were far oftener absent from her face during his inter-course with her nowadays than they had been in the earlier weeks of their acquaintance.

'Don't do that, Arabella!' he said suddenly. 'There is no harm in it, but—I don't like to see you.'

She turned and laughed. 'Lord, I didn't know you were awake!' she said. 'How countrified you are! That's nothing.'

'Where did you learn it?'

'Nowhere that I know of. They used to stay without any trouble when I was at the public-house; but now they won't. My face was fatter then.'

'I don't care about dimples. I don't think they improve a woman—particularly a married woman, and of full-sized figure like you.'

'Most men think otherwise.'

'I don't care what most men think, if they do. How do you know?'

'I used to be told so when I was serving in the tap-room.'

'Ah—that public-house experience accounts for your knowing about the adulteration of the ale when we went and had some that Sunday evening. I thought when I married you that you had always lived in your father's house.'

'You ought to have known better than that, and seen I was a little more finished than I could have been by staying where I was born. There was not much to do at home, and I was eating my head off, so I went away for three months.'

'You'll soon have plenty to do now, dear, won't you?'

'How do you mean?'

'Why, of course—little things to make.'

'Oh.'

'When will it be? Can't you tell me exactly, instead of in such general terms as you have used?'

'Tell you?'

'Yes—the date.'

'There's nothing to tell. I made a mistake.

'What?'

'It was a mistake.'

He sat bolt upright in bed and looked at her. 'How can that be?'

'Women fancy wrong things sometimes.'

'But—! Why, of course, so unprepared as I was, without a stick of furniture, and hardly a shilling, I shouldn't have hurried on our affair, and brought you to a half-furnished hut before I was ready, if it had not been for the news you gave me, which made it necessary to save you, ready or no. . . . Good God!'

'Don't take on dear. What's done can't be undone.'

'I have no more to say!'

He gave the answer simply, and lay down; and there was silence between them.

When Jude awoke the next morning he seemed to see the world with a different eye. As to the point in question he was compelled to accept her word; in the circumstances he could not have acted otherwise while ordinary notions prevailed. But how came they to prevail?

There seemed to him, vaguely and dimly, something wrong in a social ritual which made necessary a cancelling of well-formed schemes involving years of thought and labour, of foregoing a man's one opportunity of showing himself superior to the lower animals, and of contributing his units of work to the general progress of his generation, because of a momentary surprise by a new and transitory instinct which had nothing in it of the nature of vice, and could be only at the most called weakness. He was inclined to inquire what he had done, or she lost, for that matter, that he deserved to be caught in a gin[2] which would cripple him, if not her also, for the rest of a lifetime? There was perhaps something fortunate in the fact that the immediate reason of his marriage had proved to be non-existent. But the marriage remained.

I–10

The time arrived for killing the pig which Jude and his wife had fattened in their sty during the autumn months, and the butchering was timed to take place as soon as it was light in the morning, so that Jude might get to Alfredston without losing more than a quarter of a day.

The night had seemed strangely silent. Jude looked out of the window long before dawn, and perceived that the ground was covered with snow—snow rather deep for the season, it seemed, a few flakes still falling.

'I'm afraid the pig-killer won't be able to come,' he said to Arabella.

'O, he'll come. You must get up and make the water hot, if you want Challow to scald him. Though I like singeing best.'

'I'll get up,' said Jude. 'I like the way of my own county.'

He went downstairs, lit the fire under the copper, and began feeding it with bean-stalks, all the time without a candle, the blaze flinging a cheerful shine into the room; though for him the sense of cheerfulness was lessened by thoughts on the reason of that blaze—to heat water to scald the bristles from the body of an animal that as yet lived, and whose voice could be continually heard from a corner of the garden. At half-past six, the time of appointment with the butcher, the water boiled, and Jude's wife came downstairs.

2. Trap. In a later episode, the metaphor is translated into literal terms (below, p. 169).

'Is Challow come?' she asked.

'No.'

They waited, and it grew lighter, with the dreary light of a snowy dawn. She went out, gazed along the road, and returning said, 'He's not coming. Drunk last night, I expect. The snow is not enough to hinder him, surely!'

'Then we must put it off. It is only the water boiled for nothing. The snow may be deep in the valley.'

'Can't be put off. There's no more victuals for the pig. He ate the last mixing o' barleymeal yesterday morning.'

'Yesterday morning? What has he lived on since?'

'Nothing.'

'What—he has been starving?'

'Yes. We always do it the last day or two, to save bother with the innerds. What ignorance, not to know that!'

'That accounts for his crying so. Poor creature!'

'Well—you must do the sticking—there's no help for it. I'll show you how. Or I'll do it myself—I think I could. Though as it is such a big pig I had rather Challow had done it. However, his basket o' knives and things have been already sent on here, and we can use 'em.'

'Of course you shan't do it,' said Jude. 'I'll do it, since it must be done.'

He went out to the sty, shovelled away the snow for the space of a couple of yards or more, and placed the stool in front, with the knives and ropes at hand. A robin peered down at the preparations from the nearest tree, and, not liking the sinister look of the scene, flew away, though hungry. By this time Arabella had joined her husband, and Jude, rope in hand, got into the sty, and noosed the affrighted animal, who, beginning with a squeak of surprise, rose to repeated cries of rage. Arabella opened the sty-door, and together they hoisted the victim on to the stool, legs upward, and while Jude held him Arabella bound him down, looping the cord over his legs to keep him from struggling.

The animal's note changed its quality. It was not now rage, but the cry of despair; long-drawn, slow and hopeless.

'Upon my soul I would sooner have gone without the pig than have had this to do!' said Jude. 'A creature I have fed with my own hands.'

'Don't be such a tender-hearted fool! There's the sticking-knife—the one with the point. Now whatever you do, don't stick un too deep.'

'I'll stick him effectually, so as to make short work of it. That's the chief thing.'

'You must not!' she cried. 'The meat must be well bled, and to do that he must die slow. We shall lose a shilling a score[1] if the meat is red and bloody! Just touch the vein, that's all. I was brought up to it,

---

1. Twenty pounds' weight.

and I know. Every good butcher keeps un bleeding long. He ought to be eight or ten minutes dying, at least.'

'He shall not be half a minute if I can help it, however the meat may look,' said Jude determinedly. Scraping the bristles from the pig's upturned throat, as he had seen the butchers do, he slit the fat; then plunged in the knife with all his might.

' 'O damn it all!' she cried, 'that ever I should say it! You've over-stuck un! And I telling you all the time—'

'Do be quiet, Arabella, and have a little pity on the creature!'

'Hold up the pail to catch the blood, and don't talk!'

However unworkmanlike the deed, it had been mercifully done. The blood flowed out in a torrent instead of in the trickling stream she had desired. The dying animal's cry assumed its third and final tone, the shriek of agony; his glazing eyes riveting themselves on Arabella with the eloquently keen reproach of a creature recognizing at last the treachery of those who had seemed his only friends.

'Make un stop that!' said Arabella. 'Such a noise will bring somebody or other up here, and I don't want people to know we are doing it ourselves.' Picking up the knife from the ground whereon Jude had flung it, she slipped it into the gash, and slit the windpipe. The pig was instantly silent, his dying breath coming through the hole.

'That's better,' she said.

'It is a hateful business!' said he.

'Pigs must be killed.'

The animal heaved in a final convulsion, and, despite the rope, kicked out with all his last strength. A tablespoonful of black clot came forth, the trickling of red blood having ceased for some seconds.

'That's it; now he'll go,' said she. 'Artful creatures—they always keep back a drop like that as long as they can!'

The last plunge had come so unexpectedly as to make Jude stagger, and in recovering himself he kicked over the vessel in which the blood had been caught.

'There!' she cried, thoroughly in a passion. 'Now I can't make any blackpot.[2] There's a waste, all through you!'

Jude put the pail upright, but only about a third of the whole steam-ing liquid was left in it, the main part being splashed over the snow, and forming a dismal, sordid, ugly spectacle—to those who saw it as other than an ordinary obtaining of meat. The lips and nostrils of the animal turned livid, then white, and the muscles of his limbs relaxed.

'Thank God!' Jude said. 'He's dead.'

'What's God got to do with such a messy job as a pig-killing, I should like to know!' she said scornfully. 'Poor folks must live.'

'I know, I know,' said he. 'I don't scold you.'

2. Black puddings.

Suddenly they became aware of a voice at hand.

'Well done, young married volk! I couldn't have carried it out much better myself, cuss me if I could!' The voice, which was husky, came from the garden-gate, and looking up from the scene of slaughter they saw the burly form of Mr. Challow leaning over the gate, critically surveying their performance.

' 'Tis well for 'ee to stand there and glane!'[3] said Arabella. 'Owing to your being late the meat is blooded and half spoiled! 'Twon't fetch so much by a shilling a score!'

Challow expressed his contrition. 'You should have waited a bit,' he said, shaking his head, 'and not have done this—in the delicate state, too, that you be in at present, ma'am. 'Tis risking yourself too much.'

'You needn't be concerned about that,' said Arabella, laughing. Jude too laughed, but there was a strong flavour of bitterness in his amusement.

Challow made up for his neglect of the killing by zeal in the scalding and scraping. Jude felt dissatisfied with himself as a man at what he had done, though aware of his lack of common sense, and that the deed would have amounted to the same thing if carried out by deputy. The white snow, stained with the blood of his fellow-mortal, wore an illogical look to him as a lover of justice, not to say a Christian; but he could not see how the matter was to be mended. No doubt he was, as his wife had called him, a tender-hearted fool.

He did not like the road to Alfredston now. It stared him cynically in the face. The wayside objects reminded him so much of his courtship of his wife that, to keep them out of his eyes, he read whenever he could as he walked to and from his work. Yet he sometimes felt that by caring for books he was not escaping common-place nor gaining rare ideas, every working-man being of that taste now. When passing near the spot by the stream on which he had first made her acquaintance he one day heard voices just as he had done at that earlier time. One of the girls who had been Arabella's companions was talking to a friend in a shed, himself being the subject of discourse, possibly because they had seen him in the distance. They were quite unaware that the shed-walls were so thin that he could hear their words as he passed.

'Howsomever, 'twas I put her up to it! "Nothing venture nothing have," I said. If I hadn't she'd no more have been his mis'ess than I.'

' 'Tis my belief she knew there was nothing the matter when she told him she was . . . '

What had Arabella been put up to by this woman, so that he should make her his 'mis'ess,' otherwise wife? The suggestion was horridly unpleasant, and it rankled in his mind so much that instead of entering his own cottage when he reached it he flung his basket inside the

---

3. Smile or sneer (dialect).

garden-gate and passed on, determined to go and see his old aunt and get some supper there.

This made his arrival home rather late. Arabella, however, was busy melting down lard from fat of the deceased pig, for she had been out on a jaunt all day, and so delayed her work. Dreading lest what he had heard should lead him to say something regrettable to her he spoke little. But Arabella was very talkative, and said among other things that she wanted some money. Seeing the book sticking out of his pocket she added that he ought to earn more.

'An apprentice's wages are not meant to be enough to keep a wife on, as a rule, my dear.'

'Then you shouldn't have had one.'

'Come, Arabella! That's too bad, when you know how it came about.'

'I'll declare afore Heaven that I thought what I told you was true. Doctor Vilbert thought so. It was a good job for you that it wasn't so!'

'I don't mean that,' he said hastily. 'I mean before that time. I know it was not your fault; but those women friends of yours gave you bad advice. If they hadn't, or you hadn't taken it, we should at this moment have been free from a bond which, not to mince matters, galls both of us devilishly. It may be very sad, but it is true.'

'Who's been telling you about my friends? What advice? I insist upon your telling me.'

'Pooh—I'd rather not.'

'But you shall—you ought to. It is mean of 'ee not to!'

'Very well.' And he hinted gently what had been revealed to him. 'But I don't wish to dwell upon it. Let us say no more about it.'

Her defensive manner collapsed. 'That was nothing,' she said, laughing coldly. 'Every woman has a right to do such as that. The risk is hers.'

'I quite deny it, Bella. She might if no life-long penalty attached to it for the man, or, in his default, for herself; if the weakness of the moment could end with the moment, or even with the year. But when effects stretch so far she should not go and do that which entraps a man if he is honest, or herself if he is otherwise.'

'What ought I to have done?'

'Given me time. . . . Why do you fuss yourself about melting down that pig's fat to-night? Please put it away!'

'Then I must do it to-morrow morning. It won't keep.'

'Very well—do.'

I–11

Next morning, which was Sunday, she resumed operations about ten o'clock; and the renewed work recalled the conversation which had

accompanied it the night before, and put her back into the same intractable temper.

'That's the story about me in Marygreen, is it—that I entrapped 'ee?
Much of a catch you were, Lord send!' As she warmed she saw some
of Jude's dear ancient classics on a table where they ought not to have
been laid. 'I won't have them books here in the way!' she cried petulantly; and seizing them one by one she began throwing them upon
the floor.

'Leave my books alone!' he said. 'You might have thrown them aside
if you had liked, but as to soiling them like that, it is disgusting!' In
the operation of making lard Arabella's hands had become smeared
with the hot grease, and her fingers consequently left very perceptible
imprints on the book-covers. She continued deliberately to toss the
books severally upon the floor, till Jude, incensed beyond bearing,
caught her by the arms to make her leave off. Somehow, in doing so,
he loosened the fastening of her hair, and it rolled about her ears.

'Let me go!' she said.

'Promise to leave the books alone.'

She hesitated. 'Let me go!' she repeated.

'Promise!'

After a pause: 'I do.'

Jude relinquished his hold, and she crossed the room to the door,
out of which she went with a set face, and into the highway. Here she
began to saunter up and down, perversely pulling her hair into a worse
disorder than he had caused, and unfastening several buttons of her
gown. It was a fine Sunday morning, dry, clear and frosty, and the bells
of Alfredston Church could be heard on the breeze from the north.
People were going along the road, dressed in their holiday clothes; they
were mainly lovers—such pairs as Jude and Arabella had been when
they sported along the same track some months earlier. These pedestrians turned to stare at the extraordinary spectacle she now presented,
bonnetless, her dishevelled hair blowing in the wind, her bodice apart,
her sleeves rolled above her elbows for her work, and her hands reeking
with melted fat. One of the passers said in mock terror: 'Good Lord
deliver us!'

'See how he's served me!' she cried. 'Making me work Sunday mornings when I ought to be going to my church, and tearing my hair off
my head, and my gown off my back!'

Jude was exasperated, and went out to drag her in by main force.
Then he suddenly lost his heat. Illuminated with the sense that all was
over between them, and that it mattered not what she did, or he, her
husband stood still, regarding her. Their lives were ruined, he thought;
ruined by the fundamental error of their matrimonial union: that of
having based a permanent contract on a temporary feeling which had

no necessary connection with affinities that alone render a life-long comradeship tolerable.

'Going to ill-use me on principle, as your father ill-used your mother, and your father's sister ill-used her husband?' she asked. 'All you be a queer lot as husbands and wives!'

Jude fixed an arrested, surprised look on her. But she said no more, and continued her saunter till she was tired. He left the spot, and, after wandering vaguely a little while, walked in the direction of Mary-green. Here he called upon his great-aunt, whose infirmities daily increased.

'Aunt—did my father ill-use my mother, and my aunt her husband?' said Jude abruptly, sitting down by the fire.

She raised her ancient eyes under the rim of the bygone bonnet that she always wore. 'Who's been telling you that?' she said.

'I have heard it spoken of, and want to know all.'

'You med so well, I s'pose; though your wife—I reckon 'twas she—must have been a fool to open up that! There isn't much to know after all. Your father and mother couldn't get on together, and they parted. It was coming home from Alfredston market, when you were a baby—on the hill by the Brown House barn—that they had their last differ-ence, and took leave of one another for the last time. Your mother soon afterwards died—she drowned herself, in short, and your father went away with you to South Wessex, and never came here anymore.'

Jude recalled his father's silence about North Wessex and Jude's mother, never speaking of either till his dying day.

'It was the same with your father's sister. Her husband offended her, and she so disliked living with him afterwards that she went away to London with her little maid. The Fawleys were not made for wedlock: it never seemed to sit well upon us. There's sommat in our blood that won't take kindly to the notion of being bound to do what we do readily enough if not bound. That's why you ought to have hearkened to me, and not ha' married.'

'Where did father and mother part—by the Brown House, did you say?'

'A little further on—where the road to Fenworth branches off, and the handpost stands. A gibbet once stood there not onconnected with our history. But let that be.'

In the dusk of that evening Jude walked away from his old aunt's as if to go home. But as soon as he reached the open down he struck out upon it till he came to a large round pond. The frost continued, though it was not particularly sharp, and the larger stars overhead came out slow and flickering. Jude put one foot on the edge of the ice, and then the other: it cracked under his weight; but this did not deter him. He ploughed his way inward to the centre, the ice making sharp noises as he went. When just about the middle he looked around him and gave a jump. The cracking repeated itself; but he did not go down. He jumped again, but the cracking had ceased. Jude went back to the edge, and stepped upon the ground.

It was curious, he thought. What was he reserved for? He supposed he was not a sufficiently dignified person for suicide. Peaceful death abhorred him as a subject, and would not take him.

What could he do of a lower kind than self-extermination; what was there less noble, more in keeping with his present degraded position? He could get drunk. Of course that was it; he had forgotten. Drinking was the regular, stereotyped resource of the despairing worthless. He began to see now why some men boozed at inns. He struck down the hill northwards and came to an obscure public-house. On entering and sitting down the sight of the picture of Samson and Delilah on the wall caused him to recognize the place as that he had visited with Arabella on that first Sunday evening of their courtship. He called for liquor and drank briskly for an hour or more.

Staggering homeward late that night, with all his sense of depression gone, and his head fairly clear still, he began to laugh boisterously, and to wonder how Arabella would receive him in his new aspect. The house was in darkness when he entered, and in his stumbling state it was some time before he could get a light. Then he found that, though the marks of pig-dressing, of fats and scallops,[1] were visible, the materials themselves had been taken away. A line written by his wife on the inside of an old envelope was pinned to the cotton blower[2] of the fireplace:

'Have gone to my friends. Shall not return.'

All the next day he remained at home, and sent off the carcase of the pig to Alfredston. He then cleaned up the premises, locked the door, put the key in a place she would know if she came back, and returned to his masonry at Alfredston.

At night when he again plodded home he found she had not visited the house. The next day went in the same way, and the next. Then there came a letter from her.

That she had grown tired of him she frankly admitted. He was such a slow old coach, and she did not care for the sort of life he led. There was no prospect of his ever bettering himself or her. She further went on to say that her parents had, as he knew, for some time considered the question of emigrating to Australia, the pig-jobbing[3] business being a poor one nowadays. They had at last decided to go, and she proposed to go with them, if he had no objections. A woman of her sort would have more chance over there than in this stupid country.

---

1. "The stringy part of the fat which cannot be resolved into lard" (Wright's *English Dialect Dictionary*).
2. Curtain hung over fireplace to produce a current of air.
3. Dealing in pigs.

Jude replied that he had not the least objection to her going. He thought it a wise course, since she wished to go, and one that might be to the advantage of both. He enclosed in the packet containing the letter the money that had been realized by the sale of the pig, with all he had besides, which was not much.

From that day he heard no more of her except indirectly, though her father and his household did not immediately leave, but waited till his goods and other effects had been sold off. When Jude learnt that there was to be an auction of the house of the Donns he packed his own household goods into a waggon, and sent them to her at the aforesaid homestead, that she might sell them with the rest, or as many of them as she should choose.

He then went into lodgings at Alfredston, and saw in a shop-window the little handbill announcing the sale of his father-in-law's furniture. He noted its date, which came and passed without Jude's going near the place, or perceiving that the traffic out of Alfredston by the southern road was materially increased by the auction. A few days later he entered a dingy broker's shop in the main street of the town, and amid a heterogeneous collection of saucepans, a clothes-horse, rolling pin, brass candlestick, swing looking-glass, and other things at the back of the shop, evidently just brought in from a sale, he perceived a framed photograph, which turned out to be his own portrait.

It was one which he had had specially taken and framed by a local man in bird's-eye maple, as a present for Arabella, and had duly given her on their wedding-day. On the back was still to be read, '*Jude to Arabella*,' with the date. She must have thrown it in with the rest of her property at the auction.

'Oh,' said the broker, seeing him look at this and the other articles in the heap, and not perceiving that the portrait was of himself: 'It is a small lot of stuff that was knocked down to me at a cottage sale out on the road to Marygreen. The frame is a very useful one, if you take out the likeness. You shall have it for a shilling.'

The utter death of every tender sentiment in his wife, as brought home to him by this mute and undesigned evidence of her sale of his portrait and gift, was the conclusive little stroke required to demolish all sentiment in him. He paid the shilling, took the photograph away with him, and burnt it, frame and all, when he reached his lodging.

Two or three days later he heard that Arabella and her parents had departed. He had sent a message offering to see her for a formal leave-taking, but she had said that it would be better otherwise, since she was bent on going, which perhaps was true. On the evening following their emigration, when his day's work was done, he came out of doors after supper, and strolled in the starlight along the too familiar road towards the upland whereon had been experienced the chief emotions of his life. It seemed to be his own again.

He could not realize himself. On the old track he seemed to be a boy still, hardly a day older than when he had stood dreaming at the top of that hill, inwardly fired for the first time with ardours for Christminster and scholarship. 'Yet I am a man,' he said. 'I have a wife. More, I have arrived at the still riper stage of having disagreed with her, disliked her, had a scuffle with her, and parted from her.'

He remembered then that he was standing not far from the spot at which the parting between his father and his mother was said to have occurred.

A little further on was the summit whence Christminster, or what he had taken for that city, had seemed to be visible. A milestone, now as always, stood at the roadside hard by. Jude drew near it, and felt rather than read the mileage to the city. He remembered that once on his way home he had proudly cut with his keen new chisel an inscription on the back of that milestone, embodying his aspirations. It had been done in the first week of his apprenticeship, before he had been diverted from his purposes by an unsuitable woman. He wondered if the inscription were legible still, and going to the back of the milestone brushed away the nettles. By the light of a match he could still discern what he had cut so enthusiastically so long ago:

T H I T H E R
J. F.

The sight of it, unimpaired, within its screen of grass and nettles, lit in his soul a spark of the old fire. Surely his plan should be to move onward through good and ill—to avoid morbid sorrow even though he did see uglinesses in the world? *Bene agere et Lætari*—to do good cheerfully—which he had heard to be the philosophy of one Spinoza,[4] might be his own even now.

He might battle with his evil star, and follow out his original intention.

By moving to a spot a little way off he uncovered the horizon in a north-easterly direction. There actually rose the faint halo, a small dim nebulousness, hardly recognizable save by the eye of faith. It was enough for him. He would go to Christminster as soon as the term of his apprenticeship expired.

He returned to his lodgings in a better mood, and said his prayers.

---

4. Dutch philosopher (1632–1677).

Part Second: At Christminster[1]

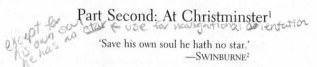

*except for
his own soul
he has no
star ← use for navigational orientation*

'Save his own soul he hath no star.'
—SWINBURNE[2]

'Notitiam primosque gradus vicinia fecit;
Tempore crevit amor.'
—OVID[3]

II–1

The next noteworthy move in Jude's life was that in which he appeared gliding steadily onward through a dusky landscape of some three years' later leafage than had graced his courtship of Arabella, and the disruption of his coarse conjugal life with her. He was walking towards Christminster City, at a point a mile or two to the south-west of it.

He had at last found himself clear of Marygreen and Alfredston: he was out of his apprenticeship, and with his tools at his back seemed to be in the way of making a new start—the start to which, barring the interruption involved in his intimacy and married experience with Arabella, he had been looking forward for about ten years.

Jude would now have been described as a young man with a forcible, meditative, and earnest rather than handsome cast of countenance. He was of dark complexion, with dark harmonizing eyes, and he wore a closely trimmed black beard of more advanced growth than is usual at his age; this, with his great mass of black curly hair, was some trouble to him in combing and washing out the stone-dust that settled on it in the pursuit of his trade. His capabilities in the latter, having been acquired in the country, were of an all-round sort, including monumental stonecutting, gothic free-stone work for the restoration of churches, and carving of a general kind. In London he would probably have become specialized and have made himself a 'moulding mason,' a 'foliage sculptor'—perhaps a 'statuary.'

He had that afternoon driven in a cart from Alfredston to the village nearest the city in this direction, and was now walking the remaining four miles rather from choice than from necessity, having always fancied himself arriving thus.

The ultimate impulse to come had had a curious origin—one more nearly related to the emotional side of him than to the intellectual, as is often the case with young men. One day while in lodgings at Alfred-

---

1. Based on the university city of Oxford.
2. From the "Prelude" to *Songs before Sunrise* (1871), by A. C. Swinburne (1837–1909), one of Hardy's favorite poets.
3. "Closeness led to awareness and the first steps: love grew with time" (*Metamorphoses* 4.59–60). Ovid is a Latin poet.

ston he had gone to Marygreen to see his old aunt, and had observed between the brass candlesticks on her mantelpiece the photograph of a pretty girlish face, in a broad hat with radiating folds under the brim like the rays of a halo. He had asked who she was. His grand-aunt had gruffly replied that she was his cousin Sue Bridehead, of the inimical branch of the family; and on further questioning the old woman had replied that the girl lived in Christminster, though she did not know where, or what she was doing.

His aunt would not give him the photograph. But it haunted him; and ultimately formed a quickening ingredient in his latent intent of following his friend the schoolmaster thither.

He now paused at the top of a crooked and gentle declivity, and obtained his first near view of the city. Grey stoned and dun-roofed, it stood within hail of the Wessex border, and almost with the tip of one small toe within it, at the northernmost point of the crinkled line along which the leisurely Thames strokes the fields of that ancient kingdom. The buildings now lay quiet in the sunset, a vane here and there on their many spires and domes giving sparkle to a picture of sober secondary and tertiary hues.

Reaching the bottom he moved along the level way between pollard willows growing indistinct in the twilight, and soon confronted the outmost lamps of the town—some of those lamps which had sent into the sky the gleam and glory that caught his strained gaze in his days of dreaming, so many years ago. They winked their yellow eyes at him dubiously, and as if, though they had been awaiting him all these years in disappointment at his tarrying, they did not much want him now.

He was a species of Dick Whittington[4] whose spirit was touched to finer issues than a mere material gain. He went along the outlying streets with the cautious tread of an explorer. He saw nothing of the real city in the suburbs on this side. His first want being a lodging he scrutinized carefully such localities as seemed to offer on inexpensive terms the modest type of accommodation he demanded; and after inquiry took a room in a suburb nick-named 'Beersheba,'[5] though he did not know this at the time. Here he installed himself, and having had some tea sallied forth.

It was a windy, whispering, moonless night. To guide himself he opened under a lamp a map he had brought. The breeze ruffled and fluttered it, but he could see enough to decide on the direction he should take to reach the heart of the place.

After many turnings he came up to the first ancient mediæval pile that he had encountered. It was a college, as he could see by the gate-

4. According to a popular legend, Whittington was a poor boy who went to London to seek his fortune, prospered in business ventures, and became Lord Mayor.
5. Town on Lake Galilee, prominent in the Gospels. Hardy's manuscript shows that he first wrote "Capernaum," the scene of Christ's Galilean ministry: Jesus spoke of the lack of faith of the people of Capernaum (Matthew 11.23).

way. He entered it, walked round, and penetrated to dark corners which
no lamplight reached. Close to this college was another; and a little
further on another; and then he began to be encircled as it were with
the breath and sentiment of the venerable city. When he passed
objects out of harmony with its general expression he allowed his eyes
to slip over them as if he did not see them.

A bell[6] began clanging, and he listened till a hundred-and-one
strokes had sounded. He must have made a mistake, he thought; it
was meant for a hundred.

When the gates were shut, and he could no longer get into the
quadrangles, he rambled under the walls and doorways, feeling with
his fingers the contours of their mouldings and carving. The minutes
passed, fewer and fewer people were visible, and still he serpentined
among the shadows, for had he not imagined these scenes through ten
bygone years, and what mattered a night's rest for once? High against
the black sky the flash of a lamp would show crocketed[7] pinnacles and
indented battlements. Down obscure alleys, apparently never trodden
now by the foot of man, and whose very existence seemed to be forgotten, there would jut into the path porticoes, oriels,[8] doorways of
enriched and florid middle-age design, their extinct air being accentuated by the rottenness of the stones. It seemed impossible that modern thought could house itself in such decrepit and superseded
chambers.

Knowing not a human being here, Jude began to be impressed with
the isolation of his own personality, as with a self-spectre, the sensation
being that of one who walked but could not make himself seen or
heard. He drew his breath pensively, and, seeming thus almost his own
ghost, gave his thoughts to the other ghostly presences with which the
nooks were haunted.

During the interval of preparation for this venture, since his wife
and furniture's uncompromising disappearance into space, he had read
and learnt almost all that could be read and learnt by one in his position, of the worthies who had spent their youth within these reverend
walls, and whose souls had haunted them in their maturer age. Some
of them, by the accidents of his reading, loomed out in his fancy dis-
proportionately large by comparison with the rest. The brushing of the
wind against the angles, buttresses, and door-jambs were as the passing
of these only other inhabitants, the tappings of each ivy leaf on its
neighbour were as the mutterings of their mournful souls, the shadows
as their thin shapes in nervous movement, making him comrades in

6. "The *Great Tom* [in Christ Church, Hardy's "Cardinal College"], one of the largest bells in
   England . . . is tolled every evening at ten minutes past nine o'clock, one hundred and one
   times . . . at the closing of college gates" (*The Oxford University and City Guide*, 1860).
7. Decorated with Gothic ornaments.
8. Projecting rooms or recesses with windows.

his solitude. In the gloom it was as if he ran against them without feeling their bodily frames.

The streets were now deserted, but on account of these things he could not go in. There were poets abroad, of early date and of late, from the friend and eulogist of Shakespear[9] down to him who has recently passed into silence,[1] and that musical one of the tribe who is still among us.[2] Speculative philosophers drew along, not always with wrinkled foreheads and hoary hair as in framed portraits, but pink-faced, slim, and active as in youth; modern divines sheeted in their surplices, among whom the most real to Jude Fawley were the founders of the religious school called Tractarian; the well-known three, the enthusiast, the poet, and the formularist,[3] the echoes of whose teachings had influenced him even in his obscure home. A start of aversion appeared in his fancy to move them at sight of those other sons of the place, the form in the full-bottomed wig, statesman, rake, reasoner, and sceptic; smoothly shaven historian so ironically civil to Christianity,[4] with others of the same incredulous temper, who knew each quad as well as the faithful, and took equal freedom in haunting its cloisters.

He regarded the statesmen in their various types, men of firmer movement and less dreamy air; the scholar, the speaker, the plodder; the man whose mind grew with his growth in years, and the man whose mind contracted with the same.

The scientists and philologists followed on in his mind-sight in an odd impossible combination, men of meditative faces, strained foreheads, and weak-eyed as bats with constant research; then official characters—such men as Governor-Generals and Lord-Lieutenants, in whom he took little interest; Chief-Justices and Lord Chancellors, silent thin-lipped figures of whom he knew barely the names. A keener regard attached to the prelates, by reason of his own former hopes. Of them he had an ample band—some men of heart, others rather men of head; he who apologized for the Church in Latin;[5] the saintly author of the Evening Hymn;[6] and near them the great itinerant preacher, hymn-writer, and zealot[7] shadowed like Jude by his matrimonial difficulties.

---

9. Ben Jonson (1572–1637). (A "key" to this and the next eighteen names alluded to is given by Hardy in a letter to Mrs. Henniker [see p. 344 below] dated November 10, 1895.)
1. Robert Browning: Hardy noted Browning's death in his diary on December 13, 1889.
2. Swinburne.
3. John Henry Newman (1801–1890), John Keble (1792–1866), and Edward Pusey (1800–1882), leaders of the Tractarian Movement (see p. 121 below).
4. Edward Gibbon (1737–1794), author of The Decline and Fall of the Roman Empire. Sceptic: Lord Bolingbroke (1678–1751).
5. Hardy's "key" has "can't remember!" against this reference. The most likely candidate is Newman: his autobiography, Apologia pro vita sua, has a Latin title but is written in English; it has been suggested that the work referred to may be the Dissertationculae quaedam critico-theologicae.
6. Bishop Ken (1637–1711).
7. John Wesley (1703–1791).

Jude found himself speaking out loud, holding conversations with them as it were, like an actor in a melodrama who apostrophizes the audience on the other side of the footlights; till he suddenly ceased with a start at his absurdity. Perhaps those incoherent words of the wanderer were heard within the walls by some student or thinker over his lamp; and he may have raised his head, and wondered what voice it was, and what it betokened. Jude now perceived that, so far as solid flesh went, he had the whole aged city to himself with the exception of a belated townsman here and there, and that he seemed to be catching a cold.

A voice reached him out of the shade; a real and local voice:

'You've been a-settin' a long time on that plinth-stone, young man. What med you be up to?'

It came from a policeman who had been observing Jude without the latter observing him.

Jude went home and to bed, after reading up a little about these men and their several messages to the world from a book or two that he had brought with him concerning the sons of the University. As he drew towards sleep various memorable words of theirs that he had just been conning seemed spoken by them in muttering utterances; some audible, some unintelligible to him. One of the spectres[8] (who afterwards mourned Christminster as 'the home of lost causes,' though Jude did not remember this) was now apostrophizing her thus:

'Beautiful city! so venerable, so lovely, so unravaged by the fierce intellectual life of our century, so serene! . . . Her ineffable charm keeps ever calling us to the true goal of all of us, to the ideal, to perfection.'

Another voice was that of the Corn Law convert,[9] whose phantom he had just seen in the quadrangle with a great bell. Jude thought his soul might have been shaping the historic words of his master-speech:

'Sir, I may be wrong, but my impression is that my duty towards a country threatened with famine requires that that which has been the ordinary remedy under all similar circumstances should be resorted to now, namely, that there should be free access to the food of man from whatever quarter it may come. . . . Deprive me of office to-morrow, you can never deprive me of the consciousness that I have exercised the powers committed to me from no corrupt or interested motives, from no desire to gratify ambition, for no personal gain.'

Then the sly author[1] of the immortal Chapter on Christianity: 'How shall we excuse the supine inattention of the Pagan and philosophic world, to those evidences [miracles] which were presented by Omnipotence? . . . The sages of Greece and Rome turned aside from the awful

8. The words quoted appear in the preface to Matthew Arnold's *Essays in Criticism: First Series* (1865).
9. Sir Robert Peel (1788–1850); the speech quoted from was delivered in the House of Commons on May 15, 1846, when Peel was prime minister.
1. Gibbon; the chapter referred to is chapter 15 of the *Decline and Fall*.

spectacle, and appeared unconscious of any alterations in the moral or physical government of the world.'

Then the shade of the poet,[2] the last of the optimists:

'How the world is made for each of us!
·   ·   ·   ·   ·
And each of the Many helps to recruit
The life of the race by a general plan.'

Then one of the three enthusiasts he had seen just now, the author of the *Apologia*:[3]

'My argument was . . . that absolute certitude as to the truths of natural theology was the result of an assemblage of concurring and converging probabilities . . . that probabilities which did not reach to logical certainty might create a mental certitude.'

The second of them,[4] no polemic, murmured quieter things:

'Why should we faint, and fear to live alone,
Since all alone, so Heaven has will'd, we die'?

He likewise heard some phrases spoken by the phantom with the short face, the genial Spectator:[5]

'When I look upon the tombs of the great, every motion of envy dies in me; when I read the epitaphs of the beautiful, every inordinate desire goes out; when I meet with the grief of parents upon a tomb-stone, my heart melts with compassion; when I see the tombs of the parents themselves, I consider the vanity of grieving for those whom we must quickly follow.'

And lastly a gentle-voiced prelate[6] spoke, during whose meek, familiar rhyme, endeared to him from earliest childhood, Jude fell asleep:

'Teach me to live, that I may dread
The grave as little as my bed.
Teach me to die . . . '

He did not wake till morning. The ghostly past seemed to have gone, and everything spoke of to-day. He started up in bed, thinking he had overslept himself, and then said:

'By Jove—I had quite forgotten my sweet-faced cousin, and that she's here all the time! . . . and my old schoolmaster, too.' His words about his schoolmaster had, perhaps, less zest in them than his words concerning his cousin.

---

2. Browning; the lines quoted are from "By the Fire-side."
3. Newman, whose autobiography is titled *Apologia pro vita sua* (1864).
4. Keble; the quotation is from his popular collection of devotional poems, *The Christian Year* (1827).
5. Joseph Addison (1672–1719); the sentence quoted (slightly inaccurately) is from his *Spectator* no. 26.
6. Bishop Ken; the lines are from his famous "Evening Hymn."

II–2

Necessary meditations on the actual, including the mean bread-and-cheese question, dissipated the phantasmal for a while, and compelled Jude to smother high thinkings under immediate needs. He had to get up, and seek for work, manual work; the only kind deemed by many of its professors to be work at all.

Passing out into the streets on this errand he found that the colleges had treacherously changed their sympathetic countenances: some were pompous; some had put on the look of family vaults above ground; something barbaric loomed in the masonries of all. The spirits of the great men had disappeared.

The numberless architectural pages around him he read, naturally, less as an artist-critic of their forms than as an artizan and comrade of the dead handicraftsmen whose muscles had actually executed those forms. He examined the mouldings, stroked them as one who knew their beginning, said they were difficult or easy in the working, had taken little or much time, were trying to the arm, or convenient to the tool.

What at night had been perfect and ideal was by day the more or less defective real. Cruelties, insults, had, he perceived, been inflicted on the aged erections. The condition of several moved him as he would have been moved by maimed sentient beings. They were wounded, broken, sloughing off their outer shape in the deadly struggle against years, weather, and man.

The rottenness of these historical documents reminded him that he was not, after all, hastening on to begin the morning practically as he had intended. He had come to work, and to live by work, and the morning had nearly gone. It was, in one sense, encouraging to think that in a place of crumbling stones there must be plenty for one of his trade to do in the business of renovation. He asked his way to the workyard of the stone-mason whose name had been given him at Alfredston; and soon heard the familiar sound of the rubbers and chisels.

The yard was a little centre of regeneration. Here, with keen edges and smooth curves, were forms in the exact likeness of those he had seen abraded and time-eaten on the walls. These were the ideas in modern prose which the lichened colleges presented in old poetry. Even some of those antiques might have been called prose when they were new. They had done nothing but wait, and had become poetical. How easy to the smallest building; how impossible to most men.

He asked for the foreman, and looked among the new traceries, mul-lions, transoms, shafts, pinnacles, and battlements standing on the bankers[1] half worked, or waiting to be removed. They were marked by precision, mathematical straightness, smoothness, exactitude: there in the old walls were the broken lines of the original idea; jagged curves, disdain of precision, irregularity, disarray.

For a moment there fell on Jude a true illumination; that here in the stone yard was a centre of effort as worthy as that dignified by the name of scholarly study within the noblest of the colleges. But he lost it under stress of his old idea. He would accept any employment which might be offered him on the strength of his late employer's recommendation; but he would accept it as a provisional thing only. This was his form of the modern vice of unrest.

Moreover he perceived that at best only copying, patching and imitating went on here; which he fancied to be owing to some temporary and local cause. He did not at that time see that mediævalism was as dead as a fern-leaf in a lump of coal; that other developments were shaping in the world around him, in which Gothic architecture and its associations had no place. The deadly animosity of contemporary logic and vision towards so much of what he held in reverence was not yet revealed to him.

Having failed to obtain work here as yet he went away, and thought again of his cousin, whose presence somewhere at hand he seemed to feel in wavelets of interest, if not of emotion. How he wished he had that pretty portrait of her! At last he wrote to his aunt to send it. She did so, with a request, however, that he was not to bring disturbance into the family by going to see the girl or her relations. Jude, a ridiculously affectionate fellow, promised nothing, put the photograph on the mantelpiece, kissed it—he did not know why—and felt more at home. She seemed to look down and preside over his tea. It was cheering—the one thing uniting him to the emotions of the living city.

There remained the schoolmaster—probably now a reverend parson. But he could not possibly hunt up such a respectable man just yet; so raw and unpolished was his condition, so precarious were his fortunes. Thus he still remained in loneliness. Although people moved round him he virtually saw none. Not as yet having mingled with the active life of the place it was largely non-existent to him. But the saints and prophets in the window-tracery, the paintings in the galleries, the statues, the busts, the gurgoyles,[2] the corbel-heads[3]—these seemed to breathe his atmosphere. Like all new comers to a spot on which the

---

1. Stone benches used by masons. "Traceries": interlaced stonework on a Gothic window or vault; "transoms": horizontal bars of stone across mullioned windows; "shafts": slender stone columns.
2. Gargoyles: projecting spouts, often in the form of grotesque human or animal figures, to carry rainwater clear of the walls of a building.
3. A corbel is a projection sticking out from a wall and supporting some weight above it; it is often carved in the form of a head.

past is deeply graven he heard that past announcing itself with an emphasis altogether unsuspected by, and even incredible to, the habitual residents.

For many days he haunted the cloisters and quadrangles of the colleges at odd minutes in passing them, surprised by impish echoes of his own footsteps, smart as the blows of a mallet. The Christminster 'sentiment,' as it had been called, ate further and further into him; till he probably knew more about those buildings materially, artistically, and historically, than any one of their inmates.

It was not till now, when he found himself actually on the spot of his enthusiasm, that Jude perceived how far away from the object of that enthusiasm he really was. Only a wall divided him from those happy young contemporaries of his with whom he shared a common mental life; men who had nothing to do from morning till night but to read, mark, learn, and inwardly digest.[4] Only a wall—but what a wall!

Every day, every hour, as he went in search of labour, he saw them going and coming also, rubbed shoulders with them, heard their voices, marked their movements. The conversation of some of the more thoughtful among them seemed oftentimes, owing to his long and persistent preparation for this place, to be peculiarly akin to his own thoughts. Yet he was as far from them as if he had been at the antipodes. Of course he was. He was a young workman in a white blouse, and with stone-dust in the creases of his clothes; and in passing him they did not even see him, or hear him, rather saw through him as through a pane of glass at their familiars beyond. Whatever they were to him, he to them was not on the spot at all; and yet he had fancied he would be close to their lives by coming there.

But the future lay ahead after all; and if he could only be so fortunate as to get into good employment he would put up with the inevitable. So he thanked God for his health and strength, and took courage. For the present he was outside the gates of everything, colleges included: perhaps some day he would be inside. Those palaces of light and leading; he might some day look down on the world through their panes.

At length he did receive a message from the stonemason's yard—that a job was waiting for him. It was his first encouragement, and he closed with the offer promptly.

He was young and strong, or he never could have executed with such zest the undertakings to which he now applied himself, since they involved reading most of the night after working all the day. First he bought a shaded lamp for four and sixpence, and obtained a good light. Then he got pens, paper, and such other necessary books as he had been unable to obtain elsewhere. Then, to the consternation of his

4. Quoted from the *Book of Common Prayer*.

landlady, he shifted all the furniture of his room—a single one for living and sleeping—rigged up a curtain on a rope across the middle, to make a double chamber out of one, hung up a thick blind that nobody should know how he was curtailing the hours of sleep, laid out his books, and sat down.

Having been deeply encumbered by marrying, getting a cottage, and buying the furniture which had disappeared in the wake of his wife, he had never been able to save any money since the time of those disastrous ventures, and till his wages began to come in he was obliged to live in the narrowest way. After buying a book or two he could not even afford himself a fire; and when the nights reeked with the raw and cold air from the Meadows he sat over his lamp in a great-coat, hat, and woollen gloves.

From his window he could perceive the spire of the Cathedral, and the ogee[5] dome under which resounded the great bell of the city. The tall tower, tall belfry windows, and tall pinnacles of the college by the bridge he could also get a glimpse of by going to the staircase. These objects he used as stimulants when his faith in the future was dim.

Like enthusiasts in general he made no inquiries into details of procedure. Picking up general notions from casual acquaintance, he never dwelt upon them. For the present, he said to himself, the one thing necessary was to get ready by accumulating money and knowledge, and await whatever chances were afforded to such an one of becoming a son of the University. 'For wisdom is a defence, and money is a defence; but the excellency of knowledge is, that wisdom giveth life to them that have it.'[6] His desire absorbed him, and left no part of him to weigh its practicability.

At this time he received a nervously anxious letter from his poor old aunt, on the subject which had previously distressed her—a fear that Jude would not be strong-minded enough to keep away from his cousin Sue Bridehead and her relations. Sue's father, his aunt believed, had gone back to London, but the girl remained at Christminster. To make her still more objectionable she was an artist or designer of some sort in what was called an ecclesiastical warehouse, which was a perfect seed-bed of idolatry, and she was no doubt abandoned to mummeries[7] on that account—if not quite a Papist. (Miss Drusilla Fawley was of her date, Evangelical.)

As Jude was rather on an intellectual track than a theological, this news of Sue's probable opinions did not much influence him one way or the other, but the clue to her whereabouts was decidedly interesting. With an altogether singular pleasure he walked at his earliest spare minutes past the shops answering to his great-aunt's description; and

5. Curved in an S shape.
6. Ecclesiastes 7.12.
7. Contemptuous term for religious rituals (the original meaning is "play acting").

beheld in one of them a young girl sitting behind a desk, who was suspiciously like the original of the portrait. He ventured to enter on a trivial errand, and having made his purchase lingered on the scene. The shop seemed to be kept entirely by women. It contained Anglican books, stationery, texts, and fancy goods: little plaster angels on brackets, Gothic-framed pictures of saints, ebony crosses that were almost crucifixes, prayer-books that were almost missals.[8] He felt very shy of looking at the girl in the desk; she was so pretty that he could not believe it possible that she should belong to him. Then she spoke to one of the two older women behind the counter; and he recognized in the accents certain qualities of his own voice; softened and sweetened, but his own. What was she doing? He stole a glance round. Before her lay a piece of zinc, cut to the shape of a scroll three or four feet long, and coated with a dead-surface paint on one side. Hereon she was designing or illuminating, in characters of Church text, the single word

ALLELUJA

'A sweet, saintly, Christian business, hers!' thought he.

Her presence here was now fairly enough explained, her skill in work of this sort having no doubt been acquired from her father's occupation as an ecclesiastical worker in metal. The lettering on which she was engaged was clearly intended to be fixed up in some chancel to assist devotion.

He came out. It would have been easy to speak to her there and then, but it seemed scarcely honourable towards his aunt to disregard her request so incontinently. She had used him roughly, but she had brought him up: and the fact of her being powerless to control him lent a pathetic force to a wish that would have been inoperative as an argument.

So Jude gave no sign. He would not call upon Sue just yet. He had other reasons against doing so when he had walked away. She seemed so dainty beside himself in his rough working-jacket and dusty trousers that he felt he was as yet unready to encounter her, as he had felt about Mr. Phillotson. And how possible it was that she had inherited the antipathies of her family, and would scorn him, as far as a Christian could, particularly when he had told her that unpleasant part of his history which had resulted in his becoming enchained to one of her own sex whom she would certainly not admire.

Thus he kept watch over her, and liked to feel she was there. The consciousness of her living presence stimulated him. But she remained more or less an ideal character, about whose form he began to weave curious and fantastic day-dreams.

8. Books, often illustrated, used in celebrating mass.

Between two and three weeks afterwards Jude was engaged with
some more men, outside Crozier College in Old-time Street, in getting
a block of worked freestone from a waggon across the pavement, before
hoisting it to the parapet which they were repairing. Standing in position the head man said, 'Spail[9] when ye heave! He-ho!' And they
heaved.

All of a sudden, as he lifted, his cousin stood close to his elbow,
pausing a moment on the bend of her foot till the obstructing object
should have been removed. She looked right into his face with liquid,
untranslatable eyes, that combined, or seemed to him to combine,
keenness with tenderness, and mystery with both, their expression, as
well as that of her lips, taking its life from some words just spoken to
a companion, and being carried on into his face quite unconsciously.
She no more observed his presence than that of the dust-motes which
his manipulations raised into the sunbeams.

His closeness to her was so suggestive that he trembled, and turned
his face away with a shy instinct to prevent her recognizing him, though
as she had never once seen him she could not possibly do so; and might
very well never have heard even his name. He could perceive that
though she was a country-girl at bottom, a latter girlhood of some years
in London, and a womanhood here, had taken all rawness out of her.

When she was gone he continued his work, reflecting on her. He
had been so caught by her influence that he had taken no count of
her general mould and build. He remembered now that she was not a
large figure, that she was light and slight, of the type dubbed elegant.
That was about all he had seen. There was nothing statuesque in her;
all was nervous motion. She was mobile, living, yet a painter might not
have called her handsome or beautiful. But the much that she was
surprised him. She was quite a long way removed from the rusticity
that was his. How could one of his cross-grained, unfortunate, almost
accursed stock, have contrived to reach this pitch of niceness? London
had done it, he supposed.

From this moment the emotion which had been accumulating in
his breast as the bottled-up effect of solitude and the poetized locality
he dwelt in, insensibly began to precipitate itself on this half-visionary
form; and he perceived that, whatever his obedient wish in a contrary
direction, he would soon be unable to resist the desire to make himself
known to her.

He affected to think of her quite in a family way, since there were
crushing reasons why he should not and could not think of her in any
other.

The first reason was that he was married, and it would be wrong.
The second was that they were cousins. It was not well for cousins to

9. Speak, shout (dialect).

fall in love even when circumstances seemed to favour the passion. The third: even were he free, in a family like his own where marriage usually meant a tragic sadness, marriage with a blood-relation would duplicate the adverse conditions, and a tragic sadness might be intensified to a tragic horror.

Therefore, again, he would have to think of Sue with only a relation's mutual interest in one belonging to him; regard her in a practical way as some one to be proud of; to talk and nod to; later on, to be invited to tea by, the emotion spent on her being rigorously that of a kinsman and well-wisher. So would she be to him a kindly star, an elevating power, a companion in Anglican worship, a tender friend.

II–3

But under the various deterrent influences Jude's instinct was to approach her timidly, and the next Sunday he went to the morning service in the Cathedral-church of Cardinal College to gain a further view of her, for he had found that she frequently attended there.

She did not come, and he awaited her in the afternoon, which was finer. He knew that if she came at all she would approach the building along the eastern side of the great green quadrangle from which it was accessible, and he stood in a corner while the bell was going. A few minutes before the hour for service she appeared as one of the figures walking along under the College walls, and at sight of her he advanced up the side opposite, and followed her into the building, more than ever glad that he had not as yet revealed himself. To see her, and to be himself unseen and unknown, was enough for him at present.

He lingered awhile in the vestibule, and the service was some way advanced when he was put into a seat. It was a louring, mournful, still afternoon, when a religion of some sort seems a necessity to ordinary practical men, and not only a luxury of the emotional and leisured classes. In the dim light and the baffling glare of the clerestory[1] windows he could discern the opposite worshippers indistinctly only, but he saw that Sue was among them. He had not long discovered the exact seat that she occupied when the chanting of the 119th Psalm in which the choir was engaged reached its second part, *In quo corriget*,[2] the organ changing to a pathetic Gregorian[3] tune as the singers gave forth:

'Wherewithal shall a young man cleanse his way?'

It was the very question that was engaging Jude's attention at this moment. What a wicked worthless fellow he had been to give vent as

---

1. Upper part of church, above arches of nave, containing windows.
2. The opening words of the Latin version of Psalm 119.9.
3. Ancient type of church music, also known as plainsong; named after Pope Gregory I.

he had done to an animal passion for a woman, and allow it to lead to such disastrous consequences; then to think of putting an end to himself; then to go recklessly and get drunk. The great waves of pedal music tumbled round the choir, and, nursed on the supernatural as he had been, it is not wonderful that he could hardly believe that the psalm was not specially set by some regardful Providence for this moment of his first entry into the solemn building. And yet it was the ordinary psalm for the twenty-fourth evening of the month.

The girl for whom he was beginning to nourish an extraordinary tenderness, was at this time ensphered by the same harmonies as those which floated into his ears; and the thought was a delight to him. She was probably a frequenter of this place, and, steeped body and soul in church sentiment as she must be by occupation and habit, had, no doubt, much in common with him. To an impressionable and lonely young man the consciousness of having at last found anchorage for his thoughts, which promised to supply both social and spiritual possibilities, was like the dew of Hermon,[4] and he remained throughout the service in a sustaining atmosphere of ecstasy.

Though he was loth to suspect it, some people might have said to him that the atmosphere blew as distinctly from Cyprus as from Galilee.[5]

Jude waited till she had left her seat and passed under the screen before he himself moved. She did not look towards him, and by the time he reached the door she was half way down the broad path. Being dressed up in his Sunday suit he was inclined to follow her and reveal himself. But he was not quite ready; and, alas, ought he to do so with the kind of feeling that was awakening in him?

For though it had seemed to have an ecclesiastical basis during the service, and he had persuaded himself that such was the case, he could not altogether be blind to the real nature of the magnetism. She was such a stranger that the kinship was affectation, and he said, 'It can't be! I, a man with a wife, must not know her!' Still Sue *was* his own kin, and the fact of his having a wife, even though she was not in evidence in this hemisphere, might be a help in one sense. It would put all thought of a tender wish on his part out of Sue's mind, and make her intercourse with him free and fearless. It was with some heartache that he saw how little he cared for the freedom and fearlessness that would result in her from such knowledge.

Some little time before the date of this service in the cathedral the pretty, liquid-eyed, light-footed young woman Sue Bridehead had an afternoon's holiday, and leaving the ecclesiastical establishment in

---

4. A high mountain, the scene of Christ's transfiguration (see Mark 9.2–9; also Psalm 133.3).
5. According to Greek legend, Aphrodite, goddess of love, emerged from the sea and landed at Paphos in Cyprus. Cyprus and Galilee here stand, respectively, for physical and spiritual love.

which she not only assisted but lodged, took a walk into the country
with a book in her hand. It was one of those cloudless days which
sometimes occur in Wessex and elsewhere between days of cold and
wet, as if intercalated by caprice of the weather-god. She went along
for a mile or two until she came to much higher ground than that of
the city she had left behind her. The road passed between green fields,
and coming to a stile Sue paused there, to finish the page she was
reading, and then looked back at the towers and domes and pinnacles
new and old.

On the other side of the stile, in the footpath, she beheld a foreigner
with black hair and a sallow face, sitting on the grass beside a large
square board whereon were fixed, as closely as they could stand, a
number of plaster statutettes, some of them bronzed, which he was re-
arranging before proceeding with them on his way. They were in the
main reduced copies of ancient marbles, and comprised divinities of a
very different character from those the girl was accustomed to see portrayed, among them being a Venus of standard pattern, a Diana, and,
of the other sex, Apollo, Bacchus, and Mars. Though the figures were
many yards away from her the south-west sun brought them out so
brilliantly against the green herbage that she could discern their contours with luminous distinctness; and being almost in a line between
herself and the church towers of the city they were awoke in her an
oddly foreign and contrasting set of ideas by comparison. The man
rose, and, seeing her, politely took off his cap, and cried 'I-i-i-mages!'
in an accent that agreed with his appearance. In a moment he dexter-
ously lifted upon his knee the great board with its assembled notabil-
ities divine and human, and raised it to the top of his head, bringing
them on to her and resting the board on the stile. First he offered her
his smaller wares—the busts of kings and queens, then a minstrel, then
a winged Cupid. She shook her head.

'How much are these two?' she said, touching with her finger the
Venus and the Apollo—the largest figures on the tray.

He said she should have them for ten shillings.

'I cannot afford that,' said Sue. She offered considerably less, and to
her surprise the image-man drew them from their wire stay and handed
them over the stile. She clasped them as treasures.

When they were paid for, and the man had gone, she began to be
concerned as to what she should do with them. They seemed so very
large now that they were in her possession, and so very naked. Being
of a nervous temperament she trembled at her enterprise. When she
handled them the white pipeclay came off on her gloves and jacket.
After carrying them along a little way openly an idea came to her, and,
pulling some huge burdock leaves, parsley, and other rank growths from
the hedge, she wrapped up her burden as well as she could in these,

so that what she carried appeared to be an enormous armful of green stuff gathered by a zealous lover of nature.

'Well, anything is better than those everlasting church fal-lals!' she said. But she was still in a trembling state, and seemed almost to wish she had not bought the figures.

Occasionally peeping inside the leaves to see that Venus's arm was not broken, she entered with her heathen load into the most Christian city in the country by an obscure street running parallel to the main one and round a corner to the side door of the establishment to which she was attached. Her purchases were taken straight up to her own chamber, and she at once attempted to lock them in a box that was her very own property; but finding them too cumbersome she wrapped them in large sheets of brown paper, and stood them on the floor in a corner.

The mistress of the house, Miss Fontover, was an elderly lady in spectacles, dressed almost like an abbess; a dab at Ritual,[6] as became one of her business, and a worshipper at the ceremonial church of St. Silas, in the suburb of Beersheba before-mentioned, which Jude also had begun to attend. She was the daughter of a clergyman in reduced circumstances, and at his death, which had occurred several years before this date, she boldly avoided penury by taking over a little shop of church requisites and developing it to its present creditable proportions. She wore a cross and beads round her neck as her only ornament, and knew the Christian Year by heart.

She now came to call Sue to tea, and, finding that the girl did not respond for a moment, entered the room just as the other was hastily putting a string round each parcel.

'Something you have been buying, Miss Bridehead?' she asked, regarding the enwrapped objects.

'Yes—just something to ornament my room,' said Sue.

'Well, I should have thought I had put enough here already,' said Miss Fontover, looking round at the Gothic-framed prints of saints, the Church-text scrolls, and other articles which, having become too stale to sell, had been used to furnish this obscure chamber. 'What is it? How bulky!' She tore a little hole, about as big as a wafer, in the brown paper, and tried to peep in. 'Why, statuary? Two figures? Where did you get them?'

'O—I bought them of a travelling man who sells casts—'

'Two saints?'

'Yes,'

'What ones?'

'St. Peter and St.—St. Mary Magdalen.'

6. An expert in High Church forms of worship (the High Anglican or Anglo-Catholic church stressed ritual and ceremony).

'Well—now come down to tea, and go and finish that organ-text, if there's light enough afterwards.'

These little obstacles to the indulgence of what had been the merest passing fancy, created in Sue a great zest for unpacking her objects and looking at them; and at bedtime, when she was sure of being undisturbed, she unrobed the divinities in comfort. Placing the pair of figures on the chest of drawers, a candle on each side of them, she withdrew to the bed, flung herself down thereon, and began reading a book she had taken from her box, which Miss Fontover knew nothing of. It was a volume of Gibbon, and she read the chapter dealing with the reign of Julian the Apostate.[7] Occasionally she looked up at the statuettes, which appeared strange and out of place, there happening to be a Calvary print hanging between them, and, as if the scene suggested the action, she at length jumped up and withdrew another book from her box—a volume of verse—and turned to the familiar poem— which she read to the end.

> 'Thou hast conquered, O pale Galilean:
> The world has grown grey from thy breath!'[8]

Presently she put out the candles, undressed, and finally extinguished her own light.

She was of an age which usually sleeps soundly, yet to-night she kept waking up, and every time she opened her eyes there was enough diffused light from the street to show her the white plaster figures, standing on the chest of drawers in odd contrast to their environment of text and martyr, and the Gothic-framed Crucifix-picture that was only discernible now as a Latin cross, the figure thereon being obscured by the shades.

On one of these occasions the church clocks struck some small hour. It fell upon the ears of another person who sat bending over his books at a not very distant spot in the same city. Being Saturday night the morrow was one on which Jude had not set his alarm clock to call him at his usually early time, and hence he had stayed up, as was his custom, two or three hours later than he could afford to do on any other day of the week. Just then he was earnestly reading from his Griesbach's text. At the very time that Sue was tossing and staring at her figures, the policeman and belated citizens passing along under his window might have heard, if they had stood still, strange syllables mumbled with fervour within—words that had for Jude an indescribable enchantment: inexplicable sounds something like these:—

'All hemin heis Theos ho Pater, ex hou ta panta, kai hemeis eis auton.'

---

7. Chapter 23 of the *Decline and Fall*. The Roman emperor Julian announced his conversion to paganism in 361; Sue displays a certain daring in reading this particular chapter.
8. From Swinburne's "Hymn to Prosperpine"; the "pale Galilean" is Christ. The reference is to Julian's supposed dying words: "Vicisti, Galilaee" ("Thou hast conquered, O Galilean").

Till the sounds rolled with reverent loudness, as a book was heard to close:—

'Kai heis Kurios Iesous Christos, di hou ta panta kai hemeis di autou!'[9]

II-4

He was a handy man at his trade, an all-round man, as artizans in country-towns are apt to be. In London the man who carves the boss or knob of leafage declines to cut the fragment of moulding which merges in that leafage, as if it were a degradation to do the second half of one whole. When there was not much Gothic moulding for Jude to run, or much window-tracery on the bankers, he would go out lettering monuments or tombstones, and take a pleasure in the change of hand-iwork.

The next time that he saw her was when he was on a ladder exe-cuting a job of this sort inside one of the churches. There was a short morning service, and when the parson entered Jude came down from his ladder, and sat with the half-dozen people forming the congrega-tion, till the prayers should be ended, and he could resume his tapping. He did not observe till the service was half over that one of the women was Sue, who had perforce accompanied the elderly Miss Fontover thither.

Jude sat watching her pretty shoulders, her easy, curiously noncha-lant risings and sittings, and her perfunctory genuflexions, and thought what a help such an Anglican would have been to him in happier circumstances. It was not so much his anxiety to get on with his work that made him go up to it immediately the worshippers began to take their leave: it was that he dared not, in this holy spot, confront the woman who was beginning to influence him in such an indescribable manner. Those three enormous reasons why he must not attempt inti-mate acquaintance with Sue Bridehead now that his interest in her had shown itself to be unmistakably of a sexual kind, loomed as stub-bornly as ever. But it was also obvious that man could not live by work alone; that the particular man Jude, at any rate, wanted something to love. Some men would have rushed incontinently to her, snatched the pleasure of easy friendship which she could hardly refuse, and have left the rest to chance. Not so Jude—at first.

But as the days, and still more particularly the lonely evenings, dragged along, he found himself, to his moral consternation, to be thinking more of her instead of thinking less of her, and experiencing a fearful bliss in doing what was erratic, informal, and unexpected.

9. A verse from the Greek New Testament: "But to us there is but one God, the Father, of whom are all things, and we in him; and one Lord Jesus Christ, by whom are all things, and we by him" (1 Corinthians 8.6).

Surrounded by her influence all day, walking past the spots she frequented, he was always thinking of her, and was obliged to own to
himself that his conscience was likely to be the loser in this battle.

To be sure she was almost an ideality to him still. Perhaps to know
her would be to cure himself of this unexpected and unauthorized
passion. A voice whispered that, though he desired to know her, he did
not desire to be cured.

There was not the least doubt that from his own orthodox point of
view the situation was growing immoral. For Sue to be the loved one
of a man who was licensed by the laws of his country to love Arabella
and none other unto his life's end, was a pretty bad second beginning
when the man was bent on such a course as Jude purposed. This conviction was so real with him that one day when, as was frequent, he
was at work in a neighbouring village church alone, he felt it to be his
duty to pray against his weakness. But much as he wished to be an
exemplar in these things he could not get on. It was quite impossible,
he found, to ask to be delivered from temptation when your heart's
desire was to be tempted unto seventy times seven. So he excused
himself. 'After all,' he said, 'it is not altogether an *erotolepsy*[1] that is
the matter with me, as at that first time. I can see that she is excep-
tionally bright; and it is partly a wish for intellectual sympathy, and a
craving for loving-kindness in my solitude.' Thus he went on adoring
her, fearing to realize that it was human perversity. For whatever Sue's
virtues, talents, or ecclesiastical saturation, it was certain that those
items were not at all the cause of his affection for her.

On an afternoon at this time a young girl entered the stone-mason's
yard with some hesitation, and, lifting her skirts to avoid draggling
them in the white dust, crossed towards the office.

'That's a nice girl,' said one of the men known as Uncle Joe.

'Who is she?' asked another.

'I don't know—I've seen her about here and there. Why, yes, she's
the daughter of that clever chap Bridehead who did all the wrought
ironwork at St. Silas' ten years ago, and went away to London afterwards. I don't know what he's doing now—not much I fancy—as she's
come back here.'

Meanwhile the young woman had knocked at the office door and
asked if Mr. Jude Fawley was at work in the yard. It so happened that
Jude had gone out somewhere or other that afternoon, which information she received with a look of disappointment, and went away
immediately. When Jude returned they told him, and described her,
whereupon he exclaimed, 'Why—that's my cousin Sue!'

He looked along the street after her, but she was out of sight. He
had no longer any thought of a conscientious avoidance of her, and

1. Literally a "love seizure." Hardy appears to have invented the word.

resolved to call upon her that very evening. And when he reached his lodging he found a note from her—a first note—one of those documents which, simple and commonplace in themselves, are seen retrospectively to have been pregnant with impassioned consequences. The very unconsciousness of a looming drama which is shown in such innocent first epistles from women to men, or *vice versa*, makes them, when such a drama follows, and they are read over by the purple or lurid light of it, all the more impressive, solemn, and in cases, terrible.

Sue's was of the most artless and natural kind. She addressed him as her dear cousin Jude; said she had only just learnt by the merest accident that he was living in Christminster, and reproached him with not letting her know. They might have had such nice times together, she said, for she was thrown much upon herself, and had hardly any congenial friend. But now there was every probability of her soon going away, so that the chance of companionship would be lost perhaps for ever.

A cold sweat overspread Jude at the news that she was going away. That was a contingency he had never thought of, and it spurred him to write all the more quickly to her. He would meet her that very evening, he said, one hour from the time of the writing, at the cross in the pavement which marked the spot of the Martyrdoms.[2]

When he had despatched the note by a boy he regretted that in his hurry he should have suggested to her to meet him out of doors, when he might have said he would call upon her. It was, in fact, the country custom to meet thus, and nothing else had occurred to him. Arabella had been met in the same way, unfortunately, and it might not seem respectable to a dear girl like Sue. However, it could not be helped now, and he moved towards the point a few minutes before the hour, under the glimmer of the newly lighted lamps.

The broad street was silent, and almost deserted, although it was not late. He saw a figure on the other side, which turned out to be hers, and they both converged towards the cross-mark at the same moment. Before either had reached it she called out to him:

'I am not going to meet you just there, for the first time in my life! Come further on.'

The voice, though positive and silvery, had been tremulous. They walked on in parallel lines, and, waiting her pleasure, Jude watched till she showed signs of closing in, when he did likewise, the place being where the carriers' carts stood in the daytime, though there was none on the spot then.

'I am sorry that I asked you to meet me, and didn't call,' began Jude with the bashfulness of a lover. 'But I thought it would save time if we were going to walk.'

2. Of Ridley, Latimer, and Cranmer, put to death in 1555–56 during the reign of Mary I.

'O—I don't mind that,' she said with the freedom of a friend. 'I have really no place to ask anybody in to. What I meant was that the place you chose was so horrid—I suppose I ought not to say horrid,—I mean gloomy and inauspicious in its associations . . . But isn't it funny to begin like this, when I don't know you yet?' She looked him up and down curiously, though Jude did not look much at her.

'You seem to know me more than I know you,' she added.

'Yes—I have seen you now and then.'

'And you knew who I was, and didn't speak? And now I am going away!'

'Yes. That's unfortunate. I have hardly any other friend. I have, indeed, one very old friend here somewhere, but I don't quite like to call on him just yet. I wonder if you know anything of him—Mr. Phillotson? A parson somewhere about the county I think he is.'

'No—I only know of one Mr. Phillotson. He lives a little way out in the country, at Lumsdon. He's a village schoolmaster.'

'Ah! I wonder if he's the same. Surely it is impossible! Only a schoolmaster still! Do you know his Christian name—is it Richard?'

'Yes—it is; I've directed books to him, though I've never seen him.'

'Then he couldn't do it!'

Jude's countenance fell, for how could he succeed in an enterprise wherein the great Phillotson had failed? He would have had a day of despair if the news had not arrived during his sweet Sue's presence, but even at this moment he had visions of how Phillotson's failure in the grand University scheme would depress him when she had gone.

'As we are going to take a walk, suppose we go and call upon him?' said Jude suddenly. 'It is not late.'

She agreed, and they went along up a hill, and through some prettily wooded country. Presently the embattled tower and square turret of the church rose into the sky, and then the schoolhouse. They inquired of a person in the street if Mr. Phillotson was likely to be at home, and were informed that he was always at home. A knock brought him to the schoolhouse door, with a candle in his hand and a look of inquiry on his face, which had grown thin and careworn since Jude last set eyes on him.

That after all these years the meeting with Mr. Phillotson should be of this homely complexion destroyed at one stroke the halo which had surrounded the schoolmaster's figure in Jude's imagination ever since their parting. It created in him at the same time a sympathy with Phillotson as an obviously much chastened and disappointed man. Jude told him his name, and said he had come to see him as an old friend who had been kind to him in his youthful days.

'I don't remember you in the least,' said the schoolmaster thoughtfully. 'You were one of my pupils you say? Yes, no doubt; but they number so many thousands by this time of my life, and have naturally changed so much, that I remember very few except the quite recent ones.'

'It was out at Marygreen,' said Jude, wishing he had not come.

'Yes. I was there a short time. And is this an old pupil, too?'

'No—that's my cousin. . . . I wrote to you for some grammars, if you recollect, and you sent them?'

'Ah—yes!—I do dimly recall that incident.'

'It was very kind of you to do it. And it was you who first started me on that course. On the morning you left Marygreen, when your goods were on the waggon, you wished me good-bye, and said your scheme was to be a University man and enter the church—that a degree was the necessary hall-mark of one who wanted to do anything as a theologian or teacher.'

'I remember I thought all that privately; but I wonder I did not keep my own counsel. The idea was given up years ago.'

'I have never forgotten it. It was that which brought me to this part of the country, and out here to see you to-night.'

'Come in,' said Phillotson. 'And your cousin, too.'

They entered the parlour of the schoolhouse, where there was a lamp with a paper shade, which threw the light down on three or four books. Phillotson took it off, so that they could see each other better, and the rays fell on the nervous little face and vivacious dark eyes and hair of Sue, on the earnest features of her cousin, and on the schoolmaster's own maturer face and figure, showing him to be a spare and thoughtful personage of five-and-forty, with a thin-lipped, somewhat refined mouth, a slightly stooping habit, and a black frock coat, which from continued frictions shone a little at the shoulder-blades, the middle of the back, and the elbows.

The old friendship was imperceptibly renewed, the schoolmaster speaking of his experiences, and the cousins of theirs. He told them that he still thought of the church sometimes, and that though he could not enter it as he had intended to do in former years he might enter it as a licentiate.[3] Meanwhile, he said, he was comfortable in his present position, though he was in want of a pupil-teacher.

They did not stay to supper, Sue having to be indoors before it grew late, and the road was retraced to Christminster. Though they had talked of nothing more than general subjects Jude was surprised to find what a revelation of woman his cousin was to him. She was so vibrant that everything she did seemed to have its source in feeling. An exciting thought would make her walk ahead so fast that he could hardly keep up with her; and her sensitiveness on some points was such that it might have been misread as vanity. It was with heart-sickness he perceived that, while her sentiments towards him were those of the frank-

---

3. One holding a license to preach, as opposed to an ordained clergyman.

est friendliness only, he loved her more than before becoming acquainted with her; and the gloom of the walk home lay not in the night overhead, but in the thought of her departure.

'Why must you leave Christminster?' he said regretfully. 'How can you do otherwise than cling to a city in whose history such men as Newman, Pusey, Ward,[4] Keble, loom so large!'

'Yes—they do. Though how large do they loom in the history of the world? . . . What a funny reason for caring to stay! I should never have thought of it!' She laughed.

'Well—I must go,' she continued. 'Miss Fontover, one of the partners whom I serve, is offended with me, and I with her; and it is best to go.'

'How did that happen?'

'She broke some statuary of mine.'

'Oh? Wilfully?'

'Yes. She found it in my room, and though it was my property she threw it on the floor and stamped on it, because it was not according to her taste, and ground the arms and the head of one of the figures all to bits with her heel—a horrid thing?'

'Too Catholic-Apostolic for her, I suppose? No doubt she called them Popish images and talked of the invocation of saints.'

'No. . . . No, she didn't do that. She saw the matter quite differently.'

'Ah! Then I am surprised!'

'Yes. It was for quite some other reason that she didn't like my patron-saints. So I was led to retort upon her; and the end of it was that I resolved not to stay, but to get into an occupation in which I shall be more independent.'

'Why don't you try teaching again? You once did, I heard.'

'I never thought of resuming it; for I was getting on as an art-designer.'

'Do let me ask Mr. Phillotson to let you try your hand in his school? If you like it, and go to a Training College, and become a first-class certificated mistress, you get twice as large an income as any designer or church artist, and twice as much freedom.'

'Well—ask him. Now I must go in. Good-bye, dear Jude! I am so glad we have met at last. We needn't quarrel because our parents did, need we?'

Jude did not like to let her see quite how much he agreed with her, and went his way to the remote street in which he had his lodging.

To keep Sue Bridehead near him was now a desire which operated without regard of consequences, and the next evening he again set out for Lumsdon, fearing to trust to the persuasive effects of a note only. The schoolmaster was unprepared for such a proposal.

---

4. W. G. Ward (1812–1882), theological writer.

'What I rather wanted was second year's transfer, as it is called,' he said. 'Of course your cousin would do, personally; but she has had no experience. O—she has, has she? Does she really think of adopting teaching as a profession?'

Jude said she was disposed to do so, he thought, and his ingenious arguments on her natural fitness for assisting Mr. Phillotson, of which Jude knew nothing whatever, so influenced the schoolmaster that he said he would engage her, assuring Jude as a friend that unless his cousin really meant to follow on in the same course, and regarded this step as the first stage of an apprenticeship, of which her training in a normal school would be the second stage, her time would be wasted quite, the salary being merely nominal.

The day after this visit Phillotson received a letter from Jude, containing the information that he had again consulted his cousin, who took more and more warmly to the idea of tuition; and that she had agreed to come. It did not occur for a moment to the schoolmaster and recluse that Jude's ardour in promoting the arrangements arose from any other feelings towards Sue than the instinct of co-operation common among members of the same family.

II–5

The schoolmaster sat in his homely dwelling attached to the school, both being modern erections; and he looked across the way at the old house in which his teacher Sue had a lodging. The arrangement had been concluded very quickly. A pupil-teacher who was to have been transferred to Mr. Phillotson's school had failed him, and Sue had been taken as stop-gap. All such provisional arrangements as these could only last till the next annual visit of H.M. Inspector, whose approval was necessary to make them permanent. Having taught for some two years in London, though she had abandoned that vocation of late, Miss Bridehead was not exactly a novice, and Phillotson thought there would be no difficulty in retaining her services, which he already wished to do, though she had only been with him three or four weeks. He had found her quite as bright as Jude had described her; and what master-tradesman does not wish to keep an apprentice who saves him half his labour?

It was a little over half-past eight o'clock in the morning, and he was waiting to see her cross the road to the school, when he would follow. At twenty minutes to nine she did cross, a light hat tossed on her head; and he watched her as a curiosity. A new emanation, which had nothing to do with her skill as a teacher, seemed to surround her this morning. He went to the school also, and Sue remained governing her class at the other end of the room, all day under his eye. She certainly was an excellent teacher.

It was part of his duty to give her private lessons in the evening, and some article in the Code made it necessary that a respectable, elderly woman should be present at these lessons when the teacher and the taught were of different sexes. Richard Phillotson thought of the absurdity of the regulation in this case, when he was old enough to be the girl's father; but he faithfully acted up to it; and sat down with her in a room where Mrs. Hawes, the widow at whose house Sue lodged, occupied herself with sewing. The regulation was, indeed, not easy to evade, for there was no other sitting-room in the dwelling.

Sometimes as she figured—it was arithmetic that they were working at—she would involuntarily glance up with a little inquiring smile at him, as if she assumed that, being the master, he must perceive all that was passing in her brain, as right or wrong. Phillotson was not really thinking of the arithmetic at all, but of her, in a novel way which somehow seemed strange to him as preceptor. Perhaps she knew that he was thinking of her thus.

For a few weeks their work had gone on with a monotony which in itself was a delight to him. Then it happened that the children were to be taken to Christminster to see an itinerant exhibition, in the shape of a model of Jerusalem, to which schools were admitted at a penny a head in the interests of education. They marched along the road two and two, she beside her class with her simple cotton sunshade, her little thumb cocked up against its stem; and Phillotson behind in his long dangling coat, handling his walking-stick genteelly, in the musing mood which had come over him since her arrival. The afternoon was one of sun and dust, and when they entered the exhibition room few people were present but themselves.

The model of the ancient city stood in the middle of the apartment, and the proprietor, with a fine religious philanthropy written on his features, walked round it with a pointer in his hand, showing the young people the various quarters and places known to them by name from reading their Bibles; Mount Moriah, the Valley of Jehoshaphat, the City of Zion, the walls and the gates, outside one of which there was a large mound like a tumulus, and on the mound a little white cross. The spot, he said, was Calvary.[1]

'I think,' said Sue to the schoolmaster, as she stood with him a little in the background, 'that this model, elaborate as it is, is a very imaginary production. How does anybody know that Jerusalem was like this in the time of Christ? I am sure this man doesn't.'

'It is made after the best conjectural maps, based on actual visits to the city as it now exists.'

'I fancy we have had enough of Jerusalem' she said, 'considering we are not descended from the Jews. There was nothing first-rate about

---

1. Scene of Christ's crucifixion.

the place, or people, after all—as there was about Athens, Rome, Alexandria, and other old cities.'

'But my dear girl, consider what it is to us!'

She was silent, for she was easily repressed; and then perceived behind the group of children clustered round the model a young man in a white flannel jacket, his form being bent so low in his intent inspection of the Valley of Jehoshaphat that his face was almost hidden from view by the Mount of Olives. 'Look at your cousin Jude,' continued the schoolmaster. 'He doesn't think we have had enough of Jerusalem!'

'Ah—I didn't see him!' she cried in her quick light voice. 'Jude— how seriously you are going into it!'

Jude started up from his reverie, and saw her. 'O—Sue!' he said, with a glad flush of embarrassment. 'These are your school-children, of course! I saw that schools were admitted in the afternoons, and thought you might come; but I got so deeply interested that I didn't remember where I was. How it carries one back, doesn't it! I could examine it for hours, but I have only a few minutes, unfortunately; for I am in the middle of a job out here.'

'Your cousin is so terribly clever that she criticizes it unmercifully,' said Phillotson, with good-humoured satire. 'She is quite sceptical as to its correctness.'

'No, Mr. Phillotson, I am not—altogether! I hate to be what is called a clever girl—there are too many of that sort now!' answered Sue sensitively. 'I only meant—I don't know what I meant—except that it was what you don't understand!'

'I know your meaning,' said Jude ardently (although he did not). 'And I think you are quite right.'

'That's a good Jude—I know *you* believe in me!' She impulsively seized his hand, and leaving a reproachful look on the schoolmaster turned away to Jude, her voice revealing a tremor which she herself felt to be absurdly uncalled for by sarcasm so gentle. She had not the least conception how the hearts of the twain went out to her at this momentary revelation of feeling, and what a complication she was building up thereby in the futures of both.

The model wore too much of an educational aspect for the children not to tire of it soon, and a little later in the afternoon they were all marched back to Lumsdon, Jude returning to his work. He watched the juvenile flock in their clean frocks and pinafores, filing down the street towards the country beside Phillotson and Sue, and a sad, dissatisfied sense of being out of the scheme of the latters' lives had possession of him. Phillotson had invited him to walk out and see them on Friday evening, when there would be no lessons to give to Sue, and Jude had eagerly promised to avail himself of the opportunity.

Meanwhile the scholars and teachers moved homewards, and the next day, on looking on the black-board in Sue's class, Phillotson was surprised to find upon it, skilfully drawn in chalk, a perspective view of Jerusalem, with every building shown in its place.

'I thought you took no interest in the model, and hardly looked at it?' he said.

'I hardly did,' said she, 'but I remembered that much of it.'

'It is more than I had remembered myself.'

Her Majesty's school-inspector was at that time paying 'surprise-visits' in this neighbourhood to test the teaching unawares; and two days later, in the middle of the morning lessons, the latch of the door was softly lifted, and in walked my gentleman, the king of terrors[2]—to pupil-teachers.

To Mr. Phillotson the surprise was not great; like the lady in the story he had been played that trick too many times to be unprepared. But Sue's class was at the further end of the room, and her back was towards the entrance; the inspector therefore came and stood behind her and watched her teaching some half-minute before she became aware of his presence. She turned, and realized that an oft-dreaded moment had come. The effect upon her timidity was such that she uttered a cry of fright. Phillotson, with a strange instinct of solicitude quite beyond his control, was at her side just in time to prevent her falling from faintness. She soon recovered herself, and laughed; but when the inspector had gone there was a reaction, and she was so white that Phillotson took her into his room, and gave her some brandy to bring her round. She found him holding her hand.

'You ought to have told me,' she gasped petulantly, 'that one of the Inspector's surprise-visits was imminent! O what shall I do! Now he'll write and tell the managers that I am no good, and I shall be disgraced for ever!'

'He won't do that, my dear little girl. You are the best teacher ever I had!'

He looked so gently at her that she was moved, and regretted that she had upbraided him. When she was better she went home.

Jude in the meantime had been waiting impatiently for Friday. On both Wednesday and Thursday he had been so much under the influence of his desire to see her that he walked after dark some distance along the road in the direction of the village, and, on returning to his room to read, found himself quite unable to concentrate his mind on the page. On Friday, as soon as he had got himself up as he thought Sue would like to see him, and made a hasty tea, he set out, notwithstanding that the evening was wet. The trees overhead deepened the gloom of the hour, and they dripped sadly upon him, impressing

2. The phrase is normally applied to death.

him with forebodings—illogical forebodings; for though he knew that he loved her he also knew that he could not be more to her than he was.

On turning the corner and entering the village the first sight that greeted his eyes was that of two figures under one umbrella coming out of the vicarage gate. He was too far back for them to notice him, but he knew in a moment that they were Sue and Phillotson. The latter was holding the umbrella over her head, and they had evidently been paying a visit to the vicar—probably on some business connected with the school work. And as they walked along the wet and deserted lane Jude saw Phillotson place his arm round the girl's waist; whereupon she gently removed it; but he replaced it; and she let it remain, looking quickly round her with an air of misgiving. She did not look absolutely behind her, and therefore did not see Jude, who sank into the hedge like one struck with a blight. There he remained hidden till they had reached Sue's cottage and she had passed in, Phillotson going on to the school hard by.

'O, he's too old for her—too old!' cried Jude in all the terrible sickness of hopeless, handicapped love.

He could not interfere. Was he not Arabella's? He was unable to go on further, and retraced his steps towards Christminster. Every tread of his feet seemed to say to him that he must on no account stand in the schoolmaster's way with Sue. Phillotson was perhaps twenty years her senior, but many a happy marriage had been made in such conditions of age. The ironical clinch to his sorrow was given by the thought that the intimacy between his cousin and schoolmaster had been brought about entirely by himself.

II–6

Jude's old and embittered aunt lay unwell at Marygreen, and on the following Sunday he went to see her—a visit which was the result of a victorious struggle against his inclination to turn aside to the village of Lumsdon and obtain a miserable interview with his cousin, in which the word nearest his heart could not be spoken, and the sight which had tortured him could not be revealed.

His aunt was now unable to leave her bed, and a great part of Jude's short day was occupied in making arrangements for her comfort. The little bakery business had been sold to a neighbour, and with the proceeds of this and her savings she was comfortably supplied with necessaries and more, a widow of the same village living with her and ministering to her wants. It was not till the time had nearly come for him to leave that he obtained a quiet talk with her, and his words tended insensibly towards his cousin.

'Was Sue born here?'

'She was—in this room. They were living here at that time. What made 'ee ask that?'

'O—I wanted to know.'

'Now you've been seeing her!' said the harsh old woman. 'And what did I tell 'ee?'

'Well—that I was not to see her.'

'Have you gossiped with her?'

'Yes.'

'Then don't keep it up. She was brought up by her father to hate her mother's family; and she'll look with no favour upon a working chap like you—a townish girl as she's become by now. I never cared much about her. A pert little thing, that's what she was too often, with her tight-strained nerves. Many's the time I've smacked her for her impertinence. Why, one day when she was walking into the pond with her shoes and stockings off, and her petticoats pulled above her knees, afore I could cry out for shame, she said: "Move on, aunty! This is no sight for modest eyes!" '

'She was a little child then.'

'She was twelve if a day.'

'Well—of course. But now she's older she's of a thoughtful, quivering, tender nature, and as sensitive as—'

'Jude!' cried his aunt, springing up in bed. 'Don't you be a fool about her!'

'No, no, of course not.'

'Your marrying that woman Arabella was about as bad a thing as a man could possibly do for himself by trying hard. But she's gone to the other side of the world, and med never trouble you again. And there'll be a worse thing if you, tied and bound as you be, should have a fancy for Sue. If your cousin is civil to you, take her civility for what it is worth. But anything more than a relation's good wishes it is stark madness for 'ee to give her. If she's townish and wanton it med bring 'ee to ruin.'

'Don't say anything against her, aunt! Don't, please!'

A relief was afforded to him by the entry of the companion and nurse of his aunt, who must have been listening to the conversation, for she began a commentary on past years, introducing Sue Bridehead as a character in her recollections. She described what an odd little maid Sue had been when a pupil at the village school across the green opposite, before her father went to London—how, when the vicar arranged readings and recitations, she appeared on the platform, the smallest of them all, 'in her little white frock, and shoes, and pink sash'; how she recited 'Excelsior,' 'There was a sound of revelry by right,' and 'The Raven',[1] how during the delivery she would knit her little brows and

---

1. Poems by, respectively, Longfellow, Byron, and Poe.

glare round tragically, and say to the empty air, as if some real creature stood there—

'Ghastly, grim, and ancient Raven, wandering from the Nightly shore, Tell me what thy lordly name is on the Night's Plutonian shore!'

'She'd bring up the nasty carrion bird that clear,' corroborated the sick woman reluctantly, 'as she stood there in her little sash and things, that you could see un a'most before your very eyes. You too, Jude, had the same trick as a child of seeming to see things in the air.'

The neighbour told also of Sue's accomplishments in other kinds:

'She was not exactly a tomboy, you know; but she could do things that only boys do, as a rule. I've seen her hit in and steer down the long slide on yonder pond, with her little curls blowing, one of a file of twenty moving along against the sky like shapes painted on glass, and up the back slide without stopping. All boys except herself; and then they'd cheer her, and then she'd say, "Don't be saucy, boys," and suddenly run indoors. They'd try to coax her out again. But 'a wouldn't come.'

These retrospective visions of Sue only made Jude the more miserable that he was unable to woo her, and he left the cottage of his aunt that day with a heavy heart. He would fain have glanced into the school to see the room in which Sue's little figure had so glorified itself; but he checked his desire and went on.

It being Sunday evening some villagers who had known him during his residence here were standing in a group in their best clothes. Jude was startled by a salute from one of them:

'Ye've got there right enough, then!'

Jude showed that he did not understand.

'Why, to the seat of l'arning—the "City of Light" you used to talk to us about as a little boy! Is it all you expected of it?'

'Yes; more!' cried Jude.

'When I was there once for an hour I didn't see much in it for my part; auld crumbling buildings, half church, half almshouse, and not much going on at that.'

'You are wrong, John; there is more going on than meets the eye of a man walking through the streets. It is a unique centre of thought and religion—the intellectual and spiritual granary of this country. All that silence and absence of goings-on is the stillness of infinite motion—the sleep of the spinning-top, to borrow the simile of a well-known writer.'

'O, well, it med be all that, or it med not. As I say, I didn't see nothing of it the hour or two I was there; so I went in and had a pot o' beer, and a penny loaf, and a ha'porth o' cheese, and waited till it was time to come along home. You've j'ined a College by this time, I suppose?'

'Ah, no!' said Jude. 'I am almost as far off that as ever.'

'How so?'

Jude slapped his pocket.

'Just what we thought! Such places be not for such as you—only for them with plenty o' money.'

'There you are wrong,' said Jude, with some bitterness. 'They are for such ones!'

Still, the remark was sufficient to withdraw Jude's attention from the imaginative world he had lately inhabited, in which an abstract figure, more or less himself, was steeping his mind in a sublimation of the arts and sciences, and making his calling and election sure to a seat in the paradise of the learned. He was set regarding his prospects in a cold northern light. He had lately felt that he could not quite satisfy himself in his Greek—in the Greek of the dramatists particularly. So fatigued was he sometimes after his day's work that he could not maintain the critical attention necessary for thorough application. He felt that he wanted a coach—a friend at his elbow to tell him in a moment what sometimes would occupy him a weary month in extracting from unanticipative, clumsy books.

It was decidedly necessary to consider facts a little more closely than he had done of late. What was the good, after all, of using up his spare hours in a vague labour called 'private study' without giving an outlook on practicabilities?

'I ought to have thought of this before,' he said, as he journeyed back. 'It would have been better never to have embarked in the scheme at all than to do it without seeing clearly where I am going, or what I am aiming at. . . . This hovering outside the walls of the colleges, as if expecting some arm to be stretched out from them to lift me inside, won't do! I must get special information.'

The next week accordingly he sought it. What at first seemed an opportunity occurred one afternoon when he saw an elderly gentleman, who had been pointed out as the Head of a particular College, walking in the public path of a parklike enclosure near the spot at which Jude chanced to be sitting. The gentleman came nearer, and Jude looked anxiously at his face. It seemed benign, considerate, yet rather reserved. On second thoughts Jude felt that he could not go up and address him; but he was sufficiently influenced by the incident to think what a wise thing it would be for him to state his difficulties by letter to some of the best and most judicious of these old masters, and obtain their advice.

During the next week or two he accordingly placed himself in such positions about the city as would afford him glimpses of several of the most distinguished among the Provosts, Wardens, and other Heads of Houses; and from those he ultimately selected five whose physiognomies seemed to say to him that they were appreciative and far-seeing men. To these five he addressed letters, briefly stating his difficulties, and asking their opinion on his stranded situation.

When the letters were posted Jude mentally began to criticize them; he wished they had not been sent. 'It is just one of those intrusive, vulgar, pushing, applications which are so common in these days,' he thought. 'Why couldn't I know better than address utter strangers in such a way? I may be an impostor, an idle scamp, a man with a bad character, for all that they know to the contrary. . . . Perhaps that's what I am!'

Nevertheless, he found himself clinging to the hope of some reply as to his one last chance of redemption. He waited day after day, saying that it was perfectly absurd to expect, yet expecting. While he waited he was suddenly stirred by news about Phillotson. Phillotson was giving up the school near Christminster, for a larger one further south, in Mid-Wessex. What this meant; how it would affect his cousin; whether, as seemed possible, it was a practical move of the schoolmaster's toward a larger income, in view of a provision for two instead of one, he would not allow himself to say. And the tender relations between Phillotson and the young girl of whom Jude was passionately enamoured effectually made it repugnant to Jude's tastes to apply to Phillotson for advice on his own scheme.

Meanwhile the academic dignitaries to whom Jude had written vouchsafed no answer, and the young man was thus thrown back entirely on himself, as formerly, with the added gloom of a weakened hope. By indirect inquiries he soon perceived clearly, what he had long uneasily suspected, that to qualify himself for certain open scholarships and exhibitions was the only brilliant course. But to do this a good deal of coaching would be necessary, and much natural ability. It was next to impossible that a man reading on his own system, however widely and thoroughly, even over the prolonged period of ten years, should be able to compete with those who had passed their lives under trained teachers and had worked to ordained lines.

The other course, that of buying himself in, so to speak, seemed the only one really open to men like him, the difficulty being simply of a material kind. With the help of his information he began to reckon the extent of this material obstacle, and ascertained, to his dismay, that, at the rate at which, with the best of fortune, he would be able to save money, fifteen years must elapse before he could be in a position to forward testimonials to the Head of a College and advance to a matriculation examination.[2] The undertaking was hopeless.

He saw what a curious and cunning glamour the neighbourhood of the place had exercised over him. To get there and live there, to move

2. Examination for admission to the university.

among the churches and halls and become imbued with the *genius loci*,[3] had seemed to his dreaming youth, as the spot shaped its charms to him from its halo on the horizon, the obvious and ideal thing to do. 'Let me only get there,' he had said with the fatuousness of Crusoe over his big boat,[4] and the rest is but a matter of time and energy.' It would have been far better for him in every way if he had never come within sight and sound of the delusive precincts, had gone to some busy commercial town with the sole object of making money by his wits, and thence surveyed his plan in true perspective. Well, all that was clear to him amounted to this, that the whole scheme had burst up, like an iridescent soap-bubble, under the touch of a reasoned inquiry. He looked back at himself along the vista of his past years, and his thought was akin to Heine's:

> 'Above the youth's inspired and flashing eyes
> I see the motley mocking fool's-cap rise!'[5]

Fortunately he had not been allowed to bring his disappointment into his dear Sue's life by involving her in this collapse. And the painful details of his awakening to a sense of his limitations should now be spared her as far as possible. After all, she had only known a little part of the miserable struggle in which he had been engaged thus unequipped, poor, and unforeseeing.

He always remembered the appearance of the afternoon on which he awoke from his dream. Not quite knowing what to do with himself, he went up to an octagonal chamber in the lantern of a singularly built theatre[6] that was set amidst this quaint and singular city. It had windows all round, from which an outlook over the whole town and its edifices could be gained. Jude's eyes swept all the views in succession, mediatively, mournfully, yet sturdily. Those buildings and their associations and privileges were not for him. From the looming roof of the great library, into which he hardly ever had time to enter, his gaze travelled on to the varied spires, halls, gables, streets, chapels, gardens, quadrangles, which composed the *ensemble* of this unrivalled panorama. He saw that his destiny lay not with these, but among the manual toilers in the shabby purlieu which he himself occupied, unrecognized as part of the city at all by its visitors and panegyrists, yet without whose denizens the hard readers could not read nor the high thinkers live.

3. Spirit of the place.
4. In Defoe's *Robinson Crusoe* the hero builds a boat with great toil, only to find that it is too heavy for him to move to the water.
5. Translation of lines from the poem "Götterdämmerung" by the German poet Heine (1797–1856).
6. The Sheldonian Theatre, designed by Wren, is not a theater in the usual sense but a building in which university ceremonies take place. It is the scene of the annual Commemoration, at which degrees are granted.

He looked over the town into the country beyond, to the trees which screened her whose presence had at first been the support of his heart, and whose loss was now a maddening torture. But for this blow he might have borne with his fate. With Sue as companion he could have renounced his ambitions with a smile. Without her it was inevitable that the reaction from the long strain to which he had subjected himself should affect him disastrously. Phillotson had no doubt passed through a similar intellectual disappointment to that which now enveloped him. But the schoolmaster had been since blest with the consolation of sweet Sue, while for him there was no consoler.

Descending to the streets, he went listlessly along till he arrived at an inn, and entered it. Here he drank several glasses of beer in rapid succession, and when he came out it was night. By the light of the flickering lamps he rambled home to supper, and had not long been sitting at table when his landlady brought up a letter that had just arrived for him. She laid it down as if impressed with a sense of its possible importance, and on looking at it Jude perceived that it bore the embossed stamp of one of the Colleges whose heads he had addressed. 'One—at last!' cried Jude.

The communication was brief, and not exactly what he had expected; though it really was from the Master in person. It ran thus:

'BIBLIOLL COLLEGE

'SIR,—I have read your letter with interest; and, judging from your description of yourself as a working-man, I venture to think that you will have a much better chance of success in life by remaining in your own sphere and sticking to your trade than by adopting any other course. That, therefore, is what I advise you to do. Yours faithfully,

'T. TETUPHENAY.[7]

'To Mr. J. FAWLEY Stone-mason.'

This terribly sensible advice exasperated Jude. He had known all that before. He knew it was true. Yet it seemed a hard slap after ten years of labour, and its effect upon him just now was to make him rise recklessly from the table, and, instead of reading as usual, to go downstairs and into the street. He stood at a bar and tossed off two or three glasses, then unconsciously sauntered along till he came to a spot called The Fourways[8] in the middle of the city, gazing abstractedly at the groups of people like one in a trance, till, coming to himself, he began talking to the policeman fixed there.

7. It has been suggested that Tetuphenay (whose name is based on a Greek verb meaning "to have struck") was modeled on Benjamin Jowett, famous classical scholar and master of Balliol College, Oxford. It has also been claimed that the letter received by Jude is a transcript of a letter sent to the young Hardy by Jowett.
8. Carfax, "a place where the four ways meet" (*The Visitor's Guide to Oxford*, 1881).

That officer yawned, stretched out his elbows, elevated himself an inch and a half on the balls of his toes, smiled, and looking humorously at Jude, said, 'You've had a wet,[9] young man.'

'No; I've only begun,' he replied cynically.

Whatever his wetness, his brains were dry enough. He only heard in part the policeman's further remarks, having fallen into thought on what struggling people like himself had stood at that Crossway, whom nobody ever thought of now. It had more history than the oldest college in the city. It was literally teeming, stratified, with the shades of human groups, who had met there for tragedy, comedy, farce; real enactments of the intensest kind. At Fourways men had stood and talked of Napoleon, the loss of America, the execution of King Charles, the burning of the Martyrs, the Crusades, the Norman Conquest, possibly of the arrival of Caesar. Here the two sexes had met for loving, hating, coupling, parting; had waited, had suffered, for each other; had triumphed over each other; cursed each other in jealousy, blessed each other in forgiveness.

He began to see that the town life was a book of humanity infinitely more palpitating, varied, and compendious than the gown life.[1] These struggling men and women before him were the reality of Christminster, though they knew little of Christ or Minster. That was one of the humours of things. The floating population of students and teachers, who did know both in a way, were not Christminster in a local sense at all.

He looked at his watch, and, in pursuit of this idea, he went on till he came to a public hall, where a promenade concert[2] was in progress. Jude entered, and found the room full of shop youths and girls, soldiers, apprentices, boys of eleven smoking cigarettes, and light women of the more respectable and amateur class. He had tapped the real Christminster life. A band was playing, and the crowd walked about and jostled each other, and every now and then a man got upon a platform and sang a comic song.

The spirit of Sue seemed to hover round him and prevent his flirting and drinking with the frolicsome girls who made advances—wistful to gain a little joy. At ten o'clock he came away, choosing a circuitous route homeward to pass the gates of the College whose Head had just sent him the note.

The gates were shut, and, by an impulse, he took from his pocket the lump of chalk which as a workman he usually carried there, and wrote along the wall:

'I have understanding as well as you; I am not inferior to you: yea, who knoweth not such things as these?'—Job xii.3.

<hr>

9. Had too much to drink.
1. The life of the university, as opposed to "town" life, that of the other residents of the city.
2. Concert at which the audience could stroll about freely.

II–7

The stroke of scorn relieved his mind, and the next morning he laughed at his self-conceit. But the laugh was not a healthy one. He re-read the letter from the Master, and the wisdom in its lines, which had at first exasperated him, chilled and depressed him now. He saw himself as a fool indeed.

Deprived of the objects of both intellect and emotion, he could not proceed to his work. Whenever he felt reconciled to his fate as a student, there came to disturb his calm his hopeless relations with Sue. That the one affined soul he had ever met was lost to him through his marriage returned upon him with cruel persistency, till, unable to bear it longer, he again rushed for distraction to the real Christminster life. He now sought it out in an obscure and low-ceiled tavern up a court which was well known to certain worthies of the place, and in brighter times would have interested him simply by its quaintness. Here he sat more or less all the day, convinced that he was at bottom a vicious character, of whom it was hopeless to expect anything.

In the evening the frequenters of the house dropped in one by one, Jude still retaining his seat in the corner, though his money was all spent, and he had not eaten anything the whole day except a biscuit. He surveyed his gathering companions with all the equanimity and philosophy of a man who has been drinking long and slowly, and made friends with several: to wit, Tinker Taylor, a decayed church-ironmonger who appeared to have been of a religious turn in earlier years, but was somewhat blasphemous now; also a red-nosed auctioneer; also two Gothic masons like himself, called Uncle Jim and Uncle Joe. There were present, too, some clerks, and a gown-and surplice-maker's assistant; two ladies who sported moral characters of various depths of shade, according to their company, nicknamed 'Bower o' Bliss' and 'Freckles'; some horsey men 'in the know' of betting circles; a travelling actor from the theatre, and two devil-may-care young men who proved to be gownless[1] undergraduates; they had slipped in by stealth to meet a man about bull-pups, and stayed to drink and smoke short pipes with the racing gents aforesaid, looking at their watches every now and then.

The conversation waxed general. Christminster society was criticized, the Dons, magistrates, and other people in authority being sincerely pitied for their shortcomings, while opinions on how they ought to conduct themselves and their affairs to be properly respected, were exchanged in a large-minded and disinterested manner.

Jude Fawley, with the self-conceit, effrontery, and *aplomb* of a strong-brained fellow in liquor, threw in his remarks somewhat per-

---

1. Undergraduates were required by university regulations to wear academic gowns after dark.

emptorily; and his aims having been what they were for so many years, everything the others said turned upon his tongue, by a sort of mechanical craze, to the subject of scholarship and study, the extent of his own learning being dwelt upon with an insistence that would have appeared pitiable to himself in his sane hours.

'I don't care a damn,' he was saying, 'for any Provost, Warden, Principal, Fellow, or cursed Master of Arts in the University! What I know is that I'd lick 'em on their own ground if they'd give me a chance, and show 'em a few things they are not up to yet!'

'Hear, hear!' said the undergraduates from the corner, where they were talking privately about the pups.

'You always was fond o' books, I've heard,' said Tinker Taylor, 'and I don't doubt what you state: Now with me 'twas different: I always saw there was more to be learnt outside a book than in; and I took my steps accordingly, or I shouldn't have been the man I am.'

'You aim at the Church, I believe?' said Uncle Joe. 'If you are such a scholar as to pitch yer hopes so high as that, why not give us a specimen of your scholarship? Canst say the Creed in Latin, man? That was how they once put it to a chap down in my country.'

'I should think so!' said Jude haughtily.

'Not he! Like his conceit!' screamed one of the ladies.

'Just you shut up, Bower o' Bliss!' said one of the undergraduates. 'Silence!' He drank off the spirits in his tumbler, rapped with it on the counter, and announced. 'The gentleman in the corner is going to rehearse the Articles of his Belief, in the Latin tongue, for the edification of the company.'

'I won't!' said Jude.

'Yes—have a try!' said the surplice-maker.

'You can't! said Uncle Joe.

'Yes, he can!' said Tinker Taylor.

'I'll swear I can!' said Jude. 'Well, come now, stand me a small Scotch cold. and I'll do it straight off.'

'That's a fair offer,' said the undergraduate, throwing down the money for the whisky.

The barmaid concocted the mixture with the bearing of a person compelled to live amongst animals of an inferior species, and the glass was handed across to Jude, who, having drunk the contents, stood up and began rhetorically, without hesitation:

'Credo in unum Deum, Patrem omnipotentem, Factorem coeli et terrae, visibilium omnium et invisibilium.'

'Good! Excellent Latin!' cried one of the undergraduates, who, however, had not the slightest conception of a single word.

A silence reigned among the rest in the bar, and the maid stood still, Jude's voice echoing sonorously into the inner parlour, where the landlord was dozing, and bringing him out to see what was going on. Jude had declaimed steadily ahead, and was continuing:

'Crucifixus etiam pro nobis: sub Pontio Pilato passus, et sepultus est. Et resurrexit tertia die, secundum Scripturas.'

'That's the Nicene,' sneered the second undergraduate. 'And we wanted the Apostles'!'[2]

'You didn't say so! And every fool knows, except you, that the Nicene is the most historic creed!'

'Let un go on, let un go on!' said the auctioneer.

But Jude's mind seemed to grow confused soon, and he could not get on. He put his hand to his forehead, and his face assumed an expression of pain.

'Give him another glass—then he'll fetch up and get through it,' said Tinker Taylor.

Somebody threw down threepence, the glass was handed, Jude stretched out his arm for it without looking, and having swallowed the liquor, went on in a moment in a revived voice, raising it as he neared the end with the manner of a priest leading a congregation:

'Et in Spiritum Sanctum, Dominum et vivificantem, qui ex Patre Filioque procedit. Qui cum Patre et Filio simul adoratur et conglori- ficatur. Qui locutus est per prophetas.

'Et unam Catholicam et Apostolicam Ecclesiam. Confitior unum Baptisma in remissionem peccatorum. Et exspecto Resurrecti onem mortuorum. Et vitam venturi saeculi. Amen.'

'Well done!' said several, enjoying the last word, as being the first and only one they had recognized.

Then Jude seemed to shake the fumes from his brain, as he stared round upon them.

'You pack of fools!' he cried. 'Which one of you knows whether I have said it or no? It might have been the Ratcatcher's Daughter[3] in double Dutch for all that your besotted heads can tell! See what I have brought myself to—the crew I have come among!'

The landlord, who had already had his license endorsed for har- bouring queer characters, feared a riot, and came outside the counter; but Jude, in his sudden flash of reason, had turned in disgust and left the scene, the door slamming with a dull thud behind him.

He hastened down the lane and round into the straight broad street, which he followed till it merged in the highway, and all sound of his late companions had been left behind. Onward he still went, under the influence of a childlike yearning for the one being in the world to

2. The Nicene and the Apostles' Creeds are declarations of faith originating from the early Christian church.
3. Popular nineteenth-century street ballad; its words are given in The Oxford Book of Light Verse, ed. W. H. Auden (1938), no. 237.

whom it seemed possible to fly—an unreasoning desire, whose ill judgment was not apparent to him now. In the course of an hour, when it
was between ten and eleven o'clock, he entered the village of Lumsdon,
and reaching the cottage, saw that a light was burning in a downstairs
room, which he assumed, rightly as it happened, to be hers.

Jude stepped close to the wall, and tapped with his finger on the
pane, saying impatiently, 'Sue, Sue!'

She must have recognized his voice, for the light disappeared from
the apartment, and in a second or two the door was unlocked and
opened, and Sue appeared with a candle in her hand.

'Is it Jude? Yes, it is! My dear, dear cousin, what's the matter?'

'O, I am—I couldn't help coming, Sue!' said he, sinking down upon
the doorstep. 'I am so wicked, Sue—my heart is nearly broken, and I
could not bear my life as it was! So I have been drinking, and blaspheming, or next door to it, and saying holy things in disreputable
quarters—repeating in idle bravado words which ought never to be
uttered but reverently! O, do anything with me, Sue—kill me—I don't
care! Only don't hate me and despise me like all the rest of the world!'

'You are ill, poor dear! No, I won't despise you; of course I won't.
Come in and rest, and let me see what I can do for you. Now lean on
me, and don't mind.' With one hand holding the candle and the other
supporting him, she led him indoors, and placed him in the only easy-
chair the meagrely furnished house afforded, stretching his feet upon
another, and pulling off his boots. Jude, now getting towards his sober
senses, could only say, 'Dear, dear Sue!' in a voice broken by grief and
contrition.

She asked him if he wanted anything to eat, but he shook his head.
Then telling him to go to sleep, and that she would come down early
in the morning and get him some breakfast, she bade him good-night
and ascended the stairs.

Almost immediately he fell into a heavy slumber, and did not wake
till dawn. At first he did not know where he was, but by degrees his
situation cleared to him, and he beheld it in all the ghastliness of a
right mind. She knew the worst of him—the very worst. How could he
face her now? She would soon be coming down to see about breakfast,
as she had said, and there would he be in all his shame confronting
her. He could not bear the thought, and softly drawing on his boots,
and taking his hat from the nail on which she had hung it, he slipped
noiselessly out of the house.

His fixed idea was to get away to some obscure spot and hide, and
perhaps pray; and the only spot which occurred to him was Marygreen.
He called at his lodging in Christminster, where he found awaiting him
a note of dismissal from his employer; and having packed up he turned
his back upon the city that had been such a thorn in his side, and
struck southward into Wessex. He had no money left in his pocket,

his small savings, deposited at one of the banks in Christminster, having fortunately been left untouched. To get to Marygreen, therefore, his only course was walking; and the distance being nearly twenty miles, he had ample time to complete on the way the sobering process begun in him.

At some hour of the evening he reached Alfredston. Here he pawned his waistcoat, and having gone out of the town a mile or two, slept under a rick that night. At dawn he rose, shook off the hayseeds and stems from his clothes, and started again, breasting the long white road up the hill to the downs, which had been visible to him a long way off, and passing the milestone at the top, whereon he had carved his hopes years ago.

He reached the ancient hamlet while the people were at breakfast. Weary and mud-bespattered, but quite possessed of his ordinary clearness of brain, he sat down by the well, thinking as he did so what a poor Christ he made.[4] Seeing a trough of water near he bathed his face, and went on to the cottage of his great-aunt, whom he found breakfasting in bed, attended by the woman who lived with her.

'What—out o' work?' asked his relative, regarding him through eyes sunken deep, under lids heavy as pot-covers, no other cause for his tumbled appearance suggesting itself to one whose whole life had been a struggle with material things.

'Yes,' said Jude heavily. 'I think I must have a little rest.'

Refreshed by some breakfast, he went up to his old room and lay down in his shirt-sleeves, after the manner of the artizan. He fell asleep for a short while, and when he awoke it was as if he had awakened in hell. It *was* hell—'the hell of conscious failure,' both in ambition and in love. He thought of that previous abyss into which he had fallen before leaving this part of the country; the deepest deep he had supposed it then; but it was not so deep as this. That had been the breaking in of the outer bulwarks of his hope: this was of his second line.

If he had been a woman he must have screamed under the nervous tension which he was now undergoing. But that relief being denied to his virility, he clenched his teeth in misery, bringing lines about his mouth like those in the Laocoön,[5] and corrugations between his brows.

A mournful wind blew through the trees, and sounded in the chimney like the pedal notes of an organ. Each ivy leaf overgrowing the wall of the churchless churchyard hard by, now abandoned, pecked its neighbour smartly, and the vane on the new Victorian-Gothic church in the new spot had already begun to creak. Yet apparently it was not always the outdoor wind that made the deep murmurs; it was a voice. He guessed its origin in a moment or two; the curate was praying with his aunt in the adjoining room. He remembered her speaking of him.

4. The reference is to John 4.6, where Christ sits "on the well."
5. Famous Roman sculpture, showing struggling figures.

Presently the sound ceased, and a step seemed to cross the landing. Jude sat up, and shouted 'Hoi!'

The step made for his door, which was open, and a man looked in. It was a young clergyman.

'I think you are Mr. Highridge,' said Jude. 'My aunt has mentioned you more than once. Well, here I am, just come home; a fellow gone to the bad; though I had the best intentions in the world at one time. Now I am melancholy mad, what with drinking and one thing and another.'

Slowly Jude unfolded to the curate his late plans and movements by an unconscious bias dwelling less upon the intellectual and ambitious side of his dream, and more upon the theological, though this had, up till now, been merely a portion of the general plan of advancement.

'Now I know I have been a fool, and that folly is with me,' added Jude in conclusion. 'And I don't regret the collapse of my University hopes one jot. I wouldn't begin again if I were sure to succeed. I don't care for social success any more at all. But I do feel I should like to do some good thing; and I bitterly regret the Church, and the loss of my chance of being her ordained minister.'

The curate, who was a new man to this neighbourhood, had grown deeply interested, and at last he said: 'If you feel a real call to the ministry, and I won't say from your conversation that you do not, for it is that of a thoughtful and educated man, you might enter the Church as a licentiate. Only you must make up your mind to avoid strong drink.'

'I could avoid that easily enough, if I had any kind of hope to support me!'

Part Third: At Melchester

'For there was no other girl, O bridegroom, like her!'
—SAPPHO (H. T. WHARTON)[1]

III–1

It was a new idea—the ecclesiastical and altruistic life as distinct from the intellectual and emulative life. A man could preach and do good to his fellow-creatures without taking double-firsts in the schools of Christminster, or having anything but ordinary knowledge. The old fancy which had led on to the culminating vision of the bishopric had not been an ethical or theological enthusiasm at all, but a mundane ambition masquerading in a surplice. He feared that his whole scheme

1. Sappho was a poet of ancient Greece. H. T. Wharton's translation was published in 1885.

had degenerated to, even though it might not have originated in, a social unrest which had no foundation in the nobler instincts; which was purely an artificial product of civilization. There were thousands of young men on the same self-seeking track at the present moment. The sensual hind[2] who ate, drank, and lived carelessly with his wife through the days of his vanity[3] was a more likable being than he.

But to enter the Church in such an unscholarly way that he could not in any probability rise to a higher grade through all his career than that of the humble curate wearing his life out in an obscure village or city slum—that might have a touch of goodness and greatness in it; that might be true religion, and a purgatorial course worthy of being followed by a remorseful man.

The favourable light in which this new thought showed itself by contrast with his foregone intentions cheered Jude, as he sat there, shabby and lonely; and it may be said to have given, during the next few days, the *coup de grâce*[4] to his intellectual career—a career which had extended over the greater part of a dozen years. He did nothing, however, for some long stagnant time to advance his new desire, occupying himself with little local jobs in putting up and lettering headstones about the neighbouring villages, and submitting to be regarded as a social failure, a returned purchase, by the half-dozen or so of farmers and other country-people who condescended to nod to him.

The human interest of the new intention—and a human interest is indispensable to the most spiritual and self-sacrificing—was created by a letter from Sue, bearing a fresh postmark. She evidently wrote with anxiety, and told very little about her own doings, more than that she had passed some sort of examination for a Queen's Scholarship, and was going to enter a Training College at Melchester to complete herself for the vocation she had chosen, partly by his influence. There was a Theological College at Melchester; Melchester was a quiet and soothing place, almost entirely ecclesiastical in its tone; a spot where worldly learning and intellectual smartness had no establishment; where the altruistic feeling that he did possess would perhaps be more highly estimated than a brilliancy which he did not.

As it would be necessary that he should continue for a time to work at his trade while reading up Divinity, which he had neglected at Christminster for the ordinary classical grind, what better course for him than to get employment at the further city, and pursue this plan of reading? That his excessive human interest in the new place was entirely of Sue's making, while at the same time Sue was to be regarded even less than formerly as proper to create it, had an ethical contra-

2. Peasant.
3. "Live joyfully with the wife whom thou lovest . . . all the days of thy vanity" (Ecclesiastes 9.9).
4. Death stroke, final blow.

dictoriness to which he was not blind. But that much he conceded to human frailty, and hoped to learn to love her only as a friend and kinswoman.

He considered that he might so mark out his coming years as to begin his ministry at the age of thirty—an age which much attracted him as being that of his exemplar[5] when he first began to teach in Galilee. This would allow him plenty of time for deliberate study, and for acquiring capital by his trade to help his aftercourse of keeping the necessary terms at a Theological College.

Christmas had come and passed, and Sue had gone to the Melchester Normal School.[6] The time was just the worst in the year for Jude to get into new employment, and he had written suggesting to her that he should postpone his arrival for a month or so, till the days had lengthened. She had acquiesced so readily that he wished he had not proposed it—she had never once reproached him for his strange conduct in coming to her that night, and his silent disappearance. Neither had she ever said a word about her relations with Mr. Phillotson.

Suddenly, however, quite a passionate letter arrived from Sue. She was quite lonely and miserable, she told him. She hated the place she was in; it was worse than the ecclesiastical designer's; worse than anywhere. She felt utterly friendless; could he come immediately?—though when he did come she would only be able to see him at limited times, the rules of the establishment she found herself in being strict to a degree. It was Mr. Phillotson who had advised her to come there, and she wished she had never listened to him.

Phillotson's suit was not exactly prospering, evidently; and Jude felt unreasonably glad. He packed up his things and went to Melchester with a lighter heart than he had known for months.

This being the turning over a new leaf he duly looked about for a temperance hotel,[7] and found a little establishment of that description in the street leading from the station. When he had had something to eat he walked out into the dull winter light over the town bridge, and turned the corner towards the Close. The day was foggy, and standing under the walls of the most graceful architectural pile in England[8] he paused and looked up. The lofty building was visible as far as the roof-ridge; above, the dwindling spire rose more and more remotely, till its apex was quite lost in the mist drifting across it.

The lamps now began to be lighted, and turning to the west front he walked round. He took it as a good omen that numerous blocks of

---

5. Jesus Christ.
6. Teachers' training college. Hardy's two sisters had been students at the teachers' college in Salisbury, the original of "Melchester."
7. One that does not serve alcohol.
8. Salisbury Cathedral, which has the tallest spire in England. It was much admired by Hardy, who frequently visited it.

stone were lying about, which signified that the cathedral was under-going restoration or repair to a considerable extent. It seemed to him, full of the superstitions of his beliefs, that this was an exercise of fore-thought on the part of a ruling Power, that he might find plenty to do in the art he practised while waiting for a call to higher labours.

Then a wave of warmth came over him as he thought how near he now stood to the bright-eyed vivacious girl with the broad forehead and pile of dark hair above it; the girl with the kindling glance, daringly soft at times—sometimes like that of the girls he had seen in engrav-ings from paintings of the Spanish school. She was here—actually in this Close—in one of the houses confronting this very west façade.

He went down the broad gravel path towards the building. It was an ancient edifice of the fifteenth century, once a palace, now a training-school, with mullioned and transomed windows, and a courtyard in front shut in from the road by a wall. Jude opened the gate and went up to the door through which, on inquiring for his cousin, he was gingerly admitted to a waiting-room, and in a few minutes she came.

Though she had been here such a short while, she was not as he had seen her last. All her bounding manner was gone; her curves of motion had become subdued lines. The screens and subtleties of convention had likewise disappeared. Yet neither was she quite the woman who had written the letter that summoned him. That had plainly been dashed off in an impulse which second thoughts had somewhat regret-ted; thoughts that were possibly of his recent self-disgrace. Jude was quite overcome with emotion.

'You don't—think me a demoralized wretch—for coming to you as I was—and going so shamefully, Sue?'

'O, I have tried not to! You said enough to let me know what had caused it. I hope I shall never have any doubt of your worthiness, my poor Jude! And I am glad you have come!'

She wore a murrey-coloured[9] gown with a little lace collar. It was made quite plain, and hung about her slight figure with clinging grace-fulness. Her hair, which formerly she had worn according to the custom of the day, was now twisted up tightly, and she had altogether the air of a woman clipped and pruned by severe discipline, an under-brightness shining through from the depths which that discipline had not yet been able to reach.

She had come forward prettily; but Jude felt that she had hardly expected him to kiss her, as he was burning to do, under other colours than those of cousinship. He could not perceive the least sign that Sue regarded him as a lover, or ever would do so, now that she knew the worst of him, even if he had the right to behave as one; and this helped on his growing resolve to tell her of his matrimonial entanglement,

9. Mulberry-colored, purple-red.

which he had put off doing from time to time in sheer dread of losing the bliss of her company.

Sue came out into the town with him, and they walked and talked with tongues centred only on the passing moments. Jude said he would like to buy her a little present of some sort, and then she confessed, with something of shame, that she was dreadfully hungry. They were kept on very short allowances in the College, and a dinner, tea, and supper all in one was the present she most desired in the world. Jude thereupon took her to an inn and ordered whatever the house afforded, which was not much. The place, however, gave them a delightful opportunity for a *tête-à-tête*, nobody else being in the room, and they talked freely.

She told him about the school as it was at that date, and the rough living, and the mixed character of her fellow-students, gathered together from all parts of the diocese, and how she had to get up and work by gas-light in the early morning, with all the bitterness of a young person to whom restraint was new. To all this he listened; but it was not what he wanted especially to know—her relations with Phillotson. That was what she did not tell. When they had sat and eaten, Jude impulsively placed his hand upon hers; she looked up and smiled, and took his quite freely into her own little soft one, dividing his fingers and coolly examining them, as if they were the fingers of a glove she was purchasing.

'Your hands are rather rough, Jude, aren't they?' she said.

'Yes. So would yours be if they held a mallet and chisel all day.'

'I don't dislike it, you know. I think it is noble to see a man's hands subdued to what he works in.[1] . . . Well, I'm rather glad I came to this Training-School, after all. See how independent I shall be after the two years' training! I shall pass pretty high, I expect, and Mr. Phillotson will use his influence to get me a big school.'

She had touched the subject at last. 'I had a suspicion, a fear,' said Jude, 'that he—cared about you rather warmly, and perhaps wanted to marry you.'

'Now don't be such a silly boy!'

'He has said something about it, I expect.'

'If he had, what would it matter? An old man like him!'

'O, come, Sue; he's not so very old. And I know what I saw him doing—'

'Not kissing me—that I'm certain!'

'No. But putting his arm round your waist.'

'Ah—I remember. But I didn't know he was going to.'

'You are wriggling out of it, Sue, and it isn't quite kind!'

Her ever-sensitive lip began to quiver, and her eye to blink, at something this reproof was deciding her to say.

---

1. Sue is recalling Shakespeare's sonnet 111.

'I know you'll be angry if I tell you everything, and that's why I don't want to!'

'Very well, then, dear,' he said soothingly. 'I have no real right to ask you, and I don't wish to know.'

'I shall tell you!' said she, with the perverseness that was part of her. 'This is what I have done: I have promised—I have promised—that I will marry him when I come out of the Training-School two years hence, and have got my Certificate; his plan being that we shall then take a large double school in a great town—he the boys' and I the girls'—as married school-teachers often do, and make a good income between us.'

'O, Sue! . . . But of course it is right—you couldn't have done better!'

He glanced at her and their eyes met, the reproach in his own belying his words. Then he drew his hand quite away from hers, and turned his face in estrangement from her to the window. Sue regarded him passively without moving.

'I knew you would be angry!' she said with an air of no emotion whatever. 'Very well—I am wrong, I suppose! I ought not to have let you come to see me! We had better not meet again; and we'll only correspond at long intervals, on purely business matters!'

This was just the one thing he would not be able to bear, as she probably knew, and it brought him round at once. 'O yes, we will,' he said quickly. 'Your being engaged can make no difference to me whatever. I have a perfect right to see you when I want to; and I shall!'

'Then don't let us talk of it any more. It is quite spoiling our evening together. What does it matter about what one is going to do two years hence!'

She was something of a riddle to him, and he let the subject drift away. 'Shall we go and sit in the Cathedral?' he asked, when their meal was finished.

'Cathedral? Yes. Though I think I'd rather sit in the railway station,' she answered, a remnant of vexation still in her voice. 'That's the centre of the town life now. The Cathedral has had its day!'

'How modern you are!'

'So would you be if you had lived so much in the Middle Ages as I have done these last few years! The Cathedral was a very good place four or five centuries ago; but it is played out now. . . . I am not modern, either. I am more ancient than mediævalism, if you only knew.'

Jude looked distressed.

'There—I won't say any more of that!' she cried. 'Only you don't know how bad I am, from your point of view, or you wouldn't think so much of me, or care whether I was engaged or not. Now there's just time for us to walk round the Close, then I must go in, or I shall be locked out for the night.'

He took her to the gate and they parted. Jude had a conviction that

his unhappy visit to her on that sad night had precipitated this marriage engagement, and it did anything but add to his happiness. Her
reproach had taken that shape, then, and not the shape of words. However, next day he set about seeking employment, which it was not so
easy to get as at Christminster, there being, as a rule, less stone-cutting
in progress in this quiet city, and hands being mostly permanent. But
he edged himself in by degrees. His first work was some carving at the
cemetery on the hill; and ultimately he became engaged on the labour
he most desired—the Cathedral repairs, which were very extensive, the
whole interior stonework having been overhauled, to be largely replaced
by new.

It might be a labour of years to get it all done, and he had confidence
enough in his own skill with the mallet and chisel to feel that it would
be a matter of choice with himself how long he would stay.

The lodgings he took near the Close Gate would not have disgraced
a curate, the rent representing a higher percentage on his wages than
mechanics of any sort usually care to pay. His combined bed and sitting
room was furnished with framed photographs of the rectories and
deaneries at which his landlady had lived as trusted servant in her time,
and the parlour downstairs bore a clock on the mantelpiece inscribed
to the effect that it was presented to the same serious-minded woman
by her fellow-servants on the occasion of her marriage. Jude added to
the furniture of his room by unpacking photographs of the ecclesiastical carvings and monuments that he had executed with his own
hands; and he was deemed a satisfactory acquisition as tenant of the
vacant apartment.

He found an ample supply of theological books in the city book-
shops, and with these his studies were recommenced in a different
spirit and direction from his former course. As a relaxation from the
Fathers, and such stock works as Paley and Butler,[2] he read Newman,
Pusey, and many other modern lights. He hired a harmonium, set it
up in his lodging, and practised chants thereon, single and double.

III–2

'To-morrow is our grand day, you know. Where shall we go?'

'I have leave from three till nine. Wherever we can get to and come
back from in that time. Not ruins, Jude—I don't care for them.'

'Well—Wardour Castle.[1] And then we can do Fonthill[2] if we like—
all in the same afternoon.'

---

2. Paley's *Evidences of Christianity* (1794) and Butler's *Analogy of Religion* (1736) were standard
theological works.
1. In Wiltshire; designed by James Paine and built in 1770–76.
2. Fonthill Abbey, built for the writer William Beckford in mock-Gothic style in 1796–1807,
was also in Wiltshire.

'Wardour is Gothic ruins—and I hate Gothic!'

'No. Quite otherwise. It is a classic building—Corinthian,[3] I think; with a lot of pictures.'

'Ah—that will do. I like the sound of Corinthian. We'll go.'

Their conversation had run thus some few weeks later, and next morning they prepared to start. Every detail of the outing was a facet reflecting a sparkle to Jude, and he did not venture to meditate on the life of inconsistency he was leading. His Sue's conduct was one lovely conundrum to him; he could say no more.

There duly came the charm of calling at the College door for her; her emergence in a nunlike simplicity of costume that was rather enforced than desired; the traipsing along to the station, the porters' 'B'your leave!' the screaming of the trains—everything formed the basis of a beautiful crystallization. Nobody stared at Sue, because she was so plainly dressed, which comforted Jude in the thought that only himself knew the charms those habiliments subdued. A matter of ten pounds spent in a drapery-shop, which had no connection with her real life or her real self, would have set all Melchester staring. The guard of the train thought they were lovers, and put them into a compartment all by themselves.

'That's a good intention wasted!' said she.

Jude did not respond. He thought the remark unnecessarily cruel, and partly untrue.

They reached the Park and Castle and wandered through the picture-galleries, Jude stopping by preference in front of the devotional pictures by Del Sarto, Guido Reni, Spagnoletto, Sassoferrato, Carlo Dolci, and others.[4] Sue paused patiently beside him, and stole critical looks into his face as, regarding the Virgins, Holy Families, and Saints, it grew reverent and abstracted. When she had thoroughly estimated him at this, she would move on and wait for him before a Lely or Reynolds.[5] It was evident that her cousin deeply interested her, as one might be interested in a man puzzling out his way along a labyrinth from which one had one's self escaped.

When they came out a long time still remained to them, and Jude proposed that as soon as they had had something to eat they should walk across the high country to the north of their present position, and intercept the train of another railway leading back to Melchester, at a station about seven miles off. Sue, who was inclined for any adventure that would intensify the sense of her day's freedom, readily agreed; and away they went, leaving the adjoining station behind them.

3. The most ornate of the three orders of Greek architecture.
4. Italian painters of the sixteenth and seventeenth centuries.
5. Sir Peter Lely (1618–1680) was principal painter to Charles II; Sir Joshua Reynolds (1723–1792) is another English painter. Their portraits of fashionable and worldly subjects are contrasted with the religious paintings admired by Jude.

It was indeed open country, wide and high. They talked and
bounded on, Jude cutting from a little covert a long walking-stick for
Sue as tall as herself, with a great crook, which made her look like a
shepherdess. About half-way on their journey they crossed a main road
running due east and west—the old road from London to Land's End.
They paused, and looked up and down it for a moment, and remarked
upon the desolation which had come over this once lively thoroughfare,
while the wind dipped to earth and scooped straws and hay-stems from
the ground.

They crossed the road and passed on, but during the next half-mile
Sue seemed to grow tired, and Jude began to be distressed for her.
They had walked a good distance altogether, and if they could not
reach the other station it would be rather awkward. For a long time
there was no cottage visible on the wide expanse of down and turnip-
land; but presently they came to a sheepfold, and next to the shepherd,
pitching hurdles. He told them that the only house near was his
mother's and his, pointing to a little dip ahead from which a faint blue
smoke arose, and recommended them to go on and rest there.

This they did, and entered the house, admitted by an old woman
without a single tooth, to whom they were as civil as strangers can be
when their only chance of rest and shelter lies in the favour of the
householder.

'A nice little cottage,' said Jude.

'O, I don't know about the niceness. I shall have to thatch it soon,
and where the thatch is to come from I can't tell, for straw do get that
dear, that 'twill soon be cheaper to cover your house wi' chainey[6] plates
than thatch.'

They sat resting, and the shepherd came in. 'Don't 'ee mind I,' he
said with a deprecating wave of the hand; 'bide here as long as ye will.
But mid you be thinking o' getting back to Melchester to-night by
train? Because you'll never do it in this world, since you don't know
the lie of the country. I don't mind going with ye some o' the ways,
but even then the train mid be gone.'

They started up.

'You can bide here, you know, over the night—can't em, mother?
The place is welcome to ye. 'Tis hard lying, rather, but volk may do
worse.' He turned to Jude and asked privately: 'Be you a married couple?'

'Hsh—no!' said Jude.

'O—I meant nothing ba'dy—not I! Well then, she can go into
mother's room, and you and I can lie in the outer chimmer[7] after
they've gone through. I can call ye soon enough to catch the first train
back. You've lost this one now.'

6. China (dialect).
7. Chamber (dialect).

On consideration they decided to close with this offer, and drew up and shared with the shepherd and his mother the boiled bacon and greens for supper.

'I rather like this,' said Sue, while their entertainers were clearing away the dishes. 'Outside all laws except gravitation and germination.'

'You only think you like it; you don't: you are quite a product of civilization,' said Jude, a recollection of her engagement reviving his soreness a little.

'Indeed I am not, Jude. I like reading and all that, but I crave to get back to the life of my infancy and its freedom.'

'Do you remember it so well? You seem to me to have nothing unconventional at all about you.'

'O, haven't I! You don't know what's inside me.'

'What?'

'The Ishmaelite.'[8]

'An urban miss is what you are.'

She looked severe disagreement, and turned away.

The shepherd aroused them the next morning, as he had said. It was bright and clear, and the four miles to the train were accomplished pleasantly. When they had reached Melchester, and walked to the Close, and the gables of the old building in which she was again to be immured rose before Sue's eyes, she looked a little scared. 'I expect I shall catch it!' she murmured.

They rang the great bell and waited.

'O, I bought something for you, which I had nearly forgotten,' she said quickly, searching her pocket. 'It is a new little photograph of me. Would you like it?'

'*Would* I!' He took it gladly, and the porter came. There seemed to be an ominous glance on his face when he opened the gate. She passed in, looking back at Jude, and waving her hand.

III–3

The seventy young women, of ages varying in the main from nineteen to one-and-twenty, though several were older, who at this date filled the species of nunnery known as the Training-School at Melchester, formed a very mixed community, which included the daughters of mechanics, curates, surgeons, shopkeepers, farmers, dairymen, soldiers, sailors, and villagers. They sat in the large school-room of the establishment on the evening previously described, and word was passed round that Sue Bridehead had not come in at closing-time.

---

8. Outcast or nonconformist: Ishmael was the "wild man," son of Abram and Hagar (Genesis 16.11–12).

'She went out with her young man,' said a second-year's student, who knew about young men. 'And Miss Traceley saw her at the station with him. She'll have it hot when she does come.'

'She said he was her cousin,' observed a youthful new girl.

'That excuse has been made a little too often in this school to be effectual in saving our souls,' said the head girl of the year, drily.

The fact was that, only twelve months before, there had occurred a lamentable seduction of one of the pupils, who had made the same statement in order to gain meetings with her lover. The affair had created a scandal, and the management had consequently been rough on cousins ever since.

At nine o' clock the names were called, Sue's being pronounced three times sonorously by Miss Traceley without eliciting an answer.

At a quarter past nine the seventy stood up to sing the 'Evening Hymn,' and then knelt down to prayers. After prayers they went in to supper, and every girl's thought was, Where is Sue Bridehead? Some of the students, who had seen Jude from the window, felt that they would not mind risking her punishment for the pleasure of being kissed by such a kindly-faced young man. Hardly one among them believed in the cousinship.

Half-an-hour later they all lay in their cubicles, their tender feminine faces upturned to the flaring gas-jets which at intervals stretched down the long dormitories every face bearing the legend 'The Weaker' upon it, as the penalty of the sex wherein they were moulded, which by no possible exertion of their willing hearts and abilities could be made strong while the inexorable laws of nature remain what they are. They formed a pretty, suggestive, pathetic sight, of whose pathos and beauty they were themselves unconscious, and would not discover till, amid the storms and strains of after-years, with their injustice, loneliness, child-bearing, and bereavement, their minds would revert to this experience as to something which had been allowed to slip past them insufficiently regarded.

One of the mistresses came in to turn out the lights, and before doing so gave a final glance at Sue's cot, which remained empty, and at her little dressing-table at the foot, which, like all the rest, was ornamented with various girlish trifles, framed photographs being not the least conspicuous among them. Sue's table had a moderate show, two men in their filigree and velvet frames standing together beside her looking-glass.

'Who are these men—did she ever say?' asked the mistress. 'Strictly speaking, relations' portraits only are allowed on these tables, you know.'

'One—the middle-aged man,' said a student in the next bed—'is the schoolmaster she served under—Mr. Phillotson.'

'And the outer—this undergraduate in cap and gown—who is he?'

'He is a friend, or was. She has never told his name.'

'Was it either of these two who came for her?'

'No.'

'You are sure 'twas not the undergraduate?'

'Quite. He was a young man with a black beard.'

The lights were promptly extinguished, and till they fell asleep the girls indulged in conjectures about Sue, and wondered what games she had carried on in London and at Christminster before she came here, some of the more restless ones getting out of bed and looking from the mullioned windows at the vast west front of the Cathedral opposite, and the spire rising behind it.

When they awoke the next morning they glanced into Sue's nook, to find it still without a tenant. After the early lessons by gas-light, in half-toilet, and when they had come up to dress for breakfast, the bell of the entrance gate was heard to ring loudly. The mistress of the dormitory went away, and presently came back to say that the Principal's orders were that nobody was to speak to Bridehead without permission.

When, accordingly, Sue came into the dormitory to hastily tidy herself, looking flushed and tired, she went to her cubicle in silence, none of them coming out to greet her or to make inquiry. When they had gone downstairs they found that she did not follow them into the dining-hall to breakfast, and they then learnt that she had been severely reprimanded, and ordered to a solitary room for a week, there to be confined, and take her meals, and do all her reading.

At this the seventy murmured, the sentence being, they thought, too severe. A round robin[1] was prepared and sent in to the Principal, asking for a remission of Sue's punishment. No notice was taken. Towards evening, when the geography mistress began dictating her subject, the girls in the class sat with folded arms.

'You mean that you are not going to work?' said the mistress at last. 'I may as well tell you that it has been ascertained that the young man Bridehead stayed out with was not her cousin, for the very good reason that she has no such relative. We have written to Christminster to ascertain.'

'We are willing to take her word,' said the head girl.

'This young man was discharged from his work at Christminster for drunkenness and blasphemy in public-houses, and he has come here to live, entirely to be near her.'

However, they remained stolid and motionless, and the mistress left the room to inquire from her superiors what was to be done.

Presently, towards dusk, the pupils, as they sat, heard exclamations from the first-year's girls in an adjoining class-room, and one rushed

1. Letter of complaint or request with signatures arranged in a circle to conceal the order in which the names were written.

in to say that Sue Bridehead had got out of the back window of the room in which she had been confined, escaped in the dark across the lawn, and disappeared. How she had managed to get out of the garden nobody could tell, as it was bounded by the river at the bottom, and the side door was locked.

They went and looked at the empty room, the casement between the middle mullions of which stood open. The lawn was again searched with a lantern, every bush and shrub being examined, but she was nowhere hidden. Then the porter of the front gate was interrogated, and on reflection he said that he remembered hearing a sort of splashing in the stream at the back, but he had taken no notice, thinking some ducks had come down the river from above.

'She must have walked through the river!' said a mistress.

'Or drowned herself,' said the porter.

The mind of the matron was horrified—not so much at the possible death of Sue as at the possible half-column detailing that event in all the newspapers, which, added to the scandal of the year before, would give the College an unenviable notoriety for many months to come.

More lanterns were procured, and the river examined; and then, at last, on the opposite shore, which was open to the fields, some little boot-tracks were discerned in the mud, which left no doubt that the too excitable girl had waded through a depth of water reaching nearly to her shoulders—for this was the chief river of the county, and was mentioned in all the geography books with respect. As Sue had not brought disgrace upon the school by drowning herself, the matron began to speak superciliously of her, and to express gladness that she was gone.

On the self-same evening Jude sat in his lodgings by the Close Gate. Often at this hour after dusk he would enter the silent Close, and stand opposite the house that contained Sue, and watch the shadows of the girls' heads passing to and fro upon the blinds, and wish he had nothing else to do but to sit reading and learning all day what many of the thoughtless inmates despised. But to-night, having finished tea and brushed himself up, he was deep in the perusal of the Twenty-ninth Volume of Pusey's Library of the Fathers, a set of books which he had purchased of a second-hand dealer at a price that seemed to him to be one of miraculous cheapness for that invaluable work. He fancied he heard something rattle lightly against his window; then he heard it again. Certainly somebody had thrown gravel. He rose and gently lifted the sash.

'Jude!' (from below).

'Sue!'

'Yes—it is! Can I come up without being seen?'

'O yes!'

'Then don't come down. Shut the window.'

Jude waited, knowing that she could enter easily enough, the front door being opened merely by a knob which anybody could turn, as in most old country towns. He palpitated at the thought that she had fled to him in her trouble as he had fled to her in his. <u>What counterparts they were!</u> He unlatched the door of his room, heard a stealthy rustle on the dark stairs, and in a moment she appeared in the light of his lamp. He went up to seize her hand, and found she was clammy as a marine deity, and that her clothes clung to her like the robes upon the figures in the Parthenon frieze.[2]

'I'm so cold!' she said through her chattering teeth. 'Can I come by your fire, Jude?'

She crossed to his little grate and very little fire, but as the water dripped from her as she moved, the idea of drying herself was absurd. 'Whatever have you done, darling?' he asked, with alarm, the tender epithet slipping out unawares.

'Walked through the largest river in the county—that's what I've done! They locked me up for being out with you; and it seemed so unjust that I couldn't bear it, so I got out of the window and escaped across the stream!' She had begun the explanation in her usual slightly independent tones, but before she had finished the thin pink lips trembled, and she could hardly refrain from crying.

'Dear Sue!' he said. 'You must take off all your things! And let me see—you must borrow some from the landlady. I'll ask her.'

'No, no! Don't let her know, for God's sake! We are so near the school that they'll come after me!'

'Then you must put on mine. You don't mind?'

'O no.'

'My Sunday suit, you know. It is close here.' In fact, everything was close and handy in Jude's single chamber, because there was not room for it to be otherwise. He opened a drawer, took out his best dark suit, and giving the garments a shake, said, 'Now, how long shall I give you?'

'Ten minutes.'

Jude left the room and went into the street, where he walked up and down. A clock struck half-past seven, and he returned. Sitting in his only arm-chair <u>he saw a slim and fragile being masquerading as himself on a Sunday</u>, so pathetic in her defencelessness that his heart felt big with the sense of it. On two other chairs before the fire were her wet <u>garments.</u> She blushed as he sat down beside her, but only for a moment.

'I suppose, Jude, it is odd that you should see me like this and all my things hanging there? Yet what nonsense! They are only a woman's

2. The famous sculptures from the temple of Athena in Athens. Hardy had seen them in the British Museum.

clothes—sexless cloth and linen. . . . I wish I didn't feel so ill and sick! Will you dry my clothes now? Please do, Jude, and I'll get a lodging by and by. It is not late yet.'

'No, you shan't, if you are ill. You must stay here. Dear, dear Sue, what can I get for you?'

'I don't know! I can't help shivering. I wish I could get warm.' Jude put on her his great-coat in addition, and then ran out to the nearest public-house, whence he returned with a little bottle in his hand. 'Here's six³ of best brandy,' he said. 'Now you drink it, dear; all of it.'

'I can't out of the bottle, can I?' Jude fetched the glass from the dressing-table, and administered the spirit in some water. She gasped a little, but gulped it down, and lay back in the arm-chair.

She then began to relate circumstantially her experiences since they had parted; but in the middle of her story her voice faltered, her head nodded, and she ceased. She was in a sound sleep. Jude, dying of anxiety lest she should have caught a chill which might permanently injure her, was glad to hear the regular breathing. He softly went nearer to her, and observed that a warm flush now rosed her hitherto blue cheeks, and felt that her hanging hand was no longer cold. Then he stood with his back to the fire regarding her, and saw in her almost a divinity.

III–4

Jude's reverie was interrupted by the creak of footsteps ascending the stairs.

He whisked Sue's clothing from the chair where it was drying, thrust it under the bed, and sat down to his book. Somebody knocked and opened the door immediately. It was the landlady.

'O, I didn't know whether you was in or not, Mr. Fawley. I wanted to know if you would require supper. I see you've a young gentleman—'

'Yes, ma'am. But I think I won't come down to-night. Will you bring supper up on a tray, and I'll have a cup of tea as well.'

It was Jude's custom to go downstairs to the kitchen, and eat his meals with the family, to save trouble. His landlady brought up the supper, however, on this occasion, and he took it from her at the door.

When she had descended he set the teapot on the hob, and drew out Sue's clothes anew; but they were far from dry. A thick woollen gown, he found, held a deal of water. So he hung them up again, and enlarged his fire and mused as the steam from the garments went up the chimney.

Suddenly she said, 'Jude!'

'Yes. All right. How do you feel now?'

3. Sixpennyworth.

'Better. Quite well. Why, I fell asleep, didn't I? What time is it? Not late surely?'

'It is past ten.'

'Is it really? What *shall* I do!' she said, starting up.

'Stay where you are.'

'Yes; that's what I want to do. But I don't know what they would say! And what will you do?'

'I am going to sit here by the fire all night, and read. To-morrow is Sunday, and I haven't to go out anywhere. Perhaps you will be saved a severe illness by resting there. Don't be frightened. I'm all right. Look here, what I have got for you. Some supper.'

When she had sat upright she breathed plaintively and said, 'I do feel rather weak still. I thought I was well; and I ought not to be here, ought I?' But the supper fortified her somewhat, and when she had had some tea and had lain back again she was bright and cheerful.

The tea must have been green, or too long drawn, for she seemed preternaturally wakeful afterwards, though Jude, who had not taken any, began to feel heavy; till her conversation fixed his attention.

'You called me a creature of civilization, or something, didn't you?' she said, breaking a silence. 'It was very odd you should have done that.'

'Why?'

'Well, because it is provokingly wrong. I am a sort of negation of it.'

'You are very philosophical. "A negation" is profound talking.'

'Is it? Do I strike you as being learned?' she asked, with a touch of raillery.

'No—not learned. Only you don't talk quite like a girl—well, a girl who has had no advantages.'

'I have had advantages. I don't know Latin and Greek, though I know the grammars of those tongues. But I know most of the Greek and Latin classics through translations, and other books too. I read Lemprière, Catullus, Martial, Juvenal, Lucian, Beaumont and Fletcher, Boccaccio, Scarron, De Brantôme, Sterne, De Foe, Smollett, Fielding, Shakespeare,[1] the Bible, and other such; and found that all interest in the unwholesome part of those books ended with its mystery.'

'You have read more than I,' he said with a sigh. 'How came you to read some of those queerer ones?'

'Well,' she said thoughtfully, 'it was by accident. My life has been entirely shaped by what people call a peculiarity in me. I have no fear of men, as such, nor of their books. I have mixed with them—one or two of them particularly—almost as one of their own sex. I mean I have not felt about them as most women are taught to feel—to be on

---

1. Writers notable, by Victorian standards, for frankness or indecency. In the latter part of 1890, Hardy had been reading "mostly the satirists," including Martial, Lucian and Smollett (*Life*, p. 230).

their guard against attacks on their virtue; for no average man—no man short of a sensual savage—will molest a woman by day or night, at home or abroad, unless she invites him. Until she says by a look "Come on" he is always afraid to, and if you never say it, or look it, he never comes. However, what I was going to say is that when I was eighteen I formed a friendly intimacy with an undergraduate at Christminster, and he taught me a great deal, and lent me books which I should never have got hold of otherwise.'

'Is your friendship broken off?'

'O yes. He died, poor fellow, two or three years after he had taken his degree and left Christminster.'

'You saw a good deal of him, I suppose?'

'Yes. We used to go about together—on walking tours, reading tours, and things of that sort—like two men almost. He asked me to live with him, and I agreed to by letter. But when I joined him in London I found he meant a different thing from what I meant. He wanted me to be his mistress, in fact, but I wasn't in love with him—and on my saying I should go away if he didn't agree to *my* plan, he did so. We shared a sitting-room for fifteen months; and he became a leader-writer for one of the great London dailies; till he was taken ill, and had to go abroad. He said I was breaking his heart by holding out against him so long at such close quarters; he could never have believed it of woman. I might play that game once too often, he said. He came home merely to die. His death caused a terrible remorse in me for my cruelty—though I hope he died of consumption and not of me entirely. I went down to Sandbourne to his funeral, and was his only mourner. He left me a little money—because I broke his heart, I suppose. That's how men are—so much better than women!'

'Good heavens!—what did you do then?'

'Ah—now you are angry with me!' she said, a contralto note of tragedy coming suddenly into her silvery voice. 'I wouldn't have told you if I had known!'

'No, I am not. Tell me all.'

'Well, I invested his money, poor fellow, in a bubble scheme, and lost it. I lived about London by myself for some time, and then I returned to Christminster, as my father—who was also in London, and had started as an art metal-worker near Long-Acre—wouldn't have me back; and I got that occupation in the artist-shop where you found me. . . . I said you didn't know how bad I was!'

Jude looked round upon the arm-chair and its occupant, as if to read more carefully the creature he had given shelter to. His voice trembled as he said: 'However you have lived, Sue, I believe you are as innocent as you are unconventional!'

'I am not particularly innocent, as you see, now that I have

"twitched the robe
From that blank lay-figure your fancy draped," [2]

said she, with an ostensible sneer, though he could hear that she was
brimming with tears. 'But I have never yielded myself to any lover, if
that's what you mean! I have remained as I began.'

'I quite believe you. But some women would not have remained as
they began.'

'Perhaps not. Better women would not. People say I must be cold-
natured,—sexless—on account of it. But I won't have it! Some of the
most passionately erotic poets have been the most self-contained in
their daily lives.

'Have you told Mr. Phillotson about this University-scholar-friend?'

'Yes—long ago. I have never made any secret of it to anybody.'

'What did he say?'

'He did not pass any criticism—only said I was everything to him,
whatever I did; and things like that.'

Jude felt much depressed; she seemed to get further and further
away from him with her strange ways and curious unconsciousness of
gender.

'Aren't you *really* vexed with me, dear Jude?' she suddenly asked, in
a voice of such extraordinary tenderness that it hardly seemed to come
from the same woman who had just told her story so lightly. 'I would
rather offend anybody in the world than you, I think!'

'I don't know whether I am vexed or not. I know I care very much
about you!'

'I care as much for you as for anybody I ever met.'

'You don't care *more*! There, I ought not to say that. Don't answer
it!'

There was another long silence. He felt that she was treating him
cruelly, though he could not quite say in what way. Her very helpless-
ness seemed to make her so much stronger than he.

'I am awfully ignorant on general matters, although I have worked
so hard,' he said, to turn the subject. 'I am absorbed in Theology, you
know. And what do you think I should be doing just about now, if you
weren't here? I should be saying my evening prayers. I suppose you
wouldn't like—'

'O no, no,' she answered, 'I would rather not, if you don't mind. I
should seem so—such a hypocrite.'

'I thought you wouldn't join, so I didn't propose it. You must
remember that I hope to be a useful minister some day.'

'To be ordained, I think you said?'

'Yes.'

2. From Browning's poem "Too Late."

'Then you haven't given up the idea?—I thought that perhaps you had by this time.'

'Of course not. I fondly thought at first that you felt as I do about that, as you were so mixed up in Christminster Anglicanism. And Mr. Phillotson—'

'I have no respect for Christminster whatever, except, in a qualified degree, on its intellectual side,' said Sue Bridehead earnestly. 'My friend I spoke of took that out of me. He was the most irreligious man I ever knew and the most moral. And intellect at Christminster is new wine in old bottles.[3] The mediævalism of Christminster must go, be sloughed off, or Christminster itself will have to go. To be sure, at times one couldn't help having a sneaking liking for the traditions of the old faith, as preserved by a section of the thinkers there in touching and simple sincerity; but when I was in my saddest, rightest mind I always felt,

"O ghastly glories of saints, dead limbs of gibbeted Gods!" ' . . .[4]

'Sue, you are not a good friend of mine to talk like that!'

'Then I won't, dear Jude!' The emotional throat-note had come back, and she turned her face away.

'I still think Christminster has much that is glorious; though I was resentful because I couldn't get there.' He spoke gently, and resisted his impulse to pique her on to tears.

'It is an ignorant place, except as to the townspeople, artizans, drunkards, and paupers,' she said, perverse still at his differing from her. 'They see life as it is, of course; but few of the people in the colleges do. You prove it in your own person. You are one of the very men Christminster was intended for when the colleges were founded; a man with a passion for learning, but no money, or opportunities, or friends. But you were elbowed off the pavement by the millionaires' sons.'

'Well, I can do without what it confers. I care for something higher.'

'And I for something broader, truer,' she insisted. 'At present intellect in Christminster is pushing one way, and religion the other; and so they stand stock-still, like two rams butting each other.'

'What would Mr. Phillotson—'

'It is a place full of fetichists and ghost-seers!'

He noticed that whenever he tried to speak of the schoolmaster she turned the conversation to some generalizations about the offending University. Jude was extremely, morbidly, curious about her life as Phillotson's *protégée* and betrothed; yet she would not enlighten him.

'Well, that's just what I am, too,' he said. 'I am fearful of life, spectre-seeing always.'

'But you are good and dear!' she murmured.

3. The phrase is from Matthew 9.17.
4. From Swinburne's "Hymn to Proserpine."

His heart bumped, and he made no reply.

'You are in the Tractarian⁵ stage just now, are you not?' she added, putting on flippancy to hide real feeling, a common trick with her. 'Let me see—when was I there?—In the year eighteen hundred and—'

'There's a sarcasm in that which is rather unpleasant to me, Sue. Now will you do what I want you to? At this time I read a chapter, and then say prayers, as I told you. Now will you concentrate your attention on any book of these you like, and sit with your back to me, and leave me to my custom? You are sure you won't join me?'

'I'll look at you.'

'No. Don't tease, Sue!'

'Very well—I'll do just as you bid me, and I won't vex you, Jude,' she replied, in the tone of a child who was going to be good for ever after, turning her back upon him accordingly. A small Bible other than the one he was using lay near her, and during his retreat she took it up, and turned over the leaves.

'Jude,' she said brightly, when he had finished and come back to her; 'will you let me make you a *new* New Testament, like the one I made for myself at Christminster?'

'O yes. How was that made?'

'I altered my old one by cutting up all the Epistles and Gospels into separate *brochures*, and re-arranging them in chronological order as written, beginning the book with Thessalonians, following on with the Epistles, and putting the Gospels much further on. Then I had the volume rebound. My University friend Mr.———but never mind his name, poor boy—said it was an excellent idea. I know that reading it afterwards made it twice as interesting as before, and twice as understandable.'

'H'm!' said Jude, with a sense of sacrilege.

'And what a literary enormity this is,' she said, as she glanced into the pages of Solomon's Song. 'I mean the synopsis at the head of each chapter, explaining away the real nature of that rhapsody. You needn't be alarmed: nobody claims inspiration for the chapter headings. Indeed, many divines treat them with contempt. It seems the drollest thing to think of the four-and-twenty elders, or bishops, or whatever number they were, sitting with long faces and writing down such stuff.'

Jude looked pained. 'You are quite Voltairean!'⁶ he murmured.

'Indeed? Then I won't say any more, except that people have no right to falsify the Bible! I *hate* such humbug as could attempt to plaster over with ecclesiastical abstractions such ecstatic, natural,

---

5. The Tractarian Movement, or Oxford Movement, flourished in England between 1833 and 1845. Its spokesmen, who included Newman, Keble, and Pusey, urged the revival of the original doctrines of the Christian church. The name is derived from a series of influential *Tracts for the Times* (1833–41).

6. Like the French philosopher Voltaire (1694–1778), noted for his "lack of respect for existing institutions and contempt for authority."

human love as lies in that great and passionate song!' Her speech had
grown spirited, and almost petulant at his rebuke, and her eyes moist.
'I *wish* I had a friend here to support me; but nobody is ever on my
side!'

'But, my dear Sue, my very dear Sue, I am not against you!' he said,
taking her hand, and surprised at her introducing personal feeling into
mere argument.

'Yes you are, yes you are!' she cried, turning away her face that he
might not see her brimming eyes. 'You are on the side of the people
in the Training School—at least you seem almost to be! What I insist
on is, that to explain such verses as this: "Whither is thy beloved gone,
O thou fairest among women?"[7] by the note: *"The Church professeth
her faith"* is supremely ridiculous!'

'Well then, let it be! You make such a personal matter of everything!
I am—only too inclined just now to apply the words profanely. You
know *you* are fairest among women to me, come to that!'

'But you are not to say it now!' Sue replied, her voice changing to
its softest note of severity. Then their eyes met, and they shook hands
like cronies in a tavern, and Jude saw the absurdity of quarrelling on
such a hypothetical subject, and she the silliness of crying about what
was written in an old book like the Bible.

'I won't disturb your convictions—I really won't!' she went on soothingly, for now he was rather more ruffled than she. 'But I did want and
long to ennoble some man to high aims; and when I saw you, and knew
you wanted to be my comrade, I—shall I confess it?—thought that
man might be you. But you take so much tradition on trust that I don't
know what to say.'

'Well, dear; I suppose one must take some things on trust. Life isn't
long enough to work out everything in Euclid[8] problems before you
believe it. I take Christianity.'

'Well, perhaps you might take something worse.'

'Indeed I might. Perhaps I have done so!' He thought of Arabella.

'I won't ask what, because we are going to be *very* nice with each
other, aren't we, and never, never, vex each other any more?' She
looked up trustfully, and her voice seemed trying to nestle in his breast.

'I shall always care for you!' said Jude.

'And I for you. Because you are single-hearted, and forgiving to your
faulty and tiresome little Sue!'

He looked away, for that epicene tenderness of hers was too harrowing. Was it that which had broken the heart of the poor leader-writer;
and was he to be the next one? . . . But Sue was so dear! . . . If he could
only get over the sense of her sex, as she seemed to be able to do so

---

7. Song of Solomon 6.1. This ancient erotic poem was interpreted by churchmen as a religious
   allegory.
8. Greek mathematician whose work on geometry was a standard textbook.

easily of his, what a comrade she would make; for their difference of opinion on conjectural subjects only drew them closer together on matters of daily human experience. She was nearer to him than any other woman he had ever met, and he could scarcely believe that time, creed, or absence, would ever divide him from her.

But his grief at her incredulities returned. They sat on till she fell asleep again, and he nodded in his chair likewise. Whenever he aroused himself he turned her things, and made up the fire anew. About six o'clock he awoke completely, and lighting a candle, found that her clothes were dry. Her chair being a far more comfortable one than his she still slept on inside his great-coat, looking warm as a new bun and boyish as a Ganymedes.[9] Placing the garments by her and touching her on the shoulder he went downstairs, and washed himself by starlight in the yard.

III–5

When he returned she was dressed as usual.

'Now could I get out without anybody seeing me?' she asked. 'The town is not yet astir.'

'But you have had no breakfast.'

'O, I don't want any! I fear I ought not to have run away from that school! Things seem so different in the cold light of morning, don't they? What Mr. Phillotson will say I don't know! It was quite by his wish that I went there. He is the only man in the world for whom I have any respect or fear. I hope he'll forgive me; but he'll scold me dreadfully, I expect!'

'I'll go to him and explain—' began Jude.

'O no, you shan't. I don't care for him! He may think what he likes— I shall do just as I choose!'

'But you just this moment said—'

'Well, if I did; I shall do as I like for all him! I have thought of what I shall do—go to the sister of one of my fellow-students in the Training School, who has asked me to visit her. She has a school near Shaston, about eighteen miles from here—and I shall stay there till this has blown over, and I get back to the Training School again.'

At the last moment he persuaded her to let him make her a cup of coffee, in a portable apparatus he kept in his room for use on rising to go to his work every day before the household was astir.

'Now a dew-bit[1] to eat with it,' he said; 'and off we go. You can have a regular breakfast when you get there.'

9. In Greek mythology, a beautiful youth who was cupbearer to the gods.
1. Food eaten by a laborer first thing in the morning, breakfast being taken after a period of work.

They went quietly out of the house, Jude accompanying her to the station. As they departed along the street a head was thrust out of an upper window of his lodging and quickly withdrawn. Sue still seemed sorry for her rashness, and to wish she had not rebelled; telling him at parting that she would let him know as soon as she got re-admitted to the Training School. They stood rather miserably together on the platform; and it was apparent that he wanted to say more.

'I want to tell you something—two things,' he said hurriedly as the train came up. 'One is a warm one, the other a cold one!'

'Jude,' she said. 'I know one of them. And you mustn't!'

'What?'

'You mustn't love me. You are too like me—that's all!'

Jude's face became so full of complicated glooms that hers was agitated in sympathy as she bade him adieu through the carriage window. And then the train moved on, and waving her pretty hand to him she vanished away.

Melchester was a dismal place enough for Jude that Sunday of her departure, and the Close so hateful that he did not go once to the Cathedral services. The next morning there came a letter from her, which, with her usual promptitude, she had written directly she had reached her friend's house. She told him of her safe arrival and comfortable quarters, and then added:—

> 'What I really write about, dear Jude, is something I said to you at parting. You had been so very good and kind to me that when you were out of sight I felt what a cruel and ungrateful woman I was to say it, and it has reproached me ever since. *If you want to love me, Jude, you may*: I don't mind at all; and I'll never say again that you mustn't!
>
> 'Now I won't write any more about that. You do forgive your thoughtless friend for her cruelty? and won't make her miserable by saying you don't—Ever,   SUE.'

It would be superfluous to say what his answer was; and how he thought what he would have done had he been free, which should have rendered a long residence with a female friend quite unnecessary for Sue. He felt he might have been pretty sure of his own victory if it had come to a conflict between Phillotson and himself for the possession of her.

Yet Jude was in danger of attaching more meaning to Sue's impulsive note than it really was intended to bear.

After the lapse of a few days he found himself hoping that she would write again. But he received no further communication; and in the intensity of his solicitude he sent another note, suggesting that he should pay her a visit some Sunday, the distance being under eighteen miles.

He expected a reply on the second morning after despatching his missive; but none came. The third morning arrived; the postman did not stop. This was Saturday, and in a feverish state of anxiety about her he sent off three brief lines stating that he was coming the following day, for he felt sure something had happened.

His first and natural thought had been that she was ill from her immersion; but it soon occurred to him that somebody would have written for her in such a case. Conjectures were put an end to by his arrival at the village school-house near Shaston on the bright morning of Sunday, between eleven and twelve o'clock, when the parish was as vacant as a desert, most of the inhabitants having gathered inside the church, whence their voices could occasionally be heard in unison.

A little girl opened the door. 'Miss Bridehead is upstairs,' she said. 'And will you please walk up to her?'

'Is she ill?' asked Jude hastily.

'Only a little—not very.'

Jude entered and ascended. On reaching the landing a voice told him which way to turn—the voice of Sue calling his name. He passed the doorway, and found her lying in a little bed in a room a dozen feet square.

'O Sue!' he cried, sitting down beside her and taking her hand. 'How is this! You couldn't write?'

'No—it wasn't that!' she answered. 'I did catch a bad cold—but I could have written. Only I wouldn't!'

'Why not?—frightening me like this!'

'Yes—that was what I was afraid of! But I had decided not to write to you any more. They won't have me back at the school—that's why I couldn't write. Not the fact, but the reason!'

'Well?'

'They not only won't have me, but they gave me a parting piece of advice—'

'What?'

She did not answer directly. 'I vowed I never would tell you, Jude—it is so vulgar and distressing!'

'Is it about us?'

'Yes.'

'But do tell me!'

'Well—somebody has sent them baseless reports about us, and they say you and I ought to marry as soon as possible, for the sake of my reputation! . . . There—now I have told you, and I wish I hadn't!'

'O poor Sue!'

'I don't think of you like that means! It did just *occur* to me to regard you in the way they think I do, but I hadn't begun to. I *have* recognized that the cousinship was merely nominal, since we met as total strangers. But my marrying you, dear Jude—why, of course, if I had reckoned upon marrying you I shouldn't have come to you so often! And I never supposed you thought of such a thing as marrying me till the other evening; when I began to fancy you did love me a little. Perhaps I ought not to have been so intimate with you. It is all my fault. Everything is my fault always!'

The speech seemed a little forced and unreal, and they regarded each other with a mutual distress.

'I was so blind at first!' she went on. 'I didn't see what you felt at all. O you have been unkind to me—you have—to look upon me as a sweetheart without saying a word, and leaving me to discover it myself! Your attitude to me has become known; and naturally they think we've been doing wrong! I'll never trust you again!'

'Yes, Sue,' he said simply; 'I am to blame—more than you think. I was quite aware that you did not suspect till within the last meeting or two what I was feeling about you. I admit that our meeting as strangers prevented a sense of relationship, and that it was a sort of subterfuge to avail myself of it. But don't you think I deserve a little consideration for concealing my wrong, very wrong, sentiments, since I couldn't help having them?'

She turned her eyes doubtfully towards him, and then looked away as if afraid she might forgive him.

By every law of nature and sex a kiss was the only rejoinder that fitted the mood and the moment, under the suasion of which Sue's undemonstrative regard of him might not inconceivably have changed its temperature. Some men would have cast scruples to the winds, and ventured it, oblivious both of Sue's declaration of her neutral feelings, and of the pair of autographs in the vestry chest of Arabella's parish church. Jude did not. He had, in fact, come in part to tell his own fatal story. It was upon his lips; yet at the hour of this distress he could not disclose it. He preferred to dwell upon the recognized barriers between them.

'Of course—I know you don't—care about me in any particular way,' he sorrowed. 'You ought not, and you are right. You belong to—Mr. Phillotson. I suppose he has been to see you?'

'Yes,' she said shortly, her face changing a little. 'Though I didn't ask him to come. You are glad, of course, that he has been! But I shouldn't care if he didn't come any more!'

It was very perplexing to her lover that she should be piqued at his honest acquiescence in his rival, if Jude's feelings of love were deprecated by her. He went on to something else.

'This will blow over, dear Sue,' he said. 'The Training School authorities are not all the world. You can get to be a student in some other, no doubt.'

'I'll ask Mr. Phillotson," she said decisively.

Sue's kind hostess now returned from church, and there was no more intimate conversation. Jude left in the afternoon, hopelessly unhappy. But he had seen her, and sat with her. Such intercourse as that would have to content him for the remainder of his life. The lesson of renunciation it was necessary and proper that he, as a parish priest, should learn.

But the next morning when he awoke he felt rather vexed with her, and decided that she was rather unreasonable, not to say capricious. Then, in illustration of what he had begun to discern as one of her redeeming characteristics there came promptly a note, which she must have written almost immediately he had gone from her:

> 'Forgive me for my petulance yesterday! I was horrid to you; I know it, and I feel perfectly miserable at my horridness. It was so dear of you not to be angry! Jude, please still keep me as your friend and associate, with all my faults. I'll try not to be like it again.
>
> 'I am coming to Melchester on Saturday, to get my things away from the T. S., &c. I could walk with you for half-an-hour, if you would like?—Your repentant SUE.'

Jude forgave her straightway, and asked her to call for him at the Cathedral works when she came.

III–6

Meanwhile a middle-aged man was dreaming a dream of great beauty concerning the writer of the above letter. He was Richard Phillotson, who had recently removed from the mixed village school at Lumsdon near Christminster, to undertake a large boys' school in his native town of Shaston, which stood on a hill sixty miles to the southwest as the crow flies.

A glance at the place and its accessories was almost enough to reveal that the schoolmaster's plans and dreams so long indulged in had been abandoned for some new dream with which neither the Church nor literature had much in common. Essentially an unpractical man, he was now bent on making and saving money for a practical purpose—that of keeping a wife, who, if she chose, might conduct one of the girls' schools adjoining his own; for which purpose he had advised her to go into training, since she would not marry him off-hand.

About the time that Jude was removing from Marygreen to Melchester, and entering on adventures at the latter place with Sue, the schoolmaster was settling down in the new schoolhouse at Shaston. All the furniture being fixed, the books shelved, and the nails driven, he had begun to sit in his parlour during the dark winter nights and re-

attempt some of his old studies—one branch of which had included
Roman-Britannic antiquities—an unremunerative labour for a
National schoolmaster[1] but a subject, that, after his abandonment of
the University scheme, had interested him as being a comparatively
unworked mine; practicable to those who, like himself, had lived in
lonely spots where these remains were abundant, and were seen to
compel inferences in startling contrast to accepted views on the civilization of that time.

A resumption of this investigation was the outward and apparent
hobby of Phillotson at present—his ostensible reason for going alone
into fields where causeways, dykes, and tumuli abounded, or shutting
himself up in his house with a few urns, tiles, and mosaics he had
collected, instead of calling round upon his new neighbours, who for
their part had showed themselves willing enough to be friendly with
him. But it was not the real, or the whole, reason, after all. Thus on a
particular evening in the month, when it had grown quite late—to
near midnight, indeed—and the light of his lamp, shining from his
window at a salient angle of the hill-top town over infinite miles of
valley westward, announced as by words a place and person given over
to study, he was not exactly studying.

The interior of the room—the books, the furniture, the schoolmaster's loose coat, his attitude at the table, even the flickering of the fire,
bespoke the same dignified tale of undistracted research—more than
creditable to a man who had had no advantages beyond those of his
own making. And yet the tale, true enough till latterly, was not
true now. What he was regarding was not history. They were historic
notes, written in a bold womanly hand at his dictation some months
before, and it was the clerical rendering of word after word that
absorbed him.

He presently took from a drawer a carefully tied bundle of letters,
few, very few, as correspondence counts nowadays. Each was in its
envelope just as it had arrived, and the handwriting was of the same
womanly character as the historic notes. He unfolded them one by one
and read them musingly. At first sight there seemed in these small
documents to be absolutely nothing to muse over. They were straightforward, frank letters, signed 'Sue B—'; just such ones as would be
written during short absences, with no other thought than their speedy
destruction, and chiefly concerning books in reading and other experiences of a Training School, forgotten doubtless by the writer with the
passing of the day of their inditing. In one of them—quite a recent
note—the young woman said that she had received his considerate
letter, and that it was honourable and generous of him to say he would
not come to see her oftener than she desired (the school being such

1. One in charge of a school established by the National Society, which had been founded in
1811 to promote the education of the poor.

an awkward place for callers, and because of her strong wish that her engagment to him should not be known, which it would infallibly be if he visited her often). Over these phrases the schoolmaster pored. What precise shade of satisfaction was to be gathered from a woman's gratitude that the man who loved her had not been often to see her? The problem occupied him, distracted him.

He opened another drawer, and found therein an envelope, from which he drew a photograph of Sue as a child, long before he had known her, standing under trellis-work with a little basket in her hand. There was another of her as a young woman, her dark eyes and hair making a very distinct and attractive picture of her, which just disclosed, too, the thoughtfulness that lay behind her lighter moods. It was a duplicate of the one she had given Jude, and would have given to any man. Phillotson brought it half-way to his lips, but withdrew it in doubt at her perplexing phrases: ultimately kissing the dead pasteboard with all the passionateness, and more than all the devotion, of a young man of eighteen.

The schoolmaster's was an unhealthy-looking, old-fashioned face, rendered more old-fashioned by his style of shaving. A certain gentlemanliness had been imparted to it by nature, suggesting an inherent wish to do rightly by all. His speech was a little slow, but his tones were sincere enough to make his hesitation no defect. His greying hair was curly, and radiated from a point in the middle of his crown. There were four lines across his forehead, and he only wore spectacles when reading at night. It was almost certainly a renunciation forced upon him by his academic purpose, rather than a distaste for women, which had hitherto kept him from closing with one of the sex in matrimony.

Such silent proceedings as those of this evening were repeated many and oft times when he was not under the eye of the boys, whose quick and penetrating regard would frequently become almost intolerable to the self-conscious master in his present anxious care for Sue, making him, in the grey hours of morning, dread to meet anew the gimlet glances, lest they should read what the dream within him was.

He had honourably acquiesced in Sue's announced wish that he was not often to visit her at the Training School; but at length, his patience being sorely tried, he set out one Saturday afternoon to pay her an unexpected call. There the news of her departure—expulsion as it might almost have been considered—was flashed upon him without warning or mitigation as he stood at the door expecting in a few minutes to behold her face; and when he turned away he could hardly see the road before him.

Sue had, in fact, never written a line to her suitor on the subject, although it was fourteen days old. A short reflection told him that this proved nothing, a natural delicacy being as ample a reason for silence as any degree of blameworthiness.

They had informed him at the school where she was living, and having no immediate anxiety about her comfort his thoughts took the direction of a burning indignation against the Training School Committee. In his bewilderment Phillotson entered the adjacent cathedral, just now in a direly dismantled state by reason of the repairs. He sat down on a block of freestone, regardless of the dusty imprint it made on his breeches; and his listless eyes following the movements of the workmen he presently became aware that the reputed culprit, Sue's lover Jude, was one amongst them.

Jude had never spoken to his former hero since the meeting by the model of Jerusalem. Having inadvertently witnessed Phillotson's tentative courtship of Sue in the lane there had grown up in the young man's mind a curious dislike to think of the elder, to meet him, to communicate in any way with him; and since Phillotson's success in obtaining at least her promise had become known to Jude, he had frankly recognized that he did not wish to see or hear of his senior any more, learn anything of his pursuits, or even imagine again what excellencies might appertain to his character. On this very day of the schoolmaster's visit Jude was expecting Sue, as she had promised; and when therefore he saw the schoolmaster in the nave of the building, saw, moreover, that he was coming to speak to him, he felt no little embarrassment; which Phillotson's own embarrassment prevented his observing.

Jude joined him, and they both withdrew from the other workmen to the spot where Phillotson had been sitting. Jude offered him a piece of sackcloth for a cushion, and told him it was dangerous to sit on the bare block.

'Yes; yes,' said Phillotson abstractedly, as he reseated himself, his eyes resting on the ground as if he were trying to remember where he was. 'I won't keep you long. It was merely that I have heard that you have seen my little friend Sue recently. It occurred to me to speak to you on that account. I merely want to ask—about her.'

'I think I know what!' Jude hurriedly said. 'About her escaping from the Training School, and her coming to me?'

'Yes.'

'Well'—Jude for a moment felt an unprincipled and fiendish wish to annihilate his rival at all cost. By the exercise of that treachery which love for the same woman renders possible to men the most honourable in every other relation of life, he could send off Phillotson in agony and defeat by saying that the scandal was true, and that Sue had irretrievably committed herself with him. But his action did not respond for a moment to his animal instinct; and what he said was, 'I am glad of your kindness in coming to talk plainly to me about it. You know what they say?—that I ought to marry her.'

'What!'

'And I wish with all my soul I could!'

Phillotson trembled, and his naturally pale face acquired a corpse-like sharpness in its lines. 'I had no idea that it was of this nature! God forbid!'

'No, no!' said Jude aghast. 'I thought you understood? I mean that were I in a position to marry her, or some one, and settle down, instead of living in lodgings here and there, I should be glad!'

What he had really meant was simply that he loved her.

'But—since this painful matter has been opened up—what really happened?' asked Phillotson, with the firmness of a man who felt that a sharp smart now was better than a long agony of suspense hereafter. 'Cases arise, and this is one, when even ungenerous questions must be put to make false assumptions impossible, and to kill scandal.'

Jude explained readily; giving the whole series of adventures, including the night at the shepherd's, her wet arrival at his lodging, her indisposition from her immersion, their vigil of discussion, and his seeing her off next morning.

'Well now,' said Phillotson at the conclusion, 'I take it as your final word, and I know I can believe you, that the suspicion which led to her rustication is an absolutely baseless one?'

'It is,' said Jude solemnly. 'Absolutely. So help me God!'

The schoolmaster rose. Each of the twain felt that the interview could not comfortably merge in a friendly discussion of their recent experiences, after the manner of friends; and when Jude had taken him round, and shown him some features of the renovation which the old cathedral was undergoing, Phillotson bade the young man good-day and went away.

This visit took place about eleven o'clock in the morning; but no Sue appeared. When Jude went to his dinner at one he saw his beloved ahead of him in the street leading up from the North Gate, walking as if in no way looking for him. Speedily overtaking her he remarked that he had asked her to come to him at the Cathedral, and she had promised.

'I have been to get my things from the College,' she said—an observation which he was expected to take as an answer, though it was not one. Finding her to be in this evasive mood he felt inclined to give her the information so long withheld.

'You have not seen Mr. Phillotson to-day?' he ventured to inquire.

'I have not. But I am not going to be cross-examined about him; and if you ask anything more I won't answer!'

'It is very odd that—' He stopped, regarding her.

'What?'

'That you are often not so nice in your real presence as you are in your letters!'

'Does it really seem so to you?' said she, smiling with quick curiosity.

'Well, that's strange; but I feel just the same about you, Jude. When you are gone away I seem such a cold-hearted—'

As she knew his sentiment towards her Jude saw that they were getting upon dangerous ground. It was now, he thought, that he must speak as an honest man.

But he did not speak, and she continued: 'It was that which made me write and say—I didn't mind you loving me,—if you wanted to, much!'

The exultation he might have felt at what that implied, or seemed to imply, was nullified by his intention, and he rested rigid till he began: 'I have never told you—'

'Yes you have,' murmured she.

'I mean, I have never told you my history—all of it.'

'But I guess it. I know nearly.'

Jude looked up. Could she possibly know of that morning performance of his with Arabella; which in a few months had ceased to be a marriage more completely than by death? He saw that she did not.

'I can't quite tell you here in the street,' he went on with a gloomy tongue. 'And you had better not come to my lodgings. Let us go in here.'

The building by which they stood was the market-house; it was the only place available; and they entered, the market being over, and the stalls and areas empty. He would have preferred a more congenial spot, but, as usually happens, in place of a romantic field or solemn aisle for his tale, it was told while they walked up and down over a floor littered with rotten cabbage-leaves, and amid all the usual squalors of decayed vegetable matter and unsaleable refuse. He began and finished his brief narrative, which merely led up to the information that he had married a wife some years earlier, and that his wife was living still. Almost before her countenance had time to change she hurried out the words,

'Why didn't you tell me before!'

'I couldn't. It seemed so cruel to tell it.'

'To yourself, Jude. So it was better to be cruel to me!'

'No, dear darling!' cried Jude passionately. He tried to take her hand, but she withdrew it. Their old relations of confidence seemed suddenly to have ended, and the antagonisms of sex to sex were left without any counterpoising predilections. She was his comrade, friend, unconscious sweetheart no longer; and her eyes regarded him in estranged silence.

'I was ashamed of the episode in my life which brought about the marriage,' he continued. 'I can't explain it precisely now. I could have done it if you had taken it differently!'

'But how can I?' she burst out. 'Here I have been saying, or writing, that—that you might love me, or something of the sort!—just out of

charity—and all the time—O it is perfectly damnable how things are!'
she said, stamping her foot in a nervous quiver.

'You take me wrong, Sue! I never thought you cared for me at all,
till quite lately; so I felt it did not matter! Do you care for me, Sue?—
you know how I mean?—I don't like "out of charity" at all!'

It was a question which in the circumstances Sue did not choose to
answer.

'I suppose she—your wife—is—a very pretty woman, even if she's
wicked?' she asked quickly.

'She's pretty enough, as far as that goes.'

'Prettier than I am, no doubt!'

'You are not the least alike. And I have never seen her for years. . . .
But she's sure to come back—they always do!'

'How strange of you to stay apart from her like this!' said Sue, her
trembling lip and lumpy throat belying her irony. 'You, such a religious
man. How will the demi-gods in your Pantheon[2]—I mean those leg-
endary persons you call Saints—intercede for you after this? Now if I
had done such a thing it would have been different, and not remarkable, for I at least don't regard marriage as a Sacrament. Your theories
are not so advanced as your practice!'

'Sue, you are terribly cutting when you like to be—a perfect Voltaire!
But you must treat me as you will!'

When she saw how wretched he was she softened, and trying to
blink away her sympathetic tears said with all the winning reproach-
fulness of a heart-hurt woman: 'Ah—you should have told me before
you gave me that idea that you wanted to be allowed to love me! I had
no feeling before that moment at the railway-station, except—' For
once Sue was as miserable as he, in her attempts to keep herself free
from emotion, and her less than half-success.

'Don't cry, dear!' he implored.

'I am—not crying—because I meant to—love you; but because of
your want of—confidence!'

They were quite screened from the Market-square without, and he
could not help putting out his arm towards her waist. His momentary
desire was the means of her rallying. 'No, no!' she said, drawing back
stringently, and wiping her eyes. 'Of course not! It would be hypocrisy
to pretend that it would be meant as from my cousin; and it can't be
in any other way.'

They moved on a dozen paces, and she showed herself recovered. It
was distracting to Jude, and his heart would have ached less had she
appeared anyhow but as she did appear; essentially large-minded and
generous on reflection, despite a previous exercise of those narrow
womanly humours on impulse that were necessary to give her sex.

2. Originally a temple devoted to all the gods.

'I don't blame you for what you couldn't help,' she said smiling. 'How should I be so foolish! I do blame you a little bit for not telling me before. But after all it doesn't matter. We should have had to keep apart, you see, even if this had not been in your life.'

'No, we shouldn't, Sue! This is the only obstacle!'

'You forget that I must have loved you, and wanted to be your wife, even if there had been no obstacle,' said Sue, with a gentle seriousness which did not reveal her mind. 'And then we are cousins, and it is bad for cousins to marry. And—I am engaged to somebody else. As to our going on together as we were going, in a sort of friendly way, the people round us would have made it unable to continue. Their views of the relations of man and woman are limited, as is proved by their expelling me from the school. Their philosophy only recognizes relations based on animal desire. The wide field of strong attachment where desire plays, at least, only a secondary part, is ignored by them—the part of— who is it?—Venus Urania.'[3]

Her being able to talk learnedly showed that she was mistress of herself again; and before they parted she had almost regained her vivacious glance, her reciprocity of tone, her gay manner, and her second-thought attitude of critical largeness towards others of her age and sex.

He could speak more freely now. 'There were several reasons against my telling you rashly. One was what I have said; another, that it was always impressed upon me that I ought not to marry—that I belonged to an odd and peculiar family—the wrong breed for marriage.'

'Ah—who used to say that to you?'

'My great-aunt. She said it always ended badly with us Fawleys.'

'That's strange. My father used to say the same to me!'

They stood possessed by the same thought, ugly enough, even as an assumption: that a union between them, had such been possible, would have meant a terrible intensification of unfitness—two bitters in one dish.

'O but there can't be anything in it!' she said with nervous lightness. 'Our family have been unlucky of late years in choosing mates—that's all.'

And then they pretended to persuade themselves that all that had happened was of no consequence, and that they could still be cousins and friends and warm correspondents, and have happy genial times when they met, even if they met less frequently than before. Their parting was in good friendship, and yet Jude's last look into her eyes was tinged with inquiry, for he felt that he did not even now quite know her mind.

---

3. Associated with intellectual as opposed to physical love.

III–7

Tidings from Sue a day or two after passed across Jude like a withering blast.

Before reading the letter he was led to suspect that its contents were of a somewhat serious kind by catching sight of the signature—which was in her full name, never used in her correspondence with him since her first note:

> 'MY DEAR JUDE,—I have something to tell you which perhaps you will not be surprised to hear, though certainly it may strike you as being accelerated (as the railway companies say of their trains). Mr. Phillotson and I are to be married quite soon—in three or four weeks. We had intended, as you know, to wait till I had gone through my course of training and obtained my certificate, so as to assist him, if necessary, in the teaching. But he generously says he does not see any object in waiting, now I am not at the Training School. It is so good of him, because the awkwardness of my situation has really come about by my fault in getting expelled.
>
> 'Wish me joy. Remember I say you are to, and you mustn't refuse!—Your affectionate cousin,
> 'SUSANNA FLORENCE MARY BRIDEHEAD.'

Jude staggered under the news; could eat no breakfast; and kept on drinking tea because his mouth was so dry. Then presently he went back to his work and laughed the usual bitter laugh of a man so confronted. Everything seemed turning to satire. And yet, what could the poor girl do? he asked himself: and felt worse than shedding tears.

'O Susanna Florence Mary!' he said as he worked. 'You don't know what marriage means!'

Could it be possible that his announcement of his own marriage had pricked her on to this, just as his visit to her when in liquor may have pricked her on to her engagement? To be sure, there seemed to exist these other and sufficient reasons, practical and social, for her decision; but Sue was not a very practical or calculating person; and he was compelled to think that a pique at having his secret sprung upon her had moved her to give way to Phillotson's probable representations, that the best course to prove how unfounded were the suspicions of the school authorities would be to marry him off-hand,[1] as in fulfilment of an ordinary engagement. She had, in fact, been placed in an awkward corner. Poor Sue!

He determined to play the Spartan;[2] to make the best of it, and support her; but he could not write the requested good wishes for a

1. Immediately.
2. The Spartans, a people of ancient Greece, had a reputation for great courage and self-control.

day or two. Meanwhile there came another note from his impatient
little dear:

> 'Jude, will you give me away? I have nobody else who could do
> it so conveniently as you, being the only married relation I have
> here on the spot, even if my father were friendly enough to be
> willing, which he isn't. I hope you won't think it a trouble? I have
> been looking at the marriage service in the Prayer-book, and it
> seems to be very humiliating that a giver-away should be required
> at all. According to the ceremony as there printed, my bridegroom
> chooses me of his own will and pleasure; but I don't choose him.
> Somebody *gives* me to him, like a she-ass or she-goat, or any other
> domestic animal. Bless your exalted views of woman, O Church-
> man! But I forget: I am no longer privileged to tease you.—Ever,
>   'SUSANNA FLORENCE MARY BRIDEHEAD.'

Jude screwed himself up to heroic key; and replied:

> 'MY DEAR SUE,—Of course I wish you joy! And also of course
> I will give you away. What I suggest is that, as you have no house
> of your own, you do not marry from your school friend's, but from
> mine. It would be more proper, I think, since I am, as you say, the
> person nearest related to you in this part of the world.
>   'I don't see why you sign your letter in such a new and terribly
> formal way? Surely you care a bit about me still!—Ever your
> affectionate,   JUDE.'

What had jarred on him even more than the signature was a little
sting he had been silent on—the phrase 'married relation'—What an
idiot it made him seem as her lover! If Sue had written that in satire,
he could hardly forgive her; if in suffering—ah, that was another thing!

His offer of his lodging must have commended itself to Phillotson
at any rate, for the schoolmaster sent him a line of warm thanks,
accepting the convenience. She also thanked him. Jude immediately
moved into more commodious quarters, as much to escape the espi-
onage of the suspicious landlady who had been one cause of Sue's
unpleasant experience as for the sake of room.

Then Sue wrote to tell him the day fixed for the wedding; and Jude
decided, after inquiry, that she should come into residence on the
following Saturday, which would allow of a ten days' stay in the city
prior to the ceremony, sufficiently representing a nominal residence of
fifteen.

She arrived by the ten o'clock train on the day aforesaid, Jude not
going to meet her at the station, by her special request, that he should
not lose a morning's work and pay, she said (if this were her true reason). But so well by this time did he know Sue that the remembrance
of their mutual sensitiveness at emotional crises might, he thought,

have weighed with her in this. When he came home to dinner she had taken possession of her apartment.

She lived in the same house with him, but on a different floor, and they saw each other little, an occasional supper being the only meal they took together, when Sue's manner was something that of a scared child. What she felt he did not know; their conversation was mechanical, though she did not look pale or ill. Phillotson came frequently, but mostly when Jude was absent. On the morning of the wedding, when Jude had given himself a holiday, Sue and her cousin had breakfast together for the first and last time during this curious interval; in his room—the parlour—which he had hired for the period of Sue's residence. Seeing, as women do, how helpless he was in making the place comfortable, she bustled about.

'What's the matter, Jude?' she said suddenly.

He was leaning with his elbows on the table and his chin on his hands, looking into a futurity which seemed to be sketched out on the tablecloth.

'O—nothing!'

'You are "father," you know. That's what they call the man who gives you away.'

Jude could have said 'Phillotson's age entitles him to be called that!' But he would not annoy her by such a cheap retort.

She talked incessantly, as if she dreaded his indulgence in reflection, and before the meal was over both he and she wished they had not put such confidence in their new view of things, and had taken breakfast apart. What oppressed Jude was the thought that, having done a wrong thing of this sort himself, he was aiding and abetting the woman he loved in doing a like wrong thing, instead of imploring and warning her against it. It was on his tongue to say, 'You have quite made up your mind?'

After breakfast they went out on an errand together moved by a mutual thought that it was the last opportunity they would have of indulging in unceremonious companionship. By the irony of fate, and the curious trick in Sue's nature of tempting Providence at critical times, she took his arm as they walked through the muddy street—a thing she had never done before in her life—and on turning the corner they found themselves close to a grey Perpendicular[3] church with a low-pitched roof—the church of St. Thomas.

'That's the church,' said Jude.

'Where I am going to be married?'

'Yes.'

'Indeed!' she exclaimed with curiosity. 'How I should like to go in and see what the spot is like where I am so soon to kneel and do it.'

3. Late medieval style of English church architecture.

Again he said to himself, 'She does not realize what marriage means!'

He passively acquiesced in her wish to go in, and they entered by the western door. The only person inside the gloomy building was a charwoman[4] cleaning. Sue still held Jude's arm, almost as if she loved him. Cruelly sweet, indeed, she had been to him that morning; but his thoughts of a penance in store for her were tempered by an ache:

> ' . . . I can find no way
> How a blow should fall, such as falls on men,
> Nor prove too much for your womanhood!'[5]

They strolled undemonstratively up the nave towards the altar railing, which they stood against in silence, turning then and walking down the nave again, her hand still on his arm, precisely like a couple just married. The too suggestive incident, entirely of her making, nearly broke down Jude.

'I like to do things like this,' she said in the delicate voice of an epicure in emotions, which left no doubt that she spoke the truth.

'I know you do!' said Jude.

'They are interesting, because they have probably never been done before. I shall walk down the church like this with my husband in about two hours, shan't I!'

'No doubt you will!'

'Was it like this when you were married?'

'Good God, Sue—don't be so awfully merciless! . . . There, dear one, I didn't mean it!'

'Ah—you are vexed!' she said regretfully, as she blinked away an access of eye moisture. 'And I promised never to vex you! . . . I suppose I ought not to have asked you to bring me in here. O I oughtn't! I see it now. My curiosity to hunt up a new sensation always leads me into these scrapes. Forgive me! . . . You will, won't you, Jude?'

The appeal was so remorseful that Jude's eyes were even wetter than hers as he pressed her hand for Yes.

'Now we'll hurry away, and I won't do it any more!' she continued humbly; and they came out of the building, Sue intending to go on to the station to meet Phillotson. But the first person they encountered on entering the main street was the schoolmaster himself, whose train had arrived sooner than Sue expected. There was nothing really to demur to in her leaning on Jude's arm; but she withdrew her hand; and Jude thought that Phillotson had looked surprised.

'We have been doing such a funny thing!' said she, smiling candidly. 'We've been to the church, rehearsing as it were. Haven't we, Jude?'

'How? said Phillotson curiously.

---

4. Woman hired for rough housework.
5. From Robert Browning's poem "The Worst of It."

Jude inwardly deplored what he thought to be unnecessary frankness; but she had gone too far not to explain all, which she accordingly
did, telling him how they had marched up to the altar.

Seeing how puzzled Phillotson seemed, Jude said as cheerfully as he
could, 'I am going to buy her another little present. Will you both
come to the shop with me?'

'No,' said Sue, 'I'll go on to the house with him;' and requesting her
lover not to be a long time she departed with the schoolmaster.

Jude soon joined them at his rooms, and shortly after they prepared
for the ceremony. Phillotson's hair was brushed to a painful extent,
and his shirt collar appeared stiffer than it had been for the previous
twenty years. Beyond this he looked dignified and thoughtful, and altogether a man of whom it was not unsafe to predict that he would make
a kind and considerate husband. That he adored Sue was obvious;
and she could almost be seen to feel that she was undeserving his
adoration.

Although the distance was so short he had hired a fly[6] from the Red
Lion, and six or seven women and children had gathered by the door
when they came out. The schoolmaster and Sue were unknown,
though Jude was getting to be recognized as a citizen; and the couple
were judged to be some relations of his from a distance, nobody supposing Sue to have been a recent pupil at the Training School.

In the carriage Jude took from his pocket his extra little wedding-
present, which turned out to be two or three yards of white tulle, which
he threw over her bonnet and all, as a veil.

'It looks so odd over a bonnet,' she said. 'I'll take the bonnet off.'

'O no—let it stay,' said Phillotson. And she obeyed.

When they had passed up the church and were standing in their
places Jude found that the antecedent visit had certainly taken off the
edge of this performance, but by the time they were half way on with
the service he wished from his heart that he had not undertaken the
business of giving her away. How could Sue have had the temerity to
ask him to do it—a cruelty possibly to herself as well as to him? Women
were different from men in such matters. Was it that they were, instead
of more sensitive, as reputed, more callous, and less romantic; or were
they more heroic? Or was Sue simply so perverse that she wilfully gave
herself and him pain for the odd and mournful luxury of practising
long-suffering in her own person, and of being touched with tender
pity for him at having made him practise it? He could perceive that
her face was nervously set, and when they reached the trying ordeal of
Jude giving her to Phillotson she could hardly command herself; rather,
however, as it seemed, from her knowledge of what her cousin must
feel, whom she need not have had there at all, than from self-

6. Light carriage.

consideration. Possibly she would go on inflicting such pains again and again, and grieving for the sufferer again and again, in all her colossal inconsistency.

Phillotson seemed not to notice, to be surrounded by a mist which prevented his seeing the emotions of others. As soon as they had signed their names and come away, and the suspense was over, Jude felt relieved.

The meal at his lodging was a very simple affair, and at two o'clock they went off. In crossing the pavement to the fly she looked back; and there was a frightened light in her eyes. Could it be that Sue had acted with such unusual foolishness as to plunge into she knew not what for the sake of asserting her independence of him, of retaliating on him for his secrecy? Perhaps Sue was thus venturesome with men because she was childishly ignorant of that side of their natures which wore out women's hearts and lives.

When her foot was on the carriage-step she turned round, saying that she had forgotten something. Jude and the landlady offered to get it.

'No,' she said, running back. 'It is my handkerchief. I know where I left it.'

Jude followed her back. She had found it, and came holding it in her hand. She looked into his eyes with her own tearful ones, and her lips suddenly parted as if she were going to avow something. But she went on; and whatever she had meant to say remained unspoken.

III–8

Jude wondered if she had really left her handkerchief behind; or whether it were that she had miserably wished to tell him of a love that at the last moment she could not bring herself to express.

He could not stay in his silent lodging when they were gone, and fearing that he might be tempted to drown his misery in alcohol he went upstairs, changed his dark clothes for his white, his thin boots for his thick, and proceeded to his customary work for the afternoon.

But in the cathedral he seemed to hear a voice behind him, and to be possessed with an idea that she would come back. She could not possibly go home with Phillotson, he fancied. The feeling grew and stirred. The moment that the clock struck the last of his working hours he threw down his tools and rushed homeward. 'Has anybody been for me?' he asked.

Nobody had been there.

As he could claim the downstairs sitting-room till twelve o'clock that night he sat in it all the evening; and even when the clock had struck eleven, and the family had retired, he could not shake off the feeling that she would come back and sleep in the little room adjoining his own, in which she had slept so many previous days. Her actions were always unpredictable: why should she not come? Gladly would he have compounded for the denial of her as a sweetheart and wife by having her live thus as a fellow-lodger and friend, even on the most distant terms. His supper still remained spread; and going to the front door, and softly setting it open, he returned to the room and sat as watchers sit on Old-Midsummer eves, expecting the phantom of the Beloved. But she did not come.

Having indulged in this wild hope he went upstairs, and looked out of the window, and pictured her through the evening journey to London, whither she and Phillotson had gone for their holiday; their rattling along through the damp night to their hotel, under the same sky of ribbed cloud as that he beheld, through which the moon showed its position rather than its shape, and one or two of the larger stars made themselves visible as faint nebulæ only. It was a new beginning of Sue's history. He projected his mind into the future, and saw her with children more or less in her own likeness around her. But the consolation of regarding them as a continuation of her identity was denied to him, as to all such dreamers, by the wilfulness of Nature in not allowing issue from one parent alone. Every desired renewal of an existence is debased by being half alloy. 'If at the estrangement or death of my lost love, I could go and see her child—hers solely—there would be comfort in it!' said Jude. And then he again uneasily saw, as he had latterly seen with more and more frequency, the scorn of Nature for man's finer emotions, and her lack of interest in his aspirations.

The oppressive strength of his affection for Sue showed itself on the morrow and following days yet more clearly. He could no longer endure the light of the Melchester lamps; the sunshine was as drab paint; and the blue sky as zinc. Then he received news that his old aunt was dangerously ill at Marygreen, which intelligence almost coincided with a letter from his former employer at Christminster, who offered him permanent work of a good class if he would come back. The letters were almost a relief to him. He started to visit Aunt Drusilla, and resolved to go onward to Christminster to see what worth there might be in the builder's offer.

Jude found his aunt even worse than the communication from the Widow Edlin had led him to expect. There was every possibility of her lingering on for weeks or months, though little likelihood. He wrote to Sue informing her of the state of her aunt, and suggesting that she might like to see her aged relative alive. He would meet her at Alfredston Road, the following evening, Monday, on his way back from Christminster, if she could come by the up-train which crossed his down-train at that station. Next morning, accordingly, he went on to Christminster, intending to return to Alfredston soon enough to keep the suggested appointment with Sue.

The City of learning wore an estranged look, and he had lost all feeling for its associations. Yet as the sun made vivid lights and shades of the mullioned architecture of the façades, and drew patterns of the crinkled battlements on the young turf of the quadrangles, Jude thought he had never seen the place look more beautiful. He came to the street in which he had first beheld Sue. The chair she had occupied when, leaning over her ecclesiastical scrolls, a hog-hair brush in her hand, her girlish figure had arrested the gaze of his inquiring eyes, stood precisely in its former spot, empty. It was as if she were dead, and nobody had been found capable of succeeding her in that artistic pursuit. Hers was now the City phantom, while those of the intellectual and devotional worthies who had once moved him to emotion were no longer able to assert their presence there.

However, here he was; and in fulfilment of his intention he went on to his former lodging in 'Beersheba,' near the ritualistic church of St. Silas. The old landlady who opened the door seemed glad to see him again, and bringing some lunch informed him that the builder who had employed him had called to inquire his address.

Jude went on to the stone-yard where he had worked. But the old sheds and bankers were distasteful to him; he felt it impossible to engage himself to return and stay in this place of vanished dreams. He longed for the hour of the homeward train to Alfredston, where he might probably meet Sue.

Then, for one ghastly half-hour of depression caused by these scenes, there returned upon him that feeling which had been his undoing more than once—that he was not worth the trouble of being taken care of either by himself or others; and during this half-hour he met Tinker Taylor, the bankrupt ecclesiastical ironmonger, at Fourways, who proposed that they should adjourn to a bar and drink together. They walked along the street till they stood before one of the great palpitating centres of Christminster life, the inn wherein he formerly had responded to the challenge to rehearse the Creed in Latin—now a popular tavern with a spacious and inviting entrance, which gave admittance to a bar that had been entirely renovated and refitted in modern style since Jude's residence here.

Tinker Taylor drank off his glass and departed, saying it was too stylish a place now for him to feel at home in, unless he was drunker than he had money to be just then. Jude was longer finishing his, and stood abstractedly silent in the, for the minute, almost empty place. The bar had been gutted and newly arranged throughout, mahogany fixtures having taken the place of the old painted ones, while at the back of the standing-space there were stuffed sofa-benches. The room was divided into compartments in the approved manner, between which were screens of ground glass in mahogany framing, to prevent topers in one compartment being put to the blush by the recognitions of those in the next. On the inside of the counter two barmaids leant over the white-handled beer-engines, and the row of little silvered taps inside, dripping into a pewter trough.

Feeling tired, and having nothing more to do till the train left, Jude sat down on one of the sofas. At the back of the barmaids rose bevel-edged mirrors, with glass shelves running along their front, on which stood precious liquids that Jude did not know the name of, in bottles of topaz, sapphire, ruby and amethyst. The moment was enlivened by the entrance of some customers into the next compartment, and the starting of the mechanical tell-tale of monies received, which emitted a ting-ting every time a coin was put in.

The barmaid attending to this compartment was invisible to Jude's direct glance, though a reflection of her back in the glass behind her was occasionally caught by his eyes. He had only observed this listlessly, when she turned her face for a moment to the glass to set her hair tidy. Then he was amazed to discover that the face was Arabella's.

If she had come on to his compartment she would have seen him. But she did not, this being presided over by the maiden on the other side. Abby was in a black gown, with white linen cuffs and a broad white collar, and her figure, more developed than formerly, was accentuated by a bunch of daffodils that she wore on her left bosom. In the compartment she served stood an electro-plated fountain of water over a spirit-lamp, whose blue flame sent a steam from the top, all this being visible to him only in the mirror behind her; which also reflected the faces of the men she was attending to—one of them a handsome, dissipated young fellow, possibly an undergraduate, who had been relating to her an experience of some humorous sort.

'O, Mr. Cockman, now! How can you tell such a tale to me in my innocence!' she cried gaily. 'Mr. Cockman, what do you use to make your moustache curl so beautiful?' As the young man was clean shaven the retort provoked a laugh at his expense.

'Come!' said he, 'I'll have a Curaçao;[1] and a light, please.'

She served the liqueur from one of the lovely bottles, and striking a match held it to his cigarette with ministering archness while he whiffed.

'Well, have you heard from your husband lately, my dear?' he asked.

'Not a sound,' said she.

'Where is he?'

'I left him in Australia; and I suppose he's there still.'

Jude's eyes grew rounder.

'What made you part from him?'

---

1. A liqueur flavored with orange peel.

'Don't you ask questions, and you won't hear lies.'

'Come then, give me my change, which you've been keeping from me for the last quarter of an hour; and I'll romantically vanish up the street of this picturesque city.'

She handed the change over the counter, in taking which he caught her fingers and held them. There was a slight struggle and titter, and he bade her good-bye and left.

Jude had looked on with the eye of a dazed philosopher. It was extraordinary how far removed from his life Arabella now seemed to be. He could not realize their nominal closeness. And, this being the case, in his present frame of mind he was indifferent to the fact that Arabella was his wife indeed.

The compartment that she served emptied itself of visitors, and after a brief thought he entered it, and went forward to the counter. Arabella did not recognize him for a moment. Then their glances met. She started; till a humorous impudence sparkled in her eyes, and she spoke.

'Well, I'm blest! I thought you were underground years ago!'

'Oh!'

'I never heard anything of you, or I don't know that I should have come here. But never mind! What shall I treat you to this afternoon? A Scotch and soda? Come, anything that the house will afford, for old acquaintance' sake!'

'Thanks, Arabella,' said Jude without a smile. 'But I don't want anything more than I've had.' The fact was that her unexpected presence there had destroyed at a stroke his momentary taste for strong liquor as completely as if it had whisked him back to his milk-fed infancy.

'That's a pity, now you could get it for nothing.'

'How long have you been here?'

'About six weeks. I returned from Sydney three months ago. I always liked this business, you know.'

'I wonder you came to this place!'

'Well, as I say, I thought you were gone to glory, and being in London I saw the situation in an advertisement. Nobody was likely to know me here, even if I had minded, for I was never in Christminster in my growing up.'

'Why did you return from Australia?'

'Oh, I had my reasons. . . . Then you are not a Don yet?'

'No.'

'Not even a Reverend?'

'No.'

'Nor so much as a Rather Reverend dissenting gentleman?'[2]

'I am as I was.'

'True—you look so.' She idly allowed her fingers to rest on the pull

---

2. Nonconformist minister (as opposed to a clergyman of the established church).

of the beer-engine as she inspected him critically. He observed that her hands were smaller and whiter than when he had lived with her, and that on the hand which pulled the engine she wore an ornamental ring set with what seemed to be real sapphires—which they were, indeed, and were much admired as such by the young men who frequented the bar.

'So you pass as having a living husband,' he continued.

'Yes. I thought it might be awkward it I called myself a widow, as I should have liked.'

'True. I am known here a little.'

'I didn't mean on that account—for as I said I didn't expect you. It was for other reasons.'

'What were they?'

'I don't care to go into them,' she replied evasively. 'I make a very good living, and I don't know that I want your company.'

Here a chappie with no chin, and a moustache like a lady's eyebrow, came and asked for a curiously compounded drink, and Arabella was obliged to go and attend to him. 'We can't talk here,' she said, stepping back a moment. 'Can't you wait till nine? Say yes, and don't be a fool. I can get off duty two hours sooner than usual, if I ask. I am not living in the house at present.'

He reflected and said gloomily, 'I'll come back. I suppose we'd better arrange something.'

'O bother arranging! I'm not going to arrange anything!'

'But I must know a thing or two; and, as you say, we can't talk here. Very well; I'll call for you.'

Depositing his unemptied glass he went out and walked up and down the street. Here was a rude flounce into the pellucid sentimentality of his sad attachment to Sue. Though Arabella's word was absolutely untrustworthy, he thought there might be some truth in her implication that she had not wished to disturb him, and had really supposed him dead. However, there was only one thing now to be done, and that was to play a straightforward part, the law being the law, and the woman between whom and himself there was no more unity than between east and west being in the eye of the Church one person with him.

Having to meet Arabella here, it was impossible to meet Sue at Alfredston as he had promised. At every thought of this a pang had gone through him; but the conjuncture could not be helped. Arabella was perhaps an intended intervention to punish him for his unauthorized love. Passing the evening, therefore, in a desultory waiting about the town wherein he avoided the precincts of every Cloister and Hall, because he could not bear to behold them, he repaired to the tavern bar while the hundred and one strokes were resounding from the Great Bell of Cardinal College, a coincidence which seemed to him gratuitous irony. The inn was now brilliantly lighted up, and the scene was

altogether more brisk and gay. The faces of the barmaidens had risen
in colour, each having a pink flush on her cheek; their manners were
still more vivacious than before—more abandoned, more excited, more
sensuous, and they expressed their sentiments and desires less euphe-
mistically, laughing in a lackadaisical tone, without reserve.

The bar had been crowded with men of all sorts during the previous
hour, and he had heard from without the hubbub of their voices; but
the customers were fewer at last. He nodded to Arabella, and told her
that she would find him outside the door when she came away.

'But you must have something with me first,' she said with great
good-humour. 'Just an early night-cap: I always do. Then you can go
out and wait a minute, as it is best we should not be seen going
together.' She drew a couple of liqueur glasses of brandy; and though
she had evidently, from her countenance, already taken in enough alcohol either by drinking or, more probably, from the atmosphere she had
breathed for so many hours, she finished hers quickly. He also drank
his, and went outside the house.

In a few minutes she came, in a thick jacket and a hat with a black
feather. 'I live quite near,' she said, taking his arm, 'and can let myself
in by a latch-key at any time. What arrangement do you want to come
to?'

'O—none in particular,' he answered, thoroughly sick and tired, his
thoughts again reverting to Alfredston, and the train he did not go by;
the probable disappointment of Sue that he was there when she
arrived, and the missed pleasure of her company on the long and lonely
climb by starlight up the hills to Marygreen. 'I ought to have gone back
really! My aunt is on her deathbed, I fear.'

'I'll go over with you to-morrow morning. I think I could get a day
off.'

There was something particularly uncongenial in the idea of Arabella, who had no more sympathy than a tigress with his relations or
him, coming to the bedside of his dying aunt, and meeting Sue. Yet
he said, 'Of course, if you'd like to, you can.'

'Well, that we'll consider. . . . Now, until we have come to some
agreement it is awkward our being together here—where you are
known, and I am getting known, though without any suspicion that I
have anything to do with you. As we are going towards the station
suppose we take the nine-forty train to Aldbrickham? We shall be there
in little more than half-an-hour, and nobody will know us for one night,
and we shall be quite free to act as we choose till we have made up
our minds whether we'll make anything public or not.'

'As you like.'

'Then wait till I get two or three things. This is my lodging. Sometimes when late I sleep at the hotel where I am engaged, so nobody
will think anything of my staying out.'

She speedily returned, and they went on to the railway, and made the half-hour's journey to Aldbrickham, where they entered a third-rate inn near the station in time for a late supper.

III–9

On the morrow between nine and half-past they were journeying back to Christminster, the only two occupants of a compartment in a third-class railway-carriage. Having, like Jude, made rather a hasty toilet to catch the train, Arabella looked a little frowsy, and her face was very far from possessing the animation which had characterized it at the bar the night before. When they came out of the station she found that she still had half-an-hour to spare before she was due at the bar. They walked in silence a little way out of the town in the direction of Alfredston. Jude looked up the far highway.

'Ah . . . poor feeble me!' he murmured at last.

'What?' said she.

'This is the very road by which I came into Christminster years ago full of plans!'

'Well, whatever the road is I think my time is nearly up, as I have to be in the bar by eleven o'clock. And as I said, I shan't ask for the day to go with you to see your aunt. So perhaps we had better part here. I'd sooner not walk up Chief Street with you, since we've come to no conclusion at all.'

'Very well. But you said when we were getting up this morning that you had something you wished to tell me before I left?'

'So I had—two things—one in particular. But you wouldn't promise to keep it a secret. I'll tell you now if you promise? As an honest woman I wish you to know it. . . . It was what I began telling you in the night— about the gentleman who managed the Sydney hotel.' Arabella spoke somewhat hurriedly for her. 'You'll keep it close?'

'Yes—yes—I promise!' said Jude impatiently. 'Of course I don't want to reveal your secrets.'

'Whenever I met him out for a walk, he used to say that he was much taken with my looks, and he kept pressing me to marry him. I never thought of coming back to England again; and being out there in Australia, with no home of my own after leaving my father, I at last agreed, and did'

'What—marry him?'

'Yes.'

'Regularly—legally—in church?'

'Yes. And lived with him till shortly before I left. It was stupid, I know; but I did! There, now I've told you. Don't round upon me! He talks of coming back to England, poor old chap. But if he does, he won't be likely to find me.'

Jude stood pale and fixed.

'Why the devil didn't you tell me last night!' he said.

'Well—I didn't. . . . Won't you make it up with me, then?'

'So in talking of "your husband" to the bar gentlemen you meant him, of course—not me!'

'Of course. . . . Come, don't fuss about it.'

'I have nothing more to say!' replied Jude. 'I have nothing at all to say about the—crime—you've confessed to!'

'Crime! Pooh. They don't think much of such as that over there! Lots of 'em do it. . . . Well, if you take it like that I shall go back to him! He was very fond of me, and we lived honourable enough, and as respectable as any married couple in the Colony! How did I know where you were?'

'I won't go blaming you. I could say a good deal; but perhaps it would be misplaced. What do you wish me to do?'

'Nothing. There was one thing more I wanted to tell you; but I fancy we've seen enough of one another for the present! I shall think over what you said about your circumstances, and let you know.'

Thus they parted. Jude watched her disappear in the direction of the hotel, and entered the railway station close by. Finding that it wanted three-quarters of an hour of the time at which he could get a train back to Alfredston, he strolled mechanically into the city as far as to the Fourways, where he stood as he had so often stood before, and surveyed Chief Street stretching ahead, with its college after college, in picturesqueness unrivalled except by such Continental vistas as the Street of Palaces in Genoa; the lines of the buildings being as distinct in the morning air as in an architectural drawing. But Jude was far from seeing or criticizing these things; they were hidden by an indescribable consciousness of Arabella's midnight contiguity, a sense of degradation at his revived experiences with her, of her appearance as she lay asleep at dawn, which set upon his motionless face a look as of one accurst. If he could only have felt resentment towards her he would have been less unhappy; but he pitied while he contemned her.

Jude turned and retraced his steps. Drawing again towards the station he started at hearing his name pronounced—less at the name than at the voice. To his great surprise no other than Sue stood like a vision before him—her look bodeful and anxious as in a dream, her little mouth nervous, and her strained eyes speaking reproachful inquiry.

'O Jude—I am so glad—to meet you like this!' she said in quick, uneven accents not far from a sob. Then she flushed as she observed his thought that they had not met since her marriage.

They looked away from each other to hide their emotion, took each other's hand without further speech, and went on together awhile, till she glanced at him with furtive solicitude. 'I arrived at Alfredston station last night, as you asked me to, and there was nobody to meet me!

But I reached Marygreen alone, and they told me aunt was a trifle better. I sat up with her, and as you did not come all night I was frightened about you—I thought that perhaps, when you found yourself back in the old city, you were upset at—at thinking I was—married, and not there as I used to be; and that you had nobody to speak to; so you had tried to drown your gloom!—as you did at that former time when you were disappointed about entering as a student, and had forgotten your promise to me that you never would again. And this, I thought, was why you hadn't come to meet me!'

'And you came to hunt me up, and deliver me, like a good angel!'

'I thought I would come by the morning train and try to find you—in case—in case—'

'I did think of my promise to you, dear, continually! I shall never break out again as I did, I am sure. I may have been doing nothing better, but I was not doing that—I loathe the thought of it.'

'I am glad your staying had nothing to do with that. But,' she said, the faintest pout entering into her tone, 'you didn't come back last night and meet me, as you engaged to!'

'I didn't—I am sorry to say. I had an appointment at nine o'clock— too late for me to catch the train that would have met yours, or to get home at all.'

Looking at his loved one as she appeared to him now, in his tender thought the sweetest and most disinterested comrade that he had ever had, living largely in vivid imaginings, so ethereal a creature that her spirit could be seen trembling through her limbs, he felt heartily ashamed of his earthliness in spending the hours he had spent in Arabella's company. There was something rude and immoral in thrusting these recent facts of his life upon the mind of one who, to him, was so uncarnate as to seem at times impossible as a human wife to any average man. And yet she was Phillotson's. How she had become such, how she lived as such, passed his comprehension as he regarded her to-day.

'You'll go back with me?' he said. 'There's a train just now. I wonder how my aunt is by this time. . . . And so, Sue, you really came on my account all this way! At what an early time you must have started, poor thing!'

'Yes. Sitting up watching alone made me all nerves for you, and instead of going to bed when it got light I started. And now you won't frighten me like this again about your morals for nothing?'

He was not so sure that she had been frightened about his morals for nothing. He released her hand till they had entered the train,—it seemed the same carriage he had lately got out of with another—where they sat down side by side, Sue between him and the window. He regarded the delicate lines of her profile, and the small, tight, apple-like convexities of her bodice, so different from Arabella's amplitudes.

Though she knew he was looking at her she did not turn to him, but kept her eyes forward, as if afraid that by meeting his own some troublous discussion would be initiated.

'Sue—you are married now, you know, like me; and yet we have been in such a hurry that we have not said a word about it!'

'There's no necessity,' she quickly returned.

'O well—perhaps not. . . . But I wish—'

'Jude—don't talk about *me*—I wish you wouldn't!' she entreated. 'It distresses me, rather. Forgive my saying it! . . . Where did you stay last night?'

She had asked the question in perfect innocence, to change the topic. He knew that, and said merely, 'At an inn,' though it would have been a relief to tell her of his meeting with an unexpected one. But the latter's final announcement of her marriage in Australia bewildered him lest what he might say should do his ignorant wife an injury.

Their talk proceeded but awkwardly till they reached Alfredston. That Sue was not as she had been, but was labelled 'Phillotson,' paralyzed Jude whenever he wanted to commune with her as an individual. Yet she seemed unaltered—he could not say why. There remained the five-mile extra journey into the country, which it was just as easy to walk as to drive, the greater part of it being uphill. Jude had never before in his life gone that road with Sue, though he had with another. It was now as if he carried a bright light which temporarily banished the shady associations of the earlier time.

Sue talked; but Jude noticed that she still kept the conversation from herself. At length he inquired if her husband were well.

'O yes,' she said. 'He is obliged to be in the school all the day, or would have come with me. He is so good and kind that to accompany me he would have dismissed the school for once, even against his principles—for he is strongly opposed to giving casual holidays—only I wouldn't let him. I felt it would be better to come alone. Aunt Drusilla, I knew, was so very eccentric; and his being almost a stranger to her now would have made it irksome to both. Since it turns out that she is hardly conscious I am glad I did not ask him.'

Jude had walked moodily while this praise of Phillotson was being expressed. 'Mr. Phillotson obliges you in everything, as he ought,' he said.

'Of course.'

'You ought to be a happy wife.'

'And of course I am.'

'Bride, I might almost have said, as yet. It is not so many weeks since I gave you to him, and—'

'Yes, I know! I know!' There was something in her face which belied her late assuring words, so strictly proper and so lifelessly spoken that they might have been taken from a list of model speeches in 'The

Wife's Guide to Conduct.' Jude knew the quality of every vibration in Sue's voice, could read every symptom of her mental condition; and he was convinced that she was unhappy, although she had not been a month married. But her rushing away thus from home, to see the last of a relative whom she had hardly known in her life, proved nothing; for Sue naturally did such things as those.

'Well, you have my good wishes now as always, Mrs. Phillotson.'

She reproached him by a glance.

'No, you are not Mrs. Phillotson,' murmured Jude. 'You are dear, free Sue Bridehead, only you don't know it! Wifedom has not yet squashed up and digested you in its vast maw as an atom which has no further individuality.'

Sue put on a look of being offended, till she answered, 'Nor has husbandom you, so far as I can see!'

'But it has!' he said, shaking his head sadly.

When they reached the lone cottage under the firs, between the Brown House and Marygreen, in which Jude and Arabella had lived and quarrelled, he turned to look at it. A squalid family lived there now. He could not help saying to Sue: 'That's the house my wife and I occupied the whole of the time we lived together. I brought her home to that house.'

She looked at it. 'That to you was what the school-house at Shaston is to me.'

'Yes; but I was not very happy there, as you are in yours.'

She closed her lips in retortive silence, and they walked some way till she glanced at him to see how he was taking it. 'Of course I may have exaggerated your happiness—one never knows,' he continued blandly.

'Don't think that, Jude, for a moment, even though you may have said it to sting me! He's as good to me as a man can be, and gives me perfect liberty—which elderly husbands don't do in general. . . . If you think I am not happy because he's too old for me, you are wrong.'

'I don't think anything against him—to you, dear.'

'And you won't say things to distress me, will you?'

'I will not.'

He said no more, but he knew that, from some cause or other, in taking Phillotson as a husband, Sue felt that she had done what she ought not to have done.

They plunged into the concave field on the other side of which rose the village—the field wherein Jude had received a thrashing from the farmer many years earlier. On ascending to the village and approaching the house they found Mrs. Edlin standing at the door, who at sight of them lifted her hands deprecatingly. 'She's downstairs, if you'll believe me!' cried the widow. 'Out o' bed she got, and nothing could turn her. What will come o't I do not know!'

On entering, there indeed by the fireplace sat the old woman, wrapped in blankets, and turning upon them a countenance like that of Sebastiano's Lazarus.[1] They must have looked their amazement, for she said in a hollow voice:

'Ah—sceered ye, have I! I wasn't going to bide up there no longer, to please nobody! 'Tis more than flesh and blood can bear, to be ordered to do this and that by a feller that don't know half as well as you do yourself! . . . Ah—you'll rue this marrying as well as he!' she added, turning to Sue. 'All our family do,—and nearly all everybody else's. You should have done as I did, you simpleton! And Phillotson the schoolmaster, of all men! What made 'ee marry him?'

'What makes most women marry, aunt?'

'Ah! You mean to say you loved the man!'

'I don't mean to say anything definite.'

'Do ye love un?'

'Don't ask me, aunt.'

'I can mind the man very well. A very civil, honourable liver; but Lord!—I don't want to wownd your feelings, but—there be certain men here and there that no woman of any niceness can stomach. I should have said he was one. I don't say so *now*, since you must ha' known better than I,—but that's what I *should* have said!'

Sue jumped up and went out. Jude followed her, and found her in the outhouse, crying.

'Don't cry, dear!' said Jude in distress. 'She means well, but is very crusty and queer now, you know.'

'O no—it isn't that!' said Sue, trying to dry her eyes. 'I don't mind her roughness one bit.'

'What is it, then?'

'It is that what she says is—is true!'

'God—what—you don't like him?' asked Jude.

'I don't mean that!' she said hastily. 'That I ought—perhaps I ought not to have married!'

He wondered if she had really been going to say that at first. They went back, and the subject was smoothed over, and her aunt took rather kindly to Sue, telling her that not many young women newly married would have come so far to see a sick old crone like her. In the afternoon Sue prepared to depart, Jude hiring a neighbour to drive her to Alfredston.

'I'll go with you to the station, if you'd like?' he said.

She would not let him. The man came round with the trap, and Jude helped her into it, perhaps with unnecessary attention, for she looked at him prohibitively.

1. *The Raising of Lazarus*, painted in 1517–18 by Sebastiano Del Piombo; Hardy had seen it in the National Gallery, London.

'I suppose—I may come to see you some day, when I am back again at Melchester?' he half-crossly observed.

She bent down and said softly: 'No, dear—you are not to come yet. I don't think you are in a good mood.'

'Very well,' said Jude. 'Good-bye!'

'Good-bye!' She waved her hand and was gone.

'She's right! I won't go!' he murmured.

He passed the evening and following days in mortifying by every possible means his wish to see her, nearly starving himself in attempts to extinguish by fasting his passionate tendency to love her. He read sermons on discipline; and hunted up passages in Church history that treated of the Ascetics of the second century.[2] Before he had returned from Marygreen to Melchester there arrived a letter from Arabella. The sight of it revived a stronger feeling of self-condemnation for his brief return to her society than for his attachment to Sue.

The letter, he perceived, bore a London postmark instead of the Christminster one. Arabella informed him that a few days after their parting in the morning at Christminster, she had been surprised by an affectionate letter from her Australian husband, formerly manager of the hotel in Sydney. He had come to England on purpose to find her; and had taken a free, fully-licensed public, in Lambeth, where he wished her to join him in conducting the business, which was likely to be a very thriving one, the house being situated in an excellent, densely populated, gin-drinking neighbourhood, and already doing a trade of £200 a month, which could be easily doubled.

As he had said that he loved her very much still, and implored her to tell him where she was, and as they had only parted in a slight tiff, and as her engagement in Christminster was only temporary, she had just gone to join him as he urged. She could not help feeling that she belonged to him more than to Jude, since she had properly married him, and had lived with him much longer than with her first husband. In thus wishing Jude good-bye she bore him no ill-will, and trusted he would not turn upon her, a weak woman, and inform against her, and bring her to ruin now that she had a chance of improving her circumstances and leading a genteel life.

III–10

Jude returned to Melchester, which had the questionable recommendation of being only a dozen and a half miles from his Sue's now permanent residence. At first he felt that this nearness was a distinct reason for not going southward at all; but Christminster was too sad a

2. Early Christians who practiced rigorous self-discipline and self-denial.

place to bear, while the proximity of Shaston to Melchester might afford him the glory of worsting the Enemy[1] in a close engagement, such as was deliberately sought by the priests and virgins of the early Church, who, disdaining an ignominious flight from temptation, became even chamber-partners with impunity. Jude did not pause to remember that, in the laconic words of the historian, 'insulted Nature sometimes vindicated her rights'[2] in such circumstances.

He now returned with feverish desperation to his study for the priest-hood—in the recognition that the single-mindedness of his aims, and his fidelity to the cause, had been more than questionable of late. His passion for Sue troubled his soul; yet his lawful abandonment to the society of Arabella for twelve hours seemed instinctively a worse thing—even though she had not told him of her Sydney husband till afterwards. He had, he verily believed, overcome all tendency to fly to liquor—which, indeed, he had never done from taste, but merely as an escape from intolerable misery of mind. Yet he perceived with despondency that, taken all round, he was a man of too many passions to make a good clergyman; the utmost he could hope for was that in a life of constant internal warfare between flesh and spirit the former might not always be victorious.

As a hobby, auxiliary to his readings in Divinity, he developed his slight skill in church-music and thorough-bass,[3] till he could join in part-singing from notation with some accuracy. A mile or two from Melchester there was a restored village church, to which Jude had orig-inally gone to fix the new columns and capitals. By this means he had become acquainted with the organist, and the ultimate result was that he joined the choir as a bass voice.

He walked out to this parish twice every Sunday, and sometimes in the week. One evening about Easter the choir met for practice, and a new hymn which Jude had heard of as being by a Wessex composer was to be tried and prepared for the following week. It turned out to be a strangely emotional composition. As they all sang it over and over again its harmonies grew upon Jude, and moved him exceedingly.

When they had finished he went round to the organist to make inquiries. The score was in manuscript, the name of the composer being at the head, together with the title of the hymn: 'The Foot of the Cross.'

'Yes,' said the organist. 'He is a local man. He is a professional musi-cian at Kennetbridge—between here and Christminster. The vicar knows him. He was brought up and educated in Christminster traditions, which accounts for the quality of the piece. I think he plays

1. The devil—here, specifically, sexual temptation.
2. Gibbon, *Decline and Fall* I.15.
3. Method of indicating harmony by figures attached to a single line of music.

in the large church there, and has a surpliced choir. He comes to Melchester sometimes, and once tried to get the Cathedral organ when the post was vacant. The hymn is getting about everywhere this Easter.'

As he walked humming the air on his way home, Jude fell to musing on its composer, and the reasons why he composed it. What a man of sympathies he must be! Perplexed and harassed as he himself was about Sue and Arabella, and troubled as was his conscience by the complication of his position, how he would like to know that man! 'He of all men would understand my difficulties,' said the impulsive Jude. If there were any person in the world to choose as a confidant, this composer would be the one, for he must have suffered, and throbbed, and yearned.

In brief, ill as he could afford the time and money for the journey, Fawley resolved, like the child that he was, to go to Kennetbridge the very next Sunday. He duly started, early in the morning, for it was only by a series of crooked railways that he could get to the town. About mid-day he reached it, and crossing the bridge into the quaint old borough he inquired for the house of the composer.

They told him it was a red brick building some little way further on. Also that the gentleman himself had just passed along the street not five minutes before.

'Which way?' asked Jude with alacrity.

'Straight along homeward from church.'

Jude hastened on, and soon had the pleasure of observing a man in a black coat and a black slouched felt hat no considerable distance ahead. Stretching out his legs yet more widely he stalked after. 'A hungry soul in pursuit of a full soul!' he said. 'I must speak to that man!'

He could not, however, overtake the musician before he had entered his own house, and then arose the question if this were an expedient time to call. Whether or not he decided to do so there and then, now that he had got here, the distance home being too great for him to wait till late in the afternoon. This man of soul would understand scant ceremony, and might be quite a perfect adviser in a case in which an earthly and illegitimate passion had cunningly obtained entrance into his heart through the opening afforded for religion.

Jude accordingly rang the bell, and was admitted.

The musician came to him in a moment, and being respectably dressed, good-looking, and frank in manner, Jude obtained a favourable reception. He was nevertheless conscious that there would be a certain awkwardness in explaining his errand.

'I have been singing in the choir of a little church near Melchester,' he said. 'And we have this week practised "The Foot of the Cross," which I understand, sir, that you composed?'

'I did—a year or so ago.'

'I—like it. I think it supremely beautiful!'

'Ah well—other people have said so too. Yes, there's money in it, if I could only see about getting it published. I have other compositions to go with it, too; I wish I could bring them out; for I haven't made a five-pound note out of any of them yet. These publishing people—they want the copyright of an obscure composer's work, such as mine is, for almost less than I should have to pay a person for making a fair manuscript copy of the score. The one you speak of I have lent to various friends about here and Melchester, and so it has got to be sung a little. But music is a poor staff to lean on—I am giving it up entirely. You must go into trade if you want to make money nowadays. The wine business is what I am thinking of. This is my forthcoming list—it is not issued yet—but you can take one.'

He handed Jude an advertisement list of several pages in booklet shape, ornamentally margined with a red line, in which were set forth the various clarets, champagnes, ports, sherries, and other wines with which he purposed to initiate his new venture. It took Jude more than by surprise that the man with the soul was thus and thus; and he felt that he could not open up his confidences.

They talked a little longer, but constrainedly, for when the musician found that Jude was a poor man his manner changed from what it had been while Jude's appearance and address deceived him as to his position and pursuits. Jude stammered out something about his feelings in wishing to congratulate the author on such an exalted composition, and took an embarrassed leave.[4]

All the way home by the slow Sunday train, sitting in the fireless waiting-rooms on this cold spring day, he was depressed enough at his simplicity in taking such a journey. But no sooner did he reach his Melchester lodging that he found awaiting him a letter which had arrived that morning a few minutes after he had left the house. It was a contrite little note from Sue, in which she said, with sweet humility, that she felt she had been horrid in telling him he was not to come to see her; that she despised herself for having been so conventional; and that he was to be sure to come by the eleven-forty-five train that very Sunday, and have dinner with them at half-past one.

Jude almost tore his hair at having missed this letter till it was too late to act upon its contents; but he had chastened himself considerably of late, and at last his chimerical[5] expedition to Kennetbridge really did seem to have been another special intervention of Providence to keep him away from temptation. But a growing impatience of faith, which he had noticed in himself more than once of late, made him pass over in ridicule the idea that God sent people on fools' errands. He longed to see her; he was angry at having missed her: and he wrote

4. This episode is said to be based on an actual event in the life of the composer Louis Spohr.
5. Based only on fancy or delusion (from the chimera, a mythical monster).

instantly, telling her what had happened, and saying he had not enough patience to wait till the following Sunday, but would come any day in the week that she liked to name.

Since he wrote a little over-ardently, Sue, as her manner was, delayed her reply till Thursday before Good Friday, when she said he might come that afternoon if he wished, this being the earliest day on which she could welcome him, for she was now assistant-teacher in her husband's school. Jude therefore got leave from the Cathedral works at the trifling expense of a stoppage of pay, and went.

Part Fourth: At Shaston

'Whoso prefers either Matrimony or other Ordinance before the Good of Man and the plain Exigence of Charity, let him profess Papist, or Protestant, or what he will, he is no better than a Pharisee.'
—J. MILTON[1]

IV–1

Shaston,[2] the ancient British Palladour,

'From whose foundation first such strange reports arise,'

(as Drayton[3] sang it), was, and is, in itself the city of a dream. Vague imaginings of its castle, its three mints, its magnificent apsidal[4] Abbey, the chief glory of South Wessex, its twelve churches, its shrines, chantries,[5] hospitals, its gabled freestone[6] mansions—all now ruthlessly swept away—throw the visitor, even against his will, into a pensive melancholy, which the stimulating atmosphere and limitless landscape around him can scarcely dispel. The spot was the burial-place of a king and a queen, of abbots and abbesses, saints and bishops, knights and squires. The bones of King Edward 'the Martyr,'[7] carefully removed hither for holy preservation, brought Shaston a renown which made it the resort of pilgrims from every part of Europe, and enabled it to maintain a reputation extending far beyond English shores. To this fair creation of the great Middle-Age the Dissolution[8] was, as historians tell us, the death-knell. With the destruction of the enormous abbey

1. From the pamphlet *Doctrine and Discipline of Divorce*.
2. For an indication of Hardy's debts in this passage to the account of Shaftesbury in Hutchins's *History and Antiquities of the County of Dorset*, see below pp. 366–67.
3. Michael Drayton (1563–1631), whose *Polyolbion* (1622), from which this line is taken, is a versified guidebook to Britain.
4. Having an apse (a semicircular arched recess at the end of a church).
5. Chapels endowed for the singing of masses for the founder's soul.
6. Sandstone or limestone that can be easily cut.
7. King of England from 975 to 978; assassinated at Corfe Castle, Dorset, and later buried at Shaftesbury.
8. Of the monasteries, by Henry VIII.

the whole place collapsed in a general ruin: the Martyr's bones met with the fate of the sacred pile that held them, and not a stone is now left to tell where they lie.

The natural picturesqueness and singularity of the town still remain; but strange to say these qualities, which were noted by many writers in ages when scenic beauty is said to have been unappreciated, are passed over in this, and one of the queerest and quaintest spots in England stands virtually unvisited to-day.

It has a unique position on the summit of a steep and imposing scarp, rising on the north, south, and west sides of the borough out of the deep alluvial Vale of Blackmoor, the view from the Castle Green over three counties of verdant pasture—South, Mid, and Nether Wessex—being as sudden a surprise to the unexpectant traveller's eyes as the medicinal air is to his lungs. Impossible to a railway, it can best be reached on foot, next best by light vehicles; and it is hardly accessible to these but by a sort of isthmus on the north-east, that connects it with the high chalk table-land on that side.

Such is, and such was, the now world-forgotten Shaston or Palladour. Its situation rendered water the great want of the town; and within living memory, horses, donkeys and men may have been seen toiling up the winding ways to the top of the height, laden with tubs and barrels filled from the wells beneath the mountain, and hawkers retailing their contents at the price of a halfpenny a bucketful.

This difficulty in the water supply, together with two other odd facts, namely, that the chief graveyard slopes up as steeply as a roof behind the church, and that in former times the town passed through a curious period of corruption, conventual and domestic, gave rise to the saying that Shaston was remarkable for three consolations to man, such as the world afforded not elsewhere. It was a place where the churchyard lay nearer heaven than the church steeple, where beer was more plentiful than water, and where there were more wanton women than honest wives and maids. It is also said that after the middle ages the inhabitants were too poor to pay their priests, and hence were compelled to pull down their churches, and refrain altogether from the public worship of God; a necessity which they bemoaned over their cups in the settles of their inns on Sunday afternoons. In those days the Shastonians were apparently not without a sense of humour.

There was another peculiarity—this a modern one—which Shaston appeared to owe to its site. It was the resting-place and headquarters of the proprietors of wandering vans, shows, shooting-galleries, and other itinerant concerns, whose business lay largely at fairs and markets. As strange wild birds are seen assembled on some lofty promontory, meditatively pausing for longer flights, or to return by the course they followed thither, so here, in this clifftown, stood in stultified silence the yellow and green caravans bearing names not local, as if surprised by a change in the landscape so violent as to hinder their further progress; and here they usually remained all the winter till they turned to seek again their old tracks in the following spring.

It was to this breezy and whimsical spot that Jude ascended from the nearest station for the first time in his life about four o'clock one afternoon, and entering on the summit of the peak after a toilsome climb, passed the first houses of the aerial town; and drew towards the school-house. The hour was too early; the pupils were still in school, humming small, like a swarm of gnats; and he withdrew a few steps along Abbey Walk, whence he regarded the spot which fate had made the home of all he loved best in the world. In front of the schools, which were extensive and stone-built, grew two enormous beeches with smooth mouse-coloured trunks, as such trees will only grow on chalk uplands. Within the mullioned and transomed windows he could see the black, brown, and flaxen crowns of the scholars over the sills, and to pass the time away he walked down to the level terrace where the Abbey gardens once had spread, his heart throbbing in spite of him.

Unwilling to enter till the children were dismissed he remained here till young voices could be heard in the open air, and girls in white pinafores over red and blue frocks appeared dancing along the paths which the abbess, prioress, sub-prioress, and fifty nuns had demurely paced three centuries earlier. Retracing his steps he found that he had waited too long, and that Sue had gone out into the town at the heels of the last scholar, Mr. Phillotson having been absent all the afternoon at a teachers' meeting at Shottsford.

Jude went into the empty schoolroom and sat down, the girl who was sweeping the floor having informed him that Mrs. Phillotson would be back again in a few minutes. A piano stood near—actually the old piano that Phillotson had possessed at Marygreen—and though the dark afternoon almost prevented him seeing the notes Jude touched them in his humble way, and could not help modulating into the hymn which had so affected him in the previous week.

A figure moved behind him, and thinking it was still the girl with the broom Jude took no notice, till the person came close and laid her fingers lightly upon his bass hand. The imposed hand was a little one he seemed to know, and he turned.

"Don't stop,' said Sue. 'I like it. I learnt it before I left Melchester. They used to play it in the Training School.'

'I can't strum before you! Play it for me.'

'O well—I don't mind.'

Sue sat down, and her rendering of the piece, though not remarkable, seemed divine as compared with his own. She, like him, was evidently touched—to her own surprise—by the recalled air; and when she had finished, and he moved his hand towards hers, it met his own half-way. Jude grasped it—just as he had done before her marriage.

'It is odd,' she said, in a voice quite changed, 'that I should care about that air; because—'

'Because what?'

'I am not that sort—quite.'

'Not easily moved?'

'I didn't quite mean that.'

'O, but you *are* one of that sort, for you are just like me at heart!'

'But not at head.'

She played on, and suddenly turned round; and by an unpremeditated instinct each clasped the other's hand again.

She uttered a forced little laugh as she relinquished his quickly. 'How funny!' she said. 'I wonder what we both did that for?'

'I suppose because we are both alike, as I said before.'

'Not in our thoughts! Perhaps a little in our feelings.'

'And they rule thoughts. . . . Isn't it enough to make one blaspheme that the composer of that hymn is one of the most commonplace men I ever met!'

'What—you know him?'

'I went to see him.'

'O you goose—to do just what I should have done! Why did you?'

'Because we are not alike,' he said drily.

'Now we'll have some tea,' said Sue. 'Shall we have it here instead of in my house? It is no trouble to get the kettle and things brought in. We don't live at the school, you know, but in that ancient dwelling across the way called Old-Grove Place. It is so antique and dismal that it depresses me dreadfully. Such houses are very well to visit, but not to live in—I feel crushed into the earth by the weight of so many previous lives there spent. In a new place like these schools there is only your own life to support. Sit down, and I'll tell Ada to bring the tea-things across.'

He waited in the light of the stove, the door of which she flung open before going out, and when she returned, followed by the maiden with tea, they sat down by the same light, assisted by the blue rays of a spirit-lamp under the brass kettle on the stand.

'This is one of your wedding-presents to me,' she said, signifying the latter.

'Yes,' said Jude.

The kettle of his gift sang with some satire in its note, to his mind; and to change the subject he said. 'Do you know of any good readable edition of the uncanonical[9] books of the New Testament? You don't read them in the school, I suppose?'

9. Those not included in the recognized canon of scripture; also known as the Apocrypha. Cowper's *Apocryphal Gospels* was published in 1874.

'O dear no!—'twould alarm the neighbourhood. . . . Yes, there is one. I am not familiar with it now, though I was interested in it when my former friend was alive. Cowper's *Apocryphal Gospels*.'

'That sounds like what I want.' His thoughts, however, reverted with a twinge to the 'former friend'—by whom she meant, as he knew, the University comrade of her earlier days. He wondered if she talked of him to Phillotson.

'The Gospel of Nicodemus is very nice,' she went on, to keep him from his jealous thoughts, which she read clearly, as she always did. Indeed when they talked on an indifferent subject, as now, there was ever a second silent conversation passing between their emotions, so perfect was the reciprocity between them. 'It is quite like the genuine article. All cut up into verses, too; so that it is like one of the other evangelists read in a dream, when things are the same, yet not the same. But, Jude, do you take an interest in those questions still? Are you getting up *Apologetica*?'[1]

'Yes. I am reading Divinity harder than ever.'

She regarded him curiously.

'Why do you look at me like that?' said Jude.

'Oh—why do you want to know?'

'I am sure you can tell me anything I may be ignorant of in that subject. You must have learnt a lot of everything from your dear dead friend!'

'We won't get on to that now!' she coaxed. 'Will you be carving out at that church again next week, where you learnt the pretty hymn?'

'Yes, perhaps.'

'That will be very nice. Shall I come and see you there? It is in this direction, and I could come any afternoon by train for half-an-hour?'

'No. Don't come!'

'What—aren't we going to be friends, then, any longer, as we used to be?'

'No.'

'I didn't know that. I thought you were always going to be kind to me!'

'No, I am not.'

'What have I done, then? I am sure I thought we two—' The *tremolo* in her voice caused her to break off.

'Sue, I sometimes think you are a flirt,' said he abruptly.

There was a momentary pause, till she suddenly jumped up; and to his surprise he saw by the kettle-flame that her face was flushed.

'I can't talk to you any longer, Jude!' she said, the tragic contralto note having come back as of old. 'It is getting too dark to stay together

1. Theological textbook.

like this, after playing morbid Good Friday tunes that make one feel
what one shouldn't! . . . We mustn't sit and talk in this way any more.
Yes—you must go away, for you mistake me! I am very much the
reverse of what you say so cruelly—O Jude, it *was* cruel to say that!
Yet I can't tell you the truth—I should shock you by letting you know
how I give way to my impulses, and how much I feel that I shouldn't
have been provided with attractiveness unless it were meant to be
exercised! Some women's love of being loved is insatiable; and so,
often, is their love of loving; and in the last case they may find that
they can't give it continuously to the chamber-office appointed by the
bishop's license to receive it. But you are so straightforward, Jude, that
you can't understand me! . . . Now you must go. I am sorry my husband
is not at home.'

'Are you?'

'I perceive I have said that in mere convention! Honestly I don't
think I am sorry. It does not matter, either way, sad to say!'

As they had overdone the grasp of hands some time sooner, she
touched his fingers but lightly when he went out now. He had hardly
gone from the door when, with a dissatisfied look, she jumped on a
form and opened the iron casement of a window beneath which he
was passing in the path without. 'When do you leave here to catch
your train, Jude?' she asked.

He looked up in some surprise. 'The coach that runs to meet it goes
in three-quarters of an hour or so.'

'What will you do with yourself for the time?'

'O—wander about, I suppose. Perhaps I shall go and sit in the old
church.'

'It does seem hard of me to pack you off so! You have thought
enough of churches, Heavens knows, without going into one in the
dark. Stay there.'

'Where?'

'Where you are. I can talk to you better like this than when you
were inside. . . . It was so kind and tender of you to give up half a day's
work to come to see me! . . . You are Joseph the dreamer of dreams,[2]
dear Jude. And a tragic Don Quixote. And sometimes you are St. Stephen, who, while they were stoning him, could see Heaven opened.[3]
O my poor friend and comrade, you'll suffer yet!'

Now that the high window-sill was between them, so that he could
not get at her, she seemed not to mind indulging in a frankness she
had feared at close quarters. 'I have been thinking,' she continued, still
in the tone of one brimful of feeling, 'that the social moulds civilization
fits us into have no more relation to our actual shapes than the con-

2. Genesis 37.5–10.
3. Acts 7.55–59. Hardy is not quite accurate: Stephen saw "the heavens opened" *before* he was
   stoned.

ventional shapes of the constellations have to the real star-patterns. I am called Mrs. Richard Phillotson, living a calm wedded life with my counterpart of that name. But I am not really Mrs. Richard Phillotson, but a woman tossed about, all alone, with aberrant passions, and unaccountable antipathies. . . . Now you mustn't wait longer, or you will lose the coach. Come and see me again. You must come to the house then.'

'Yes!' said Jude. 'When shall it be?'

'To-morrow week. Good-bye—good-bye!' She stretched out her hand and stroked his forehead pitifully—just once. Jude said goodbye, and went away into the darkness.

Passing along Bimport Street he thought he heard the wheels of the coach departing, and, truly enough, when he reached the Duke's Arms in the Market Place the coach had gone. It was impossible for him to get to the station on foot in time for this train, and he settled himself perforce to wait for the next—the last to Melchester that night.

He wandered about awhile, obtaining something to eat; and then, having another half-hour on his hands, his feet involuntarily took him through the venerable graveyard of Trinity Church, with its avenues of limes, in the direction of the schools again. They were entirely in darkness. She had said she lived over the way at Old-Grove Place, a house which he soon discovered from her description of its antiquity.

A glimmering candle-light shone from a front window, the shutters being yet unclosed. He could see the interior clearly—the floor sinking a couple of steps below the road without, which had become raised during the centuries since the house was built. Sue, evidently just come in, was standing with her hat on in this front parlour or sitting-room, whose walls were lined with wainscoting of panelled oak reaching from floor to ceiling, the latter being crossed by huge moulded beams only a little way above her head. The mantelpiece was of the same heavy description, carved with Jacobean pilasters and scroll-work. The centuries did, indeed, ponderously overhang a young wife who passed her time here.

She had opened a rosewood work-box, and was looking at a photograph. Having contemplated it a little while she pressed it against her bosom, and put it again in its place.

Then becoming aware that she had not obscured the windows she came forward to do so, candle in hand. It was too dark for her to see Jude without, but he could see her face distinctly, and there was an unmistakable tearfulness about the dark, long-lashed eyes.

She closed the shutters, and Jude turned away to pursue his solitary journey home. 'Whose photograph was she looking at?' he said. He had once given her his; but she had others, he knew. Yet it was his, surely?

He knew he should go to see her again, according to her invitation. Those earnest men he read of, the saints, whom Sue, with gentle irreverence, called his demi-gods, would have shunned such encounters if they doubted their own strength. But he could not. He might fast and pray during the whole interval, but the human was more powerful in him than the Divine.

IV–2

However, if God disposed not, woman did.[1] The next morning but one brought him this note from her:

> 'Don't come next week. On your own account don't! We were too free, under the influence of that morbid hymn and the twilight. Think no more than you can help of
>
> SUSANNA FLORENCE MARY.'

The disappointment was keen. He knew her mood, the look of her face, when she subscribed herself at length thus. But whatever her mood he could not say she was wrong in her view. He replied:

> 'I acquiesce. You are right. It is a lesson in renunciation which I suppose I ought to learn at this season.
>
> JUDE.'

He despatched the note on Easter Eve, and there seemed a finality in their decisions. But other forces and laws than theirs were in operation. On Easter Monday morning he received a message from the Widow Edlin, whom he had directed to telegraph if anything serious happened:

> 'Your aunt is sinking. Come at once.'

He threw down his tools and went. Three and a half hours later he was crossing the downs about Marygreen, and presently plunged into the concave field across which the short cut was made to the village. As he ascended on the other side a labouring man, who had been watching his approach from a gate across the path, moved uneasily, and prepared to speak. 'I can see in his face that she is dead,' said Jude. 'Poor Aunt Drusilla!'

It was as he had supposed, and Mrs. Edlin had sent out the man to break the news to him.

'She wouldn't have knowed 'ee. She lay like a doll wi' glass eyes; so it didn't matter that you wasn't here,' said he.

Jude went on to the house, and in the afternoon, when everything was done, and the layers-out[2] had finished their beer, and gone, he sat

---

1. "Man proposes, but God disposes" (found in Thomas a Kempis and other early writers).
2. Those who prepared the corpse for burial.

down alone in the silent place. It was absolutely necessary to communicate with Sue, though two or three days earlier they had agreed to mutual severance. He wrote in the briefest terms:

> 'Aunt Drusilla is dead, having been taken almost suddenly. The funeral is on Friday afternoon.'

He remained in and about Marygreen through the intervening days, went out on Friday morning to see that the grave was finished, and wondered if Sue would come. She had not written, and that seemed to signify rather that she would come than that she would not. Having timed her by her only possible train, he locked the door about midday, and crossed the hollow field to the verge of the upland by the Brown House, where he stood and looked over the vast prospect northwards, and over the nearer landscape in which Alfredston stood. Two miles behind it a jet of white steam was travelling from the left to the right of the picture.

There was a long time to wait, even now, till he would know if she had arrived. He did wait, however, and at last a small hired vehicle pulled up at the bottom of the hill, and a person alighted, the conveyance going back, while the passenger began ascending the hill. He knew her; and she looked so slender to-day that it seemed as if she might be crushed in the intensity of a too passionate embrace—such as it was not for him to give. Two-thirds of the way up her head suddenly took a solicitous poise, and he knew that she had at that moment recognized him. Her face soon began a pensive smile, which lasted till, having descended a little way, he met her.

'I thought,' she began with nervous quickness, 'that it would be so sad to let you attend the funeral alone!' And so—at the last moment—I came.'

'Dear faithful Sue!' murmured Jude.

With the elusiveness of her curious double nature, however, Sue did not stand still for any further greeting, though it wanted some time to the burial. A pathos so unusually compounded as that which attached to this hour was unlikely to repeat itself for years, if ever, and Jude would have paused, and meditated, and conversed. But Sue either saw it not at all, or, seeing it more than he, would not allow herself to feel it.

The sad and simple ceremony was soon over, their progress to the church being almost at a trot, the bustling undertaker having a more important funeral an hour later, three miles off. Drusilla was put into the new ground, quite away from her ancestors. Sue and Jude had gone side by side to the grave, and now sat down to tea in the familiar house; their lives united at least in this last attention to the dead.

'She was opposed to marriage, from first to last, you say?' murmured Sue.

'Yes. Particularly for members of our family.'

Her eyes met his, and remained on him awhile.

'We are rather a sad family, don't you think, Jude?'

'She said we made bad husbands and wives. Certainly we make unhappy ones. At all events, I do, for one!'

Sue was silent. 'Is it wrong, Jude,' she said with a tentative tremor, 'for a husband or wife to tell a third person that they are unhappy in their marriage? If a marriage ceremony is a religious thing, it is possibly wrong; but if it is only a sordid contract, based on material convenience in householding, rating, and taxing, and the inheritance of land and money by children, making it necessary that the male parent should be known—which it seems to be—why surely a person may say, even proclaim upon the housetops, that it hurts and grieves him or her?'

'I have said so, anyhow, to you.'

Presently she went on: 'Are there many couples, do you think, where one dislikes the other for no definite fault?'

'Yes, I suppose. If either cares for another person, for instance.'

'But even apart from that? Wouldn't the woman, for example, be very bad-natured if she didn't like to live with her husband; merely'— her voice undulated, and he guessed things—'merely because she had a personal feeling against it—a physical objection—a fastidiousness, or whatever it may be called—although she might respect and be grateful to him? I am merely putting a case. Ought she to try to overcome her pruderies?'

Jude threw a troubled look at her. He said, looking away; 'It would be just one of those cases in which my experiences go contrary to my dogmas. Speaking as an order-loving man—which I hope I am, though I fear I am not—I should say, yes. Speaking from experience and unbiased nature, I should say, no. . . . Sue, I believe you are not happy!'

'Of course I am!' she contradicted. 'How can a woman be unhappy who has only been married eight weeks to a man she chose freely?'

' "Chose freely!" '

'Why do you repeat it? . . . But I have to go back by the six o'clock train. You will be staying on here, I suppose?'

'For a few days to wind up aunt's affairs. This house is gone now. Shall I go to the train with you?'

A little laugh of objection came from Sue. 'I think not. You may come part of the way.'

'But stop—you can't go to-night! That train won't take you to Shaston. You must stay and go back to-morrow. Mrs. Edlin has plenty of room, if you don't like to stay here?'

'Very well,' she said dubiously. 'I didn't tell him I would come for certain.'

Jude went to the widow's house adjoining, to let her know; and returning in a few minutes sat down again.

'It is horrible how we are circumstanced, Sue—horrible!' he said
abruptly, with his eyes bent to the floor.

'No! Why?'

'I can't tell you all my part of the gloom. Your part is that you ought
not to have married him. I saw it before you had done it, but I thought
I mustn't interfere. I was wrong. I ought to have!'

'But what makes you assume all this, dear?'

'Because—I can see you through your feathers, my poor little bird!'

Her hand lay on the table, and Jude put his upon it. Sue drew hers
away.

'That's absurd, Sue,' cried he, 'after what we've been talking about!
I am more strict and formal than you, if it comes to that; and that you
should object to such an innocent action shows that you are ridiculously inconsistent!'

'Perhaps it was too prudish,' she said, repentantly. 'Only I have fancied it was a sort of trick of ours—too frequent perhaps. There, you
may hold it as much as you like. Is that good of me?'

'Yes; very.'

'But I must tell him.'

'Who?'

'Richard.'

'O—of course, if you think it necessary. But as it means nothing it
may be bothering him needlessly.'

'Well—are you sure you mean it only as my cousin?'

'Absolutely sure. I have no feelings of love left in me.'

'That's news. How has it come to be?'

'I've seen Arabella.'

She winced at the hit; then said curiously, 'When did you see her?'

'When I was at Christminster.'

'So she's come back; and you never told me! I suppose you will live
with her now?'

'Of course—just as you live with your husband.'

She looked at the window pots with the geraniums and cactuses,
withered for want of attention, and through them at the outer distance,
till her eyes began to grow moist. 'What is it?' said Jude, in a softened
tone.

'Why should you be so glad to go back to her if—if—what you used
to say to me is still true—I mean if it were true then! Of course it is
not now! How could your heart go back to Arabella so soon?'

'A special Providence, I suppose, helped it on its way.'

'Ah—it isn't true!' she said with gentle resentment. 'You are teasing
me—that's all—because you think I am not happy!'

'I don't know. I don't wish to know.'

'If I were unhappy it would be my fault, my wickedness; not that I
should have a right to dislike him! He is considerate to me in every-

thing; and he is very interesting, from the amount of general knowledge he has acquired by reading everything that comes in his way. . . . Do you think, Jude, that a man ought to marry a woman his own age, or one younger than himself—eighteen years—as I am than he?'

'It depends upon what they feel for each other.'

He gave her no opportunity of self-satisfaction, and she had to go on unaided, which she did in a vanquished tone, verging on tears:

'I—I think I must be equally honest with you as you have been with me. Perhaps you have seen what it is I want to say?—that though I like Mr. Phillotson as a friend, I don't like him—it is a torture to me to—live with him as a husband!—There, now I have let it out—I couldn't help it, although I have been—pretending I am happy.—Now you'll have a contempt for me for ever, I suppose!' She bent down her face upon her hands as they lay upon the cloth, and silently sobbed in little jerks that made the fragile three-legged table quiver.

'I have only been married a month or two!' she went on, still remaining bent upon the table, and sobbing into her hands. 'And it is said that what a woman shrinks from—in the early days of her marriage—she shakes down to with comfortable indifference in half-a-dozen years. But that is much like saying that the amputation of a limb is no afflic-tion, since a person gets comfortably accustomed to the use of a wooden leg or arm in the course of time!'

Jude could hardly speak, but he said, 'I thought there was something wrong, Sue! O, I thought there was!'

'But it is not as you think!—there is nothing wrong except my own wickedness, I suppose you'd call it—a repugnance on my part, for a reason I cannot disclose, and what would not be admitted as one by the world in general! . . . What tortures me so much is the necessity of being responsive to this man whenever he wishes, good as he is mor-ally!—the dreadful contract to feel in a particular way in a matter whose essence is its voluntariness! . . . I wish he would beat me, or be faithless to me, or do some open thing that I could talk about as a justification for feeling as I do! But he does nothing, except that he has grown a little cold since he has found out how I feel. That's why he didn't come to the funeral. . . . O, I am very miserable—I don't know what to do! . . . Don't come near me, Jude, because you mustn't. Don't—don't!'

But he had jumped up and put his face against hers—or rather against her ear, her face being inaccessible.

'I told you not to, Jude!'

'I know you did—I only wish to—console you! It all arose through my being married before we met, didn't it? You would have been my wife, Sue, wouldn't you, if it hadn't been for that?'

Instead of replying she rose quickly, and saying she was going to walk to her aunt's grave in the churchyard to recover herself, went out of the house. Jude did not follow her. Twenty minutes later he saw her cross the village green towards Mrs. Edlin's, and soon she sent a little girl to fetch her bag, and tell him she was too tired to see him again that night.

In the lonely room of his aunt's house Jude sat watching the cottage of the Widow Edlin as it disappeared behind the night shade. He knew that Sue was sitting within its walls equally lonely and disheartened; and again questioned his devotional motto that all was for the best.

He retired to rest early, but his sleep was fitful from the sense that Sue was so near at hand. At some time near two o'clock, when he was beginning to sleep more soundly, he was aroused by a shrill squeak that had been familiar enough to him when he lived regularly at Marygreen. It was the cry of a rabbit caught in a gin. As was the little creature's habit, it did not soon repeat its cry; and probably would not do so more than once or twice; but would remain bearing its torture till the morrow, when the trapper would come and knock it on the head.

He who in his childhood had saved the lives of the earthworms now began to picture the agonies of the rabbit from its lacerated leg. If it were a 'bad catch' by the hind-leg, the animal would tug during the ensuing six hours till the iron teeth of the trap had stripped the legbone of its flesh, when, should a weak-springed instrument enable it to escape, it would die in the fields from the mortification of the limb. If it were a 'good catch,' namely, by the fore-leg, the bone would be broken, and the limb nearly torn in two in attempts at an impossible escape.

Almost half-an-hour passed, and the rabbit repeated its cry. Jude could rest no longer till he had put it out of its pain, so dressing himself quickly he descended, and by the light of the moon went across the green in the direction of the sound. He reached the hedge bordering the widow's garden, when he stood still. The faint click of the trap as dragged about by the writhing animal guided him now, and reaching the spot he struck the rabbit on the back of the neck with the side of his palm, and it stretched itself out dead.

He was turning away when he saw a woman looking out of the open casement at a window on the ground floor of the adjacent cottage. 'Jude!' said a voice timidly—Sue's voice. 'It is you—is it not?'

'Yes, dear!'

'I haven't been able to sleep at all, and then I heard the rabbit, and couldn't help thinking of what it suffered, till I felt I must come down and kill it! But I am so glad you got there first. . . . They ought not to be allowed to set these steel traps, ought they!'

Jude had reached the window, which was quite a low one, so that she was visible down to her waist. She let go the casement-stay and put her hand upon his, her moonlit face regarding him wistfully.

'Did it keep you awake?' he said.

'No—I was awake.'

'How was that?'

'O, you know—now! I know you, with your religious doctrines, think that a married woman in trouble of a kind like mine commits a mortal sin in making a man the confidant of it, as I did you. I wish I hadn't, now!'

'Don't wish it, dear,' he said. 'That may have *been* my view; but my doctrines and I begin to part company.'

'I knew it—I knew it! And that's why I vowed I wouldn't disturb your beliefs. But—I am so *glad* to see you!—and, O, I didn't mean to see you again, now the last tie between us, Aunt Drusilla, is dead!'

Jude seized her hand and kissed it. 'There is a stronger one left!' he said. 'I'll never care about my doctrines or my religion any more! Let them go! Let me help you, even if I do love you, and even if you . . .'

'Don't say it!—I know what you mean; but I can't admit so much as that. There! Guess what you like, but don't press me to answer questions!'

'I wish you were happy, whatever I may be!'

'I can't be! So few could enter into my feeling—they would say 'twas my fanciful fastidiousness, or something of that sort, and condemn me. . . . It is none of the natural tragedies of love that's love's usual tragedy in civilized life, but a tragedy artificially manufactured for people who in a natural state would find relief in parting! . . . It would have been wrong, perhaps, for me to tell my distress to you, if I had been able to tell it to anybody else. But I have nobody. And I *must* tell somebody! Jude, before I married him I had never thought out fully what marriage meant, even though I knew. It was idiotic of me—there is no excuse. I was old enough, and I thought I was very experienced. So I rushed on, when I had got into that Training School scrape, with all the cock-sureness of the fool that I was! . . . I am certain one ought to be allowed to undo what one has done so ignorantly! I daresay it happens to lots of women; only they submit, and I kick. . . . When people of a later age look back upon the barbarous customs and super-stitions of the times that we have the unhappiness to live in, what *will* they say!'

'You are very bitter, darling Sue! How I wish—I wish—'

'You must go in now!'

In a moment of impulse she bent over the sill, and laid her face upon his hair, weeping, and then imprinting a scarcely perceptible little kiss upon the top of his head, withdrawing quickly, so that he could not put his arms round her, as otherwise he unquestionably would have done. She shut the casement, and he returned to his cottage.

IV–3

Sue's distressful confession recurred to Jude's mind all the night as being a sorrow indeed.

The morning after, when it was time for her to go, the neighbours saw her companion and herself disappearing on foot down the hill path which led into the lonely road to Alfredston. An hour passed before he returned along the same route, and in his face there was a look of exaltation not unmixed with recklessness. An incident had occurred.

They had stood parting in the silent highway, and their tense and passionate moods had led to bewildered inquiries of each other on how far their intimacy ought to go; till they had almost quarrelled, and she had said tearfully that it was hardly proper of him as a parson in embryo to think of such a thing as kissing her even in farewell, as he now wished to do. Then she had conceded that the fact of the kiss would be nothing: all would depend upon the spirit of it. If given in the spirit of a cousin and a friend she saw no objection: if in the spirit of a lover she could not permit it. 'Will you swear that it will not be in that spirit?' she had said.

No: he would not. And then they had turned from each other in estrangement, and gone their several ways, till at a distance of twenty or thirty yards both had looked round simultaneously. That look behind was fatal to the reserve hitherto more or less maintained. They had quickly run back, and met, and embracing most unpremeditatedly, kissed close and long. When they parted for good it was with flushed cheeks on her side, and a beating heart on his.

The kiss was a turning-point in Jude's career. Back again in the cottage, and left to reflection, he saw one thing: that though his kiss of that aerial being had seemed the purest moment of his faultful life, as long as he nourished this unlicensed tenderness it was glaringly inconsistent for him to pursue the idea of becoming the soldier and servant of a religion in which sexual love was regarded as at its best a frailty, and at its worst damnation. What Sue had said in warmth was really the cold truth. When to defend his affection tooth and nail, to persist with headlong force in impassioned attentions to her, was all he thought of, he was condemned *ipso facto*[1] as a professor of the accepted school of morals. He was as unfit, obviously, by nature, as he had been by social position, to fill the part of a propounder of accredited dogma.

Strange that his first aspiration—towards academical proficiency— had been checked by a woman, and that his second aspiration— towards apostleship—had also been checked by a woman. 'Is it,' he said, 'that the women are to blame; or is it the artificial system of things, under which the normal sex-impulses are turned into devilish

1. By that same fact.

domestic gins and springes[2] to noose and hold back those who want to progress?'

It had been his standing desire to become a prophet, however humble, to his struggling fellow-creatures, without any thought of personal gain. Yet with a wife living away from him with another husband, and himself in love erratically, the loved one's revolt against her state being possibly on his account, he had sunk to be barely respectable according to regulation views.

It was not for him to consider further: he had only to confront the obvious, which was that he had made himself quite an impostor as a law-abiding religious teacher.

At dusk that evening he went into the garden and dug a shallow hole, to which he brought out all the theological and ethical works that he possessed, and had stored here. He knew that, in this country of true believers, most of them were not saleable at a much higher price than waste-paper value, and preferred to get rid of them in his own way, even if he should sacrifice a little money to the sentiment of thus destroying them. Lighting some loose pamphlets to begin with, he cut the volumes into pieces as well as he could, and with a three-pronged fork shook them over the flames. They kindled, and lighted up the back of the house, the pigsty, and his own face, till they were more or less consumed.

Though he was almost a stranger here now, passing cottagers talked to him over the garden hedge.

'Burning up your awld aunt's rubbidge, I suppose? Ay; a lot gets heaped up in nooks and corners when you've lived eighty years in one house.'

It was nearly one o'clock in the morning before the leaves, covers, and binding of Jeremy Taylor, Butler, Doddridge, Paley, Pusey, Newman[3] and the rest had gone to ashes; but the night was quiet, and as he turned and turned the paper shreds with the fork, the sense of being no longer a hypocrite to himself afforded his mind a relief which gave him calm. He might go on believing as before, but he professed nothing, and no longer owned and exhibited engines of faith which, as their proprietor, he might naturally be supposed to exercise on himself first of all. In his passion for Sue he could now stand as an ordinary sinner, and not as a whited sepulchre.[4]

Meanwhile Sue, after parting from him earlier in the day, had gone along to the station, with tears in her eyes for having run back and let him kiss her. Jude ought not to have pretended that he was not a lover, and made her give way to an impulse to act unconventionally, if not wrongly. She was inclined to call it the latter; for Sue's logic was

2. Snares for wild creatures.
3. Standard theological authors from the seventeenth to the nineteenth centuries.
4. Hypocrite (see Matthew 23.27).

extraordinarily compounded, and seemed to maintain that before a thing was done it might be right to do, but that being done it became wrong; or, in other words, that things which were right in theory were wrong in practice.

'I have been too weak, I think!' she jerked out as she pranced on, shaking down tear-drops now and then. 'It was burning, like a lover's—O it was! And I won't write to him any more, or at least for a long time, to impress him with my dignity! And I hope it will hurt him very much—expecting a letter to-morrow morning, and the next, and the next, and no letter coming. He'll suffer then with suspense—won't he, that's all!—and I am very glad of it!'—Tears of pity for Jude's approaching sufferings at her hands mingled with those which had surged up in pity for herself.

Then the slim little wife of a husband whose person was disagreeable to her, the ethereal, fine-nerved, sensitive girl, quite unfitted by temperament and instinct to fulfill the conditions of the matrimonial relation with Phillotson, possibly with scarce any man, walked fitfully along, and panted, and brought weariness into her eyes by gazing and worrying hopelessly.

Phillotson met her at the arrival station, and, seeing that she was troubled, thought it must be owing to the depressing effect of her aunt's death and funeral. He began telling her of his day's doings, and how his friend Gillingham, a neighbouring schoolmaster whom he had not seen for years, had called upon him. While ascending to the town, seated on the top of the omnibus beside him, she said suddenly and with an air of self chastisement, regarding the white road and its bordering bushes of hazel:

'Richard—I let Mr. Fawley hold my hand a long while. I don't know whether you think it wrong?'

He, waking apparently from thoughts of far different mould, said vaguely, 'O, did you? What did you do that for?'

'I don't know. He wanted to, and I let him.'

'I hope it pleased him. I should think it was hardly a novelty.'

They lapsed into silence. Had this been a case in the court of an omniscient judge he might have entered on his notes the curious fact that Sue had placed the minor for the major indiscretion, and had not said a word about the kiss.

After tea that evening Phillotson sat balancing the school registers. She remained in an unusually silent, tense, and restless condition, and at last, saying she was tired, went to bed early. When Phillotson arrived upstairs, weary with the drudgery of the attendance-numbers, it was a quarter to twelve o'clock. Entering their chamber, which by day commanded a view of some thirty or forty miles over the Vale of Blackmoor, and even into Outer Wessex, he went to the window, and, pressing his face against the pane, gazed with hard-breathing fixity into the mysterious darkness which now covered the far-reaching scene. He was musing. 'I think,' he said at last, without turning his head, 'that I must get the Committee to change the school-stationer. All the copybooks are sent wrong this time.'

There was no reply. Thinking Sue was dozing he went on:

'And there must be a re-arrangement of that ventilator in the class-room. The wind blows down upon my head unmercifully, and gives me the earache.'

As the silence seemed more absolute than ordinarily he turned around. The heavy, gloomy oak wainscot which extended over the walls upstairs and down in the dilapidated 'Old-Grove Place,' and the mas-sive chimney-piece reaching to the ceiling, stood in odd contrast to the new and shining brass bedstead, and the new suite of birch fur-niture that he had bought for her, the two styles seeming to nod to each other across three centuries upon the shaking floor.

'Soo!' he said (this being the way in which he pronounced her name).

She was not in the bed, though she had apparently been there—the clothes on her side being flung back. Thinking she might have forgot-ten some kitchen detail and gone downstairs for a moment to see to it, he pulled off his coat and idled quietly enough for a few minutes, when, finding she did not come he went out upon the landing, candle in hand, and said again 'Soo!'

'Yes!' came back to him in her voice, from the distant kitchen quar-ter.

'What are you doing down there at midnight—tiring yourself out for nothing!'

'I am not sleepy; I am reading; and there is a larger fire here.'

He went to bed. Some time in the night he awoke. She was not there, even now. Lighting a candle he hastily stepped out upon the landing, and again called her name.

She answered 'Yes!' as before; but the tones were small and confined, and whence they came he could not at first understand. Under the staircase was a large clothes-closet, without a window; they seemed to come from it. The door was shut, but there was no lock or other fas-tening. Phillotson, alarmed, went towards it, wondering if she had sud-denly become deranged.

'What are you doing in there?' he asked

'Not to disturb you I came here, as it was so late.'

'But there's no bed, is there? And no ventilation! Why, you'll be suffocated if you stay all night!'

'O no, I think not. Don't trouble about me.'

'But—' Phillotson seized the knob and pulled at the door. She had fastened it inside with a piece of string, which broke at his pull. There being no bedstead she had flung down some rugs and made a little nest for herself in the very cramped quarters the closet afforded.

When he looked in upon her she sprang out of her lair, great-eyed and trembling.

'You ought not to have pulled open the door!' she cried excitedly. 'It is not becoming in you! O, will you go away; please will you!'

She looked so pitiful and pleading in her white night-gown against the shadowy lumber-hole that he was quite worried. She continued to beseech him not to disturb her.

He said: 'I've been kind to you, and given you every liberty; and it is monstrous that you should feel in this way!'

'Yes,' said she, weeping. 'I know that! It is wrong and wicked of me, I suppose! I am very sorry. But it is not I altogether that am to blame!'

'Who is then? Am I?'

'No—I don't know! The universe, I suppose—things in general, because they are so horrid and cruel!'

'Well, it is no use talking like that. Making a man's house so unseemly at this time o' night! Eliza will hear, if we don't mind.' (He meant the servant.) 'Just think if either of the parsons in this town was to see us now! I hate such eccentricities, Sue. There's no order or regularity in your sentiments! . . . But I won't intrude on you further; only I would advise you not to shut the door too tight, or I shall find you stifled to-morrow.'

On rising the next morning he immediately looked into the closet, but Sue had already gone downstairs. There was a little nest where she had lain, and spiders' webs hung overhead. 'What must a woman's aversion be when it is stronger than her fear of spiders!' he said bitterly.

He found her sitting at the breakfast-table, and the meal began almost in silence, the burghers walking past upon the pavement—or rather roadway, pavements being scarce here—which was two or three feet above the level of the parlour floor. They nodded down to the happy couple their morning greetings, as they went on.

'Richard,' she said all at once; 'would you mind my living away from you?'

'Away from me? Why, that's what you were doing when I married you. What then was the meaning of marrying at all?'

'You wouldn't like me any the better for telling you.'

'I don't object to know.'

'Because I thought I could do nothing else. You had got my promise a long time before that, remember. Then, as time went on, I regretted I had promised you, and was trying to see an honourable way to break it off. But as I couldn't I became rather reckless and careless about the conventions. Then you know what scandals were spread, and how I was turned out of the Training School you had taken such time and trouble to prepare me for and get me into; and this frightened me, and it seemed then that the one thing I could do would be to let the engagement stand. Of course I, of all people, ought not to have cared what was said, for it was just what I fancied I never did care for. But I was a coward—as so many women are—and my theoretic unconventionality broke down. If that had not entered into the case it would have been better to have hurt your feelings once for all then, than to marry you and hurt them all my life after. . . . And you were so generous in never giving credit for a moment to the rumour.'

'I am bound in honesty to tell you that I weighed its probability, and inquired of your cousin about it.'

'Ah!' she said with pained surprise.

'I didn't doubt you.'

'But you inquired!'

'I took his word.'

Her eyes had filled. '*He* wouldn't have inquired!' she said. 'But you haven't answered me. Will you let me go away? I know how irregular it is of me to ask it—'

'It is irregular.'

'But I do ask it! Domestic laws should be made according to temperaments, which should be classified. If people are at all peculiar in character they have to suffer from the very rules that produce comfort in others! . . . Will you let me?'

'But we married—'

'What is the use of thinking of laws and ordinances,' she burst out, 'if they make you miserable when you know you are committing no sin?'

'But you are committing a sin in not liking me.'

'I *do* like you! But I didn't reflect it would be—that it would be so much more than that. . . . For a man and woman to live on intimate terms when one feels as I do is adultery, in any circumstances, however legal. There—I've said it! . . . Will you let me, Richard?'

'You distress me, Susanna, by such importunity!'

'Why can't we agree to free each other? We made the compact, and surely we can cancel it—not legally, of course; but we can morally, especially as no new interests, in the shape of children, have arisen to be looked after. Then we might be friends, and meet without pain to either. O Richard, be my friend and have pity! We shall both be dead in a few years, and then what will it matter to anybody that you relieved me from constraint for a little while? I daresay you think me eccentric, or super-sensitive, or something absurd. Well—why should I suffer for what I was born to be, if it doesn't hurt other people?'

'But it does—it hurts *me*! And you vowed to love me.'

'Yes—that's it! I am in the wrong. I always am! It is as culpable to bind yourself to love always as to believe a creed always, and as silly as to vow always to like a particular food or drink!'

'And do you mean, by living away from me, living by yourself?'

'Well, if you insisted, yes. But I meant living with Jude.'

'As his wife?'

'As I choose.'

Phillotson writhed.

Sue continued: 'She, or he, "who lets the world, or his own portion of it, choose his plan of life for him, has no need of any other faculty than the ape-like one of imitation." J. S. Mill's words, those are.[5] I have been reading it up. Why can't you act upon them? I wish to, always.'

'What do I care about J. S. Mill!' moaned he. 'I only want to lead a quiet life! Do you mind my saying that I have guessed what never once occurred to me before our marriage—that you were in love, and are in love, with Jude Fawley!'

'You may go on guessing that I am, since you have begun. But do you suppose that if I had been I should have asked you to let me go and live with him?'

The ringing of the school bell saved Phillotson from the necessity of replying at present to what apparently did not strike him as being such a convincing *argumentum ad verecundiam*[6] as she, in her loss of courage at the last moment, meant it to appear. She was beginning to be so puzzling and unstateable that he was ready to throw in with her other little peculiarities the extremest request which a wife could make.

They proceeded to the schools that morning as usual, Sue entering the class-room, where he could see the back of her head through the glass partition whenever he turned his eyes that way. As he went on giving and hearing lessons his forehead and eyebrows twitched from concentrated agitation of thought; till at length he tore a scrap from a sheet of scribbling paper and wrote:

> 'Your request prevents my attending to work at all. I don't know what I am doing! Was it seriously made?'

He folded the piece of paper very small, and gave it to a little boy to take to Sue. The child toddled off into the class-room. Phillotson saw his wife turn and take the note, and the bend of her pretty head as she read it, her lips slightly crisped, to prevent undue expression under fire of so many young eyes. He could not see her hands, but she changed her position, and soon the child returned, bringing nothing in reply. In a few minutes, however, one of Sue's class appeared, with a little note similar to his own. These words only were pencilled therein:

> 'I am sincerely sorry to say that it was seriously made.'

Phillotson looked more disturbed than before, and the meeting-place of his brows twitched again. In ten minutes he called up the child he had just sent to her, and despatched another missive:

5. From *On Liberty* (1859), chapter 3, by John Stuart Mill (1806–1873).
6. Argument resting on an appeal to reverence for an established authority.

'God knows I don't want to thwart you in any reasonable way. My whole thought is to make you comfortable and happy. But I cannot agree to such a preposterous notion as your going to live with your lover. You would lose everybody's respect and regard; and so should I!'

After an interval a similar part was enacted in the class-room, and an answer came:

'I know you mean my good. But I don't want to be respectable! To produce "Human development in its richest diversity" (to quote your Humboldt)[7] is to my mind far above respectability. No doubt my tastes are low—in your view—hopelessly low! If you won't let me go to him, will you grant me this one request—allow me to live in your house in a separate way?'

To this he returned no answer.
She wrote again:

'I know what you think. But cannot you have pity on me? I beg you to; I implore you to be merciful! I would not ask if I were not almost compelled by what I can't bear! No poor woman has ever wished more than I that Eve had not fallen, so that (as the primitive Christians believed) some harmless mode of vegetation might have peopled Paradise. But I won't trifle! Be kind to me— even though I have not been kind to you! I will go away, go abroad, anywhere, and never trouble you.'

Nearly an hour passed, and then he returned an answer:

'I do not wish to pain you. How well you *know* I don't! Give me a little time. I am disposed to agree to your last request.'

One line from her:

'Thank you from my heart, Richard. I do not deserve your kindness.'

All day Phillotson bent a dazed regard upon her through the glazed partition; and he felt as lonely as when he had not known her.

But he was as good as his word, and consented to her living apart in the house. At first, when they met at meals, she had seemed more composed under the new arrangement; but the irksomeness of their position worked on her temperament, and the fibres of her nature seemed strained like harp-strings. She talked vaguely and indiscriminately to prevent his talking pertinently.

7. Baron Wilhelm von Humboldt (1767–1835), German scholar, author of *The Sphere and Duties of Government*. He is quoted in Mill's *On Liberty*.

IV–4

Phillotson was sitting up late, as was often his custom, trying to get together the materials for his long-neglected hobby of Roman antiquities. For the first time since reviving the subject he felt a return of his old interest in it. He forgot time and place, and when he remembered himself and ascended to rest it was nearly two o'clock.

His preoccupation was such that, though he now slept on the other side of the house, he mechanically went to the room that he and his wife had occupied when he first became a tenant of Old-Grove Place, which since his differences with Sue had been hers exclusively. He entered, and unconsciously began to undress.

There was a cry from the bed, and a quick movement. Before the schoolmaster had realized where he was he perceived Sue starting up half-awake, staring widly, and springing out upon the floor on the side away from him, which was towards the window. This was somewhat hidden by the canopy of the bedstead, and in a moment he heard her flinging up the sash. Before he had thought that she meant to do more than get air she had mounted upon the sill and leapt out. She disappeared in the darkness, and he heard her fall below.

Phillotson, horrified, ran downstairs, striking himself sharply against the newel[1] in his haste. Opening the heavy door he ascended the two or three steps to the level of the ground, and there on the gravel before him lay a white heap. Phillotson seized it in his arms, and bringing Sue into the hall seated her on a chair, where he gazed at her by the flapping light of the candle which he had set down in the draught on the bottom stair.

She had certainly not broken her neck. She looked at him with eyes that seemed not to take him in; and though not particularly large in general they appeared so now. She pressed her side and rubbed her arm, as if conscious of pain; then stood up, averting her face, in evident distress at his gaze.

'Thank God—you are not killed! Though it's not for want of trying—not much hurt I hope?'

Her fall, in fact, had not been a serious one, probably owing to the lowness of the old rooms and to the high level of the ground without. Beyond a scraped elbow and a blow in the side she had apparently incurred little harm.

'I was asleep, I think!' she began, her pale face still turned away from him. 'And something frightened me—a terrible dream—I thought I saw you—' The actual circumstances seemed to come back to her, and she was silent.

Her cloak was hanging at the back of the door, and the wretched

1. Post supporting the handrail.

Phillotson flung it round her. 'Shall I help you upstairs?' he asked drearily; for the significance of all this sickened him of himself and of everything.

'No thank you, Richard. I am very little hurt. I can walk.'

'You ought to lock your door,' he mechanically said, as if lecturing in school. 'Then no one could intrude even by accident.'

'I have tried—it won't lock. All the doors are out of order.'

The aspect of things was not improved by her admission. She ascended the staircase slowly, the waving light of the candle shining on her. Phillotson did not approach her, or attempt to ascend himself till he heard her enter her room. Then he fastened up the front door, and returning sat down on the lower stairs, holding the newel with one hand, and bowing his face into the other. Thus he remained for a long time—a pitiable object enough to one who had seen him; till, raising his head and sighing a sigh which seemed to say that the business of his life must be carried on, whether he had a wife or no, he took the candle and went upstairs to his lonely room on the other side of the landing.

No further incident touching the matter between them occurred till the following evening, when, immediately school was over, Phillotson walked out of Shaston, saying he required no tea, and not informing Sue where he was going. He descended from the town level by a steep road in a north-westerly direction, and continued to move downwards till the soil changed from its white dryness to a tough brown clay. He was now on the low alluvial beds

> 'Where Duncliffe is the traveller's mark,
> And cloty Stour's a-rolling dark'

More than once he looked back in the increasing obscurity of evening. Against the sky was Shaston, dimly visible.

> 'On the grey-topp'd height
> Of Paladore, as pale day wore
> Away . . .'[2]

The new-lit lights from its windows burnt with a steady shine as if watching him, one of which windows was his own. Above it he could just discern the pinnacled tower of Trinity Church. The air down here, tempered by the thick damp bed of tenacious clay, was not as it had been above, but soft and relaxing, so that when he had walked a mile or two he was obliged to wipe his face with his handkerchief.

Leaving Duncliffe Hill on the left he proceeded without hesitation through the shade, as a man goes on, night or day, in a district over

---

2. William Barnes [*Hardy's note*]. Both quotations are from the poem "Shaftesbury Feair." Barnes (1801–1886) was a Dorset dialect poet and scholar; Hardy knew him well and wrote a fine account of him.

which he has played as a boy. He had walked altogether about four and
a half miles

> 'Where Stour receives her strength,
> From six cleere fountains fey,'[3]

when he crossed a tributary of the Stour, and reached Leddenton—a
little town of three or four thousand inhabitants—where he went on
to the boys' school, and knocked at the door of the master's residence.

A boy pupil-teacher opened it, and to Phillotson's inquiry if Mr.
Gillingham was at home replied that he was, going at once off to his
own house, and leaving Phillotson to find his way in as he could. He
discovered his friend putting away some books from which he had been
giving evening lessons. The light of the paraffin lamp fell on Phillotson's face—pale and wretched by contrast with his friend's, who had
a cool, practical look. They had been schoolmates in boyhood, and
fellow-students at Wintoncester Training College, many years before
this time.

'Glad to see you, Dick! But you don't look well? Nothing the matter?'

Phillotson advanced without replying, and Gillingham closed the
cupboard and pulled up beside his visitor.

'Why you haven't been here—let me see—since you were married?
I called, you know, but you were out; and upon my word it is such a
climb after dark that I have been waiting till the days are longer before
lumpering[4] up again. I am glad you didn't wait, however.'

Though well-trained and even proficient masters, they occasionally
used a dialect-word of their boyhood to each other in private.

'I've come, George, to explain to you my reasons to taking a step
that I am about to take, so that you, at least, will understand my
motives if other people question them anywhen—as they may, indeed
certainly will. . . . But anything is better than the present condition of
things. God forbid that you should ever have such an experience as
mine!'

'Sit down. You don't mean—anything wrong between you and Mrs.
Phillotson?'

'I do. . . . My wretched state is that I've a wife I love, who not only
does not love me, but—but—Well, I won't say. I know her feeling! I
should prefer hatred from her!'

'Ssh!'

'And the sad part of it is that she is not so much to blame as I. She
was a pupil-teacher under me, as you know, and I took advantage of
her inexperience, and toled[5] her out for walks, and got her to agree to

3. Drayton [Hardy's note].
4. Walking heavily (dialect).
5. Persuaded (dialect).

a long engagement before she well knew her own mind. Afterwards she saw somebody else, but she blindly fulfilled her engagement.'

'Loving the other?'

'Yes; with a curious tender solicitude seemingly; though her exact feeling for him is a riddle to me—and to him too, I think—possibly to herself. She is one of the oddest creatures I ever met. However, I have been struck with these two facts; the extraordinary sympathy, or similarity, between the pair. He is her cousin, which perhaps accounts for some of it. They seem to be one person split in two! And with her unconquerable aversion to myself as a husband, even though she may like me as a friend, 'tis too much to bear longer. She has conscientiously struggled against it, but to no purpose. I cannot bear it—I cannot! I can't answer her arguments—she has read ten times as much as I. Her intellect sparkles like diamonds, while mine smoulders like brown paper. . . . She's one too many for me!'

'She'll get over it, good-now[6]?'

'Never! It is—but I won't go into it—there are reasons why she never will. At last she calmly and firmly asked if she might leave me and go to him. The climax came last night, when, owing to my entering her room by accident, she jumped out of window—so strong was her dread of me! She pretended it was a dream, but that was to soothe me. Now when a woman jumps out of window without caring whether she breaks her neck or no, she's not to be mistaken; and this being the case I have come to a conclusion: that it is wrong to so torture a fellow-creature any longer; and I won't be the inhuman wretch to do it, cost what it may!'

'What—you'll let her go? And with her lover?'

'Whom with is her matter. I shall let her go; with him certainly, if she wishes. I know I may be wrong—I know I can't logically, or religiously, defend my concession to such a wish of hers; or harmonize it with the doctrines I was brought up in. Only I know one thing: something within me tells me I am doing wrong in refusing her. I, like other men, profess to hold that if a husband gets such a so-called preposterous request from his wife, the only course that can possibly be regarded as right and proper and honourable in him is to refuse it, and put her virtuously under lock and key, and murder her lover perhaps. But is that essentially right, and proper, and honourable, or is it contemptibly mean and selfish? I don't profess to decide. I simply am going to act by instinct, and let principles take care of themselves. If a person who has blindly walked into a quagmire cries for help, I am inclined to give it, if possible.'

6. Hardy explained this dialect expression as follows: "the expression 'good now' is still much in use in the interior of this country, though it is dying away hereabout . . . its precise meaning being 'You may be sure.' . . . The Americanism 'I guess' is near it" (W. R. Rutland, *Thomas Hardy: A Study of His Writings and Their Background* [1938]).

'But—you see, there's the question of neighbours and society—what will happen if everybody—'

'O, I am not going to be a philosopher any longer! I only see what's under my eyes.'

'Well—I don't agree with your instinct, Dick!' said Gillingham gravely. 'I am quite amazed, to tell the truth, that such a sedate, plodding fellow as you should have entertained such a craze for a moment. You said when I called that she was puzzling and peculiar: I think you are!'

'Have you ever stood before a woman whom you know to be intrinsically a good woman, while she has pleaded for release—been the man she has knelt to and implored indulgence of?'

'I am thankful to say I haven't.'

'Then I don't think you are in a position to give an opinion. I have been that man, and it makes all the difference in the world, if one has any manliness or chivalry in him. I had not the remotest idea—living apart from women as I have done for so many years—that merely taking a woman to church and putting a ring upon her finger could by any possibility involve one in such a daily, continuous tragedy as that now shared by her and me!'

'Well, I could admit some excuse for letting her leave you, provided she kept to herself. But to go attended by a cavalier—that makes a difference.'

'Not a bit. Suppose, as I believe, she would rather endure her present misery than be made to promise to keep apart from him? All that is a question for herself. It is not the same thing at all as the treachery of living on with a husband and playing him false. . . . However, she has not distinctly implied living with him as wife, though I think she means to. . . . And to the best of my understanding it is not an ignoble, merely animal, feeling between the two: that is the worst of it; because it makes me think their affection will be enduring. I did not mean to confess to you that in the first jealous weeks of my marriage, before I had come to my right mind, I hid myself in the school one evening when they were together there, and I heard what they said. I am ashamed of it now, though I suppose I was only exercising a legal right. I found from their manner that an extraordinary affinity, or sympathy, entered into their attachment, which somehow took away all flavour of grossness. Their supreme desire is to be together—to share each other's emotions, and fancies, and dreams.'

'Platonic!'

'Well no. Shelleyan would be nearer to it. They remind me of—what are their names—Laon and Cythna.[7] Also of Paul and Virginia[8] a little. The more I reflect, the more *entirely* I am on their side!'

7. Lovers in Percy Bysshe Shelley's *The Revolt of Islam* (1818). Shelley was Hardy's favorite poet.
8. Types of idealized and innocent love in Bernardin de St. Pierre's novel *Paul et Virginie* (1787).

'But if people did as you want to do, there'd be a general domestic disintegration. The family would no longer be the social unit.'

'Yes—I am all abroad, I suppose!' said Phillotson sadly. 'I was never a very bright reasoner, you remember. . . . And yet, I don't see why the woman and the children should not be the unit without the man.'

'By the Lord Harry!—Matriarchy! . . . Does *she* say all this too?'

'O no. She little thinks I have out-Sued Sue in this—all in the last twelve hours!'

'It will upset all received opinion hereabout. Good God—what will Shaston say!'

'I don't say that it won't. I don't know—I don't know! . . . As I say, I am only a feeler, not a reasoner.'

'Now,' said Gillingham, 'let us take it quietly, and have something to drink over it.' He went under the stairs, and produced a bottle of cider-wine, of which they drank a rummer[9] each. 'I think you are rafted,[1] and not yourself,' he continued. 'Do go back and make up your mind to put up with a few whims. But keep her. I hear on all sides that she's a charming young thing.'

'Ah yes! That's the bitterness of it! Well, I won't stay. I have a long walk before me.'

Gillingham accompanied his friend a mile on his way, and at parting expressed his hope that this consultation, singular as its subject was, would be the renewal of their old comradeship. 'Stick to her!' were his last words, flung into the darkness after Phillotson; from which his friend answered 'Ay, ay!'

But when Phillotson was alone under the clouds of night, and no sound was audible but that of the purling tributaries of the Stour, he said, 'So Gillingham, my friend, you had no stronger arguments against it than those!'

'I think she ought to be smacked, and brought to her senses—that's what I think!' murmured Gillingham, as he walked back alone.

The next morning came, and at breakfast Phillotson told Sue:

'You may go—with whom you will. I absolutely and unconditionally agree.'

Having once come to this conclusion it seemed to Phillotson more and more indubitably the true one. His mild serenity at the sense that he was doing his duty by a woman who was at his mercy almost overpowered his grief at relinquishing her.

Some days passed, and the evening of their last meal together had come—a cloudy evening with wind—which indeed was very seldom absent in this elevated place. How permanently it was imprinted upon his vision; that look of her as she glided into the parlour to tea; a slim

9. Large drinking glass.
1. Upset (dialect).

flexible figure; a face, strained from its roundness, and marked by the pallors of restless days and nights, suggesting tragic possibilities quite at variance with her times of buoyancy; a trying of this morsel and that, and an inability to eat either. Her nervous manner, begotten of a fear lest he should be injured by her course, might have been interpreted by a stranger as displeasure that Phillotson intruded his presence on her for the few brief minutes that remained.

'You had better have a slice of ham, or an egg, or something with your tea? You can't travel on a mouthful of bread and butter.'

She took the slice he helped her to; and they discussed as they sat trivial questions of housekeeping, such as where he would find the key of this or that cupboard, what little bills were paid, and what not.

'I am a bachelor by nature, as you know, Sue,' he said, in a heroic attempt to put her at her ease. 'So that being without a wife will not really be irksome to me, as it might be to other men who have had one a little while. I have, too, this grand hobby in my head of writing "The Roman Antiquities of Wessex," which will occupy all my spare hours.'

'If you will send me some of the manuscript to copy at any time, as you used to, I will do it with so much pleasure!' she said with amenable gentleness. 'I should much like to be some help to you still—as a— friend.'

Phillotson mused, and said: 'No, I think we ought to be really sep-arate, if we are to be at all. And for this reason, that I don't wish to ask you any questions, and particularly wish you not to give me infor-mation as to your movements, or even your address. . . . Now, what money do you want? You must have some, you know.'

'O, of course, Richard, I couldn't think of having any of *your* money to go away from you with! I don't want any either. I have enough of my own to last me for a long while, and Jude will let me have—'

'I would rather not know anything about him, if you don't mind. You are free, absolutely; and your course is your own.'

'Very well. But I'll just say that I have packed only a change or two of my own personal clothing, and one or two little things besides that are my very own. I wish you would look into my trunk before it is closed. Besides that I have only a small parcel that will go into Jude's port-manteau.'

'Of course I shall do no such thing as examine your luggage! I wish you would take three-quarters of the household furniture. I don't want to be bothered with it. I have a sort of affection for a little of it that belonged to my poor mother and father. But the rest you are welcome to whenever you like to send for it.'

'That I shall never do.'

'You go by the six-thirty train, don't you? It is now a quarter to six.'

'You . . . You don't seem very sorry I am going, Richard!'

'O no—perhaps not.'

'I like you much for how you have behaved. It is a curious thing that directly I have begun to regard you as not my husband, but as my old teacher, I like you. I won't be so affected as to say I love you, because you know I don't, except as a friend. But you do seem that to me!'

Sue was for a few moments a little tearful at these reflections, and then the station omnibus came round to take her up. Phillotson saw her things put on the top, handed her in, and was obliged to make an appearance of kissing her as he wished her good-bye, which she quite understood and imitated. From the cheerful manner in which they parted the omnibus-man had no other idea than that she was going for a short visit.

When Phillotson got back into the house he went upstairs and opened the window in the direction the omnibus had taken. Soon the noise of its wheels died away. He came down then, his face compressed like that of one bearing pain; he put on his hat and went out, following by the same route for nearly a mile. Suddenly turning round he came home.

He had no sooner entered than the voice of his friend Gillingham greeted him from the front room.

'I could make nobody hear; so finding your door open I walked in, and made myself comfortable. I said I would call, you remember.'

'Yes. I am much obliged to you, Gillingham, particularly for coming to-night.'

'How is Mrs.——'

'She is quite well. She is gone—just gone. That's her tea-cup, that she drank out of only an hour ago. And that's the plate she—' Phillotson's throat got choked up, and he could not go on. He turned and pushed the tea-things aside.

'Have you had any tea, by-the-bye?' he asked presently in a renewed voice.

'No—yes—never mind,' said Gillingham, preoccupied. 'Gone, you say she is!'

'Yes. . . . I would have died for her; but I wouldn't be cruel to her in the name of the law. She is, as I understand, gone to join her lover. What they are going to do I cannot say. Whatever it may be she has my full consent to.'

There was a stability, a ballast, in Phillotson's pronouncement which restrained his friend's comment. 'Shall I—leave you?' he asked.

'No, no. It is a mercy to me that you have come. I have some articles to arrange and clear away. Would you help me?'

Gillingham assented; and having gone to the upper rooms the schoolmaster opened drawers, and began taking out all Sue's things that she had left behind, and laying them in a large box. 'She wouldn't take all I wanted her to,' he continued. 'But when I made up my mind to her going to live in her own way I did make up my mind.'

'Some men would have stopped at an agreement to separate.'

'I've gone into all that, and don't wish to argue it. I was, and am, the most old-fashioned man in the world on the question of marriage—in fact I had never thought critically about its ethics at all. But certain facts stared me in the face, and I couldn't go against them.'

They went on with the packing silently. When it was done Phillotson closed the box and turned the key.

'There,' he said. 'To adorn her in somebody's eyes; never again in mine!'

IV–5

Four-and-twenty hours before this time Sue had written the following note to Jude:

> 'It is as I told you; and I am leaving to-morrow evening. Richard and I thought it could be done with less obtrusiveness after dark. I feel rather frightened, and therefore ask you to be sure you are on the Melchester platform to meet me. I arrive at a little to seven. I know you will, of course, dear Jude; but I feel so timid that I can't help begging you to be punctual. He has been so *very* kind to me through it all!
>
> 'Now to our meeting!   S.'

As she was carried by the omnibus further and further down from the mountain town—the single passenger that evening—she regarded the receding road with a sad face. But no hesitation was apparent therein.

The up-train by which she was departing stopped by signal only. To Sue it seemed strange that such a powerful organization as a railway-train should be brought to a standstill on purpose for her—a fugitive from her lawful home.

The twenty minutes' journey drew towards its close, and Sue began gathering her things together to alight. At the moment that the train came to a standstill by the Melchester platform a hand was laid on the door and she beheld Jude. He entered the compartment promptly. He had a black bag in his hand, and was dressed in the dark suit he wore on Sundays and in the evening after work. Altogether he looked a very handsome young fellow, his ardent affection for her burning in his eyes.

'O Jude!' She clasped his hand with both hers, and her tense state caused her to simmer over in a little succession of dry sobs. 'I—I am so glad! I get out here?'

'No. I get in, dear one! I've packed. Besides this bag I've only a big box which is labelled.'

'But don't I get out? Aren't we going to stay here?'

'We couldn't possibly, don't you see. We are known here—I, at any rate, am well known. I've booked for Aldbrickham; and here's your ticket for the same place, as you have only one to here.'

'I thought we should have stayed here,' she repeated.

'It wouldn't have done at all.'

'Ah!—Perhaps not.'

'There wasn't time for me to write and say the place I had decided on. Aldbrickham is a much bigger town—sixty or seventy thousand inhabitants—and nobody knows anything about us there.'

'And you have given up your Cathedral work here?'

'Yes. It was rather sudden—your message coming unexpectedly. Strictly, I might have been made to finish out the week. But I pleaded urgency and I was let off. I would have deserted any day at your command, dear Sue. I have deserted more than that for you!'

'I fear I am doing you a lot of harm. Ruining your prospects of the Church; ruining your progress in your trade; everything!'

'The Church is no more to me. Let it lie! *I* am not to be one of

> "The soldier-saints who, row on row,
> Burn upward each to his point of bliss,"[1]

if any such there be! My point of bliss is not upward, but here.'

'O I seem so bad—upsetting men's courses like this!' said she, taking up in her voice the emotion that had begun in his. But she recovered her equanimity by the time they had travelled a dozen miles.

'He has been so good in letting me go,' she resumed. 'And here's a note I found on my dressing-table, addressed to you.'

'Yes. He's not an unworthy fellow,' said Jude, glancing at the note. 'And I am ashamed of myself for hating him because he married you.'

'According to the rule of women's whims I suppose I ought to suddenly love him, because he has let me go so generously and unexpectedly,' she answered smiling. 'But I am so cold, or devoid of gratitude, or so something, that even this generosity hasn't made me love him, or repent, or want to stay with him as his wife; although I do feel I like his large-mindedness, and respect him more than ever.'

'It may not work so well for us as if he had been less kind, and you had run away against his will,' murmured Jude.

'That *I* never would have done.'

Jude's eyes rested musingly on her face. Then he suddenly kissed her; and was going to kiss her again. 'No—only once now—please, Jude!'

'That's rather cruel,' he answered; but acquiesced. 'Such a strange thing has happened to me,' Jude continued after a silence. 'Arabella

---

1. From Browning's poem "The Statue and the Bust."

has actually written to ask me to get a divorce from her—in kindness to her, she says. She wants to honestly and legally marry that man she has already married virtually; and begs me to enable her to do it.'

'What have you done?'

'I have agreed. I thought at first I couldn't do it without getting her into trouble about that second marriage, and I don't want to injure her in any way. Perhaps she's no worse than I am, after all! But nobody knows about it over here, and I find it will not be a difficult proceeding at all. If she wants to start afresh I have only too obvious reasons for not hindering her.'

'Then you'll be free?'

'Yes, I shall be free.'

'Where are we booked for?' she asked, with the discontinuity that marked her to-night.

'Aldbrickham, as I said.'

'But it will be very late when we get there?'

'Yes. I thought of that, and I wired for a room for us at the Temperance Hotel there.'

'One?'

'Yes—one.'

She looked at him. 'O Jude!' Sue bent her forehead against the corner of the compartment. 'I thought you might do it; and that I was deceiving you. But I didn't mean that!'

In the pause which followed, Jude's eyes fixed themselves with a stultified expression on the opposite seat. 'Well!' he said. . . . 'Well!'

He remained in silence; and seeing how discomfited he was she put her face against his cheek, murmuring, 'Don't be vexed, dear!'

'Oh—there's no harm done,' he said. 'But—I understood it like that. . . . Is this a sudden change of mind?'

'You have no right to ask me such a question; and I shan't answer!' she said, smiling.

'My dear one, your happiness is more to me than anything—although we seem to verge on quarrelling so often!—and your will is law to me. I am something more than a mere—selfish fellow, I hope. Have it as you wish!' On reflection his brow showed perplexity. 'But perhaps it is that you don't love me—not that you have become conventional! Much as, under your teaching, I hate convention, I hope it *is* that, not the other terrible alternative!'

Even at this obvious moment for candour Sue could not be quite candid as to the state of that mystery, her heart. 'Put it down to my timidity,' she said with hurried evasiveness; 'to a woman's natural timidity when the crisis comes. I *may* feel as well as you that I have a perfect right to live with you as you thought—from this moment. I *may* hold the opinion that, in a proper state of society, the father of a woman's child will be as much a private matter of hers as the cut of her under-linen, on whom nobody will have any right to question her. But partly, perhaps, because it is by his generosity that I am now free, I would rather not be other than a little rigid. If there had been a rope-ladder, and he had run after us with pistols, it would have seemed different, and I may have acted otherwise. But don't press me and criticize me, Jude! Assume that I haven't the courage of my opinions. I know I am a poor miserable creature. My nature is not so passionate as yours!'

He repeated simply: 'I thought—what I naturally thought. But if we are not lovers, we are not. Phillotson thought so, I am sure. See, here is what he has written to me.' He opened the letter she had brought, and read:

'I make only one condition—that you are tender and kind to her. I know you love her. But even love may be cruel at times. You are made for each other: it is obvious, palpable, to any unbiased older person. You were all along "the shadowy third"² in my short life with her. I repeat, take care of Sue.'

'He's a good fellow, isn't he!' she said with latent tears. On reconsideration she added, 'He was very resigned to letting me go—too resigned almost! I never was so near being in love with him as when he made such thoughtful arrangements for my being comfortable on my journey, and offering to provide money. Yet I was not. If I loved him ever so little as a wife, I'd go back to him even now.'

'But you don't, do you?'

'It is true—O so terribly true!—I don't.'

'Nor me neither, I half fear!' he said pettishly. 'Nor anybody perhaps!—Sue, sometimes, when I am vexed with you, I think you are incapable of real love.'

'That's not good and loyal of you!' she said, and drawing away from him as far as she could, looked severely out into the darkness. She added in hurt tones, without turning round: 'My liking for you is not as some women's perhaps. But it is a delight in being with you, of a supremely delicate kind, and I don't want to go further and risk it by—an attempt to intensify it! I quite realized that, as woman with man, it was a risk to come. But, as me with you, I resolved to trust you to set my wishes above your gratification. Don't discuss it further, dear Jude!'

'Of course, if it would make you reproach yourself . . . but you do like me very much, Sue? say you do! Say that you do a quarter, a tenth, as much as I do you; and I'll be content!'

'I've let you kiss me, and that tells enough.'

'Just once or so!'

'Well—don't be a greedy boy.'

---

2. A phrase from Browning's poem "By the Fire-side."

He leant back, and did not look at her for a long time. That episode in her past history of which she had told him—of the poor Christminster graduate whom she had handled thus, returned to Jude's mind; and he saw himself as a possible second in such a torturing destiny.

'This is a queer elopement!' he murmured. 'Perhaps you are making a cat's-paw of me with Phillotson all this time. Upon my word it almost seems so—to see you sitting up there so prim!'

'Now you mustn't be angry—I won't let you!' she coaxed, turning and moving nearer to him. 'You did kiss me just now, you know; and I didn't dislike you to, I own it, Jude. Only I don't want to let you do it again, just yet—considering how we are circumstanced, don't you see!'

He could never resist her when she pleaded (as she well knew). And they sat side by side with joined hands, till she aroused herself at some thought.

'I can't possibly go to that Temperance Inn, after your telegraphing that message!'

'Why not?'

'You can see well enough!'

'Very well; there'll be some other one open, no doubt. I have sometimes thought, since your marrying Phillotson because of a stupid scandal, that under the affectation of independent views you are as enslaved to the social code as any woman I know!'

'Not mentally. But I haven't the courage of my views, as I said before. I didn't marry him altogether because of the scandal. But sometimes a woman's *love of being loved* gets the better of her conscience, and though she is agonized at the thought of treating a man cruelly, she encourages him to love her while she doesn't love him at all. Then, when she sees him suffering, her remorse sets in, and she does what she can to repair the wrong.'

'You simply mean that you flirted outrageously with him, poor old chap, and then repented, and to make reparation, married him, though you tortured yourself to death by doing it.'

'Well—if you will put it brutally!—it was a little like that—that and the scandal together—and your concealing from me what you ought to have told me before!'

He could see that she was distressed and tearful at his criticisms, and soothed her, saying: 'There, dear; don't mind! Crucify me, if you will! You know you are all the world to me, whatever you do!'

'I am very bad and unprincipled—I know you think that!' she said, trying to blink away her tears.

'I think and know you are my dear Sue, from whom neither length nor breadth, nor things present nor things to come, can divide me!'[3]

---

3. Adapted from Romans 8.38–39.

Though so sophisticated in many things she was such a child in others that this satisfied her, and they reached the end of their journey on the best of terms. It was about ten o'clock when they arrived at Aldbrickham, the county town of North Wessex. As she would not go to the Temperance Hotel because of the form of his telegram, Jude inquired for another; and a youth who volunteered to find one wheeled their luggage to The George further on, which proved to be the inn at which Jude had stayed with Arabella on that one occasion of their meeting after their division for years.

Owing, however, to their now entering it by another door, and to his preoccupation, he did not at first recognize the place. When they had engaged their respective rooms they went down to a late supper. During Jude's temporary absence the waiting-maid spoke to Sue.

'I think, ma'am, I remember your relation, or friend, or whatever he is, coming here once before—late, just like this, with his wife—a lady, at any rate, that wasn't you by no manner of means—jest as med be with you now.'

'O do you?' said Sue, with a certain sickness of heart. 'Though I think you must be mistaken! How long ago was it?'

'About a month or two. A handsome, full-figured woman. They had this room.'

When Jude came back and sat down to supper Sue seemed moping and miserable. 'Jude,' she said to him plaintively, at their parting that night upon the landing, 'it is not so nice and pleasant as it used to be with us! I don't like it here—I can't bear the place! And I don't like you so well as I did!'

'How fidgeted you seem, dear! Why do you change like this?'

'Because it was cruel to bring me here!'

'Why?'

'You were lately here with Arabella. There, now I have said it!'

'Dear me, why—' said Jude looking round him. 'Yes—it is the same! I really didn't know it, Sue. Well—it is not cruel, since we have come as we have—two relations staying together.'

'How long ago was it you were here? Tell me, tell me!'

'The day before I met you in Christminster, when we went back to Marygreen together. I told you I had met her.'

'Yes, you said you had met her, but you didn't tell me all. Your story was that you had met as estranged people, who were not husband and wife at all in Heaven's sight—not that you had made it up with her.'

'We didn't make it up,' he said sadly. 'I can't explain, Sue.'

'You've been false to me; you, my last hope! And I shall never forget it, never!'

'But by your own wish, dear Sue, we are only to be friends, not lovers! It is so very inconsistent of you to—'

'Friends can be jealous!'

'I don't see that. You concede nothing to me and I have to concede everything to you. After all, you were on good terms with your husband at that time.'

'No, I wasn't, Jude. O how can you think so! And you have taken me in, even if you didn't intend to.' She was so mortified that he was obliged to take her into her room and close the door lest the people should hear. 'Was it this room? Yes it was—I see by your look it was! I won't have it for mine! O it was treacherous of you to have her again! *I* jumped out of the window!'

'But Sue, she was, after all, my legal wife, if not—'

Slipping down on her knees Sue buried her face in the bed and wept.

'I never knew such an unreasonable—such a dog-in-the-manger feeling,' said Jude. 'I am not to approach you, nor anybody else!'

'O don't you *understand* my feeling! Why don't you! Why are you so gross! *I* jumped out of the window!'

'Jumped out of window?'

'I can't explain!'

It was true that he did not understand her feeling very well. But he did a little; and began to love her none the less.

'I—I thought you cared for nobody—desired nobody in the world but me at that time—and ever since!' continued Sue.

'It is true. I did not, and don't now!' said Jude, as distressed as she.

'But you must have thought much of her! Or—'

'No—I need not—you don't understand me either—women never do! Why should you get into such a tantrum about nothing?'

Looking up from the quilt she pouted provokingly: 'If it hadn't been for that, perhaps I would have gone on to the Temperance Hotel, after all, as you proposed; for I was beginning to think I did belong to you!'

'O, it is of no consequence!' said Jude distantly.

'I thought, of course, that she had never been really your wife since she left you of her own accord years and years ago! My sense of it was, that a parting such as yours from her, and mine from him, ended the marriage.'

'I can't say more without speaking against her, and I don't want to do that,' said he. 'Yet I must tell you one thing, which would settle the matter in any case. She has married another man—really married him! I knew nothing about it till after the visit we made here.'

'Married another? . . . It is a crime—as the world treats it, but does not believe.'

'There—now you are yourself again. Yes, it is a crime—as you don't hold, but would fearfully concede. But I shall never inform against her! and it is evidently a prick of conscience in her that has led her to urge me to get a divorce, that she may re-marry this man legally. So you perceive I shall not be likely to see her again.'

'And you didn't really know anything of this when you saw her?' said Sue more gently, as she rose.

'I did not. Considering all things, I don't think you ought to be angry, darling!'

'I am not. But I shan't go to the Temperance Hotel!'

He laughed. 'Never mind!' he said. 'So that I am near you, I am comparatively happy. It is more than this earthly wretch called Me deserves—you spirit, you disembodied creature, you dear, sweet, tantalizing phantom—hardly flesh at all; so that when I put my arms round you I almost expect them to pass through you as through air! Forgive me for being gross, as you call it! Remember that our calling cousins when really strangers was a snare. The enmity of our parents gave a piquancy to you in my eyes that was intenser even than the novelty of ordinary new acquaintance.'

'Say those pretty lines, then, from Shelley's "Epipsychidion" as if they meant me!' she solicited, slanting up closer to him as they stood. 'Don't you know them?'

'I know hardly any poetry,' he replied mournfully.

'Don't you? These are some of them:

"There was a Being whom my spirit oft
Met on its visioned wanderings far aloft.
    •   •   •   •   •   •
A seraph of Heaven, too gentle to be human,
Veiling beneath that radiant form of woman. . . ."[4]

O it is too flattering, so I won't go on! But say it's me!—say it's me!'

'It *is* you, dear; exactly like you!'

'Now I forgive you! And you shall kiss me just once there—not very long.' She put the tip of her finger gingerly to her cheek; and he did as commanded. 'You do care for me very much, don't you, in spite of my not—you know?'

'Yes, sweet!' he said with a sigh; and bade her good-night.

IV–6

In returning to his native town of Shaston as schoolmaster Phillotson had won the interest and awakened the memories of the inhabitants, who, though they did not honour him for his miscellaneous acquirements as he would have been honoured elsewhere, retained for him a sincere regard. When, shortly after his arrival, he brought home a pretty wife—awkwardly pretty for him, if he did not take care, they said—they were glad to have her settle among them.

For some time after her flight from that home Sue's absence did not

4. From Shelley's *Epipsychidion*.

excite comment. Her place as monitor[1] in the school was taken by another young woman within a few days of her vacating it, which substitution also passed without remark, Sue's services having been of a provisional nature only. When, however, a month had passed, and Phillotson casually admitted to acquaintance that he did not know where his wife was staying, curiosity began to be aroused; till, jumping to conclusions, people ventured to affirm that Sue had played him false and run away from him. The schoolmaster's growing languor and listlessness over his work gave countenance to the idea.

Though Phillotson had held his tongue as long as he could, except to his friend Gillingham, his honesty and directness would not allow him to do so when misapprehensions as to Sue's conduct spread abroad. On a Monday morning the chairman of the School Committee called, and after attending to the business of the school drew Phillotson aside out of earshot of the children.

'You'll excuse my asking, Phillotson, since everybody is talking of it: is this true as to your domestic affairs—that your wife's going away was on no visit, but a secret elopement with a lover? If so, I condole with you.'

'Don't,' said Phillotson. 'There was no secret about it.'

'She has gone to visit friends?'

'No.'

'Then what has happened?'

'She has gone away under circumstances that usually call for condolence with the husband. But I gave my consent.'

The chairman looked as if he had not apprehended the remark.

'What I say is quite true,' Phillotson continued testily. 'She asked leave to go away with her lover, and I let her. Why shouldn't I? A woman of full age, it was a question for her own conscience—not for me. I was not her gaoler. I can't explain any further. I don't wish to be questioned.'

The children observed that much seriousness marked the faces of the two men, and went home and told their parents that something new had happened about Mrs. Phillotson. Then Phillotson's little maid-servant, who was a schoolgirl just out of her standards, said that Mr. Phillotson had helped in his wife's packing, had offered her what money she required, and had written a friendly letter to her young man, telling him to take care of her. The chairman of committee thought the matter over, and talked to the other managers of the school, till a request came to Phillotson to meet them privately. The meeting lasted a long time, and at the end the schoolmaster came home, looking as usual pale and worn. Gillingham was sitting in his house awaiting him.

---

1. Teacher's assistant (strictly, a senior student).

'Well, it is as you said,' observed Phillotson, flinging himself down wearily in a chair. 'They have requested me to send in my resignation on account of my scandalous conduct in giving my tortured wife her liberty—or, as they call it, condoning her adultery. But I shan't resign!'

'I think I would.'

'I won't. It is no business of theirs. It doesn't affect me in my public capacity at all. They may expel me if they like.'

'If you make a fuss it will get into the papers, and you'll never get appointed to another school. You see, they have to consider what you did as done by a teacher of youth—and its effects as such upon the morals of the town; and, to ordinary opinion, your position is indefensible. You must let me say that.'

To this good advice, however, Phillotson would not listen.

'I don't care,' he said. 'I don't go unless I am turned out. And for this reason; that by resigning I acknowledge I have acted wrongly by her; when I am more and more convinced every day that in the sight of Heaven and by all natural, straightforward humanity, I have acted rightly.'

Gillingham saw that his rather headstrong friend would not be able to maintain such a position as this; but he said nothing further, and in due time—indeed, in a quarter of an hour—the formal letter of dismissal arrived, the managers having remained behind to write it after Phillotson's withdrawal. The latter replied that he should not accept dismissal; and called a public meeting, which he attended, although he looked so weak and ill that his friend implored him to stay at home. When he stood up to give his reasons for contesting the decision of the managers he advanced them firmly, as he had done to his friend, and contended, moreover, that the matter was a domestic theory which did not concern them. This they overruled, insisting that the private eccentricities of a teacher came quite within their sphere of control, as it touched the morals of those he taught. Phillotson replied that he did not see how an act of natural charity could injure morals.

All the respectable inhabitants and well-to-do fellow-natives of the town were against Phillotson to a man. But, somewhat to his surprise, some dozen or more champions rose up in his defence as from the ground.

It has been stated that Shaston was the anchorage of a curious and interesting group of itinerants, who frequented the numerous fairs and markets held up and down Wessex during the summer and autumn months. Although Phillotson had never spoken to one of these gentlemen they now nobly led the forlorn hope in his defence. The body included two cheap-jacks,[2] a shooting-gallery proprietor and the lad-

2. Traveling hawkers who claimed to offer great bargains.

ies who loaded the guns, a pair of boxing-masters, a steam-round-about manager, two travelling broom-makers, who called themselves widows, a gingerbread-stall keeper, a swing-boat owner, and a 'test-your strength' man.

This generous phalanx of supporters, and a few others of independent judgment, whose own domestic experiences had been not without vicissitude, came up and warmly shook hands with Phillotson; after which they expressed their thoughts so strongly to the meeting that issue was joined, the result being a general scuffle, wherein a black-board was split, three panes of the school-windows were broken, an inkbottle was spilled over a town-councillor's shirtfront, a church-warden was dealt such a topper with the map of Palestine that his head went right through Samaria, and many black eyes and bleeding noses were given, one of which, to everybody's horror, was the venerable incumbent's, owing to the zeal of an emancipated chimney-sweep, who took the side of Phillotson's party. When Phillotson saw the blood running down the rector's face he deplored almost in groans the unto-ward and degrading circumstances, regretted that he had not resigned when called upon, and went home so ill that next morning he could not leave his bed.

The farcical yet melancholy event was the beginning of a serious illness for him; and he lay in his lonely bed in the pathetic state of mind of a middle-aged man who perceives at length that his life, intel-lectual and domestic, is tending to failure and gloom. Gillingham came to see him in the evenings, and on one occasion mentioned Sue's name.

'She doesn't care anything about me!' said Phillotson. 'Why should she?'

'She doesn't know you are ill.'

'So much the better for both of us.'

'Where are her lover and she living?'

'At Melchester—I suppose; at least he was living there some time ago.'

When Gillingham reached home he sat and reflected, and at last wrote an anonymous line to Sue, on the bare chance of its reaching her, the letter being enclosed in an envelope addressed to Jude at the diocesan capital. Arriving at that place it was forwarded to Marygreen in North Wessex, and thence to Aldbrickham by the only person who knew his present address—the widow who had nursed his aunt.

Three days later, in the evening, when the sun was going down in splendour over the lowlands of Blackmoor, and making the Shaston windows like tongues of fire to the eyes of the rustics in that Vale, the sick man fancied that he heard somebody come to the house, and a few minutes after there was a tap at the bedroom door. Phillotson did not speak; the door was hesitatingly opened, and there entered—Sue.

She was in light spring clothing, and her advent seemed ghostly—like the flitting in of a moth. He turned his eyes upon her, and flushed; but appeared to check his primary impulse to speak.

'I have no business here,' she said, bending her frightened face to him. 'But I heard you were ill—very ill; and—and as I know that you recognize other feelings between man and woman than physical love, I have come.'

'I am not very ill, my dear friend. Only unwell.'

'I didn't know that; and I am afraid that only a severe illness would have justified my coming!'

'Yes . . . yes. And I almost wish you had not come! It is a little too soon—that's all I mean. Still, let us make the best of it. You haven't heard about the school, I suppose?'

'No—what about it?'

'Only that I am going away from here to another place. The managers and I don't agree, and we are going to part—that's all.'

Sue did not for a moment, either now or later, suspect what troubles had resulted to him from letting her go; it never once seemed to cross her mind, and she had received no news whatever from Shaston. They talked on slight and ephemeral subjects and when his tea was brought up he told the amazed little servant that a cup was to be set for Sue. That young person was much more interested in their history than they supposed, and as she descended the stairs she lifted her eyes and hands in grotesque amazement. While they sipped Sue went to the window and thoughtfully said, 'It is such a beautiful sunset, Richard.'

'They are mostly beautiful from here, owing to the rays crossing the mist of the Vale. But I lose them all, as they don't shine into this gloomy corner where I lie.'

'Wouldn't you like to see this particular one? It is like heaven opened.'

'Ah yes! But I can't.'

'I'll help you to.'

'No—the bedstead can't be shifted.'

'But see how I mean.'

She went to where a swing-glass[3] stood, and taking it in her hands carried it to a spot by the window where it could catch the sunshine, moving the glass till the beams were reflected into Phillotson's face.

'There—you can see the great red sun now!' she said. 'And I am sure it will cheer you—I do so hope it will!' She spoke with a childlike, repentant kindness, as if she could not do much for him.

---

3. Mirror mounted on a stand so that its angle can be adjusted. Hardy noted in his diary on March 22, 1881, during a long illness, that a friend "conceived the kind idea of reflecting the sun into my face by a looking-glass" so that he could watch a gorgeous sunset; the *Life* (p. 148) quotes this diary entry and notes that the incident was used in *Jude the Obscure*.

Phillotson smiled sadly. 'You are an odd creature!' he murmured as the sun glowed in his eyes. 'The idea of your coming to see me after what has passed!'

'Don't let us go back upon that!' she said quickly. 'I have to catch the omnibus for the train, as Jude doesn't know I have come; he was out when I started; so I must return home almost directly. Richard, I am so very glad you are better. You don't hate me, do you? You have been such a kind friend to me!'

'I am glad to know you think so,' said Phillotson huskily. 'No. I don't hate you!'

It grew dusk quickly in the gloomy room during their intermittent chat, and when candles were brought and it was time to leave she put her hand in his—or rather allowed it to flit through his; for she was significantly light in touch. She had nearly closed the door when he said, 'Sue!' He had noticed that, in turning away from him, tears were on her face and a quiver in her lip.

It was bad policy to recall her—he knew it while he pursued it. But he could not help it. She came back.

'Sue,' he murmured, 'do you wish to make it up, and stay? I'll forgive you and condone everything!'

'O you can't, you can't!' she said hastily. 'You can't condone it now!'

'*He* is your husband now, in effect, you mean, of course?'

'You may assume it. He is obtaining a divorce from his wife Arabella.'

'His wife! It is altogether news to me that he has a wife.'

'It was a bad marriage.'

'Like yours.'

'Like mine. He is not doing it so much on his own account as on hers. She wrote and told him it would be a kindness to her, since then she could marry and live respectably. And Jude has agreed.'

'A wife. . . . A kindness to her. Ah, yes; a kindness to her to release her altogether. . . . But I don't like the sound of it. *I* can forgive, Sue.'

'No, no! You can't have me back now I have been so wicked—as to do what I have done!'

There had arisen in Sue's face that incipient fright which showed itself whenever he changed from friend to husband, and which made her adopt any line of defence against marital feeling in him. 'I *must* go now. I'll come again—may I?'

'I don't ask you to go, even now. I ask you to stay.'

'I thank you, Richard; but I must. As you are not so ill as I thought, I *cannot* stay!'

'She's his—his from lips to heel!' said Phillotson; but so faintly that in closing the door she did not hear it. The dread of a reactionary change in the schoolmaster's sentiments, coupled, perhaps, with a faint shamefacedness at letting even him know what a slipshod lack of thoroughness, from a man's point of view, characterized her transferred allegiance, prevented her telling him of her, thus far, incomplete relations with Jude; and Phillotson lay writhing like a man in hell as he pictured the prettily dressed, maddening compound of sympathy and averseness who bore his name, returning impatiently to the home of her lover.

Gillingham was so interested in Phillotson's affairs, and so seriously concerned about him, that he walked up the hillside to Shaston two or three times a week, although, there and back, it was a journey of nine miles, which had to be performed between tea and supper, after a hard day's work in school. When he called on the next occasion after Sue's visit his friend was downstairs, and Gillingham noticed that his restless mood had been supplanted by a more fixed and composed one.

'She's been here since you called last,' said Phillotson.

'Not Mrs. Phillotson?'

'Yes.'

'Ah! You have made it up?'

'No. . . . She just came, patted my pillow with her little white hand, played the thoughtful nurse for half-an-hour, and went away.'

'Well—I'm hanged! A little hussy!'

'What do you say?'

'O—nothing!'

'What do you mean?'

'I mean, what a tantalizing, capricious little woman! If she were not your wife—'

'She is not; she's another man's except in name and law. And I have been thinking—it was suggested to me by a conversation I had with her—that, in kindness to her, I ought to dissolve the legal tie altogether; which, singularly enough, I think I can do, now she has been back, and refused my request to stay after I said I had forgiven her. I believe that fact would afford me opportunity of doing it, though I did not see it at the moment. What's the use of keeping her chained on to me if she doesn't belong to me? I know—I feel absolutely certain—that she would welcome my taking such a step as the greatest charity to her. For though as a fellow-creature she sympathizes with, and pities me, and even weeps for me, as a husband she cannot endure me—she loathes me—there's no use in mincing words—she loathes me, and my only manly, and dignified, and merciful course is to complete what I have begun. . . . And for worldly reasons, too, it will be better for her to be independent. I have hopelessly ruined my prospects because of my decision as to what was best for us, though she does not know it; I see only dire poverty ahead from my feet to the grave; for I can be accepted as teacher no more. I shall probably have enough to do to make both ends meet during the remainder of my life, now my occupation's gone;[4] and I shall be better able to bear it alone. I may as well tell you that what has suggested my letting her go is some news she brought me—the news that Fawley is doing the same.'

'O—he had a spouse too? A queer couple, these lovers!'

'Well—I don't want your opinion on that. What I was going to say is that my liberating her can do her no possible harm, and will open up a chance of happiness for her which she has never dreamt of hitherto. For then they'll be able to marry, as they ought to have done at first.'

Gillingham did not hurry to reply. 'I may disagree with your motive,' he said gently, for he respected views he could not share. 'But I think you are right in your determination—if you can carry it out. I doubt, however, if you can.'

Part Fifth: At Aldbrickham[1] and Elsewhere

'Thy aerial part, and all the fiery parts which are mingled in thee, though by nature they have an upward tendency, still in obedience to the disposition of the universe they are overpowered here in the compound mass the body.'

M. ANTONINUS (LONG)[2]

V–1

How Gillingham's doubts were disposed of will most quickly appear by passing over the series of dreary months and incidents that followed the events of the last chapter, and coming on to a Sunday in the February of the year following.

Sue and Jude were living in Aldbrickham, in precisely the same relations that they had established between themselves when she left Shaston to join him the year before. The proceedings in the Law-Courts had reached their consciousness but as a distant sound, and an occasional missive which they hardly understood.

They had met, as usual, to breakfast together in the little house with Jude's name on it, that he had taken at fifteen pounds a year, with three-pounds-ten extra for rates and taxes, and furnished with his aunt's ancient and lumbering goods, which had cost him about their full value to bring all the way from Marygreen. Sue kept house, and managed everything.

4. "Othello's occupation's gone!" (*Othello* 3.3.358).
1. Based on the Berkshire industrial town of Reading.
2. From Long's translation (1862) of the *Meditations* of Marcus Aurelius Antoninus (121–180), Roman emperor and philosopher.

As he entered the room this morning Sue held up a letter she had just received.

'Well; and what is it about?' he said after kissing her.

'That the decree *nisi* in the case of Phillotson *versus* Phillotson and Fawley, pronounced six months ago, has just been made absolute.'[3]

'Ah,' said Jude, as he sat down.

The same concluding incident in Jude's suit against Arabella had occurred about a month or two earlier. Both cases had been too insignificant to be reported in the papers, further than by name in a long list of other undefended cases.

'Now then, Sue, at any rate, you can do what you like!' He looked at his sweetheart curiously.

'Are we—you and I—just as free now as if we had never married at all?'

'Just as free—except, I believe, that a clergyman may object personally to re-marry you, and hand the job on to somebody else.'

'But I wonder—do you think it is really so with us? I know it is generally. But I have an uncomfortable feeling that my freedom has been obtained under false pretences!'

'How?'

'Well—if the truth about us had been known, the decree wouldn't have been pronounced. It is only, is it, because we have made no defence, and have led them into a false supposition? Therefore is my freedom lawful, however proper it may be?'

'Well—why did you let it be under false pretences? You have only yourself to blame,' he said mischievously.

'Jude—don't! You ought not to be touchy about that still. You must take me as I am.'

'Very well, darling: so I will. Perhaps you were right. As to your question, we were not obliged to prove anything. That was their business. Anyhow we are living together.'

'Yes. Though not in their sense.'

'One thing is certain, that however the decree may be brought about, a marriage is dissolved when it is dissolved. There is this advantage in being poor obscure people like us—that these things are done for us in a rough and ready fashion. It was the same with me and Arabella. I was afraid her criminal second marriage would have been discovered, and she punished; but nobody took any interest in her—nobody inquired, nobody suspected it. If we'd been patented nobilities we should have had infinite trouble, and days and weeks would have been spent in investigations.'

By degrees Sue acquired her lover's cheerfulness at the sense of freedom, and proposed that they should take a walk in the fields, even if

3. In English law, a court order for divorce is conditional for six months, after which it is made absolute or final, unless cause to the contrary be shown.

they had to put up with a cold dinner on account of it. Jude agreed, and Sue went upstairs and prepared to start, putting on a joyful coloured gown in observance of her liberty; seeing which Jude put on a lighter tie.

'Now we'll strut arm and arm,' he said, 'like any other engaged couple. We've a legal right to.'

They rambled out of the town, and along a path over the low-lying lands that bordered it, though these were frosty now, and the extensive, seed-fields were bare of colour and produce. The pair, however, were so absorbed in their own situation that their surroundings were little in their consciousness.

'Well, my dearest, the result of all this is that we can marry after a decent interval.'

'Yes; I suppose we can,' said Sue, without enthusiasm.

'And aren't we going to?'

'I don't like to say no, dear Jude; but I feel just the same about it now as I have done all along. I have just the same dread lest an iron contact should extinguish your tenderness for me, and mine for you, as it did between our unfortunate parents.'

'Still, what can we do? I do love you, as you know, Sue.'

'I know it abundantly. But I think I would much rather go on living always as lovers, as we are living now, and only meeting by day. It is so much sweeter—for the woman at least, and when she is sure of the man. And henceforward we needn't be so particular as we have been about appearances.'

'Our experiences of matrimony with others have not been encouraging, I own,' said he with some gloom; 'either owing to our own dissatisfied, unpractical natures, or by our misfortune. But we two—'

'Should be two dissatisfied ones linked together, which would be twice as bad as before. . . . I think I should begin to be afraid of you, Jude, the moment you had contracted to cherish me under a Government stamp, and I was licensed to be loved on the premises by you— Ugh, how horrible and sordid! Although, as you are, free, I trust you more than any other man in the world.'

'No, no—don't say I should change!' he expostulated; yet there was misgiving in his own voice also.

'Apart from ourselves, and our unhappy peculiarities, it is foreign to a man's nature to go on loving a person when he is told that he must and shall be that person's lover. There would be a much likelier chance of his doing it if he were told not to love. If the marriage ceremony consisted in an oath and signed contract between the parties to cease loving from that day forward, in consideration of personal possession being given, and to avoid each other's society as much as possible in public, there would be more loving couples than there are now. Fancy the secret meetings between the perjuring husband and wife, the denials of having seen each other, the clambering in at bedroom windows, and the hiding in closets! There'd be little cooling then.'

'Yes; but admitting this, or something like it, to be true, you are not the only one in the world to see it, dear little Sue. People go on marrying because they can't resist natural forces, although many of them may know perfectly well that they are possibly buying a month's pleasure with a life's discomfort. No doubt my father and mother, and your father and mother, saw it, if they at all resembled us in habits of observation. But then they went and married just the same, because they had ordinary passions. But you, Sue, are such a phantasmal, bodiless creature, one who—if you'll allow me to say it—has so little animal passion in you, that you can act upon reason in the matter, when we poor unfortunate wretches of grosser substance can't.'

'Well,' she sighed, 'you've owned that it would probably end in misery for us. And I am not so exceptional a woman as you think. Fewer women like marriage than you suppose, only they enter into it for the dignity it is assumed to confer, and the social advantages it gains them sometimes—a dignity and an advantage that I am quite willing to do without.'

Jude fell back upon his old complaint—that, intimate as they were, he had never once had from her an honest, candid declaration that she loved or could love him. 'I really fear sometimes that you cannot,' he said, with a dubiousness approaching anger. 'And you are so reticent. I know that women are taught by other women that they must never admit the full truth to a man. But the highest form of affection is based on full sincerity on both sides. Not being men, these women don't know that in looking back on those he has had tender relations with, a man's heart returns closest to her who was the soul of truth in her conduct. The better class of man, even if caught by airy affectations of dodging and parrying, is not retained by them. A Nemesis[4] attends the woman who plays the game of elusiveness too often, in the utter contempt for her that, sooner or later, her old admirers feel, under which they allow her to go unlamented to her grave.'

Sue, who was regarding the distance, had acquired a guilty look; and she suddenly replied in a tragic voice: 'I don't think I like you to-day so well as I did, Jude!'

'Don't you? Why?'

'O, well—you are not nice—too sermony. Though I suppose I am so bad and worthless that I deserve the utmost rigour of lecturing!'

'No, you are not bad. You are a dear. But as slippery as an eel when I want to get a confession from you.'

'O yes I am bad, and obstinate, and all sorts! It is no use your pre-

---

4. Ancient Greek goddess of retributive justice and punishment.

tending I am not! People who are good don't want scolding as I do.
. . . But now that I have nobody but you, and nobody to defend me, it
is *very* hard that I mustn't have my own way in deciding how I'll live
with you, and whether I'll be married or no!'

'Sue, my own comrade and sweetheart, I don't want to force you
either to marry or to do the other thing—of course I don't! It is too
wicked of you to be so pettish! Now we won't say any more about it,
and go on just the same as we have done; and during the rest of our
walk we'll talk of the meadows only, and the floods, and the prospect
of the farmers this coming year.'

After this the subject of marriage was not mentioned by them for
several days, though living as they were with only a landing between
them it was constantly in their minds. Sue was assisting Jude very
materially now: he had latterly occupied himself on his own account
in working and lettering headstones, which he kept in a little yard at
the back of his little house, where in the intervals of domestic duties
she marked out the letters full size for him, and blacked them in after
he had cut them. It was a lower class of handicraft than were his former
performances as a cathedral mason, and his only patrons were the poor
people who lived in his own neighbourhood, and knew what a cheap
man this 'Jude Fawley Monumental Mason' (as he called himself on
his front door) was to employ for the simple memorials they required
for their dead. But he seemed more independent than before, and it
was the only arrangement under which Sue, who particularly wished
to be no burden on him, could render any assistance.

V–2

It was an evening at the end of the month, and Jude had just
returned home from hearing a lecture on ancient history in the public
hall not far off. When he entered Sue, who had been keeping indoors
during his absence, laid out supper for him. Contrary to custom she
did not speak. Jude had taken up some illustrated paper, which he
perused till, raising his eyes, he saw that her face was troubled.

'Are you depressed, Sue?' he said.

She paused a moment. 'I have a message for you,' she answered.

'Somebody has called?'

'Yes. A woman.' Sue's voice quavered as she spoke, and she suddenly
sat down from her preparations, laid her hands in her lap, and looked
into the fire. 'I don't know whether I did right or not!' she continued.
'I said you were not at home, and when she said she would wait, I said
I thought you might not be able to see her.'

'Why did you say that, dear? I suppose she wanted a headstone. Was
she in mourning?'

'No. She wasn't in mourning, and she didn't want a headstone; and I thought you couldn't see her.' Sue looked critically and imploringly at him.

'But who was she? Didn't she say?'

'No. She wouldn't give her name. But I know who she was—I think I do! It was Arabella!'

'Heaven save us! What should Arabella come for? What made you think it was she?'

'O, I can hardly tell. But I know it was! I feel perfectly certain it was—by the light in her eyes as she looked at me. She was a fleshy, coarse woman.'

'Well—I should not have called Arabella coarse exactly, except in speech, though she may be getting so by this time under the duties of the public-house. She was rather handsome when I knew her.'

'Handsome! But yes!—so she is!'

'I think I heard a quiver in your little mouth. Well, waiving that, as she is nothing to me, and virtuously married to another man, why should she come troubling us?'

'Are you sure she's married? Have you definite news of it?'

'No—not definite news. But that was why she asked me to release her. She and the man both wanted to lead a proper life, as I understood.'

'O Jude—it was, it *was* Arabella!' cried Sue, covering her eyes with her hand. 'And I am so miserable! It seems such an ill-omen, whatever she may have come for. You could not possibly see her, could you?'

'I don't really think I could. It would be so very painful to talk to her now—for her as much as for me. However, she's gone. Did she say she would come again?'

'No. But she went away very reluctantly.'

Sue, whom the least thing upset, could not eat any supper, and when Jude had finished his he prepared to go to bed. He had no sooner raked out the fire, fastened the doors, and got to the top of the stairs than there came a knock. Sue instantly emerged from her room, which she had but just entered.

'There she is again!' Sue whispered in appalled accents.

'How do you know?

'She knocked like that last time.'

They listened, and the knocking came again. No servant was kept in the house, and if the summons were to be responded to one of them would have to do it in person. 'I'll open a window,' said Jude. 'Whoever it is cannot be expected to be let in at this time.'

He accordingly went into his bedroom and lifted the sash. The lonely street of early retiring work-people was empty from end to end save of one figure—that of a woman walking up and down by the lamp a few yards off.

'Who's there?' he asked.

'Is that Mr. Fawley?' came up from the woman, in a voice which was unmistakably Arabella's.

Jude replied that it was.

'Is it she?' asked Sue from the door, with lips apart.

'Yes, dear,' said Jude. 'What do you want, Arabella?' he inquired.

'I beg your pardon, Jude, for disturbing you,' said Arabella humbly. 'But I called earlier—I wanted particularly to see you tonight, if I could. I am in trouble, and have nobody to help me!'

'In trouble, are you?'

'Yes.'

There was a silence. An inconvenient sympathy seemed to be rising in Jude's breast at the appeal. 'But aren't you married?' he said.

Arabella hesitated. 'No, Jude, I am not,' she returned. 'He wouldn't, after all. And I am in great difficulty. I hope to get another situation as barmaid soon. But it takes time, and I really am in great distress, because of a sudden responsibility that's been sprung upon me from Australia; or I wouldn't trouble you—believe me I wouldn't. I want to tell you about it.'

Sue remained at gaze, in painful tension, hearing every word, but speaking none.

'You are not really in want of money, Arabella?' he asked, in a distinctly softened tone.

'I have enough to pay for the night's lodging I have obtained, but barely enough to take me back again.'

'Where are you living?'

'In London still.' She was about to give the address, but she said, 'I am afraid somebody may hear, so I don't like to call out particulars of myself so loud. If you could come down and walk a little way with me towards the Prince Inn, where I am staying to-night, I would explain all. You may as well, for old time's sake!'

'Poor thing!—I must do her the kindness of hearing what's the matter, I suppose,' said Jude in much perplexity. 'As she's going back to-morrow it can't make much difference.'

'But you can go and see her to-morrow, Jude! Don't go now, Jude!' came in plaintive accents from the doorway. 'O, it is only to entrap you, I know it is, as she did before! Don't, don't go, dear! She is such a low-passioned woman—I can see it in her shape, and hear it in her voice!'

'But I shall go,' said Jude. 'Don't attempt to detain me, Sue. God knows I love her little enough now, but I don't want to be cruel to her.' He turned to the stairs.

'But she's not your wife!' cried Sue distractedly. 'And I—'

'And you are not either, dear, yet,' said Jude.

'O, but are you going to her? Don't! Stay at home! Please, please stay at home, Jude, and not go to her, now she's not your wife any more than I!'

'Well, she is, rather more than you, come to that,' he said, taking his hat determinedly. 'I've wanted you to be, and I've waited with the patience of Job, and I don't see that I've got anything by my self-denial. I shall certainly give her something, and hear what it is she is so anxious to tell me; no man could do less!'

There was that in his manner which she knew it would be futile to oppose. She said no more, but, turning to her room as meekly as a martyr, heard him go downstairs, unbolt the door, and close it behind him. With a woman's disregard of her dignity when in the presence of nobody but herself, she also trotted down, sobbing articulately as she went. She listened. She knew exactly how far it was to the inn that Arabella had named as her lodging. It would occupy about seven minutes to get there at an ordinary walking pace; seven to come back again. If he did not return in fourteen minutes he would have lingered. She looked at the clock. It was twenty-five minutes to eleven. He *might* enter the inn with Arabella, as they would reach it before closing time; she might get him to drink with her; and Heaven only knew what disasters would befall him then.

In a still suspense she waited on. It seemed as if the whole time had nearly elapsed when the door was opened again, and Jude appeared.

Sue gave a little ecstatic cry. 'O, I knew I could trust you!—how good you are!'—she began.

'I can't find her anywhere in this street, and I went out in my slippers only. She has walked on, thinking I've been so hard-hearted as to refuse her requests entirely, poor woman. I've come back for my boots, as it is beginning to rain.'

'O, but why should you take such trouble for a woman who has served you so badly!' said Sue in a jealous burst of disappointment.

'But, Sue, she's a woman, and I once cared for her; and one can't be a brute in such circumstances.'

'She isn't your wife any longer!' exclaimed Sue, passionately excited. 'You *mustn't* go out to find her! It isn't right! You _can't_ join her, now she's a stranger to you. How can you forget such a thing, my dear, dear one!'

'She seems much the same as ever—an erring, careless, unreflecting fellow-creature,' he said, continuing to pull on his boots. 'What those legal fellows have been playing at in London makes no difference in my real relations to her. If she was my wife while she was away in Australia with another husband she's my wife now.'

'But she wasn't! That's just what I hold! There's the absurdity! —Well—you'll come straight back, after a few minutes, won't you, dear? She is too low, <u>too coarse for you to</u> talk to long, Jude, and was always!'

'Perhaps I <u>am coarse too</u>, worse luck! I have the germs of every human infirmity in me, I verily believe—that was why I saw it was so preposterous of me to think of being a curate. I have cured myself of drunkenness I think; but I never know in what new form a suppressed vice will break out in me! I do love you, Sue, though I have danced attendance on you so long for such poor returns! All that's best and noblest in me loves you, and your freedom from everything that's gross has elevated me, and enabled me to do what I should never have dreamt myself capable of, or any man, a year or two ago. It is all very well to preach about self-control, and the wickedness of coercing a woman. But I should just like a few virtuous people who have con-demned me in the past, about Arabella and other things, to have been in my tantalizing position with you through these late weeks!—they'd believe, I think, that I have exercised some little restraint in always giving in to your wishes—living here in one house, and not a soul between us.'

'Yes, you have been good to me, Jude; I know you have, my dear protector.'

'Well—Arabella has appealed to me for help. I must go out and speak to her, Sue, at least!'

'I can't say any more!—O, if you must, you must!' she said, bursting out into sobs that seemed to tear her heart. 'I have nobody but you, Jude, and you are deserting me! I didn't know you were like this—I can't bear it, I can't! If she were yours it would be different!'

'Or if you were.'

'Very well then—if I must I must. Since you will have it so, I agree! I will be. Only I didn't mean to! And I didn't want to marry again, either! . . . But, yes—I agree, I agree! I do love you. I ought to have known that you would conquer in the long run, living like this!'

She ran across and flung her arms round his neck. 'I am not a cold-natured, sexless creature, am I, for keeping you at such a distance? I am sure you don't think so! Wait and see! I do belong to you, don't I? I give in!'

'And I'll arrange for our marriage to-morrow, or as soon as ever you wish.'

'Yes, Jude.'

'Then I'll let her go,' said he, embracing Sue softly. 'I do feel that it would be unfair to you to see her, and perhaps unfair to her. She is not like you, my darling, and never was: it is only bare justice to say that. Don't cry any more. There; and there; and there!' He kissed her on one side, and on the other, and in the middle, and rebolted the front door.

The next morning it was wet.

'Now, dear,' said Jude gaily at breakfast; 'as this is Saturday I mean to call about the banns at once, so as to get the first publishing done to-morrow, or we shall lose a week. Banns will do? We shall save a pound or two.'

Sue absently agreed to banns. But her mind for the moment was running on something else. A glow had passed away from her, and depression sat upon her features.

'I feel I was wickedly selfish last night!' she murmured. 'It was sheer unkindness in me—or worse—to treat Arabella as I did. I didn't care about her being in trouble, and what she wished to tell you! Perhaps it was really something she was justified in telling you. That's some more of my badness, I suppose! Love has its own dark morality when rivalry enters in—at least, mine has, if other people's hasn't. . . . I wonder how she got on? I hope she reached the inn all right, poor woman.'

'O yes: she got on all right,' said Jude placidly.

'I hope she wasn't shut out, and that she hadn't to walk the streets in the rain. Do you mind my putting on my waterproof and going to see if she got in? I've been thinking of her all the morning.'

'Well—is it necessary? You haven't the least idea how Arabella is able to shift for herself. Still, darling, if you want to go and inquire you can.'

There was no limit to the strange and unnecessary penances which Sue would meekly undertake when in a contrite mood; and this going to see all sorts of extraordinary persons whose relation to her was precisely of a kind that would have made other people shun them, was her instinct ever, so that the request did not surprise him.

'And when you comeback,' he added, 'I'll be ready to go about the banns. You'll come with me?'

Sue agreed, and went off under cloak and umbrella, letting Jude kiss her freely, and returning his kisses in a way she had never done before. Times had decidedly changed. 'The little bird is caught at last!' she said, a sadness showing in her smile.

'No—only nested,' he assured her.

She walked along the muddy streets till she reached the publichouse mentioned by Arabella, which was not so very far off. She was informed that Arabella had not yet left, and in doubt how to announce herself so that her predecessor in Jude's affections would recognize her, she sent up word that a friend from Spring Street had called, naming the place of Jude's residence. She was asked to step upstairs, and on being shown into a room found that it was Arabella's bedroom, and that the latter had not yet risen. She halted on the turn of her toe till Arabella cried from the bed, 'Come in and shut the door,' which Sue accordingly did.

Arabella lay facing the window, and did not at once turn her head: and Sue was wicked enough, despite her penitence, to wish for a moment that Jude could behold her forerunner now, with the daylight full upon her. She may have seemed handsome enough in profile under the lamps, but a frowsiness was apparent this morning; and the sight of her own fresh charms in the looking-glass made Sue's manner bright, till she reflected what a meanly sexual emotion this was in her, and hated herself for it.

'I've just looked in to see if you got back comfortably last night, that's all,' she said gently. 'I was afraid afterwards that you might have met with any mishap?'

'O—how stupid this is! I thought my visitor was—your friend—your husband—Mrs. Fawley, as I suppose you call yourself?' said Arabella, flinging her head back upon the pillows with a disappointed toss, and ceasing to retain the dimple she had just taken the trouble to produce.

'Indeed I don't,' said Sue.

'O, I thought you might have, even if he's not really yours. Decency is decency, any hour of the twenty-four.'

'I don't know what you mean,' said Sue stiffly. 'He is mine, if you come to that!'

'He wasn't yesterday.'

Sue coloured roseate, and said 'How do you know?'

'From your manner when you talked to me at the door. Well, my dear, you've been quick about it, and I expect my visit last night helped it on—ha-ha! But I don't want to get him away from you.'

Sue looked out at the rain, and at the dirty toilet-cover, and at the detached tail of Arabella's hair hanging on the looking-glass, just as it had done in Jude's time; and wished she had not come. In the pause there was a knock at the door, and the chambermaid brought in a telegram for 'Mrs. Cartlett.'

Arabella opened it as she lay, and her ruffled look disappeared.

'I am much obliged to you for your anxiety about me,' she said blandly when the maid had gone; 'but it is not necessary you should feel it. My man finds he can't do without me after all, and agrees to stand by the promise to marry again over here that he has made me all along. See here! This is in answer to one from me.' She held out the telegram for Sue to read, but Sue did not take it. 'He asks me to come back. His little corner public in Lambeth would go to pieces without me, he says. But he isn't going to knock me about when he has had a drop, any more after we are spliced[1] by English law than before! . . . As for you, I should coax Jude to take me before the parson straight off, and have done with it, if I were in your place. I say it as a friend, my dear.'

1. Married (slang).

'He's waiting to, any day,' returned Sue, with frigid pride.

'Then let him, in Heaven's name. Life with a man is more business-like after it, and money matters work better. And then, you see, if you have rows, and he turns you out of doors, you can get the law to protect you, which you can't otherwise, unless he half runs you through with a knife, or cracks your noddle[2] with a poker. And if he bolts away from you—I say it friendly, as woman to woman, for there's never any know-ing what a man med do—you'll have the sticks o' furniture, and won't be looked upon as a thief. I shall marry my man over again, now he's willing, as there was a little flaw in the first ceremony. In my telegram last night which this is an answer to, I told him I had almost made it up with Jude; and that frightened him, I expect! Perhaps I should quite have done it if it hadn't been for you,' she said laughing; 'and then how different our histories might have been from to-day! Never such a tender fool as Jude is if a woman seems in trouble, and coaxes him a bit! Just as he used to be about birds and things. However, as it happens, it is just as well as if I had made it up, and I forgive you. And, as I say, I'll advise you to get the business legally done as soon as possible. You'll find it an awful bother later on if you don't.'

'I have told you he is asking me to marry him—to make our natural marriage a legal one,' said Sue, with yet more dignity. 'It was quite by my wish that he didn't the moment I was free.'

'Ah, yes—you are a oneyer[3] too, like myself,' said Arabella, eyeing her visitor with humorous criticism. 'Bolted from your first, didn't you, like me?'

'Good morning!—I must go,' said Sue hastily.

'And I, too, must up and off!' replied the other, springing out of bed so suddenly that the soft parts of her person shook. Sue jumped aside in trepidation. 'Lord, I am only a woman—not a six-foot sojer![4] . . . Just a moment dear,' she continued, putting her hand on Sue's arm. 'I really did want to consult Jude on a little matter of business, as I told him. I came about that more than anything else. Would he run up to speak to me at the station as I am going? You think not. Well, I'll write to him about it. I didn't want to write it, but never mind—I will.'

V–3

When Sue reached home Jude was awaiting her at the door to take the initial step towards their marriage. She clasped his arm, and they went along silently together, as true comrad ofttimes do. He saw that she was preoccupied, and forbore to question her.

2. Head (slang).
3. Meaning obscure: perhaps "without a husband," or "individualist."
4. Soldier.

'O Jude—I've been talking to her,' she said at last. 'I wish I hadn't! And yet it is best to be reminded of things.'

'I hope she was civil.'

'Yes. I—I can't help liking her—just a little bit! She's not an ungenerous nature; and I am so glad her difficulties have all suddenly ended.' She explained how Arabella had been summoned back, and would be enabled to retrieve her position. 'I was referring to our old question. What Arabella has been saying to me has made me feel more than ever how hopelessly vulgar an institution legal marriage is—a sort of trap to catch a man—I can't bear to think of it. I wish I hadn't promised to let you put up the banns this morning!'

'O, don't mind me. Any time will do for me. I thought you might like to get it over quickly, now.'

'Indeed, I don't feel any more anxious now than I did before. Perhaps with any other man I might be a little anxious; but among the very few virtues possessed by your family and mine, dear, I think I may set staunchness. So I am not a bit frightened about losing you, now I really am yours and you really are mine. In fact, I am easier in my mind than I was, for my conscience is clear about Richard, who now has a right to his freedom. I felt we were deceiving him before.'

'Sue, you seem when you are like this to be one of the women of some grand old civilization, whom I used to read about in my bygone, wasted, classical days, rather than a denizen of a mere Christian country. I almost expect you to say at these times that you have just been talking to some friend whom you met in the Via Sacra,[1] about the latest news of Octavia[2] or Livia[3]; or have been listening to Aspasia's[4] eloquence, or have been watching Praxiteles[5] chiselling away at his latest Venus, while Phryne[6] made complaint that she was tired of posing.'

They had now reached the house of the parish-clerk. Sue stood back, while her lover went up to the door. His hand was raised to knock when she said: 'Jude!'

He looked round.

'Wait a minute, would you mind?'

He came back to her.

'Just let us think,' she said timidly. 'I had such a horrid dream one night! . . . And Arabella—'

'What did Arabella say to you?' he asked.

'O, she said that when people were tied up you could get the law of a man better if he beat you—and how when couples quarrelled. . . . Jude, do you think that when you *must* have me with you by law, we

1. Road in ancient Rome.
2. Sister of the Emperor Augustus and wife of Mark Antony.
3. Wife of Augustus.
4. Mistress of Pericles and celebrated as an intellectual.
5. Greek sculptor.
6. Model for Praxiteles' famous statue, the Aphrodite of Cnidus.

shall be so happy as we are now? The men and women of our family are very generous when everything depends upon their good-will, but they always kick against compulsion. Don't you dread the attitude that insensibly arises out of legal obligation? Don't you think it is destructive to a passion whose essence is its gratuitousness?'

'Upon my word, love, you are beginning to frighten me, too, with all this foreboding! Well, let's go back and think it over.'

Her face brightened. 'Yes—so we will!' said she. And they turned from the clerk's door, Sue taking his arm and murmuring as they walked on homeward:

> "Can you keep the bee from ranging,
> Or the ring-dove's neck from changing?
> No! Nor fetter'd love . . ."[7]

They thought it over, or postponed thinking. Certainly they postponed action, and seemed to live on in a dreamy paradise. At the end of a fortnight or three weeks matters remained unadvanced, and no banns were announced to the ears of any Aldbrickham congregation.

Whilst they were postponing and postponing thus a letter and a newspaper arrived before breakfast one morning from Arabella. Seeing the handwriting Jude went up to Sue's room and told her, and as soon as she was dressed she hastened down. Sue opened the newspaper; Jude the letter. After glancing at the paper she held across the first page to him with her finger on a paragraph; but he was so absorbed in his letter that he did not turn awhile.

'Look!' said she.

He looked and read. The paper was one that circulated in South London only, and the marked advertisement was simply the announcement of a marriage at St. John's Church, Waterloo Road, under the names, 'CARTLETT-DONN'; the united pair being Arabella and the innkeeper.

'Well, it is satisfactory,' said Sue complacently. 'Though, after this, it seems rather low to do likewise, and I am glad—However, she is provided for now in a way, I suppose, whatever her faults, poor thing. It is nicer that we are able to think that, than to be uneasy about her. I ought, too, to write to Richard and ask him how he is getting on, perhaps?'

But Jude's attention was still absorbed. Having merely glanced at the announcement he said in a disturbed voice: 'Listen to this letter. What shall I say or do?

> "THE THREE HORNS, LAMBETH.
> "DEAR JUDE (I won't be so distant as to call you Mr. Fawley),—I send to-day a newspaper, from which useful document you will

---

7. From "Song" by Thomas Campbell (1777–1844).

learn that I was married over again to Cartlett last Tuesday. So that business is settled right and tight at last. But what I write about more particular is that private affair I wanted to speak to you on when I came down to Aldbrickham. I couldn't very well tell it to your lady friend, and should much have liked to let you know it by word of mouth, as I could have explained better than by letter. The fact is, Jude, that, though I have never informed you before, there was a boy born of our marriage, eight months after I left you, when I was at Sydney, living with my father and mother. All that is easily provable. As I had separated from you before I thought such a thing was going to happen, and I was over there, and our quarrel had been sharp, I did not think it convenient to write about the birth. I was then looking out for a good situation, so my parents took the child, and he has been with them ever since. That was why I did not mention it when I met you in Christminster, nor at the law proceedings. He is now of an intelligent age, of course, and my mother and father have lately written to say that, as they have rather a hard struggle over there, and I am settled comfortably here, they don't see why they should be encumbered with the child any longer, his parents being alive. I would have him with me here in a moment, but he is not old enough to be of any use in the bar, nor will be for years and years, and naturally Cartlett might think him in the way. They have, however, packed him off to me in charge of some friends who happened to be coming home, and I must ask you to take him when he arrives, for I don't know what to do with him. He is lawfully yours, that I solemnly swear. If anybody says he isn't, call them brimstone liars, for my sake. Whatever I may have done before or afterwards, I was honest to you from the time we were married till I went away, and I remain yours, &c.,

                                               ARABELLA CARTLETT." '

Sue's look was one of dismay. 'What will you do, dear?' she asked faintly.

Jude did not reply, and Sue watched him anxiously, with heavy breaths.

'It hits me hard!' said he in an under-voice. 'It *may* be true! I can't make it out. Certainly, if his birth was exactly when she says, he's mine. I cannot think why she didn't tell me when I met her at Christminster, and came on here that evening with her! . . . Ah—I do remember now that she said something about having a thing on her mind that she would like me to know, if ever we lived together again.'

'The poor child seems to be wanted by nobody!' Sue replied, and her eyes filled.

Jude had by this time come to himself. 'What a view of life he must have, mine or not mine!' he said. 'I must say that, if I were better off,

I should not stop for a moment to think whose he might be. I would take him and bring him up. The beggarly question of parentage—what is it, after all? What does it matter, when you come to think of it, whether a child is yours by blood or not? All the little ones of our time are collectively the children of us adults of the time, and entitled to our general care. That excessive regard of parents for their own children, and their dislike of other people's, is, like class-feeling, patriotism, save-your-own-soul-ism, and other virtues, a mean exclusiveness at bottom.'

Sue jumped up and kissed Jude with passionate devotion. 'Yes—so it is, dearest! And we'll have him here! And if he isn't yours it makes it all the better. I do hope he isn't—though perhaps I ought not to feel quite that! If he isn't, I should like so much for us to have him as an adopted child!'

'Well, you must assume about him what is most pleasing to you, my curious little comrade!' he said. 'I feel that, anyhow, I don't like to leave the unfortunate little fellow to neglect. Just think of his life in a Lambeth pothouse,[8] and all its evil influences, with a parent who doesn't want him, and has, indeed, hardly seen him, and a stepfather who doesn't know him. "Let the day perish wherein I was born, and the night in which it was said, There is a man child conceived!"[9] That's what the boy—*my* boy, perhaps, will find himself saying before long!'

'O no!'

'As I was the petitioner, I am really entitled to his custody, I suppose.'

'Whether or no, we must have him. I see that. I'll do the best I can to be a mother to him, and we can afford to keep him somehow. I'll work harder. I wonder when he'll arrive?"

'In the course of a few weeks, I suppose.'

'I wish—When shall we have courage to marry, Jude?'

'Whenever you have it, I think I shall. It remains with you entirely, dear. Only say the word, and it's done.'

'Before the boy comes?'

'Certainly.'

'It would make a more natural home for him, perhaps,' she murmured.

Jude thereupon wrote in purely formal terms to request that the boy should be sent on to them as soon as he arrived, making no remark whatever on the surprising nature of Arabella's information, nor vouchsafing a single word of opinion on the boy's paternity, nor on whether, had he known all this, his conduct towards her would have been quite the same.

8. Low-class public house.
9. Job 3.3.

In the down train that was timed to reach Aldbrickham station about
ten o'clock the next evening, a small, pale child's face could be seen
in the gloom of a third-class carriage. He had large, frightened eyes,
and wore a white woollen cravat, over which a key was suspended round
his neck by a piece of common string: the key attracting attention by
its occasional shine in the lamplight. In the band of his hat his half-
ticket was stuck. His eyes remained mostly fixed on the back of the
seat opposite, and never turned to the window even when a station
was reached and called. On the other seat were two or three passengers,
one of them a working woman who held a basket on her lap, in which
was a tabby kitten. The woman opened the cover now and then,
whereupon the kitten would put out its head, and indulge in playful
antics. At these the fellow-passengers laughed, except the solitary boy
bearing the key and ticket, who, regarding the kitten with his saucer
eyes, seemed mutely to say: 'All laughing comes from misapprehension.
Rightly looked at there is no laughable thing under the sun.'

Occasionally at a stoppage the guard would look into the compartment and say to the boy, 'All right, my man. Your box is safe in the
van.' The boy would say, 'Yes,' without animation, would try to smile,
and fail.

He was Age masquerading as Juvenility, and doing it so badly that
his real self showed through crevices. A ground swell from ancient years
of night seemed now and then to lift the child in this his morning-life,
when his face took a back view over some great Atlantic of Time, and
appeared not to care about what it saw.

When the other travellers closed their eyes, which they did one by
one—even the kitten curling itself up in the basket, weary of its too
circumscribed play—the boy remained just as before. He then seemed
to be doubly awake, like an enslaved and dwarfed Divinity, sitting passive and regarding his companions as if he saw their whole rounded
lives rather than their immediate figures.

This was Arabella's boy. With her usual carelessness she had postponed writing to Jude about him till the eve of his landing, when she
could absolutely postpone no longer, though she had known for weeks
of his approaching arrival, and had, as she truly said, visited Aldbrickham mainly to reveal the boy's existence and his near home-coming
to Jude. This very day on which she had received her former husband's
answer at some time in the afternoon, the child reached the London
Docks, and the family in whose charge he had come, having put him
into a cab for Lambeth, and directed the cabman to his mother's
house, bade him good-bye, and went their way.

On his arrival at the Three Horns, Arabella had looked him over with
an expression that was as good as saying, 'You are very much what I
expected you to be,' had given him a good meal, a little money, and,

late as it was getting, despatched him to Jude by the next train, wishing her husband Cartlett, who was out, not to see him.

The train reached Aldbrickham, and the boy was deposited on the lonely platform beside his box. The collector took his ticket and, with a meditative sense of the unfitness of things, asked him where he was going by himself at that time of night.

'Going to Spring Street,' said the little one impassively.

'Why, that's a long way from here; a'most out in the country; and the folks will be gone to bed.'

'I've got to go there.'

'You must have a fly for your box.'

'No. I must walk.'

'O well: you'd better leave your box here and send for it. There's a 'bus goes half-way, but you'll have to walk the rest.'

'I am not afraid.'

'Why didn't your friends come to meet 'ee?'

'I suppose they didn't know I was coming.'

'Who is your friends?'

'Mother didn't wish me to say.'

'All I can do, then, is to take charge of this. Now walk as fast as you can.'

Saying nothing further the boy came out into the street, looking round to see that nobody followed or observed him. When he had walked some little distance he asked for the street of his destination. He was told to go straight on quite into the outskirts of the place.

The child fell into a steady mechanical creep which had in it an impersonal quality—the movement of the wave, or of the breeze, or of the cloud. He followed his directions literally, without an inquiring gaze at anything. It could have been seen that the boy's ideas of life were different from those of the local boys. Children begin with detail, and learn up to the general; they begin with the contiguous, and gradually comprehend the universal. The boy seemed to have begun with the generals of life, and never to have concerned himself with the particulars. To him the houses, the willows, the obscure fields beyond, were apparently regarded not as brick residences, pollards, meadows; but as human dwellings in the abstract, vegetation, and the wide dark world.

He found the way to the little lane, and knocked at the door of Jude's house. Jude had just retired to bed, and Sue was about to enter her chamber adjoining when she heard the knock and came down.

'Is this where father lives?' asked the child.

'Who?'

'Mr. Fawley, that's his name.'

Sue ran up to Jude's room and told him, and he hurried down as soon as he could, though to her impatience he seemed long.

'What—is it he—so soon?' she asked as Jude came.

She scrutinized the child's features, and suddenly went away into the little sitting-room adjoining. Jude lifted the boy to a level with himself, keenly regarded him with gloomy tenderness, and telling him he would have been met if they had known of his coming so soon, set him provisionally in a chair whilst he went to look for Sue, whose super-sensitiveness was disturbed, as he knew. He found her in the dark, bending over an arm-chair. He enclosed her with his arm, and putting his face by hers, whispered, 'What's the matter?'

'What Arabella says is true—true! I see you in him!'

'Well: that's one thing in my life as it should be, at any rate.'

'But the other half of him is—*she*! And that's what I can't bear! But I ought to—I'll try to get used to it; yes, I ought!'

'Jealous little Sue! I withdraw all remarks about your sexlessness. Never mind! Time may right things. . . . And Sue, darling; I have an idea! We'll educate and train him with a view to the University. What I couldn't accomplish in my own person perhaps I can carry out through him? They are making it easier for poor students now, you know.'

'O you dreamer!' said she, and holding his hand returned to the child with him. The boy looked at her as she had looked at him. 'Is it you who's my *real* mother at last?' he inquired.

'Why? Do I look like your father's wife?'

'Well, yes; 'cept he seems fond of you, and you of him. Can I call you mother?'

Then a yearning look came over the child and he began to cry. Sue thereupon could not refrain from instantly doing likewise, being a harp which the least wind of emotion from another's heart could make to vibrate as readily as a radical stir in her own.

'You may call me mother, if you wish to, my poor dear!' she said, bending her cheek against his to hide her tears.

'What's this round your neck?' asked Jude with affected calmness.

'The key of my box that's at the station.'

They bustled about and got him some supper, and made him up a temporary bed, where he soon fell asleep. Both went and looked at him as he lay.

'He called you mother two or three times before he dropped off,' murmured Jude. 'Wasn't it odd that he should have wanted to!'

'Well—it was significant,' said Sue. 'There's more for us to think about in that one little hungry heart than in all the stars of the sky. . . . I suppose, dear, we *must* pluck up courage, and get that ceremony over? It is no use struggling against the current, and I feel myself getting intertwined with my kind. O Jude, you'll love me dearly, won't you, afterwards! I do want to be kind to this child, and to be a mother to him; and our adding the legal form to our marriage might make it easier for me.'

V–4

Their next and second attempt thereat was more deliberately made, though it was begun on the morning following the singular child's arrival at their home.

Him they found to be in the habit of sitting silent, his quaint and weird face set, and his eyes resting on things they did not see in the substantial world.

'His face is like the tragic mask of Melpomene,'[1] said Sue. 'What is your name, dear? Did you tell us?'

'Little Father Time is what they always called me. It is a nick-name; because I look so aged, they say.'

'And you talk so, too,' said Sue tenderly. 'It is strange, Jude, that these preternaturally old boys almost always come from new countries. But what were you christened?'

'I never was.'

'Why was that?'

'Because, if I died in damnation, 'twould save the expense of a Christian funeral.'

'O—your name is not Jude, then?' said his father with some disappointment.

The boy shook his head. 'Never heerd on it.'

'Of course not,' said Sue quickly; 'since she was hating you all the time!'

'We'll have him christened,' said Jude; and privately to Sue: 'The day we are married.' Yet the advent of the child disturbed him.

Their position lent them shyness, and having an impression that a marriage at a Superintendent Registrar's office was more private than an ecclesiastical one, they decided to avoid a church this time. Both Sue and Jude together went to the office of the district to give notice: they had become such companions that they could hardly do anything of importance except in each other's company.

Jude Fawley signed the form of notice, Sue looking over his shoulder and watching his hand as it traced the words. As she read the four-square undertaking, never before seen by her, into which her own and Jude's names were inserted, and by which that very voltile essence, their love for each other, was supposed to be made permanent, her face seemed to grow painfully apprehensive. 'Names and Surnames of the Parties'—(they were to be parties now, not lovers, she thought). 'Condition'—(a horrid idea)—'Rank or Occupation'—'Age'—'Dwelling at'—'Length of Residence'—'Church or Building in which the Marriage is to be solemnized'—'District and County in which the Parties respectively dwell.'

1. Greek muse of tragedy.

'It spoils the sentiment, doesn't it!' she said on their way home. 'It seems making a more sordid business of it even than signing the contract in a vestry. There is a little poetry in a church. But we'll try to get through with it, dearest, now.'

'We will. "For what man is he that hath betrothed a wife and hath not taken her? Let him go and return unto his house, lest he die in the battle, and another man take her."[2] So said the Jewish law-giver.'

'How you know the Scriptures, Jude! You really ought to have been a parson. I can only quote profane writers!'

During the interval before the issuing of the certificate Sue, in her housekeeping errands, sometimes walked past the office, and furtively glancing in saw affixed to the wall the notice of the purposed clinch to their union. She could not bear its aspect. Coming after her previous experience of matrimony, all the romance of their attachment seemed to be starved away by placing her present case in the same category. She was usually leading little Father Time by the hand, and fancied that people thought him hers, and regarded the intended ceremony as the patching up of an old error.

Meanwhile Jude decided to link his present with his past in some slight degree by inviting to the wedding the only person remaining on earth who was associated with his early life at Marygreen—the aged widow Mrs. Edlin, who had been his great-aunt's friend and nurse in her last illness. He hardly expected that she would come; but she did, bringing singular presents, in the form of apples, jam, brass snuffers,[3] an ancient pewter dish, a warming-pan, and an enormous bag of goose feathers towards a bed. She was allotted the spare room in Jude's house, whither she retired early, and where they could hear her through the ceiling below, honestly saying the Lord's Prayer in a loud voice, as the Rubric[4] directed.

As, however, she could not sleep, and discovered that Sue and Jude were still sitting up—it being in fact only ten o'clock—she dressed herself again, and came down; and they all sat by the fire till a late hour—Father Time included; though, as he never spoke, they were hardly conscious of him.

'Well, I bain't set against marrying as your great-aunt was,' said the widow. 'And I hope 'twill be a jocund wedding for ye in all respects this time. Nobody can hope it more, knowing what I do of your families, which is more, I suppose, than anybody else now living. For they have been unlucky that way, God knows.'

Sue breathed uneasily.

'They was always good-hearted people, too—wouldn't kill a fly if

<hr/>

2. Deuteronomy 20.7 (not quite accurately quoted).
3. Instrument for trimming wick of, or extinguishing, candle.
4. Instructions for conducting church services in the Book of Common Prayer used in the Church of England.

they knowed it,' continued the wedding guest. 'But things happened to thwart 'em, and if everything wasn't vitty[5] they were upset. No doubt that's how he that the tale is told of came to do what 'a did—if he *were* one of your family.'

'What was that?' said Jude.

'Well—that tale, ye know; he that was gibbeted[6] just on the brow of the hill by the Brown House—not far from the milestone between Marygreen and Alfredston, where the other road branches off. But Lord, 'twas in my grandfather's time; and it medn' have been one of your folk at all.'

'I know where the gibbet is said to have stood, very well,' murmured Jude. 'But I never heard of this. What—did this man—my ancestor and Sue's—kill his wife?'

' 'Twer not that exactly. She ran away from him, with their child, to her friends; and while she was there the child died. He wanted the body, to bury it where his people lay, but she wouldn't give it up. Her husband then came in the night with a cart, and broke into the house to steal the coffin away; but he was catched, and being obstinate, wouldn't tell what he broke in for. They brought it in burglary, and that's why he was hanged and gibbeted on Brown House Hill. His wife went mad after he was dead. But it medn' be true that he belonged to ye more than to me.'

A small slow voice rose from the shade of the fireside, as if out of the earth: 'If I was you, mother, I wouldn't marry father!' It came from little Time, and they started, for they had forgotten him.

'O, it is only a tale,' said Sue cheeringly.

After this exhilarating tradition from the widow on the eve of the solemnization they rose, and, wishing their guest good-night, retired.

The next morning Sue, whose nervousness intensified with the hours, took Jude privately into the sitting-room before starting. 'Jude, I want you to kiss me, as a lover, incorporeally,' she said, tremulously nestling up to him, with damp lashes. 'It won't be ever like this any more, will it! I wish we hadn't begun the business. But I suppose we must go on. How horrid that story was last night! It spoilt my thoughts of to-day. It makes me feel as if a tragic doom overhung our family, as it did the house of Atreus.'[7]

'Or the house of Jeroboam,'[8] said the quondam[9] theologian.

'Yes. And it seems awful temerity in us two to go marrying! I am going to vow to you in the same words I vowed in to my other husband, and you to me in the same as you used to your other wife; regard-

5. Fitting, proper (dialect).
6. Hanged on a gallows.
7. In Greek legend, the house of Atreus was under a curse and was visited by many calamities. Its story forms the subject of Aeschylus's tragic trilogy *Oresteia*.
8. God said, "I will bring evil upon the house of Jeroboam" (1 Kings 14.10).
9. At an earlier time.

less of the deterrent lesson we were taught by those experiments!'

'If you are uneasy I am made unhappy,' said he. 'I had hoped you would feel quite joyful. But if you don't, you don't. It is no use pretending. It is a dismal business to you, and that makes it so to me!'

'It is unpleasantly like that other morning—that's all,' she murmured. 'Let us go on now.'

They started arm in arm for the office aforesaid, no witness accompanying them except the Widow Edlin. The day was chilly and dull, and a clammy fog blew through the town from 'Royal-tower'd Thame.'[1] On the steps of the office there were the muddy footmarks of people who had entered, and in the entry were damp umbrellas. Within the office several persons were gathered, and our couple perceived that a marriage between a soldier and a young woman was just in progress. Sue, Jude, and the widow stood in the background while this was going on, Sue reading the notices of marriage on the wall. The room was a dreary place to two of their temperament, though to its usual frequenters it doubtless seemed ordinary enough. Law-books in musty calf covered one wall, and elsewhere were Post-Office Directories, and other books of reference. Papers in packets tied with red tape were pigeonholed around, and some iron safes filled a recess; while the bare wood floor was, like the doorstep, stained by previous visitors.

The soldier was sullen and reluctant: the bride sad and timid; she was soon, obviously, to become a mother, and she had a black eye. Their little business was soon done, and the twain and their friends straggled out, one of the witnesses saying casually to Jude and Sue in passing, as if he had known them before: 'See the couple just come in? Ha, Ha! That fellow is just out of gaol this morning. She met him at the gaol gates, and brought him straight here. She's paying for everything.'

Sue turned her head and saw an ill-favoured man, closely cropped, with a broad-faced, pock-marked woman on his arm, ruddy with liquor and the satisfaction of being on the brink of a gratified desire. They jocosely saluted the outgoing couple, and went forward in front of Jude and Sue, whose diffidence was increasing. The latter drew back and turned to her lover, her mouth shaping itself like that of a child about to give way to grief:

'Jude—I don't like it here! I wish we hadn't come! The place gives me the horrors: it seems so unnatural as the climax of our love! I wish it had been at church, if it had to be at all. It is not so vulgar there!'

'Dear little girl,' said Jude. 'How troubled and pale you look!'

'It must be performed here now, I suppose?'

'No—perhaps not necessarily.'

He spoke to the clerk, and came back. 'No—we need not marry here or anywhere, unless we like, even now,' he said. 'We can be married in

1. From Milton's poem "At a Vacation Exercise."

a church, if not with the same certificate with another he'll give us, I think. Anyhow, let us go out till you are calmer, dear, and I too, and talk it over.'

They went out stealthily and guiltily, as if they had committed a misdemeanour, closing the door without noise, and telling the widow, who had remained in the entry, to go home and await them; that they would call in any casual passers as witnesses, if necessary. When in the street they turned into an unfrequented side alley, where they walked up and down as they had done long ago in the Market-house at Melchester.

'Now, darling, what shall we do? We are making a mess of it, it strikes me. Still, *anything* that pleases you will please me.'

'But Jude, dearest, I am worrying you! You wanted it to be there, didn't you?'

'Well, to tell the truth, when I got inside I felt as if I didn't care much about it. The place depressed me almost as much as it did you—it was ugly. And then I thought of what you had said this morning as to whether we ought.'

They walked on vaguely, till she paused, and her little voice began anew: 'It seems so weak, too, to vacillate like this! And yet how much better than to act rashly a second time. . . . How terrible that scene was to me! The expression in that flabby woman's face, leading her on to give herself to that gaol-bird, not for a few hours, as she would, but for a lifetime, as she must. And the other poor soul—to escape a nominal shame which was owing to the weakness of her character, degrading herself to the real shame of bondage to a tyrant who scorned her—a man whom to avoid for ever was her only chance of salvation. . . . This is our parish church, isn't it? This is where it would have to be, if we did it in the usual way? A service or something seems to be going on.'

Jude went up and looked in at the door. 'Why—it is a wedding here too,' he said. 'Everybody seems to be on our tack[2] to-day.'

Sue said she supposed it was because Lent was just over, when there was always a crowd of marriages. 'Let us listen,' she said, 'and find how it feels to us when performed in a church.'

They stepped in, and entered a back seat, and watched the proceedings at the altar. The contracting couple appeared to belong to the well-to-do middle class, and the wedding altogether was of ordinary prettiness and interest. They could see the flowers tremble in the bride's hand, even at that distance, and could hear her mechanical murmur of words whose meaning her brain seemed to gather not at all under the pressure of her self-consciousness. Sue and Jude listened, and severally saw themselves in time past going through the same form of self-committal.

2. Doing the same as us.

'It is not the same to her, poor thing, as it would be to me doing it over again with my present knowledge,' Sue whispered. 'You see, they are fresh to it, and take the proceedings as a matter of course. But having been awakened to its awful solemnity as we have, or at least as I have, by experience, and to my own too squeamish feelings perhaps sometimes, it really does seem immoral in me to go and undertake the same thing again with open eyes. Coming in here and seeing this has frightened me from a church wedding as much as the other did from a registry one. . . . We are a weak, tremulous pair, Jude, and what others may feel confident in I feel doubts of—my being proof against the sordid conditions of a business contract again!'

Then they tried to laugh, and went on debating in whispers the object-lesson before them. And Jude said he also thought they were both too thin-skinned—that they ought never to have been born—much less have come together for the most preposterous of all joint-ventures for *them*—matrimony.

His betrothed shuddered; and asked him earnestly if he indeed felt that they ought not to go in cold blood and sign that life-undertaking again? 'It is awful if you think we have found ourselves not strong enough for it, and knowing this, are proposing to perjure ourselves,' she said.

'I fancy I do think it—since you ask me,' said Jude. 'Remember I'll do it if you wish, own darling.' While she hesitated he went on to confess that, though he thought they ought to be able to do it, he felt checked by the dread of incompetency just as she did—from their peculiarities, perhaps, because they were unlike other people. 'We are horribly sensitive; that's really what's the matter with us, Sue!' he declared.

'I fancy more are like us than we think!'

'Well, I don't know. The intention of the contract is good, and right for many, no doubt; but in our case it may defeat its own ends because we are the queer sort of people we are—folk in whom domestic ties of a forced kind snuff out cordiality and spontaneousness.'

Sue still held that there was not much queer or exceptional in them: that all were so. 'Everybody is getting to feel as we do. We are a little beforehand, that's all. In fifty, a hundred, years the descendants of these two will act and feel worse than we. They will see weltering humanity still more vividly than we do now, as

Shapes like our own selves hideously multiplied,[3]

and will be afraid to reproduce them.'

'What a terrible line of poetry! . . . though I have felt it myself about my fellow-creatures, at morbid times.'

3. From Shelley's *Revolt of Islam.*

Thus they murmured on, till Sue said more brightly:

'Well—the general question is not our business, and why should we plague ourselves about it? However different our reasons are we come to the same conclusion; that for us particular two, an irrevocable oath is risky. Then, Jude, let us go home without killing our dream! Yes? How good you are, my friend: you give way to all my whims!'

'They accord very much with my own.'

He gave her a little kiss behind a pillar while the attention of everybody present was taken up in observing the burial procession entering the vestry; and then they came outside the building. By the door they waited till two or three carriages, which had gone away for a while, returned, and the new husband and wife came into the open daylight. Sue sighed.

'The flowers in the bride's hand are sadly like the garland which decked the heifers of sacrifice in old times!'[4]

'Still, Sue, it is no worse for the woman than for the man. That's what some women fail to see, and instead of protesting against the conditions they protest against the man, the other victim; just as a woman in a crowd will abuse the man who crushes against her, when he is only the helpless transmitter of the pressure put upon him.'

'Yes—some are like that, instead of uniting with the man against the common enemy, coercion.' The bride and bridegroom had by this time driven off, and the two moved away with the rest of the idlers. 'No—don't let's do it,' she continued. 'At least just now.'

They reached home, and passing the window arm in arm saw the widow looking out at them. 'Well,' cried their guest when they entered, 'I said to myself when I zeed ye coming so loving up to the door, "They made up their minds at last, then!"'

They briefly hinted that they had not.

'What—and ha'n't ye really done it? Chok' it all, that I should have lived to see a good old saying like "marry in haste and repent at leisure" spoiled like this by you two! 'Tis time I got back again to Marygreen—sakes if tidden[5]—if this is what the new notions be leading us to! Nobody thought o' being afeard o' matrimony in my time, nor of much else but a cannon-ball or empty cupboard! Why when I and my poor man were married we thought no more o't than of a game o' dibs!'[6]

'Don't tell the child when he comes in,' whispered Sue nervously. 'He'll think it has all gone on right, and it will be better that he should not be surprised and puzzled. Of course it is only put off for reconsideration. If we are happy as we are, what does it matter to anybody?'

4. Hardy may have been recalling John Keats's "Ode on a Grecian Urn": " . . . that heifer lowing at the skies, / And all her silken flanks with garlands drest. . . ."
5. It is not.
6. Children's game played with pebbles or sheep's bones.

V–5

The purpose of a chronicler of moods and deeds does not require him to express his personal views upon the grave controversy above given. That the twain were happy—between their times of sadness— was indubitable. And when the unexpected apparition of Jude's child in the house had shown itself to be no such disturbing event as it had looked, but one that brought into their lives a new and tender interest of an ennobling and unselfish kind, it rather helped than injured their happiness.

To be sure, with such pleasing anxious beings[1] as they were, the boy's coming also brought with it much thought for the future, par- ticularly as he seemed at present to be singularly deficient in all the usual hopes of childhood. But the pair tried to dismiss, for a while at least, a too strenuously forward view.

There is in Upper Wessex an old town of nine or ten thousand souls; the town may be called Stoke-Barehills. It stands with its gaunt, unat- tractive, ancient church, and its new red brick suburb, amid the open, chalk-soiled cornlands, near the middle of an imaginary triangle which has for its three corners the towns of Aldbrickham and Wintoncester, and the important military station of Quartershot. The great western highway from London passes through it, near a point where the road branches into two, merely to unite again some twenty miles further westward. Out of this bifurcation and reunion there used to arise among wheeled travellers, before railway days, endless questions of choice between the respective ways. But the question is now as dead as the scot-and-lot freeholder,[2] the road waggoner, and the mail coach- man who disputed it; and probably not a single inhabitant of Stoke- Barehills is now even aware that the two roads which part in his town ever meet again; for nobody now drives up and down the great western highway daily.

The most familiar object in Stoke-Barehills nowadays is its cemetery, standing among some picturesque mediaeval ruins beside the railway; the modern chapels, modern tombs, and modern shrubs, having a look of intrusiveness amid the crumbling and ivy-covered decay of the ancient walls.

On a certain day, however, in the particular year which has now been reached by this narrative—the month being early June—the features of the town excite little interest, though many visitors arrive by the trains; some down trains, in especial, nearly emptying themselves here. It is the week of the Great Wessex Agricultural Show, whose vast encampment spreads over the open outskirts of the town like the tents of an investing army. Rows of marquees, huts, booths, pavilions,

1. Recalls a phrase in Thomas Gray's *Elegy Written in a Country Churchyard* (line 86).
2. Property owner subject to local tax.

arcades, porticoes—every kind of structure short of a permanent one—
cover the green field for the space of a square half-mile, and the crowds
of arrivals walk through the town in a mass, and make straight for the
exhibition ground. The way thereto is lined with shows, stalls, and
hawkers on foot, who make a market-place of the whole roadway to
the show proper, and lead some of the improvident to lighten their
pockets appreciably before they reach the gates of the exhibition they
came expressly to see.

It is the popular day, the shilling day, and of the fast arriving excursion trains two from different directions enter the two contiguous rail-
way-stations at almost the same minute. One, like several which have
preceded it, comes from London: the other by a cross line from Aldbrickham; and from the London train alights a couple; a short, rather
bloated man, with a globular stomach and small legs, resembling a top
on two pegs, accompanied by a woman of rather fine figure and rather
red face, dressed in black material, and covered with beads from bonnet
to skirt, that made her glisten as if clad in chain-mail.

They cast their eyes around. The man was about to hire a fly as some
others had done, when the woman said, 'Don't be in such a hurry,
Cartlett. It isn't so very far to the show-yard. Let us walk down the
street into the place. Perhaps I can pick up a cheap bit of furniture or
old china. It is years since I was here—never since I lived as a girl at
Aldbrickham, and used to come across for a trip sometimes with my
young man.'

'You can't carry home furniture by excursion train,' said, in a thick
voice, her husband, the landlord of The Three Horns, Lambeth; for
they had both come down from the tavern in that 'excellent, densely
populated, gin-drinking neighbourhood,' which they had occupied ever
since the advertisement in those words had attracted them thither.
The configuration of the landlord showed that he, too, like his customers, was becoming affected by the liquors he retailed.

'Then I'll get it sent, if I see any worth having,' said his wife.

They sauntered on, but had barely entered the town when her attention was attracted by a young couple leading a child, who had come
out from the second platform, into which the train from Aldbrickham
had steamed. They were walking just in front of the inn-keepers.

'Sakes alive!' said Arabella.

'What's that?' said Cartlett.

'Who do you think that couple is? Don't you recognize the man?'

'No.'

'Not from the photos I have showed you?'

'Is it Fawley?'

'Yes—of course.'

'Oh, well. I suppose he was inclined for a little sight-seeing like the
rest of us.' Cartlett's interest in Jude, whatever it might have been

when Arabella was new to him, had plainly flagged since her charms and her idiosyncrasies, her supernumerary hair-coils, and her optional dimples, were becoming as a tale that is told.[3]

Arabella so regulated her pace and her husband's as to keep just in the rear of the other three, which it was easy to do without notice in such a stream of pedestrians. Her answers to Cartlett's remarks were vague and slight, for the group in front interested her more than all the rest of the spectacle.

'They are rather fond of one another and of their child, seemingly,' continued the publican.

'*Their* child! 'Tisn't their child,' said Arabella with a curious, sudden covetousness. 'They haven't been married long enough for it to be theirs!'

But although the smouldering maternal instinct was strong enough in her to lead her to quash her husband's conjecture, she was not disposed on second thoughts to be more candid than necessary. Mr. Cartlett had no other idea than that his wife's child by her first husband was with his grandparents at the Antipodes.

'O I suppose not. She looks quite a girl.'

'They are only lovers, or lately married, and have the child in charge, as anybody can see.'

All continued to move ahead. The unwitting Sue and Jude, the couple in question, had determined to make this Agricultural Exhibition within twenty miles of their own town the occasion of a day's excursion which should combine exercise and amusement with instruction, at small expense. Not regardful of themselves alone, they had taken care to bring Father Time, to try every means of making him kindle and laugh like other boys, though he was to some extent a hindrance to the delightfully unreserved intercourse in their pilgrimages which they so much enjoyed. But they soon ceased to consider him an observer, and went along with that tender attention to each other which the shyest can scarcely disguise, and which these, among entire strangers as they imagined, took less trouble to disguise than they might have done at home. Sue, in her new summer clothes, flexible and light as a bird, her little thumb stuck up by the stem of her white cotton sunshade, went along as if she hardly touched ground, and as if a moderately strong puff of wind would float her over the hedge into the next field. Jude, in his light grey holiday-suit, was really proud of her companionship, not more for her external attractiveness than for her sympathetic words and ways. That complete mutual understanding, in which every glance and movement was as effectual as speech for conveying intelligence between them, made them almost the two parts of a single whole.

The pair with their charge passed through the turnstiles, Arabella

3. Psalms 90.9.

and her husband not far behind them. When inside the enclosure the publican's wife could see that the two ahead began to take trouble with the youngster, pointing out and explaining the many objects of interest, alive and dead; and a passing sadness would touch their faces at their every failure to disturb his indifference.

'How she sticks to him!' said Arabella. 'O no—I fancy they are not married, or they wouldn't be so much to one another as that. . . . I wonder!'

'But I thought you said he did marry her?'

'I heard he was going to—that's all, going to make another attempt, after putting it off once or twice. . . . As far as they themselves are concerned they are the only two in the show. I should be ashamed of making myself so silly if I were he!'

'I don't see as how there's anything remarkable in their behaviour. I should never have noticed their being in love, if you hadn't said so.'

'You never see anything,' she rejoined. Nevertheless Cartlett's view of the lovers' or married pair's conduct was undoubtedly that of the general crowd, whose attention seemed to be in no way attracted by what Arabella's sharpened vision discerned.

'He's charmed by her as if she were some fairy!' continued Arabella. 'See how he looks round at her, and lets his eyes rest on her. I am inclined to think that she don't care for him quite so much as he does for her. She's not a particular warm-hearted creature to my thinking, though she cares for him pretty middling[4] much—as much as she's able to; and he could make her heart ache a bit if he liked to try—which he's too simple to do. There—now they are going across to the cart-horse sheds. Come along.'

'I don't want to see the cart-horses. It is no business of ours to follow these two. If we have come to see the show let us see it in our own way, as they do in theirs.'

'Well—suppose we agree to meet somewhere in an hour's time— say at that refreshment tent over there, and go about independent? Then you can look at what you choose to, and so can I.'

Cartlett was not loth to agree to this, and they parted—he proceeding to the shed where malting processes were being exhibited, and Arabella in the direction taken by Jude and Sue. Before, however, she had regained their wake a laughing face met her own, and she was confronted by Anny, the friend of her girlhood.

Anny had burst out in hearty laughter at the mere fact of the chance rencounter. 'I am still living down there,' she said, as soon as she was composed. 'I am soon going to be married, but my intended couldn't come up here to-day. But there's lots of us come by excursion, though I've lost the rest of 'em for the present.'

4. To a moderate degree (dialect).

'Have you met Jude and his young woman, or wife, or whatever she is? I saw 'em by now.'

'No. Not a glimpse of un for years!'

'Well, they are close by here somewhere. Yes—there they are—by that grey horse!'

'O, that's his present young woman—wife did you say? Has he married again?'

'I don't know.'

'She's pretty, isn't she!'

'Yes—nothing to complain of; or jump at. Not much to depend on, though; a slim, fidgety little thing like that.'

'He's a nice-looking chap, too! You ought to ha' stuck to un, Arabella.'

'I don't know but I ought,' murmured she.

Anny laughed. 'That's you, Arabella! Always wanting another man than your own.'

'Well, and what woman don't I should like to know? As for that body with him—she don't know what love is—at least what I call love! I can see in her face she don't.'

'And perhaps, Abby dear, you don't know what she calls love.'

'I'm sure I don't wish to! . . . Ah—they are making for the Art Department. I should like to see some pictures myself. Suppose we go that way?—Why, if all Wessex isn't here, I verily believe! There's Dr. Vilbert. Haven't seen him for years, and he's not looking a day older than when I used to know him. How do you do, Physician? I was just saying that you don't look a day older than when you knew me as a girl.'

'Simply the result of taking my own pills regular, ma'am. Only two and threepence a box—warranted efficacious by the Government stamp. Now let me advise you to purchase the same immunity from the ravages of Time by following my example? Only two-and-three.'

The physician had produced a box from his waistcoat pocket, and Arabella was induced to make the purchase.

'At the same time,' continued he, when the pills were paid for, 'you have the advantage of me, Mrs.—Surely not Mrs. Fawley, once Miss Donn, of the vicinity of Marygreen?'

'Yes. But Mrs. Cartlett now.'

'Ah—you lost him, then? Promising young fellow! A pupil of mine, you know. I taught him the dead languages. And believe me, he soon knew nearly as much as I.'

'I lost him; but not as you think,' said Arabella drily. 'The lawyers untied us. There he is, look, alive and lusty; along with that young woman, entering the Art exhibition.'

'Ah—dear me! Fond of her, apparently.'

'They *say* they are cousins.'

'Cousinship is a great convenience to their feelings, I should say?'

'Yes. So her husband thought, no doubt, when he divorced her. . . . Shall we look at the pictures, too?'

The trio followed across the green and entered. Jude and Sue, with the child, unaware of the interest they were exciting, had gone up to a model at one end of the building, which they regarded with considerable attention for a long while before they went on. Arabella and her friends came to it in due course, and the inscription it bore was; 'Model of Cardinal College, Christminster; by J. Fawley and S. F. M. Bridehead.'

'Admiring their own work, said Arabella. 'How like Jude—always thinking of Colleges and Christminster, instead of attending to his business!'

They glanced cursorily at the pictures, and proceeded to the bandstand. When they had stood a little while listening to the music of the military performers, Jude, Sue, and the child came up on the other side. Arabella did not care if they should recognize her; but they were too deeply absorbed in their own lives, as translated into emotion by the military band, to perceive her under her beaded veil. She walked round the outside of the listening throng, passing behind the lovers, whose movements had an unexpected fascination for her to-day. Scrutinizing them narrowly from the rear she noticed that Jude's hand sought Sue's as they stood, the two standing close together so as to conceal, as they supposed, this tacit expression of their mutual responsiveness.

'Silly fools—like two children!' Arabella whispered to herself morosely, as she rejoined her companions, with whom she preserved a preoccupied silence.

Anny meanwhile had jokingly remarked to Vilbert on Arabella's hankering interest in her first husband.

'Now,' said the physician to Arabella, apart; 'do you want anything such as this, Mrs. Cartlett? It is not compounded out of my regular pharmacopoeia,[5] but I am sometimes asked for such a thing.' He produced a small phial of clear liquid. 'A love-philtre, such as was used by the Ancients with great effect. I found it out by study of their writings, and have never known it to fail.'

'What is it made of?' asked Arabella curiously.

'Well—a distillation of the juices of doves' hearts—otherwise pigeons'—is one of the ingredients. It took nearly a hundred hearts to produce that small bottle full.'

'How do you get pigeons enough?'

'To tell a secret, I get a piece of rock-salt, of which pigeons are inordinately fond, and place it in a dovecote on my roof. In a few hours

5. Stock of drugs.

the birds come to it from all points of the compass—east, west, north, and south—and thus I secure as many as I require. You use the liquid by contriving that the desired man shall take about ten drops of it in his drink. But remember, all this is told you because I gather from your questions that you mean to be a purchaser. You must keep faith with me?'

'Very well—I don't mind a bottle—to give some friend or other to try it on her young man.' She produced five shillings, the price asked, and slipped the phial in her capacious bosom. Saying presently that she was due at an appointment with her husband she sauntered away towards the refreshment bar, Jude, his companion, and the child having gone on to the horticultural tent, where Arabella caught a glimpse of them standing before a group of roses in bloom.

She waited a few minutes observing them, and then proceeded to join her spouse with no very amiable sentiments. She found him seated on a stool by the bar, talking to one of the gaily dressed maids who had served him with spirits.

'I should think you had enough of this business at home!' Arabella remarked gloomily. 'Surely you didn't come fifty miles from your own bar to stick in another? Come, take me round the show, as other men do their wives! Dammy, one would think you were a young bachelor, with nobody to look after but yourself!'

'But we agreed to meet here; and what could I do but wait?'

'Well, now we have met, come along,' she returned, ready to quarrel with the sun for shining on her. And they left the tent together, this pot-bellied man and florid woman, in the antipathetic, recriminatory mood of the average husband and wife of Christendom.

In the meantime the more exceptional couple and the boy still lingered in the pavilion of flowers—an enchanted palace to their appreciative taste—Sue's usually pale cheeks reflecting the pink of the tinted roses at which she gazed; for the gay sights, the air, the music, and the excitement of a day's outing with Jude, had quickened her blood and made her eyes sparkle with vivacity. She adored roses, and what Arabella had witnessed was Sue detaining Jude almost against his will while she learnt the names of this variety and that, and put her face within an inch of their blooms to smell them.

'I should like to push my face quite into them—the dears!' she had said. 'But I suppose it is against the rules to touch them—isn't it, Jude?'

'Yes, you baby,' said he: and then playfully gave her a little push, so that her nose went among the petals.

"The policeman will be down on us, and I shall say it was my husband's fault!'

Then she looked up at him, and smiled in a way that told so much to Arabella.

'Happy?' he murmured.

She nodded.

'Why? Because you have come to the great Wessex Agricultural Show—or because *we* have come?'

'You are always trying to make me confess to all sorts of absurdities. Because I am improving my mind, of course, by seeing all these steam-ploughs, and threshing-machines, and chaff-cutters, and cows, and pigs, and sheep.'

Jude was quite content with a baffle[6] from his ever evasive companion. But when he had forgotten that he had put the question, and because he no longer wished for an answer, she went on: 'I feel that we have returned to Greek joyousness, and have blinded ourselves to sickness and sorrow, and have forgotten what twenty-five centuries have taught the race since their time, as one of your Christminster luminaries[7] says. . . . There is one immediate shadow, however,—only one.' And she looked at the aged child, whom, though they had taken him to everything likely to attract a young intelligence, they had utterly failed to interest.

He knew what they were saying and thinking. 'I am very, very sorry, father and mother,' he said. 'But please don't mind!—I can't help it. I should like the flowers very very much, if I didn't keep on thinking they'd be all withered in a few days!'

v–6

The unnoticed lives that the pair had hitherto led began, from the day of the suspended wedding onwards, to be observed and discussed by other persons than Arabella. The society of Spring Street and the neighbourhood generally did not understand, and probably could not have been made to understand, Sue and Jude's private minds, emotions, positions, and fears. The curious facts of a child coming to them unexpectedly, who called Jude father, and Sue mother, and a hitch in a marriage ceremony intended for quietness to be performed at a registrar's office, together with rumours of the undefended cases in the law-courts, bore only one translation to plain minds.

Little Time—for though he was formally turned into 'Jude,' the apt nickname stuck to him—would come home from school in the evening, and repeat inquiries and remarks that had been made to him by the other boys; and cause Sue, and Jude when he heard them, a great deal of pain and sadness.

The result was that shortly after the attempt at the registrar's the pair went off—to London it was believed—for several days, hiring somebody to look to the boy. When they came back they let it be understood indirectly, and with total indifference and weariness of

6. Inconclusive or puzzling reply.
7. Probably Matthew Arnold.

mien, that they were legally married at last. Sue, who had previously been called Mrs. Bridehead, now openly adopted the name of Mrs. Fawley. Her dull, cowed, and listless manner for days seemed to substantiate all this.

But the mistake (as it was called) of their going away so secretly to do the business, kept up much of the mystery of their lives; and they found that they made not such advances with their neighbours as they had axpected to do thereby. A living mystery was not much less interesting than a dead scandal.

The baker's lad and the grocer's boy, who at first had used to lift their hats gallantly to Sue when they came to execute their errands, in these days no longer took the trouble to render her that homage, and the neighbouring artizans' wives looked straight along the pavement when they encountered her.

Nobody molested them, it is true; but an oppressive atmosphere began to encircle their souls, particularly after their excursion to the Show, as if that visit had brought some evil influence to bear on them. And their temperaments were precisely of a kind to suffer from this atmosphere, and to be indisposed to lighten it by vigorous and open statements. Their apparent attempt at reparation had come too late to be effective.

The headstone and epitaph orders fell off: and two or three months later, when autumn came, Jude perceived that he would have to return to journey-work again, a course all the more unfortunate just now, in that he had not as yet cleared off the debt he had unavoidably incurred in the payment of the law-costs of the previous year.

One evening he sat down to share the common meal with Sue and the child as usual. 'I am thinking,' he said to her, 'that I'll hold on here no longer. The life suits us, certainly; but if we could get away to a place where we are unknown, we should be lighter hearted, and have a better chance. And so I am afraid we must break it up here, however awkward for you, poor dear!'

Sue was always much affected at a picture of herself as an object of pity, and she saddened.

'Well—I am not sorry,' said she presently. 'I am much depressed by the way they look at me here. And you have been keeping on this house and furniture entirely for me and the boy! You don't want it yourself, and the expense is unnecessary. But whatever we do, wherever we go, you won't take him away from me, Jude dear? I could not let him go now! The cloud upon his young mind makes him so pathetic to me; I do hope to lift it some day! And he loves me so. You won't take him away from me?'

'Certainly I won't, dear little girl! We'll get nice lodgings, wherever we go. I shall be moving about probably—getting a job here and a job there.'

'I shall do something too, of course, till—till—Well, now I can't be useful in the lettering it behoves me to turn my hand to something else.'

'Don't hurry about getting employment,' he said regretfully. 'I don't want you to do that. I wish you wouldn't, Sue. The boy and yourself are enough for you to attend to.'

There was a knock at the door, and Jude answered it. Sue could hear the conversation:

'Is Mr. Fawley at home?. . . . Biles and Willis the building contractors sent me to know if you'll undertake the relettering of the Ten Commandments in a little church they've been restoring lately in the country near here.'

Jude reflected, and said he could undertake it.

'It is not a very artistic job,' continued the messenger. 'The clergyman is a very old-fashioned chap, and he has refused to let anything more be done to the church than cleaning and repairing.'

'Excellent old man!' said Sue to herself, who was sentimentally opposed to the horrors of over-restoration.

'The Ten Commandments are fixed to the east end,' the messenger went on, 'and they want doing up with the rest of the wall there, since he won't have them carted off as old materials belonging to the contractor, in the usual way of the trade.'

A bargain as to terms was struck, and Jude came indoors. 'There, you see,' he said cheerfully. 'One more job yet, at any rate, and you can help in it—at least you can try. We shall have all the church to ourselves, as the rest of the work is finished.'

Next day Jude went out to the church, which was only two miles off. He found that what the contractor's clerk had said was true. The tables of the Jewish law[1] towered sternly over the utensils of Christian grace,[2] as the chief ornament of the chancel end, in the fine dry style of the last century. And as their framework was constructed of ornamental plaster they could not be taken down for repair. A portion, crumbled by damp, required renewal; and when this had been done, and the whole cleansed, he began to renew the lettering. On the second morning Sue came to see what assistance she could render, and also because they liked to be together.

The silence and emptiness of the building gave her confidence, and, standing on a safe low platform erected by Jude, which she was nevertheless timid at mounting, she began painting in the letters of the first Table[3] while he set about mending a portion of the second. She was quite pleased at her powers; she had acquired them in the days she painted illumined texts for the church-fitting shop at Christmins-

1. The Ten Commandments were often painted on boards fixed to the walls inside the church.
2. Used in the Communion service.
3. The first division of the "decalogue," containing the first five commandments.

ter. Nobody seemed likely to disturb them; and the pleasant twitter of birds, and rustle of October leafage, came in through an open window, and mingled with their talk.

They were not, however, to be left thus snug and peaceful for long. About half-past twelve there came footsteps on the gravel without. The old vicar and his churchwarden entered, and, coming up to see what was being done, seemed surprised to discover that a young woman was assisting. They passed on into an aisle, at which time the door again opened, and another figure entered—a small one, that of little Time, who was crying. Sue had told him where he might find her between school-hours, if he wished. She came down from her perch, and said, 'What's the matter, my dear?'

'I couldn't stay to eat my dinner in school, because they said—' He described how some boys had taunted him about his nominal mother, and Sue, grieved, expressed her indignation to Jude aloft. The child went into the churchyard, and Sue returned to her work. Meanwhile the door had opened again, and there shuffled in with a business-like air the white-aproned woman who cleaned the church. Sue recognized her as one who had friends in Spring Street, whom she visited. The church-cleaner looked at Sue, gaped, and lifted her hands; she had evidently recognized Jude's companion as the latter had recognized her. Next came two ladies, and after talking to the char-woman they also moved forward, and as Sue stood reaching upward, watched her hand tracing the letters, and critically regarded her person in relief against the white wall, till she grew so nervous that she trembled visibly.

They went back to where the others were standing, talking in under-tones: and one said—Sue could not hear which—'She's his wife, I suppose?'

'Some say Yes: some say No,' was the reply from the charwoman.

'Not? Then she ought to be, or somebody's—that's very clear!'

'They've only been married a very few weeks, whether or no.'

'A strange pair to be painting the Two Tables! I wonder Biles and Willis could think of such a thing as hiring those!'

The churchwarden supposed that Biles and Willis knew of nothing wrong, and then the other, who had been talking to the old woman, explained what she meant by calling them strange people.

The probable drift of the subdued conversation which followed was made plain by the churchwarden breaking into an anecdote, in a voice that everybody in the church could hear, though obviously suggested by the present situation:

'Well, now, it is a curious thing, but my grandfather told me a strange tale of a most immoral case that happened at the painting of the Commandments in a church out by Gaymead—which is quite within a walk of this one. In them days Commandments were mostly done in gilt letters on a black ground, and that's how they were out where I say, before the owld church was rebuilded. It must have been somewhere about a hundred years ago that them Commandments wanted doing up, just as ours do here, and they had to get men from Aldbrickham to do 'em. Now they wished to get the job finished by a particular Sunday, so the men had to work late Saturday night, against their will, for over-time was not paid then as 'tis now. There was no true religion in the country at that date, neither among pa'sons, clerks, nor people, and to keep the men up to their work the vicar had to let 'em have plenty of drink during the afternoon. As evening drawed on they sent for some more themselves; rum, by all account. It got later and later, and they got more and more fuddled,[4] till at last they went a-putting their rum-bottle and rummers upon the Communion table, and drawed up a trestle or two, and sate round comfortable, and poured out again right hearty bumpers.[5] No sooner had they tossed off their glasses than, so the story goes, they fell down senseless, one and all. How long they bode so they didn't know, but when they came to themselves there was a terrible thunderstorm a-raging, and they seemed to see in the gloom a dark figure with very thin legs and a curious voot,[6] a-standing on the ladder, and finishing their work. When it got daylight they could see that the work was really finished, and couldn't at all mind finishing it themselves. They went home, and the next thing they heard was that a great scandal had been caused in the church that Sunday morning, for when the people came and service began, all saw that the Ten Commandments wez painted with the "Nots" left out. Decent people wouldn't attend service there for a long time, and the Bishop had to be sent for to re-consecrate the church. That's the tradition as I used to hear it as a child. You must take it for what it is wo'th, but this case to-day has reminded me o't, as I say.'

The visitors gave one more glance, as if to see whether Jude and Sue had left the Nots out likewise, and then severally left the church, even the old woman at last. Sue and Jude, who had not stopped working, sent back the child to school, and remained with out speaking; till, looking at her narrowly, he found she had been crying silently.

'Never mind, comrade!' he said. 'I know what it is!'

'I can't *bear* that they, and everybody, should think people wicked because they may have chosen to live their own way! It is really these opinions that make the best intentioned people reckless, and actually become immoral!'

'Never be cast down! It was only a funny story.'

'Ah, but we suggested it! I am afraid I have done you mischief, Jude, instead of helping you by coming!'

4. Intoxicated.
5. Glasses full to the brim.
6. Foot; the devil traditionally has a cloven foot.

To have suggested such a story was certainly not very exhilarating, in a serious view of their position. However, in a few minutes Sue seemed to see that their position this morning had a ludicrous side, and wiping her eyes she laughed.

'It is droll, after all,' she said, 'that we two, of all people, with our queer history, should happen to be here painting the Ten Commandments! You a reprobate, and I—in my condition. . . . O dear!' . . . And with her hand over her eyes she laughed again silently and intermittently, till she was quite weak.

'That's better,' said Jude gaily. 'Now we are right again, aren't we, little girl!'

'O but it is serious, all the same!' she sighed as she took up the brush and righted herself. 'But do you see they don't think we are married? They *won't* believe it! It is extraordinary!'

'I don't care whether they think so or not,' said Jude. 'I shan't take any more trouble to make them.'

They sat down to lunch—which they had brought with them not to hinder time—and having eaten it were about to set to work anew when a man entered the church, and Jude recognized in him the contractor Willis. He beckoned to Jude, and spoke to him apart.

'Here—I've just had a complaint about this,' he said, with rather breathless awkwardness. 'I don't wish to go into the matter—as of course I didn't know what was going on—but I am afraid I must ask you and her to leave off, and let somebody else finish this! It is best, to avoid all unpleasantness. I'll pay you for the week, all the same.'

Jude was too independent to make any fuss; and the contractor paid him, and left. Jude picked up his tools, and Sue cleansed her brush. Then their eyes met.

'How could we be so simple as to suppose we might do this!' said she, dropping to her tragic note, 'Of course we ought not—I ought not—to have come!'

'I had no idea that anybody was going to intrude into such a lonely place and see us! Jude returned. 'Well, it can't be helped, dear; and of course I wouldn't wish to injure Willis's trade-connection by staying.' They sat down passively for a few minutes, proceeded out of the church, and overtaking the boy pursued their thoughtful way to Aldbrickham.

Fawley had still a pretty zeal in the cause of education, and, as was natural with his experiences, he was active in furthering 'equality of opportunity' by any humble means open to him. He had joined an Artizans' Mutual Improvement Society established in the town about the time of his arrival there; its members being young men of all creeds and denominations, including Churchmen, Congregationalists, Baptists, Unitarians, Positivists, and others—Agnostics[7] had scarcely been

7. The word was coined by T. H. Huxley about 1870.

heard of at this time—their one common wish to enlarge their minds forming a sufficiently close bond of union. The subscription was small, and the room homely and Jude's activity, uncustomary acquirements, and above all, singular intuition on what to read and how to set about it—begotten of his years of struggle against malignant stars—had led to his being placed on the committee.

A few evenings after his dismissal from the church repairs, and before he had obtained any more work to do, he went to attend a meeting of the aforesaid committee. It was late when he arrived: all the others had come, and as he entered they looked dubiously at him, and hardly uttered a word of greeting. He guessed that some thing bearing on himself had been either discussed or mooted. Some ordinary business was transacted, and it was disclosed that the number of subscriptions had shown a sudden falling off for that quarter. One member—a really well-meaning and upright man—began speaking in enigmas about certain possible causes: that it behoved them to look well into their constitution; for if the committee were not respected, and had not at least, in their differences, a common standard of *conduct*, they would bring the institution to the ground. Nothing further was said in Jude's presence, but he knew what this meant; and turning to the table wrote a note resigning his office there and then.

Thus the supersensitive couple were more and more impelled to go away. And then bills were sent in, and the question arose, what could Jude do with his great-aunt's heavy old furniture, if he left the town to travel he knew not whither? This, and the necessity of ready money, compelled him to decide on an auction, much as he would have preferred to keep the venerable goods.

The day of the sale came on; and Sue for the last time cooked her own, the child's, and Jude's breakfast in the little house he had furnished. It chanced to be a wet day; moreover Sue was unwell, and not wishing to desert her poor Jude in such gloomy circumstances, for he was compelled to stay awhile, she acted on the suggestion of the auctioneer's man, and ensconced herself in an upper room, which could be emptied of its effects, and so kept closed to the bidders. Here Jude discovered her; and with the child, and their few trunks, baskets, and bundles, and two chairs and a table that were not in the sale, the two sat in meditative talk.

Footsteps began stamping up and down the bare stairs, the comers inspecting the goods, some of which were of so quaint and ancient a make as to acquire an adventitious value as art. Their door was tried once or twice, and to guard themselves against intrusion Jude wrote 'Private' on a scrap of paper, and stuck it upon the panel.

They soon found that, instead of the furniture, their own personal histories and past conduct began to be discussed to an unexpected and intolerable extent by the intending bidders. It was not till now that they really discovered what a fools' paradise of supposed unrecognition they had been living in of late. Sue silently took her companion's hand, and with eyes on each other they heard these passing remarks—the quaint and mysterious personality of Father Time being a subject which formed a large ingredient in the hints and innuendoes. At length the auction began in the room below, whence they could hear each familiar article knocked down, the highly prized ones cheaply, the unconsidered at an unexpected price.

'People don't understand us,' he sighed heavily. 'I am glad we have decided to go.'

'The question is, where to?'

'It ought to be to London. There one can live as one chooses.'

'No—not London, dear! I know it well. We should be unhappy there.'

'Why?'

'Can't you think?'

'Because Arabella is there?'

'That's the chief reason.'

'But in the country I shall always be uneasy lest there should be some more of our late experience. And I don't care to lessen it by explaining, for one thing, all about the boy's history. To cut him off from his past. I have determined to keep silence. I am sickened of ecclesiastical work now; and I shouldn't like to accept it, if offered me!'

'You ought to have learnt Classic. Gothic is barbaric art, after all. Pugin[8] was wrong, and Wren[9] was right. Remember the interior of Christminster Cathedral—almost the first place in which we looked in each other's faces. Under the picturesqueness of those Norman details one can see the grotesque childishness of uncouth people trying to imitate the vanished Roman forms, remembered by dim tradition only.'

'Yes—you have half converted me to that view by what you have said before. But one can work, and despise what one does. I must do something, if not church-gothic.'

'I wish we could both follow an occupation in which personal circumstances don't count,' she said, smiling up wistfully. 'I am as disqualified for teaching as you are for ecclesiastical art. You must fall back upon railway stations, bridges, theatres, music-halls, hotels—everything that has no connection with conduct.'

'I am not skilled in those. . . . I ought to take to bread-baking. I grew up in the baking business with aunt, you know. But even a baker must be conventional, to get customers.'

---

8. Augustus Pugin (1812–1852), architect and propagandist of the Gothic Revival, which displaced Renaissance styles in favor of imitation medievalism.
9. Sir Christopher Wren (1631–1723) designed many churches and other buildings in classical style.

'Unless he keeps a cake and gingerbread stall at markets and fairs, where people are gloriously indifferent to everything except the quality of the goods.'

Their thoughts were diverted by the voice of the auctioneer: 'Now this antique oak settle—a unique example of old English furniture, worthy the attention of all collectors!'

'That was my great-grandfather's,' said Jude. 'I wish we could have kept the poor old thing!'

One by one the articles went, and the afternoon passed away. Jude and the other two were getting tired and hungry, but after the conversation they had heard they were shy of going out while the purchasers were in their line of retreat. However, the later lots drew on, and it became necessary to emerge into the rain soon, to take on Sue's things to their temporary lodging.

'Now the next lot: two pairs of pigeons, all alive and plump—a nice pie for somebody for next Sunday's dinner!'

The impending sale of these birds had been the most trying suspense of the whole afternoon. They were Sue's pets, and when it was found that they could not possibly be kept, more sadness was caused than by parting from all the furniture. Sue tried to think away her tears as she heard the trifling sum that her dears were deemed to be worth advanced by small stages to the price at which they were finally knocked down. The purchaser was a neighbouring poulterer, and they were unquestionably doomed to die before the next market day.

Noting her dissembled distress Jude kissed her, and said it was time to go and see if the lodgings were ready. He would go on with the boy, and fetch her soon.

When she was left alone she waited patiently, but Jude did not come back. At last she started, the coast being clear, and on passing the poulterer's shop, not far off, she saw her pigeons in a hamper by the door. An emotion at sight of them, assisted by the growing dusk of evening, caused her to act on impulse, and first looking around her quickly, she pulled out the peg which fastened down the cover, and went on. The cover was lifted from within, and the pigeons flew away with a clatter that brought the chagrined poulterer cursing and swearing to the door.

Sue reached the lodging trembling, and found Jude and the boy making it comfortable for her. 'Do the buyers pay before they bring away the things;' she asked breathlessly.

'Yes, I think. Why?'

'Because, then, I've done such a wicked thing!' And she explained, in bitter contrition.

'I shall have to pay the poulterer for them, if he doesn't catch them,' said Jude. 'But never mind. Don't fret about it, dear.'

'It was so foolish of me! O why should Nature's law be mutual butchery!'

'Is it so, mother?' asked the boy intently.

'Yes!' said Sue vehemently.

'Well, they must take their chance, now, poor things,' said Jude. 'As soon as the sale-account is wound up, and our bills paid, we go.'

'Where do we go to?' asked Time, in suspense.

'We must sail under sealed orders, that nobody may trace us. . . . We mustn't go to Alfredston, or to Melchester, or to Shaston, or to Christminster. Apart from those we may go anywhere.'

'Why mustn't we go there, father?'

'Because of a cloud that has gathered over us; though "we have wronged no man, corrupted no man, defrauded no man!"[1] Though perhaps we have "done that which was right in our own eyes." '[2]

V-7

From that week Jude Fawley and Sue walked no more in the town of Aldbrickham.

Whither they had gone nobody knew, chiefly because nobody cared to know. Any one sufficiently curious to trace the steps of such an obscure pair might have discovered without great trouble that they had taken advantage of his adaptive craftsmanship to enter on a shifting, almost nomadic, life, which was not without its pleasantness for a time.

Whenever Jude heard of freestone work to be done, thither he went, choosing by preference places remote from his old haunts and Sue's. He laboured at a job, long or briefly, till it was finished; and then moved on.

Two whole years and a half passed thus. Sometimes he might have been found shaping the mullions of a country mansion, sometimes setting the parapet of a town-hall, sometimes ashlaring[1] an hotel at Sandbourne, sometimes a museum at Casterbridge, sometimes as far down as Exonbury, sometimes at Stoke-Barehills. Later still he was at Kennetbridge, a thriving town not more than a dozen miles south of Marygreen, this being his nearest approach to the village where he was known; for he had a sensitive dread of being questioned as to his life and fortunes by those who had been acquainted with him during his ardent young manhood of study and promise, and his brief and unhappy married life at that time.

1. 2 Corinthians 7.2 (with slight omissions).
2. Judges 17.6 ("every man did that which was right in his own eyes").
1. Facing a brick wall with thin slabs of stone.

At some of these places he would be detained for months, at others only a few weeks. His curious and sudden antipathy to ecclesiastical work, both episcopal and nonconformist, which had risen in him when suffering under a smarting sense of misconception, remained with him in cold blood, less from any fear of renewed censure than from an ultra-conscientiousness which would not allow him to seek a living out of those who would disapprove of his ways; also, too, from a sense of inconsistency between his former dogmas and his present practice, hardly a shred of the beliefs with which he had first gone up to Christ-minster now remaining with him. He was mentally approaching the position which Sue had occupied when he first met her.

On a Saturday evening in May, nearly three years after Arabella's recognition of Sue and himself at the Agricultural Show, some of those who there encountered each other met again.

It was the spring fair at Kennetbridge, and, though this ancient trade-meeting had much dwindled from its dimensions of former times, the long straight street of the borough presented a lively scene about midday. At this hour a light trap, among other vehicles, was driven into the town by the north road, and up to the door of a temperance inn. There alighted two women, one the driver, an ordinary country person, the other a finely built figure in the deep mourning of a widow. Her sombre suit, of pronounced cut, caused her to appear a little out of place in the medley and bustle of a provincial fair.

'I will just find out where it is, Anny,' said the widow-lady to her companion, when the horse and cart had been taken by a man who came forward: 'and then I'll come back, and meet you here; and we'll go in and have something to eat and drink. I begin to feel quite a sinking.'

'With all my heart,' said the other. 'Though I would sooner have put up at the Chequers or The Jack. You can't get much at these temperance houses.'

'Now, don't you give way to gluttonous desires, my child,' said the woman in weeds[2] reprovingly. 'This is the proper place. Very well: we'll meet in half-an-hour, unless you come with me to find out where the site of the new chapel is?'

'I don't care to. You can tell me.'

The companions then went their several ways, the one in crape[3] walking firmly along with a mien of disconnection from her miscellaneous surroundings. Making inquiries she came to a hoarding,[4] within which were excavations denoting the foundations of a building; and on the boards without one or two large posters announcing that the foundation-stone of the chapel about to be erected would be laid that

2. Mourning dress.
3. Black silk used for mourning costume.
4. Temporary wooden fence surrounding a building under construction or repair.

afternoon at three o'clock by a London preacher of great popularity among his body.[5]

Having ascertained thus much the immensely weeded widow retraced her steps, and gave herself leisure to observe the movements of the fair. By and by her attention was arrested by a little stall of cakes and gingerbreads, standing between the more pretentious erections of trestles and canvas. It was covered with an immaculate cloth, and tended by a young woman apparently unused to the business, she being accompanied by a boy with an octogenarian face, who assisted her.

'Upon my—senses!' murmured the widow to herself. 'His wife Sue—if she is so!' She drew nearer to the stall. 'How do you do, Mrs. Fawley?' she said blandly.

Sue changed colour and recognized Arabella through the crape veil.

'How are you, Mrs. Cartlett?' she said stiffly. And then perceiving Arabella's garb her voice grew sympathetic in spite of herself. 'What?—you have lost—'

'My poor husband. Yes. He died suddenly, six weeks ago, leaving me none too well off, though he was a kind husband to me. But whatever profit there is in public-house keeping goes to them that brew the liquors, and not to them that retail 'em. . . . And you, my little old man! You don't know me, I expect?'

'Yes, I do. You be the woman I thought wer my mother for a bit, till I found you wasn't,' replied Father Time, who had learned to use the Wessex tongue quite naturally by now.

'All right. Never mind. I am a friend.'

'Juey,' said Sue suddenly, 'go down to the station platform with this tray—there's another train coming in, I think.'

When he was gone Arabella continued: 'He'll never be a beauty, will he, poor chap! Does he know I am his mother really?'

'No. He thinks there is some mystery about his parentage—that's all. Jude is going to tell him when he is a little older.'

'But how do you come to be doing this? I am surprised.'

'It is only a temporary occupation—a fancy of ours while we are in a difficulty.'

'Then you are living with him still?'

'Yes.'

'Married?'

'Of course.'

'Any children?'

'Two.'

'And another coming soon, I see.'

Sue writhed under the hard and direct questioning, and her tender little mouth began to quiver.

5. Members of a congregation or denomination.

'Lord—I mean goodness gracious—what is there to cry about? Some folks would be proud enough!'

'It is not that I am ashamed—not as you think! But it seems such a terribly tragic thing to bring beings into the world—so presumptuous— that I question my right to do it sometimes!'

'Take it easy, my dear. . . . But you don't tell me why you do such a thing as this? Jude used to be a proud sort of chap—above any business almost, leave alone keeping a standing.'[6]

'Perhaps my husband has altered a little since then. I am sure he is not proud now!' And Sue's lips quivered again. 'I am doing this because he caught a chill early in the year while putting up some stone-work of a music-hall, at Quartershot, which he had to do in the rain, the work having to be executed by a fixed day. He is better than he was; but it has been a long, weary time! We have had an old widow friend with us to help us through it; but she's leaving soon.'

'Well, I am respectable too, thank God, and of a serious way of thinking since my loss. Why did you choose to sell gingerbreads?'

'That's a pure accident. He was brought up to the baking business, and it occurred to him to try his hand at these, which he can make without coming out of doors. We call them Christminster cakes. They are a great success.'

'I never saw any like 'em. Why, they are windows and towers, and pinnacles! And upon my word they are very nice.' She had helped herself, and was unceremoniously munching one of the cakes.

'Yes. They are reminiscences of the Christminster Colleges. Tracer- ied windows, and cloisters, you see. It was a whim of his to do them in pastry.'

'Still harping on Christminster—even in his cakes!' laughed Ara- bella. 'Just like Jude. A ruling passion. What a queer fellow he is, and always will be!'

Sue sighed, and she looked her distress at hearing him criticized.

'Don't you think he is? Come now; you do, though you are so fond of him!'

'Of course Christminster is a sort of fixed vision with him, which I suppose he'll never be cured of believing in. He still thinks it is a great centre of high and fearless thought, instead of what it is, a nest of commonplace schoolmasters whose characteristic is timid obsequious- ness to tradition.'

Arabella was quizzing[7] Sue with more regard of how she was speaking than of what she was saying. 'How odd to hear a woman selling cakes talk like that!' she said. 'Why don't you go back to school-keeping?'

Sue shook her head. 'They won't have me.'

'Because of the divorce, I suppose?'

6. Stall.
7. Looking at, usually with an air of mockery.

'That and other things. And there is no reason to wish it. We gave up all ambition, and were never so happy in our lives till his illness came.'

'Where are you living?'

'I don't care to say.'

'Here in Kennetbridge?'

Sue's manner showed Arabella that her random guess was right.

'Here comes the boy back again,' continued Arabella. 'My boy and Jude's!'

Sue's eyes darted a spark. 'You needn't throw that in my face!' she cried.

'Very well—though I half feel as if I should like to have him with me! . . . But Lord, I don't want to take him from 'ee—ever I should sin to speak so profane—though I should think you must have enough of your own! He's in very good hands, that I know; and I am not the woman to find fault with what the Lord has ordained. I've reached a more resigned frame of mind.'

'Indeed! I wish I had been able to do so.'

'You should try,' replied the widow, from the serene heights of a soul conscious not only of spiritual but of social superiority. 'I make no boast of my awakening, but I'm not what I was. After Cartlett's-death I was passing the chapel in the street next ours, and went into it for shelter from a shower of rain. I felt a need of some sort of support under my loss, and, as 'twas righter than gin, I took to going there regular, and found it a great comfort. But I've left London now, you know, and at present I am living at Alfredston, with my friend Anny, to be near my own old country. I'm not come here to the fair to-day. There's to be the foundation-stone of a new chapel laid this afternoon by a popular London preacher, and I drove over with Anny. Now I must go back to meet her.'

Then Arabella wished Sue good-bye, and went on.

V–8

In the afternoon Sue and the other people bustling about Kennet-bridge fair could hear singing inside the placarded hoarding further down the street. Those who peeped through the opening saw a crowd of persons in broadcloth,[1] with hymn-books in their hands, standing round the excavations for the new chapel-walls. Arabella Cartlett and her weeds stood among them. She had a clear, powerful voice, which could be distinctly heard with the rest, rising and falling to the tune, her inflated bosom being also seen doing likewise.

It was two hours later on the same day that Anny and Mrs. Cartlett having had tea at the Temperance hotel, started on their return journey across the high and open country which stretches between Kennet-

1. Black cloth of good quality.

bridge and Alfredston. Arabella was in a thoughtful mood; but her thoughts were not of the new chapel, as Anny at first surmised.

'No—it is something else,' at last said Arabella sullenly. 'I came here to-day never thinking of anybody but poor Cartlett, or of anything but spreading the Gospel by means of this new tabernacle[2] they've begun this afternoon. But something has happened to turn my mind another way quite. Anny, I've heard of un again, and I've seen *her*!'

'Who?'

'I've heard of Jude and I've seen his wife. And ever since, do what I will, and though I sung the hymns wi' all my strength, I have not been able to help thinking about 'n; which I've no right to do as a chapel member.'

'Can't ye fix your mind upon what was said by the London preacher to-day, and try to get rid of your wandering fancies that way?'

'I do. But my wicked heart will ramble off in spite of myself!'

'Well—I know what it is to have a wanton mind o' my own, too! If you on'y knew what I do dream sometimes o' nights quite against my wishes, you'd say I had my struggles!' (Anny, too, had grown rather serious of late, her lover having jilted her.)

'What shall I do about it?' urged Arabella morbidly.

'You could take a lock of your late-lost husband's hair, and have it made into a mourning brooch, and look at it every hour of the day.'

'I haven't a morsel!—and if I had 'twould be no good. . . . After all that's said about the comforts of this religion, I wish I had Jude back again!'

'You must fight valiant against the feeling, since he's another's. And I've heard that another good thing for it, when it afflicts volupshious widows, is to go to your husband's grave in the dusk of evening, and stand a long while a-bowed down.'

'Pooh! I know as well as you what I should do; only I don't do it!'

They drove in silence along the straight road till they were within the horizon of Marygreen, which lay not far to the left of their route. They came to the junction of the highway and the cross-lane leading to that village, whose church-tower could be seen athwart the hollow. When they got yet further on, and were passing the lonely house in which Arabella and Jude had lived during the first months of their marriage, and where the pig-killing had taken place, she could control herself no longer.

'He's more mine than hers!' she burst out. 'What right has she to him. I should like to know! I'd take him from her if I could!'

'Fie, Abby! And your husband only six weeks gone! Pray against it!'

'Be damned if I do! Feelings are feelings! I won't be a creeping hypocrite any longer—so there!'

---

2. Nonconformist chapel.

Arabella had hastily drawn from her pocket a bundle of tracts which she had brought with her to distribute at the fair, and of which she had given away several. As she spoke she flung the whole remainder of the packet into the hedge. 'I've tried that sort o' physic and have failed wi' it. I must be as I was born!'

'Hush! You be excited, dear! Now you come along home quiet, and have a cup of tea, and don't let us talk about un no more. We won't come out this road again, as it leads to where he is, because it inflames 'ee so. You'll be all right again soon.'

Arabella did calm herself down by degrees; and they crossed the Ridge-way. When they began to descend the long, straight hill, they saw plodding along in front of them an elderly man of spare stature and thoughtful gait. In his hand he carried a basket; and there was a touch of slovenliness in his attire, together with that indefinable something in his whole appearance which suggested one who was his own housekeeper, purveyor, confidant, and friend, through possessing nobody else at all in the world to act in those capacities for him. The remainder of the journey was down-hill, and guessing him to be going to Alfredston they offered him a lift, which he accepted.

Arabella looked at him, and looked again, till at length she spoke. 'If I don't mistake I am talking to Mr. Phillotson?'

The wayfarer faced round and regarded her in turn. 'Yes; my name is Phillotson,' he said. 'But I don't recognize you, ma'am.'

'I remember you well enough when you used to be schoolmaster out at Marygreen, and I one of your scholars. I used to walk up there from Cresscombe every day, because we had only a mistress down at our place, and you taught better. But you wouldn't remember me as I should you?—Arabella Donn.'

He shook his head. 'No,' he said politely, 'I don't recall the name. And I should hardly recognize in your present portly self the slim school child no doubt you were then.'

'Well, I always had plenty of flesh on my bones. However, I am staying down here with some friends at present. You know, I suppose, who I married?'

'No.'

'Jude Fawley—also a scholar of yours—at least a night scholar—for some little time I think? And known to you afterwards, if I am not mistaken.'

'Dear me, dear me,' said Phillotson, starting out of his stiffness. '*You* Fawley's wife? To be sure—he had a wife! And he—I understood—'

'Divorced her—as you did yours—perhaps for better reasons.'

'Indeed?'

'Well—he med have been right in doing it—right for both; for I soon married again, and all went pretty straight till my husband died lately. But you—you were decidedly wrong!'

'No,' said Phillotson, with sudden testiness. 'I would rather not talk of this, but—I am convinced I did only what was right, and just, and moral. I have suffered for my act and opinions, but I hold to them; though her loss was a loss to me in more ways than one!'

'You lost your school and good income through her, did you not?'

'I don't care to talk of it. I have recently come back here—to Marygreen, I mean.'

'You are keeping the school there again, just as formerly?'

The pressure of a sadness that would out unsealed him. 'I am there,' he replied. 'Just as formerly, no. Merely on sufferance. It was a last resource—a small thing to return to after my move upwards, and my long indulged hopes—a returning to zero, with all its humiliations. But it is a refuge. I like the seclusion of the place, and the vicar having known me before my so-called eccentric conduct towards my wife had ruined my reputation as a schoolmaster, he accepted my services when all other schools were closed against me. However, although I take fifty pounds a year here after taking above two hundred elsewhere, I prefer it to running the risk of having my old domestic experiences raked up against me, as I should do if I tried to make a move.'

'Right you are. A contented mind is a continual feast. She has done no better.'

'She is not doing well, you mean?'

'I met her by accident at Kennetbridge this very day, and she is anything but thriving. Her husband is ill, and she anxious. You made a fool of a mistake about her, I tell 'ee again, and the harm you did yourself by dirting your own nest serves you right, excusing the liberty.'

'How?'

'She was innocent.'

'But nonsense! They did not even defend the case!'

'That was because they didn't care to. She was quite innocent of what obtained you your freedom, at the time you obtained it. I saw her just afterwards, and proved it to myself completely by talking to her.'

Phillotson grasped the edge of the spring-cart, and appeared to be much stressed and worried by the information. 'Still—she wanted to go,' he said.

'Yes. But you shouldn't have let her. That's the only way with these fanciful women that chaw high[3]—innocent or guilty. She'd have come round in time. We all do! Custom does it! it's all the same in the end! However, I think she's fond of her man still—whatever he med be of her. You were too quick about her. I shouldn't have let her go! I should have kept her chained on—her spirit for kicking would have been broke soon enough! There's nothing like bondage and a stone-deaf taskmas-

3. The usual meaning of this dialect phrase is to be genteel, socially ambitious, and contemptuous of one's inferiors. Here it seems to mean "get out of hand, like to have one's own way."

ter for taming us women. Besides, you've got the laws on your side. Moses knew. Don't you call to mind what he says?'

'Not for the moment, ma'am, I regret to say.'

'Call yourself a schoolmaster! I used to think o't when they read it in church, and I was carrying on a bit. "Then shall the man be guiltless; but the woman shall bear her iniquity."⁴ Damn rough on us women; but we must grin and put up wi' it!—Haw haw!—Well; she's got her deserts now.'

'Yes,' said Phillotson, with biting sadness. 'Cruelty is the law pervading all nature and society; and we can't get out of it if we would!'

'Well—don't you forget to try it next time, old man.'

'I cannot answer you, madam. I have never known much of womankind.'

They had now reached the low levels bordering Alfredston, and passing through the outskirts approached a mill, to which Phillotson said his errand led him; whereupon they drew up, and he alighted, bidding them good-night in a preoccupied mood.

In the meantime Sue, though remarkably successful in her cakeselling experiment at Kennetbridge fair, had lost the temporary brightness which had begun to sit upon her sadness on account of that success. When all her 'Christminster' cakes had been disposed of she took upon her arm the empty basket, and the cloth which had covered the standing she had hired, and giving the other things to the boy left the street with him. They followed a lane to a distance of half a mile, till they met an old woman carrying a child in short clothes, and leading a toddler in the other hand.

Sue kissed the children, and said, 'How is he now?'

'Still better!' returned Mrs. Edlin cheerfully. 'Before you are upstairs again your husband will be well enough—don't 'ee trouble.'

They turned, and came to some old, dun-tiled⁵ cottages with gardens and fruit-trees. Into one of these they entered by lifting the latch without knocking, and were at once in the general livingroom. Here they greeted Jude, who was sitting in an arm-chair, the increased delicacy of his normally delicate features, and the childishly expectant look in his eyes, being alone sufficient to show that he had been passing through a severe illness.

'What—you have sold them all?' he said, a gleam of interest lighting up his face.

'Yes. Arcades, gables, east windows and all.' She told him the pecuniary results, and then hesitated. At last, when they were left alone, she informed him of the unexpected meeting with Arabella, and the latter's widowhood.

Jude was discomposed. 'What—is she living here?' he said.

4. Numbers 5.31 (slightly changed).
5. Roofed with dark tiles.

'No; at Alfredston,' said Sue.

Jude's countenance remained clouded. 'I thought I had better tell you?' she continued, kissing him anxiously.

'Yes. . . . Dear me! Arabella not in the depths of London, but down here! It is only a little over a dozen miles across the country to Alfredston. What is she doing there?'

She told him all she knew. 'She has taken to chapel-going,' Sue added; 'and talks accordingly.'

'Well,' said Jude, 'perhaps it is for the best that we have almost decided to move on. I feel much better to-day, and shall be well enough to leave in a week or two. Then Mrs. Edlin can go home again—dear faithful old soul—the only friend we have in the world!'

'Where do you think to go to?' Sue asked, a troublousness in her tones.

Then Jude confessed what was in his mind. He said it would surprise her, perhaps, after his having resolutely avoided all the old places for so long. But one thing and another had made him think a great deal of Christminster lately, and, if she didn't mind, he would like to go back there. Why should they care if they were known? It was over-sensitive of them to mind so much. They could go on selling cakes there, for that matter, if he couldn't work. He had no sense of shame at mere poverty; and perhaps he would be as strong as ever soon, and able to set up stone-cutting for himself there.

'Why should you care so much for Christminster?' she said pensively. 'Christminster cares nothing for you, poor dear!'

'Well, I do, I can't help it. I love the place—although I know how it hates all men like me—the so-called Self-taught,—how it scorns our laboured acquisitions, when it should be the first to respect them; how it sneers at our false quantities[6] and mispronunciations, when it should say, I see you want help, my poor friend! . . . Nevertheless, it is the centre of the universe to me, because of my early dream: and nothing can alter it. Perhaps it will soon wake up, and be generous. I pray so! . . . I should like to go back to live there—perhaps to die there! In two or three weeks I might, I think. It will then be June, and I should like to be there by a particular day.'

His hope that he was recovering proved so far well grounded that in three weeks they had arrived in the city of many memories; were actually treading its pavements, receiving the reflection of the sunshine from its wasting walls.

---

6. Confusion between long and short vowels or syllables in Latin or Greek verse.

Part Sixth: At Christminster Again

'. . . And she humbled her body greatly, and all the places of her joy she filled with her torn hair.'
—ESTHER (Apoc.)[1]

'There are two who decline, a woman and I,
And enjoy our death in the darkness here.'
—R. BROWNING[2]

VI–1

On their arrival the station was lively with straw-hatted young men, welcoming young girls who bore a remarkable family likeness to their welcomers, and who were dressed up in the brightest and lightest of raiment.

'The place seems gay,' said Sue. 'Why—it is Remembrance Day![3]— Jude—how sly of you—you came to-day on purpose!'

'Yes,' said Jude quietly, as he took charge of the small child, and told Arabella's boy to keep close to them, Sue attending to their own eldest. 'I thought we might as well come to-day as on any other.'

'But I am afraid it will depress you!' she said, looking anxiously at him up and down.

'O, I mustn't let it interfere with our business; and we have a good deal to do before we shall be settled here. The first thing is lodgings.'

Having left their luggage and his tools at the station they proceeded on foot up the familiar street, the holiday people all drifting in the same direction. Reaching the Fourways they were about to turn off to where accommodation was likely to be found when, looking at the clock and the hurrying crowd, Jude said: 'Let us go and see the procession, and never mind the lodgings just now? We can get them afterwards.'

'Oughtn't we to get a house over our heads first?' she asked.

But his soul seemed full of the anniversary, and together they went down Chief Street, their smallest child in Jude's arms, Sue leading her little girl, and Arabella's boy walking thoughtfully and silently beside them. Crowds of pretty sisters in airy costumes, and meekly ignorant parents who had known no College in their youth, were under convoy in the same direction by brothers and sons bearing the opinion written large on them, that no properly qualified human beings had lived on earth till they came to grace it here and now.

1. Esther 14.2 (Esther is one of the Apocryphal books of the Bible).
2. From Browning's poem "Too Late."
3. The annual Commemoration day at Oxford marks the end of the academic year. Hardy was in Oxford for Commemoration in June 1893.

'My failure is reflected on me by every one of those young fellows,' said Jude. 'A lesson on presumption is awaiting me to-day!—Humiliation Day for me! . . . If you, my dear darling, hadn't come to my rescue, I should have gone to the dogs with despair!'

She saw from his face that he was getting into one of his tempestuous, self-harrowing moods. 'It would have been better if we had gone at once about our own affairs, dear,' she answered. 'I am sure this sight will awaken old sorrows in you, and do no good!'

'Well—we are near; we will see it now,' said he.

They turned in on the left by the church with Italian porch,[4] whose helical[5] columns were heavily draped with creepers, and pursued the lane till there arose on Jude's sight the circular theatre[6] with that well-known lantern above it, which stood in his mind as the sad symbol of his abandoned hopes; for it was from that outlook that he had finally surveyed the City of Colleges on the afternoon of his great meditation, which convinced him at last of the futility of his attempt to be a son of the University.

To-day, in the open space stretching between this building and the nearest college, stood a crowd of expectant people. A passage was kept clear through their midst by two barriers of timber, extending from the door of the college to the door of the large building between it and the theatre.

'Here is the place—they are just going to pass!' cried Jude in sudden excitement. And pushing his way to the front he took up a position close to the barrier, still hugging the youngest child in his arms, while Sue and the others kept immediately behind him. The crowd filled in at their back, and fell to talking, joking, and laughing as carriage after carriage drew up at the lower door of the college, and solemn stately figures in blood-red robes[7] began to alight. The sky had grown overcast and livid, and thunder rumbled now and then.

Father Time shuddered. 'It do seem like the Judgment Day!' he whispered.

'They are only learned Doctors,' said Sue.

While they waited big drops of rain fell on their heads and shoulders, and the delay grew tedious. Sue again wished not to stay.

'They won't be long now,' said Jude, without turning his head.

But the procession did not come forth, and somebody in the crowd, to pass the time, looked at the façade of the nearest college, and said he wondered what was meant by the Latin inscription in its midst. Jude, who stood near the inquirer, explained it, and finding that the

4. St. Mary's, the university church, has a seventeenth-century porch in Italian style.
5. Spiral.
6. The Sheldonian.
7. The scarlet academic dress of those holding doctors' degrees. (After his death, Hardy's body was wrapped in the scarlet gown of the honorary doctorate bestowed by Cambridge University.)

people all round him were listening with interest, went on to describe the carving of the frieze (which he had studied years before), and to criticize some details of masonry in other college fronts about the city.

The idle crowd, including the two policemen at the doors, stared like the Lycaonians at Paul,[8] for Jude was apt to get too enthusiastic over any subject in hand, and they seemed to wonder how the stranger should know more about the buildings of their town than they themselves did; till one of them said: 'Why I know that man; he used to work here years ago—Jude Fawley, that's his name! Don't you mind he used to be nicknamed Tutor of St. Slums, d'ye mind?—because he aimed at that line o' business? He's married, I suppose, then, and that's his child he's carrying. Taylor would know him, as he knows everybody.'

The speaker was a man named Jack Stagg, with whom Jude had formerly worked in repairing the college masonries; Tinker Taylor was seen to be standing near. Having his attention called the latter cried across the barriers to Jude: 'You've honoured us by coming back again, my friend!'

Jude nodded.

'An' you don't seem to have done any great things for yourself by going away?'

'Except found more mouths to fill!' This came in a new voice, and Jude recognized its owner to be Uncle Joe, another mason whom he had known.

Jude replied good-humouredly that he could not dispute it; and from remark to remark something like a general conversation arose between him and the crowd of idlers, during which Tinker Taylor asked Jude if he remembered the Apostles' Creed in Latin still, and the night of the challenge in the public-house.

'But Fortune didn't lie that way?' threw in Joe. 'Yer powers wasn't enough to carry 'ee through?'

'Don't answer them any more!' entreated Sue.

'I don't think I like Christminster!' murmured little Time mournfully, as he stood submerged and invisible in the crowd.

But finding himself the centre of curiosity, quizzing, and comment, Jude was not inclined to shrink from open declarations of what he had no great reason to be ashamed of; and in a little while was stimulated to say in a loud voice to the listening throng generally:

'It is a difficult question, my friends, for any young man—that question I had to grapple with, and which thousands are weighing at the present moment in these uprising times—whether to follow uncritically the track he find himself in, without considering his aptness for it, or to consider what his aptness or bent may be, and re-shape his course accordingly. I tried to do the latter, and I failed. But I don't

8. The Lycaonians witnessed a miracle performed by St. Paul (Acts 14).

admit that my failure proved my view to be a wrong one, or that my success would have made it a right one; though that's how we appraise such attempts nowadays—I mean, not by their essential soundness, but by their accidental outcomes. If I had ended by becoming like one of these gentlemen in red and black that we saw dropping in here by now, everybody would have said: "See how wise that young man was, to follow the bent of his nature!" But having ended no better than I began they say: "See what a fool that fellow was in following a freak of his fancy!"

'However it was my poverty and not my will that consented to be beaten. It takes two or three generations to do what I tried to do in one; and my impulses—affections—vices perhaps they should be called—were too strong not to hamper a man without advantages; who should be as cold-blooded as a fish and as selfish as a pig to have a really good chance of being one of his country's worthies. You may ridicule me—I am quite willing that you should—I am a fit subject, no doubt. But I think if you knew what I have gone through these last few years you would rather pity me. And if they knew'—he nodded towards the college at which the Dons were severally arriving—'it is just possible they would do the same.'

'He do look ill and worn-out, it is true!' said a woman.

Sue's face grew more emotional; but though she stood close to Jude she was screened.

'I may do some good before I am dead—be a sort of success as a frightful example of what not to do; and so illustrate a moral story,' continued Jude, beginning to grow bitter, though he had opened serenely enough. 'I was, perhaps, after all, a paltry victim to the spirit of mental and social restlessness, that makes so many unhappy in these days!'

'Don't tell them that!' whispered Sue with tears, at perceiving Jude's state of mind. 'You weren't that. You struggled nobly to acquire knowledge, and only the meanest souls in the world would blame you!'

Jude shifted the child into a more easy position on his arm, and concluded: 'And what I appear, a sick and poor man, is not the worst of me. I am in a chaos of principles—groping in the dark—acting by instinct and not after example. Eight or nine years ago when I came here first, I had a neat stock of fixed opinions, but they dropped away one by one and the further I get the less sure I am. I doubt if I have anything more for my present rule of life than following inclinations which do me and nobody else any harm, and actually give pleasure to those I love best. There, gentlemen, since you wanted to know how I was getting on, I have told you. Much good may it do you! I cannot explain further here. I perceive there is something wrong somewhere in our social formulas: what it is can only be discovered by men or women with greater insight than mine,—if, indeed, they ever discover it—at least in our time. "For who knoweth what is good for man in this life?—and who can tell a man what shall be after him under the sun?" [9]

'Hear, hear,' said the populace.

'Well preached!' said Tinker Taylor. And privately to his neighbours: 'Why, one of them jobbing pa'sons swarming about here, that takes the services when our head Reverends want a holiday, wouldn't ha' discoursed such doctrine for less than a guinea down? Hey? I'll take my oath not one o' 'em would! And then he must have had it wrote down for 'n. And this only a working man!'

As a sort of objective commentary on Jude's remarks there drove up at this moment with a belated Doctor, robed and panting, a cab whose horse failed to stop at the exact point required for setting down the hirer, who jumped out and entered the door. The driver, alighting, began to kick the animal in the belly.

'If that can be done,' said Jude, 'at college gates in the most religious and educational city in the world, what shall we say as to how far we've got?'

'Order!' said one of the policemen, who had been engaged with a comrade in opening the large doors opposite the college. 'Keep yer tongue quiet, my man, while the procession passes.' The rain came on more heavily, and all who had umbrellas opened them. Jude was not one of these, and Sue only possessed a small one, half sunshade. She had grown pale, though Jude did not notice it then.

'Let us go on, dear,' she whispered, endeavouring to shelter him. 'We haven't any lodgings yet, remember, and all our things are at the station; and you are by no means well yet. I am afraid this wet will hurt you!'

'They are coming now. Just a moment, and I'll go!' said he.

A peal of six bells struck out, human faces began to crowd the windows around, and the procession of Heads of Houses and new Doctors emerged, their red and black gowned forms passing across the field of Jude's vision like inaccessible planets across an object glass.[1]

As they went their names were called by knowing informants; and when they reached the old round theatre of Wren a cheer rose high.

'Let's go that way!' cried Jude, and though it now rained steadily he seemed not to know it, and took them round to the Theatre. Here they stood upon the straw that was laid to drown the discordant noise of wheels, where the quaint and frost-eaten stone busts encircling the building looked with pallid grimness on the proceedings, and in particular at the bedraggled Jude, Sue, and their children, as at ludicrous persons who had no business there.

9. Ecclesiastes 6.12 (with omissions).
1. Lens in telescope or microscope nearest the object.

'I wish I could get in!' he said to her fervidly. 'Listen—I may catch a few words of the Latin speech by staying here; the windows are open.'

However, beyond the peals of the organ, and the shouts and hurrahs between each piece of oratory, Jude's standing in the wet did not bring much Latin to his intelligence more than, now and then, a sonorous word in *um* or *ibus*.

'Well—I'm an outsider to the end of my days!' he sighed after a while. 'Now I'll go, my patient Sue. How good of you to wait in the rain all this time—to gratify my infatuation! I'll never care any more about the infernal cursed place, upon my soul I won't! But what made you tremble so when we were at the barrier? And how pale you are, Sue!'

'I saw Richard amongst the people on the other side.'

'Ah—did you!'

'He is evidently come up to Jerusalem to see the festival[2] like the rest of us: and on that account is probably living not so very far away. He had the same hankering for the University that you had, in a milder form. I don't think he saw me, though he must have heard you speaking to the crowd. But he seemed not to notice.'

'Well—suppose he did. Your mind is free from worries about him now, my Sue?'

'Yes, I suppose so. But I am weak. Although I know it is all right with out plans, I felt a curious dread of him; an awe, or terror, of conventions I don't believe in. It comes over me at times like a sort of creeping paralysis, and makes me so sad!'

'You are getting tired, Sue. O—I forgot, darling! Yes, we'll go on at once.'

They started in quest of the lodging, and at last found something that seemed to promise well, in Mildew Lane—a spot which to Jude was irresistible—though to Sue it was not so fascinating—a narrow lane close to the back of a college, but having no communication with it. The little houses were darkened to gloom by the high collegiate buildings, within which life was so far removed from that of the people in the lane as if it had been on opposite sides of the globe; yet only a thickness of wall divided them. Two or three of the houses had notices of rooms to let, and the newcomers knocked at the door of one, which a woman opened.

'Ah—listen!' said Jude suddenly, instead of addressing her.

'What?'

'Why the bells—what church can that be? The tones are familiar.'

Another peal of bells had begun to sound out at some distance off.

'I don't know!' said the landlady tartly. 'Did you knock to ask that?'

2. The allusion is to Luke 2.41–42. When Jesus was twelve years old, he went to Jerusalem with his parents for the feast of the Passover.

'No; for lodgings,' said Jude, coming to himself.

The householder scrutinized Sue's figure a moment. 'We haven't any to let,' said she, shutting the door.

Jude looked discomfited, and the boy distressed. 'Now, Jude,' said Sue, 'let me try. You don't know the way.'

They found a second place hard by; but here the occupier, observing not only Sue, but the boy and the small children, said civilly, 'I am sorry to say we don't let where there are children;' and also closed the door.

The small child squared its mouth and cried silently, with an instinct that trouble loomed. The boy sighed. 'I don't like Christminster!' he said. 'Are the great old houses gaols?'

'No; colleges,' said Jude; 'which perhaps you'll study in some day.'

'I'd rather not!' the boy rejoined.

'Now we'll try again,' said Sue. 'I'll pull my cloak more round me. . . . Leaving Kennetbridge for this place is like coming from Caiaphas to Pilate![3] . . . How do I look now, dear?'

'Nobody would notice it now,' said Jude.

There was one other house, and they tried a third time. The woman here was more amiable; but she had little room to spare, and could only agree to take in Sue and the children if her husband could go elsewhere. This arrangement they perforce adopted, in the stress from delaying their search till so late. They came to terms with her, though her price was rather high for their pockets. But they could not afford to be critical till Jude had time to get a more permanent abode; and in this house Sue took possession of a back room on the second floor with an inner closet-room for the children. Jude stayed and had a cup of tea; and was pleased to find that the window commanded the back of another of the colleges. Kissing all four he went to get a few necessaries and look for lodgings for himself.

When he was gone the landlady came up to talk a little with Sue, and gather something of the circumstances of the family she had taken in. Sue had not the art of prevarication, and, after admitting several facts as to their late difficulties and wanderings, she was startled by the landlady saying suddenly:

"Are you really a married woman?"

She hesitated; and then impulsively told the woman that her husband and herself had each been unhappy in their first marriages, after which, terrified at the thought of a second irrevocable union, and lest the conditions of the contract should kill their love, yet wishing to be together, they had literally not found the courage to repeat it, though

3. Caiaphas was the Jewish high priest before whom Jesus was tried before being handed over to Pontius Pilate, the Roman governor who sentenced him to be crucified (Matthew 26–27)—hence, from bad to worse.

they had attempted it two or three times. Therefore, though in her own sense of the words she was a married woman, in the landlady's sense she was not.

The housewife looked embarrassed, and went downstairs. Sue sat by the window in a reverie, watching the rain. Her quiet was broken by the noise of some one entering the house, and then the voices of a man and woman in conversation in the passage below. The landlady's husband had arrived, and she was explaining to him the incoming of the lodgers during his absence.

His voice rose in sudden anger. 'Now who wants such a woman here? and perhaps a confinement! . . . Besides, didn't I say I wouldn't have children? The hall and stairs fresh painted, to be kicked about by them! You must have known all was not straight with 'em—coming like that. Taking in a family when I said a single man.'

The wife expostulated, but, as it seemed, the husband insisted on his point; for presently a tap came to Sue's door, and the woman appeared.

'I am sorry to tell you, ma'am, she said, 'that I can't let you have the room for the week after all. My husband objects and therefore I must ask you to go. I don't mind your staying over to-night, as it is getting late in the afternoon; but I shall be glad if you can leave early in the morning.'

Though she knew that she was entitled to the lodging for a week, Sue did not wish to create a disturbance between the wife and husband, and she said she would leave as requested. When the landlady had gone Sue looked out of the window again. Finding that the rain had ceased she proposed to the boy that, after putting the little ones to bed, they should go out and search about for another place, and bespeak it for the morrow, so as not to be so hard driven then as they had been that day.

Therefore, instead of unpacking her boxes, which had just been sent on from the station by Jude, they sallied out into the damp though not unpleasant streets, Sue resolving not to disturb her husband with the news of her notice to quit while he was perhaps worried in obtaining a lodging for himself. In the company of the boy she wandered into this street and into that; but though she tried a dozen different houses she fared far worse alone than she had fared in Jude's company, and could get nobody to promise her a room for the following day. Every house-holder looked askance at such a woman and child inquiring for accommodation in the gloom.

'I ought not to be born, ought I?' said the boy with misgiving.

Thoroughly tired at last Sue returned to the place where she was not welcome, but where at least she had temporary shelter. In her absence Jude had left his address; but knowing how weak he still was she adhered to her determination not to disturb him till the next day.

VI–2

Sue sat looking at the bare floor of the room, the house being little more than an old intramural[1] cottage, and then she regarded the scene outside the uncurtained window. At some distance opposite, the outer walls of Sarcophagus College—silent, black and windowless—threw their four centuries of gloom, bigotry, and decay into the little room she occupied, shutting out the moonlight by night and the sun by day. The outlines of Rubric College[2] also were discernible beyond the other, and the tower of a third further off still. She thought of the strange operation of a simple-minded man's ruling passion, that it should have led Jude, who loved her and the children so tenderly, to place them here in this depressing purlieu,[3] because he was still haunted by his dream. Even now he did not distinctly hear the freezing negative that those scholared walls had echoed to his desire.

The failure to find another lodging, and the lack of room in this house for his father, had made a deep impression on the boy;—a brooding undemonstrative horror seemed to have seized him. The silence was broken by his saying: 'Mother, *what* shall we do tomorrow!'

'I don't know!' said Sue despondently. 'I am afraid this will trouble your father.'

'I wish father was quite well, and there had been room for him! Then it wouldn't matter so much! Poor father!'

'It wouldn't!'

'Can I do anything?'

'No! All is trouble, adversity and suffering!'

'Father went away to give us children room, didn't he?'

'Partly.'

'It would be better to be out o' the world than in it, wouldn't it?'

'It would almost, dear.'

' 'Tis because of us children, too, isn't it, that you can't get a good lodging?'

'Well—people do object to children sometimes.'

'Then if children make so much trouble, why do people have 'em?'

'O—because it is a law of nature.'

'But we don't ask to be born?'

'No indeed.'

'And what makes it worse with me is that you are not my real mother, and you needn't have had me unless you liked. I oughtn't to have come to 'ee—that's the real truth! I troubled 'em in Australia, and I trouble folk here. I wish I hadn't been born!'

1. Built within the walls of a larger building.
2. The fictitious names are symbolically appropriate: a sarcophagus is a stone coffin; a rubric is part of a prescribed order of divine service.
3. Here a mean street off a main thoroughfare.

'You couldn't help it, my dear.'

'I think that whenever children be born that are not wanted they should be killed directly, before their souls come to 'em, and not allowed to grow big and walk about!'

Sue did not reply. She was doubtfully pondering how to treat this too reflective child.

She at last concluded that, so far as circumstances permitted, she would be honest and candid with one who entered into her difficulties liked an aged friend.

'There is going to be another in our family soon,' she hesitatingly remarked.

'How?'

'There is going to be another baby.'

'What!' The boy jumped up wildly. 'O God, mother, you've never a-sent for another; and such trouble with what you've got!'

'Yes, I have, I am sorry to say!' murmured Sue, her eyes glistening with suspended tears.

The boy burst out weeping. 'O you don't care, you don't care!' he cried in bitter reproach. 'How *ever* could you, mother, be so wicked and cruel as this, when you needn't have done it till we was better off, and father well!—To bring us all into *more* trouble! No room for us, and father a-forced to go away, and we turned out tomorrow; and yet you be going to have another of us soon! . . . 'Tis done o' purpose!— 'tis—'tis!' He walked up and down sobbing.

'Y-you must forgive me, little Jude!' she pleaded, her bosom heaving now as much as the boy's. 'I can't explain—I will when you are older. It does seem—as if I had done it on purpose, now we are in these difficulties! I can't explain, dear! But it—is not quite on purpose—I can't help it!'

'Yes it is—it must be! For nobody would interfere with us, like that, unless you agreed! I won't forgive you, ever, ever! I'll never believe you care for me, or father, or any of us any more!'

He got up, and went away into the closet adjoining her room, in which a bed had been spread on the floor. There she heard him say: 'If we children was gone there'd be no trouble at all!'

'Don't think that, dear,' she cried, rather peremptorily. 'But go to sleep!'

The following morning she awoke at a little past six, and decided to get up and run across before breakfast to the inn which Jude had informed her to be his quarters, to tell him what had happened before he went out. She arose softly, to avoid disturbing the children, who, as she knew, must be fatigued by their exertions of yesterday.

She found Jude at breakfast in the obscure tavern he had chosen as a counterpoise to the expense of her lodging; and she explained to him her homelessness. He had been so anxious about her all night, he said.

Somehow, now it was morning, the request to leave the lodgings did not seem such a depressing incident as it had seemed the night before, nor did even her failure to find another place affect her so deeply as at first. Jude agreed with her that it would not be worth while to insist upon her right to stay a week, but to take immediate steps for removal.

'You must all come to this inn for a day or two,' he said. 'It is a rough place, and it will not be so nice for the children, but we shall have more time to look round. There are plenty of lodgings in the suburbs—in my old quarter of Beersheba. Have breakfast with me now you are here, my bird. You are sure you are well? There will be plenty of time to get back and prepare the children's meal before they wake. In fact, I'll go with you.'

She joined Jude in a hasty meal, and in a quarter of an hour they started together, resolving to clear out from Sue's too respectable lodging immediately. On reaching the place and going upstairs she found that all was quiet in the children's room, and called to the landlady in timorous tones to please bring up the tea-kettle and something for their breakfast. This was perfunctorily done, and producing a couple of eggs which she had brought with her she put them into the boiling kettle, and summoned Jude to watch them for the youngsters, while she went to call them, it being now about half-past eight o'clock.

Jude stood bending over the kettle, which his watch in his hand, timing the eggs, so that his back was turned to the little inner chamber where the children lay. A shriek from Sue suddenly caused him to start round. He saw that the door of the room, or rather closet—which had seemed to go heavily upon its hinges as she pushed it back—was open, and that Sue had sunk to the floor just within it. Hastening forward to pick her up he turned his eyes to the little bed spread on the boards; no children were there. He looked in bewilderment round the room. At the back of the door were fixed two hooks for hanging garments, and from these the forms of the two youngest children were suspended, by a piece of box-cord round each of their necks, while from a nail a few yards off the body of little Jude was hanging in a similar manner. An overturned chair was near the elder boy, and his glazed eyes were slanted into the room; but those of the girl and the baby boy were closed.

Half paralyzed by the strange and consummate horror of the scene he let Sue lie, cut the cords with his pocket-knife and threw the three children on the bed; but the feel of their bodies in the momentary handling seemed to say that they were dead. He caught up Sue, who was in fainting fits, and put her on the bed in the other room, after which he breathlessly summoned the landlady and ran out for a doctor.

When he got back Sue had come to herself, and the two helpless women, bending over the children in wild efforts to restore them, and the triplet of little corpses, formed a sight which overthrew his self-command. The nearest surgeon came in, but, as Jude had inferred, his presence was superfluous. The children were past saving, for though their bodies were still barely cold it was conjectured that they had been hanging more than an hour. The probability held by the parents later on, when they were able to reason on the case, was that the elder boy, on waking, looked into the outer room for Sue, and, finding her absent, was thrown into a fit of aggravated despondency that the events and information of the evening before had induced in his morbid temperament. Moreover a piece of paper was found upon the floor, on which was written, in the boy's hand, with the bit of lead pencil that he carried:

arabella's name last '*Done because we are too menny.*'

At sight of this Sue's nerves utterly gave way, an awful conviction that her discourse with the boy had been the main cause of the tragedy, throwing her into a convulsive agony which knew no abatement. They carried her away against her wish to a room on the lower floor; and there she lay, her slight figure shaken with her gasps, and her eyes staring at the ceiling, the woman of the house vainly trying to soothe her.

They could hear from this chamber the people moving about above, and she implored to be allowed to go back, and was only kept from doing so by the assurance that, if there were any hope, her presence might do harm, and the reminder that it was necessary to take care of herself lest she should endanger a coming life. Her inquiries were incessant, and at last Jude came down and told her there was no hope. As soon as she could speak she informed him what she had said to the boy, and how she thought herself the cause of this.

'No,' said Jude. 'It was in his nature to do it. The doctor says there are such boys springing up amongst us—boys of a sort unknown in the last generation—the outcome of new views of life. They seem to see all its terrors before they are old enough to have staying power to resist them. He says it is the beginning of the coming universal wish not to live. He's an advanced man, the doctor: but he can give no consolation to—'

Jude had kept back his own grief on account of her; but he now broke down; and this stimulated Sue to efforts of sympathy which in some degree distracted her from her poignant self-reproach. When everybody was gone, she was allowed to see the children.

The boy's face expressed the whole tale of their situation. On that little shape had converged all the inauspiciousness and shadow which had darkened the first union of Jude, and all the accidents, mistakes, fears, errors of the last. He was their nodal point, their focus, their expression in a single term. For the rashness of those parents he had groaned, for their ill-assortment he had quaked, and for the misfortunes of these he had died.

When the house was silent, and they could do nothing but await the coroner's inquest, a subdued, large, low voice spread into the air of the room from behind the heavy walls at the back.

'What is it?' said Sue, her spasmodic breathing suspended.

'The organ of the College chapel. The organist practising I suppose. It's the anthem from the seventy-third Psalm; "Truly God is loving unto Israel." '

She sobbed again. 'O, O my babies! They had done no harm! Why should they have been taken away, and not I!'

There was another stillness—broken at last by two persons in conversation somewhere without.

'They are talking about us, no doubt!' moaned Sue. ' "We are made a spectacle unto the world, and to angels, and to men!" '[4]

Jude listened—'No—they are not talking of us,' he said. 'They are two clergymen of different views, arguing about the eastward position.[5] Good God—the eastward position, and all creation groaning!'[6]

Then another silence, till she was seized with another uncontrollable fit of grief. 'There is something external to us which says, "You shan't!" First it said, "You shan't learn!" Then it said, "You shan't labour!" Now it says, "You shan't love!" '

He tried to soothe her by saying, 'That's bitter of you, darling.'

'But it's true!'

Thus they waited, and she went back again to her room. The baby's frock, shoes, and socks, which had been lying on a chair at the time of his death, she would not now have removed, though Jude would fain have got them out of her sight. But whenever he touched them she implored him to let them lie, and burst out almost savagely at the woman of the house when she also attempted to put them away.

Jude dreaded her dull apathetic silences almost more than her paroxysms. 'Why don't you speak to me, Jude?' she cried out, after one of these. 'Don't turn away from me! I can't *bear* the loneliness of being out of your looks!'

'There, dear; here I am,' he said, putting his face close to hers.

'Yes. . . . O my comrade, our perfect union—our two-in-oneness—is now stained with blood!'

'Shadowed by death—that's all.'

'Ah; but it was I who incited him really, though I didn't know I was doing it! I talked to the child as one should only talk to people of

4. 1 Corinthians 4.9.
5. There was a vigorous ecclesiastical controversy in the nineteenth century whether a priest celebrating Holy Communion should face east (i.e., with his back to the congregation) or west.
6. "The whole creation groaneth" (Romans 8.22).

mature age. I said the world was against us, that it was better to be out of life than in it at this price; and he took it literally. And I told him I was going to have another child. It upset him. O how bitterly he upbraided me!'

'Why did you do it, Sue?'

'I can't tell. It was that I wanted to be truthful. I couldn't bear deceiving him as to the facts of life. And yet I wasn't truthful, for with a false delicacy I told him too obscurely.—Why was I half wiser than my fellow-women? and not entirely wiser! Why didn't I tell him pleasant untruths, instead of half realities? It was my want of self-control, so that I could neither conceal things nor reveal them!'

'Your plan might have been a good one for the majority of cases; only in our peculiar case it chanced to work badly perhaps. He must have known sooner or later.'

'And I was just making my baby darling a new frock; and now I shall never see him in it, and never talk to him any more! . . . My eyes are so swollen that I can scarcely see; and yet little more than a year ago I called myself happy! We went about loving each other too much— indulging ourselves to utter selfishness with each other! We said—do you remember?—that we would make a virtue of joy. I said it was Nature's intention, Nature's law and *raison d'être*[7] that we should be joyful in what instincts she afforded us—instincts which civilization had taken upon itself to thwart. What dreadful things I said! And now Fate has given us this stab in the back for being such fools as to take Nature at her word!'

She sank into a quiet contemplation, till she said, 'It is best, perhaps, that they should be gone.—Yes—I see it is! Better that they should be plucked fresh than stay to wither away miserably!'

'Yes,' replied Jude. 'Some say that the elders should rejoice when their children die in infancy.'

'But they don't know! . . . O my babies, my babies, could you be alive now! You may say the boy wished to be out of life, or he wouldn't have done it. It was not unreasonable for him to die: it was part of his incurably sad nature, poor little fellow! But then the others—my *own* children and yours!'

Again Sue looked at the hanging little frock and at the socks and shoes; and her figure quivered like a string. 'I am a pitiable creature,' she said, 'good neither for earth nor heaven any more! I am driven out of my mind by things! What ought to be done?' She stared at Jude, and tightly held his hand.

'Nothing can be done,' he replied. 'Things are as they are, and will be brought to their destined issue.'

_____

7. Reason for existence.

She paused. 'Yes! Who said that?' she asked heavily.

'It comes in the chorus of the *Agamemnon*.[8] It has been in my mind continually since this happened.'

'My poor Jude—how you've missed everything!—you more than I, for I did get you! To think you should know that by your unassisted reading, and yet be in poverty and despair!'

After such momentary diversions her grief would return in a wave.

The jury duly came and viewed the bodies, the inquest was held; and next arrived the melancholy morning of the funeral. Accounts in the newspapers had brought to the spot curious idlers, who stood apparently counting the window-panes and the stones of the walls. Doubt of the real relations of the couple added zest to their curiosity. Sue had declared that she would follow the two little ones to the grave, but at the last moment she gave way, and the coffins were quietly carried out of the house while she was lying down. Jude got into the vehicle, and it drove away, much to the relief of the landlord, who now had only Sue and her luggage remaining on his hands, which he hoped to be also clear of later on in the day, and so to have freed his house from the exasperating notoriety it had acquired during the week through his wife's unlucky admission of these strangers. In the afternoon he privately consulted with the owner of the house, and they agreed that if any objection to it arose from the tragedy which had occurred there they would try to get its number changed.

When Jude had seen the two little boxes—one containing little Jude, and the other the two smallest—deposited in the earth he hastened back to Sue, who was still in her room, and he therefore did not disturb her just then. Feeling anxious, however, he went again about four o'clock. The woman thought she was still lying down, but returned to him to say that she was not in her bedroom after all. Her hat and jacket, too, were missing: she had gone out. Jude hurried off to the public-house where he was sleeping. She had not been there. Then bethinking himself of possibilities he went along the road to the cemetery, which he entered, and crossed to where the interments had recently taken place. The idlers who had followed to the spot by reason of the tragedy were all gone now. A man with a shovel in his hands was attempting to earth in the common grave of the three children, but his arm was held back by an expostulating woman who stood in the half-filled hole. It was Sue, whose coloured clothing, which she had never thought of changing for the mourning he had bought, suggested to the eye a deeper grief than the conventional garb of bereavement could express.

'He's filling them in, and he shan't till I've seen my little ones again!' she cried wildly when she saw Jude. 'I want to see them once more. O

8. Line 65 of Aeschylus's tragedy.

Jude—please Jude—I want to see them! I didn't know you would let them be taken away while I was asleep! You said perhaps I should see them once more before they were screwed down; and then you didn't, but took them away! O Jude, you are cruel to me too!'

'She's been wanting me to dig out the grave again, and let her get to the coffins,' said the man with the spade. 'She ought to be took home, by the look o' her. She is hardly responsible, poor thing, seem-ingly. Can't dig 'em up again now, ma'am. Do ye go home with your husband, and take it quiet, and thank God that there'll be another soon to swage[9] yer grief.'

But Sue kept asking piteously: 'Can't I see them once more—just once! Can't I? Only just one little minute, Jude? It would not take long! And I should be so glad, Jude! I will be so good, and not disobey you ever any more, Jude, if you will let me? I would go home quietly afterwards, and not want to see them any more! Can't I? Why can't I?'

Thus she went on. Jude was thrown into such acute sorrow that he almost felt he would try to get the man to accede. But it could do no good, and might make her still worse; and he saw that it was imperative to get her home at once. So he coaxed her, and whispered tenderly, and put his arm round her to support her; till she helplessly gave in, and was induced to leave the cemetery.

He wished to obtain a fly to take her back in, but economy being so imperative she deprecated his doing so, and they walked along slowly, Jude in black crape, she in brown and red clothing. They were to have gone to a new lodging that afternoon, but Jude saw that it was not practicable, and in course of time they entered the now hated house. Sue was at once got to bed, and the doctor sent for.

Jude waited all the evening downstairs. At a very late hour the intel-ligence was brought to him that a child had been prematurely born, and that it, like the others, was a corpse.

VI–3

Sue was convalescent, though she had hoped for death, and Jude had again obtained work at his old trade. They were in other lodgings now, in the direction of Beersheba, and not far from the Church of Ceremonies—Saint Silas.

They would sit silent, more bodeful of the direct antagonism of things than of their insensate and stolid obstructiveness. Vague and quaint imaginings had haunted Sue in the days when her intellect scintillated like a star, that the world resembled a stanza or melody composed in a dream; it was wonderfully excellent to the half-aroused

9. Assuage or mitigate.

intelligence, but hopelessly absurd at the full waking; that the First Cause worked automatically like a somnambulist, and not reflectively like a sage; that at the framing of the terrestrial conditions there seemed never to have been contemplated such a development of emotional perceptiveness among the creatures subject to those conditions as that reached by thinking and educated humanity. But affliction makes opposing forces loom anthropomorphous; and those ideas were now exchanged for a sense of Jude and herself fleeing from a persecutor.

'We must conform!' she said mournfully. "All the ancient wrath of the Power above us has been vented upon us, His poor creatures, and we must submit. There is no choice. We must. It is no use fighting against God!'

'It is only against man and senseless circumstance,' said Jude.

'True!' she murmured. 'What have I been thinking of! I am getting as superstitious as a savage! . . . But whoever or whatever our foe may be, I am cowed into submission. I have no more fighting strength left; no more enterprise. I am beaten, beaten! . . . "We are made a spectacle unto the world, and to angels, and to men!" I am always saying that now.'

'I feel the same!'

'What shall we do? You are in work now; but remember, it may only be because our history and relations are not absolutely known. . . . Possibly, if they knew our marriage had not been formalized they would turn you out of your job as they did at Aldbrickham!'

'I hardly know. Perhaps they would hardly do that. However, I think that we ought to make it legal now—as soon as you are able to go out.'

'You think we ought?'

'Certainly.'

And Jude fell into thought. 'I have seemed to myself lately,' he said, 'to belong to that vast band of men shunned by the virtuous—the men called seducers. It amazes me when I think of it! I have not been conscious of it, or of any wrong-doing towards you, whom I love more than myself. Yet I *am* one of those men! I wonder if any other of them are the same purblind, simple creatures as I? . . . Yes, Sue—that's what I am. I seduced you. . . . You were a distinct type—a refined creature, intended by Nature to be left intact. But I couldn't leave you alone!'

'No, no, Jude!' she said quickly. 'Don't reproach yourself with being what you are not. If anybody is to blame it is I.'

'I supported you in your resolve to leave Phillotson; and without me perhaps you wouldn't have urged him to let you go.'

'I should have, just the same. As to ourselves, the fact of our not having entered into a legal contract is the saving feature in our union. We have thereby avoided insulting, as it were, the solemnity of our first marriages.'

'Solemnity?' Jude looked at her with some surprise, and grew conscious that she was not the Sue of their earlier time.

'Yes,' she said, with a little quiver in her words, 'I have had dreadful fears, a dreadful sense of my own insolence of action. I have thought— that I am still his wife!'

'Whose?'

'Richard's.'

'Good God, dearest!—why?'

'O I can't explain! Only the thought comes to me.'

'It is your weakness—a sick fancy, without reason or meaning! Don't let it trouble you.'

Sue sighed uneasily.

As a set-off against such discussions as these there had come an improvement in their pecuniary position, which earlier in their experience would have made them cheerful. Jude had quite unexpectedly found good employment at his old trade almost directly he arrived, the summer weather suiting his fragile constitution; and outwardly his days went on with that monotonous uniformity which is in itself so grateful after vicissitude. People seemed to have forgotten that he had ever shown any awkward aberrancies: and he daily mounted to the parapets and copings[1] of colleges he could never enter, and renewed the crumbling freestones of mullioned windows he would never look from, as if he had known no wish to do otherwise.

There was this change in him; that he did not often go to any service at the churches now. One thing troubled him more than any other; that Sue and himself had mentally travelled in opposite directions since the tragedy: events which had enlarged his own views of life, laws, customs, and dogmas, had not operated in the same manner on Sue's. She was no longer the same as in the independent days, when her intellect played like lambent lightning over conventions and formalities which he at that time respected, though he did not now.

On a particular Sunday evening he came in rather late. She was not at home, but she soon returned, when he found her silent and meditative.

'What are you thinking of, little woman?' he asked curiously.

'O I can't tell clearly! I have thought that we have been selfish, careless, even impious, in our courses, you and I. Our life has been a vain attempt at self-delight. But self-abnegation is the higher road. We should mortify the flesh—the terrible flesh—the curse of Adam!'

'Sue!' he murmured. 'What has come over you?'

'We ought to be continually sacrificing ourselves on the altar of duty! But I have always striven to do what has pleased me. I well deserved the scourging I have got! I wish something would take the evil right out of me, and all my monstrous errors, and all my sinful ways!'

1. The uppermost courses of masonry or brickwork in a wall, usually sloping.

'Sue—my own too suffering dear!—there's no evil woman in you. Your natural instincts are perfectly healthy; not quite so impassioned, perhaps, as I could wish; but good, and dear, and pure. And as I have often said, you are absolutely the most ethereal, least sensual woman I ever knew to exist without inhuman sexlessness. Why do you talk in such a changed way? We have not been selfish, except when no one could profit by our being otherwise. You used to say that human nature was noble and long-suffering, not vile and corrupt, and at last I thought you spoke truly. And now you seem to take such a much lower view!'

'I want a humble heart; and a chastened mind; and I have never had them yet!'

'You have been fearless, both as a thinker and as a feeler, and you deserved more admiration than I gave. I was too full of narrow dogmas at that time to see it.'

'Don't say that, Jude! I wish my every fearless word and thought could be rooted out of my history. Self-renunciation—that's everything! I cannot humilitate myself too much. I should like to prick myself all over with pins and bleed out the badness that's in me!'

'Hush!' he said, pressing her little face against his breast as if she were an infant. 'It is bereavement that has brought you to this! Such remorse is not for you, my sensitive plant,[2] but for the wicked ones of the earth—who never feel it!'

'I ought not to stay like this,' she murmured, when she had remained in the position a long while.

'Why not?'

'It is indulgence.'

'Still on the same tack! But is there anything better on earth than that we should love one another?'

'Yes. It depends on the sort of love; and yours—ours—is the wrong.'

'I won't have it, Sue! Come, when do you wish our marriage to be signed in a vestry?'

She paused, and looked up uneasily. 'Never,' she whispered.

Not knowing the whole of her meaning he took the objection serenely, and said nothing. Several minutes elapsed, and he thought she had fallen asleep; but he spoke softly, and found that she was wide awake all the time. She sat upright and sighed.

'There is a strange, indescribable perfume or atmosphere about you to-night, Sue,' he said. 'I mean not only mentally, but about your clothes, also. A sort of vegetable scent, which I seem to know, yet cannot remember.'

'It is incense.'

'Incense?'

'I have been to the service at St. Silas', and I was in the fumes of it.'

---

2. "The Sensitive Plant" is the title of a poem by Shelley.

'Oh—St. Silas'.'

'Yes. I go there sometimes.'

'Indeed. You go there!'

'You see, Jude, it is lonely here in the week-day mornings, when you are at work, and I think and think of—of my—' She stopped till she could control the lumpiness of her throat. 'And I have taken to go in there, as it is so near.'

'O well—of course, I say nothing against it. Only it is odd, for you. They little think what sort of chiel is amang them!'[3]

'What do you mean, Jude?'

'Well—a sceptic, to be plain.'

'How can you pain me so, dear Jude, in my trouble! Yet I know you didn't mean it. But you ought not to say that.'

'I won't. But I am much surprised!'

'Well—I want to tell you something else, Jude. You won't be angry, will you? I have thought of it a good deal since my babies died. I don't think I ought to be your wife—or as your wife—any longer.'

'What? . . . But you *are!*'

'From your point of view; but—'

'Of course we were afraid of the ceremony, and a good many others would have been in our places, with such strong reasons for fears. But experience has proved how we misjudged ourselves, and overrated our infirmities; and if you are beginning to respect rites and ceremonies, as you seem to be, I wonder you don't say it shall be carried out instantly? You certainly *are* my wife, Sue, in all but law. What do you mean by what you said?'

'I don't think I am!'

'Not? But suppose we *had* gone through the ceremony? Would you feel that you were then?'

'No. I should not feel even then that I was. I should feel worse than I do now.'

'Why so—in the name of all that's perverse, my dear?'

'Because I am Richard's.'

'Ah—you hinted that absurd fancy to me before!'

'It was only an impression with me then; I feel more and more convinced as time goes on that—I belong to him, or to nobody.'

'My good heavens—how we are changing places!'

'Yes. Perhaps so.'

Some few days later, in the dusk of the summer evening, they were sitting in the same small room downstairs, when a knock came to the front door of the carpenter's house where they were lodging, and in a few moments there was a tap at the door of their room. Before they could open it the comer did so, and a woman's form appeared.

<hr/>

3. The allusion is to a poem by Robert Burns (1759–1796), "On Captain Grose's Peregrinations Through Scotland."

'Is Mr. Fawley here?'

Jude and Sue started as he mechanically replied in the affirmative, for the voice was Arabella's.

He formally requested her to come in, and she sat down in the window bench, where they could distinctly see her outline against the light; but no characteristic that enabled them to estimate her general aspect and air. Yet something seemed to denote that she was not quite so comfortably circumstanced, nor so bouncingly attired, as she had been during Cartlett's lifetime.

The three attempted an awkward conversation about the tragedy, of which Jude had felt it to be his duty to inform her immediately, though she had never replied to his letter.

'I have just come from the cemetery,' she said. 'I inquired and found the child's grave. I couldn't come to the funeral—thank you for inviting me all the same. I read all about it in the papers, and I felt I wasn't wanted. . . . No—I couldn't come to the funeral,' repeated Arabella, who, seeming utterly unable to reach the ideal of a catastrophic manner, fumbled with iterations. 'But I am glad I found the grave. As 'tis your trade, Jude, you'll be able to put up a handsome stone to 'em.'

'I shall put up a headstone,' said Jude drearily.

'He was my child, and naturally I feel for him.'

'I hope so. We all did.'

'The others that weren't mine I didn't feel so much for, as was natural.'

'Of course.'

A sigh came from the dark corner where Sue sat.

'I had often wished I had mine with me,' continued Mrs. Cartlett. 'Perhaps 'twouldn't have happened then! But of course I didn't wish to take him away from your wife.'

'I am not his wife,' came from Sue.

The unexpectedness of her words struck Jude silent.

'O I beg your pardon, I'm sure,' said Arabella. 'I thought you were!'

Jude had known from the quality of Sue's tone that her new and transcendental views lurked in her words; but all except their obvious meaning was, naturally, missed by Arabella. The latter, after evincing that she was struck by Sue's avowal, recovered herself, and went on to talk with placid bluntness about 'her' boy, for whom, though in his lifetime she had shown no care at all, she now exhibited a ceremonial mournfulness that was apparently sustaining to the conscience. She alluded to the past, and in making some remark appealed again to Sue. There was no answer: Sue had invisibly left the room.

'She said she was not your wife?' resumed Arabella in another voice. 'Why should she do that?'

'I cannot inform you,' said Jude shortly.

'She is, isn't she? She once told me so.'

'I don't criticize what she says.'

'Ah—I see! Well, my time is up. I am staying here to-night and thought I could do no less than call, after our mutual affliction. I am sleeping at the place where I used to be barmaid, and to-morrow I go back to Alfredston. Father is come home again, and I am living with him.'

'He has returned from Australia?' said Jude with languid curiosity.

'Yes. Couldn't get on there. Had a rough time of it. Mother died of dys—what do you call it—in the hot weather, and father and two of the young ones have just got back. He has got a cottage near the old place, and for the present I am keeping house for him.'

Jude's former wife had maintained a stereotyped manner of strict good breeding even now that Sue was gone, and limited her stay to a number of minutes that should accord with the highest respectability. When she had departed Jude, much relieved, went to the stairs and called Sue—feeling anxious as to what had become of her.

There was no answer, and the carpenter who kept the lodgings said she had not come in. Jude was puzzled, and became quite alarmed at her absence, for the hour was growing late. The carpenter called his wife, who conjectured that Sue might have gone to St. Silas' church, as she often went there.

'Surely not at this time o' night?' said Jude. 'It is shut.'

'She knows somebody who keeps the key, and she has it whenever she wants it.'

'How long has she been going on with this?'

'Oh, some few weeks, I think.'

Jude went vaguely in the direction of the church, which he had never once approached since he lived out that way years before when his young opinions were more mystical than they were now. The spot was deserted, but the door was certainly unfastened; he lifted the latch without noise, and pushing to the door behind him, stood absolutely still inside. The prevalent silence seemed to contain a faint sound, explicable as a breathing, or a sobbing, which came from the other end of the building. The floor-cloth deadened his footsteps as he moved in that direction through the obscurity, which was broken only by the faintest reflected night-light from without.

High overhead, above the chancel steps, Jude could discern a huge, solidly constructed Latin cross—as large, probably, as the original it was designed to commemorate. It seemed to be suspended in the air by invisible wires; it was set with large jewels, which faintly glimmered in some weak ray caught from outside, as the cross swayed to and fro in a silent and scarcely perceptible motion. Underneath, upon the floor, lay what appeared to be a heap of black clothes, and from this was repeated the sobbing that he had heard before. It was his Sue's form, prostrate on the paving.

'Sue!' he whispered.

Something white disclosed itself; she had turned up her face.

'What—do you want with me here, Jude?' she said almost sharply. 'You shouldn't come! I wanted to be alone! Why did you intrude here?'

'How can you ask!' he retorted in quick reproach, for his full heart was wounded to its centre at this attitude of hers towards him. 'Why do I come? Who has a right to come, I should like to know, if I have not! I, who love you better than my own self—better—O far better— than you have loved me! What made you leave me to come here alone?'

'Don't criticize me, Jude—I can't bear it!—I have often told you so. You must take me as I am. I am a wretch—broken by my distractions! I couldn't *bear* it when Arabella came—I felt so utterly miserable I had to come away. She seems to be your wife still, and Richard to be my husband!'

'But they are nothing to us!'

'Yes, dear friend, they are. I see marriage differently now. My babies have been taken from me to show me this! Arabella's child killing mine was a judgment—the right slaying the wrong. What, *what* shall I do! I am such a vile creature—too worthless to mix with ordinary human beings!'

'This is terrible!' said Jude, verging on tears. 'It is monstrous and unnatural for you to be so remorseful when you have done no wrong!'

'Ah—you don't know my badness!'

He returned vehemently: 'I do! Every atom and dreg of it! You make me hate Christianity, or mysticism, or Sacerdotalism,[4] or whatever it may be called, if it's that which has caused this deterioration in you. That a woman-poet, a woman-seer, a woman whose soul shone like a diamond—whom all the wise of the world would have been proud of, if they could have known you—should degrade herself like this! I am glad I had nothing to do with Divinity—damn glad—if it's going to ruin you in this way!'

'You are angry, Jude, and unkind to me, and don't see how things are.'

'Then come along home with me, dearest, and perhaps I shall. I am over-burdened—and you, too, are unhinged just now.' He put his arm round her and lifted her; but though she came, she preferred to walk without his support.

'I don't dislike you, Jude,' she said in a sweet and imploring voice. 'I love you as much as ever! Only—I ought not to love you—any more. O I must not any more!'

'I can't own it.'

'But I have made up my mind that I am not your wife! I belong to him—I sacramentally joined myself to him for life. Nothing can alter it!'

---

4. Doctrine that priests are invested with supernatural powers by virtue of their ordination.

'But surely we are man and wife, if ever two people were in this world? Nature's own marriage it is, unquestionably!'

'But not Heaven's. Another was made for me there, and ratified eternally in the church at Melchester.'

'Sue, Sue—affliction has brought you to this unreasonable state! After converting me to your views on so many things, to find you suddenly turn to the right-about like this—for no reason whatever, confounding all you have formerly said through sentiment merely! You root out of me what little affection and reverence I had left in me for the Church as an old acquaintance. . . . What I can't understand in you is your extraordinary blindness now to your old logic. Is it peculiar to you, or is it common to woman? Is a woman a thinking unit at all, or a fraction always wanting its integer? How you argued that marriage was only a clumsy contract—which it is—how you showed all the objections to it—all the absurdities! If two and two made four when we were happy together, surely they make four now? I can't understand it, I repeat!'

'Ah, dear Jude; that's because you are like a totally deaf man observing people listening to music. You say "What are they regarding? Nothing is there." But something is.'

'That is a hard saying from you; and not a true parallel! You threw off old husks of prejudices, and taught me to do it; and now you go back upon yourself. I confess I am utterly stultified in my estimate of you.'

'Dear friend, my only friend, don't be hard with me! I can't help being as I am, I am convinced I am right—that I see the light at last. But O, how to profit by it!'

They walked along a few more steps till they were outside the building, and she had returned the key. 'Can this be the girl,' said Jude when she came back, feeling a slight renewal of elasticity now that he was in the open street; 'can this be the girl who brought the Pagan deities into this most Christian city?—who mimicked Miss Fontover when she crushed them with her heel?—quoted Gibbon, and Shelley, and Mill? Where are dear Apollo, and dear Venus now!'

'O don't, don't be so cruel to me, Jude, and I so unhappy!' she sobbed. 'I can't bear it! I was in error—I cannot reason with you. I was wrong—proud in my own conceit! Arabella's coming was the finish. Don't satirize me: it cuts like a knife!'

He flung his arms round her and kissed her passionately there in the silent street, before she could hinder him. They went on till they came to a little coffee-house. 'Jude,' she said with suppressed tears, 'would you mind getting a lodging here?'

'I will—if, if you really wish? But do you? Let me go to our door and understand you.'

He went and conducted her in. She said she wanted no supper, and went in the dark upstairs and struck a light. Turning she found that Jude had followed her, and was standing at the chamber door. She went to him, put her hand in his, and said 'Good-night.'

'But Sue! Don't we live here?'

'You said you would do as I wished!'

'Yes. Very well!. . . . Perhaps it was wrong of me to argue distastefully as I have done! Perhaps as we couldn't conscientiously marry at first in the old-fashioned way, we ought to have parted. Perhaps the world is not illuminated enough for such experiments as ours! Who were we, to think we could act as pioneers!'

'I am so glad you see that much, at any rate. I never deliberately meant to do as I did. I slipped into my false position through jealousy and agitation!'

'But surely through love—you loved me?'

'Yes. But I wanted to let it stop there, and go on always as mere lovers; until—'

'But people in love couldn't live for ever like that!'

'Women could: men can't because they—won't. An average woman is in this superior to an average man—that she never instigates, only responds. We ought to have lived in mental communion, and no more.'

'I was the unhappy cause of the change, as I have said before! . . . Well, as you will! . . . But human nature can't help being itself.'

'O yes—that's just what it has to learn—self-mastery.'

'I repeat—if either were to blame it was not you but I.'

'No—it was I. Your wickedness was only the natural man's desire to possess the woman. Mine was not the reciprocal wish till envy stimulated me to oust Arabella. I had thought I ought in charity to let you approach me—that it was damnably selfish to torture you as I did my other friend. But I shouldn't have given way if you hadn't broken me down by making me fear you would go back to her. . . . But don't let us say any more about it! Jude, will you leave me to myself now?'

'Yes. . . . But Sue—my wife, as you are!' he burst out; 'my old reproach to you was, after all, a true one. You have never loved me as I love you—never—never! Yours is not a passionate heart—your heart does not burn in a flame! You are, upon the whole, a sort of fay,[5] or sprite—not a woman!'

'At first I did not love you, Jude; that I own. When I first knew you I merely wanted you to love me. I did not exactly flirt with you; but that inborn craving which undermines some women's morals almost more than unbridled passion—the craving to attract and captivate, regardless of the injury it may do the man—was in me; and when I

5. Fairy.

found I had caught you, I was frightened. And then—I don't know how it was—I couldn't bear to let you go—possibly to Arabella again—and so I got to love you, Jude. But you see, however fondly it ended, it began in the selfish and cruel wish to make your heart ache for me without letting mine ache for you.'

'And now you add to your cruelty by leaving me!'

'Ah—yes! The further I flounder, the more harm I do!'

'O Sue!' said he with a sudden sense of his own danger. 'Do not do an immoral thing for moral reasons! You have been my social salvation. Stay with me for humanity's sake! You know what a weak fellow I am. My two Arch Enemies you know—my weakness for womankind and my impulse to strong liquor. Don't abandon me to them, Sue, to save your own soul only! They have been kept entirely at a distance since you became my guardian-angel! Since I have had you I have been able to go into any temptations of the sort, without risk. Isn't my safety worth a little sacrifice of dogmatic principle? I am in terror lest, if you leave me, it will be with me another case of the pig that was washed turning back to his wallowing in the mire!'

Sue burst out weeping. 'O but you must not, Jude! You won't! I'll pray for you night and day!'

'Well—never mind; don't grieve,' said Jude generously. 'I did suffer, God knows, about you at that time; and now I suffer again. But perhaps not so much as you. The woman mostly gets the worst of it in the long run!'

'She does.'

'Unless she is absolutely worthless and contemptible. And this one is not that, anyhow!'

Sue drew a nervous breath or two. 'She is—I fear! . . . Now Jude—good-night,—please!'

'I mustn't stay?—Not just once more? As it has been so many times—O Sue, my wife, why not!'

'No—no—not wife! . . . I am in your hands, Jude—don't tempt me back now I have advanced so far!'

'Very well. I do your bidding. I owe that to you, darling, in penance for how I over-ruled it at the first time. My God, how selfish I was! Perhaps—perhaps I spoilt one of the highest and purest loves that ever existed between man and woman! . . . Then let the veil of our temple be rent in two from this hour!'[6]

He went to the bed, removed one of the pair of pillows thereon, and flung it to the floor.

Sue looked at him, and bending over the bed-rail wept silently. 'You don't see that it is a matter of conscience with me, and not of dislike to you!' she brokenly murmured. 'Dislike to you! But I can't say any

---

6. When Jesus died, "the veil of the temple was rent in twain" (Mark 15.38).

more—it breaks my heart—it will be undoing all I have begun! Jude—good-night!'

'Good-night,' he said, and turned to go.

'O but you shall kiss me!' said she, starting up. 'I can't—bear—!'

He clasped her, and kissed her weeping face as he had scarcely ever done before, and they remained in silence till she said, 'Good-bye, good-bye!' And then gently pressing him away she got free, trying to mitigate the sadness by saying: 'We'll be dear friends just the same, Jude, won't we? And we'll see each other sometimes—Yes!—and forget all this, and try to be as we were long ago?'

Jude did not permit himself to speak, but turned and descended the stairs.

VI–4

The man whom Sue, in her mental volte-face, was now regarding as her inseparable husband, lived still at Marygreen.

On the day before the tragedy of the children, Phillotson had seen both her and Jude as they stood in the rain at Christminster watching the procession to the Theatre. But he had said nothing of it at the moment to his companion Gillingham, who, being an old friend, was staying with him at the village aforesaid, and had, indeed, suggested the day's trip to Christminster.

'What are you thinking of?' said Gillingham, as they went home. 'The University degree you never obtained?'

'No, no,' said Phillotson gruffly. 'Of somebody I saw to-day.' In a moment he added, 'Susanna.'

'I saw her, too.'

'You said nothing.'

'I didn't wish to draw your attention to her. But, as you did see her, you should have said: "How d'ye do, my dear-that-was?" '

'Ah, well. I might have. But what do you think of this: I have good reason for supposing that she was innocent when I divorced her—that I was all wrong. Yes, indeed! Awkward, isn't it?'

'She has taken care to set you right since, anyhow, apparently.'

'H'm. That's a cheap sneer. I ought to have waited, unquestionably.'

At the end of the week, when Gillingham had gone back to his school near Shaston, Phillotson, as was his custom, went to Alfredston market; ruminating again on Arabella's intelligence as he walked down the long hill which he had known before Jude knew it, though his history had not beaten so intensely upon its incline. Arrived in the town he bought his usual weekly local paper; and when he had sat down in an inn to refresh himself for the five miles' walk back, he pulled the paper from his pocket and read awhile. The account of the 'Strange suicide of a stone-mason's children' met his eye.

Unimpassioned as he was, it impressed him painfully, and puzzled him not a little, for he could not understand the age of the elder child being what it was stated to be. However, there was no doubt that the newspaper report was in some way true.

'Their cup of sorrow is now full!' he said: and thought and thought of Sue, and what she had gained by leaving him.

Arabella having made her home at Alfredston, and the schoolmaster coming to market there every Saturday, it was not wonderful that in a few weeks they met again—the precise time being just after her return from Christminster, where she had stayed much longer than she had at first intended, keeping an interested eye on Jude, though Jude had seen no more of her. Phillotson was on his way homeward when he encountered Arabella, and she was approaching the town.

'You like walking out this way, Mrs. Cartlett?' he said.

'I've just begun to again,' she replied. 'It is where I lived as maid and wife, and all the past things of my life that are interesting to my feelings are mixed up with this road. And they have been stirred up in me too, lately; for I've been visiting at Christminster. Yes; I've seen Jude.'

'Ah! How do they bear their terrible affliction?'

'In a ve-ry strange way—ve-ry strange! She don't live with him any longer. I only heard of it as a certainty just before I left; though I had thought things were drifting that way from their manner when I called on them.'

'Not live with her husband? Why, I should have thought 'twould have united them more.'

'He's not her husband, after all. She has never really married him although they have passed as man and wife so long. And now, instead of this sad event making 'em hurry up, and get the thing done legally, she's took in a queer religious way, just as I was in my affliction at losing Cartlett, only hers is of a more 'sterical sort than mine. And she says, so I was told, that she's your wife in the eye of Heaven and the Church—yours only; and can't be anybody else's by any act of man.'

'Ah—indeed? . . . Separated, have they!'

'You see, the eldest boy was mine—'

'O—yours!'

'Yes, poor little fellow—born in lawful wedlock, thank God. And perhaps she feels, over and above other things, that I ought to have been in her place. I can't say. However, as for me, I am soon off from here. I've got father to look after now, and we can't live in such a humdrum place as this. I hope soon to be in a bar again at Christminster, or some other big town.'

They parted. When Phillotson had ascended the hill a few steps he stopped, hastened back, and called her.

'What is, or was, their address?'

Arabella gave it.

'Thank you. Good afternoon.'

Arabella smiled grimly as she resumed her way, and practised dimple-making all along the road from where the pollard willows begin to the old almshouses in the first street of the town.

Meanwhile Phillotson ascended to Marygreen, and for the first time during a lengthened period he lived with a forward eye. On crossing under the large trees of the green to the humble schoolhouse to which he had been reduced he stood a moment, and pictured Sue coming out of the door to meet him. No man had ever suffered more inconvenience from his own charity, Christian or heathen, than Phillotson had done in letting Sue go. He had been knocked about from pillar to post at the hands of the virtuous almost beyond endurance; he had been nearly starved, and was now dependent entirely upon the very small stipend from the school of this village (where the parson had got ill-spoken of for befriending him). He had often thought of Arabella's remarks that he should have been more severe with Sue, that her recalcitrant spirit would soon have been broken. Yet such was his obstinate and illogical disregard of opinion, and of the principles in which he had been trained, that his convictions on the rightness of his course with his wife had not been disturbed.

Principles which could be subverted by feeling in one direction were liable to the same catastrophe in another. The instincts which had allowed him to give Sue her liberty now enabled him to regard her as none the worse for her life with Jude. He wished for her still, in his curious way, if he did not love her, and, apart from policy, soon felt that he would be gratified to have her again as his, always provided that she came willingly.

But artifice was necessary, he had found, for stemming the cold and inhumane blast of the world's contempt. And here were the materials ready made. By getting Sue back and re-marrying her on the respectable plea of having entertained erroneous views of her, and gained his divorce wrongfully, he might acquire some comfort, resume his old courses, perhaps return to the Shaston school, if not even to the Church as a licentiate.

He thought he would write to Gillingham to inquire his views, and what he thought of his, Phillotson's, sending a letter to her. Gillingham replied, naturally, that now she was gone it were best to let her be; and considered that if she were anybody's wife she was the wife of the man to whom she had borne three children and owed such tragic adventures. Probably, as his attachment to her seemed unusually strong, the singular pair would make their union legal in course of time, and all would be well, and decent, and in order.

'But they won't—Sue won't!' exclaimed Phillotson to himself. 'Gillingham is so matter-of-fact. She's affected by Christminster sentiment and teaching. I can see her views on the indissolubility of marriage well enough, and I know where she got them. They are not mine; but I shall make use of them to further mine.'

He wrote a brief reply to Gillingham. 'I know I am entirely wrong, but I don't agree with you. As to her having lived with and had three children by him, my feeling is (though I can advance no logical or moral defence of it, on the old lines) that it has done little more than finish her education. I shall write to her, and learn whether what that woman said is true or no.'

As he had made up his mind to do this before he had written to his friend, there had not been much reason for writing to the latter at all. However, it was Phillotson's way to act thus.

He accordingly addressed a carefully considered epistle to Sue, and, knowing her emotional temperament, threw a Rhadamanthine[1] strictness into the lines here and there, carefully hiding his heterodox feelings, not to frighten her. He stated that, it having come to his knowledge that her views had considerably changed, he felt compelled to say that his own, too, were largely modified by events subsequent to their parting. He would not conceal from her that passionate love had little to do with his communication. It arose from a wish to make their lives, if not a success, at least no such disastrous failure as they threatened to become, through his acting on what he had considered at the time a principle of justice, charity, and reason.

To indulge one's instinctive and uncontrolled sense of justice and right, was not, he had found, permitted with impunity in an old civilization like ours. It was necessary to act under an acquired and cultivated sense of the same, if you wished to enjoy an average share of comfort and honour; and to let crude loving-kindness take care of itself.

He suggested that she should come to him there at Marygreen.

On second thoughts he took out the last paragraph but one; and having re-written the letter he despatched it immediately, and in some excitement awaited the issue.

A few days after a figure moved through the white fog which enveloped the Beersheba suburb of Christminster, towards the quarter in which Jude Fawley had taken up his lodging since his division from Sue. A timid knock sounded upon the door of his abode.

It was evening—so he was at home; and by a species of divination he jumped up and rushed to the door himself.

'Will you come out with me? I would rather not come in. I want to—to talk with you—and to go with you to the cemetery.'

It had been in the trembling accents of Sue that these words came. Jude put on his hat. 'It is dreary for you to be out,' he said. 'But if you prefer not to come in, I don't mind.'

1. In Greek mythology, Rhadamanthus was one of the judges in the underworld and was noted for his severity.

'Yes—I do. I shall not keep you long.'

Jude was too much affected to go on talking at first; she, too, was now such a mere cluster of nerves that all initiatory power seemed to have left her, and they proceeded through the fog like Acherontic[2] shades for a long while, without sound or gesture.

'I want to tell you," she presently said, her voice now quick, now slow, 'so that you may not hear of it by chance. I am going back to Richard. He has—so magnanimously—agreed to forgive all—'

'Going back? How can you go—'

'He is going to marry me again. That is for form's sake, and to satisfy the world, which does not see things as they are. But of course I *am* his wife already. Nothing has changed that.'

He turned upon her with an anguish that was well-nigh fierce.

'But you are *my* wife! Yes, you are. You know it. I have always regretted that feint of ours in going away and pretending to come back legally married, to save appearances. I loved you, and you loved me; and we closed with each other; and that made the marriage. We still love—you as well as I—I *know* it, Sue! Therefore our marriage is not cancelled.'

'Yes; I know how you see it,' she answered with despairing self-suppression. 'But I am going to marry him again, as it would be called by you. Strictly speaking you, too,—don't mind my saying it, Jude!—you should take back—Arabella.'

'I should? Good God—what next! But how if you and I had married legally, as we were on the point of doing?'

'I should have felt just the same—that ours was not a marriage. And I would go back to Richard without repeating the sacrament, if he asked me. But "the world and its ways have a certain worth"[3] (I suppose): therefore I concede a repetition of the ceremony. . . . Don't crush all the life out of me by satire and argument, I implore you! I was strongest once, I know, and perhaps I treated you cruelly. But Jude, return good for evil! I am the weaker now. Don't retaliate upon me, but be kind. O be kind to me—a poor wicked woman who is trying to mend!'

He shook his head hopelessly, his eyes wet. The blow of her bereavement seemed to have destroyed her reasoning faculty. The once keen vision was dimmed. 'All wrong, all wrong!' he said huskily. 'Error—perversity! It drives me out of my senses. Do you care for him? Do you love him? You know you don't! It will be a fanatic prostitution—God forgive me, yes—that's what it will be!'

'I don't love him—I must, must, own it, in deepest remorse! But I shall try to learn to love him by obeying him.'

---

2. In Greek mythology, Acheron was a river of Hades (the underworld), associated with gloom and darkness.
3. From Browning's poem "The Statue and the Bust."

Jude argued, urged, implored; but her conviction was proof against all. It seemed to be the one thing on earth on which she was firm, and that her firmness in this had left her tottering in every other impulse and wish she possessed.

'I have been considerate enough to let you know the whole truth, and to tell it you myself,' she said in cut tones; 'that you might not consider yourself slighted by hearing of it at second-hand. I have even owned the extreme fact that I do not love him. I did not think you would be so rough with me for doing so! I was going to ask you . . . '

'To give you away?'

'No. To send—my boxes to me—if you would. But I suppose you won't.'

'Why, of course I will. What—isn't he coming to fetch you—to marry you from here? He won't condescend to do that?'

'No—I won't let him. I go to him voluntarily, just as I went away from him. We are to be married at his little church at Marygreen.'

She was so sadly sweet in what he called her wrong-headedness that Jude could not help being moved to tears more than once for pity of her. 'I never knew such a woman for doing impulsive penances as you, Sue! No sooner does one expect you to go straight on, as the one rational proceeding, than you double round the corner!'

'Ah, well; let that go! . . . Jude, I must say good-bye! But I wanted you to go to the cemetery with me. Let our farewell be there—beside the graves of those who died to bring home to me the error of my views.'

They turned in the direction of the place, and the gate was opened to them on application. Sue had been there often, and she knew the way to the spot in the dark. They reached it, and stood still.

'It is here—I should like to part,' said she.

'So be it!'

'Don't think me hard because I have acted on conviction. Your generous devotion to me is unparalleled, Jude! Your worldly failure, if you have failed, is to your credit rather than to your blame. Remember that the best and greatest among mankind are those who do themselves no worldly good. Every successful man is more or less a selfish man. The devoted fail. . . . "Charity seeketh not her own." '[4]

'In that chapter we are at one, ever beloved darling, and on it we'll part friends. Its verses will stand fast when all the rest that you call religion has passed away!'

'Well—don't discuss it. Good-bye, Jude; my fellow-sinner, and kindest friend!'

'Good-bye, my mistaken wife. Good-bye!'

---

4. 1 Corinthians 13.5.

VI–5

The next afternoon the familiar Christminster fog still hung over all things. Sue's slim shape was only just discernible going towards the station.

Jude had no heart to go to his work that day. Neither could he go anywhere in the direction by which she would be likely to pass. He went in an opposite one, to a dreary, strange, flat scene, where boughs dripped, and coughs and consumptions lurked, and where he had never been before.

'Sue's gone from me—gone!' he murmured miserably.

She in the meantime had left by the train, and reached Alfredston Road, where she entered the steam-tram and was conveyed into the town. It had been her request to Phillotson that he should not meet her. She wished, she said, to come to him voluntarily, to his very house and hearthstone.

It was Friday evening, which had been chosen because the school-master was disengaged at four o'clock that day till the Monday morning following. The little car[1] she hired at The Bear to drive her to Mary-green set her down at the end of the lane, half-a-mile from the village, by her desire, and preceded her to the school-house with such portion of her luggage as she had brought. On its return she encountered it, and asked the driver if he had found the master's house open. The man informed her that he had, and that her things had been taken in by the schoolmaster himself.

She could now enter Marygreen without exciting much observation. She crossed by the well and under the trees to the pretty new school on the other side, and lifted the latch of the dwelling without knocking. Phillotson stood in the middle of the room, awaiting her, as requested.

'I've come, Richard,' said she, looking pale and shaken, and sinking into a chair. 'I cannot believe—you forgive your—wife!'

'Everything, darling Susanna,' said Phillotson.

She started at the endearment, though it had been spoken advisedly without fervour. Then she nerved herself again.

'My children—are dead—and it is right that they should be! I am glad—almost. They were sin-begotten. They were sacrificed to teach me how to live!—their death was the first stage of my purification. That's why they have not died in vain! . . . You will take me back?'

He was so stirred by her pitiful words and tone that he did more than he had meant to do. He bent and kissed her cheek.

Sue imperceptibly shrank away, her flesh quivering under the touch of his lips.

1. Horse-drawn vehicle.

Phillotson's heart sank, for desire was renascent in him. 'You still have an aversion to me!'

'O no, dear—I—have been driving through the damp, and I was chilly!' she said, with a hurried smile of apprehension. 'When are we going to have the marriage? Soon?'

'To-morrow morning, early, I thought—if you really wish. I am sending round to the vicar to let him know you are come. I have told him all, and he highly approves—he says it will bring our lives to a triumphant and satisfactory issue. But—are you sure of yourself? It is not too late to refuse now if—you think you can't bring yourself to it, you know?'

'Yes, yes, I can! I want it done quick. Tell him, tell him at once! My strength is tried by the undertaking—I can't wait long!'

'Have something to eat and drink then, and go over to your room at Mrs. Edlin's. I'll tell the vicar half-past eight to-morrow, before anybody is about—if that's not too soon for you? My friend Gillingham is here to help us in the ceremony. He's been good enough to come all the way from Shaston at great inconvenience to himself.'

Unlike a woman in ordinary, whose eye is so keen for material things, Sue seemed to see nothing of the room they were in, or any detail of her environment. But on moving across the parlour to put down her muff she uttered a little 'O!' and grew paler than before. Her look was that of the condemned criminal who catches sight of his coffin.

'What?' said Phillotson.

The flap of the bureau chanced to be open, and in placing her muff upon it her eye had caught a document which lay there. 'O—only a—funny surprise!' she said, trying to laugh away her cry as she came back to the table.

'Ah! yes,' said Phillotson. 'The license. . . . It has just come.'

Gillingham now joined them from his room above, and Sue nervously made herself agreeable to him by talking on whatever she thought likely to interest him, except herself, though that interested him most of all. She obediently ate some supper, and prepared to leave for her lodging hard by. Phillotson crossed the green with her, bidding her good-night at Mrs. Edlin's door.

The old woman accompanied Sue to her temporary quarters, and helped her to unpack. Among other things she laid out a nightgown tastefully embroidered.

'O—I didn't know *that* was put in!' said Sue quickly. 'I didn't mean it to be. Here is a different one.' She handed a new and absolutely plain garment, of coarse and unbleached calico.

'But this is the prettiest,' said Mrs. Edlin. 'That one is no better than very sackcloth[2] o' Scripture!'

---

2. Coarse fabric, worn as penitential or mourning garb.

'Yes—I meant it to be. Give me the other.'

She took it, and began rending it with all her might, the tears resounding through the house like a screech-owl.

'But my dear, dear!—whatever . . . '

'It is adulterous! It signifies what I don't feel—I bought it long ago—to please Jude! It must be destroyed!'

Mrs. Edlin lifted her hands, and Sue excitedly continued to tear the linen into strips, laying the pieces in the fire.

'You med ha' give it to me!' said the widow. 'It do make my heart ache to see such pretty open-work[3] as that a-burned by the flames—not that ornamental night-rails[4] can be much use to a' ould 'ooman like I. My days for such be all past and gone!'

'It is an accursed thing—it reminds me of what I want to forget!' Sue repeated. 'It is only fit for the fire.'

'Lord, you be too strict! What do ye use such words for, and condemn to hell your dear little innocent children that's lost to 'ee! Upon my life I don't call that religion!'

Sue flung her face upon the bed, sobbing. 'O, don't, don't! That kills me!' She remained shaken with her grief, and slipped down upon her knees.

'I'll tell 'ee what—you ought not to marry this man again!' said Mrs. Edlin indignantly. 'You are in love wi' t' other still!'

'Yes I must—I am his already!'

'Pshoo! You be t' other man's. If you didn't like to commit yourselves to the binding vow again, just at first, 'twas all the more credit to your consciences, considering your reasons, and you med ha' lived on, and made it all right at last. After all, it concerned nobody but your own two selves.'

'Richard says he'll have me back, and I'm bound to go! If he had refused, it might not have been so much my duty to—give up Jude. But—' She remained with her face in the bedclothes, and Mrs. Edlin left the room.

Phillotson in the interval had gone back to his friend Gillingham, who still sat over the supper-table. They soon rose, and walked out on the green to smoke awhile. A light was burning in Sue's room, a shadow moving now and then across the blind.

Gillingham had evidently been impressed with the indefinable charm of Sue, and after a silence he said, 'Well: you've all but got her again at last. She can't very well go a second time. The pear has dropped into your hand.'

'Yes! . . . I suppose I am right in taking her at her word. I confess there seems a touch of selfishness in it. Apart from her being what she

---

3. Embroidery.
4. Nightdresses or dressing gowns.

is, of course, a luxury for a fogey[5] like me, it will set me right in the
eyes of the clergy and orthodox laity, who have never forgiven me for
letting her go. So I may get back in some degree into my old track.'

'Well—if you've got any sound reason for marrying her again, do it
now in God's name! I was always against your opening the cage-door
and letting the bird go in such an obviously suicidal way. You might
have been a school inspector by this time, or a reverend, if you hadn't
been so weak about her.'

'I did myself irreparable damage—I know it.'

'Once you've got her housed again, stick to her.'

Phillotson was more evasive to-night. He did not care to admit
clearly that his taking Sue to him again had at bottom nothing to do
with repentance of letting her go, but was, primarily, a human instinct
flying in the face of custom and profession. He said, 'Yes—I shall do
that. I know woman better now. Whatever justice there was in releasing
her, there was little logic, for one holding my views on other subjects.'

Gillingham looked at him, and wondered whether it would ever happen that the reactionary spirit induced by the world's sneers and his
own physical wishes would make Phillotson more orthodoxly cruel to
her than he had erstwhile been informally and perversely kind.

'I perceive it won't do to give way to impulse,' Phillotson resumed,
feeling more and more every minute the necessity of acting up to his
position. 'I flew in the face of the Church's teaching; but I did it without malice prepense.[6] Women are so strange in their influence, that
they tempt you to misplaced kindness. However, I know myself better
now. A little judicious severity, perhaps. . . . '

'Yes; but you must tighten the reins by degrees only. Don't be too
strenuous at first. She'll come to any terms in time.'

The caution was unnecessary, though Phillotson did not say so. 'I
remember what my vicar at Shaston said, when I left after the row that
was made about my agreeing to her elopement. "The only thing you
can do to retrieve your position and hers is to admit your error in not
restraining her with a wise and strong hand, and to get her back again
if she'll come, and be firm in the future." But I was so headstrong at
that time that I paid no heed. And that after the divorce she should
have thought of doing so I did not dream.'

The gate of Mrs. Edlin's cottage clicked, and somebody began
crossing in the direction of the school. Phillotson said 'Good-night.'

'O, is that Mr. Phillotson,' said Mrs. Edlin. 'I was going over to see
'ee. I've been upstairs with her, helping her to unpack her things; and
upon my word, sir, I don't think this ought to be!'

'What—the wedding?'

5. One with old-fashioned ideas.
6. Deliberate, premeditated.

'Yes. She's forcing herself to it, poor dear little thing; and you've no notion what she's suffering. I was never much for religion nor against it, but it can't be right to let her do this, and you ought to persuade her out of it. Of course everybody will say it was very good and forgiving of 'ee to take her to 'ee again. But for my part I don't.'

'It's her wish, and I am willing,' said Phillotson with grave reserve, opposition making him illogically tenacious now. 'A great piece of laxity will be rectified.'

'I don't believe it. She's his wife if anybody's. She's had three children by him, and he loves her dearly; and it's a wicked shame to egg her on to this, poor little quivering thing! She's got nobody on her side. The one man who'd be her friend the obstinate creature won't allow to come near her. What first put her into this mood o' mind, I wonder!'

'I can't tell. Not I certainly. It is all voluntary on her part. Now that's all I have to say.' Phillotson spoke stiffly. 'You've turned round, Mrs. Edlin. It is unseemly of you!'

'Well. I knowed you'd be affronted at what I had to say; but I don't mind that. The truth's the truth.'

'I'm not affronted, Mrs. Edlin. You've been too kind a neighbour for that. But I must be allowed to know what's best for myself and Susanna. I suppose you won't go to church with us, then?'

'No. Be hanged if I can. . . . I don't know what the times be coming to! Matrimony have growed to be that serious in these days that one really do feel afeard to move in it at all. In my time we took it more careless; and I don't know that we was any the worse for it! When I and my poor man were jined in it we kept up the junketing[7] all the week, and drunk the parish dry, and had to borrow half-a-crown to begin housekeeping!'

When Mrs. Edlin had gone back to her cottage Phillotson spoke moodily. 'I don't know whether I ought to do it—at any rate quite so rapidly.'

'Why?'

'If she is really compelling herself to this against her instincts—merely from this new sense of duty or religion—I ought perhaps to let her wait a bit.'

'Now you've got so far you ought not to back out of it. That's my opinion.'

'I can't very well put it off now; that's true. But I had a qualm when she gave that little cry at sight of the license.'

'Now, never you have qualms, old boy. I mean to give her away tomorrow morning, and you mean to take her. It has always been on my conscience that I didn't urge more objections to your letting her

7. Feasting, merrymaking.

go, and now we've got to this stage I shan't be content if I don't help you to set the matter right.'

Phillotson nodded, and seeing how staunch his friend was, became more frank. 'No doubt when it gets known what I've done I shall be thought a soft fool by many. But they don't know Sue as I do. Though so elusive, hers is such an honest nature at bottom that I don't think she has ever done anything against her conscience. The fact of her having lived with Fawley goes for nothing. At the time she left me for him she thought she was quite within her right. Now she thinks otherwise.'

The next morning came, and the self-sacrifice of the woman on the altar of what she was pleased to call her principles was acquiesced in by these two friends, each from his own point of view. Phillotson went across to the Widow Edlin's to fetch Sue a few minutes after eight o'clock. The fog of the previous day or two on the lowlands had travelled up here by now, and the trees on the green caught armfuls, and turned them into showers of big drops. The bride was waiting, ready; bonnet and all on. She had never in her life looked so much like the lily her name connoted[8] as she did in that pallid morning light. Chastened, world-weary, remorseful, the strain on her nerves had preyed upon her flesh and bones, and she appeared smaller in outline than she had formerly done, though Sue had not been a large woman in her days of rudest health.

'Prompt,' said the schoolmaster, magnanimously taking her hand. But he checked his impulse to kiss her, remembering her start of yesterday, which unpleasantly lingered in his mind.

Gillingham joined them, and they left the house, Widow Edlin continuing steadfast in her refusal to assist in the ceremony.

'Where is the church?' said Sue. She had not lived there for any length of time since the old church was pulled down, and in her preoccupation forgot the new one.

'Up here,' said Phillotson; and presently the tower loomed large and solemn in the fog. The vicar had already crossed to the building, and when they entered he said pleasantly: 'We almost want candles.'

'You do—wish me to be yours, Richard?' gasped Sue in a whisper.

'Certainly, dear: above all things in the world.'

Sue said no more; and for the second or third time he felt he was not quite following out the humane instinct which had induced him to let her go.

There they stood, five altogether: the parson, the clerk, the couple and Gillingham; and the holy ordinance was re-solemnized forthwith. In the nave of the edifice were two or three villagers, and when the clergyman came to the words, 'What God hath joined,' a woman's voice from among these was heard to utter audibly:

8. The name Susanna is derived from the Hebrew for "lily."

'God hath jined indeed!'

It was like a re-enactment by the ghosts of their former selves of the similar scene which had taken place at Melchester years before. When the books were signed the vicar congratulated the husband and wife on having performed a noble, and righteous, and mutually forgiving act. 'All's well that ends well,' he said smiling. 'May you long be happy together, after thus having been "saved as by fire." '⁹

They came down the nearly empty building, and crossed to the schoolhouse. Gillingham wanted to get home that night, and left early. He, too, congratulated the couple. 'Now,' he said in parting from Phillotson, who walked out a little way, 'I shall be able to tell the people in your native place a good round tale; and they'll all say "Well done," depend on it.'

When the schoolmaster got back Sue was making a pretence of doing some housewifery as if she lived there. But she seemed timid at his approach, and compunction wrought on him at sight of it.

'Of course, my dear, I shan't expect to intrude upon your personal privacy any more than I did before,' he said gravely. 'It is for our good socially to do this, and that's its justification, if it was not my reason.'

Sue brightened a little.

vi–6

The place was the door of Jude's lodging in the outskirts of Christminster—far from the precincts of St. Silas' where he had formerly lived, which saddened him to sickness. The rain was coming down. A woman in shabby black stood on the doorstep talking to Jude, who held the door in his hand.

'I am lonely, destitute, and houseless—that's what I am! Father has turned me out of doors after borrowing every penny I'd got, to put it into his business, and then accusing me of laziness when I was only waiting for a situation. I am at the mercy of the world! If you can't take me and help me, Jude, I must go to the workhouse, or to something worse. Only just now two undergraduates winked at me as I came along. 'Tis hard for a woman to keep virtuous where there's so many young men!'

The woman in the rain who spoke thus was Arabella, the evening being that of the day after Sue's re-marriage with Phillotson.

'I am sorry for you, but I am only in lodgings,' said Jude coldly.

'Then you turn me away?'

'I'll give you enough to get food and lodging for a few days.'

'O, but can't you have the kindness to take me in? I cannot endure going to a public-house to lodge; and I am so lonely. Please, Jude, for old times' sake!'

9. Adapted from 1 Corinthians 3.15.

'No, no,' said Jude hastily. 'I don't want to be reminded of those things; and if you talk about them I shall not help you.'

'Then I suppose I must go!' said Arabella. She bent her head against the doorpost and began sobbing.

'The house is full,' said Jude. 'And I have only a little extra room to my own—not much more than a closet—where I keep my tools, and templates,[1] and the few books I have left!'

'That would be a palace for me!'

'There is no bedstead in it.'

'A bit of a bed could be made on the floor. It would be good enough for me.'

Unable to be harsh with her, and not knowing what to do, Jude called the man who let the lodgings, and said this was an acquaintance of his in great distress for want of temporary shelter.

'You may remember me as barmaid at the Lamb and Flag formerly?' spoke up Arabella. 'My father has insulted me this afternoon, and I've left him, though without a penny!'

The householder said he could not recall her features. 'But still, if you are a friend of Mr. Fawley's we'll do what we can for a day or two— if he'll make himself answerable?'

'Yes, yes,' said Jude. 'She has really taken me quite unawares; but I should wish to help her out of her difficulty.' And an arrangement was ultimately come to under which a bed was to be thrown down in Jude's lumber-room, to make it comfortable for Arabella till she could get out of the strait she was in—not by her own fault, as she declared—and return to her father's again.

While they were waiting for this to be done Arabella said: 'You know the news, I suppose?'

'I guess what you mean; but I know nothing.'

'I had a letter from Anny at Alfredston to-day. She had just heard that the wedding was to be yesterday: but she didn't know if it had come off.'

'I don't wish to talk of it.'

'No, no: of course you don't. Only it shows what kind of woman—'

'Don't speak of her I say! She's a fool!—And she's an angel, too, poor dear!'

'If it's done, he'll have a chance of getting back to his old position, by everybody's account, so Anny says. All his well-wishers will be pleased, including the bishop himself.'

'Do spare me, Arabella.'

Arabella was duly installed in the little attic, and at first she did not come near Jude at all. She went to and fro about her own business, which, when they met for a moment on the stairs or in the passage,

1. Instruments for measuring and pattern making.

she informed him was that of obtaining another place in the occupation she understood best. When Jude suggested London as affording the most likely opening in the liquor trade, she shook her head. 'No—the temptations are too many,' she said. 'Any humble tavern in the country before that for me.'

On the Sunday morning following, when he breakfasted later than on other days, she meekly asked him if she might come in to breakfast with him, as she had broken her teapot, and could not replace it immediately, the shops being shut.

'Yes, if you like,' he said indifferently.

While they sat without speaking she suddenly observed: 'You seem all in a brood, old man. I'm sorry for you.'

'I am all in a brood.'

'It is about her, I know. It's no business of mine, but I could find out all about the wedding—if it really did take place—if you wanted to know.'

'How could you?'

'I wanted to go to Alfredston to get a few things I left there. And I could see Anny, who'll be sure to have heard all about it, as she has friends at Marygreen.'

Jude could not bear to acquiesce in this proposal; but his suspense pitted itself against his discretion, and won in the struggle. 'You can ask about it if you like,' he said. 'I've not heard a sound from there. It must have been very private, if—they have married.'

'I am afraid I haven't enough cash to take me there and back, or I should have gone before. I must wait till I have earned some.'

'O—I can pay the journey for you,' he said impatiently. And thus his suspense as to Sue's welfare, and the possible marriage, moved him to dispatch for intelligence the last emissary he would have thought of choosing deliberately.

Arabella went, Jude requesting her to be home not later than by the seven o'clock train. When she had gone he said: 'Why should I have charged her to be back by a particular time! She's nothing to me:—nor the other neither!'

But having finished work he could not help going to the station to meet Arabella, dragged thither by feverish haste to get the news she might bring, and know the worst. Arabella had made dimples most successfully all the way home, and when she stepped out of the railway carriage she smiled. He merely said 'Well?' with the very reverse of a smile.

'They are married.'

'Yes—of course they are!' he returned. She observed, however, the hard strain upon his lip as he spoke.

'Anny says she has heard from Belinda, her relation out at Marygreen, that it was very sad, and curious!'

'How do you mean sad? She wanted to marry him again, didn't she?—and he her!'

'Yes—that was it. She wanted to in one sense, but not in the other. Mrs. Edlin was much upset by it all, and spoke out her mind at Phillotson. But Sue was that excited about it that she burnt her best embroidery that she'd worn with you, to blot you out entirely. Well—if a woman feels like it, she ought to do it. I commend her for it, though others don't.' Arabella sighed. 'She felt he was her only husband, and that she belonged to nobody else in the sight of God A'mighty while he lived. Perhaps another woman feels the same about herself, too!' Arabella sighed again.

'I don't want any cant!' exclaimed Jude.

"It isn't cant,' said Arabella. 'I feel exactly the same as she!'

He closed that issue by remarking abruptly: 'Well—now I know all I wanted to know. Many thanks for your information. I am not going back to my lodgings just yet.' And he left her straightway.

In his misery and depression Jude walked to well-nigh every spot in the city that he had visited with Sue; thence he did not know whither, and then thought of going home to his usual evening meal. But having all the vices of his virtues, and some to spare, he turned into a public-house, for the first time during many months. Among the possible consequences of her marriage Sue had not dwelt on this.

Arabella, meanwhile, had gone back. The evening passed, and Jude did not return. At half-past nine Arabella herself went out, first proceeding to an out-lying district near the river where her father lived, and had opened a small and precarious pork-shop lately.

'Well,' she said to him, 'for all your rowing[2] me that night, I've called in, for I have something to tell you. I think I shall get married and settled again. Only you must help me: and you can do no less, after what I've stood 'ee.'

'I'll do anything to get thee off my hands!'

'Very well. I am now going to look for my young man. He's on the loose I'm afraid, and I must get him home. All I want you to do to-night is not to fasten the door, in case I should want to sleep here, and should be late.'

'I thought you'd soon get tired of giving yourself airs and keeping away!'

'Well—don't do the door. That's all I say.'

She then sallied out again, and first hastening back to Jude's to make sure that he had not returned, began her search for him. A shrewd guess as to his probable course took her straight to the tavern which Jude had formerly frequented, and where she had been barmaid for a brief term. She had no sooner opened the door of the 'Private Bar' than

---

2. Scolding, quarreling with.

her eyes fell upon him—sitting in the shade at the back of the compartment, with his eyes fixed on the floor in a blank stare. He was drinking nothing stronger than ale just then. He did not observe her, and she entered and sat beside him.

Jude looked up, and said without surprise: 'You've come to have something, Arabella? . . . I'm trying to forget her: that's all! But I can't; and I am going home.' She saw that he was a little way on in liquor, but only a little as yet.

'I've come entirely to look for you, dear boy. You are not well. Now you must have something better than that.' Arabella held up her finger to the barmaid. 'You shall have a liqueur—that's better fit for a man of education than beer. You shall have maraschino, or curaçoa dry or sweet, or cherry brandy. I'll treat you, poor chap!'

'I don't care which! Say cherry brandy. . . . Sue has served me badly, very badly. I didn't expect it of Sue! I stuck to her, and she ought to have stuck to me. I'd have sold my soul for her sake, but she wouldn't risk hers a jot for me. To save her own soul she lets mine go damn! . . . But it isn't her fault, poor little girl—I am sure it isn't!'

How Arabella had obtained money did not appear, but she ordered a liqueur each, and paid for them. When they had drunk these Arabella suggested another; and Jude had the pleasure of being, as it were, personally conducted through the varieties of spirituous delectation by one who knew the landmarks well. Arabella kept very considerably in the rear of Jude; but though she only sipped where he drank, she took as much as she could safely take without losing her head—which was not a little, as the crimson upon her countenance showed.

Her tone towards him to-night was uniformly soothing and cajoling; and whenever he said 'I don't care what happens to me,' a thing he did continually, she replied, 'But I do very much!' The closing hour came, and they were compelled to turn out; whereupon Arabella put her arm round his waist, and guided his unsteady footsteps.

When they were in the streets she said: 'I don't know what our landlord will say to my bringing you home in this state. I expect we are fastened out, so that he'll have to come down and let us in.'

'I don't know—I don't know.'

'That's the worst of not having a home of your own. I tell you, Jude, what we had best do. Come round to my father's—I made it up with him a bit to-day. I can let you in, and nobody will see you at all; and by to-morrow morning you'll be all right.'

'Anything—anywhere,' replied Jude. 'What the devil does it matter to me?'

They went along together, like any other fuddling³ couple, her arm still round his waist, and his, at last, round hers; though with no ama-

---

3. Intoxicated, on a drinking bout.

tory intent; but merely because he was weary, unstable, and in need of support.

'This—is th' Martyrs'—burning-place,' he stammered as they dragged across a broad street. 'I remember—in old Fuller's *Holy State*[4]—and I am reminded of it—by our passing by here—old Fuller in his *Holy State* says, that at the burning of Ridley, Doctor Smith— preached sermon, and took as his text *"Though I give my body to be burned, and have not charity, it profiteth me nothing,"*[5]—Often think of it as I pass here. Ridley was a—'

'Yes. Exactly. Very thoughtful of you, deary, even though it hasn't much to do with our present business.'

'Why, yes it has! I'm giving *my* body to be burned! But—ah—you don't understand!—it wants Sue to understand such things! And I was her seducer—poor little girl! And she's gone—and I don't care about myself! Do what you like with me! . . . And yet she did it for conscience' sake, poor little Sue!'

'Hang her!—I mean, I think she was right,' hiccupped Arabella. 'I've my feelings too, like her; and I feel I belong to you in Heaven's eye, and to nobody else, till death us do part![6] It is—hic—never too late— hic—to mend!'

They had reached her father's house, and she softly unfastened the door, groping about for a light within.

The circumstances were not altogether unlike those of their entry into the cottage at Cresscombe, such a long time before. Nor were perhaps Arabella's motives. But Jude did not think of that, though she did.

'I can't find the matches, dear,' she said when she had fastened up the door. 'But never mind—this way. As quiet as you can, please.'

'It is as dark as pitch,' said Jude.

'Give me your hand, and I'll lead you. That's it. Just sit down here, and I'll pull off your boots. I don't want to wake him.'

'Who?'

'Father. He'd make a row, perhaps.'

She pulled off his boots. 'Now,' she whispered, 'take hold of me— never mind your weight. Now—first stair, second stair—'

'But,—are we out in our old house by Marygreen?' asked the stupefied Jude. 'I haven't been inside it for years till now! Hey? And where are my books? That's what I want to know?'

'We are at my house, dear, where there's nobody to spy out how ill you are. Now—third stair, fourth stair—that's it. Now we shall get on.'

---

4. *The Holy State and the Profane State* (1642), by Thomas Fuller (1608–1661).
5. 1 Corinthians 13.3.
6. Arabella is quoting the marriage service of the Church of England: see above, p. 48.

VI-7

Arabella was preparing breakfast in the downstairs back room of this small, recently hired tenement of her father's. She put her head into the little pork-shop in front, and told Mr. Donn it was ready. Donn, endeavouring to look like a master pork-butcher, in a greasy blue blouse, and with a strap round his waist from which a steel[1] dangled, came in promptly.

'You must mind the shop this morning,' he said casually. 'I've to go and get some inwards and half a pig from Lumsdon, and to call elsewhere. If you live here you must put your shoulder to the wheel, at least till I get the business started!'

"Well, for to-day I can't say.' She looked deedily into his face. 'I've got a prize upstairs.'

'Oh?—What's that?'

'A husband—almost.'

'No!'

'Yes. It's Jude. He's come back to me.'

'Your old original one? Well, I'm damned!'

'Well, I always did like him, that I will say.'

'But how does he come to be up there?' said Donn, humour-struck, and nodding to the ceiling.

'Don't ask inconvenient questions, father. What we've to do is to keep him here till he and I are—as we were.'

'How was that?'

'Married.'

'Ah. . . . Well it is the rummest[2] thing I ever heard of—marrying an old husband again, and so much new blood in the world! He's no catch, to my thinking. I'd have had a new one while I was about it.'

'It isn't rum for a woman to want her old husband back for respectability, though for a man to want his old wife back—well, perhaps it is funny, rather!' And Arabella was suddenly seized with a fit of loud laughter, in which her father joined more moderately.

'Be civil to him, and I'll do the rest,' she said when she had recovered seriousness. 'He told me this morning that his head ached fit to burst, and he hardly seemed to know where he was. And no wonder, considering how he mixed his drink last night. We must keep him jolly and cheerful here for a day or two, and not let him go back to his lodging. Whatever you advance I'll pay back to you again. But I must go up and see how he is now, poor deary.'

Arabella ascended the stairs, softly opened the door of the first bedroom, and peeped in. Finding that her shorn Samson[3] was asleep she

---

1. Steel rod with handle, used for sharpening knives.
2. Strangest.
3. Judges 16.19. The allusion recalls the earlier references (above, pp. 39 and 59).

entered to the bedside and stood regarding him. The fevered flush on his face from the debauch of the previous evening lessened the fragility of his ordinary appearance, and his long lashes, dark brows, and curly black hair and beard against the white pillow, completed the physiognomy of one whom Arabella, as a woman of rank passions, still felt it worth while to recapture, highly important to recapture as a woman straitened both in means and in reputation. Her ardent gaze seemed to affect him; his quick breathing became suspended, and he opened his eyes.

'How are you now, dear?' said she. 'It is I—Arabella.'

'Ah!—where—O yes, I remember! You gave me shelter. . . . I am stranded—ill—demoralized—damn bad! That's what I am!'

'Then do stay there. There's nobody in the house but father and me, and you can rest till you are thoroughly well. I'll tell them at the stone-works that you are knocked up.'[4]

'I wonder what they are thinking at the lodgings!'

'I'll go round and explain. Perhaps you had better let me pay up, or they'll think we've run away?'

'Yes. You'll find enough money in my pocket there.'

Quite indifferent, and shutting his eyes because he could not bear the daylight in his throbbing eyeballs, Jude seemed to doze again. Arabella took his purse, softly left the room, and putting on her outdoor things went off to the lodgings she and he had quitted the evening before.

Scarcely half-an-hour had elapsed ere she reappeared round the corner, walking beside a lad wheeling a truck on which were piled all Jude's household possessions, and also the few of Arabella's things which she had taken to the lodging for her short sojourn there. Jude was in such physical pain from his unfortunate breakdown of the previous night, and in such mental pain from the loss of Sue and from having yielded in his half-somnolent state to Arabella, that when he saw his few chattels unpacked and standing before his eyes in this strange bedroom, intermixed with woman's apparel, he scarcely considered how they had come there, or what their coming signalized.

'Now,' said Arabella to her father downstairs, 'we must keep plenty of good liquor going in the house these next few days. I know his nature, and if he once gets into that fearfully low state that he does get into sometimes, he'll never do the honourable thing by me in this world, and I shall be left in the lurch. He must be kept cheerful. He has a little money in the savings-bank, and he has given me his purse to pay for anything necessary. Well, that will be the license; for I must have that ready at hand, to catch him the moment he's in the humour. You must pay for the liquor. A few friends, and a quiet convivial party

4. Ill.

would be the thing, if we could get it up. It would advertise the shop, and help me too.'

'That can be got up easy enough by anybody who'll afford victuals and drink. . . . Well yes—it would advertise the shop—that's true.'

Three days later, when Jude had recovered somewhat from the fearful throbbing of his eyes and brain, but was still considerably confused in his mind by what had been supplied to him by Arabella during the interval—to keep him jolly, as she expressed it—the quiet convivial gathering suggested by her, to wind Jude up to the striking point, took place.

Donn had only just opened his miserable little pork and sausage shop, which had as yet scarce any customers; nevertheless that party advertised it well, and the Donns acquired a real notoriety among a certain class in Christminster who knew not the colleges, nor their works, nor their ways. Jude was asked if he could suggest any guest in addition to those named by Arabella and her father, and in a saturnine humour of perfect recklessness mentioned Uncle Joe, and Stagg, and the decayed auctioneer, and others whom he remembered as having been frequenters of the well-known tavern during his bout therein years before. He also suggested Freckles and Bower o' Bliss. Arabella took him at his word so far as the men went, but drew the line at the ladies.

Another man they knew, Tinker Taylor, though he lived in the same street, was not invited; but as he went homeward from a late job on the evening of the party, he had occasion to call at the shop for trotters. There were none in, but he was promised some the next morning. While making his inquiry Taylor glanced into the back room, and saw the guests sitting round, card-playing, and drinking, and otherwise enjoying themselves at Donn's expense. He went home to bed, and on his way out next morning wondered how the party went off. He thought it hardly worth while to call at the shop for his provisions at that hour, Donn and his daughter being probably not up, if they caroused late the night before. However, he found in passing that the door was open, and he could hear voices within, though the shutters of the meat-stall were not down. He went and tapped at the sitting-room door, and opened it.

'Well—to be sure!' he said, astonished.

Hosts and guests were sitting card-playing, smoking, and talking, precisely as he had left them eleven hours earlier; the gas was burning and the curtains drawn, though it had been broad daylight for two hours out of doors.

'Yes!' cried Arabella, laughing. 'Here we are, just the same. We ought to be ashamed of ourselves, oughtn't we! But it is a sort of housewarming, you see; and our friends are in no hurry. Come in, Mr. Taylor, and sit down.'

The tinker, or rather reduced ironmonger, was nothing loth, and entered and took a seat. 'I shall lose a quarter, but never mind,' he said. 'Well, really, I could hardly believe my eyes when I looked in! It seemed as if I was flung back again into last night, all of a sudden.'

'So you are. Pour out for Mr. Taylor.'

He now perceived that she was sitting beside Jude, her arm being round his waist. Jude, like the rest of the company, bore on his face the signs of how deeply he had been indulging.

'Well, we've been waiting for certain legal hours to arrive, to tell the truth,' she continued bashfully, and making her spirituous crimson look as much like a maiden blush as possible. 'Jude and I have decided to make up matters between us by tying the knot again, as we find we can't do without one another after all. So, as a bright notion, we agreed to sit on till it was late enough, and go and do it off-hand.'

Jude seemed to pay no great heed to what she was announcing, or indeed to anything whatever. The entrance of Taylor infused fresh spirit into the company, and they remained sitting, till Arabella whispered to her father: 'Now we may as well go.'

'But the parson don't know?'

'Yes, I told him last night that we might come between eight and nine, as there were reasons of decency for doing it as early and quiet as possible; on account of it being our second marriage, which might make people curious to look on if they knew. He highly approved.'

'O very well: I'm ready,' said her father, getting up and shaking himself.

'Now, old darling,' she said to Jude. 'Come along, as you promised.'

'When did I promise anything?' asked he, whom she had made so tipsy by her special knowledge of that line of business as almost to have made him sober again—or to seem so to those who did not know him.

'Why!' said Arabella, affecting dismay. 'You've promised to marry me several times as we've sat here to-night. These gentlemen have heard you.'

'I don't remember it,' said Jude doggedly. "There's only one woman—but I won't mention her in this Capharnaum!"[5]

Arabella looked towards her father. 'Now, Mr. Fawley, be honourable,' said Donn. 'You and my daughter have been living here together these three or four days, quite on the understanding that you were going to marry her. Of course I shouldn't have had such goings on in my house if I hadn't understood that. As a point of honour you must do it now.'

5. The town of Capernaum (usual spelling) figures frequently in the Gospel accounts of Christ's ministry (see also p. 32 above). Hardy may here have had in mind either Matthew 4.16 ("The people who sat in darkness saw great light") or Matthew 11.23 ("And thou, Capernaum, which art exalted unto heaven, shall be brought down to hell").

'Don't say anything against my honour!' enjoined Jude hotly, stand-ing up. 'I'd marry the W—of Babylon[6] rather than do anything dis-honourable! No reflection on you, my dear. It is a mere rhetorical figure—what they call in the books, hyperbole.'

'Keep your figures for your debts to friends who shelter you,' said Donn.

'If I am bound in honour to marry her—as I suppose I am—though how I came to be here with her I know no more than a dead man—marry her I will, so help me God! I have never behaved dishonourably to a woman or to any living thing. I am not a man who wants to save himself at the expense of the weaker among us!'

'There—never mind him, deary,' said she, putting her cheek against Jude's. 'Come up and wash your face, and just put yourself tidy, and off we'll go. Make it up with father.'

They shook hands. Jude went upstairs with her, and soon came down looking tidy and calm. Arabella, too, had hastily arranged herself, and accompanied by Donn away they went.

'Don't go,' she said to the guests at parting. 'I've told the little maid to get the breakfast while we are gone; and when we come back we'll all have some. A good strong cup of tea will set everybody right for going home.'

When Arabella, Jude and Donn had disappeared on their matri-monial errand the assembled guests yawned themselves wider awake. and discussed the situation with great interest. Tinker Taylor, being the most sober, reasoned the most lucidly.

'I don't wish to speak against friends,' he said. 'But it do seem a rare curiosity for a couple to marry over again! If they couldn't get on the first time when their minds were limp, they won't the second, by my reckoning.'

'Do you think he'll do it?'

'He's been put upon his honour by the woman, so he med.'

'He'd hardly do it straight off like this. He's got no license nor any-thing.'

'She's got that, bless you. Didn't you hear her say so to her father?'

'Well,' said Tinker Taylor, re-lighting his pipe at the gas-jet. 'Take her all together, limb by limb, she's not such a bad-looking piece—particular by candlelight. To be sure, halfpence that have been in cir-culation can't be expected to look like new ones from the Mint. But for a woman that's been knocking about the four hemispheres for some time, she's passable enough. A little bit thick in the flitch[7] perhaps: but I like a woman that a puff o' wind won't blow down.'

6. Whore of Babylon, a term of abuse derived from Revelation 17 and applied by the Puritans to the Roman Catholic Church.
7. Literally, a side of pork or bacon; here, stout or heavily built.

Their eyes followed the movements of the little girl as she spread the breakfast-cloth on the table they had been using, without wiping up the slops of the liquor. The curtains were undrawn, and the expression of the house made to look like morning. Some of the guests, however, fell asleep in their chairs. One or two went to the door, and gazed along the street more than once. Tinker Taylor was the chief of these, and after a time he came in with a leer on his face.

'By Gad, they are coming! I think the deed's done!'

'No,' said Uncle Joe, following him in. 'Take my word, he turned rusty[8] at the last minute. They are walking in a very onusual way; and that's the meaning of it!'

They waited in silence till the wedding party could be heard entering the house. First into the room came Arabella boisterously; and her face was enough to show that her strategy had succeeded.

'Mrs. Fawley, I presume?' said Tinker Taylor with mock courtesy.

'Certainly. Mrs. Fawley again,' replied Arabella blandly, pulling off her glove and holding out her left hand. 'There's the padlock, see. . . . Well, he was a very nice, gentlemanly man indeed. I mean the clergyman. He said to me as gentle as a babe when all was done: "Mrs. Fawley, I congratulate you heartily," he says. "For having heard your history, and that of your husband, I think you have both done the right and proper thing. And for your past errors as a wife, and his as a husband, I think you ought now to be forgiven by the world, as you have forgiven each other," says he. Yes: he was a very nice, gentlemanly man. "The Church don't recognize divorce in her dogma, strictly speaking," he says: "and bear in mind the words of the Service in your goings out and your comings in: What God hath joined together let no man put asunder." Yes: he was a very nice, gentlemanly man.. . . .But, Jude, my dear, you were enough to make a cat laugh! You walked that straight, and held yourself that steady, that one would have thought you were going 'prentice to a judge; though I knew you were seeing double all the time, from the way you fumbled with my finger.'

'I said I'd do anything to—save a woman's honour,' muttered Jude. 'And I've done it!'

'Well now, old deary, come along and have some breakfast.'

'I want—some—more whisky,' said Jude stolidly.

'Nonsense, dear. Not now! There's no more left. The tea will take the muddle out of our heads, and we shall be as fresh as larks.'

'All right. I've—married you. She said I ought to marry you again, and I have straightway. It is true religion! Ha—ha—ha!'

8. Surly, awkward.

VI–8

Michaelmas[1] came and passed, and Jude and his wife, who had lived but a short time in her father's house after their re-marriage, were in lodgings on the top floor of a dwelling nearer to the centre of the city.

He had done a few days' work during the two or three months since the event, but his health had been indifferent, and it was now precarious. He was sitting in an arm-chair before the fire, and coughed a good deal.

'I've got a bargain for my trouble in marrying thee over again!' Arabella was saying to him. 'I shall have to keep 'ee entirely,—that's what 'twill come to! I shall have to make black-pot and sausages, and hawk 'em about the street, all to support an invalid husband I'd no business to be saddled with at all. Why didn't you keep your health, deceiving one like this? You were well enough when the wedding was!'

'Ah, yes!' said he, laughing acridly. 'I have been thinking of my foolish feeling about the pig you and I killed during our first marriage. I feel now that the greatest mercy that could be vouchsafed to me would be that something should serve me as I served that animal.'

This was the sort of discourse that went on between them every day now. The landlord of the lodging, who had heard that they were a queer couple, had doubted if they were married at all, especially as he had seen Arabella kiss Jude one evening when she had taken a little cordial; and he was about to give them notice to quit, till by chance overhearing her one night haranguing Jude in rattling terms, and ultimately flinging a shoe at his head, he recognized the note of genuine wedlock; and concluding that they must be respectable, said no more.

Jude did not get any better, and one day he requested Arabella, with considerable hesitation, to execute a commission for him. She asked him indifferently what it was.

'To write to Sue.'

'What in the name—do you want me to write to her for?'

'To ask how she is, and if she'll come to see me, because I'm ill, and should like to see her—once again.'

'It is like you to insult a lawful wife by asking such a thing!'

'It is just in order not to insult you that I ask you to do it. You know I love Sue. I don't wish to mince the matter—there stands the fact: I love her. I could find a dozen ways of sending a letter to her without your knowledge. But I wish to be quite above-board with you, and with her husband. A message through you asking her to come is at least free from any odour of intrigue. If she retains any of her old nature at all, she'll come.'

'You've no respect for marriage whatever, or its rights and duties!'

1. September 29.

'What *does* it matter what my opinions are—a wretch like me! Can it matter to anybody in the world who comes to see me for half an-hour—here with one foot in the grave! . . . Come, please write, Ara-bella!' he pleaded. 'Repay my candour by a little generosity!'

'I should think *not!*'

'Not just once?—O do!' He felt that his physical weakness had taken away all his dignity.

'What do you want *her* to know how you are for? She don't want to see 'ee. She's the rat that forsook the sinking ship!'

'Don't, don't!'

'And I stuck to un—the more fool I! Have that strumpet in the house indeed!'

Almost as soon as the words were spoken Jude sprang from the chair, and before Arabella knew where she was he had her on her back upon a little couch which stood there, he kneeling above her.

'Say another word of that sort,' he whispered, 'and I'll kill you—here and now! I've everything to gain by it—my own death not being the least part. So don't think there's no meaning in what I say!'

'What do you want me to do?' gasped Arabella.

'Promise never to speak of her.'

'Very well. I do.'

'I take your word,' he said scornfully as he loosened her. 'But what it is worth I can't say.'

'You couldn't kill the pig, but you could kill me!'

'Ah—there you have me! No—I couldn't kill you—even in a passion. Taunt away!'

He then began coughing very much, and she estimated his life with an appraiser's eye as he sank back ghastly pale. 'I'll send for her,' Ara-bella murmured, 'if you'll agree to my being in the room with you all the time she's here.'

The softer side of his nature, the desire to see Sue, made him unable to resist the offer even now, provoked as he had been; and he replied breathlessly: 'Yes, I agree. Only send for her!'

In the evening he inquired if she had written.

'Yes,' she said; 'I wrote a note telling her you were ill, and asking her to come to-morrow or the day after. I haven't posted it yet.'

The next day Jude wondered if she really did post it, but would not ask her; and foolish Hope, that lives on a drop and a crumb, made him restless with expectation. He knew the times of the possible trains, and listened on each occasion for sounds of her.

She did not come; but Jude would not address Arabella again thereon. He hoped and expected all the next day; but no Sue appeared; neither was there any note of reply. Then Jude decided in the privacy of his mind that Arabella had never posted hers, although she had written it. There was something in her manner which told it. His physical weakness was such that he shed tears at the disappointment when she was not there to see. His suspicions were, in fact, well founded. Arabella, like some other nurses, thought that your duty towards your invalid was to pacify him by any means short of really acting upon his fancies.

He never said another word to her about his wish or his conjecture. A silent, undiscerned resolve grew up in him, which gave him, if not strength, stability and calm. One midday when, after an absence of two hours, she came into the room, she beheld the chair empty.

Down she flopped on the bed, and sitting, meditated. 'Now where the devil is my man gone to!' she said.

A driving rain from the north-east had been falling with more or less intermission all the morning, and looking from the window at the dripping spouts it seemed impossible to believe that any sick man would have ventured out to almost certain death. Yet a conviction possessed Arabella that he had gone out, and it became a certainty when she had searched the house. 'If he's such a fool, let him be!' she said. 'I can do no more.'

Jude was at that moment in a railway train that was drawing near to Alfredston, oddly swathed, pale as a monumental figure in alabaster, and much stared at by other passengers. An hour later his thin form, in the long great-coat and blanket he had come with, but without an umbrella, could have been seen walking along the five-mile road to Marygreen. On his face showed the determined purpose that alone sustained him, but to which his weakness afforded a sorry foundation. By the uphill walk he was quite blown, but he pressed on; and at half-past three o'clock stood by the familiar well at Marygreen. The rain was keeping everybody indoors; Jude crossed the green to the church without observation, and found the building open. Here he stood, looking forth at the school, whence he could hear the usual sing-song tones of the little voices that had not learnt Creation's groan.

He waited till a small boy came from the school—one evidently allowed out before hours for some reason or other. Jude held up his hand, and the child came.

'Please call at the schoolhouse and ask Mrs. Phillotson if she will be kind enough to come to the church for a few minutes.'

The child departed, and Jude heard him knock at the door of the dwelling. He himself went further into the church. Everything was new, except a few pieces of carving preserved from the wrecked old fabric, now fixed against the new walls. He stood by these: they seemed akin to the perished people of that place who were his ancestors and Sue's.

A light footstep, which might have been accounted no more than an added drip to the rainfall, sounded in the porch, and he looked round.

'O—I didn't think it was you! I didn't—O Jude!' A hysterical catch in her breath ended in a succession of them. He advanced, but she quickly recovered and went back.

'Don't go—don't go!' he implored. 'This is my last time! I thought it would be less intrusive than to enter your house. And I shall never come again. Don't then be unmerciful. Sue, Sue! we are acting by the letter; and "the letter killeth"!'

'I'll stay—I won't be unkind!' she said, her mouth quivering and her tears flowing as she allowed him to come closer. 'But why did you come, and do this wrong thing, after doing such a right thing as you have done?'

'What right thing?'

'Marrying Arabella again. It was in the Alfredston paper. She has never been other than yours, Jude—in a proper sense. And therefore you did so well—O so well!—in recognizing it—and taking her to you again.'

'God above—and is that all I've come to hear? If there is any thing more degrading, immoral, unnatural, than another in my life, it is this meretricious contract with Arabella which has been called doing the right thing! And you too—you call yourself Phillotson's wife! *His* wife! You are mine.'

'Don't make me rush away from you—I can't bear much! But on this point I am decided.'

'I cannot understand how you did it—how you think it—I cannot!'

'Never mind that. He is a kind husband to me—And I—I've wrestled and struggled, and fasted, and prayed. I have nearly brought my body into complete subjection. And you mustn't—will you—wake—'

'O you darling little fool; where is your reason? You seem to have suffered the loss of your faculties! I would argue with you if I didn't know that a woman in your state of feeling is quite beyond all appeals to her brains. Or is it that you are humbugging yourself, as so many women do about these things; and don't actually believe what you pretend to, and only are indulging in the luxury of the emotion raised by an affected belief?'

'Luxury! How can you be so cruel!'

'You dear, sad, soft, most melancholy wreck of a promising human intellect that it has ever been my lot to behold! Where is your scorn of convention gone? I *would* have died game!'

'You crush, almost insult me, Jude! Go away from me!' She turned off quickly.

'I will. I would never come to see you again, even if I had the strength to come, which I shall not have any more. Sue, Sue, you are not worth a man's love!'

Her bosom began to go up and down. 'I can't endure you to say that!' she burst out, and her eye resting on him a moment, she turned back impulsively. 'Don't, don't scorn me! Kiss me, O kiss me lots of times, and say I am not a coward and a contemptible humbug—I can't bear it!' She rushed up to him and, with her mouth on his, continued: 'I must tell you—O I must—my darling Love! It has been—only a church marriage—an apparent marriage I mean! He suggested it at the very first!'

'How?'

'I mean it is a nominal marriage only. It hasn't been more than that at all since I came back to him!'

'Sue!' he said. Pressing her to him in his arms he bruised her lips with kisses: 'If misery can know happiness, I have a moment's happiness now! Now, in the name of all you hold holy, tell me the truth, and no lie. You do love me still?'

'I do! You know it too well! . . . But I *mustn't* do this!—I mustn't kiss you back as I would!'

'But do!'

'And yet you are so dear!—and you look so ill—'

'And so do you! There's one more, in memory of our dead little children—yours and mine!'

The words struck her like a blow, and she bent her head. 'I *mustn't*—I *can't* go on with this!' she gasped presently. 'But there, there, darling; I give you back your kisses; I do, I do! . . . And now I'll *hate* myself for ever for my sin!'

'No—let me make my last appeal. Listen to this! We've both remarried out of our senses. I was made drunk to do it. You were the same. I was gin-drunk; you were creed-drunk. Either form of intoxication takes away the nobler vision. . . . Let us then shake off our mistakes, and run away together!'

'No; again no! . . . Why do you tempt me so far, Jude! It is too merciless! . . . But I've got over myself now. Don't follow me—don't look at me. Leave me, for pity's sake!'

She ran up the church to the east end, and Jude did as she requested. He did not turn his head, but took up his blanket, which she had not seen, and went straight out. As he passed the end of the church she heard his coughs mingling with the rain on the windows, and in a last instinct of human affection, even now unsubdued by her fetters, she sprang up as if to go and succour him. But she knelt down again, and stopped her ears with her hands till all possible sound of him had passed away.

He was by this time at the corner of the green, from which the path ran across the fields in which he had scared rooks as a boy. He turned and looked back, once, at the building which still contained Sue; and then went on, knowing that his eyes would light on that scene no more.

There are cold spots up and down Wessex in autumn and winter weather; but the coldest of all when a north or east wind is blowing is the crest of the down by the Brown House, where the road to Alfred-

ston crosses the old Ridgeway. Here the first winter sleets and snows
fall and lie, and here the spring frost lingers last unthawed. Here in the
teeth of the north-east wind and rain Jude now pursued his way, wet
through, the necessary slowness of his walk from lack of his former
strength being insufficient to maintain his heat. He came to the milestone, and, raining as it was, spread his blanket and lay down there to
rest. Before moving on he went and felt at the back of the stone for
his own carving. It was still there; but nearly obliterated by moss. He
passed the spot where the gibbet of his ancestor and Sue's had stood,
and descended the hill.

It was dark when he reached Alfredston, where he had a cup of tea,
the deadly chill that began to creep into his bones being too much for
him to endure fasting. To get home he had to travel by a steam tram-
car, and two branches of railway, with much waiting at a junction. He
did not reach Christminster till ten o'clock.

VI–9

On the platform stood Arabella. She looked him up and down.

'You've been to see her?' she asked.

'I have,' said Jude, literally tottering with cold and lassitude.

'Well, now you'd best march along home.'

The water ran out of him as he went, and he was compelled to lean
against the wall to support himself while coughing.

'You've done for yourself by this, young man,' said she. 'I don't know
whether you know it.'

'Of course I do. I meant to do for myself.'

'What—to commit suicide?'

'Certainly.'

'Well, I'm blest! Kill yourself for a woman.'

'Listen to me, Arabella. You think you are the stronger; and so you
are, in a physical sense, now. You could push me over like a ninepin.
You did not send that letter the other day, and I could not resent your
conduct. But I am not so weak in another way as you think. I made up
my mind that a man confined to his room by inflammation of the
lungs, a fellow who had only two wishes left in the world, to see a
particular woman, and then to die, could neatly accomplish those two
wishes at one stroke by taking this journey in the rain. That I've done.
I have seen her for the last time, and I've finished myself—put an end
to a feverish life which ought never to have been begun!'

'Lord—you do talk lofty! Won't you have something warm to drink?'

'No thank you. Let's get home.'

They went along by the silent colleges, and Jude kept stopping.

'What are you looking at?'

'Stupid fancies. I see, in a way, those spirits of the dead again, on this my last walk, that I saw when I first walked here!'

'What a curious chap you are!'

'I seem to see them, and almost hear them rustling. But I don't revere all of them as I did then. I don't believe in half of them. The theologians, the apologists, and their kin the metaphysicians, the high-handed statesmen, and others, no longer interest me. All that has been spoilt for me by the grind of stern reality!'

The expression of Jude's corpse-like face in the watery lamplight was indeed as if he saw people where there was nobody. At moments he stood still by an archway, like one watching a figure walk out; then he would look at a window like one discerning a familiar face behind it. He seemed to hear voices, whose words he repeated as if to gather their meaning.

'They seem laughing at me!'

'Who?'

'O—I was talking to myself! The phantoms all about here, in the college archways, and windows. They used to look friendly in the old days, particularly Addison, and Gibbon, and Johnson, and Dr. Browne, and Bishop Ken—'[1]

'Come along do! Phantoms! There's neither living nor dead hereabouts except a damn policeman! I never saw the streets emptier.'

'Fancy! The Poet of Liberty[2] used to walk here, and the great Dissector of Melancholy there!'[3]

'I don't want to hear about 'em! They bore me.'

'Walter Raleigh[4] is beckoning to me from that lane—Wycliffe —Harvey—Hooker—Arnold[5]—and a whole crowd of Tractarian Shades——'

'I *don't want* to know their names, I tell you! What do I care about folk dead and gone? Upon my soul you are more sober when you've been drinking than when you have not!'

'I must rest a moment,' he said; and as he paused, holding to the railings, he measured with his eye the height of a college front. 'This is old Rubric. And that Sarcophagus; and up that lane Crozier and Tudor: and all down there is Cardinal with its long front, and its windows with lifted eyebrows, representing the polite surprise of the University at the efforts of such as I.'

---

1. Dr. Samuel Johnson (1709–1784) was for a short time at Pembroke College, Oxford. Sir Thomas Browne (1605–1682), physician and author, and the others named were also Oxford figures.
2. Shelley. Hardy's manuscript shows that he originally wrote "the poet of the West Wind" (alluding to Shelley's famous ode).
3. Robert Burton (1577–1640), author of *The Anatomy of Melancholy* (1621).
4. Sir Walter Raleigh (1552?–1618), poet, soldier, and voyager.
5. John Wycliffe, fourteenth-century religious reformer and translator of the Bible. William Harvey (1578–1657) discovered the circulation of the blood. Richard Hooker (1554?–1600), theological writer.

'Come along, and I'll treat you!'

'Very well. It will help me home, for I feel the chilly fog from the meadows of Cardinal as if death-claws were grabbing me through and through. As Antigone said, I am neither a dweller among men nor ghosts.[6] But, Arabella, when I am dead, you'll see my spirit flitting up and down here among these!'

'Pooh! You mayn't die after all. You are tough enough yet, old man.'

It was night at Marygreen, and the rain of the afternoon showed no sign of abatement. About the time at which Jude and Arabella were walking the streets of Christminster homeward, the Widow Edlin crossed the green, and opened the back door of the schoolmaster's dwelling, which she often did now before bedtime, to assist Sue in putting things away.

Sue was muddling helplessly in the kitchen, for she was not a good housewife, though she tried to be, and grew impatient of domestic details.

'Lord love 'ee, what do ye do that yourself for, when I've come o' purpose! You knew I should come.'

'O—I don't know—I forgot! No, I didn't forget. I did it to discipline myself. I have scrubbed the stairs since eight o'clock. I *must* practise myself in my household duties. I've shamefully neglected them!'

'Why should ye? He'll get a better school, perhaps be a parson, in time, and you'll keep two servants. 'Tis a pity to spoil them pretty hands.'

'Don't talk of my pretty hands, Mrs. Edlin. This pretty body of mine has been the ruin of me already!'

'Pshoo—you've got no body to speak of! You put me more in mind of a sperrit. But there seems something wrong to-night, my dear. Husband cross?'

'No. He never is. He's gone to bed early.'

'Then what is it?'

'I cannot tell you. I have done wrong to-day. And I want to eradicate it. . . . Well—I will tell you this—Jude has been here this afternoon, and I find I still love him—O, grossly! I cannot tell you more.'

'Ah! said the widow. 'I told 'ee how 'twould be!'

'But it shan't be! I have not told my husband of his visit; it is not necessary to trouble him about it, as I never mean to see Jude any more. But I am going to make my conscience right on my duty to Richard—by doing a penance—the ultimate thing. I must!'

'I wouldn't—since he agrees to it being otherwise, and it has gone on three months very well as it is.'

'Yes—he agrees to my living as I choose; but I feel it is an indulgence

I ought not to exact from him. It ought not to have been accepted by me. To reverse it will be terrible—but I must be more just to him. O why was I so unheroic!'

'What is it you don't like in him? asked Mrs. Edlin curiously.

'I cannot tell you. It is something . . . I cannot say. The mournful thing is, that nobody would admit it as a reason for feeling as I do; so that no excuse is left me.'

'Did you ever tell Jude what it was?'

'Never.'

'I've heard strange tales o' husbands in my time,' observed the widow in a lowered voice. 'They say that when the saints were upon the earth devils used to take husbands' forms o' nights, and get poor women into all sorts of trouble. But I don't know why that should come into my head, for it is only a tale. . . . What a wind and rain it is to-night! Well—don't be in a hurry to alter things, my dear. Think it over.

'No, no! I've screwed my weak soul up to treating him more cour-teously—and it must be now—at once—before I break down!'

'I don't think you ought to force your nature. No woman ought to be expected to.'

'It is my duty. I will drink my cup to the dregs!'

Half-an-hour later when Mrs. Edlin put on her bonnet and shawl to leave, Sue seemed to be seized with vague terror.

'No, no—don't go, Mrs. Edlin,' she implored, her eyes enlarged, and with a quick nervous look over her shoulder.

'But it is bed-time, child.'

'Yes, but—there's the little spare room—my room that was. It is quite ready. Please stay, Mrs. Edlin!—I shall want you in the morning.'

'O well—I don't mind, if you wish. Nothing will happen to my four old walls, whether I be there or no.'

She then fastened up the doors, and they ascended the stairs together.

'Wait here, Mrs. Edlin,' said Sue. 'I'll go into my old room a moment by myself.'

Leaving the widow on the landing Sue turned to the chamber which had been hers exclusively since her arrival at Marygreen, and pushing to the door knelt down by the bed for a minute or two. She then arose, and taking her nightgown from the pillow undressed and came out to Mrs. Edlin. A man could be heard snoring in the room opposite. She wished Mrs. Edlin good-night, and the widow entered the room that Sue had just vacated.

Sue unlatched the other chamber door, and, as if seized with faint-ness, sank down outside it. Getting up again she half opened the door, and said 'Richard.' As the word came out of her mouth she visibly shuddered.

The snoring had quite ceased for some time, but he did not reply.

Sue seemed relieved, and hurried back to Mrs Edlin's chamber. 'Are you in bed, Mrs. Edlin?' she asked.

'No, dear,' said the widow, opening the door. 'I be old and slow, and it takes me a long while to un-ray.[7] I hadn't unlaced my jumps[8] yet.'

'I—don't hear him! And perhaps—perhaps—'

'What, child?'

'Perhaps he's dead!' she gasped. 'And then—I should be *free*, and I could go to Jude! . . . Ah—no—I forgot *her*—and God!'

'Let's go and hearken. No—he's snoring again. But the rain and the wind is so loud that you can hardly hear anything but between whiles.'

Sue had dragged herself back. 'Mrs. Edlin, good night again! I am sorry I called you out.' The widow retreated a second time.

The strained, resigned look returned to Sue's face when she was alone. 'I must do it—I must! I must drink to the dregs!' she whispered. 'Richard!' she said again.

'Hey—what? Is that you, Susanna?'

'Yes.'

'What do you want? Anything the matter? Wait a moment.' He pulled on some articles of clothing, and came to the door. 'Yes?'

'When we were at Shaston I jumped out of the window rather than that you should come near me. I have never reversed that treatment till now—when I have come to beg your pardon for it, and ask you to let me in.'

'Perhaps you only think you ought to do this? I don't wish you to come against your impulses, as I have said.'

'But I beg to be admitted.' She waited a moment, and repeated, 'I beg to be admitted! I have been in error—even to-day. I have exceeded my rights. I did not mean to tell you, but perhaps I ought. I sinned against you this afternoon.'

'How?'

'I met Jude! I didn't know he was coming. And—'

'Well?'

'I kissed him, and let him kiss me.'

'O—the old story!'

'Richard, I didn't know we were going to kiss each other till we did!'

'How many times?'

'A good many. I don't know. I am horrified to look back on it, and the least I can do after it is to come to you like this.'

'Come—this is pretty bad, after what I've done! Anything else to confess?'

'No.' She had been intending to say: 'I called him my darling Love.'

7. Undress (dialect).
8. Stays (dialect).

But, as a contrite woman always keeps back a little, that portion of the scene remained untold. She went on: 'I am never going to see him any more. He spoke of some things of the past: and it overcame me. He spoke of—the children.—But, as I have said, I am glad—almost glad I mean—that they are dead, Richard. It blots out all that life of mine!'

'Well—about not seeing him again any more. Come—you really mean this?' There was something in Phillotson's tone now which seemed to show that his three months of re-marriage with Sue had somehow not been so satisfactory as his magnanimity or amative patience had anticipated.

'Yes, yes!'

'Perhaps you'll swear it on the New Testament?'

'I will.'

He went back to the room and brought out a little brown Testament. 'Now then: So help you God!'

She swore.

'Very good!'

'Now I supplicate you, Richard, to whom I belong, and whom I wish to honour and obey, as I vowed, to let me in.'

'Think it over well. You know what it means. Having you back in the house was one thing—this another. So think again.'

'I have thought—I wish this!'

'That's a complaisant spirit—and perhaps you are right. With a lover hanging about, a half-marriage should be completed. But I repeat my reminder this third and last time.'

'It is my wish! . . . O God!'

'What did you say O God for?'

'I don't know!'

'Yes you do! But . . . ' He gloomily considered her thin and fragile form a moment longer as she crouched before him in her nightclothes. 'Well, I thought it might end like this,' he said presently. 'I owe you nothing, after these signs; but I'll take you in at your word, and forgive you.'

He put his arm round her to lift her up. Sue started back.

'What's the matter?' he asked, speaking for the first time sternly. 'You shrink from me again?—just as formerly!'

'No, Richard—I—I—was not thinking—'

'You wish to come in here?'

'Yes.'

'You still bear in mind what it means?'

'Yes. It is my duty!'

Placing the candlestick on the chest of drawers he led her through the doorway, and lifting her bodily, kissed her. A quick look of aversion passed over her face, but clenching her teeth she uttered no cry.

Mrs. Edlin had by this time undressed, and was about to get into bed when she said to herself: 'Ah—perhaps I'd better go and see if the little thing is all right. How it do blow and rain!'

The widow went out on the landing, and saw that Sue had disappeared. 'Ah! Poor soul! Weddings be funerals 'a b'lieve nowadays. Fifty-five years ago, come Fall, since my man and I married! Times have changed since then!'

VI–10

Despite himself Jude recovered somewhat, and worked at his trade for several weeks. After Christmas, however, he broke down again.

With the money he had earned he shifted his lodgings to a yet more central part of the town. But Arabella saw that he was not likely to do much work for a long while, and was cross enough at the turn affairs had taken since her re-marriage to him. 'I'm hanged if you haven't been clever in this last stroke!' she would say, 'to get a nurse for nothing by marrying me!'

Jude was absolutely indifferent to what she said, and, indeed, often regarded her abuse in a humorous light. Sometimes his mood was more earnest, and as he lay he often rambled on upon the defeat of his early aims.

'Every man has some little power in some one direction,' he would say. 'I was never really stout enough for the stone trade, particularly the fixing. Moving the blocks always used to strain me, and standing the trying draughts in buildings before the windows are in, always gave me colds, and I think that began the mischief inside. But I felt I could do one thing if I had the opportunity. I could accumulate ideas, and impart them to others. I wonder if the Founders had such as I in their minds—a fellow good for nothing else but that particular thing? . . . I hear that soon there is going to be a better chance for such helpless students as I was. There are schemes afoot for making the University less exclusive, and extending its influence. I don't know much about it. And it is too late, too late for me! Ah—and for how many worthier ones before me!'

'How you keep a-mumbling!' said Arabella. 'I should have thought you'd have got over all that craze about books by this time. And so you would, if you'd had any sense to begin with. You are as bad now as when we were first married.'

On one occasion while soliloquizing thus he called her 'Sue' unconsciously.

'I wish you'd mind who you are talking to!' said Arabella indignantly. 'Calling a respectable married woman by the name of that—' She remembered herself and he did not catch the word.

But in the course of time, when she saw how things were going, and how very little she had to fear from Sue's rivalry, she had a fit of generosity. 'I suppose you want to see your—Sue?' she said. 'Well, I don't mind her coming. You can have her here if you like.

'I don't wish to see her again.'

'O—that's a change!'

'And don't tell her anything about me—that I'm ill, or anything. She has chosen her course. Let her go!'

One day he received a surprise. Mrs. Edlin came to see him, quite on her own account. Jude's wife, whose feelings as to where his affections were centred had reached absolute indifference by this time, went out, leaving the old woman alone with Jude. He impulsively asked how Sue was, and then said bluntly, remembering what Sue had told him: 'I suppose they are still only husband and wife in name?'

Mrs. Edlin hesitated. 'Well, no—it's different now. She's begun it quite lately—all of her own free will.'

'When did she begin?' he asked quickly.

'The night after you came. But as a punishment to her poor self. He didn't wish it, but she insisted.'

'Sue, my Sue—you darling fool—this is almost more than I can endure! . . . Mrs. Edlin—don't be frightened at my rambling—I've got to talk to myself lying here so many hours alone—she was once a woman whose intellect was to mine like a star to a benzoline lamp: who saw all *my* superstitions as cobwebs that she could brush away with a word. Then bitter affliction came to us, and her intellect broke, and she veered round to darkness. Strange difference of sex, that time and circumstance, which enlarge the views of most men, narrow the views of women almost invariably. And now the ultimate horror has come—her giving herself like this to what she loathes, in her enslavement to forms!—she, so sensitive, so shrinking, that the very wind seemed to blow on her with a touch of deference . . . [1] As for Sue and me when we were at our own best, long ago—when our minds were clear, and our love of truth fearless—the time was not ripe for us! Our ideas were fifty years too soon to be any good to us. And so the resistance they met with brought reaction in her, and recklessness and ruin on me! . . . There—this, Mrs. Edlin, is how I go on to myself continually, as I lie here. I must be boring you awfully.'

'Not at all, my dear boy. I could hearken to 'ee all day.'

As Jude reflected more and more on her news, and grew more restless, he began in his mental agony to use terribly profane language about social conventions, which started a fit of coughing. Presently there came a knock at the door downstairs. As nobody answered it Mrs. Edlin herself went down.

---

1. Reminiscent of *Hamlet* 1.2.141–42.

The visitor said blandly: 'The doctor.' The lanky form was that of Physician Vilbert, who had been called in by Arabella.

'How is my patient at present?' asked the physician.

'O bad—very bad! Poor chap, he got excited, and do blaspeam terribly, since I let out some gossip by accident—the more to my blame. But there—you must excuse a man in suffering for what he says, and I hope God will forgive him.'

'Ah. I'll go up and see him. Mrs. Fawley at home?'

'She's not in at present, but she'll be here soon.'

Vilbert went; but though Jude had hitherto taken the medicines of that skilful practitioner with the greatest indifference whenever poured down his throat by Arabella, he was now so brought to bay by events that he vented his opinion of Vilbert in the physician's face, and so forcibly, and with such striking epithets, that Vilbert soon scurried downstairs again. At the door he met Arabella, Mrs. Edlin having left. Arabella inquired how he thought her husband was now, and seeing that the doctor looked ruffled, asked him to take something. He assented.

'I'll bring it to you here in the passage,' she said. 'There's nobody but me about the house to-day.'

She brought him a bottle and a glass, and he drank. Arabella began shaking with suppressed laughter. 'What is this, my dear?' he asked, smacking his lips.

'O—a drop of wine—and something in it.' Laughing again she said: 'I poured your own love-philter into it, that you sold me at the Agricultural Show, don't you remember?'

'I do, I do! Clever woman! But you must be prepared for the consequences.' Putting his arm round her shoulders he kissed her there and then.

'Don't, don't,' she whispered, laughing good-humouredly. 'My man will hear.'

She let him out of the house, and as she went back she said to herself: 'Well! Weak women must provide for a rainy day. And if my poor fellow upstairs do go off—as I suppose he will soon—it's well to keep chances open. And I can't pick and choose now as I could when I was younger. And one must take the old if one can't get the young.'

VI–11

The last pages to which the chronicler of these lives would ask the reader's attention are concerned with the scene in and out of Jude's bedroom when leafy summer came round again.

His face was now so thin that his old friends would hardly have known him. It was afternoon, and Arabella was at the looking-glass curling her hair, which operation she performed by heating an umbrella-stay[1] in the flame of a candle she had lighted, and using it upon the flowing lock. When she had finished this, practised a dimple, and put on her things, she cast her eyes round upon Jude. He seemed to be sleeping, though his position was an elevated one, his malady preventing him lying down.

Arabella, hatted, gloved, and ready, sat down and waited, as if expecting some one to come and take her place as nurse.

Certain sounds from without revealed that the town was in festivity,[2] though little of the festival, whatever it might have been, could be seen here. Bells began to ring, and the notes came into the room through the open window, and travelled round Jude's head in a hum. They made her restless, and at last she said to herself: 'Why ever doesn't father come!'

She looked again at Jude, critically gauged his ebbing life, as she had done so many times during the late months, and glancing at his watch, which was hung up by way of timepiece, rose impatiently. Still he slept, and coming to a resolution she slipped from the room, closed the door noiselessly, and descended the stairs. The house was empty. The attraction which moved Arabella to go abroad had evidently drawn away the other inmates long before.

It was a warm, cloudless, enticing day. She shut the front door, and hastened round into Chief Street, and when near the Theatre could hear the notes of the organ, a rehearsal for a coming concert being in progress. She entered under the archway of Oldgate College, where men were putting up awnings round the quadrangle for a ball in the Hall that evening. People who had come up from the country for the day were picnicking on the grass, and Arabella walked along the gravel paths and under the aged limes. But finding this place rather dull she returned to the streets, and watched the carriages drawing up for the concert, numerous Dons and their wives, and undergraduates with gay female companions, crowding up likewise. When the doors were closed, and the concert began, she moved on.

The powerful notes of that concert rolled forth through the swinging yellow blinds of the open windows, over the house-tops, and into the still air of the lanes. They reached so far as to the room in which Jude lay; and it was about this time that his cough began again and awakened him.

As soon as he could speak he murmured, his eyes still closed: 'A little water, please.'

Nothing but the deserted room received his appeal, and he coughed

---

1. Part of metal framework of umbrella over which silk is stretched.
2. Commemoration: see above, p. 253.

to exhaustion again—saying still more feebly: 'Water—some water—Sue—Arabella!'

The room remained still as before. Presently he gasped again: 'Throat—water—Sue—darling—drop of water—please—O please!'

No water came, and the organ notes, faint as a bee's hum, rolled in as before.

While he remained, his face changing, shouts and hurrahs came from somewhere in the direction of the river.

'Ah—yes! The Remembrance games,' he murmured. 'And I here. And Sue defiled!'

The hurrahs were repeated, drowning the faint organ notes. Jude's face changed more: he whispered slowly, his parched lips scarcely moving:

'*Let the day perish wherein I was born, and the night in which it was said, There is a man child conceived.*'

('Hurrah!')

'*Let that day be darkness; let not God regard it from above, neither let the light shine upon it. Lo, let that night be solitary, let no joyful voice come therein.*'

('Hurrah!)

'*Why died I not from the womb? Why did I not give up the ghost when I came out of the belly? . . . For now should I have lain still and been quiet. I should have slept: then had I been at rest!*'

('Hurrah!')

'*There the prisoners rest together; they hear not the voice of the oppressor. . . . The small and the great are there; and the servant is free from his master. Wherefore is light given to him that is in misery, and life unto the bitter in soul?*'[3]

Meanwhile Arabella, in her journey to discover what was going on, took a short cut down a narrow street and through an obscure nook into the quad of Cardinal. It was full of bustle, and brilliant in the sunlight with flowers and other preparations for a ball here also. A carpenter nodded to her, one who had formerly been a fellow-workman of Jude's. A corridor was in course of erection from the entrance to the Hall staircase, of gay red and buff bunting. Waggon-loads of boxes containing bright plants in full bloom were being placed about, and the great staircase was covered with red cloth. She nodded to one workman and another, and ascended to the Hall on the strength of their acquaintance, where they were putting down a new floor and decorating for the dance. The cathedral bell close at hand was sounding for five o'clock service.

'I should not mind having a spin there with a fellow's arm round my

3. Job 3.

waist,' she said to one of the men. 'But Lord, I must be getting home again—there's a lot to do. No dancing for me!'

When she reached home she was met at the door by Stagg, and one or two other of Jude's fellow stone-workers. 'We are just going down to the river,' said the former, 'to see the boat-bumping.[4] But we've called round on our way to ask how your husband is.'

'He's sleeping nicely, thank you,' said Arabella.

'That's right. Well now, can't you give yourself half-an-hour's relaxation, Mrs. Fawley, and come along with us? 'Twould do you good.'

'I should like to go,' said she. 'I've never seen the boat-racing, and I hear it is good fun.'

'Come along!'

'How I *wish* I could!' She looked longingly down the street. 'Wait a minute, then. I'll just run up and see how he is now. Father is with him, I believe; so I can most likely come.'

They waited, and she entered. Downstairs the inmates were absent as before, having, in fact, gone in a body to the river where the procession of boats was to pass. When she reached the bedroom she found that her father had not even now come.

'Why couldn't he have been here!' she said impatiently. 'He wants to see the boats himself—that's what it is!'

However, on looking round to the bed she brightened, for she saw that Jude was apparently sleeping, though he was not in the usual half-elevated posture necessitated by his cough. He had slipped down, and lay flat. A second glance caused her to start, and she went to the bed. His face was quite white, and gradually becoming rigid. She touched his fingers; they were cold, though his body was still warm. She listened at his chest. All was still within. The bumping of near thirty years had ceased.

After her first appalled sense of what had happened the faint notes of a military or other brass band from the river reached her ears; and in a provoked tone she exclaimed, 'To think he should die just now! Why did he die just now!' Then meditating another moment or two she went to the door, softly closed it as before, and again descended the stairs.

'Here she is!' said one of the workmen. 'We wondered if you were coming after all. Come along; we must be quick to get a good place. . . . Well, how is he? Sleeping well still? Of course, we don't want to drag 'ee away if—'

'O yes—sleeping quite sound. He won't wake yet,' she said hurriedly.

They went with the crowd down Cardinal Street, where they presently reached the bridge, and the gay barges burst upon their view.

---

4. Races on the river.

Thence they passed by a narrow slit down to the riverside path—now dusty, hot, and thronged. Almost as soon as they had arrived the grand procession of boats began; the oars smacking with a loud kiss on the face of the stream, as they were lowered from the perpendicular.

'O, I say—how jolly! I'm glad I've come,' said Arabella. 'And—it can't hurt my husband—my being away.'

On the opposite side of the river, on the crowded barges, were gorgeous nosegays of feminine beauty, fashionably arrayed in green, pink, blue, and white. The blue flag of the Boat Club denoted the centre of interest, beneath which a band in red uniform gave out the notes she had already heard in the death-chamber. Collegians of all sorts, in canoes with ladies, watching keenly for 'our' boat, darted up and down. While she regarded the lovely scene somebody touched Arabella in the ribs, and looking round she saw Vilbert.

'That philter is operating, you know!' he said with a leer. 'Shame on 'ee to wreck a heart so!'

'I shan't talk of love to-day.'

'Why not? It is a general holiday.'

She did not reply. Vilbert's arm stole round her waist, which act could be performed unobserved in the crowd. An arch expression overspread Arabella's face at the feel of the arm, but she kept her eyes on the river as if she did not know of the embrace.

The crowd surged, pushing Arabella and her friends sometimes nearly into the river, and she would have laughed heartily at the horseplay that succeeded, if the imprint on her mind's eye of a pale, statuesque countenance she had lately gazed upon had not sobered her a little.

The fun on the water reached the acme of excitement; there were immersions, there were shouts: the race was lost and won, the pink and blue and yellow ladies retired from the barges, and the people who had watched began to move.

'Well—it's been awfully good,' cried Arabella. 'But I think I must get back to my poor man. Father is there, so far as I know; but I had better get back.'

'What's your hurry?'

'Well, I must go. . . . Dear, dear, this is awkward!'

At the narrow gangway where the people ascended from the riverside path to the bridge the crowd was literally jammed into one hot mass— Arabella and Vilbert with the rest; and here they remained motionless, Arabella exclaiming, 'Dear, dear!' more and more impatiently; for it had just occurred to her mind that if Jude were discovered to have died alone an inquest might be deemed necessary.

'What a fidget you are, my love,' said the physician, who, being pressed close against her by the throng, had no need of personal effort for contact. 'Just as well have patience: there's no getting away yet!'

It was nearly ten minutes before the wedged multitude moved sufficiently to let them pass through. As soon as she got up into the street Arabella hastened on, forbidding the physician to accompany her further that day. She did not go straight to her house; but to the abode of a woman who performed the last necessary offices for the poorer dead; where she knocked.

'My husband has just gone, poor soul,' she said. 'Can you come and lay him out?'

Arabella waited a few minutes; and the two women went along, elbowing their way through the stream of fashionable people pouring out of Cardinal meadow, and being nearly knocked down by the carriages.

'I must call at the sexton's about the bell, too,' said Arabella. 'It is just round here, isn't it? I'll meet you at my door.'

By ten o'clock that night Jude was lying on the bedstead at his lodging covered with a sheet, and straight as an arrow. Through the partly opened window the joyous throb of a waltz entered from the ball-room at Cardinal.

Two days later, when the sky was equally cloudless, and the air equally still, two persons stood beside Jude's open coffin in the same little bedroom. On one side was Arabella, on the other the Widow Edlin. They were both looking at Jude's face, the worn old eyelids of Mrs. Edlin being red.

'How beautiful he is!' said she.

'Yes. He's a 'andsome corpse,' said Arabella.

The window was still open to ventilate the room, and it being about noontide the clear air was motionless and quiet without. From a distance came voices; and an apparent noise of persons stamping.

'What's that?' murmured the old woman.

'Oh, that's the doctors in the Theatre, conferring Honorary degrees on the Duke of Hamptonshire and a lot more illustrious gents of that sort. It's Remembrance Week, you know. The cheers come from the young men.'

'Ay; young and strong-lunged! Not like our poor boy here.'

An occasional word, as from some one making a speech, floated from the open windows of the Theatre across to this quiet corner, at which there seemed to be a smile of some sort upon the marble features of Jude; while the old, superseded, Delphin editions of Virgil and Horace, and the dog-eared Greek Testament on the neighbouring shelf, and the few other volumes of the sort that he had not parted with, roughened with stone-dust where he had been in the habit of catching them up for a few minutes between his labours, seemed to pale to a sickly cast at the sounds. The bells struck out joyously; and their reverberations travelled around the bedroom.

Arabella's eyes removed from Jude to Mrs. Edlin. 'D'ye think she will come?' she asked.

'I could not say. She swore not to see him again.'

'How is she looking?'

'Tired and miserable, poor heart. Years and years older than when you saw her last. Quite a staid, worn woman now. 'Tis the man;—she can't stomach un, even now!'

'If Jude had been alive to see her, he would hardly have cared for her any more, perhaps.'

'That's what we don't know. . . . Didn't he ever ask you to send for her, since he came to see her in that strange way?'

'No. Quite the contrary. I offered to send, and he said I was not to let her know how ill he was.'

'Did he forgive her?'

'Not as I know.'

'Well—poor little thing, 'tis to be believed she's found forgiveness somewhere! She said she had found peace!'

'She may swear that on her knees to the holy cross upon her necklace till she's hoarse, but it won't be true!' said Arabella. 'She's never found peace since she left his arms, and never will again till she's as he is now!'

BACKGROUNDS AND CONTEXTS

Composition, Publication, and Text

RICHARD LITTLE PURDY

[Composition and Serialization of the Novel]†

* * *

Jude the Obscure was first printed serially in *Harper's New Monthly Magazine* from December 1894 to November 1895. The American and European editions were published simultaneously in New York and London, the latter the American sheets bound up with English advertisements in an English wrapper. The first instalment appeared under the title *The Simpletons*; with the second instalment the title was altered to *Hearts Insurgent* and the following note was published in explanation: 'The author's attention having been drawn to the resemblance between the title "The Simpletons" and that of another English novel [presumably Charles Reade's *A Simpleton*, published in *Harper's*, 1872–3], he has decided to revert to the title originally selected, viz., "Hearts Insurgent," which will therefore be used in future parts of the story.' The monthly instalments ran as follows (chapter numbers differing, because of the subsequent division into Parts, from the book form—here indicated in brackets): December, Chaps. 1–6 [I, 1–6]; January, Chaps. 7–11 [I, 7–11]; February, Chaps. 12–16 [II, 1–4]; March, Chaps. 17–21 [II, 6–III, 3]; April, Chaps. 22–25 [III, 4–7]; May, Chaps. 26–29 [III, 8–IV, 2]; June, Chaps. 30–32 [IV, 3–5]; July, Chaps. 33–36 [IV, 6–V, 3]; August, Chaps. 37–40 [V, 4–7]; September, Chaps. 41–44 [V, 8–VI, 3]; October, Chaps. 45–48 [VI, 4–7]; November, Chaps. 48(*cont.*)–51 [VI, 7(*cont.*)–11]. Chaps. 28 and 49 were divided for book publication, making 53 chapters in all. The novel was 'abridged and modified' to meet the demands of *Harper's*. Jude's relations with Arabella and Sue were fundamentally altered, and numerous passages of considerable extent excised altogether, with amazing sacrifice of art and credibility. This did not pass completely undetected.

† From Richard Little Purdy, *Thomas Hardy: A Bibliographical Study* (Oxford: Oxford UP, 1954) 87–90. Reprinted by permission of Oxford University Press.

The *Athenaeum* remarked, 'Complaint has been made by readers of Mr. Hardy's novel in *Harper's Magazine* of the miraculous and perplexing appearance of a child on the scene in the current chapters of the story. We are informed that this was due to an oversight of the author's in modifying the manuscript for the American public, whereby he omitted to substitute some other reason for the child's advent after deleting the authentic reason—its illegitimate birth.'

With each of the 12 monthly instalments appeared an illustration by W. Hatherell. They gave Hardy great satisfaction. He wrote to the artist in admiration of the last, 'Jude at the Mile-stone', that it was 'a tragedy in itself: and I do not remember ever before having an artist who grasped a situation so thoroughly', and he had the whole set of 12 (as reproduced for the American edition) framed and hung over the mantel of his study at Max Gate.

The MS. of *Jude the Obscure* is written on 377 leaves of ruled paper, measuring 8⅛" (Chaps. 30–40, 7¾") × 10½". These have been numbered 1–436 by Hardy, but some are fragmentary and 59 scattered leaves are wanting altogether. The MS., dated 'March. 1895' at the end, is much altered and revised and does not show the usual marks of the compositor, instalments presumably being set from typescript. Some cancelled passages of interest remain in spite of Hardy's usual procedure of cutting them away. At the head of the MS., but deleted, are the words 'The Simpletons / Part First / Hearts Insurgent / A Dreamer.' Jude Fawley's name was at first Jack and Head, Hopeson, Stan, and Stancombe; Marygreen was originally Shawley and Fawn Green. On the first page Hardy has written, 'Note. Alterations and deletions in blue and green are for serial publication only: and have no authority beyond.' This note is repeated at intervals for new instalments, but a few of the alterations are retained in the definitive text nevertheless. Some of the missing leaves correspond to bowdlerizations—8 leaves missing, for instance, at the end of Chap. 32.

The MS. is bound in three-quarters blue morocco and was presented to the Fitzwilliam Museum, Cambridge, in October 1911 when Hardy, through Sydney Cockerell (then Director of the Fitzwilliam), was distributing his MSS. among various public collections.

* * * *Jude the Obscure* was Hardy's last novel and brings to a close, save for a short story or two and the revision of *The Pursuit of the Well-Beloved*, his long career in the field of prose fiction. In the Preface to the first edition, dated August 1895, he is more explicit about the genesis of the novel than was his custom. 'The scheme was jotted down in 1890, from notes made in 1887 and onwards, some of the circumstances being suggested by the death of a woman in the former year. The scenes were revisited in October 1892; the narrative was written

in outline in 1893 and the spring of 1893, and at full length, as it now appears, from August 1893 onwards into the next year; the whole, with the exception of a few chapters, being in the hands of the publisher by the end of 1894.' From the date at the end of the MS. it appears the novel was finished in March 1895.

Serial publication had been agreed upon with Harper & Brothers before the end of 1893, Hardy choosing his American publishers and *Harper's Magazine* (with its European edition in the hands of Osgood, McIlvaine) to obviate the difficulties of simultaneous publication. In reply to a gentle stipulation that the proposed novel should 'be in every respect suitable for a family magazine', Hardy had written 'that it would be a tale that could not offend the most fastidious maiden', but as composition progressed he had serious misgivings and 7 April 1894 wrote to Harper's asking to be allowed to cancel the agreement altogether, confessing that 'the development of the story was carrying him into unexpected fields and he was afraid to predict its future trend.' The agreement was not cancelled, but with the first instalments in hand H. M. Alden the editor protested, and Hardy consented to revise and bowdlerize, along lines thrice familiar to him by now. Alden wrote to him later (29 August 1894), 'You are right. My objections are based on a purism (not mine, but our readers'), which is undoubtedly more rigid here than in England. Our rule is that the Magazine must contain nothing which could not be read aloud in any family circle. To this we are pledged. You will see for yourself our difficulty, and we fully appreciate the annoyance you must feel at being called upon to modify work conscientiously done, and which is best as it left your hands, from an artist's point of view. I assure you that I felt properly ashamed for every word of protest I had to write to you about the second instalment of "The Simpletons." In the portraiture of the situation there was an artistic excellence surpassing anything I have seen in the fiction of today. . . . It is a pity that you should touch a word of the story, but you have been very good to lend yourself so kindly and so promptly to our need, when the task is in itself so ungraceful. I did not much deprecate the pig-killing scene [modified, nevertheless], and my objection was based upon the indignation shown by many of our readers because of a recent sketch by Owen Wister, exposing most frankly the cruelty to animals in our Western ranches.'

The novel was restored to its original form and sent off to the publishers with a Preface in August 1895, Hardy commenting in his diary, 'On account of the labour of altering *Jude the Obscure* to suit the magazine, and then having to alter it back, I have lost energy for revising and improving the original as I meant to do.'

328

JOHN PATERSON

[Hardy's Change of Direction]†

The manuscript of Hardy's *Jude the Obscure* discloses that the novel must have undergone, in the very first stages of its composition, a basic reorganization in conception. It discloses that the situation with which the novel now opens and out of which the action now develops was antedated by a situation so markedly different in its minor and major details as to suggest a novel strikingly at variance with that which was finally to materialize. The indications are, in fact, that what was undertaken as a critical examination of the educational system in Hardy's time came inadvertently, in its working out, to take in an equally critical examination of the sacrament and institution of marriage.

In its definitive form, *Jude the Obscure* opens with the departure of the schoolmaster, Richard Phillotson, for the university city of Christminster. Inspired by his memory and example, the orphaned Jude (who has been the ward of his aunt Drusilla in Marygreen for close to a year) comes to nourish a nearly hopeless passion for Christminster and, during the remainder of the novel's Part I, seeks painfully to qualify himself for admission to the celestial city. Although intermittently and briefly alluded to, Sue Bridehead, the heroine of the novel, does not appear on the scene until early in Part II when Jude arrives as a young man in the heavenly Jerusalem of his imagination. It has been intimated, in the meanwhile, that with the failure of her parents' marriage, Sue has been taken as a child to London and has later found her own way to the university city.

The manuscript makes clear, however, that the novel originally was predicated upon a radically different set of terms and circumstances. For one thing, where Jude is now said to have been in Marygreen for a year, he was initially said to have been in Marygreen for only a month. For another, where Sue is now conceived as the child of divorced parents and as having been taken up to London either by her father or her mother, she was earlier conceived as an orphan who had been adopted by the provost of a college at Christminster. More crucially, the schoolmaster who now enters the novel in the first chapter was not, according to Hardy's original plan, to have entered it until much later, if indeed he was meant to enter it at all. At the same time, the heroine who does not appear until the early stages of Part II was formerly scheduled to appear in the very first chapters of Part I. As a result, where Jude's passion for Christminster is now motivated by the

_____

† From John Paterson, "The Genesis of *Jude the Obscure*," *Studies in Philology* 57 (1960): 87–88. Copyright © 1960 by the University of North Carolina Press. Used by permission of the publisher.

example of the schoolmaster, it was, according to the original terms of the novel, to have been motivated by the example of the precocious Sue Bridehead.

ROBERT C. SLACK

[Hardy's Revisions]†

The textual history of *Jude the Obscure*, as of any Hardy novel, is a complicated matter. * * *

Even the "first edition" text of this novel offers complications, since there were actually two "first editions," one English and one American. The company of Osgood and McIlvaine published the true first edition in London on November 1, 1895. On November 9, the American first edition of the novel was published by Harpers. There are many insignificant textual differences between these two editions. Besides changing to American spelling, the Harper edition uses closer punctuation throughout and contains a number of minor textual changes, many of which may have been errors by Harper's typesetters. However, though the textual differences between these two editions are numerous, they are trifling in nature.

Eight years later, in 1903, a "New Edition" of *Jude* was issued by Hardy's new English publishers, Macmillan and Company. That edition contained almost thirty instances of textual revision.

The most striking revision was Hardy's tempering of the scene branded by Mrs. Oliphant as "more brutal in depravity than anything which the darkest slums could bring forth." It is the scene in which Arabella first makes Jude's acquaintance by flinging the pizzle of a pig at him as he is walking along dreaming of becoming a learned Doctor of Divinity. The whole tone of the relationship between the coarse, sensual Arabella and her idealistic victim is perfectly established by her choice of missile, and this tone is strongly maintained throughout the scene as it was originally written. Hardy, no doubt sensitive to the many outcries like Mrs. Oliphant's, deliberately emasculated the passage in his revision. The scene is worth quoting at length.

> [Jude was walking along home dreaming of his future, saying to himself, "Yes, Christminster shall be my Alma Mater; and I'll be her beloved son," when a clammy substance struck him in the ear. Perceiving what the object was, he mounted the bank of a stream and saw on the other side three girls washing pigs' chitterlings in the running water.]

† From Robert C. Slack, "The Text of Hardy's *Jude the Obscure*," *Nineteenth Century Fiction* 11 (1957): 261–75. Reprinted by permission of the publisher.

"Thank you!" said Jude severely.

"I *didn't* throw it, I tell you!" asserted one girl to her neighbour, as if unconscious of the young man's presence.

"Nor I," the second answered.

"O, Anny, how can you!" said the third.

"If I had thrown anything at all,

[OM'95] it shouldn't have been such an indecent thing as that!"

[M'o3] it shouldn't have been that!"

"Pooh! I don't care for him!" And they laughed and continued their work, without looking up, still ostentatiously accusing each other.

Jude grew sarcastic

[OM'95] as he wiped the spot where the clammy flesh had struck him.

[M'o3] as he wiped his face, and caught their remarks.

"You didn't do it—O no!" he said to the up-stream one of the three.

She whom he addressed was a fine dark-eyed girl, not exactly handsome, but capable of passing as such at a little distance, despite some coarseness of skin and fibre. She had a round and prominent bosom, full lips, perfect teeth, and the rich complexion of a Cochin hen's egg. She was a complete and

[OM'95] substantial female human—

[M'o3] substantial female animal—

no more, no less; and Jude was almost certain that to her was attributable

[OM'95] the enterprise of throwing the lump of offal at him, the bladder, from which she had obviously just cut it off, lying close beside her.

[M'o3] the enterprise of attracting his attention from dreams of the humaner letters to what was simmering in the minds around him.

"That you'll never be told," said she deedily.

"Whoever did it was wasteful of other people's property."

[OM'95] "O, that's nothing. The pig is my father's."

"But you want it back, I suppose?"

"O yes; if you like to give it me."

"Shall I throw it across, or will you come to the plank above here for me to hand it to you?"

[M'o3] "O, that's nothing.

"But you want to speak to me, I suppose?"

"O yes; if you like to."

"Shall I clamber across, or will you come to the plank above here?"

Perhaps she foresaw an opportunity; for somehow or other the eyes of the brown girl rested in his own when he said the words, and there was a momentary flash of intelligence, a dumb announcement of affinity *in pose*, between herself and him, which, so far as Jude Fawley was concerned, had no sort of premeditation in it. She saw that he had singled her out from the three, as a woman is singled out in such cases, for no reasoned purpose of further acquaintance, but in commonplace obedience to conjunctive orders from headquarters, unconsciously received by unfortunate men when the last intention of their lives is to be occupied with the feminine.

Springing to her feet, she said:

[OM'95] "Don't throw it! Give it to me."	[M'o3] "Bring back what is lying there."
Jude was now aware that the intrinsic value of the missile had nothing to do with her request. He set down his basket of tools, raked out with his stick the slip of flesh from the ditch, and got over the hedge.	Jude was now aware that no message on any matter connected with her father's business had prompted her signal to him. He set down his basket of tools, beat a pathway for himself with his stick, and got over the hedge.

They walked in parallel lines, one on each bank of the stream, towards the small plank bridge. As the girl drew nearer to it, she gave, without Jude perceiving it, an adroit little suck to the interior of each of her cheeks in succession, by which curious and original manoeuvre she brought as by magic upon its smooth and rotund surface a perfect dimple, which she was able to retain there as long as she continued to smile. This production of dimples at will was a not unknown operation, which many attempted, but only a few succeeded in accomplishing.

They met in the middle of the plank, and

[OM'95] Jude held out his stick with the fragment of pig dangling therefrom, looking elsewhere the while, and faintly colouring.	[M'o3] Jude, tossing back her missile, seemed to expect her to explain why she had audaciously stopped him by this novel artillery instead of by hailing him.
She, too, looked in another direction, and took the piece as though ignorant of what her hand was doing. She hung it temporarily on the rail of the bridge, and then, by a species of mutual curiosity, they both turned, and regarded it.	But she, slily looking in another direction, swayed herself backwards and forwards on her hand as it clutched the rail of the bridge; till, moved by amatory curiosity, she turned her eyes critically upon him.

"You don't think I threw it?"

"O no."

It belongs to father, and he med have been in a taking if he had wanted it. He makes it into dubbin."

"You don't think I would shy things at you?"

"O no."

"We are doing this for my father, who doesn't want anything thrown away."

"What made either of the others throw it, I wonder?" Jude asked, politely accepting her assertion, though he had very large doubts as to its truth.

"Impudence. Don't tell folk it was I, mind!"

"How can I? I don't know your name."

"Ah, no. Shall I tell it to you?"

"Do!"

"Arabella Donn. I'm living here."

"I must have known it if I had often come this way. But I mostly go straight along the high-road."

"My father is a pig-breeder, and these girls are helping me wash the innerds for

[OM'95] black-puddings and chitterlings."

[M'o3] black-puddings and such like."

They talked a little more and a little more,

[OM'95] as they stood regarding the limp object dangling across the handrail of the bridge.

[M'o3] as they stood regarding each other and leaning against the handrail of the bridge.

The unvoiced call of woman to man, which was uttered very distinctly by Arabella's personality, held Jude to the spot against his intention—almost against his will, and in a way new to his experience. . . .

[They talked a while longer, and Jude obtained permission to call on her the next day.]

She brightened with a little glow of triumph, swept him almost tenderly with her eyes in turning,

[OM'95] and throwing the offal out of the way upon the grass, rejoined her companions.

[M'o3] and retracing her steps down the brookside grass, rejoined her companions.

[After Jude left, the girls talked together about him. One of them said:]

" . . . he's as simple as a child. I could see it as you courted

[OM'95] on the bridge, wi' that piece o' the pig hanging between ye—haw-haw! What a proper thing to court over!

[M'o3]on the bridge, when he looked at 'ee as if he had never seen a woman before in his born days.

Well, he's to be had by any woman who can get him to care for her a bit, if she likes to set herself to catch him the right way."

In his revision, Hardy consistently shied away from "that piece o' the pig," and the scene is of course weakened. But Hardy several times before this—for magazine publication, at any rate—had made similar artistic concessions to editors and to public taste. By comparison this was a minor yielding.

In this scene, and in the other revisions for the Macmillan 1903 "New Edition," Hardy was as economical as an author can be. Macmillan reused the original plates of the Osgood, McIlvaine edition of 1895, and the textual alterations were made usually by inserting a changed word or phrase in the old line of type. Hardy cooperated by choosing substitute words or phrases of the same physical length almost to the letter. This resulted in a certain awkwardness, at times, in the revised passages; but apparently Hardy was more concerned with meaning, in these revisions, than with style.

Other than recasting the foregoing scene, Hardy made twenty-eight isolated changes in the text of the novel, most of them minor corrections of fact.

A striking oversight had appeared in the first edition of the novel. As the Osgood, McIlvaine 1895 edition tells the story, Jude is torn between the desire to keep his appointment with Arabella and the desire to study his Greek Testament. Arabella of course finally wins out, and—

Η ΚΑΙΝΗ ΔΙΑΘΗΚΗ was suddenly closed, and the predestinate Jude sprang up and across the room.

After his outing he returns home feeling guilty, to experience a dramatically effective but factually impossible chastisement.

He went upstairs without a light, and the dim interior of his room accosted him with sad inquiry. There lay his book open, just as he had left it, and the capital letters on the title-page regarded him with fixed reproach in the grey starlight, like the unclosed eyes of a dead man:

Η ΚΑΙΝΗ ΔΙΑΘΗΚΗ.

In the Macmillan 1903 edition, the book was never closed; Hardy corrected the passage to read:

Η ΚΑΙΝΗ ΔΙΑΘΗΚΗ was no more heeded, and the predestinate Jude sprang up and across the room.

* * *

In 1912 Macmillan and Company published their definitive "Wessex Edition" of Hardy's works. In his Preface to the *Jude* of that edition, Hardy wrote:

> Nor am I able, across the gap of years since the production of the novel, to exercise more criticism upon it of a general kind than extends to a few verbal corrections. . . .

The "few" verbal corrections amounted to quite a few. There are 206 variants between the Macmillan 1903 text and the Macmillan 1912 text. No one of the changes is extensive or very significant in itself; yet their number shows that Hardy gave the text of *Jude* a careful going-over for his final, definitive edition. This constitutes a second revision of the text.

The most numerous changes are those which appear to have been made for stylistic reasons. For instance, Hardy no doubt wished to remove the *double-entendre* that originally appeared as "A new-made wife can usually manage to look interesting for a few weeks." This was changed to "A new-made wife can usually manage to excite interest for a few weeks." In places Hardy has added nonintegral material to the text, to heighten the effectiveness of a passage. In the scuffle which developed over the attempt to force Phillotson to resign his post at Shaston after Sue had left him, the 1903 passage has "an inkbottle spilled over a town-councillor's shirt-front, and some black eyes and bleeding noses given" (p. 311). The 1912 revision contains an interesting addition: "an inkbottle was spilled over a town-councillor's shirt-front, a church-warden was dealt such a topper with the map of Palestine that his head went right through Samaria, and many black eyes and bleeding noses were given" (p. 299). Such changes and nonintegral additions as these appear to have been made to the text for general stylistic reasons.

Almost a third of the total number of changes are ones in which Hardy makes details more explicit. In the 1903 book, Sue ran back to Jude and they merely "kissed each other" (p. 272); whereas in the 1912 version they "kissed close and long" (p. 261). In the earlier book the waiting-maid at the George tells Sue that Jude had been to that very hotel a month or two before with "A handsome, full-figured woman" (p. 304). In the later reading the maid adds to her remark: "A handsome, full-figured woman. They had this room" (p. 291). In the 1903 text, when Jude and the pregnant Sue are hunting a lodging in Christminster, before refusing them, "The householder scrutinized Sue a moment" (p. 415). In the 1912 version Hardy says explicitly what he wants to: "The householder scrutinized Sue's figure a moment" (p. 397).

Other changes include correction of facts (such as the correction of a quotation from Poe's "The Raven") and a few alterations which appear to be printer's errors.

But the most interesting of the revisions are a small group which change the affective meaning of a detail or of a passage. These differ from simple alteration of facts in that they reflect a different interpretation of characters or events on the part of the author. Many of these are concerned with Sue Bridehead. Perhaps Hardy felt that his original drawing of her was somewhat harsh, that he had made her a bit too rigid, for these changes tend to give her more human sympathy than the original Sue possessed. Since this is the one group of revisions from the 1903 edition which has a consistent direction, it is worthwhile to examine them.

The most pronounced of these changes occurs when Sue is leaving Phillotson, who has so generously given her her freedom. So that the omnibusman would not suspect she was leaving him, Phillotson "was obliged to make an appearance of kissing her as he wished her good-bye, though she shrank even from that." Thus, in Hardy's earlier version, Sue is seen to be so wrapped up in her own reactions that she is callously inconsiderate of the man who is acting so generously toward her. In the revision, this passage reads: "to make an appearance of kissing her as he wished her good-bye, which she quite understood and imitated." This is a different Sue.

Surely no male reader of this novel will deny the force of Jude's impatient outburst at Sue the night she attempts to prevent him from going to Arabella: "I do love you, Sue, though I have danced attendance on you so long for such poor returns! . . . I should just like a few virtuous people who have condemned me in the past, about Arabella and other things, to have been in my tantalizing position with you through these late weeks!" She has never once given him even a "candid declaration that she loved or could love him."

To prevent Jude's going to Arabella, Sue agrees to live intimately with him. She cries:

MACMILLAN 1903	MACMILLAN 1912
" . . . But, yes—I agree, I agree! I ought to have known that you would conquer in the long run, living like this!" (p. 334)	" . . . But, yes—I agree, I agree! I do love you. I ought to have known that [etc.]" (p. 321)

The change is slight, but the words *I do love you* make a world of difference to Jude.

There are other, more subtle, changes of this nature which show Sue capable of a bit more womanly sympathy.

Macmillan 1903	—Macmillan 1912
[After Jude tells Sue of his marriage to Arabella, she is, at first angry; then she cries, and says:] "I am—not crying—because I love you; but because of your want of—confidence!" (p. 207)	"I am—not crying—because I meant to—love you; but because [etc.]" (p. 200)
[Sue has met Jude on the train and told him that she did not mean to live with him as he had understood. He is disappointed, and she says to him:] "You did kiss me just now, you know; and I didn't dislike you to, very much, Jude. . . ." (p. 302)	" . . . I didn't dislike you to, I own it, Jude. . . ." (p. 289)
[After the death of the children, Sue decides to live apart from Jude. He analyzes her thus:] " . . . Yours is not a passionate heart—your heart does not burn in a flame! You are, upon the whole, cold,—a sort of fay, or sprite—not a woman!" (p. 445)	" . . . You are, upon the whole, a sort of fay, or sprite—not a woman!" (p. 426)

The revision of a speech of Jude's tends to soften one of the harsher aspects of Sue's character. She has the habit of blowing hot and cold, of telling and then wishing she hadn't, of putting Jude off by her actions and then impulsively writing a note that leaves him all in a glow. In the Macmillan 1903 text, Jude refers to this habit in blunt terms: " . . . you are never so nice in your real presence as you are in your letters!" Hardy softened the statement in his revision to: " . . . you are often not so nice in [etc.]"

A little humanizing touch is given to Sue's character when she is proposing to Phillotson that she leave him to live with Jude. Originally she quotes John Stuart Mill like a professor:

> "She, or he, 'who lets the world, or his own portion of it, choose his plan of life for him, has no need of any other faculty than the ape-like one of imitation.' J. S. Mill's words, those are. Why can't you act upon them? I wish to, always."

In the revision, after the quotation, Sue says: "J. S. Mill's words, those are. I have been reading it up. Why can't you [etc.]" One likes Sue

better for admitting that she has been "reading up" Mill; this reminder
of human fallibility appeals to our sympathy.

When Phillotson is about to remarry Sue, he sums up her character
for his friend Gillingham. He says.

MACMILLAN 1903	MACMILLAN 1912
"No doubt when it gets known what I've done I shall be thought a soft fool by many. But they don't know Sue as I do. Hers is such a straight and open nature that I don't think she has ever done anything against her conscience...." (p. 464)	"... But they don't know Sue as I do. Though so elusive, hers is such an honest nature at bottom that I don't think she has ever done anything against her conscience...." (p. 445)

Hardy has pointedly changed Phillotson's concept of Sue. A "straight
and open" (and rather inconsiderate) nature is seen in the revision as
one which is elusive, but honest at bottom. "Elusive" allows a kind of
charm which "straight and open" seems to prohibit.

All these textual changes which pertain to Sue are slight, and each
one in itself is of minor importance. But the cumulative effect of all
of them does somewhat alter a reader's concept of her. She has become
more of a daughter of Eve than she was before; she is a shade more
sympathetic, more elusive, more charming.

Hardy's Nonfictional Writings

From Hardy's Autobiography†

[The two-volume "biography" of Hardy which was published soon after his death with his widow's name on the title pages is now known to be almost entirely an autobiography, written during the last ten years of his life and making extensive use of old diaries, notebooks, and letters. The autobiography was originally issued as *The Early Life of Thomas Hardy* (1928) and *The Later Years of Thomas Hardy* (1930). Since 1962 it has been available as a single volume, *The Life of Thomas Hardy, 1840–1928* (London: Macmillan & Co.).]

One or two more characteristics of his personality at this childhood-time can be recounted. In those days the staircase at Bockhampton (later removed) had its walls coloured Venetian red by his father, and was so situated that the evening sun shone into it, adding to its colour a great intensity for a quarter of an hour or more. Tommy used to wait for this chromatic effect, and, sitting alone there, would recite to himself 'And now another day is gone' from Dr. Watts's Hymns, with great fervency, though perhaps not for any religious reason, but from a sense that the scene suited the lines.

It is not therefore to be wondered at that a boy of this sort should have a dramatic sense of the church services, and on wet Sunday mornings should wrap himself in a tablecloth, and read the Morning Prayer standing in a chair, his cousin playing the clerk with loud Amens, and his grandmother representing the congregation. The sermon which followed was simply a patchwork of sentences used by the vicar. Everybody said that Tommy would have to be a parson, being obviously no good for any practical pursuit; which remark caused his mother many misgivings.

One event of this date or a little later stood out, he used to say, more distinctly than any. He was lying on his back in the sun, thinking how useless he was, and covered his face with his straw hat. The sun's rays streamed through the interstices of the straw, the lining having disappeared. Reflecting on his experiences of the world so far as he had

† From F. E. Hardy, *The Life of Thomas Hardy, 1840–1928* (London: Macmillan, 1962) 15–16, 207–8, 268–69, 270, 274, 277–80, 392. Reprinted by permission of Macmillan Press Ltd.

got, he came to the conclusion that he did not wish to grow up. Other boys were always talking of when they would be men; he did not want at all to be a man, or to possess things, but to remain as he was, in the same spot, and to know no more people than he already knew (about half a dozen). Yet this early evidence of that lack of social ambition which followed him through life was shown when he was in perfect health and happy circumstances.

* * *

April 28. A short story of a young man—"who could not go to Oxford"—His struggles and ultimate failure. Suicide. [Probably the germ of *Jude the Obscure*]. There is something [in this] the world ought to be shown, and I am the one to show it to them—though I was not altogether hindered going, at least to Cambridge, and could have gone up easily at five-and-twenty.[1]

* * *

[At the end of the summer of 1895, Hardy][2] was 'restoring the MS. of *Jude the Obscure* to its original state'—on which process he sets down an undated remark, probably about the end of August, when he sent off the restored copy to the publishers:

'On account of the labour of altering *Jude the Obscure* to suit the magazine, and then having to alter it back, I have lost energy for revising and improving the original as I meant to do.'

* * *

The onslaught upon *Jude* started by the vituperative section of the press—unequalled in violence since the publication of Swinburne's *Poems and Ballads* thirty years before—was taken up by the anonymous writers of libellous letters and post-cards, and other such gentry. It spread to America and Australia, whence among other appreciations he received a letter containing a packet of ashes, which the virtuous writer stated to be those of his iniquitous novel.

Thus, though Hardy with his quick sense of humour could not help seeing a ludicrous side to it all, and was well enough aware that the evil complained of was what these 'nice minds with nasty ideas' had read into his book, and not what he had put there, he underwent the strange experience of beholding a sinister lay figure of himself constructed by them, which had no sort of resemblance to him as he was, and which he, and those who knew him well, would not have recognized as being meant for himself if it had not been called by his name. Macaulay's remark in his essay on Byron was well illustrated by,

---

1. An extract from Hardy's diary, April 28, 1888 [*Editor*].
2. This bracketed phrase added by the editor of this Norton Critical Edition.

Thomas Hardy's experience at this time: 'We know of no spectacle so ridiculous as the British public in one of its periodical fits of morality.'

* * *

When they got back to Dorchester during December Hardy had plenty of time to read the reviews of *Jude* that continued to pour out. Some paragraphists knowingly assured the public that the book was an honest autobiography, and Hardy did not take the trouble to deny it till more than twenty years later, when he wrote to an inquirer with whom the superstition still lingered that no book he had ever written contained less of his own life, which of course had been known to his friends from the beginning. Some of the incidents were real in so far as that he had heard of them, or come in contact with them when they were occurring to people he knew; but no more. It is interesting to mention that on his way to school he did once meet with a youth like Jude who drove the bread-cart of a widow, a baker, like Mrs. Fawley, and carried on his studies at the same time, to the serious risk of other drivers in the lanes; which youth asked him to lend him his Latin grammar. But Hardy lost sight of this featful student, and never knew if he profited by his plan.

Hardy makes a remark on one or two of the reviews:

'Tragedy may be created by an opposing environment either of things inherent in the universe, or of human institutions. If the former be the means exhibited and deplored, the writer is regarded as impious; if the latter, as subversive and dangerous; when all the while he may never have questioned the necessity or urged the nonnecessity of either. . . . '

* * *

[Hardy and his wife spent the 1896 'season' in London.]

* * * at the very height of the season the Bishop of Wakefield announced in a letter to the papers that he had thrown Hardy's novel into the fire. Knowing the difficulty of burning a thick book even in a good fire, and the infrequency of fires of any sort in summer, Hardy was mildly sceptical of the literal truth of the bishop's story; but remembering that Shelley, Milton, and many others of the illustrious, reaching all the way back to the days of Protagoras, had undergone the same sort of indignity at the hands of bigotry and intolerance he thought it a pity in the interests of his own reputation to disturb the episcopal narrative of adventures with *Jude*. However, it appeared that, further,—to quote the testimony in the Bishop's *Life*—the scandalized prelate was not ashamed to deal a blow below the belt, but 'took an envelope out of his paperstand and addressed it to W. F. D. Smith, Esq., M.P. The result was the quiet withdrawal of the book from the library, and an assurance that any other books by the same author would be carefully examined before they were allowed to be circulated.' Of this precious conspiracy Hardy knew nothing, or it might have moved a mind which the burning could not stir to say a word on literary garrotting. In his ignorance of it he remained silent, being fully aware of one thing, that the ethical teaching of the novel, even if somewhat crudely put, was as high as that of any of the bishop's sermons— (indeed, Hardy was afterwards reproached for its being 'too much of a sermon'). And thus feeling quite calm on the ultimate verdict of Time he merely reflected on the shallowness of the episcopal view of the case and of morals generally, which brought to his memory a witty remark he had once read in a *Times* leading article, to the effect that the qualities which enabled a man to become a bishop were often the very reverse of those which made a good bishop when he became one.

The only sad feature in the matter to Hardy was that if the bishop could have known him as he was, he would have found a man whose personal conduct, views of morality, and of the vital facts of religion, hardly differed from his own.

Possibly soured by all this he wrote a little while after his birthday:

'Every man's birthday is a first of April for him; and he who lives to be fifty and won't own it is a rogue or a fool, hypocrite or simpleton.'

* * *

It has been remarked above that Hardy with his quick sense of humour could not help seeing a ludicrous side to his troubles over *Jude*, and an instance to that effect now occurred. The *New York World* had been among those papers that fell foul of the book in the strongest terms, the critic being a maiden lady who expressed herself thus:

'What has happened to Thomas Hardy? . . . I am shocked, appalled by this story! . . . It is almost the worst book I ever read. . . . I thought that *Tess of the d'Urbervilles* was bad enough, but that is milk for babes compared to this. . . . It is the handling of it that is the horror of it. . . . I do not believe that there is a newspaper in England or America that would print this story of Thomas Hardy's as it stands in the book. Aside from its immorality there is coarseness which is beyond belief. . . . When I finished the story I opened the windows and let in the fresh air, and I turned to my bookshelves and I said: "Thank God for Kipling and Stevenson, Barrie and Mrs. Humphry Ward. Here are four great writers who have never trailed their talents in the dirt".'

It was therefore with some amazement that in the summer, after reading the above and other exclamations grossly maligning the book and the character of its author, to show that she would not touch him with a pair of tongs, he received a letter from the writer herself. She was in London, and requested him to let her interview him 'to get your side of the argument'. He answered:

'SAVILE CLUB,
'July 16, 1896

'MY DEAR MADAM:

'I have to inform you in answer to your letter that ever since the publication of *Jude the Obscure* I have declined to be interviewed on the subject of that book; and you must make allowance for human nature when I tell you I do not feel disposed to depart from this rule in favour of the author of the review of the novel in the *New York World*.

'I am aware that the outcry against it in America was only an echo of its misrepresentation here by one or two scurrilous papers which got the start of the more sober press, and that dumb public opinion was never with these writers. But the fact remains that such a meeting would be painful to me and, I think, a disappointment to you.

'Moreover, my respect for my own writings and reputation is so very slight that I care little what happens to either, so that the rectification of judgements, etc., and the way in which my books are interpreted, do not much interest me. Those readers who, like yourself, could not see that *Jude* (though a book quite without a "purpose" as it is called) makes for morality more than any other book I have written, are not likely to be made to do so by a newspaper article, even from your attractive pen.

'At the same time I cannot but be touched by your kindly wish to set right any misapprehension you may have caused about the story. Such a wish will always be cherished in my recollection, and it removes from my vision of you some obviously unjust characteristics I had given it in my mind. This is, at any rate on my part, a pleasant gain from your letter, whilst I am "never the worse for a touch or two on my speckled hide" as the consequence of your review.

'Believe me, dear Madam,
'Yours sincerely,
'THOMAS HARDY

'TO MISS JEANNETTE GILDER'

It may be interesting to give Miss Gilder's reply to this:

'HOTEL CECIL,
'July 17, '96.

'DEAR MR. HARDY,

'I knew that you were a great man, but I did not appreciate your goodness until I received your letter this morning.

'Sincerely yours,
'JEANNETTE L. GILDER.

Hardy must indeed have shown some magnanimity in condescending to answer the writer of a review containing such contumelious misrepresentations as hers had contained. But, as he said, she was a woman, after all—one of the sex that makes up for lack of justice by excess of generosity—and she had screamed so grotesquely loud in her article that Hardy's sense of the comicality of it had saved his feelings from being much hurt by the outrageous slurs.

*   *   *

On October 30[3] the following was written at his request:
'In reply to your letter I write for Mr. Hardy, who is in bed with a chill, to say that he cannot furnish you with any biographical details. ... To your inquiry if *Jude the Obscure* is autobiographical, I have to answer that there is not a scrap of personal detail in it, it having the least to do with his own life of all his books. The rumour, if it still persists, was started some years ago. Speaking generally, there is more autobiography in a hundred lines of Mr. Hardy's poetry than in all the novels.'

It is a tribute to Hardy's powers of presentation that readers would not for many years believe that such incidents as Jude's being smacked when bird-keeping, his driving a baker's cart, his working as a journeyman mason, as also many situations described in verse, were not actual transcripts from the writer's personal experience, although the briefest reference to biographical date-books would have shown the impossibility of anything of the sort.

Comments from Hardy's Letters[†]

To Sir George Douglas[1]

October 8, 1892

As you know, or guess, I have passed through glooms such as I hope you will never see: & I cannot say they were ever the result of material surroundings.

To Mrs. Florence Henniker[2]

September 16, 1893

I have already jotted down a few notes for the next long story—which I hope may be big as well as long.

---

3. 1919 [*Editor*].
† *The Collected Letters of Thomas Hardy*, ed. Richard Little Purdy and Michael Millgate (Oxford: Clarendon Press) Vol. 1 (1978) 285; Vol. 2 (1980) 32, 38, 43, 47, 70, 84, 93, 94, 99, 100, 103, 105, 122–23. All notes are by the editor of this Norton Critical Edition.
1. Douglas, Scottish baronet and man of letters, met Hardy in 1881; they became close friends, visited each other frequently, and exchanged many letters.
2. The Honourable Florence Ellen Hungerford Henniker, society hostess and writer of fiction, met Hardy in May 1893, or possibly earlier. They quickly became friends, collaborated in the

October 22, 1893

What name shall I give to the heroine of my coming long story when I get at it? I don't quite know when that will be, though it must be this winter.

December 1, 1893

I am not sure that I feel so keen about the, alas, unwritten, long story as I should do. I feel more inclined just now to write short ones. However, as it is one I planned a couple of years ago I shall, I think, go on with it, and probably shall warm up.

January 15, 1894

I am creeping on a little with the long story, and am beginning to get interested in my heroine as she takes shape and reality; though she is very nebulous at present.

To Sir George Douglas

March 3, 1895

Please don't read it in the magazine, for I have been obliged to make many changes, omissions, & glosses. It will be restored to its original shape in the volume.

To Mrs. Florence Henniker

August 4, 1895

I am impatient to restore and revise the serial story for the volume, and this [illness] has been a vexing hindrance.

August 12, 1895

I am restoring the MS. of the Harper story to its original state. Fortunately I wrote the alterations and abridgments in blue ink—which makes it easy to recover the first form. Curiously enough, I am more interested in the Sue story than in any I have written.

---

tale "The Spectre of the Real" in October 1893, wrote frequently to each other, and remained friends until her death in 1923. It has been claimed that she inspired some of Hardy's poems and that Sue Bridehead was in part modeled on her (note that one of Sue's names is Florence).

November 10, 1895

My hesitating to send *Jude* was not because I thought you narrow—
but because I had rather bored you with him during the writing of
some of the story, or thought I had.

I am rather indifferent about his reception by the public: and you
may, *of course*, criticize quite freely without offending me. Though not
a novel with a purpose, I think it turns out to be a novel which 'makes
for' humanity—more than any other I have written: an opinion that
will probably surprise you. I suppose I have missed the mark in the pig-
killing scene the papers are making such a fuss about: I fully expected
that, though described in that particular place for the purely artistic
reason of bringing out A[rabella]'s character, it might serve a humane
end in showing people the cruelty that goes on unheeded under the
barbarous *régime* we call civilization.

It is curious that some papers consider the story a sort of manifesto
on the marriage question, though it is really one about two persons
who, by a hereditary curse of temperament, peculiar to their family,
are rendered unfit for marriage, or think they are. The tragedy is really
addressed to those into whose souls the iron of adversity has deeply
entered at some time of their lives, and can hardly be congenial to self-
indulgent persons of ease and affluence. Indeed, there is something
bizarre in the tragedy of *Jude* coming out as the last fashionable novel.
But one cannot choose one's readers. I think you will admit that, if the
story had to be told, it c[oul]d not be told with more reticence.

To Sir Edmund Gosse[3]

November 10, 1895

. . . Your review [of *Jude the Obscure*] is the most discriminating that
has yet appeared. It required an artist to see that the plot is almost
geometrically constructed—I ought not to say *constructed*, for, beyond
a certain point, the characters necessitated it, and I simply let it come.
As for the story itself, it is really sent out to those into whose souls the
iron has entered, and has entered deeply at some time of their lives.
But one cannot choose one's readers.

It is curious that some of the papers should look upon the novel as
a manifesto on 'the marriage question' (although, of course, it involves
it), seeing that it is concerned first with the labours of a poor student
to get a University degree, and secondly with the tragic issues of two
bad marriages, owing in the main to a doom or curse of hereditary
temperament peculiar to the family of the parties. The only remarks
which can be said to bear on the *general* marriage question occur in

---

3. Gosse (1849–1928), prolific man of letters and influential reviewer, is now best remembered
   for his autobiographical *Father and Son*. He corresponded frequently with Hardy.

dialogue, and comprise no more than half a dozen pages in a book of five hundred. And of these remarks I state (p. 362) that my own views are not expressed therein. I suppose the attitude of these critics is to be accounted for by the accident that, during the serial publication of my story, a sheaf of "purpose" novels on the matter appeared.

You have hardly an idea how poor and feeble the book seems to me, as executed, beside the idea of it that I had formed in prospect. * * *

P.S. One thing I did not answer. The "grimy" features of the story go to show the contrast between the ideal life a man wished to lead, and the squalid real life he was fated to lead. The throwing of the pizzle, at the supreme moment of his young dream, is to sharply initiate this contrast. But I must have lamentably failed, as I feel I have, if this requires explanation and is not self-evident. The idea was meant to run all through the novel. It is, in fact, to be discovered in *everybody's* life, though it lies less on the surface perhaps than it does in my poor puppet's.

November 20, 1895

You are quite right; there is nothing perverted or depraved in Sue's nature. The abnormalism consists in disproportion, not in inversion, her sexual instinct being healthy as far as it goes, but unusually weak and fastidious. Her sensibilities remain painfully alert notwithstanding, as they do in nature with such women. One point illustrating this I could not dwell upon: that, though she has children, her intimacies with Jude have never been more than occasional, even when they were living together (I mention that they occupy separate rooms, except towards the end), and one of her reasons for fearing the marriage ceremony is that she fears it would be breaking faith with Jude to withhold herself at pleasure, or altogether, after it; though while uncontracted she feels at liberty to yield herself as seldom as she chooses. This has tended to keep his passion as hot at the end as at the beginning, and helps to break his heart. He has never really possessed her as freely as he desired.

Sue is a type of woman which has always had an attraction for me, but the difficulty of drawing the type has kept me from attempting it till now.

Of course the book is all contrasts—or was meant to be in its original conception. Alas, what a miserable accomplishment it is, when I compare it with what I meant to make it!—e.g. Sue and her heathen gods set against Jude's reading the Greek testament; Christminster academical, Christminster in the slums; Jude the saint, Jude the sinner; Sue the Pagan, Sue the saint; marriage, no marriage; &c., &c.

As to the "coarse" scenes with Arabella, the battle in the schoolroom, etc., the newspaper critics might, I thought, have sneered at them for their Fieldingism rather than for their Zolaism. But your everyday critic knows nothing of Fielding. I am read in Zola very little, but have felt akin locally to Fielding, so many of his scenes having been laid down this way, and his home near.

Did I tell you I feared I should seem too High-Churchy at the end of the book where Sue recants? You can imagine my surprise at some of the reviews.

To Sir George Douglas

December 9, 1895

Yes, "Jude" is doing very well. I find that London society is not at all represented by the shocked critics.***I have really not been much upset by their missiles heaved at the poor book, not nearly so much as by my own opinion on its shortcomings. Somehow I feel that the critics are not sincere: everybody knows that silence is the remedy in the case of immoral works. But they advertise it with sensational headings because that advertises their newspapers, a far more important matter with them than so-called immorality.

One wonders why, in a book of 516 pages, they shd. dwell exclusively on portions which wd. not fill the odd 16. For moral reasons, doubtless, also. Someday perhaps it will be seen that the purpose of the story was no ignoble one, though in this, as in others, I have let the moral take care of itself—as it always will, if one writes sincerely.

I hear that a rival novelist in *Blackwood* sneers at my letting *Jude* appear in Harper's. As a matter of fact I tried to withdraw it, & asked them to cancel the contract; but it was found impracticable.

To Messrs. Harper and Brothers

December 24, 1895

I write for the moment on another question respecting *Jude*. I am much surprised, and I may say distressed, by the nature of the attack on it in the N. Y. *World*, which has just come into my hands. This is the only American notice of the novel I have yet seen, except Mr. Howells's in the WEEKLY. I do not know how far the *World* is representative of American feeling and opinion. But it is so much against my wish to offend the tastes of the American public, or to thrust any book of mine upon readers there, that if it should be in your own judgment advisable, please withdraw the novel.

You will probably know that it has been received here with about equal voices for and against—somewhat as was *Tess* received. All sensible readers here see at least that the intention of the book is honest and good. I myself thought it was somewhat overburdened with the interests of morality.

To Sir Edmund Gosse

January 4, 1896

The rectangular lines of the story were not premeditated, but came by chance: except, of course, that the involutions of four lives must necessarily be a sort of quadrille. The only point in the novel on which I feel sure is that it makes for morality; and that delicacy or indelicacy in a writer is according to his object. If I say to a lady "I met a naked woman", it is indelicate. But if I go on to say "I found she was mad with sorrow", it ceases to be indelicate. And in writing Jude my mind was fixed on the ending.

To Mrs. Florence Henniker

June 1, 1896

The unexpected result of *Jude* is that I am overwhelmed with requests for stories to an extent that I have never before experienced— though I imagined before publishing it that it w[oul]d considerably lower my commercial value. By the way, I have been offended with you for some time, though I have forgotten to say so, for what you said— that I was an advocate for 'free love.' I hold no theory whatever on the subject,—except by way of experimental remarks at tea parties, and seriously I don't see any possible scheme for the union of the sexes that w[oul]d be satisfactory.***There is a feeble attack on *Jude* in this month's *Fortnightly*. How much better I c[oul]d cut it up myself!

The Tree of Knowledge†

[Hardy contributed the following short essay to *The New Review* in May 1894, while the composition of *Jude the Obscure* was in progress. It formed part of a symposium on questions of marriage and sexual morality.]

To your first inquiry I would answer that a girl should certainly not be allowed to enter into matrimony without a full knowledge of her probable future in that holy estate, and of the possibilities which may lie in the past of the elect man.

I have not much faith in an innocent girl's "discovery of the great mysteries of life" by means of "the ordinary intercourse of society." Incomplete presentations, vicious presentations, meretricious and seductive presentations, are not unlikely in pursuing such investigations through such a channel.

† Reprinted in E. Brennecke, Jr., *Life and Art by Thomas Hardy* (New York, 1925) 118–19.

What would seem to be the most natural course is the answer to your second question: that a plain handbook on natural processes, specially prepared, should be placed in the daughter's hands, and, later on, similar information on morbid contingencies. Innocent youths should, I think, also receive the same instruction; for (if I may say a word out of my part) it has never struck me that the spider is invariably male and the fly invariably female.

As your problems are given on the old lines so I take them, without entering into the general question whether marriage, as we at present understand it, is such a desirable goal for all women as it is assumed to be; or whether civilisation can escape the humiliating indictment that, while it has been able to cover itself with glory in the arts, in literatures, in religions, and in the sciences, it has never succeeded in creating that homely thing, a satisfactory scheme for the conjunction of the sexes.

The Profitable Reading of Fiction†

*   *   *

It may seem something of a paradox to assert that the novels which most conduce to moral profit are likely to be among those written without a moral purpose. But the truth of the statement may be realized if we consider that the didactic novel is so generally devoid of *vraisemblance*[1] as to teach nothing but the impossibility of tampering with natural truth to advance dogmatic opinions. Those, on the other hand, which impress the reader with the inevitableness of character and environment in working out destiny, whether that destiny be just or unjust, enviable or cruel, must have a sound effect, if not what is called a good effect, upon a healthy mind.

Of the effects of such sincere presentation on weak minds, when the courses of the characters are not exemplary, and the rewards and punishments ill adjusted to deserts, it is not our duty to consider too closely. A novel which does moral injury to a dozen imbeciles, and has bracing results upon a thousand intellects of normal vigor, can justify its existence; and probably a novel was never written by the purest-minded author for which there could not be found some moral invalid or other whom it was capable of harming.

*   *   *

It is unfortunately quite possible to read the most elevating works of imagination in our own or any language, and, by fixing the regard

---

† These extracts are taken from Hardy's essay "The Profitable Reading of Fiction," originally published in the New York journal *Forum* in March 1888 and reprinted in *Thomas Hardy's Personal Writings*, ed. H. Orel (London, 1967).
1. Plausibility [*Editor*].

on the wrong sides of the subject, to gather not a grain of wisdom from them, nay, sometimes positive harm. What author has not had his experience of such readers?—the mentally and morally warped ones of both sexes, who will, where practicable, so twist plain and obvious meanings as to see in an honest picture of human nature an attack on religion, morals, or institutions. Truly has it been observed that "the eye sees that which it brings with it the means of seeing."[2]

---

2. Quoted from Thomas Carlyle's *The French Revolution* [*Editor*].

Hardy's Poems[†]

Hardy's *Complete Poems* contains nearly a thousand short poems, written over a period of more than sixty years. As a young man he sent poems to magazine editors, and they were rejected without exception. After he turned to prose, his quarter-century's labors as a writer of fiction left him little time for verse; but a few poems survive from the seventies and eighties, and his first volume of poetry (*Wessex Poems*, 1898) followed quickly after his abandonment of the novel. He wrote a great deal of poetry, and little else (apart from his autobiography), during the last thirty years of his life. Between Hardy's prose and his verse there exists a considerable degree of continuity of ideas and emotional range; on occasion he even rendered the same or similar material twice over, in prose and verse. The following poems have been selected on account of their closeness to elements and passages in *Jude the Obscure*.

Childhood Among the Ferns[1]

I sat one sprinkling day upon the lea,
Where tall-stemmed ferns spread out luxuriantly,
And nothing but those tall ferns sheltered me.

The rain gained strength, and damped each lopping[2] frond,
Ran down their stalks beside me and beyond,
And shaped slow-creeping rivulets as I conned,

With pride, my spray-roofed house. And though anon
Some drops pierced its green rafters, I sat on,
Making pretence I was not rained upon.

The sun then burst, and brought forth a sweet breath
From the limp ferns as they dried underneath:
I said: "I could live on here thus till death";

---

† Text from *The Complete Poems of Thomas Hardy*, ed. James Gibson (London: Macmillan, 1976). All notes are by the editor of this Norton Critical Edition.
1. First published a few weeks after Hardy's death in the *Daily Telegraph* (March 29, 1928). Compare with this poem both the passage in the *Life* reproduced on pp. 339–40 and the passage in the second chapter of the novel (p. 17).
2. Drooping.

And queried in the green rays as I sate:
"Why should I have to grow to man's estate,
And this afar-noised World perambulate?"

A Necessitarian's Epitaph

A world I did not wish to enter
Took me and poised me on my centre,
Made me grimace, and foot, and prance,
As cats on hot bricks have to dance
Strange jigs to keep them from the floor,
Till they sink down and feel no more.

The Masked Face

I found me in a great surging space,
        At either end a door,
And I said: "What is this giddying place,
        With no firm-fixéd floor,
        That I knew not of before?"
"It is Life," said a mask-clad face.

I asked: "But how do I come here,
        Who never wished to come;
Can the light and air be made more clear,
        The floor more quietsome,
        And the doors set wide? They numb
Fast-locked, and fill with fear."

The mask put on a bleak smile then,
        And said, "O vassal-wight,
There once complained a goosequill pen
        To the scribe of the Infinite
        Of the words it had to write
Because they were past its ken."

Thoughts of Phena[3]

At News of Her Death

Not a line of her writing have I,
        Not a thread of her hair,

3. Hardy's cousin Tryphena Sparks; see below, p. 370.

No mark of her late time as dame in her dwelling, whereby
   I may picture her there;
  And in vain do I urge my unsight
    To conceive my lost prize
At her close, whom I knew when her dreams were upbrimming
     with light,
   And with laughter her eyes.

  What scenes spread around her last days,
    Sad, shining, or dim?
Did her gifts and compassions enray and enarch her sweet ways
    With an aureate nimb?
   Or did life-light decline from her years,
    And mischances control
Her full day-star; unease, or regret, or forebodings, or fears
    Disennoble her soul?

  Thus I do but the phantom retain
    Of the maiden of yore
As my relic; yet haply the best of her—fined in my brain
    It may be the more
   That no line of her writing have I,
    Nor a thread of her hair,
No mark of her late time as dame in her dwelling, whereby
   I may picture her there.

March 1890

The Son's Portrait

  I walked the streets of a market town,
   And came to a lumber-shop,
  Which I had known ere I met the frown
    Of fate and fortune,
   And habit led me to stop.

  In burrowing mid this chattel and that,
   High, low, or edgewise thrown,
  I lit upon something lying flat—
    A fly-flecked portrait,
   Framed. 'Twas my dead son's own.

  "That photo? . . . A lady—I know not whence—
   Sold it me, Ma'am, one day,
  With more. You can have it for eighteenpence:

　　　　The picture's nothing;
　　　　It's but for the frame you pay."

　　　He had given it her in their heyday shine,
　　　　　When she wedded him, long her wooer:
　　　And then he was sent to the front-trench-line,
　　　　　And fell there fighting;
　　　　And she took a new bridegroom to her.

　　　I bought the gift she had held so light,
　　　　　And *buried it*—as 'twere he.—
　　　Well, well! Such things are trifling, quite,
　　　　　But when one's lonely
　　　How cruel they can be!

Lausanne

In Gibbon's Old Garden: 11–12 P.M.

JUNE 27, 1897

(The 110th Anniversary of the Completion of the "Decline and Fall" at the Same Hour and Place)

　　　A spirit seems to pass,
　　Formal in pose, but grave withal and grand:
　　He contemplates a volume in his hand,
And far lamps fleck him through the thin acacias.

　　　Anon the book is closed,
　　With "It is finished!" And at the alley's end
　　He turns, and when on me his glances bend
As from the Past comes speech—small, muted, yet composed.

　　　"How fares the Truth now?—Ill?
　　—Do pens but slily further her advance?
　　May one not speed her but in phrase askance?
Do scribes aver the Comic to be Reverend still?

　　　"Still rule those minds on earth
　　At whom sage Milton's wormwood words were hurled:
　　*'Truth like a bastard comes into the world
Never without ill-fame to him who gives her birth'?*"[4]

4. Adapted from a passage in Milton's prose work *The Doctrine and Discipline of Divorce*. Hardy used another quotation from this work as the epigraph to part four of *Jude the Obscure* (above, p. 157).

The Young Glass-Stainer

"These Gothic windows, how they wear me out
With cusp[5] and foil, and nothing straight or square,
Crude colours, leaden borders roundabout,
And fitting in Peter here, and Matthew there!

"What a vocation! Here do I draw now
The abnormal, loving the Hellenic norm;
Martha I paint, and dream of Hera's brow.
Mary, and think of Aphrodite's[6] form."

Nov. 1893

The Conformers

Yes; we'll wed, my little fay,
And you shall write you mine,
And in a villa chastely gray
        We'll house, and sleep, and dine.
        But those night-screened, divine,
        Stolen trysts of heretofore,
We of choice ecstasies and fine
                Shall know no more.

The formal-faced cohue[7]
Will then no more upbraid
With smiting smiles and whisperings two
        Who have thrown less loves in shade.
        We shall no more evade
        The searching light of the sun,
Our game of passion will be played,
                Our dreaming done.

We shall not go in stealth
To rendezvous unknown,
But friends will ask me of your health,
        And you about my own.
        When we abide alone,
        No leapings each to each,

5. Projecting point between the small arcs or "foils" in Gothic stonework.
6. Martha and Mary appear in the Gospels; Hera and Aphrodite are figures in Greek mythology
   (Hera was associated with women and marriage, and Aphrodite was the goddess of sexual love).
   The contrast between Christianity and paganism—"Hebraism" and "Hellenism," in Matthew
   Arnold's terms—is prominent in the novel, especially in the exchanges between Jude and Sue.
7. Throng, mob (French word).

But syllables in frigid tone
          Of household speech.

          When down to dust we glide
          Men will not say askance,
As now: "How all the country side
          Rings with their mad romance!"
          But as they graveward glance
          Remark: "In them we lose
A worthy pair, who helped advance
          Sound parish views."

The Recalcitrants[8]

Let us off and search, and find a place
Where yours and mine can be natural lives,
Where no one comes who dissects and dives
And proclaims that ours is a curious case,
Which its touch of romance can scarcely grace.

You would think it strange at first, but then
Everything has been strange in its time.
When some one said on a day of the prime
He would bow to no brazen god again
He doubtless dazed the mass of men.

None will see in us a pair whose claims
To righteous judgment we care not making;
Who have doubted if breath be worth the taking,
And have no respect for the current fames
Whence the savour has flown while abide the names.

We have found us already shunned, disdained,
And for re-acceptance have not once striven;
Whatever offence our course has given
The brunt thereof we have long sustained.
Well, let us away, scorned, unexplained.

To a Motherless Child

Ah, child, thou art but half thy darling mother's;
          Hers couldst thou wholly be,

8. According to R. L. Purdy, this poem was written shortly after 1893. *The Recalcitrants* was one
of Hardy's earlier titles for *Jude the Obscure*: he suggests it in a letter to his publishers dated
November 5, 1894.

My light in thee would outglow all in others;
    She would relive to me.
But niggard Nature's trick of birth
    Bars, lest she overjoy,
Renewal of the loved on earth
    Save with alloy.

The Dame has no regard, alas, my maiden,
    For love and loss like mine—
No sympathy with mindsight memory-laden;
    Only with fickle eyne.[9]
To her mechanic artistry
    My dreams are all unknown,
And why I wish that thou couldst be
    But One's alone!

Midnight on the Great Western

In the third-class seat sat the journeying boy,
    And the roof-lamp's oily flame
Played down on his listless form and face,
Bewrapt past knowing to what he was going,
    Or whence he came.

In the band of his hat the journeying boy
    Had a ticket stuck; and a string
Around his neck bore the key of his box,
That twinkled gleams of the lamp's sad beams
    Like a living thing.

What past can be yours, O journeying boy
    Towards a world unknown,
Who calmly, as if incurious quite
On all at stake, can undertake
    This plunge alone?

Knows your soul a sphere, O journeying boy,
    Our rude realms far above,
Whence with spacious vision you mark and mete[1]
This region of sin that you find you in,
    But are not of?

9. Eyes.
1. Measure, appraise.

To a Lady

Offended by a Book of the Writer's

Now that my page is exiled,—doomed, maybe,
Never to press thy cosy cushions more,
Or wake thy ready Yeas as heretofore,
Or stir thy gentle vows of faith in me:

Knowing thy natural receptivity,
I figure that, as flambeaux[2] banish eve,
My sombre image, warped by insidious heave
Of those less forthright, must lose place in thee.

So be it. I have borne such. Let thy dreams
Of me and mine diminish day by day,
Any yield their space to shine of smugger things;
Till I shape to thee but in fitful gleams,
And then in far and feeble visitings,
And then surcease.[3] Truth will be truth alway.

2. Torches.
3. Die.

Locale

NORMAN PAGE

Settings and Sources†

Jude is the most restless of all Hardy's heroes; and, as the titles of its six "parts" indicate, the novel is constructed around his wanderings. From Marygreen he makes his long-desired journey to Christminster; subsequently he lives in Melchester, Shaston, Aldbrickham, "and elsewhere"; and he returns to Christminster to die. All of these correspond to actual places (see map, pp. 2–3), and all are evoked with a powerful sense of the physical environment—not, however, the rural environment of the earlier novels, but (with the exception of Marygreen) urban settings in which the most powerful elements are the architectural qualities of their buildings and the awareness that they have been the scenes of multitudinous lives in the past.

For some of these settings Hardy drew directly on personal experience. Marygreen is based on the village of Great Fawley in Berkshire; Hardy's paternal grandmother had lived there as a child, and he visited the spot in October 1892 when he was beginning to plan the novel (see extracts below from the *Life*). Hardy also knew "Melchester" well: it is the cathedral city of Salisbury in Wiltshire, and was familiar both on account of its architectural attractions and because his sisters had trained as teachers at the Church of England college there.

The account of "Shaston" (Shaftesbury in Dorset) places more emphasis on the history of the town than on its present-day appearance, and for this material Hardy went to a printed source. The parallel passages given below suggest the extent of his debt to Hutchins's county history. But it is "Christminster" which dominates the novel: its streets and buildings, colleges and slums, are described with precision and feeling, down to the very texture of the crumbling medieval stonework. Hardy visited Oxford in June 1893, shortly before he began to write the novel "at full length": he was a conscientious sightseer, and this was a working holiday in quest of material for the novel, though his information seems to be derived from guide-books and his-

† All bracketed words and phrases have been added by the editor of this Norton Critical Edition.

ERNEST PIGOTT'S Fresh Butter Delivered to all Parts of the City Daily.

33 & 34 THE MARKET. AVENUE 4, HIGH STREET END.

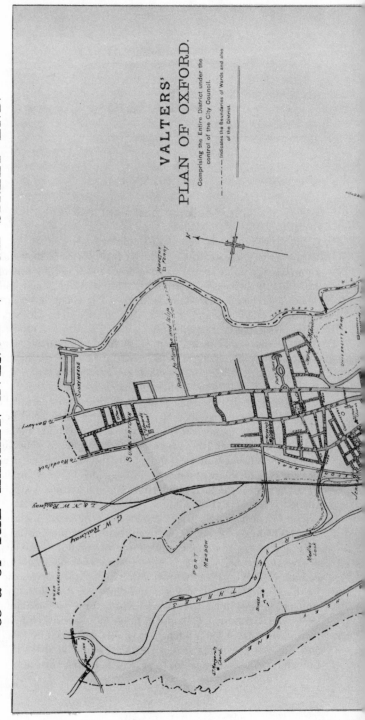

VALTERS'
PLAN OF OXFORD.

Comprising the Entire District under the
control of the City Council.

—·—·—·— Indicates the Boundaries of Wards and also
of the District.

A. BALLARD,

15 QUEEN STREET, OXFORD,

Practical Watch and Clock Maker

and Working Jeweller.

Noted House for Wedding and Keeper Rings.

A Large Stock of Electro and Silver Plate.

OPTICIAN TO THE OXFORD EYE HOSPITAL.

Published by J. C. VALTER, 30 James Street, Oxford.

Entered at Stationers' Hall.

VALTER'S PLAN OF OXFORD

Issued in 1891. Hardy may have used this map, or one very much like it, when he explored Oxford in 1893.

tories as well as from personal impressions. In spite of his later insistence on the fictitious element in Christminster, the picture of late-Victorian Oxford is both detailed and accurate.

Marygreen

'*October*. At Great Fawley, Berks. Entered a ploughed vale which might be called the Valley of Brown Melancholy. The silence is remarkable. . . . Though I am alive with the living I can only see the dead here, and am scarcely conscious of the happy children at play.'[1]

[During Hardy's last visit to Oxford, in June 1923] they paused also at Fawley, that pleasant Berkshire village described in [*Jude the Obscure*] under the name of Marygreen. Here some of Hardy's ancestors were buried, and he searched fruitlessly for their graves in the little churchyard. His father's mother, the gentle, kindly grandmother who lived with the family at Bockhampton during Hardy's childhood, had spent the first thirteen years of her life here as an orphan child, named Mary Head, and her memories of Fawley were so poignant that she never cared to return to the place after she had left it as a young girl. The surname of Jude was taken from this place.[2]

Christminster

[In June 1893] Hardy was at Oxford. It was during the Encaenia, with the Christ Church and other college balls, garden-parties, and suchlike bright functions, but Hardy did not make himself known, his object being to view the proceedings entirely as a stranger. * * * He viewed the Commemoration proceedings from the undergraduates' gallery of the Sheldonian, his quarters while at Oxford being at the Wilberforce Temperance Hotel.[3]

Lord Rosebery took occasion in a conversation to inquire 'why Hardy had called Oxford "Christminister".' Hardy assured him that he had not done anything of the sort, 'Christminster' being a city of learning that was certainly suggested by Oxford, but in its entirety existed nowhere else in the world but between the covers of the novel under discussion. The answer was not so flippant as it seemed, for Hardy's idea had been, as he often explained, to use the difficulty of a poor man's acquiring learning at that date merely as the 'tragic mischief' (among others) of a dramatic story, for which purpose an old-fashioned university at the very door of the poor man was the most striking

1. Hardy's diary, October 1892, quoted in *Life*, pp. 250–51.
2. *Life*, p. 420.
3. *Life*, p. 257.

method; and though the architecture and scenery of Oxford were the best in England adapted for this, he did not slavishly copy them; indeed in some details he departed considerably from whatever of the city he took as a general model. It is hardly necessary to add that he had no feeling in the matter, and used Jude's difficulties of study as he would have used war, fire, or shipwreck for bringing about a catastrophe.[4]

There is in existence a sheet of notepaper on which, in Hardy's own hand, are written most of the place-names in *Jude*, and then, after the words *approximates* to, the real place-names in a parallel column; part of this list is as follows:[5]

Beersheba	the purlieu called Jericho.
St. Silas	St. Barnabas.
Chief St.	High St.
Fourways	Carfax.
Meeting place of Jude & Sue	Cross in pavement, Broad St.
Crozier Coll.	Oriel?
Old Time Street	Oriel Lane?
Rubric Coll.	Brazenose.
Cardinal Coll.	Christ Church Coll.
The Cathedral	Christchurch.
Cardinal Street	St. Aldates St.
Ch(urch) with Italian Porch	St. Mary's.
Theatre of Wren	Sheldonian.
The octagonal chamber (p. 141)	Cupola of Sheldonian.
Oldgate Coll.	New Coll.
The riverside path	The towing path.[6]

Melchester

* * * Salisbury, a place in which he was never tired of sojourning, partly from personal associations and partly because its graceful cathedral pile was the most marked instance in England of an architectural intention carried out to the full.[7]

At Salisbury they stopped for a little while to look at the Cathedral, as Hardy always loved doing, and various old buildings, including the Training College which he had visited more than fifty years before when his two sisters were students there, and which is faithfully described in *Jude the Obscure*.[8]

4. *Life*, pp. 278–79.
5. Reproduced in facsimile in *Thomas Hardy*, by Clive Holland, p. 144 [*Rutland's* note].
6. W. R. Rutland, *Thomas Hardy: A Study of His Writings and Their Background* (New York: Russell & Russell, 1938) 246–47.
7. *Life*, p. 295.
8. *Life*, p. 420, referring to the 1923 journey.

Shaston

Jude the Obscure, part IV, chapter 1, contains an elaborate description of Shaston. As the following parallel passages show, Hardy's source for much of his information was John Hutchins's *The History and Antiquities of the County of Dorset,* first published in 1774. Hardy used the third edition, "corrected, augmented, and improved," issued in four large volumes in 1861–70; his annotated copy is now in the Thomas Hardy Memorial Collection in Dorset County Museum.

(a)   [Hardy] Shaston, the ancient British Palladour * * *

[Hutchins] In British it is called Caer Palladur, * * * The supposed British names Caer Palladur, or Palledour, seem to be mere invention, alluding to a temple of Pallas, which some have placed here, though that deity was unknown to the ancient Britons. [A footnote adds:] Shaftesbury might by the Britons have been called Paladur, from the British Pal a dur, distant from water.

(b)   [Hardy] * * * rising on the north, south, and west sides of the borough out of the deep alluvial Vale of Blackmoor, the view from the Castle Green over three counties of verdant pasture— South, Mid, and Nether Wessex * * * the medicinal air * * * Its situation rendered water the great want of the town; and within living memory, horses, donkeys and men may have been seen toiling up the winding ways to the top of the height, laden with tubs and barrels filled from the wells beneath the mountain, and hawkers retailing their contents at the price of a halfpenny a bucketful.

[Hutchins] On the south and west you have a very extensive prospect over the counties of Dorset, Somerset, and Wilts * * * The air * * * is pure and healthy * * * on the north, south, and west, the vale of Blakemore, a deep country * * * Few places have been more distressed for water than Shaftesbury, the situation being so high * * * 'Naturally it has in it no water; but round about on the edge of the hill are pleasant springs, from which the towne's uses are supplied, and brought up by hands, or on horses' backs.'9 * * * A great many people formerly got their living by carrying water, for which they had three-halfpence or two-pence a load, according to the part of the town they carried it to; and a farthing or a halfpenny a pail, if fetched upon the head.

9. Quoted by Hutchins from a map of 1615.

(c) [Hardy] The bones of King Edward 'the Martyr,' carefully removed hither for holy preservation, brought Shaston a renown which made it the resort of pilgrims from every part of Europe * * *

[Hutchins] St. Edward the Martyr * * * This unfortunate king being esteemed a martyr and canonized a saint, his shrine was much resorted to by superstitious pilgrims * * *

(d) [Hardy] * * * its magnificent apsidal Abbey, the chief glory of South Wessex * * * its shrines, chantries, hospitals * * * To this fair creation of the great Middle-Age the Dissolution was, as historians tell us, the death-knell.

[Hutchins] [The Abbey was] the glory and ornament of the town * * * It was a most magnificent building * * * It seems to have been ruined immediately upon the Dissolution * * * [Among those buried there are] King Edward the Martyr; Elfgiva, wife of Edmund, King of the West Saxons * * * Cecilia Fovent, abbess; Joan Formage, abbess * * * the choir and presbytery, which terminated to the east in a semicircular apse * * * [Hutchins adds a list of chantries, also "The Priory or Hospital of St. John Baptist."]

Influences on the Novel

C. J. WEBER

[Autobiographical Elements]†

In *The Later Years* Mrs. Hardy is quoted as having written a letter at Hardy's request and obviously at his dictation: 'To your inquiry if *Jude the Obscure* is autobiographical, I have to answer that there is not a scrap of personal detail in it, it having the least to do with his own life of all his books.' This assertion is so obviously untrue that one wonders why Hardy made it.

* * *

Hardy was born two miles from Stinsford ('Mellstock') and Jude Fawley 'comes from Mellstock, down in South Wessex'. 'Hardy was a born bookworm,' and in *Jude* 'the boy is crazy for books, that he is'. Once upon a time Hardy was stopped in Dorchester by a boy who drove a baker's cart; the boy wanted to borrow Hardy's Latin grammar. In the novel Jude asks 'for some grammars, if you recollect', and is described as having 'driven old Drusilla Fawley's breadcart'. When young Tom Hardy became old enough to take his studies seriously, he taught himself Homer by using Clarke's edition of the *Iliad*, just as Jude Fawley 'dabbled in Clarke's *Homer*'. In February 1860, while he was still studying architecture under John Hicks, Hardy acquired a copy of Griesbach's edition of the New Testament in Greek (it was sold on May 26, 1938, in Lot 22 at the sale of Hardy's library). He studied the book diligently in order to fit himself for carrying on arguments about infant baptism with the Perkins boys, the sons of the Baptist minister at Dorchester. In *Jude the Obscure* young Fawley obtains 'by post from a second-hand bookseller' a copy of the 'New Testament in the Greek, . . . Griesbach's text', in which he was later described as 'earnestly reading'. In 1863 Hardy bought a copy of Buckley's translation of *Aeschylus*, from which he lifted the 'Aeschylean phrase' which so annoyed some

† From C. J. Weber, *Hardy of Wessex: His Life and Literary Career*, rev. ed. (New York: Columbia UP, 1965) 200–203. Copyright © 1965, Columbia University Press. Reprinted with permission of the publisher.

readers of *Tess of the D'Urbervilles*. In *Jude* (Chapter VI, 2) Fawley quoted from that same book, citing (from the *Agamemnon*): 'Things are as they are, and will be brought to their destined issue.'

On June 20, 1873, Hardy went to Cambridge and spent a night at Queens' College as the guest of his friend Horace M. Moule, just as Jude Fawley calls on Phillotson at Oxford. Jude thinks of 'entering the Church' and 'keeping the necessary terms at a Theological College' exactly as Hardy, in August 1865, had thought of 'keeping terms' at Cambridge with a view to fitting himself for 'a curacy in a country village'—a career 'towards which he had long had a leaning.' By this time Hardy had grown a dark beard, and in *Jude* (Chapter III, 3) Fawley wears a dark beard. Jude shares Hardy's view that Salisbury Cathedral is 'the most graceful architectural pile in England,' and (in Chapter II, 3) 'the great waves of pedal music' which 'tumbled round the choir' of Oxford Cathedral affected Jude precisely as the organ music had affected Thomas Hardy on June 22, 1875, when he listened to it in Wimborne Minster. In *Jude* (Chapter IV, 5) Fawley quotes Hardy's favourite poem by Browning, 'The Statue and the Bust', and (in Chapter II, 6) shows himself to be familiar with Hardy's favourite *Book of Job*.

In view of this multiplicity of proved and reliable echoes, we are probably justified in surmising that in the novel we hear further echoes out of Hardy's own past. In Chapter III, 6, Jude remarks to Sue: 'We are cousins, and it is bad for cousins to marry', and (in II, 6) Jude is told: 'Don't you be a fool about her! . . . If your cousin is civil to you, take her civility for what it is worth, but anything more than a relation's good wishes it is stark madness for 'ee to give her'. One wonders whether Hardy was here recalling remarks made to him in 1868 when he was 'walking out' with his cousin Tryphena Sparks. In *Jude* (Chapter III, 8), after Sue had announced her intention to marry Phillotson, Fawley 'projected his mind into the future' and imagined his cousin Sue 'with children . . . around her.' However, 'the consolation of regarding them as a continuation of her identity was denied to him . . . by the wilfulness of Nature in not allowing issue from one parent alone'. Was this Thomas Hardy's own thought when, in 1877, his cousin Tryphena married Charles Gale? Their daughter, also called Tryphena, was born in 1878. After Hardy's cousin had died in 1890, he went to call on her daughter. In Chapter III, 8, Jude Fawley remarks: 'If at the . . . death of my lost love I could go and see her child—hers solely—there would be comfort in it.'

* * *

Hardy made similar use of the experience of other members of his family. His sisters, Mary and Katherine ('Kate'), had gone to a Teachers' Training School at Salisbury; he had once visited them there. In

1891 he visited the Training College for Schoolmistresses at White-lands, and was reminded by that visit of the painful restrictions to which his sisters had been subjected during their period of training. Out of these memories came his description of that 'species of nunnery known as the Training School at Melchester' to which Sue Bridehead goes.

Hardy also drew on other family associations. His father had died in 1892—just a year before the novelist went to explore Oxford. This bereavement was the first time death had visited Hardy's immediate family since he was a boy. His grandmother Hardy had died when he was seventeen. She is the 'One We Knew' in the 1907 poem of that title. Hardy recalled his grandmother's stories of the first dozen years of her life, when, as a little girl named Mary Head, she had endured such hardships at Great Fawley in Berkshire, near Oxford, that she had never been willing to return to that spot after she had once left it. Hardy himself went to take a look at Great Fawley in October 1892 when the story of Jude was taking shape in his imagination. He decided to call his ambitious boy Fawley, and to rename the place where Mary Head had spent her girlhood 'Marygreen'.

W. R. RUTLAND

[Hardy, Parnell, and Ibsen]†

Properly to understand the main subject of *Jude the Obscure*, it is necessary to glance at something that was happening in England in the early 'nineties.***The whole question of marriage and divorce was brought to the forefront of public attention in 1890 by the Parnell case. In December 1889, Captain O'Shea filed a petition for divorce from his wife on the ground of her adultery with Charles Stewart Par-nell, the Irish political leader. The case came into Court in November 1890; and a decree nisi, with costs against Parnell, was pronounced. Although Parnell's Irish followers publicly declared their continued allegiance to him, the English Liberal party, of which the backbone was nonconformity, refused to overlook the matter. On November 24th, Gladstone wrote a famous open letter to John Morley, saying that:

> notwithstanding the splendid services rendered by Mr. Parnell to his country, his continuance at the present time in the leadership would be productive of consequences disastrous in the highest degree to the cause of Ireland.

† From W. R. Rutland, *Thomas Hardy, a Study of His Writings and Their Background* (1938; reprint ed., New York: Russell and Russell, 1962) 249–53.

A storm of controversy ensued, which cost Parnell his leadership, his reputation, his health and his life; he died in 1891.

This *cause célèbre* let loose a flood of discussion and polemic upon the whole question of love, marriage and divorce; and of this *Jude the Obscure* formed a part. To consider here only two examples pertinent to this novel. With the *Fortnightly Review* Hardy had at that time close connections. In the course of 1891, that periodical published 'A Midnight Baptism,' the episode from *Tess* which the *Graphic* refused to print, as well as Hardy's short story, 'For Conscience' Sake,' a study in the results of illicit sexual relationship. The same volume of the *Fortnightly* contains an article occasioned by the Parnell case, entitled 'Public Life and Private Morals.' One paragraph discusses the grounds for regarding marriage as sacred:

> Now what are these grounds? If we say that they are merely grounds of civil contract, we entirely deceive ourselves. Marriage, merely as a civil contract is a contract which the parties concerned in it are, by mutual consent, at perfect liberty to break. But let us suppose for a moment that this was not the case. Let us suppose that this contract had something so special about it, that each party was not only bound to fulfil its conditions if the other demanded, but that each, whether they willed it or no, was bound to demand the fulfillment of them. Let us suppose further that marriage was literally a lottery—that men and women were bound to each other who had neither love nor sympathy, who were suited neither by age nor by temperament. What should we say of the sanctity of marriage then? Would it not seem hateful rather than sacred? . . . The sanctity of marriage depends, not on its being a contract, but on its being a willing contract. It depends also on the willingness of the contracting parties being the result of dispositions which will enable them to live together happily. If love and marriage were essentially incompatible, would marriage in that case have ever seemed sacred to anybody? Most of its sanctity is gone when they are bound to be incompatible practically. The legal aspect of the union is merely its husk and shell. Its real sanctity is like the sanctity of friendship; it lies far deeper than any law can reach and depends on circumstances of which no law can take account.

Later in the same year, the same periodical published another article entitled 'Marriage and Freethought,' which was a powerful plea for reasoned consideration of the whole question. A striking passage in this ran:

> Could any scientific discovery in these days be discredited, even for a moment, by the authority of a biblical text? Would a text, no matter how plain, do anything towards arresting any popular

reform or change? The answer to both these questions, as we are all aware, is no. . . . But the liberal and progressive thought of this country, the moment it is brought to bear on this one social question (Marriage) becomes doggedly false to every one of its boasted principles . . . while indignantly refusing to recognise the vows that bind the nun, it refuses even to consider the relaxation of those that may be killing the wife; and whilst ridiculing the idea that any other contract is inviolable . . . it treats this contract of marriage, which constantly works so miserably, as a contract which no one may violate, though every one concerned is willing, and which it is a kind of blasphemy to attempt to regulate better.

For some years past, Hardy had had strong and bitter feelings about marriage, as may be seen in *The Woodlanders*. Then the whole question became the most discussed subject in the country. When we remember that Hardy was a contributor to the periodical in which both these articles appeared, and that it was just at this time that *Jude the Obscure* was taking shape in his mind, we need no further commentary upon one aspect of that novel. Although it does not seem to have been even mentioned by any of the critics, such is the background to the book which has written upon its title-page: 'The letter killeth.'

Another matter has also to be mentioned in this connection, which also appears to have been overlooked. It was at this time that the plays of Ibsen first began to appear on the English stage. Between 1889 and 1896 there raged a bitter controversy over the Scandinavian dramatist. Hardy, Meredith and George Moore were among the first members of an Independent Theatre Association founded in 1891 to sponsor the production of Ibsen's plays. This cause was also sponsored by the *Fortnightly Review*, which published an article on the Independent Theatre Association by William Archer. Edmund Gosse, a close personal friend of Hardy's at this time, was another leading spirit among the English advocates of Ibsen. The English versions of the Norwegian plays which were published by him and by Archer did much to popularize them in this country. Without going into lengthy comparisons, it is easy to see that *Jude the Obscure* owes something to Ibsen. It is not surprising to learn that in the course of 1893, when the novel was being written, Hardy went to performances of *Hedda Gabler*, *Rosmersholm* and *The Master Builder*. Readers of *Jude* will suspect that he also knew something of *The Doll's House* and of *Ghosts*. The less perspicacious critics accused Hardy of imitating Zola, whom they, like Mrs. Oliphant, had never read themselves. Time need not be wasted upon this comparison; nothing could well be further apart than the aims of that particular French realist, and the aims with which Hardy wrote *Jude*. But the influence of Ibsen is certainly to be seen in that novel; which is not the same thing as saying that Hardy 'imitated' Ibsen. He was in no need to imitate anybody.

In one of three letters about *Jude* which Hardy wrote to Gosse, he denied that the book was 'a manifesto on the marriage question, although, of course, it involves it.'[1] The distinction is a very fine one, if it exists at all; but there is little doubt that the ridiculous and scandalous uproar of which he became the subject made Hardy lose his head a little at the time. It may be that the 'general remarks' upon marriage only fill a few pages; but no one who has read it impartially can deny that marital relationships are one of the main subjects of the book. The horrible penance of Sue, in which that theme culminates, was deliberately contrived to sear the minds of his readers with the evil of unhappy marriage; as, indeed, was the whole plot. In the original preface dated August 1895, Hardy very clearly stated the objects of his last novel:

> to deal unaffectedly with the fret and fever, derision and disaster, that may press in the wake of the strongest passion known to humanity; to tell without a mincing of words, of deadly war waged between flesh and spirit; and to point the tragedy of unfulfilled aims.

Jude's attempt on Christminster, in all its implications, is the third of these. The deadly war waged between spirit and flesh hinges entirely upon two unhappy marriages. The facts do not admit of any denial that Hardy made it so on purpose, partly urged on thereto by the controversy raging in the country when he was planning the novel.

1. See above, p. 346.

CRITICISM

Contemporary Reception

WILLIAM DEAN HOWELLS

From Harper's Weekly (December 7, 1895)†

The story is a tragedy, and tragedy almost unrelieved by the humorous touch which the poet is master of. The grotesque is there abundantly, but not the comic; and at times this ugliness heightens the pathos to almost intolerable effect. But I must say that the figure of Jude himself is, in spite of all his weakness and debasement, one of inviolable dignity. He is the sport of fate, but he is never otherwise than sublime; he suffers more for others than for himself. The wretched Sue who spoils his life and her own, helplessly, inevitably, is the kind of fool who finds the fool in the poet and prophet so often, and brings him to naught. She is not less a fool than Arabella herself; though of such exaltation in her folly that we cannot refuse her a throe of compassion, even when she is most perverse. All the characters, indeed, have the appealing quality of human creatures really doing what they must while seeming to do what they will. It is not a question of blaming them or praising them; they are in the necessity of what they do and what they suffer. One may indeed blame the author for presenting such a conception of life; one may say that it is demoralizing if not immoral; but as to his dealing with his creations in the circumstance which he has imagined, one can only praise him for his truth.

The story has to do with some things not hitherto touched in fiction, or Anglo-Saxon fiction at least; and there cannot be any doubt of the duty of criticism to warn the reader that it is not for all readers. But not to affirm the entire purity of the book in these matters would be to fail of another duty of which there can be as little doubt. I do not believe any one can get the slightest harm from any passage of it; only one would rather that innocence were not acquainted with all that virtue may know. Vice can feel nothing but self-abhorrence in the presence of its facts.

---

† Howells (1837–1920), the American novelist, was a friend of Hardy. He was active as a literary journalist and magazine editor.

The old conventional personifications seem drolly factitious in their reference to the vital reality of this strange book. I suppose it can be called morbid, and I do not deny that it is. But I have not been able to find it untrue, while I know that the world is full of truth that contradicts it. The common experience, or perhaps I had better say the common knowledge of life contradicts it. Commonly, the boy of Jude's strong aspiration and steadfast ambition succeeds and becomes in some measure the sort of man he dreamed of being. Commonly, a girl like Sue flutters through the anguish of her harassed and doubting youth and settles into acquiescence with the ordinary life of women, if not acceptance of it. Commonly, a boy like the son of Jude, oppressed from birth with the sense of being neither loved nor wanted, hardens himself against his misery, fights for the standing denied him, and achieves it. The average Arabella has no reversion to her first love when she has freed herself from it. The average Phillotson does not give up his wife to the man she says she loves, and he does not take her back knowing her loathing for himself. I grant all these things; and yet the author makes me believe that all he says to the contrary inevitably happened.

I allow that there are many displeasing things in the book, and few pleasing. Arabella's dimple-making, the pig-killing, the boy suicide and homicide; Jude's drunken second marriage; Sue's wilful self-surrender to Phillotson: these and other incidents are revolting. They make us shiver with horror and grovel with shame, but we know that they are deeply founded in the condition, if not in the nature of humanity. There are besides these abhorrent facts certain accusations against some accepted formalities of civilization, which I suppose most readers will find hardly less shocking. But I think it is very well for us to ask from time to time the reasons of things, and to satisfy ourselves, if we can, what the reasons are. If the experience of Jude with Arabella seems to arraign marriage, and it is made to appear not only ridiculous but impious that two young, ignorant, impassioned creatures should promise lifelong fealty and constancy when they have no real sense of what they are doing, and that then they should be held to their rash vow by all the forces of society, it is surely not the lesson of the story that any other relation than marriage is tolerable for the man and woman who live together. Rather it enforces the conviction that marriage is the sole solution of the question of sex, while it shows how atrocious and heinous marriage may sometimes be.

I find myself defending the book on the ethical side when I meant chiefly to praise it for what seems to me its artistic excellence. It has not only the solemn and lofty effect of a great tragedy; a work far faultier might impart this; but it has unity very uncommon in the novel, and especially the English novel. So far as I can recall its incidents there are none but such as seem necessary from the circumstances and the characters. Certain little tricks which the author sometimes uses to help himself out, and which give the sense of insincerity or debility, are absent here. He does not invoke the playful humour which he employs elsewhere. Such humour as there is tastes bitter, and is grim if not sardonic. This tragedy of fate suggests the classic singleness of means as well as the classic singleness of motive.

MARGARET OLIPHANT

From Blackwood's Magazine (January 1896)†

* * *

I do not know, however, for what audience Mr. Hardy intends his last work, which has been introduced, as he tells us, for the last twelve months, into a number of decent houses in England and America, with the most shameful portions suppressed.[1] How they could be suppressed in a book whose tendency throughout is so shameful I do not understand; but it is to be hoped that the conductors and readers of *Harper's Magazine* were so protected by ignorance as not to understand what the writer meant then—though he now states it with a plainness beyond mistake.

* * *

The present writer does not pretend to a knowledge of the works of Zola,[2] which perhaps she ought to have before presuming to say that nothing so coarsely indecent as the whole history of Jude in his relations with his wife Arabella has ever been put in English print—that is to say, from the hands of a Master. There may be books more disgusting, more impious as regards human nature, more foul in detail, in those dark corners where the amateurs of filth find garbage to their taste; but not, we repeat, from any Master's hand. It is vain to tell us that there are scenes in Shakespeare himself which, if they were picked out for special attention, would be offensive to modesty. There is no need for picking out in the work now referred to. Its faults do not lie in mere suggestion, or any *double entendre*, though these are bad enough. In the history of Jude, the half-educated and by no means

† Mrs. Margaret Oliphant was a prolific novelist and reviewer. Her attack on Hardy's novel appears in an article titled "The Anti-Marriage League," which also discusses Grant Allen's controversial novel *The Woman Who Did* (1895). For Hardy's views on Mrs. Oliphant, see N. Page, "Hardy, Mrs. Oliphant, and *Jude the Obscure*," *Victorian Newsletter* 46 (1974): 22–24. All notes are by the editor of this Norton Critical Edition.

1. The reference is to the serialization of the novel in *Harper's New Monthly Magazine.*

2. Emile Zola (1840–1902), French novelist, was widely attacked by English critics and moralists for the alleged immorality of his realistic fictions. The publisher Henry Vizetelly had been successfully prosecuted in 1888 for issuing translations of some of Zola's novels.

uninteresting hero in whose early self-training there is much that is admirable—Mr. Hardy has given us a chapter in what used to be called the conflict between vice and virtue. The young man, vaguely aspiring after education, learning, and a position among the scholars and students of the land, with a piteous ignorance of the difficulties before him, yet that conviction of being able to triumph over them, which, as we know, has often in real life succeeded in doing so—is really an attractive figure at his outset. He is virtuous by temperament, meaning no evil; bent upon doing more than well, and elevating himself to the level which appears to him the highest in life. But he falls into the hands of a woman so completely animal that it is at once too little and too much to call her vicious. She is a human pig, like the beast whom in a horrible scene she and her husband kill, quite without shame or consciousness of any occasion for shame, yet not even carried away by her senses or any overpowering impulse for their gratification, so much worse than the sow, that it is entirely on a calculation of profit that she puts forth her revolting spell. After the man has been subjugated, a process through which the reader is required to follow him closely (and Jude's own views on this subject are remarkable), he is made for the rest of his life into a puppet flung about between them by two women—the fleshly animal Arabella and the fantastic Susan, the one ready to gratify him in whatever circumstances they may meet, the other holding him on the tiptoe of expectation, with a pretended reserve which is almost more indecent still. In this curious dilemma the unfortunate Jude, who is always the puppet, always acted upon by the others, never altogether loses our esteem. He is a very poor creature, but he would have liked much better to do well if they would have let him, and dies a virtuous victim of the eternal feminine, scarcely ever blameable, though always bearing both the misery and the shame.

We can with difficulty guess what is Mr. Hardy's motive in portraying such a struggle. It can scarcely be said to be one of those attacks upon the institution of Marriage, which is the undisguised inspiration of some of the other books before us. It is marriage indeed which in the beginning works Jude's woe; and it is by marriage, or rather the marrying of himself and others, that his end is brought about. We rather think the author's object must be, having glorified women by the creation of Tess, to show after all what destructive and ruinous creatures they are, in general circumstances and in every development, whether brutal or refined. Arabella, the first—the pig-dealer's daughter, whose native qualities have been ripened by the experiences of a barmaid—is the Flesh, unmitigated by any touch of human feeling except that of merciless calculation as to what will be profitable for herself. She is the native product of the fields, the rustic woman, exuberant and overflowing with health, vanity and appetite. The colloquy between her and her fellows in their disgusting work, after her first almost equally disgusting interview with Jude, is one of the most unutterable foulness—a shame to the language in which it is recorded and suggested; and the picture altogether of the country lasses at their outdoor work is more brutal in depravity than anything which the darkest slums could bring forth, as are the scenes in which their good advice is carried out. Is it possible that there are readers in England to whom this infamy can be palatable, and who, either in inadvertence or in wantonness, can *make it pay*? Mr. Hardy informs us[3] he has taken elaborate precautions to secure the double profit of the serial writer, by subduing his colours and diminishing his effects, in the presence of the less corrupt, so as to keep the perfection of filthiness for those who love it. It would be curious to compare in this unsavoury traffic how much of the sickening essence of his story Mr. Hardy has thought his first public could stomach, and how many edifying details he has put in for the enlightenment of those who have no squeamish scruples to get over. The transaction is insulting to the public, with whom he trades the viler wares under another name, with all the suppressed passages restored, as old-book dealers say in their catalogues, recommending their ancient scandal to the amateurs of the unclean. It is not the first time Mr. Hardy has adopted this expedient. If the English public supports him in it, it will be to the shame of every individual who thus confesses himself to like and accept what the author himself acknowledges to be unfit for the eyes—not of girls and young persons only, but of the ordinary reader—the men and women who read the Magazines, the public whom we address in these pages. That the prophets should prophesy falsely is not the most important fact in national degradation: it is only when the people love to have it so that the climax is attained.

The other woman—who makes virtue vicious by keeping the physical facts of one relationship in life in constant prominence by denying, as Arabella does by satisfying them, and even more skilfully and insistently than Arabella—the fantastic *raisonneuse*,[4] Susan, completes the circle of the unclean. She marries to save herself from trouble; then quits her husband, to live a life of perpetual temptation and resistance with her lover; then marries, or professes to marry him, when her husband amiably divorces her without the reason he supposes himself to have; and then, when a selfish conscience is tardily awakened, returns to the husband, and ends in ostentatious acceptance of the conditions of matrimony at the moment when the unfortunate Jude, who has also been recaptured by the widowed Arabella, dies of his cruel misery. This woman we are required to accept as the type of high-toned purity. It is the women who are the active agents in all this unsavoury imbroglio: the story is carried on, and life is represented as carried on, entirely by

3. The reference seems to be to the second paragraph of Hardy's "Preface to the First Edition."
4. Woman who reasons or argues.

their means. The men are passive, suffering, rather good than otherwise, victims of these and of fate. Not only do they never dominate,
but they are quite incapable of holding their own against these
remorseless ministers of destiny, these determined operators, manag-
ing all the machinery of life so as to secure their own way. This is one
of the most curious developments of recent fiction. It is perhaps natural that it should be more or less the case in books written by women,
to whom the mere facility of representing their own sex acts as a primary reason for giving them the chief place in the scene. But it has
now still more markedly, though much less naturally, become the
method with men, in the hands of many of whom women have
returned to the *rôle* of the temptress given to them by the old monkish
sufferers of ancient times, who fled to the desert, like Anthony, to get
free of them, but even there barely escaped with their lives from the
seductions of the sirens, who were so audacious as to follow them to
the very scene of the macerations and miseries into which the unhappy
men plunged to escape from their toils. In the books of the younger
men, it is now the woman who seduces—it is no longer the man.

This, however, is a consideration by the way. I have said that it is
not clear what Mr. Hardy's motive is in the history of Jude: but, on
reconsideration, it becomes more clear that it is intended as an assault
on the stronghold of marriage, which is now beleaguered on every side.
The motto is, 'The letter killeth'; and I presume this must refer to the
fact of Jude's early and unwilling union to Arabella, and that the lesson
the novelist would have us learn is, that if marriage were not exacted,
and people were free to form connections as the spirit moves them,
none of these complications would have occurred, and all would have
been well. 'There seemed to him, vaguely and dimly, something wrong
in a social ritual which made necessary the cancelling of well-formed
schemes involving years of thought and labour, of foregoing a man's
one opportunity of showing himself superior to the lower animals, and
of contributing his units of work to the general progress of his generation, because of a momentary surprise by a new and transitory instinct
which had nothing in it of the nature of vice, and could be only at the
most called weakness.' This is the hero's own view of the circumstances
which, in obedience to the code of honour prevalent in the countryside,
compelled his marriage. Suppose, however, that instead of upsetting
the whole framework of society, Jude had shown himself superior to
the lower animals by not yielding to that new and transitory influence,
the same result could have been easily attained: and he might then
have met and married Susan and lived happy ever after, without
demanding a total overthrow of all existing laws and customs to prevent him from being unhappy. Had it been made possible for him to
have visited Arabella as long as the new and transitory influence lasted,
and then to have lived with Susan as long as she pleased to permit him

to do so, which was the best that could happen were marriage abol-
ished, how would that have altered the circumstances? When Susan
changed her mind would he have been less unhappy? When Arabella
claimed him again would he have been less weak?

Mr. Hardy's solution of the great insoluble question of what is to be
the fate of children in such circumstances brings this nauseous tragedy
suddenly and at a stroke into the regions of pure farce—which is a
surprise of the first quality, only too grotesque to be amusing. There
are children, as a matter of course: a weird little imp, the son of Arabella, and two babies of Susan's. What is the point of the allegory
which Mr. Hardy intends us to read in the absurd little gnome, nick-
named Old Father Time, who is the offspring of the buxom country
lass, is a secondary subject upon which we have no light: but it is by
the means of this strange creature that the difficulty is settled. In a
moment of dreadful poverty and depression, Susan informs her step-
son, whom she loves and is very kind to, of the severe straits in which
she is. The child—he is now fourteen—asks whether himself and the
others are not a great burden upon the parents who are already so poor;
and she consents that life would be easier without them. The result is
that when she comes in after a short absence she can find no trace of
the children, until she perceives what seems to be, at first, suits of their
clothes hanging against the wall, but discovers to be the children themselves, all hanged, and swinging from the clothes-pegs: the elder boy
having first hanged them and then himself to relieve the parent's
hands. Does Mr. Hardy think this is really a good way of disposing of
the unfortunate progeny of such connections? does he recommend it
for general adoption? It is at least a clean and decisive cut of the knot,
leaving no ragged ends; but then there is no natural provision in families of such a wise small child to get its progenitors out of trouble.
* * * Mr. Hardy knows, no doubt as everybody does, that the children
are a most serious part of the question of the abolition of marriage. Is
this the way in which he considers it would be resolved best?

EDMUND GOSSE

From Cosmopolis (January 1896)†

* * *

In *Jude the Obscure*, [Hardy][1] has aimed, in all probability, higher
than he ever aimed before, and it is not to be maintained that he has
been equally successful in every part of his design.

---

† On Gosse, see above, p. 346. Hardy's letters to Gosse, mentioning this review, are given above, on pp. 346–48. All notes are by the editor of this Norton Critical Edition.
1. Added by the editor of this Norton Critical Edition.

Before these pages find a reader, everybody will be familiar with *Jude the Obscure*, and we may well be excused, therefore, from repeating the story in detail. It will be remembered that it is a study of four lives, a rectangular problem in failures, drawn with almost mathematical rigidity. The tragedy of these four persons is constructed in a mode almost as geometrical as that in which Dr. Samuel Clarke[2] was wont to prove the existence of the Deity. It is difficult not to believe that the author set up his four ninepins in the wilds of Wessex, and built up his theorem round them. Here is an initial difficulty. Not quite thus is theology or poetry conveniently composed; we like to conceive that the relation of the parts was more spontaneous, we like to feel that the persons of a story have been thrown up in a jet of enthusiasm, not put into a cave of theory to be slowly covered with stalactite. In this I may be doing Mr. Hardy an injustice, but a certain hardness in the initial conception of *Jude the Obscure* cannot, I believe, be denied. Mr. Hardy is certainly to be condoled with upon the fact that his novel, which has been seven years in the making, has appeared at last at a moment when a sheaf of 'purpose' stories on the 'marriage question' (as it is called) have just been irritating the nerves of the British Patron. No serious critic, however, will accuse Mr. Hardy of joining the ranks of these deciduous troublers of our peace.

We come, therefore, without prejudice to his chronicle of four unnecessary lives. There are the poor village lad, with his longing for the intellectual career; the crude village beauty, like a dahlia in a cottage-garden; the neurotic, semi-educated girl of hyper-sensitive instincts; and the dull, earthy, but not ungenerous schoolmaster. On these four failures, inextricably tied together and dragging one another down, our attention is riveted—on Jude, Arabella, Sue and Phillotson. Before, however, we discuss their characteristics, we may give a little attention to the scene in which these are laid. Mr. Hardy, as all the world knows, has dedicated his life's work to the study of the old province of Wessex. * * * That he is never happy outside its borders is a commonplace; it is not quite so clearly perceived, perhaps, that he is happiest in the heart of it. When Mr. Hardy writes of South Wessex (Dorsetshire) he seldom goes wrong; this country has been the theatre for all his most splendid successes. From Abbot's Cornal to Budmouth Regis, and wherever the wind blows freshly off Egdon Heath, he is absolute master and king. But he is not content with such a limited realm; he claims four other counties, and it must be confessed that his authority weakens as he approaches their confines.

Jude the Obscure is acted in North Wessex (Berkshire) and just across the frontier, at Christminster (Oxford), which is not in Wessex at all. We want our novelist back among the rich orchards of the Hintocks,

2. Metaphysician and moralist, author of "A Demonstration of the Being and Attributes of God" (1704).

and where the water-lilies impede the lingering river at Shottsford Ash. Berkshire is an unpoetical county, 'meanly utilitarian', as Mr. Hardy confesses; the imagination hates its concave, loamy cornfields and dreary, hedgeless highways. The local history has been singularly tampered with in Berkshire; it is useless to speak to us of ancient records where the past is all obliterated, and the thatched and dormered houses replaced by modern cottages. In choosing North Wessex as the scene of a novel Mr. Hardy wilfully deprives himself of a great element of his strength. Where there are no prehistoric monuments, no ancient buildings, no mossed and immemorial woodlands, he is Samson shorn. In Berkshire, the change which is coming over England so rapidly, the resignation of the old dreamy elements of beauty, has proceeded further than anywhere else in Wessex. Pastoral loveliness is to be discovered only here and there, while in Dorsetshire it still remains the master-element. All this combines to lessen the physical charm of *Jude the Obscure* to those who turn from it in memory to *Far from the Madding Crowd* and *The Return of the Native*.

But, this fortuitous absence of beauty being acknowledged, the novelist's hand shows no falling off in the vigour and reality of his description. It may be held, in fact, to be a lesser feat to raise before us an enchanting vision of the valley of the Froom, than successfully to rivet our attention on the prosaic arable land encircling the dull hamlet of Marygreen. Most attractive Mr. Hardy's pictures of purely country life have certainly been—there is no picture in *Jude* to approach that of the life on the dairy farm in *Tess*—but he has never treated rural scenes with a more prodigious mastery and knowledge. It is, in fact, in knowledge, that Mr. Hardy's work of this class is so admirable. Mere observation will not produce this illusion of absolute truth. * * * we are never more happy than when he allows us to overhear the primitive Wessex speech. Our only quarrel with Mr. Hardy, indeed, in this respect, is that he grows now impatient of retailing to us the axiomatic humour, the crafty and narrow dignity of the villager.

To pass from the landscape to the persons, two threads of action seem to be intertwined in *Jude the Obscure*. We have, first of all, the contrast between the ideal life the young peasant of scholarly instincts wished to lead, and the squalid real life into which he was fated to sink. We have, secondly, the almost rectilinear puzzle of the sexual relations of the four principal characters. Mr. Hardy has wished to show how cruel destiny can be to the eternal dream of youth, and he has undertaken to trace the lamentable results of unions in a family exhausted by intermarriage and poverty. Some collision is apparent between these aims; the first seems to demand a poet, the second a physician. The Fawleys are a decayed and wasted race, in the last of whom, Jude, there appears, with a kind of flicker in the socket, a certain intellectual and artistic brightness. In favourable surroundings, we feel that this young man might have become fairly distinguished as a scholar, or as a sculptor. But at the supreme moment, or at each supreme moment, the conditions hurl him back into insignificance. When we examine clearly what these conditions are, we find them to be instinctive. He is just going to develop into a lad of education, when Arabella throws her hideous missile at him, and he sinks with her into a resigned inferiority.

So far, the critical court is with Mr. Hardy; these scenes and their results give a perfect impression of truth. Later on, it is not quite evident whether the claim on Jude's passions, or the inherent weakness of his inherited character, is the source of his failure. Perhaps both. But it is difficult to see what part Oxford has in his destruction, or how Mr. Hardy can excuse the rhetorical diatribes against the university which appear towards the close of the book. Does the novelist really think that it was the duty of the heads of houses to whom Jude wrote his crudely pathetic letters to offer him immediately a fellowship? We may admit to the full the pathos of Jude's position—nothing is more heart-rending than the obscurity of the half-educated—but surely, the fault did not lie with Oxford.

The scene at Commemoration (Part VI) is of a marvellous truth and vividness of presentment, but it would be stronger, and even more tragic, if Mr. Hardy did not appear in it as an advocate taking sides with his unhappy hero. In this portion of his work, it seems to me, Mr. Hardy had but to paint—as clearly and as truthfully as he could—the hopes, the struggles, the disappointments of Jude, and of these he has woven a tissue of sombre colouring, indeed, and even of harsh threads, but a tapestry worthy of a great imaginative writer. It was straightforward poet's work in invention and observation, and he has executed it well.

But in considering the quadruple fate of the four leading characters, of whom Jude is but one, we come to matter of a different order. Here the physician, the neuropathist, steps in, and takes the pen out of the poet's hand. Let us for a moment strip to its barest nomination this part of the plot. Jude, a neurotic subject in whom hereditary degeneracy takes an idealist turn, with some touch, perhaps, of what the new doctors call megalomania, has been warned by the local gossips not to marry. But he is physically powerful and attractive, and he engages the notice of Arabella, a young woman of gross instincts and fine appearance, who seduces and marries him. He falls from his scholastic dream to the level of a labourer, and is only saved by the fact that Arabella wearies of him and leaves him. He goes to Oxford, and, gradually cultivating the dream again, seems on the first rung of the ladder of success, when he comes across his own cousin Sue, and loves her. But she has promised to marry Phillotson, a weary middle-aged schoolmaster, and marry him she will, although she loves Jude, and has forced him to compromise her. But she finds Phillotson intolerable, and leaves him to join Jude, only to find herself equally unhappy and unsatisfying, dragging Jude once more down to mediocrity. Arabella crosses Jude's life again, and jealousy forces Sue to some semblance of love for Jude. Sue becomes the mother of several children, who are killed in a fit of infantile mania by a boy, the son of Jude and Arabella, whose habitual melancholy, combined with his hereditary antecedents, has prepared us for an outbreak of suicide, if not of murder. This horrible event affects Sue by producing religious mania. She will live no longer with Jude, although both couples have got their divorce, but fatally returns to be the slave of her detested schoolmaster, while Jude, in a paroxysm of drunken abandonment, goes back to Arabella and dies.

It is a ghastly story, especially when reduced to this naked skeleton. But it does not appear to me that we have any business to call in question the right of a novelist of Mr. Hardy's extreme distinction to treat what themes he will. We may wish—and I for my part cordially wish—that more pleasing, more charming plots than this could take his fancy. But I do not feel at liberty to challenge his discretion. One thing, however, the critic of comparative literature must note. We have, in such a book as *Jude the Obscure*, traced the full circle of propriety. A hundred and fifty years ago, Fielding and Smollett brought up before us pictures, used expressions, described conduct, which appeared to their immediate successors a little more crude than general reading warranted. In Miss Burney's hands and in Miss Austen's, the morals were still further hedged about. Scott was even more daintily reserved. We came at last to Dickens, where the clamorous passions of mankind, the coarser accidents of life, were absolutely ignored, and the whole question of population seemed reduced to the theory of the gooseberry bush. This was the *ne plus ultra* of decency; Thackeray and George Eliot relaxed this intensity of prudishness; once on the turn, the tide flowed rapidly, and here is Mr. Hardy ready to say any mortal thing that Fielding said, and a good deal more too.

So much we note, but to censure it, if it calls for censure, is the duty of the moralist and not the critic. Criticism asks how the thing is done, whether the execution is fine and convincing. To tell so squalid and so abnormal a story in an interesting way is in itself a feat, and this, it must be universally admitted, Mr. Hardy has achieved. *Jude the Obscure* is an irresistible book; it is one of those novels into which we descend and are carried on by a steady impetus to the close, when we return, dazzled, to the light of common day. The two women, in particular, are surely created by a master. Every impulse, every speech, which reveals to us the coarse and animal, but not hateful Arabella, adds to the solidity of her portrait. We may dislike her, we may hold her intrusion into our consciousness a disagreeable one, but of her reality there can be no question: Arabella lives.

It is conceivable that not so generally will it be admitted that Sue

Bridehead is convincing. Arabella is the excess of vulgar normality; every public bar and village fair knows Arabella, but Sue is a strange and unwelcome product of exhaustion. The *vita sexualis*[3] of Sue is the central interest of the book, and enough is told about it to fill the specimen tables of a German specialist. Fewer testimonies will be given to her reality than to Arabella's because hers is much the rarer case. But her picture is not less admirably drawn; Mr. Hardy has, perhaps, never devoted so much care to the portrait of a woman. She is a poor, maimed 'degenerate', ignorant of herself and of the perversion of her instincts, full of febrile, amiable illusions, ready to dramatize her empty life, and play at loving though she cannot love. Her adventure with the undergraduate has not taught her what she is; she quits Phillotson still ignorant of the source of her repulsion; she lives with Jude, after a long, agonizing struggle, in a relation that she accepts with distaste, and when the tragedy comes, and her children are killed, her poor extravagant brain slips one grade further down, and she sees in this calamity the chastisement of God. What has she done to be chastised? She does not know, but supposes it must be her abandonment of Phillotson, to whom, in a spasm of self-abasement, and shuddering with repulsion, she returns without a thought for the misery of Jude. It is a terrible study in pathology, but of the splendid success of it, of the sustained intellectual force implied in the evolution of it, there cannot, I think, be two opinions.

One word must be added about the speech of the author and of the characters in *Jude the Obscure*. Is it too late to urge Mr. Hardy to struggle against the jarring note of rebellion which seems growing upon him? It sounded in *Tess*, and here it is, more roughly expressed, further acerbated. What has Providence done to Mr. Hardy that he should rise up in the arable land of Wessex and shake his fist at his Creator? He should not force his talent, should not give way to these chimerical outbursts of philosophy falsely so called. His early romances were full of calm and lovely pantheism; he seemed in them to feel the deep-hued country landscapes full of rural gods, all homely and benign. We wish he would go back to Egdon Heath and listen to the singing in the heather. And as to the conversations of his semi-educated characters, they are really terrible. Sue and Jude talk a sort of University Extension jargon that breaks the heart. 'The mediaevalism of Christminster must go, be sloughed off, or Christminster will have to go', says Sue, as she sits in a pair of Jude's trousers, while Jude dries her petticoat at his garret-fire. Hoity-toity, for a minx! the reader cries, or, rather, although he firmly believes in the existence of Sue, and in the truth of the episode, he is convinced that Mr. Hardy is mistaken in what he heard her say. She *could* not have talked like that.

3. Sex life.

D. F. HANNIGAN

From the Westminster Review (January 1896)†

* * * The history of Jude's ineffectual efforts to obtain a University education is intensely pathetic. If Samuel Johnson could come back to earth and read this portion of Mr. Hardy's last novel, I venture to think that he would have found it hard to keep back his tears, stern Briton though he was; and, but for the miserable priggery of this tail-end of the nineteenth century, the first part of *Jude the Obscure* would be held up by the critics as one of the most touching records in all literature. This story of crushed aspirations can only be appreciated by those who have the power of true sympathy. Unfortunately, we live in an age when nearly all human beings are concerned only with their material success in life. The word 'failure' makes them tremble; and, no doubt, Mr. Hardy's apparent pessimism is distasteful to the innumerable throng of vulgar-minded aspirants whose only gospel is to 'get on' by hook or by crook. How could we expect the modern young man, whose thoughts are fixed solely on the Woolsack or on the results of a suc-cessful experiment on the Turf or the Stock Exchange, to enter into the feelings of a poor rustic stone-cutter who dreamed of taking out his degree and becoming a clergyman! The love-affairs of so obscure an individual may excite the attention of the unambitious middle-aged man, but not of the youthful prig of our day. The relations between Sue and her cousin will necessarily appear impure to those who see nothing but uncleanness in the relations of a married man and a woman who is not his wife. But Mr. Hardy is not to blame for the brutishness of some of his readers' minds any more than Miranda (to borrow a favourite illustration of Mr. Ruskin) is to blame for Caliban's beastly thoughts about her.

The 'plot' (hideous word!) of *Jude the Obscure* has been sketched, and, indeed, misrepresented, by so many of the smug journalistic critics of this book, that it is better to let all intelligent and honest readers find out the true history of Jude Fawley for themselves by reading the novel. It is certainly 'strong meat', but there is nothing prurient, noth-ing artificial in this work; it is *human* in the widest sense of that com-prehensive word. The tragic chapter with which the novel closes is perhaps the finest specimen of pure narrative that Mr. Hardy has ever given us—there is nothing equal to it in *Tess of the D'Urbervilles*. The character of Sue is nearly as fascinating as that of Elfride in *A Pair of Blue Eyes*. In concentrated power the novel, as a whole, is inferior to *Tess*, and it lacks the fresh, sweet atmosphere which makes *The Wood-*

† Denis F. Hannigan was a reviewer and the translator of several French novels.

landers one of the most delightful of books. In Arabella we have a faithful portrait of a foul-minded woman whom we can compare to no other female personage in Mr. Hardy's novels. Some of the language put into the mouth of Phillotson, the husband of Sue, is a little incongruous, for it is scarcely likely that a village schoolmaster would talk about 'the matriarchal system'.

But in spite of certain defects of form which are perhaps inevitable, having regard to the intricacies of a story involving matrimonial complications, *Jude the Obscure* is the best English novel which has appeared since *Tess of the D'Urbervilles*. Mr. George Meredith's epigrammatic cleverness cannot atone for his poverty of invention, his lack of incident, his fantastic system of misreading human nature, and, if the word 'novelist' means a writer of human history, Mr. Hardy is incomparably superior to his supposed rival. I would class the author of *Tess* with Fielding, Balzac, Flaubert, Turgenev, George Eliot and Dostoievsky; while Mr. Meredith is the literary brother of Bulwer Lytton, Peacock and Mérimée. The mosquito-like criticism of the day need not trouble a novelist who has already won fame. He is the greatest living English writer of fiction. In intensity, in grip of life, and, above all, in the artistic combination of the real and the ideal, he surpasses any of his French contemporaries. *Jude the Obscure* is not his greatest work; but no other living novelist could have written it.

W. W. HOW, BISHOP OF WAKEFIELD

Letter to the Yorkshire Post (June 9, 1896)†

SIR,

Will you allow me publicly to thank you for your outspoken leader in your to-day's issue denouncing the intolerable grossness and hateful sneering at all that one most reveres in such writers as Thomas Hardy?

On the authority of one of those reviews which you justly condemn for their reticence, I bought a copy of one of Mr. Hardy's novels, but was so disgusted with its insolence and indecency that I threw it into the fire. It is a disgrace to our great public libraries to admit such garbage, clever though it may be, to their shelves.

I am, Sir

Yours, etc.

WILLIAM WALSHAM WAKEFIELD

† On June 8, 1896, the *Yorkshire Post*, a daily newspaper widely read in the north of England, published a leading article denouncing Hardy's work in general and *Jude the Obscure* in particular. The following day it published this letter from W. W. How, Bishop of Wakefield; for Hardy's account of it, see p. 341.

HAVELOCK ELLIS

From the Savoy Magazine (October 1896)†

*   *   *

To sum up, *Jude the Obscure* seems to me—in such a matter one can only give one's own impressions for what they are worth—a singularly fine piece of art, when we remember the present position of the English novel. It is the natural outcome of Mr. Hardy's development, along lines that are genuinely and completely English. It deals very subtly and sensitively with new and modern aspects of life, and if, in so doing, it may be said to represent Nature as often cruel to our social laws, we must remark that the strife of Nature and Society, the individual and the community, has ever been the artist's opportunity. 'Matrimony have growed to be that serious in these days', Widow Edlin remarks, 'that one really do feel afeard to move in it at all.' It is an affectation to pretend that the farmyard theory of life still rules unquestioned, and that there are no facts to justify Mrs. Edlin. If anyone will not hear her, let him turn to the Registrar-General. Such facts are in our civilization today. We have no right to resent the grave and serious spirit with which Mr. Hardy, in the maturity of his genius, has devoted his best art to picture some of these facts. In *Jude the Obscure* we find for the first time in our literature the reality of marriage clearly recognized as something wholly apart from the mere ceremony with which our novelists have usually identified it. Others among our novelists may have tried to deal with the reality rather than with its shadow, but assuredly not with the audacity, purity and sincerity of an artist who is akin in spirit to the great artists of our best dramatic age, to Fletcher and Heywood and Ford, rather than to the powerful though often clumsy novelists of the eighteenth century.

There is one other complaint often brought against this book, I understand, by critics usually regarded as intelligent, and with the mention of it I have done. 'Mr. Hardy finds that marriage often leads to tragedy,' they say, 'but he shows us no way out of these difficulties; he does not tell us his own plans for the improvement of marriage and the promotion of morality.' Let us try to consider this complaint with due solemnity. It is true that the artist is god in his own world; but being so he has too fine a sense of the etiquette of creation to presume to offer suggestions to the creator of the actual world, suggestions

---

† Ellis (1859–1939) was both a scientist and a literary scholar and critic. The publication of the first volume of his *Studies in the Psychology of Sex* in 1897 led to a prosecution for obscenity. The text extracted below forms the concluding section of a long essay, "Concerning *Jude the Obscure*."

which might be resented, and would almost certainly not be adopted. An artist's private opinions concerning the things that are good and bad in the larger world are sufficiently implicit in the structure of his own smaller world; the counsel that he should make them explicit in a code or rules and regulations for humanity at large is a counsel which, as every artist knows, can only come from the Evil One. This complaint against *Jude the Obscure* could not have arisen save among a generation which has battened on moral and immoral tracts thrown into the form of fiction by ingenious novices.

Modern Criticism

IRVING HOWE

["A Distinctively Modern Novel"]†

* * * By 1895, the year *Jude* came out, Hardy was in his mid-fifties, an established writer who had composed two great novels and several of distinction. But he was more than a famous or honored writer. For the English-speaking world he had become a moral presence genuinely affecting the lives of those who read him.

When Hardy first printed *Jude the Obscure* as a monthly serial in *Harper's Magazine* between December 1894 and November 1895, he agreed to cut some of its most vital parts: those which showed Jude to be harried by sexual desire, others reporting that Jude and Sue Bridehead did finally go to bed together, and still others displaying Hardy's gift for a muted but humorous earthiness. In the serial Jude and Sue did not have a child; more demurely, they adopted one. Arabella, when she got Jude back and flooded him with liquor, ended the evening by tucking him into bed in a spare room. Today such mutilations by a serious writer would provoke an uproar of judgment; but Hardy, not being the kind of man who cared to languish in a garret, did what he had to do in order to sell the serial rights. In any case, he knew that his true novel, the one later generations would read and judge him by, was soon to appear in hard covers.

Some months later, when the book came out, it stirred up a storm of righteousness. Many of the reviewers adopted a high moral tone, denouncing Hardy's apparent hostility to the institution of marriage while choosing to neglect the sympathy he showed toward people caught up in troublesome relationships, whether in or out of marriage. One true-blooded Englishman, the Bishop of Wakefield, publicly announced that he "was so disgusted with [the book's] insolence and indecency that I threw it into the fire." To which Hardy added that probably the bishop had chosen to burn the book because he could not burn the author.

† From Irving Howe, *Thomas Hardy* (New York: The Macmillan Company, 1967) 132–46. Reprinted by permission. Bracketed page numbers refer to this Norton Critical Edition.

Later, writing to his friend Edmund Gosse, Hardy denied that the novel was "a manifesto on the marriage question, although, of course, it involves it." This is precisely the kind of distinction that most of the contemporary reviewers neither could nor wished to understand: they were, like most reviewers of any age, blunt-minded journalists who demanded from a work of art that it confirm the settled opinions they already had. What Hardy was getting at in his letter to Gosse is an idea now commonly accepted by serious writers: that while a work of fiction may frequently raise social and moral problems, the artist's main intention is to explore them freely rather than take hard-and-fast public positions. In his 1895 preface to *Jude the Obscure* Hardy make quite clear his larger purpose in composing the book:

> . . . to deal unaffectedly with the fret and fever, derision and disaster, that may press in the wake of the strongest passion known to humanity; to tell, without a mincing of words, of a deadly war waged between flesh and spirit; and to point the tragedy of unfulfilled aims. [5]

Nor were these new concerns for Hardy. In his earlier novels he had already shown what a torment an ill-suited marriage can be; he had known himself, through much of his first marriage, the dumb misery that follows upon decayed affections. By the 1890s, when England was beginning to shake loose from the grip of Victorian moralism, the cultivated minority public was ready for his gaunt honesty, even if the bulk of novel readers was not. That marriage had become a *problem*, that somehow it was in crisis and need of reform, was an idea very much in the air. During the 1890s the notorious Parnell case, involving an adultery suit against the leader of Irish nationalism, split the English-speaking world into hostile camps but also forced a relatively candid discussion of the realities of conjugal life. The plays of Ibsen were being performed in English translation during the years *Jude* was written, and their caustic inquiry into the evasions and repressions of middle-class marriage may have found an echo in Hardy's book. And through the late 1880s Hardy had been reading the work of Schopenhauer and von Hartmann, pessimistic German philosophers who had recently been translated into English; he did not need their help, or anyone else's, in order to reach his "twilight view" of man's diminished place in the universe, but he did find in their philosophic speculations a support—he might have said a confirmation—for his own temperamental bias.

Hardy's last novel was not quite the outcry of a lonely and embittered iconoclast that it has sometimes been said to be, *Jude* displeased official opinion, both literary and moral; it outraged the pieties of middle-class England to an extent few of Hardy's contemporaries were inclined to risk; but it also reflected the sentiments of advanced intellectual circles in the 1890s. Thus while it is true that *Jude* was not meant to be "a manifesto on the marriage question," the book could hardly have been written fifteen or twenty years earlier. Coming at the moment it did, *Jude* played a part in the modern transformation of marriage from a sacred rite to a secular and thereby problematic relationship—just as those nineteenth century writers who tried to salvage Christianity by scraping it of dogma and superstitution unwittingly helped to undermine the whole structure of theism.

Jude the Obscure is Hardy's most distinctly "modern" work, for it rests upon a cluster of assumptions central to modernist literature: that in our time men wishing to be more than dumb clods must live in permanent doubt and intellectual crisis; that for such men, to whom traditional beliefs are no longer available, life has become inherently problematic; that in the course of their years they must face even more than the usual allotment of loneliness and anguish; that in their cerebral overdevelopment they run the danger of losing those primary appetites for life which keep the human race going; and that courage, if it is to be found at all, consists in a readiness to accept pain while refusing the comforts of certainty. If Hardy, excessively thin-skinned as he was, suffered from the attacks *Jude* brought down upon his head, he should have realized—as in his moments of shrewdness he did— that attack was precisely what he had to expect. For he had threatened his readers not merely in their opinions but in their deepest unspoken values: the first was forgivable, the second not.

In its deepest impress *Jude the Obscure* is not the kind of novel that compels one to reflect upon the idea of history, certainly not in the ways that Tolstoy's *War and Peace* or Stendhal's *The Red and the Black* do. Nor is it the kind of novel that draws our strongest attention to the causes, patterns and turnings of large historical trends as these condition the lives of a few centered characters. The sense *Jude* leaves one with, the quality of the pain it inflicts, has mostly to do with the sheer difficulty of human beings living elbow to elbow and heart to heart; the difficulty of being unable to bear prolonged isolation or prolonged closeness; the difficulty, at least for reflective men, of getting through the unspoken miseries of daily life. Yet to grasp the full stringencies of Jude's private ordeal, one must possess a strong historical awareness.

The English working class, coming to birth through the trauma of the Industrial Revolution, suffered not merely from brutality, hunger and deprivation, but from an oppressive snobbism, at times merely patronizing and at other times proudly violent, on the part of the "superior" social classes. By the middle of the nineteenth century a minority of intellectuals and reformers had begun to display an active sympathy for the workers: they could not live in peace while millions of country men lived in degradation. But meanwhile, and going as far back as the late eighteenth century, something far more important had begun to happen among the English workers themselves—the first stirrings of intellectual consciousness, the first signs of social and moral solidarity. Working-men began to appear who sought to train their minds, to satisfy their parched imaginations, to grasp for themselves a fragment of that traditional culture from which Western society had coldly locked them out.

The rise of the self-educated proletarian is one of the most remarkable facts in nineteenth century English history. Frequently this new man discovered himself through the trade union and socialist movements, which brought to him a sense of historical mission, an assignment of destiny and role; but he could also be found elsewhere. Struggling after long hours of labor to master the rudiments of learning, he flourished in the dissident chapels which had shot up in England beyond the privileged ground of the Anglican Church; in the lecture courses and night schools that were started by intellectual missionaries; in little reading "circles" that were formed amidst the degradation of the slums. For some of these men education meant primarily a promise of escape from their cramped social position; for others, no doubt a minority, it could approximate what it meant to Jude Fawley—a joy, pure and disinterested, in the life of the mind.[1]

English fiction was slow to absorb this remarkable new figure, just as it was slow to deal with the life of the working class as a whole. There are glimpses of the self-educated worker in the novels of George Gissing; he appears a bit more fully in the "Five Towns" fiction of Arnold Bennett, and still more impressively in D. H. Lawrence's early novels; and in recent years, as he begins to fade from the social scene, he is looked back upon with nostalgia in novels about the early English Labor movement written by Raymond Williams and Walter Allen.

Now Jude Fawley is not himself a character within this tradition. But he is close to it, a sort of rural cousin of the self-educated worker; and I think it can be said that unless the latter had begun to seem a significant type in late nineteenth century England, Hardy could not have imagined as strongly as he did the intellectual yearnings of Jude. That in his last novel Hardy should have turned to a figure like Jude is itself evidence of a major shift in outlook. The fixity of Hardy's rural attachments was, in the previous Wessex novels, so deep as to provide him with something equivalent to a moral absolute, a constant of moral security through which to set off—yet keep at a manageable distance—those of his characters troubled by unrest. But Hardy, by the point he

1. In 1912 Hardy remarked, with forgivable pride, that "some readers thought . . . that when Ruskin College was . . . founded it should have been called the College of Jude the Obscure." Ruskin College at Oxford was the first English college designed to enable needy but gifted working-class boys to attend a university.

had reached in *Jude the Obscure*, could no longer find in the world of Wessex a sufficient moral and emotional support. His feelings had come to a pained recognition that Wessex and all it stood for was slipping out of his fingers, changing shape beyond what he remembered from his youth, receding into history. And as for Jude, though he comes from the country, he spends most of his life in the towns. The matters upon which Jude's heart and mind must feed, the matter which rouses him to excitement and then leaves him broken, is the intellectual disturbance of modern life—and that, for good or bad, can be found only in the towns. Not born a worker, and without the political interests which usually spurred the self-educated proletarian to read and study, Jude nevertheless shares in the latter's passion for self-improvement, as well as in the pathos of knowing that never can he really know enough. Jude is Hardy's equivalent of the self-educated worker: the self-educated worker transplanted into the Wessex world. So that when Hardy first conceived of Jude in that notable clause, "a young man who could not go to Oxford," he was foreshadowing not merely one man's deprivation but the turmoil of an entire social group.

Socially, Jude hovers somewhere between an old-fashioned artisan and a modern worker. The kind of work he does, restoring old churches, pertains to the traditional English past, but the way he does it, hiring himself out for wages, points to the future. His desire for learning, both as a boy trying to come by a Greek grammar and then as a man walking awestruck through the chill streets of Christminster (Oxford), is portrayed by Hardy with enormous sympathy. But to stress this sympathy is not at all to share the view of some critics that Hardy is so deeply involved with Jude's yearnings, he cannot bring to bear upon them any critical irony. What but somberly ironic is the incident in which Jude receives a crushing reply from the Christminster master to whom he has applied for advice, and what but devastatingly ironic is the scene in which Jude drunkenly flaunts his Latin before the good-natured uncomprehending artisans at the Christminster tavern? Jude is a thoroughly individualized figure, an achievement made possible by Hardy's balance of sympathy and distance; but Jude's personal drama is woven from the materials of historical change, the transformation and uprooting of traditional English life.

The same holds true for Sue Bridehead. She is a triumph of psychological portraiture—and to that we shall return. But the contours of her psychology are themselves shaped by a new historical situation. She could not possibly appear in a novel by Jane Austen or Dickens or Thackeray; her style of thought, her winsome charms and maddening indecisions, are all conditioned by the growth of intellectual skepticism and modernist sensibility. She is the first major anticipation in the English novel of that profoundly affecting and troublesome creature: the modern girl. If she could not appear in an earlier nineteenth century novel, she certainly could in a twentieth century one—the only difference would probably be that now, living in her neat brownstone apartment in Manhattan or stylish flat in London and working for a publishing house or television company, she would have learned to accept a "healthier" attitude toward sex. Or at the least, she would have learned to pretend it.

In the last third of the nineteenth century, the situation of women changed radically: from subordinate domesticity and Victorian repression to the first signs of emancipation, leading often enough to the poignant bewilderments of a Sue Bridehead. So that while Sue, like Jude, is an intensely individualized figure, she is also characteristic of a moment in recent history; indeed, the force with which Hardy has made her so uniquely alive depends a great deal on the accuracy with which he has placed her historically.

Between Jude and Sue there is a special closeness, and this too has been historically conditioned. It is the closeness of lovers, but more than that. It is the closeness of intellectual companions, but more again. In Jane Austen's *Pride and Prejudice* Elizabeth Bennet and Mr. Darcy make their way past comic misunderstandings to a happy marriage, for they share a sense of superior cultivation and, with the additional advantage of status, can expect to keep themselves in a semi-protected circle, a little apart from the dull but worthy people surrounding them. At home in their society, they can yet maintain a comfortable distance from it. In Emily Brontë's *Wuthering Heights* Heathcliff and Cathy, in their moments of ecstasy, cut themselves off from common life, neither accepting nor rebelling against society, but refusing the very idea of it. In George Eliot's *Middlemarch* Dorothea Brooke and Lydgate, the two figures who should come together but through force of circumstances and vanity do not, envision a union in which they would struggle in behalf of those serious values their society disdains. They know the struggle would be difficult, but do not regard it as impossible. But by *Jude the Obscure* there is neither enclave nor retreat, evasion nor grasped opportunity for resistance. Jude and Sue are lost souls; they have no place in the world they can cherish or to which they can retreat; their goals are hardly to be comprehended in worldly terms at all. Lonely, distraught, rootless, they cling to one another like children in the night. Exposed to the racking sensations of homelessness, they become prey to a kind of panic whenever they are long separated from each other. The closeness of the lost—clutching, solacing and destroying one another—is a closeness of a special kind, which makes not for heroism or tragedy or even an exalted suffering, but for that somewhat passive "modern" sadness which suffuses *Jude the Obscure*.

Now it would be foolish to suppose that the social history of nineteenth century England can be neatly registered in this sketch of changing assumptions from Jane Austen to Thomas Hardy—though by 1900 there was, I think, good reason for cultivated persons to feel more estranged from their society than their great-grandparents might have felt in 1800. What can plausibly be assumed is that there were serious historical pressures behind the increasingly critical attitudes that nineteenth century English novelists took toward their society. Hardy comes at the end of one tradition, that of the solid extroverted English novel originating mostly with Henry Fielding; but he also comes at the beginning of another tradition, that of the literary "modernism" which would dominate the twentieth century. In personal background, novelistic technique, choice of locale and characters, Hardy remains mostly of the past; but in his distinctive sensibility, he is partly of the future. He moves somewhat beyond, though he does not quite abandon, the realistic social novel such as George Eliot and Thackeray wrote, and by *Jude the Obscure* he is composing the kind of fiction about which one is tempted to employ such terms as expressionist, stylized, grotesque, symbolic distortion and a portrait of extreme situations. None of these is wholly to the point, yet all suggest that this last of Hardy's novels cannot be fully apprehended if read as a conventional realistic work. Not by its fullness or probability as a rendering of common life, but by its power and coherence as a vision of modern deracination—so must the book be judged. It is not a balanced or temperate work; it will not satisfy well-adjusted minds content with the blessings of the wholesome; it does not pretend to show the human situation in its many-sidedness. Committed to an extreme darkness of view, a promethean resistance to fatality, *Jude the Obscure* shares in the spirit of the Book of Job, whose author seems also to have been a pessimist. In the history of Hardy criticism *Jude the Obscure* provides a touchstone of taste: the older and more traditional critics, loving Hardy for the charm and comeliness of his Wessex portraiture, have usually disparaged the book as morbid, while the more recent and modern critics are inclined to regard its very starkness as a sign of truth.

To present *Jude the Obscure* as a distinctively modern novel is surely an exaggeration; but it is an exaggeration I think valuable to propose, since it helps to isolate those elements which make the book seem so close to us in spirit. There is, in regard to *Jude the Obscure*, an experience shared by many of its readers: we soon notice its fragility of structure, we are likely to be troubled by its persistent depressiveness and its tendency to prompt a fate already more than cruel, yet at the end we are forced to acknowledge that the book has moved and shaken us. This seeming paradox is almost impossible to explain if *Jude* is regarded as a conventional realistic novel; it becomes easier to account for if the book is read as a dramatic fable in which the traditional esthetic criteria of unity and verisimilitude are subordinated to those of a distended expressiveness.

In Hardy's earlier novels, as in most of nineteenth century English fiction, characters tend to be presented as fixed and synthesized entities, as knowable public events. They function in a social medium; they form the sum or resultant of a set of distinguishable traits; they act out, in their depicted conduct, the consequences and implications of these traits; and their very "meaning" as characters in a novel derives from the action to which they are entirely bound. In a book like *The Mayor of Casterbridge* the central figure, Michael Henchard, becomes known to us through his action: what he does is what he is. It would be impudent to suppose that in writing *The Mayor* Hardy did not realize that human beings have a complex inner life, or that there are discrepancies between one's inner and outer, private and public, experience. Of course he knew this, and so did such novelists as Fielding, Jane Austen and Thackeray. But in their work, as a rule, the inner life of the characters is to be inferred from their public behavior, or from the author's analytic synopses.

By *Jude the Obscure* Hardy is beginning to move away from this mode of characterization. He is still quite far from that intense hovering scrutiny to which James subjects his figures, nor does he venture upon that dissolution of public character into a stream of psychic notation and event which can be found in Virginia Woolf and James Joyce. Yet we are made aware, while reading *Jude the Obscure*, that human character is being regarded as severely problematic, open to far-reaching speculative inquiry, and perhaps beyond certain knowledge; that the character of someone like Sue Bridehead must be seen not as a coherent force realizing itself in self-consistent public action, but as an amorphous and ill-charted arena in which irrational impulses conflict with one another; and that behind the interplay of events occupying the foreground of the novel there is a series of distorted psychic shadows which, with some wrenching, can be taken to provide the true "action" of the book.

Thinking, for example, of Jude Fawley, we are inclined to see him as a man whose very being constitutes a kind of battlefield and who matters, consequently, more for what happens within him than for what happens to him. He is racked by drives he cannot control, drives he barely understands. Powerfully sexed, drawn immediately to Arabella's hearty if somewhat soiled physical life, Jude is in constant revolt against his own nature. (That revolt comprises a major portion of the novel's inner action "behind" its visible action.) Jude responds far more spontaneously to Arabella than to Sue, for Arabella is unmistakably female and every now and then he needs a bit of wallowing in sex and drink to relieve him from the strain of his ambition and spirituality. At the same time Jude is forever caught up with Sue, who represents an equivalent or extension of his unsettled consciousness, quick and brittle as he is slow and cluttered, and therefore all the more attractive to him, as a vivid bird might be to a bear. The two of them are linked in seriousness, in desolation, in tormenting kindness, but above all, in an overbred nervousness. Theirs is a companionship of the nerves.

At least in part, Jude seems an anticipation of modern rationality struggling to become proudly self-sufficient and thereby cutting itself off from its sources in physical life. Though he is born in the country and lives mostly in towns, Jude could soon enough adapt himself to the twentieth century city: his mental life, in its creasing divisions and dissociations, is that of the modern metropolis. Destined to the role of stranger, he stops here and rests there, but without community, place or home. His frustration derives not so much from a denial of his desires as from their crossing and confusion; and as he struggles to keep in harmony his rumbling sensuality, his diffused ambition and his high ethical intent, one is reminded a little of St. Augustine's plaint to God: "Thou has counselled a better course than thou hast permitted."

Even more than Jude, Sue Bridehead invites psychological scrutiny; indeed, she is one of the great triumphs of psychological portraiture in the English novel. Sue is that terrifying specter of our age, before whom men and cultures tremble: she is an *interesting* girl. She is promethean in mind but masochist in character; and the division destroys her, making a shambles of her mind and a mere sterile discipline of her character. She is all intellectual seriousness, but without that security of will which enables one to live out the consequences of an idea to their limit. She is all feminine charm, but without body, without flesh or smell, without femaleness. Lacking focused sexuality, she casts a vaguely sexual aura over everything she touches. Her sensibility is kindled but her senses are mute. Quite without pride in status or self, she is consumed by vanity, the vanity of the sufferer who takes his suffering as a mark of distinction and bears a cross heavier than even fate might demand. Sue cannot leave anything alone, neither her men nor herself: she needs always to be tampering and testing, communicating and quivering. D. H. Lawrence, quick to see in Sue Bridehead the antithesis of his idea of the woman, writes of her with a fascinated loathing:

> She is the production of the long selection by man of the woman in whom the female is subordinate to the male principle. . . .
> Her female spirit did not wed with the male spirit. . . . Her spirit submitted to the male spirit, owned the priority of the male spirit, wished to become the male spirit. . . .
> One of the supremest products of our civilization is Sue, and a product that well frightens us. . . .
> She must, by the constitution of her nature, remain quite physically intact, for the female was atrophied in her, to the enlargement of the male activity. Yet she wanted some quickening for

this atrophied female. She wanted even kisses. That the new rousing might give her a sense of life. But she could only *live* in the
mind . . .

Here, then, was her difficulty: to find a man whose vitality could
infuse her and make her live, and who would not, at the same
time, demand of her a return of the female impulse into him.
What man could receive this drainage, receiving nothing back
again? He must either die or revolt.

Yet one thing more, surely the most important, must be said about
Sue Bridehead. As she appears in the novel itself, rather than in the
grinder of analysis, she is an utterly charming and vibrant creature. We
grasp directly, and not merely because we are told, why Jude finds
himself unable to resist Sue. Hardy draws her with a marvelous plas-
ticity, an affectionate yet critical attentiveness. She is happily charming
when she first encounters Jude at the martyr's cross: " 'I am not going
to meet you just there, for the first time in my life! Come farther on' ".
[81] She is pathetically charming when she escapes the training school
and, dripping wet, comes to Jude's chambers. And there is even charm
of a morbid kind when she rehearses in church with Jude the wedding
she is soon to seal with Phillotson. " 'I like to do things like this,' " she
tells him, "in the delicate voice of an epicure in emotions" [138]—
and in that remark lies a universe of unrest and perversity.

What has been said here about the distinctively "modern" element
in *Jude the Obscure* holds not merely for its characterization but also
for its narrative structure. The novel does not depend primarily on a
traditional plot, by means of which there is revealed and acted out a
major destiny, such as Henchard's in *The Mayor of Casterbridge*. A plot
consists of an action purposefully carved out of time, that is, provided
with a beginning, sequence of development and climax, so that it will
create the impression of completeness. Often this impression comes
from the sense that the action of a novel, as given shape by the plot,
has exhausted its possibilities of significant extension; the problems
and premises with which it began have reached an appropriate termi-
nus. Thus we can say that in the traditional kind of novel it is usually
the plot which carries or releases a body of meanings: these can be
profound or trivial, comic or tragic. *The Mayor of Casterbridge* contains
a plot which fulfills the potential for self-destruction in the character
of Henchard—but it is important to notice that in *this* kind of novel
we would have no knowledge of that potential except insofar as we can
observe its effects through an action. Plot here comes to seem inseparable from meaning, and meaning to inhere in plot.

When a writer works out a plot, he tacitly assumes that there is a
rational structure in human conduct, that this structure can be ascertained, and that doing so he is enabled to provide his work with a
sequence of order. But in "modernist" literature these assumptions

come into question. In a work written on the premise that there is no secure meaning in the portrayed action, or that while the action can hold our attention and rouse our feelings, we cannot be certain, indeed must remain uncertain, as to the possibilities of meaning—in such a characteristically modern work what matters is not so much the plot but a series of *situations*, some of which can be portrayed statically, through tableaux, set-pieces, depth psychology, and others dynamically, through linked episodes, stream of consciousness, etc. Kafka's fiction, Joyce's novels, some of Faulkner's, like *The Sound and the Fury*—these all contain situations rather than plots. *Jude the Obscure* does not go nearly so far along the path of modernism as these works, but it goes as far as Hardy could. It is consequently a novel in which plot does not signify nearly so much as in his more traditional novels.

With a little trouble one could block out the main lines of a plot in *Jude the Obscure*: the protagonist, spurred by the dominant needs of his character, becomes involved in a series of complications, and these, in turn, lead to a climax of defeat and death. Yet the curve of action thus described would not, I think, bring one to what is most valuable and affecting in the novel—as a similar kind of description would in regard to *The Mayor of Casterbridge*. What is essential in *Jude*, surviving and deepening in memory, is a series of moments rather than a sequence of actions. These moments—one might also call them panels of representation—tend to resemble snapshots rather than moving pictures, concentrated vignettes rather than worked-up dramatic scenes. They center upon Jude and Sue at critical points of their experience, at the times they are together, precious and intolerable as these are, and the times they are apart, necessary and hateful as these are. Together, Jude and Sue anticipate that claustrophobic and self-destructive concentration on "personal relationships" which is to be so pervasive a theme in the twentieth century novel. They suffer, as well, from another "modern" difficulty: that of thoughtful and self-reflective persons who have become so absorbed with knowing their experience, they become unable to live it. Their predicament is "tragic" in that deeply serious and modern sense of the word which teaches us that human waste, the waste of spirit and potential, is a terrible thing. Yet a tragedy in any classical sense *Jude* is not, for it directs our attention not to the fateful action of a looming protagonist but to the inner torments of familiar contemporaries. In classical tragedy, the hero realizes himself through an action. In the modern novel, the central action occurs within the psyche of the hero. And *Jude*, in the last analysis, is a novel dominated by psychology.

It is not the kind of book that can offer the lure of catharsis or the relief of conciliation. It does not pretend to satisfy the classical standard of a composure won through or after suffering: for the quality it communicates most strongly is that of naked pain. Awkward, subjective, overwrought and embittered, *Jude the Obscure* contains moments of intense revelation, at almost any point where the two central figures come together, and moments of glaring falsity, as in the botched incident of Father Time's death. (Botched not in conception but in execution: it was a genuine insight to present the little boy as one of those who were losing the will to live, but a failure in tact to burden him with so much philosophical weight.) Such mixtures of psychological veracity and crude melodrama are characteristic of Hardy, a novelist almost always better in parts than the whole. Yet the final impact of the book is shattering. Here, in its first stirrings, is the gray poetry of modern loneliness, which Jude brings to apotheosis in the terrible words, *"Let the day perish wherein I was born, and the night in which it was said, There is a man child conceived."*

ARTHUR MIZENER

Jude the Obscure as a Tragedy†

* * *

Jude the Obscure is, then, the history of a worthy man's education. Part One, for example, is primarily an account of Jude's youth up to the moment he departs for Christminster in search of learning. From the very beginning, however, Jude and the world through which he moves are presented as they appear to the eyes of one who has accepted the view of things which will be the end-product of Jude's education. In so far as Jude understands this view of things, he is not dramatized; he is the author. In so far as, in his innocence, he ignores the necessities and their implications which this view sees, he is dramatized, objectified by Hardy's irony. Hardy's narrative is, then, secondarily, a demonstration of the consequences of Jude's innocent ignorance of "Nature's logic"—in Part One in the matter of sex. Nature takes its revenge by entangling Jude irretrievably with Arabella. Hardy gives this demonstration a complex poetic elaboration, and it is easy to suppose as a consequence that his narrative is fundamentally symbolic, the pitting of two different views of experience—Jude's and Arabella's—against each other in a neutral arena. That it is not is evident from the fact that Hardy as the narrator takes advantage of every opportunity to support Jude's attitude. Furthermore, this part cannot, as symbolic narrative, be fitted into any pattern which runs through the book as a whole, for the only pattern *Jude* has is the pattern of history.

† "*Jude the Obscure* as a Tragedy," *Southern Review* 6 (1940–41): 203–13. Some of the author's notes have been omitted. Bracketed page numbers refer to this Norton Critical Edition.

Nevertheless the poetic elaboration of this episode is interesting as an example, characteristic of the procedure of the book as a whole, of how Hardy's idea, striving to establish a form which will make sense of it, is constantly breaking through the limits of the naturalistic form. The meeting of Arabella and Jude, for example, is brought about by Arabella's hitting Jude with a pig's pizzle. No better image for what drew Arabella and Jude together could be found, and, a symbol of their meeting, the pig's pizzle hangs on the bridge rail between them throughout their first meeting. Thereafter, Arabella scarcely appears in this part unaccompanied by pigs. In the same way Jude's dream of an education which will take him through Christminster to a career as a philanthropic bishop is associated with a vision of Christminster as seen from the roof of the old Brown House against the blaze of the setting sun, like the heavenly Jerusalem, as the child Jude says solemnly to the tiler. It is also associated with the New Testament. The New Testament, in its strictly moral aspect, is the textbook of Hardy's humanitarian morality, and in so far as Jude values its morality he is demonstrating his instinctively humanitarian feelings. But Jude's Testament represents for him also religion and, in that it is a Greek text, learning; and in valuing it on these counts he is demonstrating his illusions.

During the wooing of Arabella by Jude there are sporadic recrudescences of these symbols. For example, Hardy is constantly bringing the two lovers to the rise on which the old Brown House stands, from which Jude had once seen his vision of the heavenly Jerusalem and where, under the influence of an impulse rather awkwardly explained on the narrative level, he had also once knelt and prayed to Apollo and Diana, the god and goddess of learning and chastity. Under the influence of Arabella, Jude "passed the spot where he had knelt to Diana and Phoebus without remembering that there were any such people in the mythology, or that the sun was anything else than a useful lamp for illuminating Arabella's face" [38]. Hardy carefully notes, too, that a picture of Samson and Delilah hangs on the wall of the tavern where the two lovers stop for tea but instead, partly at Arabella's suggestion, drink beer. The linkage of Arabella and liquor (she had been a barmaid) is valuable to Hardy not only as a piece of naturalism but because it makes Arabella an incarnation of what Jude later calls "my two Arch Enemies . . . my weakness for women and my impulse to strong liquor" [278].

Yet these symbols, effective as they are, are sporadic and unsystematized. Hardy never deserts his naturalistic narrative and commits his meaning to them completely, and so the reader never feels to the full in him what Henry James once so beautifully called the renewal "in the modern alchemist [of] something like the old dream of the secret of life." Hardy never thought of himself as a modern alchemist but only as a historian. This fact is plain enough in the climactic scene of this part, the pig-killing scene, for here the pig is not primarily a symbol but an object at the naturalistic level. Arabella takes toward it, as such, an attitude perfectly consistent with the attitude she has maintained throughout. Her concern is for the salableness of the meat, and even her urging that Jude kill the pig quickly when it cries out is determined by her conventional fear lest the cry reveal to the neighbors that the Fawley's have sunk to killing their own pig. "Poor folks must live"[54], she says when Jude protests against the inhumanity of slowly bleeding the pig to death. And though Hardy's description of the incident precludes any sympathy for Arabella, this statement is profoundly true within the limits of the world Arabella is aware of.

In direct contrast to Arabella's practical view of this killing, Hardy sets Jude's idealistic view of it: "The white snow, stained with the blood of his fellow-mortal, wore an illogical look to him as a lover of justice, not to say a Christian; . . ." [55]. There is irony here, of course, but it is directed solely to the point that Hardy "could not see how the matter was to be mended," not at all to the point that in one very real sense— the sense that Arabella understood—it could and ought never to be mended. This is so because Hardy is in fact and, as a consequence, by the form he has chosen committed to Jude's view of this incident. That commitment is clear in every word Hardy himself writes about the pig; for example: "The dying animal's cry assumed its third and final tone, the shriek of agony; his glazing eyes rivetting themselves on Arabella with the eloquently keen reproach of a creature recognizing at last the treachery of those who had seemed his only friends."

The consequence of the author's putting the full weight of his authority in this way behind one of the conflicting views of the events is to take the ground out from under the other. The events are presented only as Jude saw them, so that Arabella's view of them seems to the reader simply inexplicably hard-hearted, however commonplace. Hardy can see that Arabella's attitude, in its complete ignorance of Jude's, is grimly funny: " ' 'Od damn it all!' she cried, 'that ever I should say it! You've over stuck un! And I telling you all the time—' " [54]. But he cannot see that it is in any sense justified. The result of this commitment of the author is that the scene as a whole becomes sentimental; and it is difficult to resist the temptation to read it as "a burlesque of the murder of Duncan" with the pig substituted for the king ("Well—you must do the sticking—there's no help for it. I'll show you how. Or I'll do it myself—I think I could") [53].

This pig-killing scene is of course meant to connect in the reader's mind with the earlier episode where Farmer Troutham whips Jude for allowing the rooks to eat his corn. For Jude the rooks "took upon them more and more the aspect of gentle friends and pensioners. . . . A magic thread of fellow-feeling united his own life with theirs. Puny and sorry as those lives were, they much resembled his own [14]."[1] Here again Hardy presents these birds and Jude only as Jude sees them. For all his knowledge of "the defence and salvation of the body" he signally fails to do justice to Farmer Troutham's view of them, just as he fails to do justice to Arabella's view of Jude and the pig, because he cannot present two kinds of truth in a naturalistic novel. * * *

Part Two (at Christminster) brings Hardy's spiritual Whittington to his London where he is taught that his desire for learning had been only "a social unrest which had no foundation in the nobler instincts; which was purely an artificial product of civilization" [103]. At the very beginning he catches a glimpse of the truth: "For a moment there fell on Jude a true illumination; that here in the stone-yard was a centre of effort as worthy as that dignified by the name of scholarly study within the noblest of the colleges."[2] Apart from his narrative function, Phillotson is used in this part to foreshadow Jude's discovery of this truth and to reveal what happens to a weaker person at such a disappointment. Arabella's temporary conversion after Cartlett's death has the same kind of formal relation to Sue's conversion, with the additional irony that Sue's conversion involves a return to active sexual life which she hates, Arabella's a loss of it which she cannot endure. Jude's discovery of the fraudulence of learning leaves him only his Christianity; that he will discover this too is "as dead as a fern-leaf in a lump of coal" Hardy tells us directly. That it has been replaced by a German-Gothic fake he suggests by his references to the tearing down of the "hump-backed, wood-turreted, and quaintly hipped" Marygreen church and to the "tall new building of modern-Gothic design" [12] erected in its place.

Meanwhile Jude meets his cousin Sue, whom Hardy always keeps before the reader as Jude first saw her in the picture at Marygreen, "in a broad hat, with radiating folds under the brim like the rays of a halo" [63], not only because she remains always for Jude a saint but because, by a terrible irony, she literally becomes one at the end of the book. Sue has twice Jude's quickness of wit and half his strength of character. She therefore saw from the beginning that there was nothing in the universe except "Nature's law"; but because of her lack of real profun-

---

1. Birds also occasionally achieve the status of symbols in Hardy—"All are caged birds; the only difference lies in the size of the cage" (*The Early Life*, p. 224). Thus the pair of pigeons which Jude and Sue are forced to sell to the poulterer and which Sue later surreptitiously releases are an image of Jude and Sue caged and sold by society for reasons quite independent of their own feelings and worth.

     Hardy would not, of course, have used these birds at all if he had not thought their dilemma terrible in its own right. In other words, their primary meaning is still their naturalistic meaning. The same thing is true of the trapped rabbit.

2. This passage is an example of what Henry James called "the platitude of statement." Hardy indulged in it constantly, both in the prose and the poems, without, apparently, any sense that it was destructive of the life of his representation. Like his description of the objects of his narrative from Jude's point of view, it is an outgrowth of his inability to see how necessary it was for him not to commit himself as author to one view of things.

dity, she thought also that it was "Nature's . . . *raison d'être*, that we should be joyful in what instincts she afforded us . . ." [266]. When she discovered that nature had no *raison d'être* and that paganism was as false as Christianity had seemed to her, she did not have the strength to face it and went back to conventional wifehood and conventional Christianity. All this, even the impermanence of Sue's paganism (the figures of Venus and Apollo are plaster and come off on her gloves and jacket), is implicit in the episode of the images in Chapter II and in the recollections of Sue's childhood in Chapter VI. By a fine piece of irony—since Sue is, while her strength lasts, a saint of Hardy's human-itarian faith—Hardy has Jude focus not only his physical but his reli-gious feelings on Sue. Gradually he learns from her and experience the omnipotence of Nature's law. But meanwhile Jude sees this imperfect saint of humanitarianism as an Anglican saint. Of the irony of this illusion Hardy makes much, and in incident after incident, until Jude unlearns his Christianity, he reëmphasizes the irony of this love between the pagan and delicately sexed Sue and the Christian and passionate Jude.

 In Part Three Jude, having realized that learning is vain and that only his "altruistic feeling" had any "foundation in the nobler instincts," goes to Melchester, partly because it is "a spot where worldly learning and intellectual smartness had no establishment" [103], partly because Sue is there. There follows a series of episodes which represent the conflict between Sue's daring humanitarian faith and her weak conventional conduct, on the one hand, and Jude's "Tractarian" faith and courageously honest conduct, on the other. In the end, of course, Hardy arranges events so as to demonstrate the omnipotence of "the artificial system of things, under which the normal sex-impulses are turned into devilish domestic gins and springes to noose and hold back those who want to progress," and Sue marries Phillotson. In Part Four Jude's education is almost lost sight of in the welter of narrative detail. Occasionally its progress is marked for the reader, as when Jude replies to Sue's question whether she ought to continue to live with Phillot-son: "Speaking as an order-loving man—which I hope I am, though I fear I am not—I should say yes. Speaking from experience and unbi-assed nature, I should say no" [166]. Though Sue and Jude determine to sacrifice their love to right conduct, their coming together on the occasion of their aunt's death at Marygreen finally forces Jude to rec-ognize the evil of the church's marriage system and Sue to realize that she must leave Phillotson for Jude. Sue tries at first to avoid marriage and an active sexual life, but Arabella's return, ironically, forces her to yield to Jude in order to hold him.[3]

<hr>

3. On the marriage question, from Sue's point of view: " . . . she fears it would be breaking faith with Jude to withhold herself at pleasure, or altogether, after it; though while uncontracted

There follows in Part Five a period when "the twain were happy—between their times of sadness . . ." [227]. Hardy shows them as devoted lovers at the Great Wessex Agricultural Show, where they are carefully contrasted with the conventional married couple Arabella and Cartlett (Chapter V). But the pressure of the conventional world on them as unmarried lovers forces them down and down until Jude, "still haunted by his dream," brings Sue and the children to a "depressing purlieu of Christminster. Here Jude makes a speech, from the cross, as it were, to the Roman soldiers of Christminster in which he states the result of his education: "I perceive there is something wrong somewhere in our social formulas: what it is can only be discovered by men or women with greater insight than mine—if, indeed, they ever discover it—at least, in our time" [256].

It is here at Christminster that Hardy makes the most extreme use of his one completely symbolic character, Father Time.[4] All through Part Five he has been used to strike the ominous note which reminds us that Sue and Jude's moderate happiness is a snare and a delusion. Now, under the influence of his perfectly arbitrary melancholy and the misinterpretation of something Sue says, he kills all the children, including himself. Father Time is Jude and Arabella's son brought up by Jude and Sue, in order that Hardy may say:

> On that little shape had converged all the inauspiciousness and shadow which had darkened the first union of Jude, and all the accidents, mistakes, fears, errors of the last. He was their nodal point, their focus, their expression in a single term. For the rashness of those parents he had groaned, for their ill-assortment he had quaked, and for the misfortunes of these he had died. [265]

The effect of this incident on Jude and Sue is to place each of them in the position from which the other had started at the beginning of the book:

> One thing troubled him more than any other, that Sue and himself had mentally travelled in opposite directions since the tragedy: events which had enlarged his own views of life, laws, customs, and dogmas, had not operated in the same manner on Sue's. She

---

she feels at liberty to yield herself as seldom as she chooses. This has tended to keep his passions as hot at the end as at the beginning, and helps to break his heart. He has never really possessed her as freely as he desired" (*The Later Years*, p. 42). Hardy confessed that the delicacy of public sentiment in the period prevented his dwelling on this point as he wished to, made it impossible for him to show clearly, for example, that Jude's spending the night with Arabella when they met unexpectedly in Melchester was a demonstration of how powerfully sheer desire was fighting against suppression in him.

4. Father Time is an excellent illustration of the kind of sensational sentimentality which results from trying to represent the essence of life's squalor in a naturalistic narrative: "The doctor says [says Jude] there are such boys springing up amongst us—boys of a sort unknown in the last generation—the outcome of new views of life . . . He says it is the beginning of the coming universal wish not to live" [264].

was no longer the same as in the independent days, when her intellect played like lambent lightning over conventions and formalities which he had at that time respected, thought he did not now. [270]

Sue returns to Christianity and Phillotson as a consequence of this change; and Jude, partly because of a kind of stunned indifference (he takes to drink), and partly because of Arabella's predatory sexuality, returns to his first wife. It is perfectly apparent that in Hardy's opinion Sue has done an unforgivably inhuman thing to save a perfectly imaginary soul.

But Hardy is at least willing to suggest a conflict in Sue between her affection for Jude and her religious belief, even if he is capable of seeing only one right in that conflict. Thus, when Jude departs from their last meeting, to which he had gone knowing that he was committing suicide, "in a last instinct of human affection, even now unsubdued by her fetters, she sprang up as if to go and succor him. But she knelt down again, and stopped her ears with her hands till all possible sound of him had passed away." On his way home Jude feels "the chilly fog from the meadows of Cardinal as if death-claws were grabbing me through and through"[310]; Hardy catches the whole complex of "stern reality" in this symbolic statement by Jude. College, church, social convention, the very things which Jude had at the beginning believed in as the representatives of his ideal, have killed him, either by betraying him directly or by teaching Sue to betray him.

When Hardy comes to Jude's actual death, he also presents Arabella with a choice, the choice of staying with the dying Jude or going to the Remembrance games. The representation of her here is perhaps the best brief illustration in the book of the melodramatic effect which resulted from Hardy's exclusive attitude toward his material. There is not the slightest sign of conflict in Arabella over her choice; she goes without question to the games, flirts with the quack physician Vilbert, and is upset only by the thought that "if Jude were discovered to have died alone an inquest might be deemed necessary" [320]. As in the pig-killing scene Arabella is shown as feeling only brute passion and fear of convention; she is the parody villainess of melodrama, not the mighty opposite of tragedy. Thus the immediate pathos of Jude's death in part derives from Arabella's villainous neglect of him; like the cheers of the Remembrance-day crowd which are counterpointed against Jude's dying quotation from *Job*, however, this neglect illustrates only the complete indifference of society to Jude's dream of an ideal life. The rest of the pathos derives from Jude's uncertainty as to why he had been born at all. But the meaning of his death, in so far as it has one, derives from such conviction as Hardy can muster that Jude's life has not been in vain, but the unfortunate life of a man who had tried to live the ideal life several generations before the world was reformed enough to allow him to. Jude's death is not, therefore, in our ordinary understanding of the word, tragic; since it is the result of a conflict between the ideal life a man wished to lead and the only temporarily squalid real life which he was forced to lead.

Jude the Obscure is then, not a tragedy, not a carefully devised representation of life the purpose of which is to contrast, at every turn, the permanently squalid real life of man, with the ideal life (or, if you wish, man's dream of an ideal life). It is the history of how an obscure but worthy man, living a life which Hardy conceived to be representative, learned gradually "that the social moulds civilization fits us into have no more relation to our actual shapes than the conventional shapes of the constellations have to the real star-patterns," learned what the true morality of "unbiassed nature" is. In the process of learning this optimistic morality he discovered also that neither nature nor society even recognized it, to say nothing of living by it. In so far as Hardy gave him hope at the end that in time they would, he denied what he otherwise saw so clearly, that earth's conditions are ingrained; in so far as he did not give Jude this hope he denied the possibility of the only ideal life he could conceive and made his hero's life and death essentially meaningless.

The instructive comparison to *Jude* is of course *Hamlet*. For Shakespeare too saw most profoundly the horror of life's ingrained conditions. But because he could also understand and represent the attitude of those who sought to adjust themselves to life's conditions, he saw that the only hope he could give his hero was for that consummation he so devoutly wished, and death is the only felicity Hamlet ever deems possible. Hamlet's death is not death in a universe in which there is no place without bad dreams; neither is it a death justified by a hope that some day the world's ingrained conditions will come unstuck. Jude's death is a little bit of both.

Hardy says in the preface to *Jude* that it "is simply an endeavor to give shape and coherence to a series of seemings, or personal impressions, the question of their consistency or their discordance . . . being regarded as not of the first moment" [5]. In that the feeling of the presented life in *Jude* has a powerful coherence this is a justified defense of it. But it is precisely because Hardy never really posed for himself the question of how the meaning of his impressions could be coherent without being consistent that *Jude*, for all the power of its presented life, is not a tragedy.

D. H. LAWRENCE

[Male and Female]†

*   *   *

One of the supremest products of our civilization is Sue, and a product that well frightens us. It is quite natural that, with all her mental alertness, she married Phillotson without ever considering the physical quality of marriage. Deep instinct made her avoid the consideration. And the duality of her nature made her extremely liable to self-destruction. The suppressed, atrophied female in her, like a potent fury, was always there, suggesting to her to make the fatal mistake. She contained always the rarest, most deadly anarchy in her own being.

It needed that she should have some place in society where the clarity of her mental being, which was in itself a form of death, could shine out without attracting any desire for her body. * * * the atrophied female in her would still want the bodily male.

She attracted to herself Jude. His experience with Arabella had for the time being diverted his attention altogether from the female. His attitude was that of service to the pure male spirit. But the physical male in him, that which knew and belonged to the female, was potent, and roused the female in Sue as much as she wanted it roused, so much that it was a stimulant to her, making her mind the brighter.

It was a cruelly difficult position. She must, by the constitution of her nature, remain quite physically intact, for the female was atrophied in her, to the enlargement of the male activity. Yet she wanted some quickening for this atrophied female. She wanted even kisses. That the new rousing might give her a sense of life. But she could only *live* in the mind.

Then, where could she find a man who would be able to feed her with his male vitality, through kisses, proximity, without demanding the female return? For she was such that she could only receive quickening from a strong male, for she was herself no small thing. Could she then find a man, a strong, passionate male, who would devote himself entirely to the production of the mind in her, to the production of male activity, or of female activity critical to the male?

She could only receive the highest stimulus, which she must inevitably seek, from a man who put her in constant jeopardy. Her essentiality rested upon her remaining intact. Any suggestion of the physical

† From *Phoenix: The Posthumous Papers of D. H. Lawrence*, ed. E. D. McDonald (New York: Viking Press, 1936) 497–510. Copyright 1936 by Frieda Lawrence, renewed © 1964 by The Estate of Frieda Lawrence Ravagli. Reprinted by permission of Laurence Pollinger Ltd, Viking Penguin, a division of Penguin Putnam Inc., and the Estate of Frieda Lawrence Ravagli. Lawrence wrote his *Study of Thomas Hardy*, from the ninth chapter of which this extract is taken, in the latter part of 1914. Most of the book remained unpublished until after his death in 1930. All notes are by the editor of this Norton Critical Edition.

was utter confusion to her. Her principle was the ultra-Christian principle—of living entirely according to the Spirit, to the One, male spirit
which knows, and utters, and shines, but exists beyond feeling, beyond
joy or sorrow, or pain, exists only in Knowing. In tune with this, she
was herself. Let her, however, be turned under the influence of the
other dark, silent, strong principle, of the female, and she would break
like a fine instrument under discord.

Yet, to live at all in tune with the male spirit, she must receive the
male stimulus from a man. Otherwise she was as an instrument without a player. She must feel the hands of a man upon her, she must be
infused with his male vitality, or she was not alive.

Here then was her difficulty: to find a man whose vitality could
infuse her and make her live, and who would not, at the same time,
demand of her a return, the return of the female impulse into him.
What man could receive this drainage, receiving nothing back again?
He must either die, or revolt.

One man had died. She knew it well enough. She knew her own
fatality. She knew she drained the vital, male stimulus out of a man,
producing in him only knowledge of the mind, only mental clarity:
which man must always strive to attain, but which is not life in him,
rather the product of life.

*   *   *

Now Jude, after Arabella, and following his own *idée fixe*,[1] haunted
this mental clarity, this knowing, above all. What he contained in himself, of male and female impulse, he wanted to bring forth to draw into
his mind, to resolve into understanding, as a plant resolves that which
it contains into flower.

This Sue could do for him. By creating a vacuum, she could cause
the vivid flow which clarified him. By rousing him, by drawing from
him his turgid vitality, made thick and heavy and physical with Arabella, she could bring into consciousness that which he contained. For
he was heavy and full of unrealized life, clogged with untransmuted
knowledge, with accretion of his senses. His whole life had been till
now an indrawing, ingestion. Arabella had been a vital experience for
him, received into his blood. And how was he to bring out all this
fulness into knowledge or utterance? For all the time he was being
roused to new physical desire, new life-experience, new sense-
enrichening, and he could not perform his male function of transmit-
ting this into expression, or action. The particular form his flowering
should take, he could not find. So he hunted and studied, to find the
call, the appeal which should call out of him that which was in him.

And great was his transport when the appeal came from Sue. She
wanted, at first, only his words. That of him which could come to her

1. Fixed idea, obsession.

through speech, through his consciousness, her mind, like a bottomless gulf, cried out for. She wanted satisfaction through the mind, and cried out for him to satisfy her through the mind.

Great, then, was his joy at giving himself out to her. He gave, for it was more blessed to give than to receive. He gave, and she received some satisfaction. But where she was not satisfied, there he must try still to satisfy her. He struggled to bring it all forth. She was, as himself, asking himself what he was. And he strove to answer, in a transport.

And he answered in a great measure. He singled himself out from the old matrix of the accepted idea, he produced an individual flower of his own.

It was for this he loved Sue. She did for him quickly what he would have done for himself slowly, through study. By patient, diligent study, he would have used up the surplus of that turgid energy in him, and would, by long contact with old truth, have arrived at the form of truth which was in him. What he indeed wanted to get from study was, not a store of learning, nor the vanity of education, a sort of superiority of educational wealth, though this also gave him pleasure. He wanted, through familiarity with the true thinkers and poets, particularly with the classic and theological thinkers, because of their comparative sensuousness, to find conscious expression for that which he held in his blood. And to do this, it was necessary for him to resolve and to reduce his blood, to overcome the female sensuousness in himself, to transmute his sensuous being into another state, a state of clarity, of consciousness. Slowly, laboriously, struggling with the Greek and the Latin, he would have burned down his thick blood as fuel, and have come to the true light of himself.

This Sue did for him. In marriage, each party fulfils a dual function with regard to the other: exhaustive and enrichening. The female at the same time exhausts and invigorates the male, the male at the same time exhausts and invigorates the female. The exhaustion and invigoration are both temporary and relative. The male, making the effort to penetrate into the female, exhausts himself and invigorates her. But that which, at the end, he discovers and carries off from her, some seed of being, enrichens him and exhausts her. Arabella, in taking Jude, accepted very litte from him. She absorbed very little of his strength and vitality into herself. For she only wanted to be aware of herself in contact with him, she did not want him to penetrate into her very being, till he moved her to her very depths, till she loosened to him some of her very self for his enrichening. She was intrinsically impotent. * * *

So that in her Jude went very little further in Knowledge, or in Self-Knowledge. He took only the first steps: of knowing himself sexually, as a sexual male. That is only the first, the first necessary, but rudimentary, step.

When he came to Sue, he found her physically impotent, but spiritually potent. That was what he wanted. Of Knowledge in the blood he had a rich enough store: more than he knew what to do with. He wished for the further step, of reduction, of essentializing into Knowledge. Which Sue gave to him.

So that his experience with Arabella, plus his first experience of trembling intimacy and incandescent realization with Sue made one complete marriage: that is, the two women added together made One Bride.

When Jude had exhausted his surplus self, in spiritual intimacy with Sue, when he had gained through her all the wonderful understanding she could evoke in him, when he was clarified to himself, then his marriage with Sue was over. Jude's marriage with Sue was over before he knew her physically. She had, physically, nothing to give him.

Which, in her deepest instinct, she knew. She made no mistake in marrying Phillotson. She acted according to the pure logic of her nature. Phillotson was a man who wanted no marriage whatsoever with the female. Sexually, he wanted her as an instrument through which he obtained relief, and some gratification: but, really, relief. Spiritually, he wanted her as a thing to be wondered over and delighted in, but quite separately from himself. He knew quite well he could never marry her. He was a human being as near to mechanical function as a human being can be. The whole process of digestion, masticating, swallowing, digesting, excretion, is a sort of super-mechanical process. And Phillotson was like this. He was an organ, a function-fulfilling organ, he had no separate existence. He could not create a single new movement or thought or expression. Everything he did was a repetition of what had been. All his study was a study of what had been. It was a mechanical, functional process. He was a true, if small, form of the *Savant*. He could understand only the functional laws of living, but these he understood honestly. He was true to himself, he was not overcome by any cant or sentimentalizing. So that in this he was splendid. But it is a cruel thing for a complete, or a spiritual, individuality to be submitted to a functional organism.

The Widow Edlin said that there are some men no woman of any feeling could touch, and Phillotson was one of them. If the Widow knew this, why was Sue's instinct so short?

But Mrs. Edlin was a full human being, creating life in a new from through her personality. She must have known Sue's deficiency. It was natural for Sue to read and to turn again to:

> Thou hast conquered, O pale Galilean!
> The world has grown grey from Thy breath.[2]

---

2. See above, p. 78.

In her the pale Galilean had indeed triumphed. Her body was as insentient as hoar-frost. She knew well enough that she was not alive in the ordinary human sense. She did not, like an ordinary woman, receive all she knew through her senses, her instincts, but through her consciousness. The pale Galilean had a pure disciple in her: in her He was fulfilled. For the senses, the body, did not exist in her; she existed as a consciousness. And this is so much so, that she was almost an Apostate. She turned to look at Venus and Apollo. As if she could know either Venus or Apollo, save as ideas. Nor Venus nor Aphrodite had anything to do with her, but only Pallas and Christ.

She was unhappy every moment of her life, poor Sue, with the knowledge of her own non-existence within life. She felt all the time the ghastly sickness of dissolution upon her, she was as a void unto herself.

So she married Phillotson, the only man she could, in reality, marry. To him she could be a wife: she could give him the sexual relief he wanted of her, and supply him with the transcendence which was a pleasure to him; it was hers to seal him with the seal which made an honourable human being of him. For he felt, deep within himself, something a reptile feels. And she was his guarantee, his crown.

Why does a snake horrify us, or even a newt? Why was Phillotson like a newt? What is it, in our life or in our feeling, to which a newt corresponds? Is it that life has the two sides, of growth and of decay, symbolized most acutely in our bodies by the semen and the excreta? Is it that the newt, the reptile, belong to the putrescent activity of life; the bird, the fish to the growth activity? Is it that the newt and the reptile are suggested to us through those sensations connected with excretion? And was Phillotson more or less connected with the decay activity of life? Was it his function to reorganize the life-excreta of the ages? At any rate, one can honour him, for he was true to himself.

Sue married Phillotson according to her true instinct. But being almost pure Christian, in the sense of having no physical life, she had turned to the Greeks, and with her mind was an Aphrodite-worshipper. In craving for the highest form of that which she lacked, she worshipped Aphrodite.[3] There are two sets of Aphrodite-worshippers: daughters of Aphrodite and the almost neutral daughters of Mary of Bethany.[4] Sue was, oh, cruelly far from being a daughter of Aphrodite. She was the furthest alien from Aphrodite. She might excuse herself through her Venus Urania[5]—but it was hopeless.

Therefore, when she left Phillotson, in whose marriage she consummated her own crucifixion, to go to Jude, she was deserting the God

3. Greek goddess of sexual love.
4. According to the New Testament (John 12.3), she anointed the feet of Jesus with precious ointment and wiped them with her hair.
5. Greek goddess of spiritual love.

of her being for the God of her hopeless want. How much could she become a living, physical woman? But she would get away from Phillotson.

She went to Jude to continue the spiritual marriage, bodiless. That was all very well, if he had been satisfied. If he had been satisfied, they might have lived in this spiritual intimacy, without physical contact, for the rest of their lives, so strong was her true instinct for herself.

He, however, was not satisfied. He reached the point where he was clarified, where he had reduced from his blood into his consciousness all that was uncompounded before. He had become himself as far as he could, he had fulfilled himself. All that he had gathered in his youth, all that he had gathered from Arabella, was assimilated now, fused and transformed into one clear Jude.

Now he wants that which is necessary for him if he is to go on. He wants, at its lowest, the physical, sexual relief. For continually baulked sexual desire, or necessity, makes a man unable to live freely, scotches him, stultifies him. And where a man is roused to the fullest pitch, as Jude was roused by Sue, then the principal connexion becomes a necessity, if only for relief. Anything else is a violation.

Sue ran away to escape physical connexion with Phillotson, only to find herself in the arms of Jude. But Jude wanted of her more than Phillotson wanted. This was what terrified her to the bottom of her nature. Whereas Phillotson always only wanted sexual relief of her, Jude wanted the consummation of marriage. He wanted that deepest experience, that penetrating far into the unknown and undiscovered which lies in the body and blood of man and woman, during life. He wanted to receive from her the quickening, the primitive seed and impulse which should start him to a new birth. And for this he must go back deep into the primal, unshown, unknown life of the blood, the thick source-stream of life in her.

And she was terrified lest he should find her out, that it was wanting in her. This was her deepest dread, to see him inevitably disappointed in her. She could not bear to be put into the balance, wherein she knew she would be found wanting.

For she knew in herself that she was cut off from the source and origin of life. For her, the way back was lost irrevocably. And when Jude came to her, wanting to retrace with her the course right back to the springs and the welling-out, she was more afraid than of death. For she could not. She was like a flower broken off from the tree, that lives a while in water, and even puts forth. So Sue lived sustained and nourished by the rarefied life of books and art, and by the inflow from the man. But, owing to centuries and centuries of weaning away from the body of life, centuries of insisting upon the supremacy and bodilessness of Love, centuries of striving to escape the conditions of being and of striving to attain the condition of Knowledge, centuries of pure Christianity, she had gone too far. She had climbed and climbed to be near the stars. And now, at last, on the topmost pinnacle, exposed to all the horrors and magnificence of space, she could not go back. Her strength had fallen from her. Up at that great height, with scarcely any foothold, but only space, space all round her, rising up to her from beneath, she was like a thing suspended, supported almost at the point of extinction by the density of the medium. Her body was lost to her, fallen away, gone. She existed there as a point of consciousness, no more, like one swooned at a great height, held up at the tip of a fine pinnacle that drove upwards into nothingness.

Jude rose to that height with her. But he did not die as she died. Beneath him the foothold was more, he did not swoon. There came a time when he wanted to go back, down to earth. But she was fastened like Andromeda.[6]

Perhaps, if Jude had not known Arabella, Sue might have persuaded him that he too was bodiless, only a point of consciousness. But she was too late; another had been before her and given her the lie.

Arabella was never so jealous of Sue as Sue of Arabella. How shall the saint that tips the pinnacle, Saint Simon Stylites thrust on the highest needle that pricks the heavens, be envied by the man who walks the horizontal earth? But Sue was cruelly anguished with jealousy of Arabella. It was only this, this knowledge that Jude wanted Arabella, which made Sue give him access to her own body.

When she did that, she died. The Sue that had been till then, the glimmering, pale, star-like Sue, died and was revoked on the night when Arabella called at their house at Aldbrickham, and Jude went out in his slippers to look for her, and did not find her, but came back to Sue, who in her anguish gave him then the access to her body. Till that day, Sue had been, in her will and in her very self, true to one motion, to Love, to Knowledge, to the Light, to the upward motion. Phillotson had not altered this. When she had suffered him, she had said: "He does not touch me; I am beyond him."

But now she must give her body to Jude. At that moment her light began to go out, all she had lived for and by began to turn into a falseness, Sue began to nullify herself.

She could never become physical. She could never return down to earth. But there, lying bound at the pinnacle-tip, she had to pretend she was lying on horizontal earth, prostrate with a man.

It was a profanation and a pollution, worse than the pollution of Cassandra[7] or of the Vestals.[8] Sue had her own form: to break this form

6. Ethiopian princess in classical legend, chained to a rock as an offering to a sea monster and rescued by the hero Perseus.
7. Daughter of Priam, King of Troy; a virgin gifted with the power of prophecy.
8. In ancient Rome, attendants at the temple of Vesta, goddess of the hearth; if they broke their vow of chastity, they were buried alive.

was to destroy her. Her destruction began only when she said to Jude,
"I give in."

As for Jude, he dragged his body after his consciousness. His instinct
could never have made him actually desire physical connexion with
Sue. He was roused by an appeal made through his consciousness. This
appeal automatically roused his senses. His consciousness desired Sue.
So his senses were forced to follow his consciousness.

But he must have felt, in knowing her, the *frisson*[9] of sacrilege, something like the Frenchman who lay with a corpse. Her body, the body
of a Vestal, was swooned into that state of bloodless ecstasy wherein
it was dead to the senses. Or it was the body of an insane woman,
whose senses are directed from the disordered mind, whose mind is
not subjected to the senses.

But Jude was physically undeveloped. Altogether he was medieval.
His senses were vigorous but not delicate. He never realized what it
meant to *him*, his taking Sue. He thought he was satisfied.

But if it was death to her, or profanation, or pollution, or breaking,
it was unnatural to him, blasphemy. How could he, a living, loving
man, warm and productive, take with his body the moonlit cold body
of a woman who did not live to him, and did not want him? It was
monstrous, and it sent him mad.

She knew it was wrong, she knew it should never be. But what else
could she do? Jude loved her now with his will. To have left him to
Arabella would have been to destroy him. To have shared him with
Arabella would have been possible to Sue, but impossible to him, for
he had the strong, purist idea that a man's body should follow and be
subordinate to his spirit, his senses should be subordinate to and subsequent to his mind. Which idea is utterly false.

So Jude and Sue are damned, partly by their very being, but chiefly
by their incapacity to accept the conditions of their own and each
other's being. If Jude could have known that he did not want Sue
physically, and then have made his choice, they might not have wasted
their lives. But he could not know.

If he could have known, after a while, after he had taken her many
times, that it was wrong, still they might have made a life. He must
have known that, after taking Sue, he was depressed as she was
depressed. He must have known worse than that. He must have felt
the devastating sense of the unlivingness of life, things must have
ceased to exist for him, when he rose from taking Sue, and he must
have felt that he walked in a ghastly blank, confronted just by space,
void.

But he would acknowledge nothing of what he felt. He must feel
according to his idea and his will. Nevertheless, they were too truthful

9. Shiver, thrill.

ever to marry. A man as real and personal as Jude cannot, from his deeper religious sense, marry a woman unless indeed he can marry her, unless with her he can find or approach the real consummation of marriage. And Sue and Jude could not lie to themselves, in their last and deepest feelings. They knew it was no marriage; they knew it was wrong, all along; they knew they were sinning against life, in forcing a physical marriage between themselves.

How many people, man and woman, live together, in England, and have children, and are never, never asked whether they have been through the marriage ceremony together? Why then should Jude and Sue have been brought to task? Only because of their own uneasy sense of wrong, of sin, which they communicated to other people. And this wrong or sin was not against the community, but against their own being, against life. Which is why they were, the pair of them, instinctively disliked.

They never knew happiness, actual, sure-footed happiness, not for a moment. That was incompatible with Sue's nature. But what they knew was a very delightful but poignant and unhealthy condition of lightened consciousness. They reacted to each other to stimulate the consciousness. So that, when they went to the flower-show, her sense of the roses, and Jude's sense of the roses, would be most, most poignant. There is always this pathos, this poignancy, this trembling on the verge of pain and tears, in their happiness.

"Happy?" he murmured. She nodded.

The roses, how the roses glowed for them! The flowers had more being than either he or she. But as their ecstasy over things sank a little, they felt, the pair of them, as if they themselves were wanting in real body, as if they were too unsubstantial, too thin and evanescent in substance, as if the other solid people might jostle right through them, two wandering shades as they were.

This they felt themselves. Hence their uncertainty in contact with other people, hence their abnormal sensitiveness. But they had their own form of happiness, nevertheless, this trembling on the verge of ecstasy, when, the senses strongly roused to the service of the consciousness, the things they contemplated took flaming being, became flaming symbols of their own emotions to them.

So that the real marriage of Jude and Sue was in the roses. Then, in the third state, in the spirit, these two beings met upon the roses and in the roses were symbolized in consummation. The rose is the symbol of marriage-consummation in its beauty. To them it is more than a symbol, it is a fact, a flaming experience.

They went home tremblingly glad. And then the horror when, because of Jude's unsatisfaction, he must take Sue sexually. The flaming experience became a falsity, or an *ignis fatuus* leading them on.

They exhausted their lives, he in the consciousness, she in the body. She was glad to have children, to prove she was a woman. But in her it was a perversity to wish to prove she was a woman. She was no woman. And her children, the proof thereof, vanished like hoar-frost from her.

It was not the stone-masonry that exhausted him and weakened him and made him ill. It was this continuous feeding of his consciousness from his senses, this continuous state of incandescence of the consciousness, when his body, his vital tissues, the very protoplasm in him, was being slowly consumed away. For he had no life in the body. Every time he went to Sue, physically, his inner experience must have been a shock back from life and from the form of outgoing, like that of a man who lies with a corpse. He had no life in the senses: he had no inflow from the source to make up for the enormous wastage. So he gradually became exhausted, burned more and more away, till he was frail as an ember.

And she, her body also suffered. But it was in the mind that she had had her being, and it was in the mind she paid her price. She tried and tried to receive and to satisfy Jude physically. She bore him children, she gave herself to the life of the body.

But as she was formed she was formed, and there was no altering it. She needed all the life that belonged to her, and more, for the supplying of her mind, since such a mind as hers is found only, healthily, in a person of powerful vitality. For the mind, in a common person, is created out of the surplus vitality, or out of the remainder after all the sensuous life has been fulfilled.

She needed all the life that belonged to her, for her mind. It was her form. To disturb that arrangement was to make her into somebody else, not herself. Therefore, when she became a physical wife and a mother, she forswore her own being. She abjured her own mind, she denied it, took her faith, her belief, her very living away from it.

It is most probable she lived chiefly in her children. They were her guarantee as a physical woman, the being to which she now laid claim. She has forsaken the ideal of an independent mind.

She would love her children with anguish, afraid always for their safety, never certain of their stable existence, never assured of their real reality. When they were out of her sight, she would be uneasy, uneasy almost as if they did not exist. There would be a gnawing at her till they came back. She would not be satisfied till she had them crushed on her breast. And even then, she would not be sure, she would not be sure. She could not be sure, in life, of anything. She could only be sure, in the old days, of what she saw with her mind. Of that she was absolutely sure.

Meanwhile Jude became exhausted in vitality, bewildered, aimless, lost, pathetically nonproductive.

Again one can see what instinct, what feeling it was which made Arabella's boy bring about the death of the children and of himself. He, sensitive, so bodiless, so selfless as to be a sort of automaton, is very badly suggested, exaggerated, but one can see what is meant. And he feels, as any child will feel, as many children feel today, that they are really anachronisms, accidents, fatal accidents, unreal, false notes in their mothers' lives, that, according to her, they have no being: that, if they have being, then she has not. So he takes away all the children.

And then Sue ceases to be: she strikes the line through her own existence, cancels herself. There exists no more Sue Fawley. She cancels herself. She wishes to cease to exist, as a person, she wishes to be absorbed away, so that she is no longer self-responsible.

For she denied and forsook and broke her own real form, her own independent, cool-lighted mind-life. And now her children are not only dead, but self-slain, those pledges of the physical life for which she abandoned the other.

She has a passion to expiate, to expiate, to expiate. Her children should never have been born: her instinct always knew this. Now their dead bodies drive her mad with a sense of blasphemy. And she blasphemed the Holy Spirit, which told her she is guilty of their birth and their death, of the horrible nothing which they are. She is even guilty of their little, palpitating sufferings and joys of mortal life, now made nothing. She cannot bear it—who could? And she wants to expiate, doubly expiate. Her mind, which she set up in her conceit, and then forswore, she must stamp it out of existence, as one stamps out fire. She would never again think or decide for herself. The world, the past, should have written every decision for her. The last act of her intellect was the utter renunciation of her mind and the embracing of utter orthodoxy, where every belief, every thought, every decision was made ready for her, so that she did not exist self-responsible. And then her loathed body, which had committed the crime of bearing dead children, which had come to life only to spread nihilism like a pestilence, that too should be scourged out of existence. She chose the bitterest penalty in going back to Phillotson.

There was no more Sue. Body, soul, and spirit, she annihilated herself. All that remained of her was the will by which she annihilated herself. That remained fixed, a locked centre of self-hatred, life-hatred so utter that it had no hope of death. It knew that life is life, and there is no death for life.

Jude was too exhausted himself to save her. He says of her she was not worth a man's love. But that was not the point. It was not a question of her worth. It was a question of her being. If he had said she was not capable of receiving a man's love as he wished to bestow it, he might have spoken nearer the truth. But she practically told him this. She made it plain to him what she wanted, what she could take. But he overrode her. She tried hard to abide by her own form. But he forced her. He had no case against her, unless she made the great appeal for him, that he should flow to her, whilst at the same time she could not take him completely, body and spirit both.

She asked for what he could not give—what perhaps no man can give: passionate love without physical desire. She had no blame for him: she had no love for him. Self-love triumphed in her when she first knew him. She almost deliberately asked for more, far more, than she intended to give. Self-hatred triumphed in the end. So it had to be.

As for Jude, he had been dying slowly, but much quicker than she, since the first night she took him. It was best to get it done quickly in the end.

And this tragedy is the result of over-development of one principle of human life at the expense of the other; an over-balancing; a laying of all the stress on the Male, the Love, the Spirit, the Mind, the Consciousness; a denying, a blaspheming against the Female, the Law, the Soul, the Senses, the Feelings. But she is developed to the very extreme, she scarcely lives in the body at all. Being of the feminine gender, she is yet no woman at all, nor male; she is almost neuter. He is nearer the balance, nearer the centre, nearer the wholeness. But the whole human effort, towards pure life in the spirit, towards becoming pure Sue, drags him along; he identifies himself with this effort, destroys himself and her in his adherence to this identification.

But why, in casting off one or another form of religion, has man ceased to be religious altogether? Why will he not recognize Sue and Jude, as Cassandra was recognized long ago, and Achilles, and the Vestals, and the nuns, and the monks? Why must being be denied altogether?

Sue had a being, special and beautiful. Why must not Jude recognize it in all its speciality? Why must man be so utterly irreverent, that he approaches each being as if it were no-being? Why must it be assumed that Sue is an "ordinary" woman—as if such a thing existed? Why must she feel ashamed if she is specialized? And why must Jude, owing to the conception she is brought up in, force her to act as if she were his "ordinary" abstraction, a woman?

She was not a woman. She was Sue Bridehead, something very particular. Why was there no place for her? Cassandra had the Temple of Apollo. Why are we so foul that we have no reverence for that which we are and for that which is amongst us? If we had reverence for our life, our life would take at once religious form. But as it is, in our filthy irreverence, it remains a disgusting slough, where each one of us goes so thoroughly disguised in dirt that we are all alike and indistinguishable.

If we had reverence for what we are, our life would take real form, and Sue would have a place, as Cassandra had a place, she would have a place which does not yet exist, because we are all so vulgar, we have nothing.

ALBERT J. GUERARD

[Hardy's Portrait of Sue Bridehead]†

[Hardy] dealt amusingly with extreme psychic oddities, but floundered badly when he tried to dramatize familiar and very real neuroses. * * * even Jude Fawley's erotic history is sadly incomplete. The great exception to the general failure in sexual psychology is the portrait of Sue Bridehead, which remains one of the most impressive in all fiction of a neurotic and sexually maladjusted woman—a living portrait rather than a case study, but with a case study's minute responsibility. Hardy's determination to tell the whole truth at last, and his overconfident assumption that the reading public had greatly matured since 1870 or 1880, are not sufficient to explain the startling advance over earlier novels. The fact that he had contemplated such a character for many years is much more important. "Sue is a type of woman which has always had an attraction for me, but the difficulty of drawing the type has kept me from attempting it till now." Hardy could have said, more accurately, that he had never attempted a detailed portrait of the epicene woman as such. * * * The sexual life of his early heroines was a subject on which Hardy had necessarily remained evasive. But how much of *their* evasiveness may not have had its origin in sexual repugnance: the inconsequence of Elfride, the fickleness of Fancy Day, the discretion of Anne Garland, the masculinity of Ethelberta? Sue Bridehead is perhaps a development from these earlier heroines, rather than a single and anomalous creation.

It is important to recall at once that Sue is not a Lesbian; there is no reason to quarrel with Hardy's own definition:

> You are quite right; there is nothing perverted or depraved in Sue's nature. The abnormalism consists in disproportion, not in inversion, her sexual instinct being healthy as far as it goes, but unusually weak and fastidious. Her sensibilities remain painfully alert notwithstanding, as they do in nature with such women. One point illustrating this I could not dwell upon: that, though she has children, her intimacies with Jude have never been more than occasional, even when they were living together (I mention that

† From Albert J. Guerard, *Thomas Hardy: The Novels and Stories* (Cambridge: Harvard UP, 1949) 108–14. Reprinted by permission of the author. The author's notes have been omitted. Bracketed page numbers refer to this Norton Critical Edition.

they occupy separate rooms, except towards the end), and one of her reasons for fearing the marriage ceremony is that she fears it would be breaking faith with Jude to withhold herself at pleasure, or altogether, after it; though while uncontracted she feels at liberty to yield herself as seldom as she chooses.

The omission of Jude and Sue's first years together (the years during which their children were born) raises again the book's most complex formal problem. The unbendingly realistic critic must deplore not merely the incompleteness of Sue's sexual history but also the passing over in a few lines of what must have been the only reasonably happy years in Jude's life. The answer to the second objection is that *Jude the Obscure* is not realism but tragedy and like all tragedy is symbolic; it is a vision of things and a reading of life, and according to that vision happiness is but an "occasional episode in a general drama of pain." The novel formally and austerely selects only those incidents in Jude's life which are meaningful, which lead in fact to the most meaningful act of his life: his curse of the night when a man child was conceived. But even the first objection, the incompleteness of Sue's sexual history, is arguable. The few readers who do not understand after three hundred and fifty pages that Sue would be sexually reticent with any man are likely to have understood nothing in the book. In any event, the dramatic necessity to leave some aspects of character in shadow (not in ambiguity) might have demanded the omission. Otherwise the picture of Sue's adult sexual life is fairly full.

Sue combines, with her sexlessness and even repugnance to the "gross" sexual act, a very strong impulse to arouse sexual desire in men. She never outgrows her childhood oscillations between the tomboy and the coquette. She reënacts them with a Christminster undergraduate when she is eighteen and twenty, and later with Phillotson and Jude—and wrecks the nerves of all three. Jealousy prompts her to marry Phillotson and almost to marry Jude; she wants Jude to avoid Arabella not merely because sexuality is gross, but because she wants Jude to desire only herself. Her own happiness, as she half realizes at last, depends on reënactment of this pattern: to live with a man in an ostensibly sexless and fraternal intimacy, arouse his sexual desire, lead him on, reject him, and then do penance for the suffering she thus has caused. She marries Phillotson not merely to spite Jude but to punish herself for having made the schoolmaster suffer; she marries him a second time, when her self-punishing has become almost hysterical. Like all such persons, she *wants* to subject herself to punishment and horror; her religious and social scruples are the most transparent of disguises. But her horror of the sexual act is very real. The subject has been treated more extensively by twentieth-century novelists, but by none of them with more harrowing directness and economy.

Sexual maladjustment is not, to be sure, an isolated phenomenon like red hair or blue eyes; it is also, to use the jargon of the day, the product of psychic and social misemployment. Hardy saw this clearly enough and tried to relate Sue's sexual difficulties to the "disease of modern unrest." She was a pagan on theoretical grounds, not quite sure why she bought the statues of Venus and Apollo and turning automatically from Gibbon on Julian the Apostate to Swinburne on the pale Galilean. She was an "epicure in emotions" and a brilliant woman reduced to teaching children their ABC's and to fencing with the dull intellects of Phillotson and Jude. Hardy's effort to equate Sue's sexual disorders with the nervous disorders of the age nevertheless failed—perhaps because he conceived too sharp a contrast between the disoriented present and the calm stable past. Sue wanders among the various inadequacies of her own life, the experiences which cannot use her energies; but also rather too obviously between the dead world and the world waiting to be born. Her critiques of Christminster and of the Song of Solomon seem gratuitous, given her more fundamental isolation and difficulty. She is at her best when she frets against the Victorian atmospheres of her boardinghouse and of the Melchester Normal School, rather than when she doubts the authenticity of texts. Hardy's failure is nevertheless far more impressive than the obvious successes of his age. How many novelists in our own day have succeeded in dramatizing both isolated neurosis and neurosis as the product of social forces?

The origin of Sue's epicene reticence lies somewhere in her childhood, of which Hardy tells us almost nothing; the origin of her moral masochism lies there also. We are left, in fact, with two very slight clues: at the age of twelve she went in wading and was consciously, tauntingly immodest; and she was often smacked for her impertinence. Hardy variously attributes Sue's sense of guilt to an incomplete emancipation from orthodox religion, to the suffering she causes by refusing to give herself, and to the shock of her children's murder. But he nowhere attributes either the masochism or the sexual repugnance to childhood experience, as he would probably have done had he been born fifty years later. He was nevertheless distinctly ahead of his time in recognizing subconscious self-destruction at all, both here and in *The Mayor of Casterbridge*, and in understanding Sue's desire "to get back to the life of my infancy and its freedom" [111]. The self-punishing impulse first reveals itself sharply when she demands that Jude give her away in marriage and that they rehearse the ceremony without Phillotson. "Was Sue simply so perverse that she willfully gave herself and him pain for the odd and mournful luxury of practising long-suffering in her own person, and of being touched with tender pity for him at having made him practise it?" [139]. Later she feels obliged to tell Phillotson that Jude held her hand and thus humiliate the listener as well as herself. Her self-flagellation becomes intense after the death of the children, for which she feels responsible: "I cannot humiliate myself too much. I should like to prick myself all over with pins, and bleed out the badness that's in me!" [271]. She prostrates herself on the stone pavement of St. Silas' and feels "too worthless to mix with ordinary human beings." Eventually she forces herself to go back to Phillotson and does the final penance of demanding to share his bed. Her guilt works itself out in the very characteristic gesture of unnecessary housework. This, as André Gide was later to remark of his wife, is a typical feminine effort to destroy the hated self.

So summarized, Sue Bridehead may seem a monstrously unpleasant person, as unpleasant as most fictional neurotics. But she is, as it happens, one of Hardy's most appealing heroines; charming and alive from her first impulsive words to Jude waiting at the martyr's cross: "I am not going to meet you just there, for the first time in my life! Come farther on" [81]. It was difficult to make attractive such a stolid and passive sufferer as Tess; it must have been even more difficult to make Sue attractive in spite of her neurotic complexities. The survival can be explained partly by Hardy's success with dialogue and with characteristic gestures (the thumb on the parasol, removing Phillotson's arm, allowing Jude to hold her hand, etc.) and also no doubt by the starkness of her greatest sufferings. Most of all, Sue is alive not as a victim, but as a young and cheerful person immersed in daily existence, without ambition or vague dreams and with no pride beyond her feminine pride in the moment itself; a lover of outings and totally absorbed by whatever outing she happens to be on; her life naïvely and exclusively given over to the pursuit of happiness in a very gray world. She is haunted far more than most of Hardy's characters by the ghosts of guilt and the threats of future punishment. But she tries, more perhaps than any of his characters, to live in the immediate present. This is the clue to Hardy's sympathy toward Sue—and to much that seems indefinable in the appeal of his books. In very distinct contrast to Conrad, Hardy wanted people to be happy rather than good; he sympathized with their every effort to live and enjoy.

ROBERT GITTINGS

[Sue as "a Girl of the 1860s"]†

* * *

Writing to Edmund Gosse in 1895, Hardy said, of his spiritual heroine, Sue Bridehead, that

† From Robert Gittings, *Young Thomas Hardy*. (London: Heinemann, 1975) 93–95. Reprinted by permission. Bracketed page numbers refer to this Norton Critical Edition.

> Sue is a type of woman which has always had an attraction for
> me, but the difficulty of drawing the type has kept me from
> attempting it till now.[1]

"Always" is a vague word; but it indicates an early experience of such
a woman. None of Hardy's known early loves—for example, two and
eventually three Sparks girls—resembles in the slightest way the intellectual Sue. Hardy, of course, combined many elements in his drawing
of Sue, as he did, even more, in his portrayal of Jude; but one striking
element in the early character of Sue is her rationalism and anti-
Church bias. Hardy, in fact, ironically contrasts this with her money-
earning employment, which is designing illuminated texts for
churches, an idea left over from a minor theme he had used in *The
Poor Man and the Lady*. Sue herself, however, is wedded to the new
historical criticism of the Bible, which Hardy had found expounded by
Jowett in *Essays and Reviews*.[2] In pursuit of this, she makes herself
what she calls "a *new* New Testament" [121] on historical lines. She
achieves this by chopping up the Epistles and Gospels, as she explains,
"into separate *brochures*" [121], and rearranging them into their probable order of composition, thus beginning the new book with the Epistle to the Thessalonians. It was against this Epistle that Hardy wrote,
in his own Bible, "H. Lond[n]"; it seems then more than likely that the
London girl of the initials was responsible for this action by Sue
Bridehead.

The character of Sue Bridehead was seized on by critics in the 1890s
as representing "the New Woman" of that era, restless, intellectual
and in some ways unfeminine. In reality, she is very much more what
was called "The Girl of the Period" in the 1860s. The genuine New
Woman of the 1890s was likely to have political affiliations with socialism, to play some part in opening the professions to women, and probably to have received some sort of university training. Sue is still back
in a period some thirty years before that, when a band of enthusiasts
in London ran *The Englishwoman's Journal*, and aired, for practically
the first time, the independent views of women. The works of John
Stuart Mill, whom Hardy had just seen on his way to be elected for
Parliament, were their standard reading, and the editor of *The Englishwoman's Journal*, Bessie Rayner Parkes, wrote two long articles
expounding his principles. By the 1890s, Mill was out of date, superseded by the new socialism; but Sue reads and quotes Mill even obses-
sively. "What do I care about J. S. Mill!" moans her poor husband, "I
only want to lead a quiet life!" [177]. Sue's intellectualism is very much

---

1. *The Life of Thomas Hardy*, p. 272.
2. Widely discussed collection of controversial essays on religious topics, published in 1860.
   Hardy read the book, and discussed it with his friends, as soon as it appeared (*Life*, p. 33).
   The celebrated Oxford scholar Benjamin Jowett was one of the contributors [*Editor*].

that of the 1860s; she is not attached to party politics, nor is she striving for male professional qualifications, nor economic independence. She accepts the very minor jobs then allotted to women.

Still more typical of the 1860s is Sue's own loss of faith, and the idea she finds as a substitute for it. She is never quite explicit about this; but, in fact, the terms she uses show her to be a follower of the Positive Philosophy of Auguste Comte, made fashionable in the 1860s among English intellectuals by Mill's exposition of it in the 1840s, and Harriet Martineau's two-volume abridged translation of it in the 1850s. In her religious arguments with Jude, Sue mocks him by using terms that would be familiar to any reader of Comte. When Jude is in his phase of studying to be a clergyman, as Hardy was in 1865, she ridicules the theology of Oxford which, she says, is anti-intellectual. She condemns Oxford and its orthodox religious beliefs as "a place full of fetich-ists"[120]. Here she is using the language of Comte, or rather of the Harriet Martineau translation. For Comte believed that mankind passed through religion in its early history, to arrive, via metaphysics, at scientific or "positive" philosophy, which was the "religion" of the future. He analysed, at great length, the history of religion itself, and found its origins in the "fetichist" superstitions of primitive tribes: hence Sue's expression. Sue then mocks Jude as merely himself being in a later era of Comte's tracing of religious history—"You are in the Tractarian stage just now . . . Let me see—when was I there?—In the year eighteen hundred and—" [121]. She thus shocks Jude, by assuming that, even in slow process, he will grow out of religion itself, as she has already done. Finally, like Comte, she believes in a secular "pantheon" of intellectuals, rather than one of saints.

In all this, Hardy is clearly modelling Sue, in her anti-religious, rationalist, and scientific "positive" phase, on a girl of the 1860s, and not on one of the 1890s when he was writing. By 1890, Positivism in England was virtually dead, except for small groups in London and in Liverpool. Although its handful of believers were constant to its general principles, it had been disastrously split in the 1870s into two groups, represented in London by those who congregated at Newton Hall, off Fetter Lane, and those who worshipped at the hall in Chapel Street, off Lamb's Conduit Street. For Comte, feeling the need for a spiritual element in his rationalist philosophy, had come in later stages of it to construct a system very like the Catholic Church, in which he had originally been brought up, with a hierarchy of scientists, philosophers, and humanists instead of saints—Sue's "pantheon"—and an actual worship of what was vaguely called "Humanity", with some sort of service resembling a Catholic Mass without Christ. This split the already tiny number of English positivists, never more than a few hun-dred, into two even smaller groups, those who stuck to the original "positive" philosophic principles, and those whose need for a substitute

Christianity made them welcome the later more "religious" form of
Positivism. No new intellectual woman in the 1890s would have been
a positivist. Sue is, once more, a girl of the 1860s. * * *

FREDERICK P. W. McDOWELL

[Imagery and Symbolism in *Jude the Obscure*]†

*   *   *

The first function of the images, symbols, and symbolic or parallel
incidents in *Jude the Obscure* is to deepen and reinforce the realistic
and psychological aspects of the narrative, our impressions of the characters who figure in it, and the various developments arising from it.
A number of images, first encountered in the early part of the novel,
operate in this way. There is, for example, the well at Marygreen into
whose depths Jude peered as a boy. Its "long circular perspective" [11]
indicates the path of Jude's own existence which many times converges
circularly upon Marygreen. In somewhat the same manner, the schoolmaster Phillotson returns recurrently to Marygreen, where he had first
been a teacher. The well also suggests infinity, and conveys an impression of the continuity of nature and of life itself. It hints at psychic
and spiritual renewal and acts, therefore, as a counterweight to many
of the death-connoting images in the novel. The well is in part a natural
phenomenon and as such will survive man-made objects: thus it has
outlasted the old church which has been supplanted by a newer, less
aesthetically pleasing structure. Along with the suggestion of infinity,
the well had given to the young Jude intimations of sadness and of the
inscrutability of life; these impressions are, of course, heightened in
him and us by his destiny.

The well has possible sexual connotations, too, and suggests the
darkness, the mystery, the security, and the fertile energies of the
womb. It thus reinforces the animal imagery which betokens physical
sexuality and which is especially prominent in the early part of the
novel. There are the copulating earthworms which Jude as a boy tries
to avoid crushing in a wet pasture. They are responding to the same
natural force motivating the peasant youths and maidens who make
love in upland privacy and populate thereby the neighboring villages.
Somewhat later, Jude and Arabella become such lovers themselves.
Arabella is, of course, associated with pigs throughout the novel; she

† From "Hardy's 'Seemings or Personal Impressions': The Symbolical Use of Image and Contrast
in *Jude the Obscure*," *Modern Fiction Studies* 6 (1960): 236–45. Copyright © 1960, Purdue
Research Foundation, West Lafayette, IN 47907. Reprinted by permission. Bracketed page
numbers refer to this Norton Critical Edition.

is twice referred to as a "tiger" [46], and at the Aldbrickham hotel
when Sue visits her, she springs from bed like a beast from its lair. The
most celebrated of the animal images is the pig's pizzle which Arabella
throws at Jude to attract his attention when, at the brookside, she is
washing a slaughtered pig for her father. One of the most arresting
scenes is the subsequent flirtation on the bridge, after Arabella hangs
on the rail the pizzle which Jude surrenders to her in a ritualistic yielding of his own virginity to her. The coarse and sensual nature of their
soon developing affair is explicit, then, from its outset.

The first of a group of images and incidents relating to music appears
early in the book. In the opening section Phillotson has difficulty getting a piano moved which he has never learned to play. His failure to
master it is linked with his inability to play, subtly and potently, upon
the keyboard of a woman's sensibility; with the defeat of his other
aspirations, social, intellectual, and spiritual; and with the absence of
emotional depths in his nature. While Sue is Phillotson's wife at Shaston, she and Jude are brought together when he plays upon this piano
a newly written hymn which appeals with power to both of them.
Almost from the first, then, Sue and Jude share, to Phillotson's detri-
ment, experiences from which he is excluded. In addition to his sexual
magnetism, Jude has greater spiritual reserves, in general, than Phillotson. Thus Jude achieves considerable distinction in church music at
Melchester singing with deep feeling the church chants while he
accompanies himself with ease on a harmonium.

Events at Christminster are often subtly developed by references to
music. Jude is greatly moved by the Gregorian chant which he hears
at the cathedral church of Cardinal College: "Where-withal shall a
young man cleanse his way?" [74]. At this point he has begun struggling against his feeling for Sue, and the chant seems to have a special
significance for him as sinner. His feeling of guilt disappears when he
sees Sue in the cathedral and becomes conscious that they are both
steeped in the same exalted harmonies. As Jude leaves Christminster
in despair at the defeat of his intellectual ambitions, he cannot respond
to the gay promenade concert. Some years later upon his return to
Christminster he is much more susceptible to spirited music which,
on Remembrance Day, peals from the theater organ. The spell exerted
by Christminster upon Jude is greater, therefore, than the bitterness
engendered in him by his failure to become part of the university. In
ironic counterpoint to the tragedy at Christminster when little Father
Time hangs himself and the Fawley children is the joyous tumult of
the organ sounding from a nearby chapel ("Truly God is loving unto
Israel" [265]) after the bodies have been discovered. The same incon-
gruity obtrudes on the second Remembrance Day when the lilting
strains of a waltz from Cardinal College penetrate the chamber where
Jude has just died. Sue's early view of ultimate reality, in part Hardy's

own, is expressed by a musical metaphor. She had thought that "the world resembled a stanza or melody composed in a dream" [268], full of ineffable suggestion to the half-perceiving mind but "absurd" to the completely awakened intelligence. Sue's later distress, of course, involves a retreat from this position to a less aesthetically satisfying concept of God as an anthropomorphic being who does not hesitate to punish those who flout convention.

Images in the novel drawn from the Bible also serve to intensify its realism and the psychic impulsions of its characters. The relationship between Jude and Arabella is given by the picture of Samson and Delilah at the inn where the lovers decide to get tea during their courtship and are forced to get beer instead. As Holland observes, Arabella thereby combines the two forces which undermine Jude, his passion for women and his developing taste for strong drinks.[1] When he is duped a second time into marrying Arabella, she appropriately thinks of him as "her shorn Samson" [297]. Biblical and ecclesiastical images are also associated with Sue Bridehead, who looks like a saint with a halo of light in her portrait at Marygreen and who is engaged in an apparently saintly occupation at Christminster. She is an artist for an ecclesiastical warehouse and is designing, when Jude first sees her through the shop window, the word *Alleluia* in zinc. Without knowing her "Voltairean" propensities, he feels that she would be a sweet companion for him in the Anglican worship, opening for him new social and spiritual possibilities and soothing him "like the dew of Hermon" [75]. In her marital difficulties she identifies herself with the Christian drama in Eden. Writing to Phillotson from her school room, she wishes that Eve had not fallen, so that a more delicate mode of reproduction than sex might have peopled Paradise. In her developing asceticism after the death of her children, she regards the flesh as "the curse of Adam" [270]. If, as she had said previously, she was "the Ishmaelite" [111] as a result of her disregard of convention, she feels still more of an outcast after she tries to expiate her tragedy by mortification of the flesh.

In view of his devotion to Christianity in the first half of the novel, Jude is linked even more firmly with Biblical incident than is Sue. At Shaston Sue describes Jude as "Joseph, the dreamer of dreams" [162] and as "St. Stephen who, while they were stoning him, could see heaven opened" [162]. Here Sue refers, at least by implication, to Jude's scarcely practicable dreams, first of entering Christminster and then of becoming an altruistic licentiate, to his early vision of Christminster as a "heavenly Jerusalem" [18], and to the scorn merged with indifference which his unusual ambition arouses among his Marygreen and Christminster acquaintances. When Jude gets to Christminster,

1. *Nineteenth Century Fiction* 9 (June 1954): 51.

he is fascinated by a model of ancient Jerusalem while Sue as a skeptic is indifferent to it. This model of Jerusalem anticipates that made by Jude and Sue some years later of his "new Jerusalem" [20], Cardinal College, for the Great Wessex Agricultural Show at Stoke-Barehills.

The completeness of Jude's defeat at Christminster is implied when he climbs into the octagonal lantern of the theater and sees the city spread out before his eyes as if it were a Pisgah view of the Promised Land which he is never to reach. He then leaves the town, broken in spirit, and returns to Marygreen, "a poor Christ" [101]. When he comes back to Christminster in the last part of the novel, he lingers nostalgically outside the theater where he had first realized that study at Christminster was impossible for a man of his resources. Like Jude, the New Testament scribe who sought to reclaim his lapsed contemporaries to the love of Christ by citing the punishments meted to those in the Old Testament who defied God, Jude Fawley is a prophetic figure, seeing further than most of his contemporaries and deploring the placid indifference of most of them to the demands of Christian charity. As a stranger, too, to people in his own class, he is likened the last time at Christminster to Paul among the Lycaonians. Jude at this point is translating a Latin inscription and describing a carving to assembled strangers from the town side of Christminster. Jude, "the Tutor of St. Slums"[255], had been thrust out of Christminster as Paul had been from Lystra; and like Paul, who returns to the city after persecution to preach again his gospel, Jude later comes back to Christminster to voice his radical social ideas to the crowd. On this return to his old haunts, he observes that leaving Kennetbridge for Christminster was like going from Caiaphas to Pilate. There is, by implication, no place anywhere for a man of his talents from his humble class.

Images drawn from pagan and classical sources also heighten character and incident. Pagan allusions gather around Sue early in the novel: the atmosphere surrounding her "blew as distinctly from Cyprus as from Galilee" [75]. A vivid scene occurs when she is walking on a hill outside Christminster and sees some statuary of classical deities, carved by an itinerant foreigner, spread out before her and half obliterating the distant towers of the city. Sue's pagan skepticism gets between her and the Christian traditions of the city which from the first secure Jude's allegiance. Her Pisgah view of the city shows her that the secular is fast encroaching upon the religious and indeed must continue to do so if the University is ever to recover intellectual leadership.

A pagan in her sympathies, Sue purchases statues of Venus and Apollo which upon nearer view seem to her embarrassingly large and naked. In theory, then, she embraces a pagan abandon which, in the actuality, discomposes her. She wraps the statues in leaves and brings her "heathen load" [77] into the Christian city, much to the later horror of Miss Fontover, Sue's pious employer, who grinds one of the images with her heel and breaks its arm. Like ecclesiastical Christianity, then, pagan humanism is an incomplete philosophy for the modern age and its survival even more precarious, since its enlarged perspectives so often go counter to convention. Sue's own paganism is imperfect, possibly transient: the clay of the statues rubs off easily. At night she places candles before them as before Christian icons and communes with them raptly. At one such time she reads Swinburne, who expresses her own regret that "the pale Gailean" [78] has conquered. While she peruses Swinburne and Gibbon, Jude in his lodging is studying the Greek New Testament. In the diffused light the statues stand out commandingly against the wall ornaments: Christian texts, pictures of martyrs, and a gothic framed Latin cross, the figure on which is shrouded by shadows. This obscurely seen cross, which signifies the present abeyance of Christian sentiment in Sue, is in complete contrast to the brightly jeweled Latin cross in the church of St. Silas under which Jude finds Sue toward the end of the novel when, as a result of personal tragedy, Christian conventions become prominent in her life.

After Sue escapes from the training school at Melchester, where she had previously appeared "nunlike" [105] to Jude, she seems to him "clammy as a marine deity" [115] from having forded the river behind the school. Like a latter-day Venus Anadyomene, she seems to have materialized spontaneously out of the waters. If in this sequence she brings to mind the pagan goddess of love, Sue is no sensual Pandemos-like deity but the Venus Urania of heavenly love with whom she somewhat later identifies herself. Her garments also cling to her "like the robes upon the figures in the Parthenon frieze" [115]. In her most expansive moods, she seems to Jude, after they live together at Aldbrickham, to be a serene Roman matron or an enlightened woman from Greece who may have just been watching Praxiteles carving his latest Venus. Later, of course, Sue renounces Greek joyousness for Christian asceticism, and "the pale Galilean" in actuality does conquer.

Although Jude is most often seen in a Christian ambience, he is sometimes described in terms of the pagan past. As a devout young aspirant to intellectual culture who momentarily forgets his Christianity before his first sojourn at Christminster, he repeats the "Carmen Saeculare" [29] and invokes on his knees the gods of moon and sun in parallel sequence to Sue's later worship of her statues at night. When Jude returns defeated from Christminster, he is described as a Laocöon contorted by grief; the pagan image implies that the bonds of Christian orthodoxy are loosening even now, primarily as a result of his unpermitted passion for Sue. He is also sensitive to the pessimistic, as well as to the harmonious aspects, of classical antiquity. After the Widow Edlin in Aldbrickham has told the lovers of their ill-fated ancestor who had been hanged as the ultimate result of a marital quarrel, Sue feels that the curse of the house of Atreus hangs over the family, and Jude then compares its doom to that haunting the house of Jeroboam. Later in the novel, however, it is Jude who resorts to the *Agamemnon* to demonstrate that Sue's premonition concerning the ancestral curse hanging over the Fawleys had been correct: "Things are as they are, and will be brought to their destined issue" [266]. After their tragedy, the lovers are seen to be, as they move through the Christminster fog, "Acherontic shades" [283]. When the seriously ill Jude perceives the ghosts of the Christminster worthies a second time (after his final trip to Marygreen), he poignantly quotes *Antigone* to signify his own anomalous and wretched situation: "I am neither a dweller among men nor ghosts" [310]. Despite his discouragement and enervation, Jude's persisting moral force resembles that of a stolid, stoic man of antiquity. This is suggested when he is described on his final trip to Marygreen as being "pale as a monumental figure in alabaster" [305], or when he is seen by Arabella to be "pale" and "statuesque" in death with his features like "marble" [321].

Another group of symbolic incidents is concerned with action taking place at windows or casements. At Melchester, Sue jumps from a window at the training college in order to escape the hateful discipline imposed there; at Shaston she jumps from a window to escape from Phillotson and the regimentation imposed by marriage. When Sue springs from the window at the Melchester school and wades neck-deep through the river to escape, she is making a sharp break with her past and is being borne into another life with Jude at its center. Her break for freedom takes her to the lodgings of the man she loves, but destiny prevents her then from seeing where her affections are centered. Hearing from Jude that he had been married previously, she is precipitated into her union with Phillotson, an impulsive action toward Phillotson in contrast with her later bold jump through the window away from him at Shaston. When Jude comes to visit her at Shaston, she talks to him from a casement, strokes his forehead, and calls him a dreamer; a similar episode takes place at Marygreen a few weeks later after Jude mercifully kills a maimed rabbit caught in a gin. She then leans far out of the window at Mrs. Edlin's and lays her tear-stained face on his hair. Seen so often from a relatively inaccessible casement, Sue is in part the immured enchanted maiden, also a kind of inverted Juliet talking to her ardent lover from the safety of a balcony, to which she does not invite him. Somewhat later Jude, living at Aldbrickham with Sue, talks to Arabella from an upper window of the house when she comes to tell him of the existence of the child, Father Time. Whereas Sue had to this time kept the passionate Jude at a distance, the walls of this house—primly erected upon Sue's inconsistent adher-

ence to the conventions she affects to despise—are hardly proof against
Arabella's frankly competitive, more direct animal energies. Afraid of
losing Jude to Arabella, Sue yields at last to his ardor to possess her.

Other images or symbolic episodes give the novel a richer texture
than that usually found in a realistic narrative. Thus the agonies of
jealousy experienced by Sue's lovers at various points in the novel gain
strength by being counterpointed with each other. Jude is tortured
after the marriage at Melchester by the thought that any children born
to Sue would be half Phillotson's. After Sue's visit to him in an illness
following her departure from him, Phillotson himself is in jealous agony
at the thought of Jude as Sue's physical lover (at this point he is not,
so Phillotson's jealousy is wasted). Sue also experiences momentary
discomfiture when she first sees Father Time, the child of Jude and
Arabella, and thinks that he is as much Arabella's as Jude's. In his
distressing final interview with Sue at Marygreen, what sustains Jude
is her declaration that she is a wife to Phillotson only in name, whereas
what later breaks him down is the Widow Edlin's report to him that
Sue has physically become Phillotson's wife as a punishment for having
returned Jude's kisses with passion. Sue's statement that she was the
only mourner to attend the funeral of her early Christminster lover
gathers poignancy when one remembers her absence from the deathbed of the man whom she has loved even more. When she excludes
Jude from their bedroom at Christminster, the scene is made intense
by his ritualistic gesture of farewell: he flings his pillow to the floor, an
act which signifies, he says, the rending of the veil of the temple of
their marriage.

Sue, in effect, says farewell to the passions of the flesh in a similarly
poignant scene toward the end of the novel. By mistake she had
brought with her to Marygreen a beautifully embroidered nightgown.
She impulsively tears it and throws the tatters into the fire, thus fig-
uratively eliminating from her nature all stain of unpermitted earthly
passion. In its place she will wear a plain nightdress, which impresses
the Widow Edlin as similar to the sackcloth which Sue, in her passion
for self-centered suffering, would now like to wear. The destruction of
the nightgown also recalls another strong incident, Jude's burning his
divinity books on a kind of funeral pyre to his religious aspirations when
he realizes at Marygreen that he can no longer be licentiate in the
church and continue to love Sue. In burning the nightgown Sue
aspires, almost successfully, to invalidate the flesh; in burning the
books, Jude relinquishes, to the stronger call of the flesh, his aspirations. He decides that he will give up all for love, but he later finds
with a kind of hopeless irony that Sue has not fully reciprocated. Jude's
destruction of his books also anticipates Arabella's thrusting her religious pamphlets into the hedge when as Cartlett's widow she decides
she is still in love with Jude; in both cases, formal religion is unable to

restrain a powerful passion. Arabella, moreover, seems to act as a kind of catalyst in the varying relationships between Sue and Jude. The effect of her first visit to the married couple at Aldbrickham is to thrust Sue into Jude's arms and to bring about the consummation of their union. Her second visit to the couple, after the tragedy to the children, confirms Sue in her opinion that she is no longer Jude's and must return to Phillotson, since she has come to the orthodox view that her early marriage is indissoluble.

The images and symbolic patterns in the novel not only deepen its significance, but give it scope and amplitude. The full and extended representations of locale help give the novel its broadened perspectives and take it again beyond the unadorned content of most naturalistic novels. In Hardy's evocation the physical Christminster is replete with Gothic grace and charming if irregular architectural harmonies. Shaston, "the ancient British Palladour" [157], is described as "the city of a dream" and its past glories are suggested as they would now appeal to the sensitive beholder of the picturesque town. Melchester with its towering cathedral is presented with similar immediacy, though no set description of town or cathedral is given.

Although Marygreen is a desolate and remote spot, Hardy savored its uniqueness and quaintness. In particular, the features of the spacious countryside nearby are assimilated effectively into the action of the novel. The highway ascending the downs from Alfredston to Marygreen is one of the most consistently used topographical images in the novel. This is the road that Jude walks with Arabella in the early days of their relationship, it is along this road that the newly married pair settle, and it is by this road that Jude returns several times to his native village. Along this road occurs the fateful kiss between Jude and Sue; here Arabella, as the "volupshious widow" [248] of Cartlett, relives the early days with Jude and determines to get him back. Phillotson's history is also intimately connected with the highway. The surrounding landscape is full of associations for Jude: the field where he chased the crows for Farmer Troutham, the Brown House from which he first had his view of Christminster in the distance, the milestone upon which he carved the word *thither* and an arrow pointing toward Christminster, and the gibbet upon which one of his ancestors was reputed to have been hanged. The sequence at Melchester when Jude and Sue climb the downs about Wardour Castle inevitably recalls the courtship walks with Arabella across the heights near Marygreen. One instance of Hardy's skilled use of these topographical images occurs at the novel's close. Jude's inscription on the milestone at Marygreen has now been almost effaced by moss: the implication is that Jude's aspirations have been slowly undermined with the years and are soon to be extinguished in his approaching death.

Other types of nature imagery similarly enlarge the realistic frame-work of the novel by suggesting that the life of nature underlies the social life of man even when that life is led in urban rather than in rural surroundings. Thus weather becomes as important as the terrain in establishing the emotional impress of *Jude the Obscure*. The Christ-minster fog, for example, hangs over the last sequences of the novel and adds to their chill and depressing effect. In one of these scenes, Jude in effect commits suicide by going back to Marygreen in a driving rain after he has begun to show symptoms of consumption. He also lies down to rest by the milestone near the Brown House where wind and rain are fiercest and coldest. Wind and storm continue when Sue that evening forces herself to yield to her husband. In ironic counter-point to the brilliance of the sun and to the happy Remembrance Day games going on outside, Jude comes to his solitary shadowed end at Christminster. The classical and Biblical allusions, previously analyzed, also give the novel wider reference than a chronicle of contemporary events would normally possess, by suggesting that situations in the present somehow reach back through time and are comparable to con-ditions at remote dates in the history of humanity.

PENNY BOUMELHA *Jude & Sue*

[A "Double Tragedy"]†

Jude the Obscure is Hardy's final double tragedy. In his previous ver-sions of the double tragedy of a man and of a woman, the woman's tragedy has resulted from her sexual nature, while the man's has been more involved with intellectual ideals and ideological pressures. There has been a polarity of nature and culture which has meant that the protagonists have rivalled one another for the centre of the novel, pull-ing it in different directions and making it hard for him to use marital or sexual relationship as the crucial point of the divergence. In *Jude*, however, Hardy gives for the first time an intellectual component to the tragedy of the woman—Sue's breakdown from an original, incisive intellect to the compulsive reiteration of the principles of conduct of a mid-Victorian marriage manual—and, to the man's, a sexual com-ponent which resides not in simple mismatching, but in the very fact of his sexuality. There is no sense that Jude and Sue inhabit different ideological structures as there is in the cases of Clym and Eustacia, or even Angel and Tess. Indeed, for all the emphasis on the 'enigma' of

---

† From Penny Boumelha, *Thomas Hardy and Women: Sexual Ideology and Narrative Form* (Brighton: Harvester Press, 1982) 140–50. Reprinted by permission. Bracketed page numbers refer to this Norton Critical Edition.

Sue's logic and motivation, there is an equal stress—and this is something new in Hardy—on her similarity to Jude. The fact of their cousinship, besides contravening the exogamy rule and so adding an
incestuous *frisson* to their sense of an impending and hereditary doom,
serves to highlight their similarities;[1] there are episodes which quite
openly draw attention to this, either by careful counterpointing of plot
(Jude, in his distress, spending the night at Sue's lodging, balanced by
Sue, in hers, spending a night in Jude's room) or by means of images
such as that of Sue's appearance in Jude's clothes as a kind of double.
Again, the discussion between the two after Jude's impulsive visit to
the hymn-writer turned wine-merchant points up their own sense of
sameness between them; and Phillotson justifies his action in letting
Sue go partly in terms of ' "the extraordinary sympathy, or similarity,
between the pair. He is her cousin, which perhaps accounts for some
of it. They seem to be one person split in two!" (p. 245) [182]. Their
lives follow a very similar course. Both make a mistaken marriage as a
result of sexual vulnerability, as is evident in an interesting ms. revision:
when Jude, on his first outing with Arabella, visits an inn, he sees on
the wall a painting of Samson and Delilah, a clear symbol of his male
sexuality under threat; but the picture had originally been a painting
of Susannah and the Elders, a symbol of female sexuality under threat,
which corresponds very closely to the roles of Sue and Phillotson. Both
Sue and Jude escape these first marriages, become parents, lose their
jobs, their children, and their lover. Yet Sue is destroyed, while Jude is
even at the end able to talk of dying ' "game" ' (p. 394) [306]. Jude
offers explanations for this phenomenon—'The blow of her bereavement seemed to have destroyed her reasoning faculty' (p. 368) [283]—
and raises questions about it—' "What I can't understand in you is
your extraordinary blindness now to your old logic. Is it peculiar to you,
or is it common to woman? Is a woman a thinking unit at all, or a
fraction always wanting its integer?" ' (p. 359) [276]. Sue's actions and
reactions are constantly faced, whether by Jude, by the narrator, or by
Sue herself, with this alternative: either she must be peculiar, or she
must be representative of her sex.[2] It is worth noting, in passing, that
this alternative is one which certain critical readings continue to
enforce upon the text; a recent example can be found in John Lucas'
argument that 'we need more in the way of women than the novel
actually gives us' in order to judge whether Sue is to be seen as a
'pathological case' or as a 'representative woman'.[3] This apart, it is

1. Cousin, or brother and sister, relationships were widely used in feminist fiction to contrast
   the treatment and expectations and experiences of sex-differentiated pairs; e.g. in Elizabeth
   Barrett Browning's *Aurora Leigh* (1856), and Sarah Grand's *The Heavenly Twins* (1893).
2. Cf. John Goode, 'Sue Bridehead and the New Woman,' in *Women Writing and Writing about
   Women*, ed. Mary Jacobus (London, 1979), pp. 100–13.
3. John Lucas, *The Literature of Change: Studies in the Nineteenth-Century Provincial Novel*
   (Hassocks, Sussex, 1977), pp. 188–91.

noticeable that Sue's life follows almost exactly the course of the 'after-
years' marked out for the female sex in the earlier and notorious passage about the 'inexorable laws of nature' and the 'penalty of the sex':
that is, 'injustice, loneliness, child-bearing, and bereavement' (pp. 160–
I) [112]. It seems to me that Sue is to be seen as a representative of
her sex in this sense alone, that her sexuality is the decisive element
in her collapse. It has become a critical reflex to refer to Sue Bridehead
as sexless or frigid, whether as an accusation of her, in the Lawrentian
tradition, or as an accusation of Hardy, as in Kate Millett.[4] There is
much in the literature of the New Woman that appears to support
such an assumption: their concern with the double-standard, for
instance, takes almost invariably the form of a demand for male chastity, and some of the more successful problem novels, such as Sarah
Grand's *The Heavenly Twins*, turn on the terrible injuries wreaked on
women by libidinous and venereally-diseased husbands. *Jude* itself provides some evidence for this argument also, in Sue's rather absurd wish
' "that Eve had not fallen, so that . . . some harmless mode of vegetation might have peopled Paradise" ' (p. 241) [178], or in the numerous
revisions in which Hardy removes expressions referring to Sue's warmth
and spontaneity and substitutes references to her reserve or coolness.
In one scene, for instance, her reply to Jude's worries that he may have
offended her reads thus in the serial text: ' "Oh, no, no! You said
enough to let me know what had caused it. I have never had the least
doubt of your worthiness, dear, dear Jude! How glad I am you have
come!" '. In the first edition, however, she is considerably less affectionate and spontaneous: ' "O, I have tried not to! You said enough to
let me know what had caused it. I hope I shall never have any doubt
of your worthiness, my poor Jude! And I am glad you have come!" '.
As she comes to meet Jude, the serial text runs: 'She had come forward
so impulsively that Jude felt sure a moment later that she had half-
unconsciously expected him to kiss her.' The revised text, on the other
hand, reads: 'She had come forward prettily; but Jude felt that she had
hardly expected him to kiss her.'[5]

It is simplistic, however, to equate such changes with a total absence
of sexual feeling, or with frigidity. They should be seen, rather, as her
response to the complexities and difficulties of her sexuality and its
role in her relationships than as a straightforward denial of it. Hardy
subjects Sue's sexuality to some of the same ironies which undercut
Diana Warwick's sexual self-possession in *Diana of the Crossways*, and
for some of the same reasons. It is intimately connected in both cases
with the woman's sense of selfhood, and the reserve is, to quote John

4. D. H. Lawrence, 'Study of Thomas Hardy,' in *Phoenix: The Posthumous Papers of D. H. Lawrence*, ed. Edward D. McDonald (1936; rpt. London, 1961), pp. 495–510; and Kate Millett, *Sexual Politics* (London, 1971), pp. 130–4.
5. *Harper's*, European ed. 29 (1895), 576; and *Jude the Obscure* (London, 1895), p. 161.

Goode, 'not a "defect" of "nature", but . . . a necessary stand against being reduced to the "womanly" '.[6] A refusal of the sexual dimension of relationships can seem the only rational response to a dilemma; in revolt against the double bind by which female-male relationships are invariably interpreted as sexual and by which, simultaneously, sexuality is controlled and channelled into a single legalised relationship, Sue is forced into a confused and confusing situation in which she wishes at one and the same time to assert her right to a non-sexual love and her right to a non-marital sexual liaison.[7] It is the conflict of the two contradictory pressures that makes her behaviour so often seem like flirtation. Diana Warwick is a victim of the same dilemma, for her unconventionality and intelligence lead her to despise the taboo placed on friendships with men, and yet any and every sexual advance, whatever the state of her feelings toward the man, is felt as at once an insult, a threat, and an attack. 'The freedom of one's sex' is a double-edged concept.

In the case of Sue Bridehead, her diagnosis of marriage as constraint implies as its apparent corollary the equation of non-marriage and freedom. The myth of the free individual subject leads her to see her life, provided it lies outside sexual coercion, as an affair of personal choices freely made. Telling Jude of her unhappiness, she does not perceive the irony in his repetition of her phrase:

> "How can a woman be unhappy who has only been married eight weeks to a man she chose freely?"
> " 'Chose freely!' "
> "Why do you repeat it?" (p. 227) [166].

Her tragedy takes in part the form of her gradual confrontation with the fact of her non-freedom, with the knowledge that she is no less constrained and reduced by her denial of her sexuality than by Phillotson's legal or Jude's emotional demands upon it. She must learn that sexuality lies to a large degree outside the control of rationality, will, choice. The serene confidence with which she tells Jude of her sexless liaison with the undergraduate and draws from it the general conclusion that ' "no average man—no man short of a sensual savage—will molest a woman by day or night, at home or abroad, unless she invites him" ' (p. 167) [118], is a fantasy of freedom and control which she will not willingly surrender. Hardy states in a letter to Edmund Gosse what the novel itself also implies, that it is irrevocable sexual commitment which she fears and abhors, and that she has attempted

6. John Goode, 'Woman and the Literary Text,' in *The Rights and Wrongs of Women*, ed. Juliet Mitchell and Ann Oakley (Harmondsworth, 1976), p. 242.
7. See her comments on p. 186 [134] (' "Their philosophy only recognises relations based on animal desire" ') and p. 222 [162] (' "they can't give it continuously to the chamber-officer appointed by the bishop's licence to receive it." ').

to retain control of her sexuality by a straightforward restriction of her sexual availability:

> "One point illustrating this I could not dwell upon: that, though she has children, her intimacies with Jude have never been more than occasional, even when they were living together . . . , and one of her reasons for fearing the marriage ceremony is that she fears it would be breaking faith with Jude to withhold herself at plea-sure, or altogether, after it; though while uncontracted she feels at liberty to yield herself as seldom as she chooses" (*Later Years*, p. 42).

The final, ironic twist is that when she can no longer fail to recognise the limitations upon her freedom—the moment is clearly marked for us in her identification of the three commandments of the ' "some-thing external" ' which ironically mock the Hebraic Ten Command-ments (p. 347) [265]—she simply re-makes the equation in reverse, preserving the polar opposition of marriage and non-marriage. In her re-marriage with Phillotson, she subjects herself fully to the legalistic and Hebraic codes of the ideology of marriage.

Sue, then, undergoes an exploration of the limits of a liberationist impulse, the demands of a Millian individualism, not in terms of bio-logical destiny (although, at a time when contraception and abortion were still very limited of access and widely abhorred, the biological 'destiny' of motherhood is a very formidable 'given' indeed), but in terms of the impossibility of the free individual. This is, in a sense, a response to certain feminist and anti-marriage novels of the period, where the conversion of marriage into a civil contract varying in indi-vidual circumstances (as in Mona Caird), or the levelling 'up' of the double standard (as in *The Heavenly Twins*), or the replacement of marriage by the free union (as in *The Woman Who Did*), are seen as potential guarantees of the freedom of women; symptoms of the oppression of women are taken for the very structures of that oppres-sion, and a perspective of equal rights is seen as not merely a necessary, but a sufficient programme for liberation.

Nevertheless, there is a very important sense in which Sue is right to equate her refusal of a sexual relationship with her freedom, in that it avoids the surrender to involuntary physiological processes which her pregnancies entail. It is in this respect that women are at the very junction of the 'flesh and spirit'; the point where mind and body are in potential conflict—this is the crucial area of that dominance of the material over the intellectual in the duality which is characteristic of the ideology of the period. It is Sue, and not Jude, who is the primary site of that 'deadly war waged between flesh and spirit' of which Hardy speaks in his Preface (p. 27) [5].[8] In Jude, the two are constantly juxtaposed, the dominance of his sexuality displacing the dominance of his intellectual ambitions and vice-versa in a continuing series. Jude's sexuality is a disruptive force in a way that it has not previously been for Hardy's male characters; there is no question here—except in Jude's tortured self-questioning after the death of his children—of a predatory male sexuality destroying a weaker and more vulnerable female through her sexuality, but rather of a sexual nature in itself disturbing, partly because it is so largely beyond the conscious processes of decision and intention. When Jude first meets Arabella his intentions and wishes are overmastered by his sexual attraction toward her; the phrase used in ms. is 'in the authoritative operation of a natural law' but this is cancelled and a less scientific phrase finally substituted—'in commonplace obedience to conjunctive orders from headquarters' [34]. It is this episodic 'battle' of Jude's which gives the novel its similarly episodic form, in which there is a repeated pattern of the abrupt confrontation of his inner life with his material situation: his meditation over the well is broken by the strident tones of his aunt [11], his sympathies with the hungry birds are interrupted by Farmer Troutham's clacker [14], and his recitation of his intellectual attainments is answered by the slap of a pig's penis against his ear (p. 61); from this point on, the dons of Christminster temporarily give way to the Donnes of Cresscombe. Jude's attempt to unite the two through his marriage founders with the significant image of Arabella's fingermarks, hot and greasy from lard-making, on the covers of his classic texts. His wavering thereafter between the two women enacts the alteration of dominance within himself. Points of crisis and transition are marked by Jude's personalised *rites de passage*: his burning of his books, auctioning of his furniture, removing his pillow from the double bed, and so on.[9]

Kate Millett argues that Sue is the 'victim of a cultural literary convention (Lily and Rose)' that cannot allow her to have both a mind and sexuality.[1] The very persistence with which Jude attempts to bring Sue to admit her sexuality into their relationship suggests that this is too simple an account of the self-evident contrast of Sue and Arabella. Hardy seems to have been making conscious use of the convention *within* the figure of Sue; her name means 'lily', and there is symbolism in the scene in which Jude playfully forces her into contact with the roses of which she says ' "I suppose it is against the rules to touch them" ' (p. 308)[2] [233]. It is interesting to note, by the way, that in

8. Cf. Geoffrey Thurley, *The Psychology of Hardy's Novels: The Nervous and the Statuesque* (St. Lucia, Queensland, 1975), p. 191.
9. Cf. William H. Marshall, *The World of the Victorian Novel* (London, 1967), pp. 404–24.
1. *Sexual Politics*, p. 133.
2. Cf. Mary Jacobus, 'Sue the Obscure,' *Essays in Criticism*, 25 (1975), 304–28.

the year of *Jude's* publication, Hardy was collaborating with Florence
Henniker on a story where the heroine's name, Rosalys, seems consciously to draw together the two symbolic traditions.[3]

For Sue, mind and body, intellect and sexuality, are in a complex
and disturbing interdependence, given iconic representation in her
twin deities, Apollo and Venus, which she transmutes for Miss Fontover—prefiguring the later collapse of her intellect and repudiation of
her sexuality—into the representative of religious orthodoxy, St. Peter,
and the repentant sexual sinner, St. Mary Magdalen. Further, there
are the complementary images of Sue as 'a white heap' on the ground
after her desperate leap from her bedroom window (p. 242) [179], and
as a 'heap of black clothes' on the floor of St. Silas after the death of
her children (p. 358) [274]; as victim of her sexuality and as victim of
religious ideology, she is the arena of their conflict. Her intellectual
education throughout the novel runs alongside her emotional involve-
ments: the undergraduate who lent her his books and wanted her to
be his mistress; Phillotson who gives her chaperoned private lessons in
the evenings; and, of course, Jude, with whom she spends much of her
time in discussion. But in each case, sexuality is a destructive, divisive
force, wrecking the relationship and threatening the precarious balance
in Sue's life between her intellectual adventurousness and her sexual
reserve. Her relationship with Jude involves her in the involuntary physiological processes of conception, pregnancy and childbirth, and these
in turn enforce upon her a financial and emotional dependence on
Jude which is destructive for both of them.

Sue, then, is at the centre of this irreconcilability of 'flesh' and
'spirit'; yet she is constantly distanced from the novel's centre of consciousness by the careful manipulation of points of view. A variety of
interpreters interpose between her and the reader—Phillotson, Widow
Edlin, even Arabella; but chiefly, of course, Jude. There is a kind of
collusion between him and the narrator, which is most evident in the
scene of Jude's first walk round Christminster, when he sees the phantoms of past luminaries of the university; the actual names are withheld
from the reader as if to convey the sense of a shared secret between
narrator and character. This collusion enables us to follow the movements of Jude's thoughts and actions—the narrator's examination of
his consciousness is authoritative. Sue, on the other hand, is, as John
Bayley remarks, consistently *exhibited*;[4] she is pictorialised, rendered
in a series of visual images which give some accuracy to Vigar's descrip-
tions of the novel as employing a ' "snapshot" method'.[5] Sue's consciousness is opaque, filtered as it is through the interpretations of

3. 'The Spectre of the Real,' in *In Scarlet and Grey: Stories of Soldiers and Others* (London, 1896), pp. 164–208.
4. John Bayley, *An Essay on Hardy* (Cambridge, 1978), p. 201.
5. Penelope Vigar, *The Novels of Thomas Hardy: Illusion and Reality* (London, 1974), p. 193.

Jude, with all their attendant incomprehensions and distortions; it is this that makes of her actions impulses, of her confused and complex emotions flirtation, and of her motives 'one lovely conundrum' (p. 156) [109].[6] The histories of Jude and Sue are, in some respects, remarkably similar, and yet she is made the instrument of Jude's tragedy, rather than the subject of her own. In a sense the reader's knowledge of her exists only through the perceiving consciousness of Jude, and so it is that after his death, she is not shown at all; Arabella takes on Jude's role of interpreting her to us. The effect of this distancing is to give what is openly a man's picture of a woman; there is no attempt, as there is with Tess Durbeyfield, to make her consciousness and experience transparent, accessible to authoritative explanation and commentary. She is resistant to appropriation by the male narrator, and so the partiality of the novel is not naturalised.

It is often said that Sue's 'frigidity' brings about not only her own tragedy, but also—and in this view more importantly—Jude's.[7] In fact, this tragedy follows upon not merely the sexual consummation of their relationship, but Sue's assimilation, through her parenthood, into a pseudo-marriage. Once she has children, she is forced to live with Jude the economic life of the couple, and gradually to reduce her opposition to marriage to formalism by pretending to marry Jude and adopting his name. It is motherhood—her own humiliation by the respectable wives who hound her and Jude from their work, Little Father Time's taunting by his schoolmates—that convinces her that ' "the world and its ways have a certain worth" ' (p. 368) [283]; this is an insertion in the first edition), and so begins her collapse into ' "enslavement to forms" ' (p. 405) [315]. For the anti-marriage theme of the novel is not entirely concerned with legally or sacramentally defined marriage, though these play a significant role, and it differs again here from most of the contemporary New Woman fiction. In most cases (as in Grant Allen, for example) it is merely the legal aspect that is attacked, while a 'free union' which duplicates the marital relationship in every respect but this is seen as a radical alternative. Even for a radical feminist theorist like Mona Caird, it is the inequality of the terms on which the contract is based that is the root of the problem:

> The injustice of obliging two people, on pain of social ostracism, either to accept the marriage-contract as it stands, or to live apart, is surely self-evident. . . . [I]f it were to be decreed that the woman, in order to be legally married, must gouge out her right eye, no sane person would argue that the marriage-contract was

6. Cf. Elizabeth Langland, 'A Perspective of One's Own: Thomas Hardy and the Elusive Sue Bridehead,' Studies in the Novel, 12 (1980), 12–28.
7. E.g. Shalom Rachman, 'Character and Theme in Hardy's Jude the Obscure,' English, 22, No. 113 (1973), 45–53; and T. B. Tomlinson, The English Middle-Class Novel (London, 1976), pp. 121–4.

perfectly just, simply because the woman was at liberty to remain
single if she did not relish the conditions. Yet this argument is
used on behalf of the present contract, as if it were really any
sounder in the one case than in the other.[8]

Her solution is to propose a more flexible and personalised contractual
relationship. Jude and Sue experience the same sense that predeter-
mined social forms, however they may be for other people, cannot suit
' "the queer sort of people we are" ' they regard themselves unequiv-
ocally as the argument from exception, despite various intimations that
they are simply precursors of a general change of feeling. It is curious
that this argument contradicts the general tendency of the attack on
marriage, for if they are exceptional in their relationship, it is in their
'perfect . . . reciprocity' [161], their ' "extraordinary sympathy, or similarity" ' [182]. Their Shelleyan vision of themselves as twin souls, two
halves of a single whole, is a version of Romanticism which is in conflict
with the attack on marriage as enforcing a continuing and exclusive
commitment; the same contradiction is apparent in Shelley's *Epipsychidion* itself, an important source for *Jude*.[9] Sue and Jude see
themselves as giving freely just this kind and degree of commitment,
embodying in a 'purer', because unconstrained, form the very ideal of
marriage; indeed, they often talk of their relationship precisely *as* a
marriage, and refer to each other as 'husband' and 'wife'. Other relationships of this kind are perceived by them as invariably gross and
degrading—the cowed and pregnant bride who marries her seducer
' "to escape a nominal shame which was owing to the weakness of her
character" ', the boozy, pock-marked woman marrying ' "for a lifetime" ' the convict whom she really wants ' "for a few hours" '
(pp. 297–8) [224]. Their own relationship, however, they perceive as
refined and singled out, its sexuality as merely the symbol of its spirituality. But, in the course of the novel, they are forced to recognise
that their relationship is not transcendant of time, place, and material
circumstance, as they have tried to make it; their Romantic delusion
gives way, leaving Jude cynical, but in Sue's case leading on into the
ideology of legalised and sacramental marriage that her experiences
have led her to respect. Ironically, it is a debased Romantic version
that concludes the book, through Arabella's final statement that
' "She's never found peace since she left his arms, and never will again
till she's as he is now!" ' [322]. Sue comes to see in Phillotson her
husband in law, as Tess comes to see in Alec her husband in nature;
the logic is only apparently opposite, for in both cases it is underpinned

8. Mona Caird, 'The Future of the Home,' in *The Morality of Marriage and Other Essays on
the Status and Destiny of Woman* (London, 1897), p. 117.
9. For an interesting account of the Shelleyan motif in the novel, see Michael E. Hassett,
'Compromised Romanticism in *Jude the Obscure,' Nineteenth-Century Fiction,* 25 (1971),
432–43.

by that sense of the irrevocability of commitment which is inculcated by the ideology of marriage. *Jude* illustrates how a relationship conceived by its protagonists as in opposition to marriage cannot help becoming its replica—that it is in the lived texture of the relationship that the oppression resides, and not in the small print of the contract. The 'alternative' relationship proves ultimately no alternative at all, for its material situation presses upon it to shape it into a pre-existing form. Jude and Sue escape none of the oppressions of marriage, but they incur over and above these the penalties reserved for transgressors against it. There is no form for the relationship to take except those named and determined by the very form that they seek to transcend: unless it is marriage, it is adultery or fornication. It is in this sense that Jude comes to see that he too is one of ' "that vast band of men shunned by the virtuous—the men called seducers" ' (p. 352) [269].

F. B. PINION

[*Jude the Obscure* as Autobiography]†

Hardy's life was relatively uneventful, and but for his creative imagination and literary successes it would not have been very exciting; it certainly was not very sensational, apart from the effect on the public of works such as *Tess of the d'Urbervilles* and *Jude the Obscure*. Why a story of dreams or aspirations and continual failure, of inveiglement into marriage by seduction, of broken marriages, unmarried lovers who live together and rear children only to find them hanged, of marriages which please God in the eyes of the Church and lead to suicide and spiritual death—why *Jude the Obscure*, in short—should have led early reviewers to deduce that it was 'honest autobiography' must surely occasion some surprise. Not until nearly twenty-four years later, when he was roused by a letter from 'an inquirer with whom the superstition still lingered', did Hardy trouble to reply, dictating a letter to his wife Florence, who wrote: 'To your enquiry if *Jude the Obscure* is autobiographical, I have to answer that there is not a scrap of personal detail in it, it having the least to do with his own life of all his books.' When, in the course of preparing his *Life*, he reached the period ending with the 1895–96 reviews of *Jude*, he reverted to this letter, and added:

> Some of the incidents were real in so far as that he had heard of them, or come in contact with them when they were occurring to people he knew; but no more. It is interesting to mention that on his way to school he did once meet with a youth like Jude who

† From F. B. Pinion, *"Jude the Obscure*: Origins in Life and Literature," *Thomas Hardy Annual No.4*, ed. N. Page (London: Macmillan, 1986) 148–55. Reprinted by permission. Bracketed page numbers refer to this Norton Critical Edition.

drove the bread-cart of a widow, a baker, like Mrs Fawley, and carried on his studies at the same time, to the serious risk of other drivers in the lanes; which youth asked him to lend him his Latin grammar.[1]

One can sympathize with Hardy, for the frenetic itch to read auto-biography into this novel has never been more blatantly indulged than in recent years. Of course, Hardy was too absolute; there are scraps of personal detail in it, but details only, and not very considerable. Three examples come to mind: Hardy's childhood wish not to grow up, as he lay with the sun's rays streaming through the interstices of his straw hat, more accurately reproduced in *Jude* than in 'Childhood Among the Ferns'; Hardy and Jude's reading of the same portions of the *Iliad* in their teens; and the placing of a looking-glass by the window to give the invalid Hardy a view of a glorious sunset, repeated by Sue for Phil-lotson, as Hardy remembered in his *Life* long before denying autobi-ographical inclusions in his novel. The letter of rejection from T. Tetuphenay of Biblioll College (his Greek name implying the 'hard slap' he administered to Jude) presents a fourth possibility, reported evidence indicating that it could have been a transcript of a reply to Hardy from Benjamin Jowett of Balliol. The probability is that such recollections and adaptations from the author's life comprise less than one-per-cent of the text.

How much of a writer enters the thoughts, feelings, and actions of his characters, of either sex, can never be assessed. Speaking from expe-rience in 'The Three Voices of Poetry', T. S. Eliot declares his convic-tion that the author not only 'imparts something of himself to his characters' but 'is influenced by the characters he creates'. Hardy's views on marriage were not fixed; he indulges them, no doubt, through Phillotson and Sue, but precisely what his views were, and how far they were turned or moulded by the pressures of imaginative circumstance, no one can say. Undoubtedly the intellectual enfranchisement of the Sue whose intellect 'scintillated like a star' found expression in those Hardyan views which had culminated in his theory of the Unfulfilled Intention:

> that the First Cause worked automatically like a somnambulist, and not reflectively like a sage; that at the framing of the terrestrial conditions there seemed never to have been contemplated such a development of emotional perceptiveness among the creatures subject to those conditions as that reached by thinking and edu-cated humanity.

Whether Jude's silly lovesick dream, on losing Sue to Phillotson, of her having children in her own likeness reflects one of Hardy's thoughts,

1. See F. E. Hardy, *The Life of Thomas Hardy* (London, 1962), 274, 392. [See above, p. 339— Editor.]

as the poem 'To a Motherless Child' seems to suggest, is uncertain; he published the poem as a whimsy, and he must have known that the same idea came to the maudlin hero of Tennyson's 'Locksley Hall'. It is not known whether the poem was written before or after *Jude.*

An imaginative novelist may in some respect, at some stage or other, draw from people he has known in depicting some of his characters. Hardy acknowledged (as Florence told Lady Hoare) that he had one of his uncles in mind when he created Jude; this was John Antell, a Puddletown shoemaker, and a self-educated classical scholar who was occasionally the worse for drink. Nor should Horace Moule, another inebriate, be forgotten; like Jude he was a classical scholar with 'Christminster' connections; according to his friend Hardy, he may have had a bastard son who was brought up in Australia; and like Jude he committed suicide after being irrevocably parted from the woman he loved.

How much of Sue ever existed outside Hardy's imagination is a much more interesting question. The training-college which his two sisters attended at Salisbury ('Melchester') provided the background for one of his sensational episodes. (How fact and fiction can combine to create tradition was illustrated during my first visit to the college nearly twenty years ago, when I was told by a young part-time lecturer, who had become an enthusiastic volunteer guide, that one of Hardy's sisters had been an unsatisfactory student and made her escape by wading through the river. Eventually, after a further visit and more correspondence, I was sent copies of Mary and Kate Hardy's college certificates; there was only one word, term after term, for the conduct of both, and not surprisingly it was 'Good'.) Hardy's close kinship with Mary made him acquainted with the College of Sarum St Michael, but it was from his younger sister Kate, years later, in 1877–78, that he heard more about its institutional hardships and restrictions. He revived his training-college impressions by visits to two London colleges for women in 1891, one of them Stockwell College, where his cousin Tryphena Sparks had been trained. Perhaps he owed something to recollections of her experience there: and her early teaching with the headmaster in the boys' half of the schools at Puddletown may have given him the idea of placing Sue with Phillotson in a similar position at 'Shaston' (Shaftesbury).

On the train to London in March 1890 Hardy began the ambiguously titled poem 'Thoughts of Phena'. 'It was a curious instance of sympathetic telepathy', he afterwards thought, for at the time of his recalling her Tryphena was dying, as he learned soon after her death. Perhaps one of the precursors of those disharmonies which marred the last twenty years of his married life with Emma had brought back the memory of the girl whose affection and gaiety now assured him that she was another of his lost prizes. The thought (the recurring image of the elusive 'well-beloved') and wakened interest in Tryphena Sparks influenced Hardy's last two novels. In the first preface to *Jude the Obscure* he writes: 'The scheme was jotted down in 1890, from notes made in 1887 and onwards, some of the circumstances being suggested by the death of a woman in the former year.' When the lonely Jude muses sadly on Old Midsummer Eve, hoping to see 'the phantom of the Beloved', and regretting Nature's wilfulness in not allowing issue from one parent only, he expresses the thought of 'To a Motherless Child': 'If at the estrangement or death of my lost love, I could go and see her child—hers solely', he says.[2] Before beginning *Jude the Obscure*, Hardy had turned this notion to ridicule and bitter satire in the fantasy of *The Well-Beloved*, where daughter and grand-daughter have the first Avice's likeness, and all in turn attract the love of the artistic Jocelyn Pierston. The serial of 1892 anticipates *Jude* in its criticism of the marriage law, but more significantly in the physical revulsion of the third Avice towards her elderly husband Jocelyn, and in the Phillotson-like humanity with which he releases her from marital bondage. It is in *The Well-Beloved* rather than in *Jude* that Tryphena's fictional memorial is found, most patently, and with hardly any disguise, in the effect of the first Avice's death on Jocelyn:

> He loved the woman dead and inaccessible as he had never loved her in life. He had thought of her at distant intervals during the twenty years since that parting occurred, and only as somebody he could have wedded. Yet now the times of youthful friendship with her, in which he had learnt every note of her innocent nature, flamed up into a yearning and passionate attachment, embittered by regret beyond words. . . . She had been another man's wife almost the whole time since he was estranged from her, and now she was a corpse. Yet the absurdity did not make his grief the less: and the consciousness of the intrinsic, almost radiant, purity of this new-sprung affection for a flown spirit forbade him to check it.[3]

Jude the Obscure was postponed, partly because Hardy's life was too busy and unsettled; mainly, I suspect, because he was unable to plan the novel to his satisfaction. Although he had drawn up an outline, he had to make a structural alteration of the opening after embarking on full-length composition, and it was not until 1894 that the novel began to warm up; in January he was 'creeping on a little' and becoming interested in his heroine as she took 'shape and reality', though she was still 'very nebulous'. So he informed Florence Henniker, with whom his friendship began in May 1893, when he and Mrs Hardy were the guests of her widowed brother, the second Lord Houghton, Viceroy of Ireland. Mrs Henniker was his hostess, and Hardy, not on good terms

2. *Jude* 3.8.
3. *Life* p. 272.

with Emma at the time, found Florence Henniker a 'charming, *intuitive* woman'. An ambitious young novelist, she was not reluctant to encourage his friendship and literary patronage; he was only too ready to give her literary advice and encouragement. At first it was difficult for Hardy to adjust himself socially, but their friendship was based on mutual esteem, and lasted until her death. Beautiful and fascinating, she not surprisingly went to Hardy's head; victim of almost inevitable imaginings, he soon thought he was in love with her. She is the 'one rare fair woman' of 'Wessex Heights', where he tells us that she never knew how much he loved her. Just how the memory of Tryphena Sparks would have helped to create the heroine in *Jude*, had she not, as a result of time and chance, been displaced imaginatively by Mrs Henniker in the creation and development of Sue's character, will never be known. In 1896 Hardy told his friend Edward Clodd that Mrs Henniker had been his 'model' for Sue; his second wife Florence told Professor Purdy that Sue Bridehead was 'in part drawn from Mrs Henniker'. Sue is presented as an epicene intellectual, sexually cold and fastidious but tantalizingly attractive, a type which had always fascinated Hardy, and which he would have attempted to draw earlier had he not found it so difficult, he told Edmund Gosse.[4] The growing attractiveness of her personality and the progressiveness of her views (not Mrs Henniker's) took charge, the story carrying its author into such 'unexpected fields' that he was uncertain of its future by April 1894, when he urged the cancellation of a publishing contract which had led him to promise 'a tale that could not offend the most fastidious maiden'. When the novel was published in November 1895, he told Gosse that it had not altogether been *constructed*, 'for, beyond a certain point, the characters necessitated it, and I simply let it come'. The way it developed had much to do with Mrs Henniker.

Some of Hardy's thoughts about her are clearly transferred to Jude. Hardy discovered that he and Mrs Henniker had been reading Shelley's 'Epipsychidion' simultaneously, and attributed this coincidence to their 'mutual influence'. At one point in the novel (IV.v) [194] Jude quotes the poem with reference to Sue:

> A seraph of Heaven, too gentle to be human,
> Veiling beneath that radiant form of woman . . .

Earlier (III.ix) [149] he sees her in terms of the same poem, 'so ethereal a creature that her spirit could be seen trembling through her limbs'. Before the first flush of his imaginative love had waned, Hardy had endowed Mrs Henniker with this Shelleyan spirituality, a hint of it occurring in a letter of 18 December 1893: one great gain of seeing her recently, he tells her, is that 'certain nice and dear features' in her

4. *The Well-Beloved* 2.3.

character, 'half-forgotten, through their being of that etheral intangible sort', are now revived. Reverting to the passage just quoted from *Jude*, we can see how Florence Henniker existed for Hardy at the time of writing: 'the sweetest and most disinterested comrade that he had ever had, living largely in vivid imaginings'. Sue and Jude have 'complete mutual understanding'; they are 'almost the two parts of a single whole' [149], almost the ideal union Hardy had expressed a yearning for at the end of the fifth chapter of *Tess*. Elsewhere in *Jude* he writes: 'That the one affined soul he had ever met was lost to him . . . returned upon him with cruel persistency . . . '. The tragic irony of this reflection is evident in the title-page epigraph Hardy wrote, his own marriage much in mind, in August 1895, for a new edition of *The Woodlanders*:

> 'Not boskiest bow'r,
> When hearts are ill affin'd,
> Hath tree of pow'r
> To shelter from the wind!'

'What name shall I give to the heroine of my coming long story when I get at it?' he asked Mrs Henniker when he wrote on Sunday, 22 October 1893. What he wished may be guessed from the appearance of 'Florence' in the signature of Sue's more distant letters to Jude about the time of her first marriage to Phillotson.

It should be stressed that, though she resembles Hardy's impressions of Mrs Henniker in some respects, Sue developed pre-eminently in his imagination. Yet there is one other passage in Jude (III.iv) [122–23] which not only reflects Florence Henniker but bears on the tragic resolution of the novel: 'that epicene tenderness of hers was too harrowing. . . . If he could only get over the sense of her sex . . . what a comrade she would make. . . . She was nearer to him than any other woman he had ever met, and he could scarcely believe that time, creed, or absence, would ever divide him from her.' Hardy and Mrs Henniker differed profoundly in creed; she was Anglo-Catholic and proof against his protestations that as a writer she needed to be intellectually twenty-five years ahead of her time. How could she, the daughter of Shelley's champion, he asked, allow herself 'to be enfeebled to a belief in ritualistic ecclesiasticism'? He would have to trust to imagination for a woman enfranchised from 'retrograde superstitions'. This, of course, was Sue before tragedy made her retrogressive. Hardy, as a passage (III.iii) [112] on women students in training at Melchester shows— and this is based on observations made at Whitelands Training College (*Life*, p. 235)—believed that women are the weaker sex, not as well endowed as men to endure suffering and shock. The loss of her children is seen by Sue as a sign of God's anger that she and Jude have ignored ecclesiastical conformity, or 'lived in sin', as the popular saying goes. Her prostration below the Cross in the 'ceremonial' church of St Silas,

and her declaration that 'Arabella's child killing mine was a judgment—the right slaying the wrong' made Jude explode with hatred of
'Christianity, or mysticism, or Sacerdotalism, or whatever it may be
called'. Her physical self-sacrifice and spiritual death in remarriage to
Phillotson, which is presented as her crucifixion, is not quite Hardy's
last comment on the superstition that sanctifies lasting wedlock for
incompatible couples whom 'God hath joined together': Jude's remarriage is a grotesque satire on the subject. Both are crazed by their losses:
one 'creed-drunk', the other 'gin-drunk'. How *Jude the Obscure* would
have reached its tragic endings had Hardy not found Mrs Henniker
intractably unemancipated in her religious beliefs is one of those insoluble questions which are worth asking.

By influencing the character and role of Sue, Hardy's new friendship
seems to have contributed a more exciting creative element to *Jude*
than any other factor.

* * *

RICHARD DELLAMORA

[Sexuality and Scandal]†

The tightening constraints [of the 1890s] did not affect only male
homosexuals and those involved with them. Sexually conventional
men, lesbians, and New Women also were vulnerable. In 1895, likewise, literary scandal attended publication in book form of Thomas
Hardy's *Jude the Obscure*. Hardy's writing, like that of Wilde and contemporary feminists, subverted male privilege in marriage. That arbiter
of public decency, the *Pall Mall Gazette*, in a review of November 12
called the novel "Jude the Obscene"; and the London *World* ran its
review "under the title 'Hardy the Degenerate.' " Mrs. Oliphant
reviewed the book as a polemic against marriage. Most spectacularly,
Bishop William Walsham How of Wakefield burned the book—then
added injury to insult by instigating "the withdrawal of the novel from
W. H. Smith's huge circulating library."[1]

Hardy's novel was, however, offensive in other ways as well. *Jude the
Obscure* is notable for the weakness within it of same-sex bonding—
at least for its protagonists, Jude and Sue. Jude has no male friends;
he has no entry into the male homosocial enclaves to which he is so

† From Richard Dellamora, *Masculine Desire: The Sexual Politics of Victorian Aestheticism*
(Chapel Hill: U of North Carolina P, 1990) 212–15. © 1990 by the University of North
Carolina Press. Used by permission of the publisher.
1. Michael Millgate, *Thomas Hardy: A Biography* (New York: Random House, 1982), pp. 369,
371, 372.

strongly drawn, especially Oxford. And he repeatedly fails in attempts to achieve a mentor-protégé relationship. His one relationship of the kind, with a village schoolteacher named Phillotson, proves to be disastrous for both men. And Hardy is mordant about the putative solidarity that exists among working-class males. In focusing on a man whose life is characterized by exclusion from male homosocial ties, Hardy implicitly condemns institutions like Oxford, where a cherished sense of belonging was purchased at the price of a snobbish exclusivity. Hardy might also be seen as demythologizing the figure of the gentleman, since in humble, diffuse ways Jude seeks entry into an occupation that would make him a simulacrum of a gentleman. Hardy points out the cruelty to which Jude's naive pursuit of this substitute ambition exposes him. Again not surprisingly, gentlemanly reviewers reacted against the novel. In his life of Hardy, Michael Millgate points out that Hardy was especially aggrieved at "fellow members of the Savile Club" who wrote "hostile reviews" in the 1890s. Millgate remarks that Hardy's dismay "reflected his sense, ingrained from childhood, that friendship was inseparable from loyalty, and also his bitter realization that his years of investment in clubbability and *bonhomie* were not, after all, standing him in good stead."[2] *Jude* repudiates such affiliations; instead, the novel reaffirms Hardy's awareness of himself as an outsider and asserts his fellowship with someone as estranged as Jude Fawley.

Hardy was especially upset by his friend Edmund Gosse's ambivalent review of the novel on November 8.[3] And though Gosse gave as his reason the bleakness of the book, other causes of concern lay close to hand. Like Hardy, Gosse was a clubman; like Hardy, he also felt a need to belong to a number of male elites: to a circle of eminent writers, to another of journalists, and to the social world of the aristocracy.[4] Yet like Hardy himself, Gosse, though a man of letters, was not a university man. And despite the fact that he had advanced far, receiving offers of professorships from Yale, Harvard, and Johns Hopkins universities and winning appointment to the Clark Lectureship at Cambridge University in 1884, he fell victim to attack by a former friend, John Churton Collins, in the *Quarterly Review*.[5] Gosse's penchant for hasty and erroneous research made him vulnerable, and even though establishment support carried him through, "as a serious scholar he was now irrevocably handicapped."[6] Gosse had good reason to be troubled by a novel that traces the decline and fall of a book-loving young man unable to enter the university world.

Especially only six months after the Wilde trials, Gosse had further reason for discomfort, reason divined by Hardy himself, in the non-

2. Ibid., p. 373.
3. Ibid., p. 370.
4. Ann Thwaite, *Edmund Gosse: A Literary Landscape* (London: Secker & Warburg, 1984).
5. Ibid., Chapter 10.
6. Ibid., p. 295.

conformity of Sue Bridehead, the novel's heroine. Gosse, who was an acquaintance of Wilde and a heterosexual by choice rather than by inclination, panicked at the time of the trial and wrote a letter asking his and Wilde's mutual friend, Robert Ross, to stay away from the Gosse household.[7] Gosse's long and ardent friendship with the sculptor Hamo Thornycroft depended for its stability on the conscious suppression of desire on Gosse's part.[8] As it turns out, the Thornycrofts were visitors to Hardy at Max Gate in September 1895. Writing to Gosse shortly after publication of the review, Hardy specifically raises the question of sexual inversion—but in such a way as to allay, if possible, Gosse's anxiety. There is, Hardy writes, "nothing perverted or depraved in Sue's nature. The abnormalism consists in disproportion; not in inversion."[9]

In a well-known passage from the postscript to the 1912 edition of *Jude the Obscure*, Hardy suggests that Sue may reasonably be regarded as a type of "the woman of the feminist movement—the slight pale 'bachelor' girl—the intellectualized, emancipated bundle of nerves that modern conditions were producing, mainly in cities as yet."[1] Feminist critics, however, are not so sure that Sue is a feminist. Penny Boumelha for one suggests that if Sue is a type, she resembles not so much the turn-of-the-century feminist as the phenomenon of the New Woman, a figure drawn from contemporary life but also prominent in the popular press and in a number of novels that have been described as New Woman fiction. While neither the type nor the fiction are uniform, the New Woman is self-consciously critical of marriage; and her novel is often "dominated" by the ideal of " 'free union,' " a monogamous relationship "based on the notion of substituting the sanction of personal feeling for the degrading economic [and, one might add, sexual] basis of legal marriage."[2] Hardy and Sue are at one in resisting marriage as a license "to be loved on the premises."[3]

In truth, Sue's ideal, frustrated in the novel, affiliates her with both the New Woman and with feminism as well as with the critique of marriage in writers like Symonds and Kains-Jackson. Earlier feminists like Harriet Taylor and John Stuart Mill had attacked the idea, still prevalent in the 1890s, of the conjugal rights of husbands.[4] And contemporary feminists like Elizabeth Wolstenholme Elmy and Francis

7. Ibid., pp. 359–60.
8. Ibid., pp. 320–22.
9. Letter of November 20, 1895, quoted by Millgate, *Thomas Hardy*, p. 354.
1. See Penny Boumelha, *Thomas Hardy and Women* (Brighton: Harvester Press, 1982), Chapters 4, 7; Elaine Showalter, *A Literature of Their Own* (Princeton, N.J.: Princeton University Press, 1977), Chapter 7; Lloyd Fernando, *"New Women" in the Late Victorian Novel* (University Park: Pennsylvania State University Press, 1977); Gail Cunningham, *The New Woman in the Victorian Novel* (New York: Barnes & Noble, 1978).
2. Hardy, *Jude the Obscure* (see above, p. 442).
3. J. S. Mill, *The Subjection of Women*, see above, Chapter 2.
4. Sheila Jeffreys, *The Spinster and Her Enemies* (London: Pandora, 1985), p. 30.

Swiney emphasize "woman's right to physical integrity and self-determination."[5] These writers resisted male control of women's bodies—whether as the object of sexual advances or as bearers of children. Male homosexual polemicists, New Women, and feminists in their different ways all posed a challenge to male prerogatives and to the appropriation of women's bodies for purposes of social production.

One of the significant questions of contemporary women's history is how it came about that feminism, prominent in the 1890s, had by 1930 given way to reconfirmed ideals of the biological basis of women's roles and to a militant conviction that women's destiny lay in monogamous marriage.[6] One element lies in the professional development of sexology, for despite the fact that turn-of-the-century sexologists regarded themselves as intellectually and socially liberal and although in many respects they were—for instance, in supporting "the removal of penal laws against homosexuality"—in other respects their work was all too evidently reactive. In particular, they tended to confirm conventional gender roles on the ground that the bourgeois construction of gender was "natural," i.e., that it is biologically and not socially based. Weeks comments: "Their achievement has been to *naturalise* sexual patterns and identities and thus obscure their historical genealogy."[7] Taking this tack, sexologists labeled individuals who resisted conventional gender expectations—individuals like New Women or feminists or fictional characters like Sue Bridehead—as abnormal, neurotic, or even perverse. When Hardy in 1912 refers to Sue as the " 'bachelor' girl of modern urban experience," he reflects the bias of contemporary sexology, a field with which his earlier use of the word "inversion" in relation to Sue indicates his familiarity. Since, unlike the actual "bachelor" girls of the turn of the century, Sue is unable to compete with men for suitable work or to find a flat for herself in a large city, she seems an unsuitable object for Hardy's epithet.

As well, Hardy's attraction to a free-love relationship and his revulsion from marriage do not comprise a repudiation of compulsory heterosexuality. Instead his comment on Sue's "disproportion" implies a principle of indwelling proportion in gender. In the novel he enforces upon her what Rich sees as one prime element of compulsory heterosexuality, namely "the socialization of women to feel that male sexual 'drive' amounts to a right."[8] There is a glaring contrast between Hardy's ability to empathize with Jude's point of view and his inability at times to enter imaginatively into Sue's. And this observation holds even

5. George Chauncey, "From Sexual Inversion to Homosexuality," *Salmagundi*, 58–59 (Fall 1982–Winter 1983), pp. 114–46; Sheila Jeffreys, *The Spinster and Her Enemies*; Jeffrey Weeks, *Sexuality and Its Discontents* (London: Routledge & Kegan Paul, 1985).
6. Jeffrey Weeks, *Sexuality and Its Discontents*, pp. 71, 80 and Chapter 4.
7. Adrienne Rich, "Compulsory Heterosexuality and Lesbian Existence," *Signs*, 5 (1980), pp. 631–60.
8. Martha Vicinus, *Independent Women* (Chicago: University of Chicago Press, 1985).

though Sue faces choices in some ways like Jude's. In the late Victorian period, professional achievement for women usually meant a celibate life shared in a community of women.⁹ But for Sue, Hardy sketches only two alternatives: a disabling normalcy or degrees of deviance. His position foreshadows the formulation of the lesbian type two years later by Havelock Ellis. Signs of gender inversion in Sue's behavior and later criticism of her as "frigid" make her a fictional occasion of scandal. The more authentic base of scandal, however, exists in the fact that for as long as she can, she speaks intellectually and that she aspires to be a different sort of woman—even if neither she nor Hardy can say what feminine difference means.

MARJORIE GARSON

[Jude's Idealism]†

Jude Fawley wants; Jude Fawley is wanting. We know Jude through the rhythm of desire, repulsion, and renunciation which constitutes his inner life; we know him through those he wants, through Sue and Arabella and Christminster; and we know *them* in terms of their ability or inability to fulfil his desires. Jude is wanting: he is constituted in lack, defined from the first pages of the novel as 'a hungry soul in pursuit of a full soul'. His emptiness is dramatized in the action—even in the part-titles—of the novel, as he moves from place to place in search of the fulfilment which continually eludes him. Jude's wanting provides the plot, the characters, and the emotional tone of the novel.

Jude wants Sue, and he wants a university education. Examination of Hardy's manuscripts has shown that the marriage problem was part of his conception of the novel from the very beginning, and that in his first draft it was Sue who was to have been the motivation for Jude's desire to visit Christminster. Though Phillotson later replaced Sue in this capacity, there remain in the novel as it stands strong links between Jude's desire for Sue and his desire for Christminster. Sue is living in the city of his dreams, and reaching it involves discovering her. Desiring in her not only the woman but the cultivation she embodies—the kind of culture which exposure to Christminster has apparently already given to her—Jude attributes to her many of the values which he has attributed to the city, imagining them both as bodiless, visionary pres-

9. Elaine Showalter, "Syphilis, Sexuality, and the Fiction of the Fin de Siècle," in *Sex, Politics and Science in the Nineteenth-Century Novel*, ed. Ruth Bernard Yeazell (Baltimore, Md.: Johns Hopkins University Press, 1986).

† From Marjorie Garson, *Hardy's Fables of Integrity: Woman, Body, Text* (Oxford: Clarendon Press, 1991) 152–58. © Marjorie Garson 1991. Reprinted by permission of Oxford University Press. Bracketed page numbers refer to this Norton Critical Edition. The author's notes have been omitted.

ences, as shining forms encircled by haloes of light. Jude is temperamentally logocentric: he naïvely believes in the reality of the idealized images he has constructed from inherited materials. Christminster is to be the heavenly Jerusalem of Revelation, Sue is to be the haloed apparition in his aunt's photograph. However, both will remain hauntingly elusive: despite his obsession about staying close to the university and to Sue, Jude discovers that it does not necessarily help to be 'on the spot' [10]. For the truth is that both the desired woman and the desired city exist in their luminous purity only in Jude's imagination: by the very nature of his dreams, he is doomed to disappointment.

What particularly marks this novel, indeed, is the tone of what might be called 'logocentric wistfulness'. Like many of Hardy's heroes, Jude is a reader, but a reader of printed texts rather than of the signs of nature. The fact that it is the Bible which lies behind the language and imagery of the novel seems related to the stubbornness with which he insists upon a transcendent reality behind words and signs. And Jude's author shares his logocentric desire. When Hardy presents his protagonist as a Christ-figure, there may be a degree of irony in the identification; but he treats Jude's analogous fantasies without disabling irony. Though we know from the beginning that Jude is going to be mistaken about Christminster and about Sue, we are to think more of him for his idealism, and less of those beings which fail to live up to his image of them. Christminster ought to be the City of Light, and if it is not, it is the city which is to blame; Sue ought to be 'worthy' of Jude's devotion. Both equally deserve his suggestively worded reproach to Sue: 'you are . . . not so nice in your real presence as you are in your letters' [131].

Indeed, what Jude wants is implicit in his view of language. As a child, Jude imagines that there is a key which will render the whole of language transparent—undo Babel. When he finds that no such key exists, that he cannot master the whole, he starts to plug away at the parts. But his vision of identity is rather endorsed than otherwise, and the fantasy of wholeness underlies the text: the desire for magical translation into a state of pure presence, the desire to be lifted above competing voices, absorbed into a unified community. This dream seems to be presented as a legitimate desire, a vision betrayed by the social organization of contemporary Oxford and by Victorian views of marriage.

Jude's Christminster is created for him by words, by printed books. Although the notion of a blessed place is suggested by Phillotson, the shape that place takes in his imagination derives from images which are essentially literary. Jude knows Christminster through the Bible, as the heavenly Jerusalem; through his study of Latin, as his 'Alma Mater' [32]; and through the written words of her sons, who speak to him of 'her ineffable charm' [66] more kindly and clearly than Christminster ever speaks in person. These patriarchal texts testify with an authority which implies the reality of what they describe. But it is clear from the opening pages of the novel that the very terms in which Jude has conceived his desire preclude its fulfilment.

The famous opening to the second part of the novel, which has Jude listening to the 'ghostly presences' [64] of Christminster, suggests why this is so. These voices of Oxford seem stilted, 'got up' by Hardy, but the very awkwardness of the passage is part of its meaning. The episode raises in paradigmatic form some of the issues of autobiographical fiction, since the quotations Jude remembers have of course been culled from Hardy's own reading. Hardy's awareness of their miscellaneous, even arbitrary character is reflected in the way the narrator accounts for them: they are supposed to be from 'a book or two [Jude] had brought with him concerning the sons of the University' [66], evidently tourist-guide anthologies of 'purple passages'. The attribution suggests that Jude is not as well read as Hardy (the quotations are not collected by *him*) but on the other hand absolves Jude of the kind of jejune self-satisfaction implied by their assemblage. The passage dramatizes the alienation it presents, its uneasy tone a perfectly accurate register of both the pride and the defensiveness of the autodidact. Its ironies make clear that print can provide no unmediated, unproblematical contact with culture as a whole or with the mind or spirit of the writers of the past.

Indeed, the episode raises the question of the relationship between the written and the spoken word, for though their resonant words seem 'spoken by them in muttering utterances' [66], Jude has been introduced to the 'voices' through the printed pages 'he had just been conning' [66], and their rhetoric (even that of Sir Robert Peel's Corn Law speech) is very much *écriture*. Jude dreams of appropriating what these voices represent, but they undo him even as they address him: as he listens to them, he begins to feel more ghostly, less substantial, than they. Each of these writers uses the first person pronoun; each one has a powerful ego and a confident, totalizing vision of human experience. Yet, speaking together, the voices depict a Christminster which must remain incoherent, not only because (as Jude himself realizes) it has always generated a wide range of conflicting opinions but also because it is constituted by the (inevitably) fragmentary reading of an (inevitably) partially educated individual. Jude seeks to be made whole, but it is clear that his very vision of Christminster must preclude the consummation he desires.

What Jude does for a living is relevant to these issues. A country stonemason who practises his craft 'holistically', he can turn his hand to a number of tasks, in contrast to the urban workers, who master one technique only. Jude's versatility recalls while it parodies Ruskin's vision of Gothic. The values Ruskin imputes to the old architecture are seen as illusory, yet the presence in the novel of bastardized Victorian Gothic nevertheless implies *degrees* of authenticity and hints at a nostalgia for origin which the text at other times seems to debunk. (At times Hardy seems to suggest that Jude, in desiring a university education, is betraying a kind of Ruskinian vision of honest craftsmanship.) It is emblematic of this contradiction that Sue should dismiss the Gothic style as 'barbaric' [241], and yet at the same time be 'sentimentally opposed to the horrors of over-restoration' [236]; it is not entirely clear whether this is supposed to be one of her many contradictions (as the narrator's adverb 'sentimentally' would seem to suggest) or whether the inconsistencies in Hardy's feelings shape her 'character' (for the noun 'horrors' may not be Sue's but the narrator's).

For Hardy seems to endorse Jude's impulses by showing them as instinctively directed towards wholeness, while at the same time presenting that wholeness as an impossible dream. Is it because Jude is a working man, or simply because he is a human being, that he has to begin his apprenticeship laboriously and fragmentedly, by learning to shape one letter at a time? The process is analogous to the way he has to struggle with the heavy medium of the classical languages, alone and without help. The dream is of a whole which will at some moment add up to more than the sum of its parts, which will become monumental, permanent, resonant with interconnected meaning; which will make the individual whole, and unite him creatively with an organic community. But I would argue that the text is not entirely clear about whether it is Jude's class position which victimizes him, or whether this dream is by definition a hopeless one.

In my reading, the text is shaped even more radically by Hardy's feelings about the body than by his feelings about social class. It seems to me that Jude's desire—for a wholeness of a quasi-spiritual type, a wholeness which completely transcends the body, does not depend upon the body—is intrinsically unrealizable, and that the class theme in the novel is as much 'vehicle' as it is 'tenor'. Take for example Jude's occupation. The facts that he, like Hardy's father, is a stone-mason and that his dusty working clothes make him invisible to the upper-class undergraduates who pass him on the street suggest that it is his class position which is decisive. On the other hand, there is something idiosyncratically Hardyan about the way Jude's craft is presented. It is suggestive that Jude is a worker in stone, the deadest and most intractable of materials, and that he sees himself as in the business of supplying dead bodies, helping to provide 'the carcases that contained the scholar souls' [30]—for while this ought to be a perfectly legitimate aim, and would be in Ruskin's terms, it is one which, in Hardy's world, cannot be achieved with impunity.

Embodiment means death; stone itself means death. His work chills Jude and makes him vulnerable to the lung infection which eventually kills him; the dust marks him and makes him invisible to those who look through his body as through a pane of glass. But these literal details only mask the deeper, figurative import of the stonemasonry. Its implications are crystallized in the famous moment when Jude cuts into a stone the word THITHER [61]—an inscription which, we know, will remain to mock him. The act of embodying an aim in a word, and cutting that word in stone, is perfectly emblematic of Jude's logocentric desire. His aim is to make the word real—to ensure its fulfilment—by giving it a body. But in Hardy's world the opposite happens. When the word falls into matter, becomes incarnate in paper or stone, it partakes of the exigencies of material existence, and becomes sinister, mocking, dangerous. The common ('touch-wood') superstition that expressing satisfaction at a situation can reverse it is given an idiosyncratic slant by Hardy, who suggests that the real danger lies in inscribing the word, giving it a material body. The incarnate word takes the place of what it signifies, precludes its fulfilment. Incarnation means betrayal in this novel: to give or to take a body is to fall away from reality, to be involved in death.

Thomas Hardy: A Chronology

1840 (June 2) Born in the house built by his grandfather (Thomas Hardy), in Higher Bockhampton, in the parish of Stinsford, Dorset, first child of Thomas and Jemima Hardy. (A brother and two sisters follow, none of whom marries.)

1848 Attends school at Lower Bockhampton, but in the next year is moved by his mother to a school in Dorchester, three miles from his home.

1856 Leaves school and is apprenticed to a Dorchester architect, John Hicks.

1862 Moves to London, where he works as an architect. Attempts unsuccessfully to get his poetry published.

1863 Is awarded an essay prize by the Royal Institute of British Architects.

1865 Publishes a short, humorous sketch, "How I Built Myself a House."

1867 Returns to Dorset and resumes work for Hicks. Begins a novel, *The Poor Man and the Lady* (never published and later destroyed).

1869 Works as an architect in Weymouth, Dorset.

1870 While on architectural business in Cornwall, meets and falls in love with Emma Lavinia Gifford.

1871 *Desperate Remedies* published anonymously.

1872 *Under the Greenwood Tree*.

1873 Suicide of Hardy's close friend and mentor, Horace Moule. *A Pair of Blue Eyes*. (From this point on, all Hardy's novels appear initially as serials: dates given below refer to first appearance in volume form.) Abandons architecture to become a full-time writer.

1874 *Far from the Madding Crowd*. Marries Emma Gifford; honeymoon spent in France.

1876 The Hardys visit Holland and Germany.

1878 *The Return of the Native*.

1880 *The Trumpet-Major*. Seriously ill.

1881 *A Laodicean*.

1882 *Two on a Tower*.

1885 Moves into Max Gate, a large house built to his own designs

on the outskirts of Dorchester; it remains his home for the rest
of his life, though until 1911 he and his wife regularly spend
part of each year in London.

1886 *The Mayor of Casterbridge.*

1887 *The Woodlanders.* The Hardys visit France and Italy.

1888 *Wessex Tales,* Hardy's first collection of short stories.

1889 Several publishers reject the opening portion of *Tess of the d'Urbervilles.*

1891 *A Group of Noble Dames* (short stories) and *Tess of the d'Urbervilles.*

1892 Death of Hardy's father.

1893 Visits Ireland and meets Mrs. Florence Henniker, to whom he forms a close attachment.

1894 *Life's Little Ironies* (short stories).

1895 *Jude the Obscure.* The first collected edition of Hardy's novels appears as "Wessex Novels" in 1895–96.

1897 *The Well-Beloved* is published (an earlier version had appeared as a serial in 1892).

1898 *Wessex Poems,* with Hardy's own illustrations: his first collection of verse, it signals his abandonment of the novel in favor of poetry.

1901 *Poems of the Past and the Present.*

1904 Death of Hardy's mother. Part 1 of *The Dynasts,* an epic-drama about the Napoleonic Wars (the second part follows in 1906, the third and final part in 1908).

1909 *Time's Laughingstocks* (poems).

1910 Awarded the Order of Merit by King George V.

1912 Death of Emma Hardy: the great sequence "Poems of 1912–13" is written during the next few months. The Wessex Edition of Hardy's writings begins publication.

1913 Revisits Cornwall, the scene of his courtship of Emma, early in the year. *A Changed Man* (short stories).

1914 Marries Florence Emily Dugdale (1879–1937). *Satires of Circumstance* (poems).

1915 Death of Hardy's sister Mary.

1916 *Selected Poems,* his own selection from his work to date.

1917 *Moments of Vision* (poems).

1922 *Late Lyrics and Earlier.*

1923 Hardy's play, *The Famous Tragedy of the Queen of Cornwall.* The Prince of Wales, later Edward VIII, visits Hardy at Max Gate.

1925 *Human Shows* (poems).

1928 (January 11) Hardy dies at Max Gate. Later in the year *Winter Words* (poems) and *The Early Life of Thomas Hardy* are published; the latter, though issued under the name of Florence Hardy, is in effect an autobiography, compiled during the last decade of Hardy's life. (A second volume, *The Later Years of Thomas Hardy*, follows in 1930.)

Selected Bibliography

● indicates works included or excerpted in this Norton Critical Edition.

BIBLIOGRAPHIES

Davis, W. Eugene, and Helmut E. Gerber. *Thomas Hardy; An Annotated Bibliography of Writings About Him, Vol. 11: 1970–1978 and Supplement for 1871–1969*. De Kalb, Ill.: Northern Illinois UP, 1983.

Draper, Ronald P., and Martin S. Ray. *An Annotated Critical Bibliography of Thomas Hardy*. London and New York: Macmillan, 1989.

Gerber, H. E., and W. E. Davis. *Thomas Hardy: An Annotated Bibliography of Writings About Him*. De Kalb, Ill.: Northern Illinois UP, 1973.

Millgate, Michael. "Thomas Hardy." *Victorian Fiction: A Second Guide to Research*. Ed. George H. Ford. New York: Modern Language Assn. of America, 1978.

● Purdy, Richard Little.*Thomas Hardy: A Bibliographical Study*. Oxford: Clarendon Press, 1954.

BIOGRAPHIES

Gibson, James.*Thomas Hardy: A Literary Life*. London: Macmillan, 1996.

● Gittings, Robert. *Young Thomas Hardy*. London: Heinemann, 1975.

———. *The Older Hardy*. London: Heinemann, 1978.

Hands, Timothy. *A Hardy Chronology*. London: Macmillan, 1992.

Millgate, Michael. *Thomas Hardy: A Biography*. New York: Random House, 1982.

O'Sullivan, Timothy. *Thomas Hardy: An Illustrated Biography*. London: Macmillan, 1975.

GENERAL CRITICISM

Bayley, John. *An Essay on Hardy*. Cambridge: Cambridge UP, 1978.

● Boumelha, Penny. *Thomas Hardy and Women: Sexual Ideology and Narrative Form*. Brighton: Harvester Press, 1982.

Brown, Douglas. *Thomas Hardy*. Rev. ed. London: Longman, 1961.

Cox, R. G. *Thomas Hardy: The Critical Heritage*. London: Routledge, 1970.

● Garson, Marjorie. *Hardy's Fables of Integrity: Woman, Body, Text*. Oxford: Clarendon, 1991.

Gregor, Ian. *The Great Web: The Form of Hardy's Major Fiction*. Totowa, N.J.: Rowman & Littlefield, 1974.

● Guerard, Albert J. *Thomas Hardy: The Novels and Stories*. Cambridge, Mass.: Harvard UP, 1949.

Hands, Timothy. *Thomas Hardy*. London: Macmillan, 1995.

Holloway, John. *The Victorian Sage*. New York: Archon, 1962.

● Howe, Irving. *Thomas Hardy*. New York: Macmillan, 1967.

Ingham, Patricia, ed. *Thomas Hardy: Feminist Readings*. Hemel Hempstead: Harvester Wheatsheaf, 1989.

Langbaum, Robert. *Thomas Hardy in Our Time*. London: Macmillan, 1995.

Miller, J. Hillis. *Thomas Hardy: Distance and Desire*. Cambridge, Mass.: Harvard UP, 1970.

Millgate, Michael. *Thomas Hardy: His Career as a Novelist*. London: Bodley Head, 1971.

Morgan, Rosemarie. *Women and Sexuality in the Novels of Thomas Hardy*. London: Routledge, 1988.

Page, Norman. *Thomas Hardy*. London: Routledge, 1977.

Pinion, F. B. *A Hardy Companion*. London: Macmillan, 1968.

● Rutland, W. R. *Thomas Hardy: A Study of His Writings and Their Background*. 1938. New York: Russell and Russell, 1962.

Stubbs, Patricia. *Woman and Fiction: Feminism and the Novel, 1880–1920*. Brighton: Harvester, 1979.

• Weber, C. J. *Hardy of Wessex: His Life and Literary Career*. Rev. ed. New York: Columbia UP, 1965.

Wing, George. *Thomas Hardy*. Edinburgh: Oliver & Boyd, 1963.

Wright, T. R. *Hardy and the Erotic*. London: Macmillan, 1989.

ON *JUDE THE OBSCURE*

Brooke-Rose, Christine. "Ill Wit and Sick Tragedy: *Jude the Obscure*." *The Alternative Hardy*. Ed. Lance St. John Butler. London: Macmillan, 1989. 26–48.

Cunningham, A. R. "The 'New Woman' Fiction of the 1890's." *Victorian Studies* 17 (1973): 177–86.

De Laura, David J. " 'The Ache of Modernism' in Hardy's Later Novels." *Journal of English Literary History* 34 (1956): 380–90.

• Dellamora, Richard. *Masculine Desire: The Sexual Politics of Victorian Aestheticism*. Chapel Hill: U of North Carolina P, 1990. 212–15.

Draper, R. P. "Hardy's Comic Tragedy: *Jude the Obscure*." *Critical Essays on Thomas Hardy: The Novels*. Ed. Dale Kramer and Nancy Marck. Boston: Hall, 1990. 243–54.

Goode, John. "Sue Bridehead and the New Woman." *Women Writing and Writing about Women*. Ed. Mary Jacobus. London: Croom Helm, 1979.

Heilman, Robert B. "Hardy's Sue Bridehead." *Nineteenth-Century Fiction* 20 (1966): 307–23.

Holland, Norman. "*Jude the Obscure*: Hardy's Symbolic Indictment of Christianity." *Nineteenth-Century Fiction* 9 (1954): 50–60.

Hyde, W. J. "Hardy's Response to Critics of *Jude*." *Victorian Newsletter* 9 (1961): 1–5.

Ingham, Patricia. "The Evolution of *Jude the Obscure*." *Review of English Studies*, n.s.27 (1976): 27–37, 159–69.

Langland, Elizabeth. "Becoming a Man in *Jude the Obscure*." *The Sense of Sex: Feminist Perspectives on Hardy*. Ed. Margaret R. Higonnet. Urbana and Chicago: U of Illinois P, 1993. 32–48.

• Lawrence, D. H. *Phoenix: The Posthumous Papers of D. H. Lawrence*. Ed. E. D. McDonald. New York: Viking, 1936. See Chapter 9.

• McDowell, Frederick P. "Hardy's 'Seemings or Personal Impressions': The Symbolical Use of Image and Contrast in *Jude the Obscure*." *Modern Fiction Studies* 6 (1960): 236–45.

———. "In Defense of Arab...la: A Note on *Jude the Obscure*." *English Language Notes* 1 (1964): 274–80.

Mallett, Phillip. "Sexual Ideology and Narrative Form in *Jude the Obscure*." *English* 38 (1989): 211–24.

Millett, Kate. *Sexual Politics*. New York: Doubleday, 1970. See especially pp. 130–34.

• Mizener, Arthur. "*Jude the Obscure* as a Tragedy." *Southern Review* 6 (1940–41): 203–13.

• Paterson, John. "The Genesis of *Jude the Obscure*." *Studies in Philology* 57 (1960): 87–98.

• Pinion, F. B. *Jude the Obscure*: Origins in Life and Literature." *Thomas Hardy Annual No. 4*. London, 1986. 148–55.

Simpson, Anne B. "Sue Bridehead Revisited." *Victorian Literature and Culture* 19 (1991): 55–66.

• Slack, Robert C. "The Text of Hardy's *Jude the Obscure*." *Nineteenth-Century Fiction* 11 (1957): 261–75.

Steig, Michael. "Sue Bridehead." *Novel* 1 (1968): 260–66.

Sutherland, John. "A Note on the Teasing Narrator in *Jude the Obscure*." *English Literature in Transition* 17 (1974): 159–62.

Taylor, Dennis. "The Chronology of *Jude the Obscure*." *Thomas Hardy Journal* 12.3 (October 1996): 65–68.

Watts, Cedric. *Thomas Hardy: "Jude the Obscure*." Penguin Critical Studies. London: Penguin, 1992.

Wright, Janet B. "Hardy and His Contemporaries: The Literary Context of *Jude the Obscure*." *Inscape* 14 (1980): 135–50.